Family Issues in the 21st Century Series

HANDBOOK OF PARENTING: STYLES, STRESSES AND STRATEGIES

FAMILY ISSUES IN THE 21ST CENTURY SERIES

Handbook of Parenting: Styles, Stresses and Strategies
Pacey H. Krause and Tahlia M. Dailey (Editors)
ISBN: 978-1-60741-766-8

Family Issues in the 21st Century Series

HANDBOOK OF PARENTING: STYLES, STRESSES AND STRATEGIES

PACEY H. KRAUSE

AND

TAHLIA M. DAILEY

EDITORS

Nova Science Publishers, Inc.
New York

NOTICE TO THE READER

The Publisher has taken reasonable care in the preparation of this book, but makes no expressed or implied warranty of any kind and assumes no responsibility for any errors or omissions. No liability is assumed for incidental or consequential damages in connection with or arising out of information contained in this book. The Publisher shall not be liable for any special, consequential, or exemplary damages resulting, in whole or in part, from the readers' use of, or reliance upon, this material. Any parts of this book based on government reports are so indicated and copyright is claimed for those parts to the extent applicable to compilations of such works.

Independent verification should be sought for any data, advice or recommendations contained in this book. In addition, no responsibility is assumed by the publisher for any injury and/or damage to persons or property arising from any methods, products, instructions, ideas or otherwise contained in this publication.

This publication is designed to provide accurate and authoritative information with regard to the subject matter covered herein. It is sold with the clear understanding that the Publisher is not engaged in rendering legal or any other professional services. If legal or any other expert assistance is required, the services of a competent person should be sought. FROM A DECLARATION OF PARTICIPANTS JOINTLY ADOPTED BY A COMMITTEE OF THE AMERICAN BAR ASSOCIATION AND A COMMITTEE OF PUBLISHERS.

LIBRARY OF CONGRESS CATALOGING-IN-PUBLICATION DATA
Handbook of parenting styles, stresses, and strategies / [edited by] Pacey H. Krause and Tahlia M. Dailey.
    p. cm.
  Includes index.
  ISBN 978-1-60741-766-8 (hardcover)
  1. Parenting--Handbooks, manuals, etc. 2. Parenting--Psychological aspects--Handbooks, manuals, etc. 3. Parent and child--Handbooks, manuals, etc. 4. Parent and child--Psychological aspects--Handbooks, manuals, etc. I. Krause, Pacey H. II. Dailey, Tahlia M.
  HQ755.8.H3336 2009
  155.6'46--dc22
                                                                                    2009025479

Published by Nova Science Publishers, Inc. ✦ *New York*

CONTENTS

PREFACE

Families and parents have the most central and enduring influence on children's lives. Parenthood is not instinctive, but is rather an evolutionary procedure throughout the child's life-course. This book looks at the pattern of family structures, which has evolved as a result of social, cultural and economic changes. An overview of parental monitoring and the development of two new retrospective monitoring scales is examined. This book also focuses on certain parenting styles, stressors, and practices which promote positive and negative child behaviors. The goodness-of-fit concept is emphasized, which concentrates specifically on how a poor fit between the temperament behaviors of infants and young children and parents' expectations and parenting skills can stress and challenges the parent-child relationship and potentially lead to poor child outcomes. Among other issues, this book addresses the relations of maternal emotional availability with infant smiling and crying, the importance of measuring parental brain and physiological systems, the effect of working class mothers on their emotional availability to their children, and the variety of patterns that a parent must adopt in daily life to cope with situations of conflict to promote processes of emotional and social adaptation in their children.

Chapter 1 - Families and parents have the most central and enduring influence on children's lives. Parenthood is not instinctive, but is rather an evolutionary procedure throughout the child's life. In most settings parents are not prepared to raise children just after childbirth. In order to become effective at their tasks they follow advice given by expert professionals such as paediatricians, teachers, or even psychologists and psychiatrists; through books, articles, and interviews; or by seeking their friends' or family's advice. In addition, the parenting role is improved by increasingly receiving love and pleasure from their children, their creation. This reciprocal relation and affection develops over time.

Chapter 2 - Efforts to understand the socialization of adaptive emotional functioning in children have largely focused upon both laboratory observations and parents' self-report of their emotion socialization strategies. While some studies have also taken biological mechanisms into account, these have focused on children's physiological responding (e.g., cardiac vagal tone). However, parental biological state and the manner by which this may impact their children's functioning have only begun to be examined. In this commentary, the importance of measuring parental brain and physiological systems is examined. This gap in the research literature may shed light on the indirect mechanisms by which parenting behaviors may affect children's emotional development.

Chapter 3 - This chapter presents an overview of parental monitoring and describes the development of two new retrospective monitoring scales. Parental monitoring has been defined as a concern for the regulation, supervision, and management of behavior, such that parents are aware of and regulatory of their children's whereabouts, companions, and activities (Pettit, Laird, Dodge, Bates, & Criss, 2001), or, more simply, as supervision of youth and communication between parent and youth (Stanton et al., 2000). Monitoring is associated with fewer behavioral and drug problems among children. Currently, there are no convenient, retrospective scales of parental monitoring in general or of television monitoring in particular that would allow a more complete understanding of this construct, including how it might relate to subsequent behaviors.

To test some of the ideas summarized in this chapter, a report was developed of two retrospective scales, the Parental Monitoring Scale (PMS) and the Television Monitoring Scale (TMS). College students (N = 205) completed surveys regarding their family of origin and individual characteristics and behaviors. The PMS and the TMS appear to have acceptable internal consistency (alphas= .79 and .84, respectively). Scores on the PMS significantly correlated with more healthy family functioning, and more intimacy and autonomy in one's family of origin. Furthermore, scores on both the PMS and TMS correlated negatively with three measures of recent drinking, suggesting that young adults who remembered more monitoring while growing up have decreased chances of developing drinking problems in college. This study presents two new retrospective scales that measure parental monitoring and television monitoring by parents. Both scales were internally consistent and free from social desirability. Preliminary validity was established for the Parental Monitoring Scale by showing it is indeed associated with healthier family functioning as well as less subsequent drinking among college students. Limitations are discussed, as are implications for use of these new scales and ideas for related future research.

Chapter 4 - In the past few decades, there has been increasing research on the relationship between parenting behaviors and children's developmental outcomes. Within this body of literature, scholars have identified that certain parenting styles (e.g., parental warmth, support) promote positive child behaviors, whereas harsh and authoritative parenting practices are associated with negative child outcomes such as increases in aggression and externalizing disorders (e.g., Bendersky et al., 2006; Krenichyn, Saegert, & Evans, 2001; Patterson, 1992).

Chapter 5 - A substantial number of families participating in parent training interventions do not benefit and instead experience negative treatment outcomes such as dropout, mediocre engagement, and/or a lack of positive gains following intervention (Assemany & McIntosh, 2002). Spoth, Goldberg, and Redman (1999) found that 44% of families assigned to a 5-week parenting intervention and 51% of families assigned to a 7-week parenting intervention failed to attend any session. Gross and Grady (2002) reported that 26% of parents assigned to attend group parenting sessions attended fewer than 10% of the sessions and subsequently dropped out of the program. These data suggest that many participants find it difficult to attend and completely adhere to programs consisting of training sessions, possibly due to conflicting obligations. Researchers aimed at improving parenting skills and practices face the question of how best to engage and retain their participants when many are working parents who may also be highly involved in their communities and active with their children's education and extracurricular activities. In fact, Gross and Grady (2002) found that 32% of participants enrolled in a 12-week parenting program reported that it was difficult for them to attend and 50% found the weekly assignments difficult to complete. It is likely that many participants perceive parent training as one more demand in an already stressful lifestyle.

Chapter 6 - Antenatal education is a crucial component of antenatal care, yet practice and research demonstrate that women and men now seek far more than the traditional approach of a labor and birth focused program attended in the final weeks of pregnancy. This study was designed to determine whether a new antenatal education program, designed from a needs based assessment of expectant and new parents, with increased parenting content, could improve parenting outcomes when compared to a traditional program.

A randomized control trial conducted at a specialist referral maternity hospital in Sydney, Australia, measured the pre and postnatal outcomes of 170 women birthing at the hospital who attended the hospital antenatal education programs and their male partners. The intervention, a new *Having a Baby* program, was tested against the traditional hospital program which acted as the control. The primary outcome measure was perceived parenting self-efficacy, with worry and perceived knowledge also being measured.

The results revealed the perceived maternal self-efficacy scores of women and men in the experimental program were significantly higher than those in the control program and worry scores were lower, but they did not reach statistical significance. Birth outcomes were similar. The new program improved parenting knowledge and self-efficacy. Parenting programs which continue in the early postnatal period may be beneficial.

This chapter will provide a description of the randomized control trial as well as a summary of the key elements of the new program. It will be of interest to midwives, physical therapists and all involved in antenatal and postnatal education.

Chapter 7 - This review focuses on the goodness-of-fit concept, concentrating specifically on how a poor fit between the temperament behaviors of infants and young children and parents' expectations and parenting skills can stress and challenge the parent-child relationship and potentially lead to poor child outcomes. The role of the child, the parent, and the context in establishing, maintaining, and modifying the goodness of fit between children's temperament and their parents' behaviors and in determining child outcomes are considered. This is all concluded by presenting findings from a recent analysis of 629 mothers and their children that illustrates the special challenges of parenting slow-to-warm-up infants using the goodness-of-fit perspective.

Chapter 8 - In this observational study, relations of maternal emotional availability with infant smiling and crying, two behaviors that represent infants' principal social communicative functions were examined. Fifty-four mother–infant dyads were analyzed using two independent observation systems: (a) the infant socioemotional behaviors and (b) the Emotional Availability Scales. The amount of infant smiling differentiated dyads with different levels of maternal emotional availability. The more infants smile, the greater the odds that their mothers will be more emotionally available. By contrast, no association for cry was found with maternal emotional availability. These results are consistent with the burgeoning literature on the Emotional Availability construct that stresses the importance of expressed positive emotions as determinants of the quality of mother-infant interaction.

Chapter 9 - Drawing on material from my book (Marginalised Mothers: Exploring Working Class Experiences of Parenting) this paper explores how the experiences and meaning making processes of working class mothers are grounded in specific social and material realities. In particular the focus will be on how these situated understandings allow such mothers to generate crucial resources for their children. This work is based on detailed case study analysis of 14 mothers, all of whom have low incomes, lack formal educational qualifications, and live in disadvantaged communities I begin by considering the status and significance these women attach to motherhood. In spite of unremittingly negative public portrayals of disadvantaged parents, most of the women forged an extremely positive identity around mothering, emphasising satisfaction, pleasure and competence. In a context of deprivation and struggle, being a mother was valued and prioritised and was characterised by resilience and determination. The significance of home for the mothers in the study is underlined through a focus on the emotional resources made available to children.

Chapter 10 - Parenting is a process of creation: the parent's creation of a child, and the child's creation of a parent. This chapter will focus on the notion that this creation arises from the dialectical tension that emerges in the space between parent and child. The basic tension present in parenthood, the tension between parent and child, is a particular example of the basic existential tension existing between a person and an "Other" or, in other words, the tension between one subject and another. This tension between two subjects receives intense expression when the need of the one, at any particular moment, is different from the need of the other. The moment in which this acute dialectical tension between the two is created, which sometimes also involves sharp tension within each subject, is a potential moment of growth and development. Any solution that attempts to eliminate this tension quickly, so that the need of the one overpowers the need of the other, results in the constriction of the space that enables the process of creation and development. The tension between desires, between perceptions and impulses that conflict with each other in the context of intimate relations is not, a negative element that sullies relationship or mars development, as is sometimes believed. On the contrary, this tension is likely to contribute not only to the development of significant and rich relations, but also to the development of each individual within the relationship. According to this outlook, beneficial parenting does not seek to reduce conflicts or difference, or to avoid them, nor does it view conflict as a "necessary evil," but rather as an opportunity for growth and creativity.

Chapter 11 - U.S. adolescents are spending an increasing amount of time in extracurricular activities. Some adolescents who are spending an increased amount of time in extracurricular activities are experiencing behavior problems (i.e. anxiety, stress; Ginsburg & The Committee on Communications and Committee on Psychosocial Aspects of Child and Family Health, 2007). It is not clear, however, why involvement in extracurricular activities is associated with behavior problems for some, but not all adolescents. The purpose of this chapter is to propose a conceptual model to further understand the mechanisms underlying adolescent mental health problems among adolescents who spend increased amount of time in extracurricular activities. The proposed model investigates bidirectional effects among (a) the amount of time an adolescent spends in extracurricular activities, (b) parental stress, (c) parental warmth/control, and (d) adolescent behavior problems.

Chapter 12 - In Japan the rate of multiple births has been increasing since 1975 because of the wide spread of fertility treatment. Currently more than 1% of all births are multiples. The rapid increase of multiple births is now a common public health concern in developed countries. Multiple birth babies are more likely to be born preterm and of low birthweight, adding to the many pressures of coping with two or more babies. The nurturing of multiples entails a physically, mentally and economically higher burden than that of singletons, and multiple birth families surely expect appropriate information to facilitate the healthy growth of their children. Multiples tend to lag behind singletons in their physical growth and motor and language development. Multiples are reported to be one of the risk factors for maternal depression and child abuse. Good preparation and advice during or even before pregnancy is essential. After the birth, parents need continuing support and access to care from health professionals who understand their different and special needs. Therefore, there is an increasing need for appropriate information to be provided to parents and health professionals regarding the growth and development of multiples, tips on child bearing, and social resources for families. However, little information is available, especially in Japan. Multidisciplinary collaboration is essential to resolve these themes surrounding multiple birth families. Moreover, population-based or at least large-scale epidemiologic studies to assess the long-term health, social and psychological impact of multiple births on the family, children and society are crucial to provide a scientific basis and to persuade policymakers of the importance of supporting families with multiples.

The author has adopted three main strategies to resolve these problems. The first strategy is monitoring and reanalyzing vital statistics concerning multiple births, and providing an objective macroscopic vision of public health problems related to multiple births. The second strategy is to provide evidence-based information to health professionals and policymakers as well as multiple birth families. A large-scale database of multiples, mainly twins, has been organized since 1984. The third strategy is to construct a human network and family support system at the prefectural level by means of a population-approach method. The goals of these projects are to contribute to the development of welfare programs for families with multiples as well as to coordinate research useful for both maternal and child health and human genetics.

Chapter 13 - This chapter reviews the literature, with the addition of some recent unpublished findings from this group's studies, on the relationship between childhood obesity management and family-based factors. The objective was to better understand the impact of socioeconomic status (SES), family size, family functioning and parenting style on the outcomes of pediatric obesity management programs. Original research and reviews published between 1995 and 2008 were identified by searching Medline, PsycINFO, Agricola and Lexis-Nexis. The literature shows that parents from families of lower SES may underestimate the health risk of excess weight to their children; these families may also be less available for the intensive efforts and supportive interaction needed to address excess weight in their children. Moreover, psychological disturbances, lower family functioning and a permissive parenting style were some of the factors reported to be associated with less success in family-based weight loss programs among families from lower SES as well as larger families.

Chapter 14 - The role of the family in Autistic Spectrum Conditions (ASC) has a controversial history, but current research has identified a number of key relationships between the behaviors of the child with ASC and parenting stress and styles. The current review highlights a number of relationships between parenting stress, parenting behaviors, and child behavior problems in ASC samples, and identifies areas where current research is lacking. In particular, the following concerns need to be addressed: whether high parenting stress levels impact negatively on child outcomes following interventions for ASC; the nature of the relationship between parenting stress and child behavior problems over time; whether parenting stress impacts on parenting behaviors, and the types of parenting behaviors that are influential for subsequent child behavior problems in the context of ASC; whether any association between parenting behaviors and child behavior problems is a direct one; and whether the contact and communication experiences of parents with professionals leading up to, and during, the diagnostic process is of particular significance. The results of such examinations may well have practical implications for the development of future interventions for ASC.

Chapter 15 - Research shows that 20% to 38% of women experience domestic violence during their lifetime (Tjaden & Thoennes, 2000), and women may be particularly vulnerable to partner abuse during the childbearing years. As such, millions of young children are exposed to DV and are parented primarily by battered women. The notable prevalence of DV indicates that its effect on parenting outcomes requires close examination. As one might expect, existing research has found that DV generally has a devastating impact on parenting capacities (Holden et al., 1998; Levendosky & Graham-Bermann, 2000; 2001).

A few studies that have examined the impact of DV on parenting during the perinatal period have found that parenting is already compromised during pregnancy and shortly after birth as a result of DV (Dayton, Levendosky, Davidson, & Bogat, 2007; Huth-Bocks, Levendosky, Theran, & Bogat, 2004). Similarly, other studies have found that DV negatively impacts mothers' displays of sensitivity, encouragement, and guidance during parent-infant interactions (Sokolowski et al., 2008). These results suggest that DV interferes with an adaptive transition to parenthood and the earliest forms of parenting, which are known to affect long-term childhood outcomes. A number of studies have also found that mothers of preschool and school-age children who are exposed to DV report significantly higher parenting stress compared to non-battered women (Holden et al., 1998; Levendosky & Graham-Bermann, 1998; 2000; Ritchie & Holden, 1998). Parenting stress, in turn, is associated with more negative and less positive parenting behaviors (e.g., Holden et al., 1998, Huth-Bocks & Hughes, 2008) and poor child outcomes (Levendosky & Graham-Bermann, 1998). Not surprisingly, DV is also associated with other parenting deficits such as less supportive behaviors, less parenting effectiveness and child-centeredness (Graham-Bermann & Levendosky, 1998a; Levendosky & Graham-Bermann, 2001), and greater parent-child hostility and aggression (Holden et al., 1998) during the preschool and school-age years, although there appear to be a subset of women who are resilient and don't experience impairments in parenting.

In conclusion, research has demonstrated that DV is surprisingly common among mothers and has deleterious effects on a variety of parenting outcomes in most battered women. This chapter includes a thorough review of the empirical literature documenting the relationship between DV and parenting outcomes beginning in pregnancy and lasting throughout childhood.

Chapter 16 - Few pictures are as pervasive and powerful in human culture as that of a parent and child together. Whether the child is swaddled on a parent's back in Mongolia, reading a book with her father in the United States (U.S.), or walking through a market with her mother in Kenya, the activities that parents and children share together are a critical component of parenting and how a child comes to know and trust the world. In recent years, researchers have put forward various theories related to parenting. Some investigators have considered parenting styles (e.g., Baumrind, 1971)—that is, dimensions of caregiving that vary along the axes of warmth, nurturance, and responsivity. Other researchers have assessed parents' attitudes, beliefs, and goals related to childrearing, and still others have sought to examine the various categories of parenting practices such as teaching, supporting language, monitoring, and providing resources (Brooks-Gunn & Markman, 2005). This chapter focuses on parenting practices, specifically those related to learning outcomes in the early years.

Chapter 17 - A large corpus of evidence shows the effectiveness of authoritative parenting, in comparison with authoritarian, neglectful, and indulgent educational styles, on adolescents' personal and social development. However, few studies have examined the influence of authoritative parenting on adolescents' social identity and future plans. In this contribution ($N = 400$) examined were the role of warmth, strictness, and autonomy granting – the core dimensions of parenting– in influencing adolescents' social identity, measured as family collective self-esteem, and expectations for the future, in terms of stable intimate relationships and fulfillment of personal goals. Also tested the role of family collective self-esteem in mediating the influence of parenting style dimensions on expectations for the future. Besides confirming that authoritative parenting leads to better outcomes than the other educational styles, this study sheds light for the first time on the distinct contribution of different parenting dimensions on adolescents' social identity and expectations for the future.

Chapter 18 - Despite their strong presence in North America, Central American refugees have been identified as the most critically understudied Hispanic group. Relatively little is known about their cultural and familial adaptation (Dona & Berry, 1994; Guarnaccia, 1997; Organista, 2007). The cultural life of Central Americans is centered on the family and community rather than on the rugged individualism of North American society. Family and community relationships tend to have a hierarchical power structure with associated mores for interaction, in contrast to an egalitarian arrangement (Hernandez, 2005; Organista; Sue & Sue, 2008). Transmission of the culture of origin to one's children is a key focus among Central American families (Hernandez; Organista). Refugee parents have been found to have a heightened attachment to their heritage culture due to the forced rather than voluntary nature of their resettlement process in the host society (Roizblatt & Pilowsky, 1996). However, intergenerational cultural transmission may be compromised by the pressures that adolescents experience to assimilate with peers in the new socio-cultural environment. Parents may use youth's behavior and ethnic identity to gauge the effectiveness of their parenting ability and strategies, with signs of weak ethnic identity or Western cultural influence generating stress in the childrearing process (Baptiste, 1993; Hernandez; Sue & Sue). Existing research suggests that Central American mothers and fathers may play different roles in the cultural socialization of children (Harwood, Leyendecker, Carlson, Asencio, & Miller, 2002; Phinney & Vedder, 2006; Sue & Sue), implying a possible variance in indicators of adolescents' cultural stance that may serve as predictors of stress for parents of each gender.

This chapter describes a research study investigating relationships between parenting stress and adolescent ethnic identity development, adolescents' openness to behavior changes towards Western norms, and adolescents' age of migration among 100 Central American refugee families. Close to one-third of the participating parents reported high or clinically significant stress levels. Stepwise Multiple Regression Analysis revealed that in combination, adolescents' age of arrival in Canada and level of openness to behavior changes towards Western norms accounted for 37 percent of the variance in mothers' stress scores. Adolescent ethnic identity development was the only significant predictor of fathers' stress levels, accounting for 12 percent of the variance in fathers' stress scores. Relationships between these variables and maternal and paternal stress are discussed considering each parent's role in adolescents' cultural socialization. Recommendations for assisting with the parenting process across two cultures are also presented.

Chapter 19 - For decades, there has been the generalized view that cultural differences from the country of origin and the host country threaten family relations and exacerbate the risk for immigrant youth to engage in unhealthy and risky behaviors. It has been argued that immigrant families' values, beliefs, and parenting practices are different from the ones found in the host country or are forced to change during the process of adaptation to the host culture, thus, affecting children's developmental outcomes (Isralowitz & Slonim-Nevo, 2002; Nauck, 2001). In the particular case of Hispanic immigrant youth, alarming official statistics on risky sexual behaviors appear to support this notion. Hispanic youth are reported to be at an increased risk for STDs, having sexual intercourse before age 13, and having four or more sexual partners (CDC, 2000; YRBS, 2004). Yet, limited scholarship exists on how parenting processes and perceived stress (e.g., limited social networks, unreceptive school environment) predict risky sexual behaviors across generations of Hispanic immigrant adolescents.

Using a subsample from the National Longitudinal Study of Adolescent Health (Add Health; Waves I & II), the current study examined the potential changes over time in parenting practices (e.g., monitoring, support, and communication) and stress (e.g., psychological well-being, perceived social support, perceived school stress) across 1st and 2nd generation immigrant Hispanic youth (N= 2,016) and their relationships to risky sexual behaviors. Even though GLM results show that maternal parenting and stress constructs indeed changed over time, changes were not significantly different across generational groups. In addition, maternal monitoring, maternal support, and measures of stress emerged as key predictors of risky sexual behaviors across both 1st and 2nd generation Hispanic immigrant youth over time, whereas no moderation effects were found by immigration status on developmental processes across generational groups. Therefore, findings suggest that even though cultural adaptation to the host culture might represent a stressful process as documented by previous literature (e.g., Pérez & Padilla, 2000; Rueschenberg & Buriel, 1989), immigration and stress do not appear to significantly affect parenting behaviors over time or their links to risky sexual behaviors across generations of Hispanic immigrant youth.

In: Handbook of Parenting: Styles, Stresses & Strategies ISBN 978-1-60741-766-8
Editor: Pacey H. Krause and Tahlia M. Dailey © 2009 Nova Science Publishers, Inc.

Chapter 1

PARENTING PRACTICES AND CHILD MENTAL HEALTH OUTCOMES

Ippolyti Vassi, Alexandra Veltsista and Chryssa Bakoula

First Department of Paediatrics, Athens University, Aghia Sophia Children's Hospital,
Athens, Greece

Families and parents have the most central and enduring influence on children's lives. Parenthood is not instinctive, but is rather an evolutionary procedure throughout the child's life. In most settings parents are not prepared to raise children just after childbirth. In order to become effective at their tasks they follow advice given by expert professionals such as paediatricians, teachers, or even psychologists and psychiatrists; through books, articles, and interviews; or by seeking their friends' or family's advice. In addition, the parenting role is improved by increasingly receiving love and pleasure from their children, their creation. This reciprocal relation and affection develops over time.

In recent decades, the pattern of family structures has evolved as a result of social, cultural and economic changes, with a rise in the number of single-parent families, reconstructed or blended families, partnerships and foster families, while intact (with two biological parents) setups have become more nuclear [1]. However, no matter what its structure, the general principles of family and parenting remain more or less the same through generations: to attend to the physical and psychological needs of its members, especially the children.

Families provide a structured environment in which a child lives, while parents serve as role models and influence their development, attitudes and values [1]. Another important perspective of parenting is the influence of parenting styles on child development. "Authoritative" parents are more likely to have happy, creative, and cooperative children, with high self-esteem, who generally do well academically and socially. This parenting style involves a combination of affection and attentive responsiveness to children's needs, along with clear, firm expectations for developmentally appropriate, socially responsible behavior. On the other hand, "authoritarian" parenting adversely affects children's development, including self-esteem and academic achievement. It tends to be less warm and responsive and more inconsistent and punitive [1].

During adolescence, as a result of the physical, cognitive and social changes undergone, parenting styles need to adapt to new circumstances. The supervision of a young child has a very different meaning from that of a teenager or adolescent [2]. In this peculiar stage of life, events and experiences have significant implications and consequences for later life. As they develop, adolescents adopt new roles of social responsibility; they acquire skills and access opportunities necessary for functioning in adult life. The health and, even more importantly, the knowledge, attitudes and practices of adolescents are regarded as essential factors when predicting the process of epidemiological transition of a population. Current lifestyles of adolescents are crucial for the health and disease patterns that will be observed in the future. Nevertheless, during these formative years, adolescents are subject to many influences dominating their internal and external environment. These include parents, teachers, peer groups, health care providers, media, and religious and cultural norms in the community. Knowledge of the significant rapid physical, mental and social changes occurring during this critical stage of life helps both adolescents and their parents to absorb and adapt to these changes and enables the former to avoid becoming victims of any serious illnesses or to develop inappropriate behaviours [3]. Reasonably, physical and social changes are more obvious to parents, while mental health changes are rather unpredictable and astonishing sometimes to adolescents themselves.

Mental health problems account for 60–70% of disability-adjusted life years (DALY) in 12- to 24-year-old youths worldwide [4, 5] and comprise a public health issue affecting up to 20% of children, including preschool-aged children, in modern Western societies [6]. Early mental health problems often continue through childhood and adolescence into adulthood [6]. Consequently, adolescent mental health is a determining factor in their quality of life as adults [7]. Additionally, the health and well-being of children are inextricably linked to their parents' physical, emotional and social health, social circumstances, and child-rearing practices [1].

Within the framework of a Greek longitudinal population-based study from birth to 18 years of age, we examined to what extent parental roles and practices influence the emotional and behavioral health of children up to adolescence. According to relevant indices, Greek society has undergone significant social shifts during the later decades of the twentieth century. Therefore, the changing parental roles in a changing society constitute an appropriate matrix for biosocial studies over the time.

GREEK NATIONAL LONGITUDINAL STUDY: BIRTH TO 18 YEARS

Our study population consisted of all consecutive births between the 1st and the 30th of April 1983 throughout Greece (11,048 newborns). In 1983, questionnaires were addressed both to mothers and supervisors of delivery in order to collect information about family as well as pregnancy, labor and the newborn. Families of those children were reached again when children were seven years old, through their schools (1990). During the first follow-up, questionnaires addressed to parents and teachers were sent out and 8,158 of those were returned completed. Questions on family life, parents' and children's physical and mental health, lifestyle and school were included. In 2001, children were reached again at the age of 18 years, the threshold of adulthood. During the second follow-up, 3,500 pairs of parent and child questionnaires were returned, which assessed family, physical and mental health, lifestyle and academic issues. Finally, after the matching procedure, a data set for 2,695 children for each one of the three time periods was created. For the present study, we used data from the ages of seven and 18 years. Sensitivity analysis showed that this sub-population was representative of the initial birth cohort [8].

Physical punishment, parental monitoring, and extensive consumerism were used as indicative variables of the three major parenting attitudes: authoritarian, authoritative and permissive. Severe physical punishment was investigated by asking parents whether or not they believe and use physical punishment as a means of discipline, while a further question attempted to estimate the frequency that a child was physically punished during the preceding year. Children's subjective perception of parental monitoring was derived at both follow-up periods. Finally, extensive consumerism, as identified in 1990 by asking the number of pairs of shoes bought for the child during the preceding year, and the amount of pocket money provided to the adolescent, were included to give a better picture of parental provision or deprivation.

We studied the impact of the above parameters on children's mental health status during childhood and late adolescence. The independent variables derived from the 1990 survey were examined cross-sectionally and longitudinally, while variables derived from the 2001 survey were only examined cross-sectionally.

At the ages of 7 and 18 years, we used the Rutter A2 parents total, emotional and conduct scale scores [9] and the Youth Self Report (YSR) total, internalizing and externalizing scale scores [10, 11], respectively, to determine youths' mental health status. The sex-specific cut-off point of about the 98th percentile of the distribution of the symptom scores in the present sample for the total and subscales scores on the Rutter's Parent Questionnaire A2 and the YSR was used to indicate a high level of symptom loading.

A series of logistic regression models was conducted to test the unadjusted and adjusted odds of scoring above the cut-off point on the problem scales (outcome) for the variables studied.

FINDINGS

Table 1 shows the characteristics of the study population at both follow-up periods.

At 7 years of age, the odds for scoring above cut-off on the total, emotional and behavioural problems scales increased with frequent physical punishment. A trend towards higher scores on the total and behavioural problems scale was found for lack of parental monitoring. The group of children being offered two pairs of shoes only per year was found to have a lower likelihood to present total problems at 7 years. In addition, at 7 years of age socioeconomic indicators, such as single parenting and absence of siblings, were associated with a higher likelihood for emotional problems (Table 3).

When applying the long-term regression model, often use of physical punishment in pre-school years predicted behavioral deviation at the age of 18. Being a child of a single parent family predicted emotional and total problems in late adolescence. On the contrary, the cohabitating with siblings during childhood was protective of behavioral problems at 18 years (Table 3).

Finally, participants with a higher likelihood to present mental health problems at 18 years were those who lacked or had poor parental monitoring, those who received more pocket money per week, came from a single parent family, lived in an extended family, and had a mother with low education (Table 4).

Table 1. Characteristics of the population at the age of 7 and 18 years

	1990 (7 years) N (%)		2001 (18 years) N (%)	
Physical punishment				
Often	1005	(12.4%)	—	
Occasionally	4520	(55.7%)	—	
Never	2586	(31.9%)	—	
Parental monitoring				
Always	1104	(14.1%)	1943	(69.1%)
Sometimes	6326	(80.5%)	729	(25.9%)
Almost never	425	(5.4%)	139	(4.9%)
Extensive offering—shoes				
1	150	(1.9%)	—	
2	1629	(20.7%)	—	
3	2821	(35.9%)	—	
4	1991	(25.4%)	—	
5+	1262	(16.1%)	—	
Pocket money				
>20€ per week	—		1133	(40.3%)
<20€ per week	—		1681	(59.7%)
Marital status				
Married	7791	(97.2%)	2741	(88.7%)
Single parent family	228	(2.8%)	349	(11.3%)
Maternal education				
≤6 years	2837	(35.3%)	1752	(37.7%)
6–12 years	3300	(41.1%)	2011	(43.3%)
>12 years	1899	(23.6%)	881	(19.0%)
Number of siblings				
0	800	(9.9%)	158	(5.6%)
1	4986	(61.5%)	1706	(60.8%)
2	1758	(21.7%)	669	(23.9%)
3+	567	(7.0%)	272	(9.7%)
Living with grandparents				
Yes	2188	(27.0%)	499	(17.8%)
No	5923	(73.0%)	2299	(82.2%)

Table 2. Univariate logistic regression for emotional behavioural and total problems at 7 and 18 years old of variables at 7 and 18 years respectively.

Problems Variables	1990 OR (p)			2001 OR (p)		
	Emotional	Behavioural	Total	Emotional	Behavioural	Total
Gender						
Boys	NS	NS	NS	NS	NS	NS
Girls	*Reference Group*			*Reference Group*		
Physical punishment						
Often	2.77(<0.001)	12.89(<0.001)	10.75(<0.001)	—	—	—
Sometimes	NS	1.62(0.088)	1.75(0.007)	—	—	—
Never	*Reference Group*			*Reference Group*		
Parental monitoring						
Almost never	NS	3.77(<0.001)	2.82(<0.001)	4.85(<0.001)	3.46(0.007)	3.92(0.002)
Sometimes	NS	NS	NS	2.08(0.013)	2.04(0.021)	NS
Always	*Reference Group*			*Reference Group*		
Extensive offering-shoes						
5+	NS	NS	NS	—	—	—
4	NS	NS	NS	—	—	—
3	NS	NS	NS	—	—	—
2	NS	NS	0.34(0.014)	—	—	—
1	*Reference Group*			*Reference Group*		
Pocket money						
>20€ per week	—	—	—	1.60(0.076)	3.18(<0.001)	2.22(0.006)
<20€ per week	*Reference Group*			*Reference Group*		
Marital status						
Single parent family	2.22(0.017)	NS	NS	NS	NS	2.16(0.042)
Married	*Reference Group*			*Reference Group*		

Table 2. (Continued)

Maternal education					
>12	NS	NS	0.48(<0.001)	NS	NS
≤6	NS	2.04(<0.001)	NS	NS	NS
6–12	Reference Group				
Number of siblings					
0	NS	NS	NS	NS	NS
1	NS	NS	NS	NS	NS
2	NS	NS	NS	NS	0.49(0.065)
3+	Reference Group				
Living with grandparents					
No	NS	0.78(0.078)	0.54(0.041)	NS	NS
Yes	Reference Group				

Table 3. Multivariate logistic regression for emotional behavioural and total problems at 7 and 18 years old of variables at 7.

Problems Variables	1990 OR (p)			2001 OR (p)		
	Emotional	Behavioural	Total	Emotional	Behavioural	Total
Gender						
Boys	NS	NS	0.72(0.020)	NS	NS	NS
Girls	Reference Group			Reference Group		
Physical punishment						
Often	2.78(<0.001)	15.15(<0.001)	11.60(<0.001)	NS	3.18(0.036)	NS
Sometimes	NS	1.87(0.050)	2.01(0.002)	NS	NS	NS
Never	Reference Group			Reference Group		
Parental monitoring						
Almost never	NS	2.15(0.048)	1.73(0.067)	NS	NS	NS
Sometimes	NS	NS	NS	NS	NS	NS
Always	Reference Group			Reference Group		
Extensive offering—shoes						
5+	NS	NS	NS	NS	NS	NS
4	NS	NS	NS	NS	NS	NS
3	NS	NS	NS	NS	NS	NS
2	NS	NS	0.39(0.034)	NS	NS	NS
1	Reference Group			Reference Group		
Marital status						
Single parent family	1.95(0.068)	NS	NS	7.36(0.018)	6.76(0.086)	16.67(0.002)
Married	Reference Group			Reference Group		
Maternal education						
>12	NS	NS	0.61(0.024)	NS	NS	NS
≤6	NS	1.82(0.004)	NS	NS	NS	NS
6–12	Reference Group			Reference Group		

Table 3. (Continued)

Number of siblings						
0	2.16(0.060)	NS	NS	NS	NS	NS
1	NS	NS	NS	NS	0.25(0.006)	NS
2	NS	NS	NS	NS	0.24(0.018)	NS
3+	Reference Group			RG		
Living with grandparents						
Yes	NS	NS	NS	NS	NS	NS
No	Reference Group			Reference Group		

Table 4. Multivariate logistic regression for emotional, behavioural and total problems at 18 years old

| Problems | 2001 OR (p) | | |
Variables	Emotional	Behavioural	Total
Gender			
Boys	0.45(0.010)	NS	0.46(0.019)
Girls	*Reference group*		
Parental monitoring			
Almost never	6.56(<0.001)	2.55(0.074)	4.65(0.001)
Sometimes	2.38(0.006)	1.76(0.089)	1.80(0.088)
Always	*Reference Group*		
Pocket money			
>20€ per week	NS	3.00(0.001)	2.02(0.024)
<20€ per week	*Reference Group*		
Marital status			
Single parent family	NS	NS	2.19(0.043)
Married	*Reference Group*		
Maternal education			
>12	NS	NS	NS
≤6	NS	NS	1.99(0.060)
6–12	*Reference Group*		
Number of siblings			
0	NS	NS	NS
1	NS	NS	NS
2	NS	NS	NS
3+	*Reference Group*		
Living with grandparents			
Yes	2.15(0.013)	NS	2.19(0.043)
No	*Reference Group*		

COMMENTS

Throughout childhood, *physical punishment* has been related to several negative outcomes [12]. In our study frequent use of physical punishment was found to be associated with emotional and total problems at the age of 7 and behavioural deviation at the age of 7 and 18 years. Fergusson concluded that it results in 1.5 times higher overall rates of mental disorder compared to rare or absence of exposure to such violent parental behaviors [13]. More specifically, as a harsh and inconsistent means of discipline, it is considered a common risk factor for internalizing, hyperactive, disruptive, antisocial, oppositional, even aggressive or delinquent behavior in children [2, 12].

Apart from the immediate effects, it has been suggested that the use of cruel parenting behaviors may alter the development of a child's personality and self-esteem, which may in turn have an impact on adult psychopathology [14]. There appears to be a significant relationship between receiving harsh discipline as a child and the development of psychiatric disorders in adulthood, which our study confirmed only for behavioral deviation in late adolescence [14-16]. Other studies also found an association with depression, anxiety disorders, criminal and antisocial behavior, smoking, alcohol and drug abuse or dependence, aggression and violence towards others, risky sexual behaviours and post traumatic stress disorders [14, 15, 17, 18]. On the other hand, confounding social and familial factors associated with both the experience of child harsh punishment and greater risk of disorder may link even mild physical abuse to a greater vulnerability for psychiatric illness [8, 12]. These include dysfunctional family environments and poverty [14, 16], a finding which was partly confirmed in our study. Therefore, it can be assumed that preventing violence against children can contribute to a decrease in a much broader range of biosocial diseases beyond generations [15, 19].

Several researchers argue that it is not just parental physical punishment that acts on children's behavior. The converse influence is also very significant, as children's difficult behavior can be a predictor of physical punishment [14, 20], highlighting a significant interaction between parent and child behavior [2]. Previous studies suggest that violence against children is related to: contemporary family structure, large family size, parental stress, poverty, social isolation, and the use of violence as a means of conflict resolution [14, 15, 21, 22].

Monitoring is a parenting action that involves directly asking children questions about their life that they cannot directly observe themselves (i.e., school, outdoors activities, friends). It also involves setting limits that may prevent unacceptable or dangerous behaviors. An overall supervision of children's lives may teach them how to integrate in the society, make the best decisions and cope in life [23]. In the present study, absence or inconsistency in monitoring resulted in various forms of problem behavior during adolescence and in behavioral and total problems during childhood. These findings are in accordance to other studies and support that lack of supervision may lead to disruptive, delinquent, or violent behavior and alcohol use [2, 24].

The impact of *extensive consumerism* during childhood on mental health is unclear in the literature [25]. According to our findings, affluence in adolescence seems to be significantly associated with adolescents' psychological status. Family income is strongly related to children's health, and family's financial resources are closely tied to changes in family structure. Parents with low incomes are more commonly socially isolated and, thus, have fewer social supports and role models. Parental stress and poverty are often associated with longer working hours and in turn with difficulty in communicating with children and lower quality of parent-child relations [1].

Moreover, extensive consumerism triggered mainly by the media has harmed children according to studies in former eastern countries [25-27] and has been the subject of best sellers under the title of "Affluenza" [28]. The association between consumerism and affluence with mental health needs further investigation. Attitudes, such as we can and must pursue our needs rather than our wants to ensure our mental health, may need to be established.

The data presented here show that, in our country too, unfavorable mental health outcomes in childhood were strongly related to family structure. Although family-related variables, social indicators and family dynamics may vary during the study period, the effects of the social, cultural and economic changes in Western countries on the traditional family structure are also well known and documented in Greece [29].

CONCLUSION

In modern families, parents take into account children's opinions and include them in decision-making processes in order to become independent and increase their self-esteem [27]. However, in order to reach this stage of communication, much progress needs to be achieved in parenting practices. Advances in parenting during the early years could reduce the overall level of risk for the family and, moreover, improve long-term parenting and, consequently, the family's communication and function [23]. As children become adolescents, behavioral routines and expectations, good or bad, of one another become more established and resistant to change [2]. From this resistance, the so-called generation gap may emerge and the degree of family influence may vary.

Paediatricians are often parents' first source for help when problems in the family occur, and should be aware that the patient gives them a good picture of the family configuration. Parents also feel that they can share with the paediatrician their children's psychosocial problems, although their physical needs are more usually discussed. Nevertheless, paediatricians can offer advice on parenting behaviours that may result in short- and long-term improvement in family life [1].

Successful parenting strategies propose minimization of hostility in parents' behavior, and nurturing practices that disapprove of unpleasant child behavior but never of the child itself [2, 12]. Perceptions against parental monitoring constitute a myth, since adolescents themselves prefer to have limits in their behaviour and believe that values and principles in their life promote emotional stability. Problems arise when impulsive parental responses break the limits and attain authoritarian characteristics [23]. Permissive or authoritarian roles should be replaced with more thoughtful parental decisions, which are successful when they are age and development appropriate. Children could and should participate in the formation of some rules. Parents should be fair and consistent, and on occasion may need to be flexible. Rewarding positive behaviors is important, but children should never be made to feel that parental love is contingent on good behaviour [18].

REFERENCES

[1]   American, Academy, of, Pediatrics. Family Pediatrics: Report of the Task Force on the Family. *Pediatrics* 2003;111:1541-71.

[2]   Burke J.D, Pardini D.A, Loeber R. Reciprocal Relationships Between Parenting Behavior and Disruptive Psychopathology from Childhood Through Adolescence. *Journal of Abnormal Child Psychology* 2008;36:679-92.

[3]   Omran AR, Al-Hafez G. Health Education for Adolescents: Guidelines for Parents, Teachers, Health Workers and the Media EMRO Nonserial Publication WHO Regional Office for the Eastern Meditarranean 2006

[4]   WHO. Constitution. Geneva, Switzerland.

[5]   Patel V, Flisher A, Hetric S, P. M. Mental health of young people: a global public-health challenge. *Lancet* 2007 369:1302-13.

[6]   Bayer J, Hiscock H, UkoumunneO, Price A, Wake M. Early childhood aetiology of mental health problems: a longitudinal population-based study. *Journal of Child Psychology and Psychiatry*2008.

[7]   Chen H, Cohen P, Kasen S, Johnson GJ, Berenson K, Gordon K. Impact of adolescent mental disorders and physical illnesses on quality of life 17 years later. . *Archives of Pediatric and Adolescent Medicine* 2006;160:93-9.

[8]   Stefanis N.C, Delespaul P, Henquet C, Bakoula C, Stefanis CN, Van Os J. Early adolescent cannabis exposure and positive and negative dimentions of psychosis *Addiction*2004;99:1333-41.

[9]   Rutter M, Tizard J, Whitemore K, editors. *Education, health and behaviour*. London: Longman; 1970.

[10]   Achenbach TM, editor. *Manual for the Youth Self-Report and 1991 Profile*. Burlington: University of Vermont, Department of Psychiatry 1991.

[11]   Roussos A, Francis K, Zoubou V, Kyprianos S, Prokopiou A, Richardson C. The standardization of Achenbach's YSR in Greece in a national sample of high school students. *European Child and Adolescent Psychiatry* 2001;10:47-53.

[12]   Straus M.A, Mouradian VE. Impulsive Corporal Punishment by Mothers and Antisocial Behavior and Impulsiveness of Children. *Behavioral Sciences and the Law* 1998;16:353-74.

[13]   Fergusson D. M, Boden J.M, Horwood LJ. Exposure to childhood sexual and physical abuse and adjustment in early adulthood. *Child Abuse & Neglect* 2008;32:607-19.

[14]   Afifi T.O, Brownridge D.A., Cox B.J, Sareen J. Physical punishment, childhood abuse and psychiatric disorders. *Child Abuse & Neglect* 2006;30 1093-103.

[15]   Buntain-Ricklifs J.J, Kemper K.J, Bell M, Babonis T. Punishments:What predicts adults approval. *Child Abuse & Neglect* 1994;18:945-55.

[16]   MacMillan H.L, Boyle M.H, Wong M.Y.-Y, Duku E.K, Fleming J.E, Walsh CA. Slapping and spanking in childhood and its association with lifetime prevalence of psychiatric disorders in a general population sample. *CMAJ* 1999;161(7):805-9.

[17]   Spatz-Widom C, DuMont K, Czaja SJ. A Prospective Investigation of Major Depressive Disorder and Comorbidity in Abused and Neglected Children Grown Up. *Archives of General Psychiatry* 2007;64:49-56.

[18]   Ateah C.A, Secco M.L, Woodgate RL. The Risks and Alternatives to Physical Punishment Use With Children *Journal of Pediatric Health Care* 2003;17:126-32.

[19]   WHO. Prevention of child maltreatment. WHO scales up child maltreatment prevention activities 2008 [19-08-2008].

[20]   Woodward L.J FDM. Parent, Child, and Contextual Predictors of Childhood Physical Punishment. *Infant and Child Development*2002;11:213-35.

[21]   Straus MA, & , Smith C. Family patterns and child abuse. In: Straus M GRM, editor. *Physical violence in American families: Risk factors and adaptations to violence in 8,145 families*. New Brunswick NJ: Transaction Publishers 1990.

[22]   Crouch J.L, Behl LB. Relationships among parental beliefs in corporal punishment, reported stress, and physical child abuse potential. *Child Abuse & Neglect* 2001;25:413-9.

[23]   Carothers Bert S, J.R F, J.G. B. Parent Training: Implementation Strategies for Adventures in Parenting. *Journal of Primary Prevention* 2008;29:243-61.

[24] Fulkerson J.A, Pasch K.E, Perry C.L, Komro K. Relationships Between Alcohol-related Informal Social Control, Parental Monitoring and Adolescent Problem Behaviors Among Racially Diverse Urban Youth. *Journal of Community Health* 2008;33:425-33.

[25] Piko B. Psychosocial health and materialism among Hungarian youth. *Journal of Health Psychology* 2006;11:827-31.

[26] Utter J, Scragg R, Schaaf D. Associations between television viewing and consumption of commonly advertised foods among New Zealand children and young adolescents. *Public Health Nutrition* 2006;9:606-12.

[27] Valkenburg PM. Media and Youth Consumerism. *Journal of Adolescent Health* 2000;27S:52–6.

[28] Olive J, editor. Affluenza. Vermilion ed. London: *The Sunday Times*.

[29] Vassi I, Veltsista A, Lagona E, Gika A, Kavadias G, Bakoula C. The generation gap in numbers: parent-child disagreement on youth's emotional and behavioural problems. A Greek community based-survey *Social Psychiatry Psychiatric Epidemiology* 2008; 2008;43:1008-1013

In: Handbook of Parenting: Styles, Stresses & Strategies   ISBN 978-1-60741-766-8
Editor: Pacey H. Krause and Tahlia M. Dailey   © 2009 Nova Science Publishers, Inc.

Chapter 2

THE IMPORTANCE OF BRAIN AND PHYSIOLOGICAL SYSTEMS RESEARCH IN THE STUDY OF PARENTING BEHAVIORS

Susan B. Perlman[1] and Linda A. Camras[2]
[1] Yale University, Yale Child Study Center, USA
[2] DePaul University, Department of Psychology, USA

Efforts to understand the socialization of adaptive emotional functioning in children have largely focused upon both laboratory observations and parents' self-report of their emotion socialization strategies. While some studies have also taken biological mechanisms into account, these have focused on children's physiological responding (e.g., cardiac vagal tone). However, parental biological state and the manner by which this may impact their children's functioning have only begun to be examined. In this commentary, we argue for the importance of measuring parental brain and physiological systems. This gap in the research literature may shed light on the indirect mechanisms by which parenting behaviors may affect children's emotional development.

To date, multiple studies have examined children's sympathetic, parasympathetic, and hormonal systems in relation to both their own interaction with their caregivers and their caregivers' parenting behaviors. For example, Porter (2003) found that infants who participate in attuned face to face interaction with their mothers possess higher levels of resting cardiac vagal tone than non-synchronous mother-infant pairs, indicative of adaptive emotional regulation abilities (Porges, 1995). At a later age, insecurely attached/avoidant infants showed higher cortisol levels when separated from their caregiver during the strange situation paradigm than did more securely attached infants (Spangler & Grossmann, 1993), indicating a higher level of stress and a possible lack of effective emotion regulation skills. Similarly, Burgess, Marshall, Rubin, and Fox (2003) found that insecure-avoidant attachment in infancy predicted vagal tone at 4 years of age. Specifically, insecure-avoidant infants were more likely to display slower heart rate and higher resting vagal tone at the age of 4, which the authors believe to indicate the possibility that an avoidant mother-child relationship in infancy influences the development of an under-aroused autonomic profile in early childhood.

These examples indicate that distinct psychophysiological profiles likely underlie different types of parent-child relationships.

Studies have also examined child psycholphysiological variables in the context of a diathesis-stress model for parental emotion socialization. Katz and Gottman (1995, 1997) found that biological variables predicted children's vulnerability to conflict within their home. Specifically, increased marital hostility predicted lesser emotion regulation abilities in children along with increased negative affect and behavior problems, but only in children with low cardiac vagal tone. Similarly, El-Sheik and Harger (2001) reported that marital conflict predicted increased child anxiety, and both internalizing and externalizing problems in children with low vagal tone. Finally, in recent research, Hastings and De (2008) found that cardiac vagal tone moderated the relationship between maternal and paternal socialization and children's emotional behavior in early childhood. Specifically, parental emotion socialization was more associated with preschool adjustment for children with less parasympathetic regulatory capacities than for those displaying more adept levels of physiological regulation.

However, with the important exception of the child maltreatment literature (Frodi & Lamb, 1980), it is rare that researchers choose to look to parental physiological and brain systems as an indirect mechanism for socialization of the developing child. New research from our laboratory (Perlman, Camras, & Pelphrey, 2008) indicates that it might be fruitful to consider the importance of a parent's biological systems in understanding both their self-reported parenting behaviors and their child's developmental progress. First, we collected a sample of parents' resting vagal tone and correlated it with their self-reported parental socialization behaviors. We found that parents who had higher resting vagal tone, indicative of optimal physiological regulation, were more likely to report a balanced display of positive and negative emotions in their home. They also reported more desirable emotion socialization behaviors such as coaching their children to display positive emotions. In addition, we measured child basal vagal tone and children's understanding of emotional situations through a computer game in which the children matched affective facial expressions to emotional stories. We found that children's own physiological regulation was unrelated to both their emotion knowledge and their parent's vagal tone. However, parents' own resting vagal tone was related to their children's emotion knowledge, as was their reported balance of positive and negative emotions in the home. This research is the first to indicate that a parent's own physiological regulatory abilities may influence their child's emotional development through mechanisms other than shared genes. We believe this research suggests at an indirect pathway by which parents own emotion regulation abilities affect the emotional development of their children through their parents' socialization behaviors.

A small set of brain imaging studies also has begun to probe the neural mechanisms that may underly parenting behaviors (see Swain, Lorberbaum, Kose, & Strathearn, 2007 for a review). For example, Lorberbaum et al. (2002) found that mothers of newborn infants produced a greater emotional brain response to the sound of an infant cry than that of a control sound. ERP results indicated that this effect is stronger for mothers than for control women (Purhonen et al., 2001), pointing to increased parental arousal and attention to a potentially relevant environmental stimulus. Bartels and Zeki (2004) showed mothers pictures of their own infants and unfamiliar infants during fMRI scanning. Their results revealed that, while emotional regions were engaged during viewing of all infants, mothers showed greater affective brain activation in response to photos of their own babies. These results may indicate brain mechanisms underlying the development of early mother-infant attachment.

Although brain imaging studies have not yet included parent socialization behaviors, this would be an important area of future research.

We suggest that future parenting research employ psychophysiological, hormonal, and fMRI studies to better understand the means by which parenting behaviors develop and the manner in which these behaviors can affect the growing child. As biopsychological technology becomes more readily available, researchers may be able to discover indirect pathways through which parents' biology contributes to the emotional development of their children. In the future, researchers should consider measurement of both parent and child biological data, as it may prove to be imperative to our understanding of parent-child relationships and emotional development.

REFERENCES

Bartels, A., & Zeki, S. (2004). The neural correlates of maternal and romantic love. *NeuroImage*, 21, 1155–1166.

Burgess, K.B., Marshall, P.J., Rubin, K.H., & Fox, N.A. (2003). Infant attachment and temperament as predictors of subsequent externalizing problems and cardiac physiology. *Journal of Child Psychology and Psychiatry*, 44, 819-831.

El-Sheikh, M., & Harger, J. (2001). Appraisals of marital conflict and children's achievement, health, and physiological reactivity. *Developmental Psychology*, 37, 875–885.

Frodi, A.M., & Lamb, M.E. (1980). Child abusers' responses to infant smiles and cries. *Child Development*, 51, 238–241.

Katz, L. F., & Gottman, J. M. (1995). Vagal tone protects children from marital conflict. *Development and Psychopathology*, 7, 83–92.

Katz, L. F., & Gottman, J. M. (1997). Buffering children from marital conflict and dissolution. *Journal of Clinical Psychology*, 26, 157–171.

Lorberbaum, J.P., Newman, J.D., Horwitz, A.R., Dubno, J.R., Lydiard, R.B., Hamner, M.B., Bohning, D.E., & George, M.S. (2002). A potential role for thalamocingulate circuitry in human maternal behavior. *Biological Psychiatry*, 51, 431–445.

Porges, S.W. (1995). Cardiac vagal tone: A physiological index of stress. *Neuroscience and Biobehavioral Reviews*, 19, 225-233.

Porter, C.L. (2003). Coregulation in mother-infant dyads: Links to infants' cardiac vagal tone. *Psychological Reports,* 92, 307-319.

Purhonen, M., Kilpelainen-Lees, R., Paakkonen, A., Ypparila, H., Lehtonen, J., & Karhu, J. (2001). Effects of maternity on auditory event-related potentials to human sound. NeuroReport, 12, 2975–2979.

Spangler, G., & Grossmann, K.E. (1993). Biobehavioral organization in securely and insecurely attached infants. *Child Development*, 64(5), 1439-1450.

In: Handbook of Parenting: Styles, Stresses & Strategies   ISBN 978-1-60741-766-8
Editor: Pacey H. Krause and Tahlia M. Dailey   © 2009 Nova Science Publishers, Inc.

Chapter 3

PARENTAL MONITORING: OVERVIEW AND THE DEVELOPMENT OF TWO RETROSPECTIVE SCALES

Lisa Thomson Ross[1] and Maribeth L. Veal[2]

1) College of Charleston, South Carolina, USA
2) The Citadel, South Carolina, USA

This chapter presents an overview of parental monitoring and describes the development of two new retrospective monitoring scales. Parental monitoring has been defined as a concern for the regulation, supervision, and management of behavior, such that parents are aware of and regulatory of their children's whereabouts, companions, and activities (Pettit, Laird, Dodge, Bates, & Criss, 2001), or, more simply, as supervision of youth and communication between parent and youth (Stanton et al., 2000). Monitoring is associated with fewer behavioral and drug problems among children. Currently, there are no convenient, retrospective scales of parental monitoring in general or of television monitoring in particular that would allow a more complete understanding of this construct, including how it might relate to subsequent behaviors.

To test some of the ideas summarized in this chapter, we report on the development of two retrospective scales, the Parental Monitoring Scale (PMS) and the Television Monitoring Scale (TMS). College students (N = 205) completed surveys regarding their family of origin and individual characteristics and behaviors. The PMS and the TMS appear to have acceptable internal consistency (alphas= .79 and .84, respectively). Scores on the PMS significantly correlated with more healthy family functioning, and more intimacy and autonomy in one's family of origin. Furthermore, scores on both the PMS and TMS correlated negatively with three measures of recent drinking, suggesting that young adults who remembered more monitoring while growing up have decreased chances of developing drinking problems in college. This study presents two new retrospective scales that measure parental monitoring and television monitoring by parents. Both scales were internally consistent and free from social desirability. Preliminary validity was established for the Parental Monitoring Scale by showing it is indeed associated with healthier family functioning as well as less subsequent drinking among college students. Limitations are discussed, as are implications for use of these new scales and ideas for related future research.

INTRODUCTION

What is Monitoring?

Parental monitoring has been recognized as an important influence on children's development. It has been defined as a concern for the regulation, supervision, and management of behavior, such that parents are aware of and regulatory of their children's whereabouts, companions, and activities (Pettit et al., 2001), or, more simply, as supervision of youth and communication between parent and youth (Stanton et al., 2000). Caprara, Scabini, Barbaranelli, and Bandura (2004) conceptualize parental monitoring as a component of perceived collective efficacy, or beliefs about how the family system functions as a whole unit. Other researchers conceptualize monitoring as a key element of attachment, such that more monitoring promotes the child's tendency to feel secure (Parker & Benson, 2004; Sroufe & Waters, 1977). Dishion and McMahon (1998) propose that "adequate parental monitoring is a necessary but not sufficient condition for effective parenting and for improved adaptation for the child" (p. 61).

High levels of monitoring are thought to promote more parental enjoyment of the parent-adolescent relationships (Laird, Pettit, Dodge, & Bates, 2003). Research by McCoy, Frick, Loney and Ellis (1999) suggests that poor parental monitoring may be part of a constellation of dysfunctional parenting practices. More specifically, poorer supervision and monitoring has been shown to associate with less positive involvement with children, less positive forms of parenting (e.g., rarely praising child if he or she behaves well) more inconsistent discipline, and more corporal punishment (Dadds, Maujean, & Fraser, 2003). Others have replicated the link between poor supervision and inconsistent discipline in samples of Australian parents of 4-9 year olds and Canadian parents of 5-12 year olds (Elgar, Waschbusch, Dadds, & Sigvaldason, 2007).

Monitoring is Developmental

It is natural for parenting to take different forms of supervision and monitoring depending on the age of the child. Infants need intense amounts and forms of attention and care, due to their helplessness. This intensity wanes somewhat as children develop some self-sufficiency for their amusement, if not their self-care and safety. It is natural for children entering adolescence to become more entrenched in peer groups (Larson & Richards, 1991), resulting in less time spent with parents and weaker emotional ties with parents (Steinberg & Silverberg, 1986). Crouter and colleagues (1990) note the developmental process of monitoring when they ponder "At what point in the school-age years does the child have sufficient autonomy that parental monitoring becomes important? When in the school-age or adolescent years does the importance of monitoring begin to wane? (p. 656)" Findings by Smetana and Asquith (1994) suggest that as adolescents grow older, they are less likely to believe that parental control is legitimate. Thus, as children mature, "parents' efforts to effectively monitor and support their children may be increasingly thwarted" (Forehand & Jones, 2002, p. 464). Harris (1998) contends that parents have much less influence on children than previously thought (beyond genetic contributions), and furthermore a substantial portion of parental influence is indirect and due to parents selecting peer and social contexts for the child.

Not only does the *level* of monitoring vary with the age of the child, it appears to have a different *impact* depending on the age of the child. Parents' monitoring and supervision predicted conduct problems among children aged 10-12 and 13-17, however among younger children (ages 6- 9) monitoring was a weak predictor of conduct problems (Frick, Christian, & Wooten, 1999). Perhaps at such young ages fewer children are engaging in such problem behaviors, or perhaps children in the youngest group are being monitored at relatively high levels.

Monitoring is Bi-Directional

Recently, researchers have recognized that both parents' and adolescents' contribute to parental monitoring, and that monitoring is a process (Crouter, MacDermid, McHale, & Perry Jenkins, 1990; Kerr & Stattin, 2000; Stattin & Kerr, 2001). In a study of Scandanavian teenagers, Berg-Nelson, Vikan, and Dahl (2003) found parents of adolescents in treatment for behavior disorders reported more difficulties with monitoring compared to parents whose children were in treatment for emotional disorders or whose children were not in treatment. Kerr & Stattin (2003) studied Swedish adolescents, and their research suggests that parents' behaviors were *reactions* to the youth's problem behavior rather than *influences* of it.

Does Monitoring Relate to Gender?

A few studies have suggested that parents monitor their sons and daughters differently. Veal and Ross (2006) found sex differences in college students' retrospective recall of parental monitoring, with women reporting more general parental monitoring than males while growing up. Note that there was no specific age parameter given to the college students. Veal and Ross (2006) concluded parents are more protective of daughters than sons.

This may be due in part to the norms and gender roles that our society holds for men and women, i.e., that girls/women are gentle, fragile, and need taking care of, whereas boys/men are strong and brave and must learn to take care of themselves and others. Fear of pregnancy may also cause parents to monitor girls more closely than boys (Veal and Ross, p. 49).

Results of a study by Svensson (2003) concur, as daughters aged 14 to 18 reported being more highly monitored (i.e., their parents knew where they were and whom they were with when they went out in the evenings) than did similarly aged sons. Similarly, Kerr & Stattin (2000) found that 14-year old girls scored higher on perceptions of parents' knowledge than their male peers.

However, Flannery and colleagues (1999) found the opposite among sixth and seventh graders, in that boys reported more monitoring than girls. Thus it appears that age may matter, with boys reporting more monitoring at younger ages (e.g., middle school) and girls reporting more monitoring at older ages (e.g., high school). Additional research is necessary to confirm this possible interaction of sex and age.

Does monitoring differ based on the sex of the parent? Whether or not there is a difference between mothers and fathers levels of monitoring (as reported by each parent) is not known. One study showed that, when it comes to daily activities, mothers were better monitors than fathers, that is, mothers' reports more closely resembled their children's reports, compared to fathers' reports (Crouter et al., 1990). Two studies actually found a sex of parent by sex of child interaction. Hagan and Kuebli (2007) observed parental monitoring behaviors as their preschoolers engaged in two physical gymnastics-like tasks. They found that mothers did not differentiate their monitoring level based on sex of their child, but that fathers monitored their sons' actions less closely than their daughters' actions. A second interaction study by Webb and colleagues (2002) found that adolescent daughters reported more perceived monitoring (i.e., the parent more often knows what is going on) than adolescent sons, but only concerning maternal monitoring; interestingly, fathers did not appear to monitor males and females differently.

How is Monitoring Measured?

Often, research on parental monitoring queries either the parent or the child about recent activities. Self-rating surveys are relatively inexpensive and easy to administer. For example, children may be asked questions such as "Do your parents know where you are? Do your parents know who you are with?" (Weintraub & Gold, 1991, p. 272). Or parents may be asked questions such as "Do you know how your child got home from school today? *If so:* How?" (Crouter et al., 1990).

The Alabama Parenting Questionnaire contains a subscale on parental supervision and monitoring (Shelton, Frick, & Wotton, 1996) that contains ten items (e.g., your child is out with friends you do not know) that parents rate on a 5-point scale from never to always. The Ghent Parenting Behavior Scale (Van Leeuwen & Vermulst, 2004) includes monitoring along with 4 other dimensions of parenting skills (involvement, discipline, positive reinforcement, and problem solving), all of which are measured based on behaviors parents do or don't do. Van Leeuwen & Vermulst (2004) point out that a key shortcoming of self ratings is that we must assume that such measures are valid and indicate real parenting behavior. Reliability may be an issue as well. Few researchers have assessed the temporal stability of parental monitoring. One exception is a study by Metzler, Biglan, Ary, and Li (1998). They assessed fifth through seventh graders' assessments of parental monitoring (amongst other parenting factors) at three points across 9 months and found the reports were stable over time.

Kerr & Stattin (2000) have attempted to measure both parent and child reports in a more sophisticated way. They investigated three potential sources of parental knowledge: the extent to which the child freely and willingly disclosed information; the degree to which parents asked their children, their child's peers, or the parents of their child's peers about information (defined as "parental solicitation"); and the degree to which parents controlled their child's freedom, e.g., requiring permission or explanations regarding their activities and whereabouts (defined as "parental control"). Kerr and Stattin (2000) found, as have others, that knowledge is associated with a variety of ways of measuring healthy or good adjustment, however, these effects are due to children's spontaneous disclosure of information rather than what is traditionally thought of as monitoring. They conclude "Across adjustment measures, gender, and informant, control and solicitation made relatively unimportant unique contributions to the prediction of adjustment. Furthermore, they were sometimes significantly linked to poorer, rather than better, adjustment. Child disclosure, in contrast, was always linked to better adjustment, and all but one of these relations were significant" (p. 373).

Dishion and McMahon (1998) acknowledge the difficulty of maintaining a consistent definition of parental monitoring across studies that vary in children's' ages and ecologies and outcomes of interest (safety, delinquency, substance use, etc.). They write "although the specific methods and foci of monitoring change at different developmental periods, the function of these activities is essentially the same: to facilitate parental awareness of the child's activities and to communicate to the child that the parent is concerned about, and aware of, the child's activities" (p.65).

Television Monitoring

Television monitoring, the extent to which parents oversee what or how much their children watch on TV, may be an important domain of parental monitoring. Nathanson has conducted research on television monitoring, termed parental mediation, and its relationship to aggressive behavior in children. Nathanson found that when children and parents watch violent television together, a type of mediation termed coviewing, children perceive their parents are endorsing the televised messages (2001) and this is associated with an increase in children's aggression (Nathanson, 2002). In contrast, when parents either place restrictions on their child's viewing (termed restrictive mediation) or openly criticize the content of televised violence (termed active negative mediation), their children exhibited less aggression (Nathanson, 2002).

In another study, however, even parents criticizing televised characters' body size and appearance was associated with stronger negative emotions and more body image disturbance among their adolescent children (Nathanson & Botta, 2003). Valkenburg, Krcmar, Peeters, & Marseille found that restrictive mediation was employed more often by mothers than by fathers, by parents of higher educational backgrounds, by parents of younger as opposed to older children, and by parents who are more concerned about television-induced aggression and fright in the children (1999). Existing monitoring measures investigate concurrent television monitoring as reported by parents (Holman & Braithwaite, 1982; Valkenburg et al., 1999) or adolescents (Austin, 1993). Currently, there is no known retrospective scale of parent monitoring in general (or of television monitoring in particular) that would allow a more complete understanding of the construct.

Parent-Child Discrepancies in Reports of Monitoring

In some studies, monitoring is defined as the extent to which parental reports and child reports about the child's activities are in agreement (Crouter et al., 1990; Patterson & Stouthamer-Loeber, 1984). "Measures that provide judgments of both parents and children are scarce" (Van Leeuwen & Vermulst, 2004, p. 284). Interestingly, research has shown that parents' reports and their children's reports of monitoring are often discrepant. Cottrell and colleagues found no correlation between parent and teen reports of parental monitoring in a sample of 270 parent-child pairs (2003). Ross and her colleagues (1997) found that the correlations between parents' and children's reports of parenting practices were fairly low. Parents, especially fathers, reported more monitoring than did their children.

Others have found parent-child discrepancies pertaining to television monitoring. Compared to their children's reports, parents claim lower levels of viewing by their children, stricter house rules about TV viewing, more co-viewing, and lower susceptibility to commercials in their children (Xiaoming, Stanton, & Feigelman, 2000). In addition, this idealized exaggeration by parents may increase with social class, suggesting an underlying social desirability bias in the basic pattern of parents' reports of monitoring (Rossiter & Robertson, 1975). Thus, compared to parents' reports, children's reports on monitoring may be more reliable and, therefore, a better predictor of behaviors and adjustment.

Monitoring is Associated with Fewer Behavior Problems

There is a link between less parental monitoring and offspring who struggle with behavioral disorders. For example, Elgar and colleagues (2007) found Canadian mothers and fathers who reported poorer supervision also reported their children had either oppositional defiant disorder or conduct disorder. Similarly, Berg-Nielsen, Vikan, and Dahl (2003) found less monitoring reported by Norwegian parents whose children had a behavioral disorder, compared to parents whose children either did not have a disorder or had an emotional disorder. Furthermore, they stated "Insufficient monitoring is the only parenting dimension of mothers and fathers associated with both daughters' and sons' anger" (p. 144). In another study, less parental monitoring and supervision (as measured by the Alabama Parenting Questionnaire) was correlated with higher conduct problem scores (Dadds et al., 2003).

When parents monitor their adolescents more closely, adolescents appear less likely to engage in risky or problem behaviors, even when the behaviors are not severe enough to warrant a diagnosis (Crouter & Head, 2002; Leventhal & Brooks-Gunn, 2000; Li, Stanton, & Feigelman, 2000). Metzler and colleagues (1998) found students' assessments of parental monitoring consistently predicted deviant peer associations and antisocial behavior amongst fifth, sixth, and seventh graders. Patterson and Stouthamer-Loeber (1984) assessed the degree to which mothers knew of their sons' activities: this aspect of monitoring strongly correlated with seventh and tenth graders' delinquency, moreso than the other aspects of parenting measured (i.e., reinforcing prosocial behavior, consistent discipline, and effective problem solving). Flannery, Williams, and Vazsonyi (1999) found that less parental monitoring was associated with a variety of problems for sixth and seventh graders, including more aggressive behavior and more delinquent behavior. Some researchers (Forehand, Miller, Dutra, & Chance, 1997) suggest that appropriate monitoring and supervision may be especially critical for preventing conduct problems in African-American families.

Pettit, Bates, Dodge, and Meece (1999) conducted longitudinal research and found weak parental monitoring, along with unsafe neighborhoods and unsupervised peer contact, predicted externalizing problems amongst seventh graders, after controlling for existing behavior problems and family risk factors. They concluded that the adolescents at greatest risk were those from low-monitoring homes who lived in unsafe neighborhoods. Also, mothers who reported less parental monitoring also reported their young adolescent spent more after-school time unsupervised with his or her peers (Pettit et al.), which helps explain the process by which less monitoring results in more problem behaviors. Crouter and colleagues (1990) note that the interaction of insufficient parental monitoring and having both parents working outside the home is particularly troublesome for boys' problem behavior. Of course, this could mean the family is struggling financially to make ends meet, or it could mean a family is higher in socioeconomic status and has two busy parents who both work outside the home. Among children in grades five through nine, "latchkey" teenagers appear less vulnerable to peer pressure providing their parents know where they are. Similarly, McCoy and colleagues (1999) suggest that poor parental monitoring mediates the relationship between low socioeconomic status and the development of children's conduct problems. Dishion, Patterson, Stoolmiller, and Skinner (1991) followed middle school students over time: poor parental monitoring predicted which children subsequently became more involved in a deviant peer network, above and beyond the initial levels of antisocial behavior and peer rejection.

One particular area of concern among researchers who investigate adolescent deviance is substance use. Several studies show support for the relation of greater parental monitoring to less substance use (Cottrell et al., 2003; Flannery et al., 1999; Guo, Hawkins, Hill, & Abbott, 2001; Metzler et al., 1998; Ross et al., 1997; Veal & Ross, 2006). Chassin et al. (1993) found low levels of paternal monitoring were a stronger predictor of adolescent substance abuse than low levels of maternal monitoring. Not only do well-monitored adolescents drink less, they also appear less likely to engage in a variety of alcohol-related risk behaviors (Beck, Boyle, & Boekeloo, 2003).

Much of the monitoring-substance use research is based on longitudinal designs. For example, Xiaoming, Stanton, and Feigelman (2000) report that the perception of being monitored by a parent is related to lower levels of alcohol consumption over a four-year period. Beck, Boyle, and Boekeloo (2004) followed teenagers over one year and found adolescents with strong parental monitoring were less likely to report alcohol consumption, even after statistically controlling for gender, age, and level of drinking at baseline. Simons-Morton, Chen, Abroms, and Haynie (2004) followed sixth graders over four years and found parental monitoring (along with parental involvement and expectations) protected against smoking both directly and indirectly, via limiting children's number of friends who smoke.

Drinking alcohol at a young age is a risk factor for developing alcoholism (Grant, Stinson, & Harford, 2001). Not surprisingly, then, parental monitoring has also been associated with the diagnosis of alcoholism. Guo, Hawkins, Hill, and Abbot (2001) found that both clear family rules and strong parental monitoring were significantly predictive of lower probabilities of alcohol abuse and/or dependence in adolescents, based on adolescents' reports. Furthermore, these factors were influential as early as elementary school and remained influential throughout high school. Clark, Neighbors, Lesnick, Lynch, and Donovan (1998) found that teens with an alcohol use disorder and teens with a psychiatric illness both report less monitoring than their peers with neither diagnosis. Of course, this association does not test which comes first, low monitoring or developing alcoholism or a mental illness.

Parental monitoring may act as a mediator (helping to explain the correlation between two variables) or a moderator (mitigating the effect of a second variable) for understanding adolescent substance use. Dishion and colleagues have demonstrated that lower parental monitoring is a mediator between parental drug use and adolescent drug use (Dishion, Patterson, & Reid, 1988). Parents who used drugs had impaired monitoring of their child's behavior and activities, which in turn increased the child's chances of sampling drugs. Similarly, Chassin et al (1993) compared 10-15 year olds with and without an alcoholic parent and found that weaker parental monitoring mediated the relation between having an alcoholic parent and adolescent substance use. Dick and colleagues (2007) found a moderating effect of monitoring on adolescent smoking. Among teens with less parental monitoring, genetic influences were stronger predictors of smoking, yet among teens with more parental monitoring, smoking was more strongly related to environmental influences.

It would seem likely that television monitoring, like parental monitoring, would relate to lower levels of alcohol consumption. The American Academy of Pediatrics explicitly states that excess television viewing is bad for children, exposing them to more than 20,000 commercials each year, including those for beer and tobacco products (2004). Given that heavy television viewers (and poorly monitored children) are frequently exposed to these powerful forms of advertising, the possibility that these messages are partially responsible for adolescent drinking should be explored. Although heavy television viewers are more likely than light or moderate viewers to drink heavily and regularly (Tucker, 1985), at present there is a dearth of research on this relationship and whether such associations occur in younger viewers. Furthermore, there is little research on the association between parental television monitoring and alcohol consumption. One exception is a study by Veal and Ross (2006) who examined monitoring, biological sex, and drinking: men who recalled less television monitoring growing up also reported more frequent drinking and binge drinking in college.

Monitoring has been linked to areas other than behavior problems and substance use. For example, Cottrell and others (2003) found teen perceptions of low monitoring correlated with more sexual activity. In another study, higher monitoring was associated with more psychosocial well-being among African American teens (Salem, Zimmerman, & Notaro, 1998). Monitoring has also been linked to academic functioning as well: Crouter and colleagues (1990) found that boys who were less well monitored had lower grades in school, compared to their peers who were either female or boys who had more monitoring.

In an attempt to understand parental monitoring, we conducted research to develop retrospective scales of the construct and provide preliminary construct validity. In the remaining section of the chapter we describe the development of these scales and how scores related to family functioning and binge drinking. We hypothesized that both parental monitoring and television monitoring would positively correlate with overall family functioning. Finally, we hypothesized that both types of monitoring would be negatively correlated with drinking.

METHOD OF THE CURRENT STUDY

Our participants were 205 psychology students at a medium-sized, liberal arts and sciences college in the Southeastern United States. There were 65 male and 140 female participants; the majority (79%) was Caucasian, whereas 12% identified themselves as African American and 9% reported other ethnic identities. The mean age was 19.8, with a total range of 18-50 yrs. Students received research credit or extra credit toward their class for participating, and there were comparable alternatives for earning extra or research credit for those students who were not interested in research participation. The research protocol was approved by the Institutional Review Board at the college. Students completed a survey anonymously, either in class or in group sessions outside of class. Informed consent was obtained and all participants were debriefed upon survey completion.

Students answered retrospective questions from Hovestadt's (1985) Family of Origin Scale (FOS) to assess family functioning. All 40 questions from the scale were used in their original format. The FOS contains two subscales that measure autonomy (i.e. claiming one's own identity) and intimacy (i.e. maintaining closeness), components within the family that relate to better family functioning overall. Autonomy was assessed by such questions as "family members were allowed to speak for themselves." Intimacy was measured by questions like "family members are sensitive to one another." Combining these two scales yields an overall score of family functioning, whereby higher scores reflect healthier family functioning. In the present sample, the overall scale and the autonomy and intimacy subscales were found to be reliable (Cronbach's alpha = .97, .93, and .95, respectively).

Students responded to 22 retrospective questions generated by the research team to assess general and television monitoring by parents while growing up. There were 11 pertaining to parental monitoring (e.g.," My parents knew how much homework I had to do each day") and 11 pertaining to television monitoring (e.g., "My parents pre-approved the television shows they let me watch."). Higher scores on each reflect more monitoring. As discussed in the results section, the use of factor analysis and reliability analysis helped determine the final 7 items for each of these two scales.

In addition, students completed a short form of the Marlow-Crowne Social Desirability Scale (Strahan & Gerbasi, 1972) to assess proneness to social desirability (i.e., responding to questions in a way that is socially accepted as the right thing). Questions include "I'm always willing to admit it when I make a mistake" and "I have never intensely disliked someone." Higher scores reflect more susceptibility to social desirability. In the present sample, the Social Desirability scale had relatively low reliability (Cronbach's alpha = .64).

Students also answered demographic questions and three alcohol consumption questions (from Hilton & Clark, 1987). Alcohol frequency was measured with the question "How many days in the past 30 did you drink beer, wine, wine coolers, or liquor?" Alcohol quantity was measured with the question "Think of one drink as meaning 12 ounces of beer, 4 ounces of wine, a 10 ounce wine cooler, or one ounce of liquor. On the days that you drank alcohol in the past 30 days, how many drinks did you usually have per day?" Binge drinking frequency was measured with the question "On the days that you drank alcohol in the past 30 days, on how many days did you drink 5 or more drinks?" Non-drinkers were assigned a zero score for the quantity variable and the binge drinking variable.

RESULTS: DEVELOPING NEW SCALES

An iterative series of factor analyses and reliability analyses determined which of the original items to keep in the final scales. The factor analyses were conducted with Varimax rotation and the analysis was constrained to two factors. Three items were deleted because they loaded above .30 on both factors. The final Parental Monitoring Scale (PMS) contained 7 items and demonstrated acceptable internal consistency (Cronbach's alpha = .79). The final Television Monitoring Scale (TMS) contained 7 items and also demonstrated acceptable internal consistency (Cronbach's alpha =. 84). One item had a primary loading of .48 and a secondary loading of .39, however it was included in the final version because deleting it did not improve the internal consistency. All final items for each survey are found in the Appendix. Neither the PMS or the TMS correlated with social desirability, rs = .058 and .025, ns, respectively. Both types of monitoring were correlated with each other, r (193) = .40, p < .001, but not so highly correlated that they were measuring the same facet of the proposed monitoring construct. Thus, the initial goal of constructing these two scales was met.

RESULTS: MONITORING AND FAMILY FUNCTIONING

The correlations among parental and television monitoring, family functioning, and drinking are summarized in Table 1. PMS scores were positively correlated with overall healthy family functioning, as well as with increased intimacy and autonomy.

Table 1. Relationships Among Television Monitoring, Parental Monitoring, Family Functioning, and Binge Drinking (Listwise N = 171)

	TMS	PMS	Aut.	Intimacy	Function	Freq.	Quant.	Binge
TMS	1							
PMS	.37**	1						
Autonomy	-.02	.31**	1					
Intimacy	-.03	.34**	.91**	1				
Family Functioning	-.03	.34**	.97**	.98**	1			
Alcohol Frequency	-.19*	-.19*	.05	.10	.08	1		
Alcohol Quantity	-.10	-.22**	.07	.09	.08	.49**	1	
Binge Frequency	-.18*	-.20**	.08	.13	.11	.77**	.62**	1
M	3.21	4.30	3.74	3.93	3.83	6.32	3.46	3.31
SD	1.27	1.08	.69	.72	.69	7.03	3.44	5.17

** $p < 0.01$ level (2-tailed).
• $p < 0.05$ level (2-tailed).

Note: PMS = Parental Monitoring Scale & TMS = Television Monitoring Scale

However, TMS scores were not significantly correlated with these three measures of family functioning. Thus, the first hypothesis that parental monitoring and television monitoring would correlate with overall family functioning was partially supported.

RESULTS: MONITORING AND DRINKING

Overall, both PMS scores and TMS scores were negatively correlated with recent drinking (see Table 1). Higher scores on both PMS and TMS correlated with drinking on fewer days in the past month and with binge drinking on fewer days in the past month. Only PMS scores correlated with the typical quantity consumed in the past month. Therefore, the second hypothesis that both types of monitoring would correlate negatively with drinking was supported. It is interesting to note that overall family functioning did not correlate with drinking, nor did scores on the autonomy and intimacy subscales.

CONCLUSION

This chapter has summarized the research on parental monitoring and presents two new retrospective scales related to parental monitoring and television monitoring. Both scales for parental monitoring and television monitoring were internally consistent and free from social desirability. Preliminary validity was established for the Parental Monitoring Scale by showing it is indeed associated with healthier family functioning. More parental monitoring also indicated more intimacy and autonomy in one's family of origin. It makes intuitive sense that students recalling more parental monitoring in their families of origin would also recall more closeness (i.e., intimacy) in their families. This reinforces the conceptualization of monitoring as relevant to a secure family attachment (Parker & Benson, 2004; Sroufe & Waters, 1977).

The association between monitoring and autonomy is less intuitive; parents allowing their children to claim their identity and assert their uniqueness may seem contradictory to parents' knowing their children's friends and whereabouts. Also, there was not a particular time frame for describing childhood monitoring, therefore the autonomy-monitoring link may reflect older adolescence, when adolescents might perceive too much traditional monitoring as a threat to their autonomy (Smetana & Asquith, 1994). However, parental monitoring and autonomy may both share underlying variance associated with overall healthier family functioning. Or, perhaps monitoring sets up a structure or scaffold for parenting, and within that structure parents can encourage their children to develop their sense of selves.

Interestingly, the Television Monitoring Scale did not correlate with overall family functioning or with autonomy or intimacy, failing to support our expectation that television monitoring would also be negatively correlated with family dysfunction. At best this seems to be an indirect relationship, as television monitoring relates to parental monitoring, which in turn relates to family functioning. Thus, the first hypothesis was supported with regards to overall parental monitoring but not at all supported with regards to television monitoring.

Higher levels of both parental and television monitoring related to less frequent drinking and less frequent binge drinking, supporting the second hypothesis. Parental monitoring was associated with less quantity of alcohol consumption as well. This is consistent with prior findings on parental monitoring and drinking (Pettit et al., 2001, and Guo et al., 2000). Presumably, those with less television monitoring also view more television, an interpretation consistent with prior research that heavy viewers drink more (Tucker, 1985). For additional details on gender differences in the monitoring-drinking relationship, see Veal and Ross (2006).

It is important to note that the relationships between parental monitoring and drinking were modest, which would be expected for at least two reasons. First, there are numerous influences on older adolescents' drinking. Second, as children grow from childhood to adolescence and again from adolescence to adulthood, the influence of one's parents naturally diminishes over time as children become more entrenched in peer groups (Larson & Richards, 1991) and have somewhat weaker emotional ties with their parents (Steinberg & Silverberg, 1986). Interestingly, healthier family functioning, and the subscales autonomy and intimacy, did not relate to drinking, which is inconsistent with previous research (Loveland-Cherry et al., 1999; McKay, Murphy, & Rivinus, 1991). These results imply that more healthy parental involvement, characterized by higher levels of both types of monitoring, may decrease the risk of adolescent drinking. Perhaps adolescents with more involved parents are less vulnerable to harmful peer pressure and media messages to drink, or perhaps these adolescents have better mental health and are therefore less likely to cope with feelings of anxiety or depression by drinking.

There are several caveats pertaining to the data to consider. First, as with all research, correlation does not equal causation. Although parental monitoring relates to both family dysfunction and binge drinking, there is no way to infer from the study's design that one factor causes another. This is true even though monitoring and functioning assessments were retrospective and drinking measures referred to the prior month. Secondly, the use of college students as participants does not offer a representative sample of the population of older adolescents, as they are limited in age and life experiences. This sample does not include adolescents who are old enough to attend college but do not do so, or who are younger and still live at home. Furthermore, the sample is comprised of predominantly white females, which further restricts generalizability. Research based on a sample of adolescents that is more diverse, with regards to age, ethnicity, gender and non-college attendance, will yield more comprehensive findings on the present issues. Finally, the use of retrospective questions in the survey may be cause for bias in the students' answers since biases are known to exist in recall of earlier events (McNally, 2003).

The newly generated scales for parental and television monitoring, as well as the finding that both types of monitoring are related to drinking, allows for new avenues of research. For example, the new scales for parental and television monitoring derived from this study may prove to be a very useful tool to researchers interested in parental and television influences on adolescents, including their drinking behaviors, risky sexual behaviors, and other forms of risk taking. In addition, researchers may wish to modify the PMS or the TMS to create a concurrent version to assess possible effects of recent parental or television monitoring. These suggestions for additional research generated by the new scales are pivotal, as they offer the possibility of discovering exciting new ways to decrease and even prevent problem behaviors among adolescents, including binge drinking.

Parents must be educated on the importance of monitoring their children, as it relates to raising healthy children. Beck and colleagues state: "The need to enhance parental monitoring as a proactive protective parental response is indicated." (2003, p. 108). Flannery and colleagues (1999) noted that being home alone after school is a particularly vulnerable time of day for problem behaviors to develop among adolescents; they note that "while latchkey children go home to an empty house and spend time alone, they may still be "available" to monitoring by parents, who can reach them at home and who presumably know where they are and what they are doing" (p. 250). Dishion and McMahon (1998) point out the need to promote monitoring in order to prevent negative outcomes among offspring; they claim "It is a variable that shows promise as a malleable risk and/or protective factor that could also serve as an intervention target" (p. 61).

ACKNOWLEDGMENTS

The authors would like to thank Thomas P. Ross for helpful editorial comments.

REFERENCES

American Academy of Pediatrics (2004). Television and the family. Retrieved January 22, 2004 from http://www.aap.org//family/tv1.htm.

Austin, E.W. (1993). Exploring the effects of active parental mediation of television content. *Journal of Broadcasting & Electronic Media, 37,* 147-158.

Beck, K.H., Boyle, J.R., & Boekeloo, B.O. (2003). Parental monitoring and adolescent alcohol risk in a clinic population. *American Journal of Health Behavior, 27,* 108-115.

Beck, K.H., Boyle, J.R., & Boekeloo, B.O. (2004). Parental monitoring and adolescent drinking: Results of a 12-month follow-up. *American Journal of Health Behavior, 28,* 272-279.

Berg-Nielsen, T.S., Vikan, A., & Dahl, A. A. (2003). Specific parenting problems when adolescents have emotional and behavioural disorders. *Nordic Journal of Psychiatry, 57,* 139-146.

Caprara, R. Scabini, E., Barbaranelli, C., & Bandura, A. (2004). Assessment of filial, parental, marital, and collective family efficacy beliefs. *European Journal of Psychological Assessment, 20,* 247-261.

Chassin, L., Pillow, D.R., Curran, P.J, Molina, B.S. G., & Barrera, M. (1993). Relation of parental alcoholism to early adolescent substance use: A test of three mediating mechanisms. *Journal of Abnormal Psychology, 102,* 3-19.

Clark, D. B., Neighbors, B. D., Lesnick, L. A., Lynch, K. G. & Donovan, J.E. (1998). Family functioning and adolescent alcohol use disorders. *Journal of Family Psychology, 12,* 81-92.

Cottrell, L., Li, X., Harris, C., D'Alessandri, D., Atkins, M., Richardson, B., & Stanton, B. (2003). Parent and adolescent perceptions of parental monitoring and adolescent risk involvement. *Parenting: Science and Practice, 3,* 179-195.

Crouter, A.C., MacDermid, S.M., McHale, S.M., & Perry-Jenkins, M. (1990). Parental monitoring and perceptions of children's school performance and conduct in dual- and single-earner families. *Developmental Psychology, 26,* 649-657

Dadds, M.R., Maujean, A., & Fraser, J.A. (2003). Parenting and conduct problems in children: Australian data and psychometric properties of the Alabama Parenting Questionnaire. *Australian Psychologist, 38,* 238-241.

Dick, D. M., Viken, R., Purcell, S., Kaprio, J., Pulkkinen, L., & Rose, R. J. (2007). Parental monitoring moderates the importance of genetic and environmental influences on adolescent smoking. *Journal of Abnormal Psychology, 116*, 213-218.

Dishion, T. J., Patterson, G. R., & Reid, J. R. (1988). Parent and peer factors associated with drug sampling in early adolescence: Implications for treatment. In E. R. Rahdert & J. Grabowski (Eds.), *Adolescent drug abuse: Analyses of treatment research* (NIDA Research Monograph No. 77, DHHS Publication No. ADM88-1523) (pp. 69–93). Rockville, MD: National Institute on Drug Abuse.

Dishion, T.J., Patterson, G.R., Stoolmiller, M., & Skinner, M.L. (1991). Family, school, and behavioral antecedents to early adolescent involvement with antisocial peers. *Developmental Psychology, 27,* 172-180.

Dishion, T.J. & McMahon, R.J. (1998) Parental monitoring and the prevention of child and adolescent problem behavior: A conceptual and empirical formulation. *Clinical Child and Family Psychology Review, 1,* 61-75.

Elgar, F.J., Waschbusch, D.A., Dadds, M.R., & Sigvaldason, N. (2007). Development and validation of a short form of the Alabama Parenting Questionnaire. *Journal of Child and Family Studies, 16*, 243–259.

Flannery, D.J., Williams, L.L., & Vazsonyi, A.T. (1999). Who are they with and what are they doing? Delinquent behavior, substance use, and early adolescents' after-school time. *American Journal of Orthopsychiatry, 69*, 247-253.

Forehand, R. & Jones, D.J. (2002). The stability of parenting: A longitudinal analysis of inner-city African-American mothers. *Journal of Child and Family Studies, 11*, 469-483.

Frick, P.J. Christian, R.E., & Wooton, J.M. (1999). Age trends in association between parenting practices and conduct problems. *Behavior Modification, 23*, 106-128.

Grant, B. F., Stinson, F.S., & Harford, T.C. (2001). Age at *onset* of alcohol use and DSM-IV alcohol abuse and dependence: A 12-year follow-up. *Journal of Substance Abuse, 13*, 493-504.

Guo, J., Hawkins, J.D., Hill, K.G., & Abbott, R.D. (2001). Childhood and adolescent predictors of alcohol abuse and dependence in young adulthood. *Journal of Studies on Alcohol, 62,* 754-762.

Hagan, L. K. & Kuebli, J. (2007). Mothers' and fathers' socialization of preschoolers' physical risk taking. *Journal of Applied Developmental Psychology, 28*, 2–14.

Harris, J. R. (1998). *The Nurture Assumption.* New York: Free Press.

Hilton, M.E. & Clark, W.B. (1987). Changes in American drinking patterns and problems, 1967-1984. *Journal of Studies on Alcohol, 48*, 515-522.

Holman, J, & Braithwaite, V.A. (1982). Parental lifestyles and children's television viewing. *Australian Journal of Psychology, 34,* 375-382.

Hovestadt, A.J. (1985). A Family of Origin Scale. *Journal of Marital and Family Therapy, 11*, 287-297.

Johnston, L.D., O'Malley, P.M., Bachman, J.G., & Schulenberg, J.E. (2005). *Monitoring the Future national survey results on drug use, 1975-2004: Volume II, College students and adults aged 19-45.* (NIH publication No. 05-5728). Bethesda, MD: National Institute on Drug Abuse.

Kerr, M., & Stattin, H. (2000). What parents know, how they know it, and several forms of adolescent adjustment: Further support for a reinterpretation of monitoring. *Developmental Psychology, 36*, 366-380

Kerr, M., & Stattin, H. (2003). Parenting of adolescents: Action or reaction? In A.C. Crouter and A. Booth (Eds). *Children's influence on family dynamics: The neglected side of family relationships,* 121-151. Mahwah, NJ: Lawrence Erlbaum Associates.

Laird, R.D., Pettit, G.S., Dodge, K. A., & Bates, J.E. (2003). Change in parents' monitoring knowledge: Links with parenting, relationship quality, adolescent beliefs, and antisocial behavior. *Social Development, 12,* 401-419.

Larson, R., & Richards, M.H. (1991). Daily companionship in late childhood and early adolescence: Changing developmental contexts. *Child Development, 62,* 284-300.

Leventhal, T. & Brooks-Gunn, J. (2000). The effects of neighborhood residences on child and adolescent outcomes. *Psychological Bulletin, 126,* 309-337.

Loveland-Cherry, C.J., Ross, L.T., & Kaufman, S.R. (1999). Effects of a home-based family intervention on adolescent use and misuse. *Journal of Studies on Alcohol, 13,* 94-102.

McCoy, M.G., Frick, P.J., Loney, B.R., & Ellis, M.L. (1999). The potential mediating role of parenting practices in the development of conduct problems in a clinic-referred sample. *Journal of Child and Family Studies, 8,* 477-494.

McKay, J.R., Murphy, R.T., & Rivinus, T.R., (1991). Family dysfunction and alcohol and drug use in adolescent psychiatric patients. *Journal of the American Academy of Child and Adolescent Psychiatry, 30,* 967-972.

McNally, R.T. (2003). Recovering memories of trauma: A view from the laboratory. *Current Directions in Psychological Science, 12,* 32-35.

Metzler, C.W, Biglan, A., Ary, D.V., & Li, F. (1998). The stability and validity of early adolescents' reports of parenting constructs. *Journal of Family Psychology, 12,* 600-619.

Nathanson, A.I. (2001). Parent and child perspectives on the presence and meaning of parental television mediation. *Journal of Broadcasting and Electronic Media, 45,* 201-220.

Nathanson, A.I. (2002). The unintended effects of parental mediation of television on adolescents. *Mediapsychology, 4,* 207-230.

Nathanson, A.I. & Botta, R.A. (2003). Shaping the effects of television on adolescents' body image disturbance: The role of parental mediation. *Communication Research, 30,* 304-331.

Parker, J.S. & Benson, M.J. (2004). Parent-adolescent relations and adolescent functioning: self-esteem, substance abuse, and delinquency *Adolescence, 39,* 519-530.

Patterson, G.R., & Stouthamer-Loeber, M. (1984). The forrelation of family management practices and delinquency. *Child Development, 55,* 1299-1307.

Pettit, G.S., Laird, R.D., Dodge, K.A., Bates, J.E., & Criss, M.M. (2001). Antecedents and behavior-problem outcomes of parental monitoring and psychological control in early adolescence. *Child Development, 72,* 583-598.

Pettit, G.S., Bates, J.E., Dodge, K.A., & Meece, D.W. (1999). The impact of after-school peer contact on early adolescent externalizing problems is moderated by parental monitoring, perceived neighborhood safety, and prior adjustment. *Child Development, 70,* 768-778.

Ross, L.T., Leech, S.L., & Loveland-Cherry, C. (1997, April). *Parenting practices and substance use: Child and parent agreement.* Poster presented at the Society for Research in Child Development meeting, Washington D.C.

Rossiter, J.R. & Robertson, T.S. (1975). Children's television viewing: An examination of parent-child consensus. *Sociometry, 38,* 308-326.

Salem, D.A., Zimmerman, M.A. & Notaro, P.C. (1998). Effects of family structure, family process, and father involvement on psychosocial outcomes among African American adolescents. *Family Relations, 47*, Special issue: The family as a context for health and well-being, 331-341.

Shelton, K.K., Frick, P.J., & Wotton, J. (1996). Assessment of parenting practices in families of elementary school-age children. *Journal of Child Clinical Psychology, 25*, 317-129.

Simons-Morton, B., Chen, R., Abroms, L., & Haynie, D. L. (2004). Latent growth curve analyses of peer and parent influences on smoking progression among early adolescents. *Health Psychology, 23*, 612-621.

Smetana, J. G. & Asquith, P, (1994). Adolescents' and parents' conceptions of parental authority and personal autonomy. *Child Development, 65*, 1147-1162.

Stanton, B.F., Li, X., Galbraith, J., Cornick, G., Feigelman, S., Kaljee, L., & Zhou, Y. (2000). Parental underestimates of adolescent risk behavior: A randomized, controlled trial of a parental monitoring intervention. *Journal of Adolescent Health, 26*, 18-26.

Steinberg, L. (1986). Latchkey children and the susceptibility to peer pressure: An ecological analysis. *Developmental Psychology,22*, 433-439.

Steinberg, L. & Silverberg, S.B. (1986). The vicissitudes of autonomy in early adolescence. *Child Development, 57*, 841-851.

Strahan, R. & Gerbasi, K.C. (1972). Short, homogeneous versions of the Marlow-Crowne Social Desirability Scale. Journal of Clinical Psychology, 28, 191-193.

Sroufe, L.A. & Waters, E. (1977). Attachment as an organizational construct. *Child Development, 48, 1184-1199.*

Tucker, L.A. (1985). Television's role regarding alcohol use among teenagers. *Adolescence, 20*, 593-598.

Svensson, R. (2003). Gender differences in adolescent drug use: The impact of parental monitoring and peer deviance. *Youth & Society, 34*, 300-329.

Valkenburg, P.M., Krcmar, M., Peeters, A.L., & Marseille. N.M. (1999). Developing a scale to assess three styles of television mediation: "Instructive Mediation," "Restrictive Mediation," and "Social Coviewing." *Journal of Broadcast and Electronic Media, 43*, 52-66.

Van Leeuwen, K.G. & Vermulst, A.A. (2004). Some psychometric properties of the Ghent Parental Behavior Scale. *European Journal of Psychological Assessment, 20, 283–298.*

Veal, M.L. & Ross, L.T. (2006). Gender, alcohol consumption, and parental monitoring. *Journal of Psychology, 140, 41-52.*

Webb, J.A., Bray, J.H., Getz, J.G., & Adams, G. (2002). Gender, perceived parental monitoring and behavioral adjustment: Influences on adolescent alcohol use. *American Journal of Orthopsychiatry, 72*, 392-400.

Weintraub, K.J. & Gold, M. (1991). Monitoring and delinquency. *Criminal Behaviour and Mental Health, 1*, 268-281.

Xiaoming, L., Stanton, B. & Feigelman, S. (2000). Impact of perceived parental monitoring on adolescent risk behavior over 4 years. *Journal of Adolescent Health, 27*, 49-56.

APPENDIX

Please answer the following questions according to this scale. Base your responses on your family life while you were growing up (i.e., up to age 18).

1	2	3	4	5	6
strongly agree	moderately agree	mildly agree	mildly disagree	moderately disagree	strongly disagree

PMS

1. My parents knew where I was during my free time (i.e., not in school or at work). _____

2. My parents knew how I spent the money I had saved. _____

3. My parents knew who I was with during my free time (i.e., not at school or work). _____

4. My parents had restrictions about how old I had to be in order to date. _____

5. I had a curfew (i.e., I had to be back home in the evening or at night by a certain time). _____

6. My parents knew how much homework I had to do each day. _____

7. My parents knew when I had tests, papers, or projects due at school. _____

TMS

1. My parents set either daily or weekly limits on the amount of television I could watch. _____

2. I was allowed to watch as much television as I pleased. (R) _____

3. I was not allowed to watch certain shows because my parents thought they had inappropriate content (e.g., violence, sex, swearing, or drug use). _____

4. I was allowed to stay up at night and watch television if I wanted to. (R) _____

5. My parents pre-approved the television shows they let me watch. _____

6. My parents let me watch the television shows they were watching, regardless of the content. (R) _____

7. My parents let me watch whatever television shows I wanted. (R) _____

(R) these items are recoded so 1=6, 2=5, 3=4, 4=3, 5=2, 6=1

In: Handbook of Parenting: Styles, Stresses & Strategies   ISBN 978-1-60741-766-8
Editor: Pacey H. Krause and Tahlia M. Dailey   © 2009 Nova Science Publishers, Inc.

Chapter 4

PARENTING IN THE CONTEXT OF MARGINALIZATION: MOVING TOWARDS A COMPREHENSIVE FRAMEWORK[*]

Kelly E. McShane[1] and Nicole Schaefer-McDaniel[2]

1) Department of Psychology, Ryerson University
Toronto Ontario Canada M5B 2K3
2) Centre for Research on Inner City Health, St. Michael's Hospital,
Toronto, Ontario Canada M5B 1W8

PARENTING IN THE CONTEXT OF MARGINALIZATION: MOVING TOWARDS A COMPREHENSIVE FRAMEWORK

In the past few decades, there has been increasing research on the relationship between parenting behaviors and children's developmental outcomes. Within this body of literature, scholars have identified that certain parenting styles (e.g., parental warmth, support) promote positive child behaviors, whereas harsh and authoritative parenting practices are associated with negative child outcomes such as increases in aggression and externalizing disorders (e.g., Bendersky et al., 2006; Krenichyn, Saegert, & Evans, 2001; Patterson, 1992).

Our discussion on parenting styles, stressors, and practices focuses on child aggression, an umbrella term we use to refer to any "acting-out" or externalizing behaviors including violent behaviors and acts of delinquency. This commentary draws upon insights from individual, family, and contextual-level research on parenting and Bronfenbrenner's (1977; 1979; 1989) ecological systems theory to set future directions for scholars examining parenting and child aggression among marginalized populations. We advocate that researchers should contextualize children and their families not only in relation to factors within the child or parent, but also in relation to the neighborhoods in which they live, the

---

[*] Disclaimer: The views expressed in this chapter are the views of the authors and do not necessarily reflect the views of the Ontario Ministry of Health and Long-Term Care.
[1] 350 Victoria Street, Phone: 416-979-5000, x 2051, Email: kmcshane@psych.ryerson.ca

schools they attend, and other influential contexts of which the child and family are not directly a part. Such a comprehensive approach is necessary when examining parenting in marginalized populations as it has the potential to more accurately capture the multifaceted stressors faced by this population.

INDIVIDUAL AND FAMILY APPROACHES TO PARENTING AND CHILDREN'S AGGRESSION

Developmental psychologists have devoted considerable time to the study of aggression and other forms of externalizing problems. Particular attention has been paid to the study of predictors of the development of aggression, perhaps in part because aggression is relatively stable from early childhood onwards (Rubin et al., 2003). Based on writings by Hinde (1976; 1987; 1989) and Rubin and colleagues (2003), factors related to externalizing problems or aggression are often grouped into three categories: (1) internal factors (gender, temperament, regulatory process); (2) socialization factors (parenting style, attachment, peers); and (3) external factors (socioeconomic status, family structure). Most research has focused on the first two sets of factors and more recently on the combination of these issues.

Research examining internal factors related to aggression has found that being male (Cairns & Cairns, 2000) and having a difficult or reactive temperament[2] are linked to aggression. Children with a difficult or reactive temperament show high negative affectivity; they become easily frustrated, showing anger or irritability (Rothbart & Putnam, 2002). With technological advances, researchers have been able to examine neurobiological and physiological markers in children to further identify individual factors related to aggression. Gordis and colleagues (2006) gathered data on two neurobiological markers relevant to stress in children which have previously been linked to aggression; α-amylase (A-A) and salivary cortisol. A-A is considered a measure of sympathetic nervous system activity and represents the body's "fight or flight" response (Cannon, 1914), whereby elevated levels are indicative of increased activity when faced with stress (Nater et al., 2005). Low levels of salivary cortisol are hypothesized to signal low inhibition, anxiety, and fear, thereby making aggression responses more likely (Van de Wiel et al., 2006). In a sample of adolescents who were exposed to stress in a laboratory setting, low A-A and low salivary cortisol responses were associated with increased parent-reported adolescent aggression. The links between these neurobiological markers and aggression held true even after accounting for adolescents' gender and maltreatment status.

The link between aggression and socialization factors has also received significant attention in the literature. In particular, the associations between parenting styles and dimensions, and aggression are well established. In brief, negative parental behaviors, including low warmth, high directiveness, and high physical and/or verbal punishment have been linked to increased aggression and hostility in children (Rubin & Burgess, 2002).

---

[2] Temperament is defined as an individual's level of emotional and physical (i.e., motor) reactivity during a challenging situation (Degnan, Calkins, Keane, & Hill-Soderlund, 2008). In particular, it is the nature of the reactivity and the regulation of the reactivity that are essential.

When both internal and socialization factors are investigated simultaneously, the combination of negative maternal behaviors and emotional dysregulation[3] is associated with aggression in toddlers (Rubin et al., 2003). It is particularly challenging to identify which of the factors (internal vs. socialization) has the "ultimate" impact on the development of aggression; however, longitudinal research with preschoolers has found that a dysregulated child may predict negative parental behaviors, which in turn can lead to aggression (Rubin et al., 1999). Such a transactional model of child and parent characteristics is at the core of Patterson's (1982) coercion model of antisocial behavior. The model posits that children's aggressive or hostile behaviors are reinforced throughout a series of harsh and punitive actions between parents and children. Over time, conflicts escalate and parents submit to their children's coercive demands, thereby reinforcing the aggressive behavior. Results from a large longitudinal study examining family and child characteristics on the development of aggression concluded that both maternal coercive behavior and child temperament were linked to aggression; however it was not possible exclude the possibility of a reciprocal effect between these two factors (Tremblay et al., 2005). Other research suggests that there is an additive effect of child and parent characteristics on the development of aggression in preschoolers. A population-based study examined parenting and child temperament and found that both negative emotionality (similar to difficult or reactive temperament) and harsh parenting were jointly associated with reactive aggression (Vitaro, Barker, Boivin, Brendgen, & Tremblay, 2006).

Researchers have also studied the links between internal and external factors. In a meta-analysis of studies examining aggression during childhood and adolescence, a medium effect size was calculated between gender and direct aggression, with more direct aggression noted in boys (Card, Stucky, Sawalani, & Little, 2008). Other studies have examined pre-existing internal factors: Bendersky, Bennett, and Lewis (2006) examined the effects of prenatal exposure to cocaine, gender, and environmental risk on preschoolers' aggression. Research has suggested that cocaine disrupts the development of the dopaminergic neuronal circuit, which is relevant to reactivity, arousal modulation and attention regulation (Anderson-Brown, Slotkin, & Seidler, 1990). Other research has found that deficits in this circuit are associated with aggressive behavior (Damasio et al., 1994). Further research has indicated that gender may moderate the associations, such that the links hold for boys alone (Delaney-Black et al., 2000). Suffice to say, the links between cocaine exposure and aggression are complex, but have nevertheless been supported by research. The research by Bendersky and colleagues also examined the effects of environmental risk, as evidenced by family chaos, maternal social support and life stress. Aggression at age 5 was associated with being male, increased environmental risk, and prenatal exposure to cocaine.

In sum, there is evidence to suggest that internal factors such as child gender, intrauterine environment, neurobiological markers, and certain socialization factors including negative parenting harshness behaviors are linked with aggression in children and adolescents. However, the relationships are not strictly unidirectional, as suggested by Patterson's model, and the associations are not simply limited to internal or socialization factors. The findings from Bendersky et al. (2006) point to the need to include and accurately account for other factors, namely "external factors", which Rubin and colleagues delineate as encompassing

---

[3] Negativity affectivity or difficult/reactive temperament is conceptualized as a predisposing factor for emotional dysregulation (Berdan, Keane, & Calkins, 2008)

socioeconomic status and family structure. In the broader field of social science, theory and research on such factors is well established and have been conceptualized as contextual or ecological approaches.

CONTEXTUAL APPROACHES TO PARENTING AND CHILDREN'S AGGRESSION

In recent years, social science research has shifted focus from studying the family as an individual unit to studying parenting and family life at an ecological level. This shift coincided with theoretical advances, most notably Urie Bronfenbrenner's ecological systems theory. By suggesting that behavior is "embedded in the larger social structures of community, society, economics, and politics" (Moen, 1995, p. 1), Bronfenbrenner noted that we live in a dynamic system of interconnected settings or contexts, each with its own set of rules and norms. Recognizing the impact and interaction of these settings is essential for understanding human development and behavior.

Bronfenbrenner's theory (1977; 1979; 1989) especially emphasizes the following four contexts: *Microsystems* are settings of which a person is a part such as the home or school and with which the person comes into regular, direct contact. *Mesosystems* are an extension of microsystems and refer to the connections and interactions of the major settings in a person's life (e.g., the connection between the school and home). Mesosystems are thus concerned with how well various microsystems work together. *Exosystems* refer to the larger formal and informal structures that do not include the person directly but can nevertheless influence a person. Examples for this context include a parent's workplace, governmental policies, or the welfare system. Lastly, *macrosystems* refer to the larger socio-cultural beliefs, values, laws, and practices of a community of which a person is a part. Bronfenbrenner's theory also highlights the transactional capabilities of people and contexts so that systems not only affect people's actions but people alter settings as well.

Bronfenbrenner's model clearly accounts for some of the more "distal" factors and their influence on children's behaviors. For example, although there is some evidence to suggest that internal or child factors have a greater impact on aggression, the evidence is not equivocal. Ho, Bluestein, and Jenkins (2008) analyzed data from the National Longitudinal Study of Children and Youth in Canada, including a total of 14,990 families from European, East Asian, South Asian, Caribbean, and Aboriginal backgrounds. Parental harshness and teacher-reported children's aggression were positively associated for European Canadian families and negatively associated for South Asian Canadian families. Thus, focusing on the child and family level factors alone (the microsystem) creates an over-simplification of the association with aggression; by acknowledging the impact of external factors such as culture (the macrosystem), a more complete and accurate perspective emerges.

Residential neighborhood environments have also received growing attention as a microsystem in recent years. While Bronfenbrenner's theory (1977) originally suggested that neighborhoods function as an exosystem, researchers currently argue that neighborhoods can be considered a microsystem since residents come into direct contact with it on a daily basis (Brooks-Gunn, Duncan, & Aber, 1997). This is particularly true for children and young people who spend a significant time outside exploring their neighborhoods (Chawla, 2002;

Hart, 1979; Lynch, 1977; Proshansky & Fabian, 1987). After all, children and adolescents are the primary consumers of the neighborhood (Holaday, Swan, & Turner-Henson, 1997) and it is more or less their "turf" (Burton & Price-Spratlen, 1999, p. 78) where they can get together and socialize. Consequently, neighborhood research has been gaining momentum demonstrating, for example, that children growing up in lower income neighborhoods are more likely to drop out of school and develop behavioral and mental health problems than young people in wealthier neighborhoods (for a review see Leventhal & Brooks-Gunn, 2000; Sellström & Brembers, 2006).

The neighborhood literature has been growing steadily in demonstrating these "direct" effects that link area of family residence to child outcomes, however, studies that explore neighborhood factors in relation to family processes are only slowly emerging (Burton & Jarrett, 2000; Meyers & Miller, 2004; Plybon & Kliewer, 2001; Roosa et al., 2003). As Burton and Jarrett (2000) correctly note, the role of parenting and family life remains "in the mix, yet on the margins" in neighborhood research. It is also interesting that the neighborhood literature has been focused almost exclusively on inner-city marginalized populations or subgroups of society who experience widespread systematic discrimination. Marginalized populations share common determinants related to social exclusion, have unequal access to social and economic power and resources in society, and experience greater inequality and disadvantage than the general population. While marginalization is an umbrella term that captures various distinct but not mutually exclusive groups (e.g., low-income individuals, people in poverty, single parents, ethnic and religious minorities, immigrants and refugees, women, indigenous populations), the vast majority of neighborhood, parenting and child development research has been centered on lower-income and minority populations.

In the early 1990s, a small body of qualitative research emerged that examined the effects of living in different types of neighborhoods on parents' abilities to raise and supervise their children. In one of the first investigations, Furstenberg (1993) found that young mothers residing in poor neighborhoods tend to isolate themselves and their children from others. While this parenting strategy greatly increased parents' sense of safety, it also cut them off from social relationships and supports with neighbors.

In a review of qualitative literature on parenting in poor African American neighborhoods, Jarrett (1995) found that parents make use of a range of successful parenting strategies in lower-income neighborhoods. For example, some parents draw on extended adult family members for additional support in resource-poor settings; others prohibit their families from interacting with neighbors whose lifestyles they may not condone; some implement rigorous curfews for their children and tightly supervise their everyday movements; and others rely on local organizations or institutions (e.g., after-school, recreational programs) to engage and supervise their children. Based on qualitative research in Chicago, Jarret and Jefferson (2003) suggest that parents can off-set the detrimental effects of growing up in poor neighborhoods through protective parenting behaviors such as careful child monitoring and supervision, managing dangerous situations, and heightening children's awareness of dangerous situations (see also Jarrett, 1997).

There has not been a lot of quantitative research examining neighborhood factors in relation to parenting behaviors. Contrary to most of the qualitative literature, this research demonstrates the detrimental effect living in poor neighborhoods can have on parents' abilities to raise their children. For example, researchers demonstrate that parents residing in dangerous, resource-poor, and lower-income neighborhoods are more likely to use harsh parenting practices (Earls et al., 1994; Klebanov et al., 1994; Leventhal & Brooks-Gunn, 2000). Kotchick, Dorsey and Heller (2005) found that neighborhood stress defined in terms of mothers' perceptions of neighborhood crime, noise, and poor housing conditions increases maternal psychological distress over time which in turn results in less engaging parenting practices among poor African American mothers.

While quantitative neighborhood studies have been criticized for focusing on limited aspects of parenting and family life (Jarrett, 1995; McDonell, 2006), a few studies demonstrate the important role parent factors play in explaining the relationship between neighborhood context and child aggressive behaviors. For example, Sampson and Laub (1993) found that supervision of adolescents and good parenting skills mediated the effects of neighborhood influences on adolescent delinquency. The influential role of parenting quality is also demonstrated by Simons and colleagues (1996) whose research suggests that parents in poor quality neighborhoods demonstrated lower quality parenting skills and were less likely to supervise their children, which predicted adolescent delinquency. Paschall and Hubbard (1998) found that families in poorer neighborhoods reported more family stress and conflict which explained adolescents' violent behaviors. In weakly organized neighborhoods, Gorman-Smith, Tolan, and Henry (2000) related harsh and punitive parenting practices with greater risk for adolescent delinquency. Research by Plybon and Kliewer (2002) highlights the role of family cohesion in terms of protecting children in poor neighborhoods from behavior problems.

REVISED ECOLOGICAL MODEL: ACCOUNTING FOR MARGINALIZATION

An ecological model, which accounts for internal, family, and external or environmental characteristics is particularly important for research with marginalized populations. The very axes or factors which make groups marginalized can accurately be accounted for with such a model. Our definition of marginalization is a group that faces unequal access to power and resources, or faces systemic discrimination (Morgan, 2006). We note that these groups often experience social exclusion and poverty. In North America, populations at risk of being marginalized would include: racial or ethnic minorities; immigrants and refugees; individuals with substance use and/or mental health problems; individuals with HIV/AIDS; sex trade workers; homeless and under-housed persons; people with a low SES poverty; single parents; and gay, lesbian, bisexual, or transgendered individuals. We recognized that membership to one or more of the above-mentioned groups does not necessarily equate to marginalization as the experience of exclusion and poverty will vary between individuals.

To advance work on parenting and child aggression among marginalized populations, we need to integrate individual, family, and contextual models to examine structural, physical, and social effects of each context as well as their moderating and mediating associations. Similar to previous scholars (Aisenberg & Ell, 2005; Luster & Okagaki, 1993), we propose a paradigm shift from focusing on individual level determinants of parenting and child aggression to taking a contextual approach in which the importance of factors inside *and* outside of the child and home are recognized.

While our commentary highlights that parenting and child externalizing behaviors are beginning to be studied from individual and contextual perspectives, a conceptual framework or overarching model uniting both perspectives is much needed, particularly for work with marginalized populations in order to contextualize their everyday experiences and stressors. It has been suggested that individual factors as compared to contextual characteristics are stronger predictors of aggression (Patterson, 1982; Butler et al., 2007). However, without properly accounting for the contextual factors, it is difficult to make such statements as it is conceivable that individual factors are in part a product of the social environment. For example, stress as a result of unemployment, lack of social support, or neighborhood violence affects parenting. Thus, environmental factors that cause stress will likely have direct impacts on parenting and indirect impacts on children's aggression.

To address this gap, we propose a revised ecological approach beyond family and neighborhood contexts rooted in Bronfenbrenner's theory (1977; 1979; 1989). Our proposed model emphasizes the role of intrapersonal characteristics and highlights the importance of recognizing *structural, physical, and social dimensions* within each context. In line with Bronfenbrenner's ecological model, we differentiate between different contexts (primarily for illustrative purposes) and highlight that parenting and child development are influenced by the interactive nature of such contexts. We try to reconcile the struggle between models of context without development, and models of development without context, as Bronfenbrenner (1989) has highlighted.

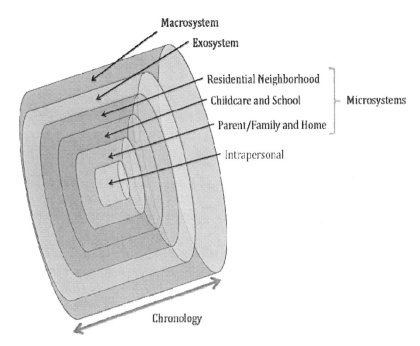

Note. Based on Bronfenbrenner (1977; 1979; 1986). The 3-D dimension of the revised ecological model is intended to reflect not only the multiple layers but also the fact that each setting captures multi-dimensional attributes i.e. structural, physical, and social characteristics.

Figure 1. Revised Ecological Framework.

INTRAPERSONAL CHARACTERISTICS

Bronfenbrenner's model provides a cursory account of the various characteristics within the child that influence his or her development. Based on the reviewed literature presented early on in this commentary, important intrapersonal factors to be noted include prenatal environment, child gender, temperament, and neurobiological/ physiological markers.

Parent/Family and Home Characteristics[4]

The next setting is concerned with the impact of parent and home characteristics. In line with Bronfenbrenner's original conceptualization, we place emphasis on the home as an important microsystem. For example, it is important to recognize physical dimensions such as crowding, housing stability or transience, actual and perceived safety, and structural characteristics such as presence of lead paint.

In terms of family dimensions, it is necessary to consider parental characteristics such as health and well-being. If parents experience chronic or acute physical health, mental health, alcohol or substance (ab)use problems, this is likely to affect parents' abilities to supervise their children, which in turn can influence child behavioral outcomes. Similarly, educational attainment, employment and poverty status, and food (in)security are likely to play important roles. In addition to these structural characteristics, it is important to note a family's social environment, for example, whether the child is being reared in a "traditional" two-parent heterosexual household or whether additional stressors related to growing up in a single-parent or same-sex parents household are present. This last set of factors was alluded to in Bronfenbrenner's later writings as the "new demography", along with some features included in the childcare setting (e.g., private vs. public schooling). Further, the degree of family relationships and the quality of such interactions between child(ren) and parents as well as among other siblings is noteworthy (i.e. parental attachments, social supports, family cohesion and integration). Again, we highlight the importance of exploring the bi-directional nature of such relationships, which is essential for conceptual models on parenting and child behavior (Aisenberg & Ell, 2005).

Childcare and School Features

The childcare and school environment forms the next important layer in our revised ecological model. In childcare and school settings, there are important structural and physical attributes that are likely to affect a developing child and his parents. For instance, the type of school or childcare setting (public vs. private), demographic make-up of teachers and students (in terms of socioeconomic status, gender, and ethnicity), as well as the quality and resources within a school/childcare setting (e.g., teachers' experience and qualifications, low funding status such as Title 1 schools in the U.S., sufficient school supplies and facilities) are

---

[4] We recognize that a number of children are raised by adults other than their parents. For ease of reading, we refer to them collectively as "parents," although we acknowledge that this can include grandparents, aunts, uncles, and any other adults that act as the child's primary caregivers.

important dimensions that need to be recognized. School crowding and school conditions (e.g., presence of lead paint, structural damages, lack of heating/cool air), and school and classroom size, are often common concerns among inner-city schools that are likely to affect children's learning and development (e.g., see Kozol, 1992; 2005). In addition, the location or neighborhood of the school is noteworthy. The social environment also deserves attention, for example, in terms of students' relationships with each others and their teachers, interactions between parents and teachers, parents' involvement in school life, and school social capital[5].

Residential Neighborhood Characteristics

The next layer in our ecological model consists of neighborhood features in which families reside. Important structural and physical characteristics to consider are residents' characteristics such as socioeconomic and employment status, age, gender, and ethnicity; degree of neighborhood safety, violence, crime, and gang activity; presence of employment opportunities and institutional or recreational resources (e.g. after-school programs); as well as physical neighborhood problems such as dilapidated housing, presence of garbage and litter, and physical abandonment (see also Sampson & Raudenbush, 2004). Important social dimensions of neighborhood and community life that need to be considered include the degree of social cohesion and support among residents, collective efficacy and level of neighborhood social capital.

We incorporate Bronfenbrenner's theory to emphasize the important role of external systems that do not include the child or family directly. The *Exosystem* is a distal context beyond the child's and family's control that nevertheless has an important effect on parenting behaviors and child behavioral outcomes. For example, rules and regulations surrounding a parent's place of employment, governmental policies around poverty and welfare, and financial supports for institutional and recreational resources can play important roles in parents' abilities to raise children and child behavioral outcomes.

Next, the *Macrosystem* refers to the broader and larger societal influences and norms such as cultural and religious believes and values, practices of a community, as well as the larger political climate. For instance, discrimination and racism could directly affect both parents and children, particularly families from marginalized communities.

Chronological Factors

Bronfenbrenner (1986) added the chronosystem at a later point into his original framework and we integrate it here as well. This system refers to a recognition of a person's experiences and histories, for example, important life transitions such as marriage, divorce, or parental death. Although not directly included in the chronosystem, Bronfenbrenner (1988, as cited in Bronfenbrenner,1989) reports on some of his work linking low birth weight infants with contextual characteristics of the mother (e.g., residing in central sections of major city). His research also found that early access to prenatal care can decrease the percentage of low

---

[5] We apply Robert Putnam's (2000) definition of social capital as the "connections among individuals – social networks and the norms of reciprocity and trustworthiness that arise from them" (p. 19).

birth weight babies. Although he doesn't extrapolate beyond this discussion about the impact from a chronological or longitudinal perspective of inadequate prenatal care, it certainly draws attention to different contextual factors.

Researchers in the field of public health and health promotion have suggested that individuals' health is greatly influenced by their early years. Specifically, Barker (1998) has suggested that events and exposures during fetal life have a lasting effect and contribute to health problems at a later time. Thus, inadequate health care, poor social support, food insecurity, and other contextual and/or environmental factors experienced by a pregnant woman could all play an indirect role in determining the health and wellbeing of a child. In fact, a review of intergenerational studies found that economically-marginalized parents with a history of aggressive childhood behaviors tended to experience continued social, behavioral and health difficulties, as did their children (Serbin & Karp, 2003). Specifically, parents who grew up in a poor neighborhood and were aggressive as a children have children who accessed emergency care more often than other children and were more likely to suffer from asthma (also associated with maternal smoking).

Some studies are already engaged in such ecological research that examines the impact of different microsettings such as the home and neighborhood. For example, Knoester and Haynie (2005) used national US data to show that adolescents in neighborhoods with higher percentages of single parents and lower degrees of family integration were more likely to commit violent acts. Furthermore, they found that family integration can moderate the relationship between neighborhood type and aggression so that family integration is less successful in preventing young people from committing violence in neighborhoods that contain more single parents.

Butler et al (2007) examined adolescents' anti-social cognitions, relationship quality (attachment with parents), and social-family context in a sample of young offenders. Social-family context included seven domains of risk; including criminal history, substance use, educational problems, family problems, peer relationship problems, neighborhood problems, and psychological problems. Relationship quality, specifically adolescent alienation, was associated with adolescents' aggression. This association was more powerful than the links for anti-social cognitions and social-contextual risk. This suggests that the parent/family microsystem exerts a greater influence than adolescents' individual characteristics (anti-social cognitions) and the combined family and neighborhood risk. However, it is unclear what association exists, transactional or otherwise, between parenting and family/neighbourhood context. For example, it is conceivable that parents choose to reside in neighborhoods with similar-minded families (i.e. role models) or that other aspects neighborhood of community life affect parenting practices in such a way as to make them similar.

Simons et al (2002) found that individual and neighborhood level factors are largely dependent on each other. They examined the importance of family integration and cohesion as a potential buffer to protect children growing up in disadvantaged neighborhoods against negative outcomes. Surprisingly, their research showed that parental controlling behaviors are not successful in preventing antisocial behaviors in lower-income and high risk neighborhoods. In fact, their work supports their "evaporation hypothesis," namely that a buffering effect of positive parenting practices is weaker in neighborhoods in which deviant behaviors are tolerated.

While studies such as these are promising and can shed insight into factors that affect not only parenting behaviors but also child and adolescent aggressive outcomes, they are limited in two primary ways. First, studies such as these remain too narrowly focused on neighborhood and home characteristics and fail to explore individual child characteristics like those outlined at the beginning of our commentary. Similarly, more distal contexts such as the effects of a parent's place of work and the overall political and policy climate receive limited attention. Second, these studies are generally conducted using quantitative methods and analysis. Little attention has focused on in-depth pilot work (perhaps of a qualitative nature) to inform study design and the conceptualization of measures.

Studies exploring parenting and child aggression through a wholistic ecological perspective such as the one proposed here require much effort. First, we view such research to be beyond the scope of any single discipline and thus advocate for cross-disciplinary collaboration. Specifically, we believe the fields of psychology, sociology, public health, and law, to name a few, have much to contribute to this topic. Cross-disciplinary collaboration such as interdisciplinary, transdisciplinary, and community-based participatory work bring many benefits but are also not without their problems. For example, they are generally much more time-consuming and labor-intensive and can bring about problems related to group dynamics (see Stokols, 2006). Nevertheless, we believe that the future of problem-focused and applied research lies in such cross-disciplinary and cross-sectoral work. In line with this recommendation, we also suggest that researchers draw on multiple methods to fully contextualize the lives and experiences of marginalized families.

CONCLUSION

The objective of our commentary was to build necessary bridges between developmental psychology and social science research in an attempt to enhance Bronfenbrenner's ecological model to better capture the factors affecting parenting in marginalized populations. Although the current discussion was limited to child aggression as an outcome measure, we envision the revised model being applicable to children's development and wellbeing more broadly.

For marginalized populations, the macro system plays both direct and indirect roles in a child's development. Specifically, the social and political climate establishes resource sharing and a context for systemic discrimination, and which then determine the choices parents have for their prenatal health care, neighborhood, child's education, recreational activities, and so on. It is our hope that by accounting, perhaps more directly, for these factors, a comprehensive framework will emerge that can more accurately conceptualize the factors affecting the development of marginalized children's.

REFERENCES

Aisenberg, E., & Ell, K. (2005). Contextualizing community violence and its effects: An ecological model of parent-child interdependent coping. *Journal of Interpersonal Violence, 20 (7)*, 855-871.

Anderson-Brown, T., Slotkin, T. A., & Seidler, F. J. (1990). Cocaine acutely inhibits DNA synthesis in developing rat brain regions: Evidence for direct actions. *Brain Research, 537*, 197-202.

Barker, D. J. P. (1998). *Mothers, babies, and health in later life*. Edinburgh, UK: Churchill Livingstone.

Bendersky, M., Bennett, D., & Lewis, M. (2006). Aggression at age 5 as a function of prenatal exposure to cocaine, gender and environmental risk. *Journal of Pediatric Psychology, 31*, 71-84.

Berdan, L. E., Keane, S. P., & Calkins, S. D. (2008). Temperament and externalizing behavior: Social preference and perceived accuracy as protective factors. *Developmental Psychology, 44*, 957-968.

Bronfenbrenner, U. (1977). Toward an experimental ecology of human development. *American Psychologist 32*, 513-531.

Bronfenbrenner, U. (1979). *The Ecology of Human Development: Experiments by Nature and Design*. Cambridge, MA: Harvard University Press.

Bronfenbrenner, U. (1986). Ecology of the family as a context for human development: Research perspectives. *Developmental Psychology, 22*, 723-742.

Bronfenbrenner, U. (1989). Ecological systems theory, in Vasta, R. (ed.) *Annals of Child Development – Six Theories of Child Development: Revised Formulations and Current Issues* (pp. 1-103). Greenwich, CT: JAI.

Brooks-Gunn, J., Duncan, G.J., & Aber, J.L. (1997). *Neighborhood Poverty: Context and Consequences for Children*. New York: Russell Sage Foundation.

Burton, L.M., & Jarrett, R.L. (2000). In the mix, yet on the margins: The place of families in urban neighborhood and child development research. *Journal of Marriage and the Family, 62 (4)*, 1114-1135.

Burton, L.M., & Price-Spratlen, T. (1999). Through the eyes of children: An ethnographic perspective on neighborhoods and child development. In Masten, A.S. (ed.), *Cultural Processes in Child Development. Vol. 29*. Mahwah, NJ: Lawrence Erlbaum Associates.

Butler, S., Fearon, P., Atkinson, l., & Parkers, K. (2007). Testing an interactive model of symptom severity in conduct disordered youth: Family relationship, antisocial cognitions, and social-contextual risk. *Criminal Justice and Behavior, 34*, 721-738.

Cairns, R., & Cairns, B. (2000). Natural history and developmental functions of aggression. In A. Sameroof, M. Lewis, & S. Miller (Eds.), *Handbook of developmental psychopathology* (2nd ed., pp. 403-429). New York: Kluwer/Plenum.

Cannon, W. B. (1914). The interrelations of emotions as suggested by recent physiological researches. *American Journal of Psychology, 25*, 256-282.

Card, N. A., Stucky, B. D., Sawalani, G M., & Little, T. D. (2008). Direct and indirect aggression in childhood and adolescence: A meta-analytic review of gender differences, intercorrelations, and relations to maladjustment. *Child Development, 79*, 1185-1229.

Chawla, L. (2002). *Growing Up in an Urbanizing World*. London: Earthscan Unicef.

Cummings, E. M., Goeke-Morey, M. C., & Papp, L. M. (2004). Everyday marital conflict and child aggression. *Journal of Abnormal Child Psychology, 32*, 191-202.

Damasio, H., Grabowski, T., Frank, R., Galaburda, A., & Damasio, A. (1994). The return of Phineas Gage: Clues about the brain from the skull of a famous patient. *Science, 264*, 1102-1105.

Degnan, K. A., Calkins, S. D., Keane, S. P., & Hill-Soderlund, A. L. (2008). Profiles of disruptive behavior across early childhood: Contributions of frustration reactivity, physiological regulation, and maternal behavior. *Child Development, 79*, 1357-1376.

Delaney-Black, V., Covington, C., Templin, T., Ager, J., Nordstrom-Klee, B., Martier, S., et al. (2000). Teacher-assess behavior of children prenatally exposed to cocaine. *Pediatrics, 106*, 782-791.

Earls, F., McGuire, J., & Shay, S. (1994). Evaluating a community intervention to reduce the risk of child abuse: Methodological strategies in conducting neighborhood surveys. *Child Abuse & Neglect, 18,* 473-485.

Furstenberg, F. (1993). How families manage risk and opportunity in dangerous neighborhoods. In W.J. Wilson (Ed.), *Sociology and the Public Agenda* (pp. 231-258). Newbury Park, CA: Sage.

Gordis, E. B., Granger, D. A., Susman, E. J., & Trickett, P. K. (2006). Asymmetry between salivary cortisol and α-amylase reactivity to stress: Relation to aggressive behavior in adolescents. *Psychoneuroendocrinology, 31*, 976-987.

Gorman-Smith, D., Tolan, P.H., & Henry, D. (2000). A development-ecological model of the relation of family functioning to patterns of delinquency. *Journal of Quantitative Criminology, 16 (2),* 169-198.

Hart, R. (1979). *Children's Experience of Place.* New York: Irvington.

Hinde, R. A. (1976). On describing relationships. *Journal of Child Psychology and Psychiatry, 17*, 1-19.

Hinde, R. A. (1987). *Individuals, relationships, and culture*. Cambridge, England: Cambridge University Press.

Hinde, R. A. (1989). Temperament as an intervening variable. In G. A. Kohnstamm, J. E. Bates, & M. K. Rothbart (Eds.), *Temperament in childhood* (pp. 27-33). Chichester, England: Wiley.

Ho, C., Bluestein, D. N., & Jenkins, J. M. (2008). Cultural differences in the relationship between parenting and children's behavior. *Developmental Psychology, 44*, 507-522.

Holaday, B., Swan, J.H., & Turner-Henson, A. (1997). Images of the neighborhood and activity patterns of chronically ill schoolage children. *Environment & Behavior, 29 (3),* 348-373.

Jarrett, R.L. (1995). Growing up poor: The family experiences of socially mobile youth in low-income African American neighborhoods. *Journal of Adolescent Research, 10 (1),* 111-135.

Jarrett, R.L. (1997). African American family and parenting strategies in impoverished neighborhoods. *Qualitative Sociology, 20 (2),* 275-288.

Jarrett, R.L., & Jefferson, S.R. (2003). 'A good mother got to fight for her kids:' Maternal management strategies in a high-risk, African American neighborhood. *Journal of Children & Poverty, 9 (1),* 21-39.

Klebanov, P.K., Brooks-Gunn, J., & Duncan, G.J. (1994). Does neighborhood and family poverty affect mothers' parenting, mental health, and social support? *Journal of Marriage and the Family, 56,* 441-455.

Knoester, C., & Haynie, D.L. (2005). Community context, social integration into family, and youth violence. *Journal of Marriage and Family, 67,* 767-780.

Kotchick, B.A., Dorsey, S., & Heller, L. (2005). Predictors of parenting in single African American mothers: Personal and contextual factors. *Journal of Marriage and the Family, 67,* 448-460.

Kozol, J. (1992). *Savage Inequalities: Children in America's Schools*. New York: Harper Perennial.

Kozol, J. (2005). *The Shame of the Nation: The Restoration of Apartheid Schooling in America*. New York: Three Rivers Press.

Krenichyn, K., Saegert, S., & Evans. G. W. (2001) Parents as moderators of psychological and physiological correlates of inner-city children's exposure to violence. *Applied Developmental Psychology, 22*, 581-602.

Leventhal, T., & Brooks-Gunn, J. (2000). The neighborhoods they live in: The effects of neighborhood residence on child and adolescent outcomes. *Psychological Bulletin, 126 (2),* 309-337.

Luster, T., & Okagaki, L. (1993). Multiple influences on parenting: Ecological and Life-Course perspectives, in Luster, T., & Okagaki, L. (Eds.) *Parenting: An Ecological Perspectives* (pp. 227-250). Hillsdale, NJ: Lawrence Erlbaum.

Lynch, K. (1977). *Growing Up in Cities*. Cambridge, MA: MIT Press.

McDonell, J.R. (2007). Neighborhood Characteristics, Parenting, and Children's Safety. *Social Indicators Research, 83 (1)*, 177-199

Meyers, S.A., & Miller, C. (2004). Direct, mediated, moderated, and cumulative relations between neighborhood characteristics and adolescent outcomes. *Adolescence, 39 (153),* 121-144.

Moen, P. (1995). Introduction, in Moen, P., Elder, G., & Lüscher, K. (Eds.) *Examining Lives in Context: Perspectives on the Ecology of Human Development* (pp. 1-11). Washington, DC: American Psychological Association.

Morgan, M. (2006). *Value chain development and marginalized populations*. Paper presented at the 2006 SEEP Conference. Presentation retrieved November 28, 2008 from http://www.seepnetwork.org/files/4677_file__1_Value_Chain_Development_Marginalized_Populations.ppt

Nater, U. M., La Marca, R., Florin, L., Moses, A., Langhans, W., Koller, M. M., & Ehlert, U. (2006). Stress-induced changes in human salivary alpha-amylase activity-associations with adrenergic activity. *Psychoneuroendocrinology, 31*, 49-58.

Paschall, M.J., & Hubbard, M.L. (1998). Effects of neighborhood and family stressors on African American male adolescents' self worth and propensity for violent behavior. *Journal of Consulting and Clinical Psychology, 66 (5),* 825-831.

Plybon, L.E., & Kliewer, W. (2001). Neighborhood types and externalizing behavior in urban school-age children: Tests of direct, mediated, and moderated effects. *Journal of Child and Family Studies, 10 (4),* 419-437.

Proshansky, H.M., & Fabian, A.K. (1987). The development of place identity in the child, in C.S. Weinstein & T.G. David (eds.), *Spaces for Children*. New York: Plenum Press, pp. 21-40.

Putnam, R. D. (2000) *Bowling Alone. The collapse and revival of American community*, New York: Simon and Schuster.

Roosa, M.W., Jones, S., Tein, J., & Cree, W. (2003). Prevention science and neighborhood influences on low-income children's development: Theoretical and methodological issues. *American Journal of Community Psychology, 31 (1/2),* 55-72.

Rubin, K. H., Burgess, K. B., Dwyer, K. M., & Hastings, P. D. (2003). Predicting preschoolers' externalizing behaviors from toddler temperament, conflict, and maternal negativity. *Developmental Psychology, 39*, 164-176.

Sampson, R. J., & Raudenbush, S.W. (2004). Seeing disorder: Neighborhood stigma and the social construction of "broken windows." *Social Psychology Quarterly, 67*, 319-342.

Sampson, R.J., & Laub, J.H. (1993). *Crime in the Making: Pathways and Turning Points Through Life*. Cambridge, MA: Harvard University Press.

Sellström, E., & Brembers, S. (2006). The significance of neighbourhood context to child and adolescent health and well-being: A systematic review of multilevel studies. *Scandinavian Journal of Public Health, 34*, 544-554.

Serbin, L., & Karp, J. (2003). Intergenerational studies of parenting and the transfer of risk from parent to child. *Current Directions in Psychological Science, 12*, 138-142.

Simons, R.L., Johnson, C., Beaman, J., Conger, R.D., & Whitbeck, L.B. (1996). Parents and peer group as mediators of the effects of community structure on adolescent problem behavior. *American Journal of Community Psychology, 24*, 145-171

Simons, R.L., Lin, K., Gordon, L.C., Murry, V., & Conger, R.D. (2002). Community differences in the association between parenting practices and child conduct problems. *Journal of Marriage and Family, 64*, 331-345.

Stokols, D. (2006). Towards a science of transdisciplinary action research. *American Journal of Community Psychology*, 38, 63-77.

Tremblay, R., E., et al., (2005). Physical aggression during childhood: Trajectories and predictors. *The Canadian Child and Adolescent Psychiatry Review, 14*, 3-9.

Van de Wiel, N., van Goosen, S., Matthys, W., Snoek, H., & van Engeland, H., (2004). Cortisoal and treatment effect in children with disruptive behavior disorders: A preliminary study. *Journal of the American Academy of Child and Adolescent Psychiatry, 43*, 1011-1018.

Vitaro, F., Barker, E. D., Boivin, M., Brendgen, M., & Tremblay, R. E. (2006). Do early temperament and harsh parenting differentially predict reactive and proactive aggression? *Journal of Abnormal Child Psychology, 34*, 685-695.

In: Handbook of Parenting: Styles, Stresses & Strategies   ISBN 978-1-60741-766-8
Editor: Pacey H. Krause and Tahlia M. Dailey   © 2009 Nova Science Publishers, Inc.

Chapter 5

ADDRESSING ATTRITION RATES: NEW DIRECTIONS IN ADMINISTERING PARENT TRAINING

Shannon S.C. Bert[1] and Jaelyn R. Farris[2]
1) University of Oklahomal OK, USA
2) University of Notre Dame, Indiana, USA

A substantial number of families participating in parent training interventions do not benefit and instead experience negative treatment outcomes such as dropout, mediocre engagement, and/or a lack of positive gains following intervention (Assemany & McIntosh, 2002). Spoth, Goldberg, and Redman (1999) found that 44% of families assigned to a 5-week parenting intervention and 51% of families assigned to a 7-week parenting intervention failed to attend any session. Gross and Grady (2002) reported that 26% of parents assigned to attend group parenting sessions attended fewer than 10% of the sessions and subsequently dropped out of the program. These data suggest that many participants find it difficult to attend and completely adhere to programs consisting of training sessions, possibly due to conflicting obligations. Researchers aimed at improving parenting skills and practices face the question of how best to engage and retain their participants when many are working parents who may also be highly involved in their communities and active with their children's education and extracurricular activities. In fact, Gross and Grady (2002) found that 32% of participants enrolled in a 12-week parenting program reported that it was difficult for them to attend and 50% found the weekly assignments difficult to complete. It is likely that many participants perceive parent training as one more demand in an already stressful lifestyle.

The elevated rates of attrition, characteristic of parent training interventions, suggest that there are situational and/or motivational factors that may influence participant retention and engagement (Reips, 2002). As further parent training research is undertaken, there is growing awareness of the importance of understanding the influence that participant circumstances such as the availability of time and access to childcare may have on participation rates and intervention effects (Nixon, 2002; Orrell-Valente, Pinderhughes, Valente, & Laird, 1999). In particular, contextual factors such as socioeconomic disadvantage, parent psychopathology, parenting stress, child behavior problems, and marital discord have each been shown to serve as risk factors for participant dropout rates and/or barriers serving to keep participants from experiencing intervention effects (e.g., Halpern, 1992, Orrell-Valente et al., 1999). Parenting programs that are designed to be sensitive to individual differences in parenting and life circumstances hold promise for future parent training initiatives (Duncan, White, & Nicholson, 2003).

WEB-BASED INSTRUCTION AS AN ALTERNATIVE APPROACH TO PARENT TRAINING

The delivery of parent training has evolved over the years with the primary aim of increasing the cost-effectiveness of services for the largest number of families (Nixon, 2002; Sanders, Mazzucchelli, & Studman, 2004). As an alternative to face-to-face instruction, Endo and colleagues (1991) suggested the use of self-instructional materials, which are relatively inexpensive and can potentially help parents with a number of child behavior problems. Other examples of alternative treatments that have been used in parenting interventions are telephone-administered interventions, audiotaped and videotaped parenting programs, booklets, and computer mediated learning.

In particular, the Internet may provide a unique opportunity to minimize the influence of situational constraints on participation rates. The Internet can do so by bringing the program into participants' homes at a time when it is convenient for them to participate. Unique features of Internet-based groups, as compared to traditional groups, are that they are generally open to the public and provide opportunities to participate for individuals who are unable or unwilling to leave their homes to attend a traditional group (Weinberg, Schmale, Uken, & Wessel, 1995). Furthermore, computer-mediated communication is capable of promoting positive relational effects among group members, which may in some situations be superior to those obtained from face-to-face interactions as in traditional group settings (Alexander, Peterson, & Hollingshead, 2003).

AN INNOVATIVE APPROACH TO PARENT TRAINING

In 2001, the National Institute of Child Health and Human Development (NICHD) published *Adventures in Parenting*, a 62-page informational booklet designed to educate parents about basic principles of parenting. The booklet, based on decades of research on parenting and child development, offers five principles that parents can use to develop a cognitive model of how they want to parent their children. The underlying assumption guiding the booklet's development was that a cognitive model based on these five empirically supported principles – Responding, Preventing, Monitoring, Mentoring, and Modeling (RPM3) – would facilitate the translation of research findings into daily parenting behaviors. We launched a study at the University of Notre Dame in 2004 to assess whether dissemination of the *Adventures in Parenting* booklet could facilitate positive parenting practices and decrease the likelihood of child maladaptation or whether supplemental intervention would be necessary in order to bring about substantial effects. The program was unique in testing web-based parent training as an alternative to group-based training sessions.

Design and Measures

Participants were 134 mothers recruited from the South Bend, IN area through the use of pediatricians, family practice centers, and local daycare centers that had volunteered to hand out flyers and collect response cards. Special importance was placed on recruiting families that were from both low and well-to-do socioeconomic statuses and who had a child between the ages of 2 and 3 years old, based on the notions that all families could benefit from the *Adventures in Parenting* program but that a cognitive model of parenting would be easier to develop and more effective if introduced to parents while their children are young. On average, participants were 30.74 years of age (*SD* = 5.87). Most participants were European-American (81.6%), 10.7% were African-American, 4.9% were Asian-American, and 4.1% were Latina (numbers add up to more than 100% because some participants were multiracial). The majority of participants were married (71.4%) and reported that their target child's father was part of his/her life (93.8%). Sex of the children was approximately equally represented (47% of the children were male).

The design of the study included an initial assessment followed by random assignment to one of three conditions: (1) booklet only – these mothers received the Adventures in Parenting booklet without any supplemental intervention, (2) booklet + face-to-face training sessions – these mothers were administered the booklet as well as invited to attend a series of 12 weekly group-based training sessions held at a university setting, and (3) booklet + web-based training sessions – these mothers were administered the booklet as well as invited to view a series of 12 weekly web-based training sessions. The post-intervention assessment was completed 3 months after the initial assessment in order to allow time for the 12-week training sessions offered to participants in the face-to-face and web-based conditions. Participants' knowledge of the RPM3 principles and evaluations of the program (Program Evaluation Form) were assessed at 3-month. Although a complete description of the design and measures is beyond the scope of this paper, the interested reader is referred to Bert, Farris, and Borkowski (2008) for more details.

The primary question driving this project revolved around whether there would be differential gains in and/or maintenance of RPM3 knowledge based on the level of intervention to which the participants were randomly assigned. Three measures were designed to address this question. First, the RPM3 Open-Ended Questionnaire was a 5-item measure in which participants reported in their own words how they would define each of the RPM3 principles as they relate to parenting. All responses were scored 0 (incorrect), 1 (somewhat correct), or 2 (correct) by a pair of trained research assistants. Scores could range from 0-10, with higher scores representing greater knowledge of the RPM3 principles. Second, the RPM3 Multiple-Choice Questionnaire was also comprised of five items. Scores were determined by assigning one point for each correct answer; thus, scale scores could range from 0-5, with higher scores representing greater knowledge of the RPM3 principles. Third, the RPM3 True/False Questionnaire was also comprised of five items. One point was awarded for each correct answer; thus, scale scores could range from 0-5, with higher scores representing greater knowledge of the RPM3 principles. Scores from the Open-Ended, Multiple-Choice, and True/False Questionnaires were summed to provide an RPM3 Total Score that could range from 0-20, with higher scores representing greater knowledge of the RPM3 principles. The RPM3 Total Score had good internal consistency with a total test coefficient alpha of .77 at the initial assessment. Participants were excluded from analyses if they were missing scores for any of the items on these scales.

The Program Evaluation Form, administered post-intervention (i.e., 3 months after the initial assessment), was designed to assess participants' reactions to and opinions about the *Adventures in Parenting* booklet, group-based sessions, and web-sessions. Specific questions asked whether participants read the booklet and attended sessions (when applicable), the proportion of the booklet that they read, the number of session they attended/viewed, and the reasons as to why they may or may not have read the booklet and/or attended sessions. Response options to the questions were designed to be on a continuum. For example, response options to the question "If you read the booklet, did you find it useful?" included "no," "not really," "somewhat," "mostly," and "yes."

Results

Attrition

From the original sample of 134, 106 participants completed the 3-month assessment. The highest rate of attrition was found in the face-to-face condition (35.6%), followed by web-based (30.0%) and booklet conditions (14.3%), respectively. This finding indicated that attrition became more likely as more demands were placed on participants and highlights an advantage of web-based, as compared to face-to-face, training. Despite differential attrition rates between intervention groups, no significant differences were found on any demographic or outcome measures for those who stayed in the study versus those who withdrew. Of most importance, an examination of the interaction between intervention condition and dropped status for demographics and initial outcomes revealed that dropping from the study did not depend on group membership. Also, following random assignment to the three conditions, ANOVA and chi-square analyses revealed no significant differences between intervention conditions for participants' age, education level, financial satisfaction, father involvement, gender of child, and marital status.

Engagement in the Intervention

Of the 45 participants invited to attend face-to-face groups, 29 of them attended at least one session. Attendance ranged from 1 to 11 sessions, with a mean of 4.93 (SD = 3.16). Although the overall proportion of mothers who participated in at least one session was lower in the web-based group, the average number of sessions viewed was higher than the average number of face-to-face sessions that were attended. Specifically, of the 40 participants invited to view the web-based sessions, 16 viewed at least one session. Participation ranged from 1 to 12 sessions, with a mean of 8.06 (*SD* = 4.54). These findings suggested that there may have been more barriers to becoming involved in the web-based than face-to face sessions, but if the initial barriers were overcome then engagement was notably better in the web-based group.

Participants' Perceptions of the ntervention: Session Evaluations

Overall, participants in both the face-to-face and web-based groups reported positive experiences with the intervention. When asked to rate and describe their experiences with the intervention, 54.1% of participants in the face-to-face group rated the program as "excellent," 43.2% rated the program as "good," and 2.7% rated the program as "fair." None of these participants rated the program as "poor." When asked to describe the most helpful aspects of the face-to-face intervention, participants gave responses which indicated that the social support aspects of the program were most beneficial. For example:

- "Being able to talk with other parents about situations, and having a leader with grown children to help with ideas to solving problems."
- "Being with adults and learning how to handle different problems."
- "Being with other parents who are going thru the same things I am. You really feel you are not alone in what you are experiencing with the age group."

When asked to describe what could be improved, responses suggested that the limited meeting times, the 12-week length of the program, and the lack of consistent attendance of many mothers were their most substantial concerns. For example:

- "Different meeting times, I was unable to attend most of them. Maybe offer options by phone, 2 or 3 times, evenings and mornings."
- "Reviewing more information in each session for fewer over-all sessions."
- "Everything was great. More moms in the class would have been more helpful."

When asked to rate and describe their experiences with the intervention, 50.0% of participants in the web-based group rated the program as "excellent," 40.0% rated the program as "good," and 10.0% rated the program as "fair." None of these participants rated the program as "poor." When asked to describe the most helpful aspects of the web-based intervention, participants indicated that it was beneficial to be given a review of basic parenting practices, to be prompted to think about how to be a better parent, and that the web-based format was positive. For example:

- "It gave me some things to think about and try to apply to make myself a better parent."
- "Just reinforcing the basics, reminding me of what SHOULD happen."
- "To be able to do this over the Internet!"

When asked to describe what could be improved, responses suggested that not having internet access at home or encountering technical issues were problematic. Moreover, because the web-based scenarios were not personalized, some participants reported boredom with encountering the same type of generalized scenarios during every session. For example:

- "The situations. They need to not be the same for every lesson."
- "The Internet has been difficult for me to use. It is inconvenient because I don't have it in my home and the site has given me trouble."
- "I don't have the Internet at home and yet I was selected to be on the Internet group. This made it somewhat difficult for me."

Knowledge of the RPM3 Principles as a Function of the Intervention

Regression analyses showed that the number of parent-training sessions that participants attended predicted post-intervention RPM3 knowledge, with participants who attended a higher number of sessions scoring better on the RPM3 measures than those who attended fewer sessions (Bert, Farris, & Borkowski, 2008). At the 3-month assessment, participants in the face-to-face group had the highest post-intervention mean RPM3 Total Scores (M = 10.29, SD = 2.28), followed by participants in the web-based (M = 9.78, SD = 2.02) and booklet groups (M = 8.60, SD = 3.18). Participants in the booklet group had the lowest mean scores on the post-intervention RPM3 Total Score, indicating that they were less able to define and accurately answer questions about the RPM3 principles. ANCOVA analyses revealed a significant omnibus effect, suggesting that the various levels of intervention were associated with differential gains in knowledge of the RPM3 principles, $F(2,96)$ = 4.50, p < .05. Post-hoc contrasts suggested that participants in the more intensive intervention conditions (i.e., face-to-face or web-based groups) had significantly greater knowledge of the RPM3 principles at the 3-month assessment than participants who received only the booklet, $F(1,80)$ = 4.67, p < .05.

Paired-samples t-tests were conducted to test for changes over time in each group (Bert et al., 2008). Mean RPM3 Total Scores for the booklet condition remained stable from pretest to posttest, whereas RPM3 Total scores for the face-to-face and web-based conditions showed significant improvements over time, $t(1, 20)$ = 1.93, p < .05 and $t(1, 22)$ = 2.25, p < .05, respectively. In summary, average RPM3 Total Scores remained stable in the booklet condition from pretest to posttest, but increased in the face-to-face and web-based conditions, suggesting that receiving a more intensive intervention was associated with significantly greater gains in knowledge of the RPM3 principles.

FINAL THOUGHTS

It is important for parenting interventions to find ways of reaching those who find it difficult to meet the participation demands of the program as well as those most in need of parental services (Orrell-Valente et al., 1999; Petersson, Petersson, & Hakansson, 2004). In addressing the individual needs of participants, programs must consider not only program characteristics (e.g., participant motivation, the nature of the relationship between trainer and parent, the extent to which the parent likes the program and finds relevance in its content), but also situational constraints of the participants themselves such as unreliable transportation, competing obligations, and family stresses such as unemployment, single-parent status, and low socioeconomic status. Since drop-out rates often reach 50% in family-based interventions (Orrell-Valente et al., 1999), it is imperative that researchers look for ways to minimize the impact of situational constraints in an effort to maximize parent participation. In this concluding section we offer suggestions on ways to retain participation rates among traditional parent training programs, as well as discuss our "lessons learned" on the advantages and disadvantages of conducting web-based parent training. We end this commentary with a discussion of possible research directions for future web-based parent training initiatives.

Findings from our *Adventures in Parenting* program corroborated results from other studies, suggesting a strong effect of parent-training on changes in parenting knowledge because of the educational experience (e.g., Hamiliton & MacQuiddy, 1984; Reid, Webster-Stratton, & Beauchaine, 2001). Of particular interest was the finding that gains in knowledge were statistically equal across the face-to-face and web-based conditions, suggesting that the web-based intervention was equally as effective as the face-to-face intervention in enhancing knowledge of the program's principles.

Reid and colleagues (2001) suggested that the interactive and collaborative nature of parenting sessions contributes to their success within parenting interventions. The interactive format of both the face-to-face and web-based sessions allowed the standard structure of *Adventures in Parenting* to be tailored more closely to each participant's situation and background, subsequently relating to how the RPM3 principles were presented and taught. As a result, participants with different parenting styles and values were taught to incorporate program principles into their own belief system (Reid et al., 2001), with greater benefits noted in the face-to-face and web-based groups as compared to the group who received the booklet without any form of supplemental intervention.

As was shown in our *Adventures in Parenting* project, a possible way of minimizing the impact of situational constraints on participation rates could be to introduce computer mediated components into existing parent training programs. Our research suggests that new or different kinds of learning can be enhanced with the use of technology, particularly the Internet. Of equal importance is the acknowledgment of other strategies utilized in *Adventures in Parenting* to minimize attrition across all groups which included: postcard, telephone, and email reminders, the collection of detailed contact information, childcare services provided during assessments and face-to-face training sessions, self-administered assessments through the mail (when necessary), transportation assistance, and incentives for participation; each of which contributed to the success of the *Adventures in Parenting* program. We highly recommend that these strategies be taken into consideration by future parent training initiatives as a means of accommodating barriers to attendance among those assigned to traditional group-based parenting classes.

Advantages of Web-Based Instruction.

The *Adventures in Parenting* booklet, supplemented by web-based training sessions, resulted in positive gains for participant's overall knowledge of RPM3 principles; thereby addressing Nixon (2002) and Duncan and colleagues' (2003) call for researchers to take advantage of the growing access of consumers to the Internet as a way to increase the accessibility of parenting programs. In addition to convenient access to parenting sessions, the utility of the Internet can be extended to include data collection, interpretation, and immediate feedback to participants on their progress (Byers, 2001). In addition, Shields (2003) found the quality of web-based data collection to be comparable to face-to-face data collection techniques. Analyses of data collected over the web showed that some of the inhibitions and self-censoring that may be present during other forms of data collection had been minimized in the web-based collection process (Shields, 2003).

In addition to their obvious benefits such as increased participant disclosure, flexible delivery, and non-judgmental environment, web-based parenting interventions likely minimize situational constraints that have been shown to interfere with participation. Web-based sessions have the ability to facilitate participation from families in rural and remote areas who typically have less access to professional services (Sanders et al., 2004). Furthermore, it is possible that the results of our parent training program are related to the novel, animated, interactive nature of web-based sessions (MacKenzie & Hilgedick, 1999). Participants who were assigned to the web-based condition may have found the Internet an engaging and convenient format that helped them maintain their levels of enthusiasm for learning (MacKenzie & Hilgedick, 1999).

In short, the use of web-based environments provides adequate means to optimize assessment activities (more frequent and more convenient data collection through online data collection, quiz scoring, survey application, analyses and graphic display results), and also make available other resources to enhance learning and teaching (Byers, 2001). The benefits of utilizing the Internet for parent-training interventions are enormous and include but are not limited to: standardized and controlled presentation of stimuli, accurate measures of response times, reduction of the tendency to respond in a socially desirable way, and avoidance of experimenter biases and demand characteristics (Byers, 2001; Reips, 2002). Taken together, researchers are encouraged to utilize the Internet as a beneficial and cost-effective means of delivering parent training.

Disadvantages of Web-Based Instruction

Despite the documented advantages of web-based instruction, there are several obstacles that need to be considered and/or addressed prior to implementing a parent-training program via the Internet and/or computer. We caution researchers of 5 concerns and offer possible suggestions and/or rebuttals.

(1) Privacy

Research through the Internet has raised many ethical issues regarding privacy. It is imperative that security measures are set in place to protect the privacy, anonymity, and the confidentiality of participants.

(2) Limited Interaction/Interconnection

A common criticism of web-based instruction is the lack of interactivity, or connectivity, between participants and staff. The underlying assumption is that there is an inherent reduction in the type and level of interaction between the instructor and students (Lavooy & Newlin, 2003, p. 158). However, Lavooy and Newlin (2003) found that computer mediated instruction resulted in an increase, not a decrease, in student-student and instructor-student interactivity through the use of course web pages, electronic bulletin boards where participants and staff are able to post messages, chat-rooms, and/or through e-mail messages. They contend that web-based and web-enhanced courses, especially the use of computer mediated communication (emails and web- pages), can produce very effective learning environments with high levels of interactivity.

(3) Technical Difficulties and/or Malfunctions

It is inevitable that there will be server failures, overloaded circuits, "dead" links, and/or issues with computer processing speeds. Researchers must pilot their training sites to test for possible technical difficulties and continually be aware of the possibility of server failures and slower computer processing speeds.

(4) Costs

A well-developed web-based training site taxes both the time and finances of researchers. A significant amount of time will be devoted to developing and maintaining sites; while technical training and support can be expensive.

(5) Internet Availability and Accessibility

Participants may complain that they do not have access to the Internet. In the *Adventures in Parenting* program we offered participants the ability to access training session using our computers and/or suggested that they use the Internet at their local public library.

Future Directions

Findings from the *Adventures in Parenting* project have indicated that web-based training can be equally as effective as more expensive and demanding forms of face-to-face parent training. Participants' comments suggested that the benefits of web-based training could be enhanced even further through the use of a more sophisticated website, options such as chat sessions with experts, and more interactive and personalized web-based training scenarios. In the meantime, it can be concluded that web-based training is a good alternative to traditional parent training approaches. Moreover, web-based training is consistent with the field's growing emphasis on translational research because it allows for efficient, widespread dissemination of empirical research. The challenge for future researchers will be not only to disseminate information via the Internet, but also to make the general public aware of how to locate credible online programs like *Adventures in Parenting* and encourage consumers to use the programs.

REFERENCES

Alexander, S.C., Peterson, J.L., & Hollingshead, A.B. (2003). Help is at your keyboard: Support groups on the Internet. In L.R. Frey (Ed.), *Group communication in context: Studies of bona fide groups (2ⁿᵈ ed.)* (pp. 309-334). Mahwah, NJ: Lawrence Erlbaum Associates.

Assemany, A. E., & McIntosh, D. E. (2002). Negative treatment outcomes of behavioral parent training programs. *Psychology in the Schools, 39,* 209 – 219.

Bates, A.W. (2000). *Managing technological change: Strategies for college and university leaders.* San Francisco: Jossey-Bass.

Bert, S. C., Farris, J.R., & Borkowski, J.G. (2008). Parent training: Implementation strategies for Adventures in Parenting. *Journal of Primary Prevention*, 29 (3), 243-261.

Byers, C. (2001). Interactive assessment: An approach to enhance teaching and learning. *Journal of Interactive Learning Research*, 12, 359-374.

Duncan, D. F., White, J. B., & Nicholson, T. (2003). Using Internet-based surveys to reach hidden populations: Case of nonabusive illicit drug users. *American Journal of Health Behavior, 27,* 208 – 218.

Endo, G.T., Sloane, H.N., Hawkes, T.W., McLoughlin, C., & Jenson, W.R. (1991). Reducing child tantrums through self-instructional parent training materials. *School Psychology International*, 12, 95-109.

Gross, D., & Grady, J. (2002). Group-based parent training for preventing mental health disorders in children. *Issues in Mental Health Nursing*, 23, 367-383.

Halpern, R. (1992). Issues of program design and implementation. In M. Larner, R. Halpern, & O. Harkavy (Eds.), *Fair start for children: Lessons learned from seven demonstration projects* (pp. 179 – 197). New Haven, CT: Yale University Press.

Lavooy, M.J., & Newlin, M.H. (2003). Computer mediated communication: Online instruction and interactivity. *Journal of Interactive Learning Research*, 14, 157-165.

MacKenzie, E.P., & Hilgedick, J.M. (1999). The Computer-Assisted Parenting Program (CAPP): The use of a computerized behavioral parent training program as an educational tool. *Child & Family Behavior Therapy*, 21, 23-43.

Nixon, R.D.V. (2002). Treatment of behavior problems in preschoolers: A review of parent training programs. *Clinical Psychology Review*, 22, 525-546.

Orell-Valente, J.K., Pinderhughes, E.E., Valente, E., & Laird, R.D. (1999). If its offered, will they come? Influences on parents' participation in a community-based conduct problems prevention program. *American Journal of Community Psychology*, 27, 753-783.

Petersson, K., Petersson, C., & Hakansson, A. (2004). What is good parental education? Interviews with parents who have attended parental education sessions. *Scandinavian Journal of Caring Sciences*, 18, 82-89.

Reid, M. J., Webster-Stratton, C., and Beauchaine, T.P. 2001. Parent Training in Head Start: A comparison of program response among African American, Asian American, Caucasian, and Hispanic mothers. *Prevention Science*, 2, 209-227.

Reips, U.D. (2002). Internet-based psychological experiments: Five does and five don'ts. *Social Science Computer Review, 20 (3)*, 241-249.

Sanders, M.R., Mazzucchelli, T.G., & Studman, L.J. (2004). Stepping Stones Triple P: The theoretical basis and development of an evidences-based positive parenting program for families with a child who has a disability. *Journal of Intellectual & Developmental Disability*, 29, 265-283.

Shields, C.M. (2003). 'Giving voice' to students: Using the Internet for data collection. *Qualitative Research*, 3 (3), 397-414.

Spoth, R., Goldberg, C., & Redman, C. (1999). Engaging families in longitudinal preventive intervention research: Discrete-time survival analysis of socioeconomic and social-emotional risk factors. *Journal of Consulting and Clinical Psychology*, 67, 157-163.

Weinberg, N., Schmale, J.D., Uken, J., & Wessel, K. (1995). Computer-mediated support groups. *Social Work With Groups, 17*, 43-54.

In: Handbook of Parenting: Styles, Stresses & Strategies   ISBN 978-1-60741-766-8
Editor: Pacey H. Krause and Tahlia M. Dailey   © 2009 Nova Science Publishers, Inc.

Chapter 6

ANTENATAL EDUCATION: PREPARING FOR PARENTHOOD

Jane Svensson

Royal Hospital for Women, Sydney Australia

ABSTRACT

Antenatal education is a crucial component of antenatal care, yet practice and research demonstrate that women and men now seek far more than the traditional approach of a labor and birth focused program attended in the final weeks of pregnancy. This study was designed to determine whether a new antenatal education program, designed from a needs based assessment of expectant and new parents, with increased parenting content, could improve parenting outcomes when compared to a traditional program.

A randomized control trial conducted at a specialist referral maternity hospital in Sydney, Australia, measured the pre and postnatal outcomes of 170 women birthing at the hospital who attended the hospital antenatal education programs and their male partners. The intervention, a new *Having a Baby* program, was tested against the traditional hospital program which acted as the control. The primary outcome measure was perceived parenting self-efficacy, with worry and perceived knowledge also being measured.

The results revealed the perceived maternal self-efficacy scores of women and men in the experimental program were significantly higher than those in the control program and worry scores were lower, but they did not reach statistical significance. Birth outcomes were similar. The new program improved parenting knowledge and self-efficacy. Parenting programs which continue in the early postnatal period may be beneficial.

This chapter will provide a description of the randomized control trial as well as a summary of the key elements of the new program. It will be of interest to midwives, physical therapists and all involved in antenatal and postnatal education.

INTRODUCTION

This chapter describes a randomized controlled study which investigated the effect a new antenatal education program had on parenting self-efficacy and worry of the expectant women and men who attended. The new program focused more on parenting issues when compared to the traditional birth-oriented antenatal education program, and was delivered based on adult learning principles [1].

This chapter provides the background to the program, an outline the study, describes the program and provides the results from both the women and men who participated.

BACKGROUND

Historically antenatal education programs were developed in an attempt to decrease pain in labor and improve birth outcomes, and they have been based on the theories of Lamaze [2], Grantly Dick-Read [3] and others [4]. Research investigating the impact of antenatal education has, therefore, primarily focused on labor and birth outcomes and/or patterns of attendance. This research suggests that programs rarely have an impact on pain relief or childbirth outcomes [5-9], and that women attend programs for reasons in addition to gaining information [10, 11].

More recently, parenting information has been added to some antenatal education programs, but the impact of baby care and parenting information being provided during pregnancy on knowledge, confidence, worry or ability to parent has infrequently been examined. Indeed an appropriate adjustment to parenthood measure has long been sought by researchers and clinicians. Corwin [12], in her evaluation of an antenatal education program which had parenting integrated through the program, designed and used a Prenatal Parenting Scale pre and post intervention. This scale, similar to one used by Rolls and Cutts [13], tested knowledge pre and post intervention in experimental and control groups. Rolls and Cutts only measured postnatal outcomes.

Further, research measuring the outcomes of antenatal and postnatal education has focused on the women, with few exceptions. Barclay et al [14] in an earlier study on men's experiences, found men 'endured' rather than 'enjoyed' antenatal classes. Diemer [15] found that men who attended a father-focused discussion in perinatal classes showed an improvement in spousal relations than those in traditional classes. Schmied et al [16] found men liked having a single gender component in antenatal education. Galloway et al [17] found, however, that only sixteen percent of the men they questioned wanted a father's only session.

Information in pregnancy can be gained from numerous sources, but what is learned and retained as knowledge and skills is affected by many factors, including the method by which the learning occurs. An important feature of the new *Having a Baby* program tested in this randomized control trial was the inclusion of problem-solving activities related to labor, birth, baby care and parenting, aimed at increasing participant's confidence in their innate problem solving skills, and enhancing their own self-confidence.

Self-efficacy, according to social learning theory, is an individual's belief that she or he has the ability to perform a given task. A strong sense of self-efficacy is needed for a sense of personal well-being and it allows for preserving in efforts towards success [18]. As Reece and Harkless state, 'those persons with greater self-perceptions of efficacy are able to channel their attention and resources toward mastering the situation at hand' [19]. Parenting self-efficacy was therefore selected as a useful measure of adjustment to parenthood to be used in this research. The Parent Expectations Survey, was selected as a tool to measure parenting self efficacy because it is a scale with demonstrated reliability and validity [20] and it has been used for samples of men and women.

Research demonstrates stress is inversely related to self-efficacy. Women who are perceived by health professionals as having a 'normal' pregnancy can exhibit 'worry' [21], so there was a need to measure worry as an outcome in this study. General anxiety measures, such as the State Trait Anxiety Scale, were not appropriate because this research specifically wanted to examine worry about parenting and labor. The Cambridge Worry Scale [22] was therefore selected as the tool to measure concerns and fears related to pregnancy, labor, caring for a baby, relationships and socio-economic issues. It had been used in a large study of pregnant women [23, 24] and had face validity for men. The Cambridge Worry Scale also has demonstrated validity and reliability.

The aim of this randomized control trial was to test whether the new *Having a Baby* program designed from the needs assessment data, and conducted within current resources, improved perceived parenting self efficacy and knowledge, and decreased worry about the baby eight weeks after birth. The new *Having a Baby* was the experimental program, with the conventional antenatal education program acting as the control.

METHOD

Design

A randomized control trial of two antenatal education programs for first time parents was conducted. Self-report surveys were used to collect data on commencement of the program, on completion of the program and at approximately eight weeks postnatal. Repeated measures analysis of variance was used to examine differences between the groups on perceived parenting self efficacy, perceived parenting knowledge, and worry about the baby.

Setting

All primiparous, English-speaking clients who booked for an evening antenatal education program at a specialist referral maternity hospital in Sydney, Australia were informed of the study. The clients who were willing to participate in the research were randomly allocated, by random number generation, to an experimental or control group on their preferred night of attendance by a booking clerk. Participants were not informed whether they were attending experimental or control programs. Clients who did not give consent were allocated to the program of their choice. A power calculation indicated that a total sample size of 90 was required to determine change of clinical significance in parenting self-efficacy, with a power of 80 and an alpha of 0.05. A sample of 160 women was recruited to allow for a 40% dropout rate at eight weeks post birth.

The programs were provided in two physically separate venues within the hospital, thereby minimizing the probability of interaction between experimental and control groups during study. Ethics approval was obtained from both the Hospital and the University Research Ethics Committee prior to commencement of the study. Informed written consent was obtained from all participants.

Intervention

The experimental *Having a Baby* program was the same length as the control program. That is seven x 2 hour sessions before the birth and a reunion meeting approximately six weeks after birth. The maximum number of couples enrolled in both the experimental and control programs were eleven, with the majority (80%) enrolling ten couples. This was the accepted maximum number of couples attending programs in Australia and was based on figures from state-wide reviews of maternity services [25, 26] and adult learning literature [27, 28].

The broad topic areas covered in experimental and control programs were similar, but they differed in their order and importantly, in their method of presentation. All of the methods included were recommended by expectant and new parents themselves during the comprehensive needs assessment conducted prior to this randomized control trial. The results of the needs assessment are reported elsewhere [1, 29-31].

The experimental *Having a Baby* program differed from the control program in the following ways:

- Pregnancy, labor and the early parenting experience were each regarded as a microcosm of the childbearing experience, rather than identified or taught as isolated events. For example, the first hours of a baby's life outside the uterus was discussed alongside the birth of the placenta and the other processes that occur in the third and fourth stages of labor. This integrated approach aimed to unify the childbearing experience and promote having a baby as a life transition.
- Relaxation, comfort and distraction strategies such as massage, positioning, movement, water and heat, traditionally taught as skills for labor, were presented as life skills able to be used at any time.
- Parenting activities were integral to each session of the program. Some of the activities were presented as icebreakers at the beginning of a session, others were presented during a session to change its focus, and some as homework activities for discussion between sessions.
- Two couples came to the second last session of the program to share their experience as first-time parents. The two couples were from a previous program during the course of which they had offered to do this feedback/peer learning segment. Subsequent experience has demonstrated that this segment is highly regarded by all participants and that it is sometimes difficult to draw it to a close at the end of the one hour allocated time.

- The program included the bath of a baby on the Postnatal Ward so that participants could observe the behavior of a newborn, and also ask the Mother questions about her experience.
- The program had a problem solving, proactive approach to learning and an emphasis on experiential learning. The experiential and mastery nature of these strategies aimed to increase the confidence and competence of women and their partners in the early weeks with a new baby, and therefore enhance self-efficacy.
- Many small and large group discussions focused on psychosocial and emotional issues, such as 'What for you is the worst thing that could happen during labor?', 'As a laboring women I would like…', and 'How do you feel about becoming a mother and a father?'. The needs assessment and anecdotal evidence demonstrates that childbearing women and their partners value an expression and discussion on issues of concern.

The Educators

Both the experimental and control programs were facilitated by educators who were contracted by the hospital to conduct antenatal education programs. They had a variety of professional backgrounds, six were midwives, three were independent childbirth educators and one was a physical therapist. They were employed on a contract basis and paid a State Health In-service Educator's award. The majority (80%) had facilitated antenatal education programs for at least eight years. Prior to the trial commencing all of the educators had attended the Health Area Basic Group Skills training program, providing a sample as homogenous as possible in their ability to facilitate groups as possible.

DATA COLLECTION

In this study women and men were asked to complete three self-report surveys. Survey One was mailed to participants with their program booking confirmation letter, Survey Two was distributed and completed during the final session of the Having a Baby program, Survey Three was posted to participants approximately six weeks after birth. Participants who had not returned Survey Three within four weeks were given a follow-up telephone call and sent a copy of Survey Three if required. The majority of women completed Survey Three eight–ten weeks after the birth, with the mean age of the baby being 9.69 weeks.

To reduce the chance of incorrect survey distribution, for example experimental surveys being given to control group participants, all surveys were color coded according to group and gender of participant. The researcher coordinated distribution and collection of surveys with assistance from the educators facilitating the programs. Each survey was tested by forty participants who gave consent during a pilot study of the programs. No modification of surveys was required.

Variables

Perceived Maternal Self-Efficacy

Adjustment to parenthood, in this study, was measured by maternal and paternal perceived self-efficacy pre-program and postnatal. The 25-item Pre and Postnatal Parent Expectations Survey [20] is a self-report survey, which examines perceived self-efficacy in relation to tasks they will perform in caring for their baby, their role as a parent and their relationship with their partner. Participants are asked to rate the confidence they have on a scale of 0 (cannot do) to 10 (certain can do) in their ability as a parent on twenty-five affirmative statements. *'I will be able to manage the feeding of my baby'* and *'I will be able to tell when my baby is sick'* are examples of statements to be rated by the parent. In the prenatal scale each statement has the prefix *'I will'*, and in the postnatal scale the prefix is *'I can'*. The total score is calculated by summing the rating on each statement and dividing by the number of items, that is by twenty-five. The Parent Expectation Scale has demonstrated reliability and validity and has been used to measure perceived self-efficacy with women and men.

The fact that the scale had been used for men in previous research studies was one of the reasons it was used as a measure in this trial. The wording of all items in the scale, except item 14, was suitable for men. The wording of statement 14 in both pre and postnatal surveys was changed for the men's survey. *'I will easily be able to get the baby and myself out for a visit to the Early Childhood Health Centre'* was changed to *'I will be able to get the baby and myself out for a visit to friends.'* This change was made because the majority of men attending antenatal education programs were not primary carer of the baby and/or unable to visit the Early Childhood Health Centre during hours of operation.

Maternal and Paternal Worry

The Cambridge Worry Scale [24, 32] was selected to measure maternal and paternal worry for several reasons. These include it measures concerns and fears related to pregnancy, labor, caring for a baby, relationships and socio-economic issues and it has demonstrated reliability and validity [23]. It can be modified to more accurately measure worry in a specific population, can be administered pre and postnatal. It can also be used by women and men. With the Cambridge Worry Scale participants are asked to rate their degree of concern about 10 items on a 5-point likert scale from 0 (not a worry) to 5 (a major worry). The rating they give to each item is summed to give the total score. In this trial Cambridge Worry Scale was divided into three subsets which were worry about baby, life and self.

ASSESSMENT OF PERCEIVED KNOWLEDGE

An Assessment of Perceived Knowledge Scale designed and used for quality assurance purposes at the hospital, and subsequently by colleagues across the state of New South Wales, was used to measure knowledge related to labour, infant care and the role of a parent. Participants are asked to rate their perceived knowledge on 11 topics covered in a program on a 5-point likert scale from 1 (very poor) to 5 (very good). In this study four topics related to labor and birth, one to hospital services, one to rights and responsibilities, and five to postnatal issues. The postnatal topics, of particular interest in this study, were 'your feelings after baby is born', 'caring for your baby', and 'feeding your baby' and 'life as a mother' in the women's survey. The rating given to each item was summed to give the total score.

Demographic, Pregnancy, Labor, Birth and Postnatal Details

In addition to the above measures, demographic data was collected in Survey One, and pregnancy, labor, birth and postnatal outcomes were collected in Survey Three. The outcomes measured included:

- Date of birth of their baby;
- How many weeks pregnant when their baby was born;
- Pregnancy related health problems;
- How labor started i.e. spontaneous or induction;
- Use of nitrous oxide, pethidine and epidural in labour;
- Type of birth i.e. natural or assisted;
- Length of labor in hours;
- Length of postnatal hospitalisation in days;
- Method of infant feeding;
- Problems with health of baby.

DATA ANALYSIS

The statistical software package SPSS (Version 14) was used for data analysis. Only data from participants who had completed every question in the three surveys was analysed. An independent researcher checked 10% of the SPSS data entry for accuracy. Data analysis commenced during data collection, but was not reported to the educators or the working party to decrease the chance of the results influencing the facilitation style of each educator.

Simple descriptive statistics, frequencies, means, χ^2 and independent sample t-test, were used to measure nominal and ordinal data and differences between group means, for example, demographic details, labor, birth and postnatal outcomes. Fishers exact, rather than χ^2 was used for cells that had a count less than five, and Yates continuity correction was used for 2x2 tables. Statistical significance set at $\alpha = 0.05$.

The responses to every item on the three primary outcome measures, perceived self-efficacy, worry and assessment of perceived knowledge were totaled. Repeated measures analysis of variance was performed to determine whether perceived self-efficacy, worry and perceived knowledge scores varied with group. The assumptions were tested and not violated.

RESULTS

Two hundred and ninety women and their partners, referred to as 'couples', were approached to participate in the research, see Figure 1. Forty-two refused or were unable to participate. The reasons for non-participation were 'did not want to participate' (n=15) and for twenty-seven there were no vacancies in programs on their preferred night, which meant they had to attend the alternate program.

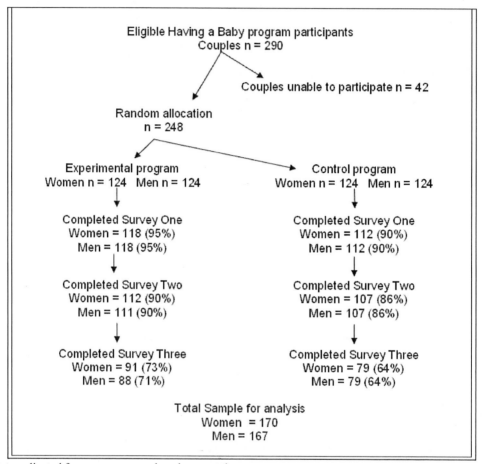

* Data collected from men was analyzed separately

Figure 1: Flow chart identifying sample size from eligibility to final sample.

Ultimately 248 couples were recruited to the study, 124 couples were randomly allocated to the experimental program and 124 couples to the control program. With the women ninety-five percent (n=118) of the experimental group and 90% (n=112) of the control group completed

Survey One. Ninety percent (n = 112) of the experimental group and 86% (n=107) of the control group completed Survey Two. Seventy-three percent (n = 91) of the experimental and 64% (n=79) of control group completed Survey Three. The response rate of the men was similar as can be seen in Figure 1.

Women and men in the final sample of both groups were included irrespective of whether they received the entire program. The response rates for the groups were tested and found not to be significantly different. There were no observable differences in age, parity, or education between women or men participating in this study, and the program attendees who did not agree to participate in the research.

Demographic Details and Pregnancy Characteristics

There was no significant difference in age, country of birth, level of education, family income or pregnancy complications between **women** in experimental and control groups. Frequencies, proportions, means, and test of significance are presented in Table 1. The age range of the women in the study was 19 to 41 years, (mean 30.26 years, SD 4.26), with all women expecting their first baby. Ninety-eight percent of participants (166/170) spoke English at home, with the country of birth of women in the study being representative of the women who gave birth at the Hospital. Sixty-six percent of participants (112/170) were born in Australia, 15% (25/170) were born in the United Kingdom and 9% (15/170) born in Asia. The majority of the women were educated with 84% (142/170) having a tertiary level of education, and 73% (123/170) had a family income greater than $60,000 per annum. The majority of women went into labor at term, with a mean gestation of 40 weeks and range of 35–42 weeks.

With the **men** there was no significant difference in age, country of birth, level of education or family income between those in experimental and control groups. The age range of the men in the study was 19 to 45 years, (mean 31.31 years, SD 4.41), with all men expecting their first baby. Ninety-seven percent of men (162/167) spoke English at home, with the country of birth of men in the study being similar to the men who attend the participating hospital with their partner. Sixty-seven percent of participants (112/167) were born in Australia, 17% (29/167) were born in the United Kingdom and 6% (10/167) born in Asia. The majority of the men were educated with 75% (126/167) having a tertiary level of education, and 73% (122/167) had a family income greater than $60,000 per annum. Twenty-five percent of men (442/167) had a major stress in the twelve months prior to the study. Ninety-two percent (153/167) were employed in paid work, with 85% (142/167) working > 20 hours per week.

Labor, Birth and Postnatal Outcomes

There was no significant difference between experimental and control groups in the proportion of **women** who had induction of labor, spontaneous vaginal birth and instrumental delivery, perineal trauma, length of labor, satisfaction with birth, feeling in control during the birth and use of medical pain relief during labor. Frequencies, proportions, means, and test of significance are presented in Table 2. There was no significant difference in the length of postnatal hospital stay, method of infant feeding, health problems of mother or baby, or paid work hours of women in experimental and control groups.

Table 1. Maternal demographic details and pregnancy characteristics by allocated group

	Total Sample n = 170	Experimental n = 91 number (%)	Control n = 79 number (%)	Statistic / Sig
Mean age in years (SD)	30.26 (4.26)	30.08 (4.33)	30.47 (4.19)	t = -.596
Range in years	19 - 41	21 - 41	19 - 39	p = 0.55
Nulliparous	170 (100)	91 (100)	79 (100)	
English spoken at home	166 (97.6)	87 (95.6)	79 (100)	Fishers exact =3.09 p = 0.25
Country of birth				
Australia and NZ	112 (65.9)	59 (64.8)	53 (67.1)	χ^2 = 3.02
United Kingdom	25 (14.7)	13 (14.3)	12 (15.2)	p = 0.39
Asia	15 (8.8)	11 (12.1)	4 (5.1)	
Other	18 (10.6)	8 (8.8)	10 (12.7)	
Highest level of education				
Degree	80 (47.1)	43 (47.3)	37 (46.8)	
Diploma	62 (36.5)	34 (37.4)	28 (35.4)	χ^2 = 0.33
Apprentice	15 (8.8)	7 (7.7)	8 (10.1)	p = 0.95
Secondary	13 (7.6)	7 (7.7)	6 (7.6)	
Family Income				
<40,000	13 (7.6)	7 (7.7)	6 (7.6)	χ^2 = 0.099
40,001-60,000	34 (20.0)	19 (20.9)	15 (19.0)	p= 0.95
>60,000	123 (72.4)	65 (71.4)	58 (73.4)	
Major stress in last 12 months	59 (34.7)	31 (34.1)	28 (35.4)	χ^2 = .001 p = 0.98
Pregnancy Characteristics				
Multiple pregnancy	2 (1.2)	2 (2.2)	0 (0)	
Pregnancy complication	49 (28.8)	27 (29.7)	22 (27.8)	χ^2 = .008 p = 0.93
Mean gestation labor-weeks	39.7	39.82	39.56	t = 1.27
Range (SD)	35-42 (1.37)	37–42 (1.30)	35-42 (1.43)	p = 0.21

Independent sample t-test was used to test difference between groups for interval data. Chi-square and Fishers exact were used to test difference between groups on nominal variables. Yates continuity correction was used for 2x2 tables. Statistical significance set at α = 0.05.

With the **women** the mean satisfaction with the childbirth experience, measured on a scale 0 (totally unsatisfactory) to 10 (absolutely wonderful) was 6.54 (SD 2.40). Mann-Whitney U test demonstrated there was no significant difference between the satisfaction of women in experimental and control groups (z = -0.085 p=0.932). Ninety-three percent (85/91) of women in the experimental group and 86% (68/79) in the control group felt they were given a say in making decision in labor 'most of the time'.

With the **men,** the mean satisfaction with the childbirth experience, measured on a scale 0 (totally unsatisfactory) to 10 (absolutely wonderful), was 7.94 (SD 1.93). Mann-Whitney U test demonstrated there was no significant difference between the satisfaction of men in experimental and control groups z = -1.814 p=0.07. Eighty-five percent (75/88) of men in the experimental group and 80% (63/79) in the control group felt they were given a say in making decision in labor 'most of the time'. Ninety-four percent (158/167) of men felt in control during their wife's labor.

Table 2. Maternal labor and birth outcomes by allocated group

	Total Sample n = 170	Experimental n = 91 number (%)	Control n = 79 number (%)	Statistic / Sig
Induction of labor	56 (32.9)	27 (29.7)	29 (36.7)	χ^2 =0.657 p = 0.42
Birth outcome				
Spontaneous vaginal	91 (53.5)	49 (53.8)	42 (53.2)	
Assisted vaginal	36 (21.2)	18 (19.8)	18 (22.8)	χ^2 =0.317
Emergency C/S	31 (18.2)	17 (18.7)	14 (17.7)	p = 0.96
Elective C/S	12 (7.1)	7 (7.7)	5 (6.3)	
Drugs used in labor *				
Nitrous Oxide	87/158 (55.1)	46/84 (54.8)	41/74 (55.4)	χ^2 = 0.000 p = 1.00
Pethidine	61/158 (38.6)	29/84 (34.5)	32/74 (43.2)	χ^2 =0.921 p = 0.34
Epidural	66/158 (41.8)	34/84 (40.5)	32/74 (43.2)	χ^2 =0.036 p = 0.85
No drugs in labor *	21/158 (13.3)	9/84 (10.7)	12/74 (16.2)	χ^2 =0.61 p=0.43
Caesarean section				
Epidural	41/43 (95.3)	24/24 (100)	17/19 (89.5)	χ^2 = 0.81 p =0.37
Perineal trauma #				
Episiotomy	36/127 (28.3)	18/67 (26.9)	18/60 (30.0)	χ^2 =0.038 p= 0.85
Mean length of labor (SD) #	10.43 (5.27)	10.13 (5.08)	10.77 (5.51)	t = -0.673 p=0.502
Range in hours	2 - 27	2 - 22	3 -27	
Mean satisfaction childbirth (SD)	6.54 (2.40)	6.60 (2.34)	6.47 (2.47)	z = -0.085 p=0.932
Control in labor				
Most of the time	126 (74.1)	67 (73.6)	59 (74.7)	χ^2 =0.000
Hardly at all	44 (25.9)	24 (26.4)	20 (25.3)	p = 1.00

*Sample excluded women who had an elective caesarean section. Women were asked to identify all drugs used. # Sample excluded women who had a caesarean section. Independent sample t-test, Chi-square and Mann-Whitney U were used to test difference between groups on the variables. Fisher's exact was used when expected count <5. Yates Continuity Correction for 2x2 tables. Statistical significance set at α = 0.05.

Maternal Perceived Self-Efficacy

The 25 item Prenatal Parent Expectations Scale asks participants to rate how they feel about their ability to perform 25 skills relating baby care, interaction with baby and life as a mother on a scale 0 (cannot do) to 10 (certain can do). This scale was administered pre-program (Survey One) and postnatal (Survey Three). The pre-program mean score by group was 6.88 (SD 1.29) for the experimental group and 6.98 (SD 1.16) for the control group. T-test for independent means was used to measure the difference between experimental and control group means. There was no statistically significant difference between the pre-program self-efficacy mean scores for women in experimental and control groups (t = -0.527, p=0.599).

The 25-item Postnatal Parent Expectations Scale measures the same skills as the prenatal scale, prefacing each skill with 'I am' rather than 'I will'. Distributed to study participants by mail approximately six weeks after the birth of their baby, the majority were returned by 9 weeks, with a range of 5 to 12 weeks. The mean postnatal perceived self-efficacy score for the experimental group was 8.61 (SD 0.87) and 7.94 (SD 0.92) for the control group. There was a statistically significant difference, measured by t-test for independent group means, between the postnatal mean scores of women in experimental and control groups (t = 4.84, p= 0.000).

To determine the effect of group and time on perceived maternal self-efficacy, a repeated measures ANOVA was performed. Perceived self-efficacy increased over time (df 1,168, F = 170.09, p = .000), as shown in Figure 2, with the difference in perceived self-efficacy scores between the antenatal and postnatal period being greater for women in the experimental group than the control group (df 1,168, F = 13.99, p = .000). That is the new *Having a baby* program had an increased beneficial effect on maternal perceived self-efficacy.

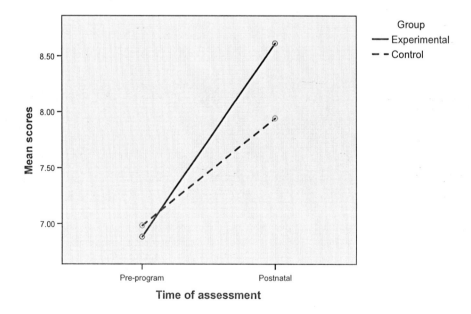

Figure 2. Maternal perceived parenting self-efficacy by group and time of assessment

Paternal Perceived Self-Efficacy

With the **men**, the pre-program mean score by group was 6.85 (SD 1.19) for the experimental group and 6.73 (SD 1.21) for the control group. T-test for independent means was used to measure the difference between experimental and control group means. There was no statistically significant difference between the pre-program self-efficacy mean scores for men in experimental and control groups (t = 0.63, p=0.527).

The mean postnatal perceived self-efficacy score for the experimental group was 8.29 (SD 0.96) and 7.48 (SD 0.99) for the control group. There was a statistically significant difference, measured by t-test for independent group means, between the postnatal mean scores of men in experimental and control groups (t = 5.32, p= 0.000).

To determine the effect of group and time on perceived paternal self-efficacy, a repeated measures ANOVA was performed. Perceived self-efficacy increased over time (df 1,165, F = 115.87, p = .000), with the difference in perceived self-efficacy scores between the antenatal and postnatal period greater for men in the experimental group than in the control group (df 1,165, F = 11.38, p = .001), as shown in Figure 3.

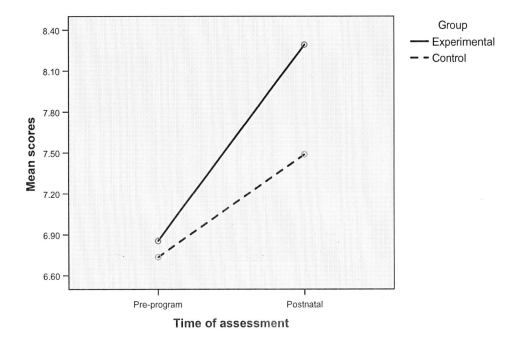

Figure 3: Paternal perceived parenting self-efficacy by group and time of assessment.

Maternal Worry abut the Baby

The outcome of interest in this trial from the Cambridge Worry Scale was worry pertaining to the baby. The mean scores prenatal for this subsection of the scale were 5.66 (SD 3.2) for the experimental group and 5.99 (SD 3.23) for the control group. Mean postnatal scores were 2.04 (2.49) experimental and 2.14 (SD 2.51) for the control group.

A repeated measure ANOVA demonstrated worry about the baby scores in both groups decreased over time, see Figure 4, with the difference between Survey One and Survey Three being significant (df 1,168, F = 177.804, p = .000). The difference between groups was not statistically significant (df 1,168, F = .173, p = .678). That is the experimental and control programs did not differ in their effect on worry about the baby.

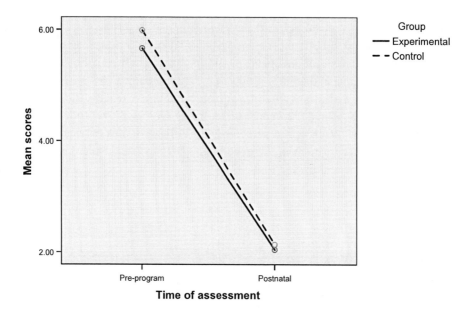

Figure 4. Maternal worry about baby by group and time of assessment.

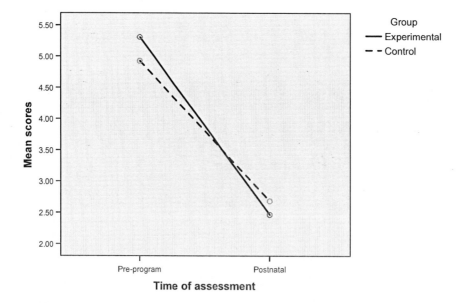

Figure 5. Paternal worry about baby by group and time of assessment.

Paternal Worry

With the men, the mean prenatal scores for the Cambridge Worry Scale were 5.30 (SD 3.14) for the experimental group and 4.92 (SD 3.75) for the control group, (see Figure 5). Mean postnatal scores were 2.46 (SD 3.09) experimental and 2.68 (SD 2.55) for control group.

A repeated measure ANOVA demonstrated worry about the baby scores decreased over time, the difference being significant (df 1,165, $F = 67.585$, $p = .000$). There was no statistically significant difference between the groups over time (df 1,165, $F = .944$, $p = .333$).

Maternal Assessment of Perceived Knowledge

An assessment of perceived knowledge, relating to issues covered in the *Having a Baby* program, was performed pre-program, post-program and postnatal. Mean scores demonstrated an increase in assessment of perceived knowledge scores between pre and post-program for women in both programs, with a decrease in perceived knowledge occurring after the birth of the baby.

To determine the effect of group on perceived knowledge of childbirth and parenting, two knowledge subscales were examined. Sub-scale One related to aspects of parenting knowledge and Subscale Two related to labor and birth. A repeated measures ANOVA was performed on the both of the sub-scales.

Assessment of Parenting Knowledge

A significant difference in the learning processes of the experimental and control programs was the integration of parenting topics and skills throughout the *Having a Baby* program, with labor and birth being presented as a life transition. Less direct lectures and more self-directed activities were used in the new program. Therefore, assessment of group differences of perceived parenting knowledge was of particular interest. The pre-program mean scores by group were 12.407 (SD 2.78) for the experimental group and 13.215 (SD 2.95) for the control group. T-test for independent means was used to measure the difference between experimental and control group means. There was no statistically significant difference between the pre-program mean scores for women in the experimental and control groups ($t=-1.84$ $p=0.068$).

Perceived parenting knowledge scores for both groups increased post-program as shown in Figure 6. The means scores measured by Survey Two were 16.79 (SD 2.06) for the experimental group and 16.07 (SD 2.31) for the control group.

To determine the effect of group on parenting knowledge scores a repeated measures ANOVA was performed on pre-program (Survey One) and post-program scores (Survey Two). Perceived parenting knowledge for both groups increased over the time between Survey One and Survey Two (df 1,168, $F=219.511$, $p=.000$) with the increase for women in the experimental group being greater than those in the control group (df 1,168, $F=9.710$, $p=.002$).

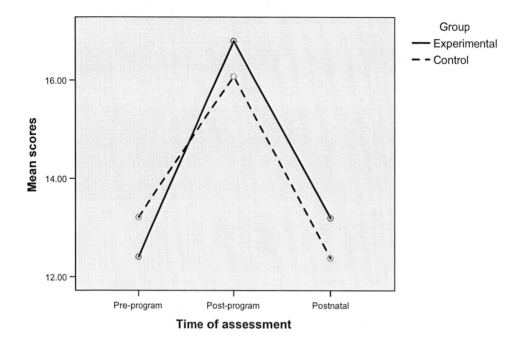

Figure 6. Maternal assessment of perceived parenting knowledge by group and time.

Perceived parenting knowledge scores for both groups decreased after the birth. Means scores measured by Survey Three were 13.20 (SD3.60) for the experimental group and 12.38 (3.90) for the control group. The mean postnatal score for each group demonstrated that perceived knowledge for women in the experimental group remained above the pre-program score (Survey One), whereas for the women in the control group it decreased.

A repeated measures ANOVA conducted on the pre-program (Survey One) and postnatal scores (Survey Three) demonstrated that there was a significant interaction between group and time. That is, women in the experimental group increased their level of perceived parenting knowledge 8 weeks after the birth of the baby compared to pre program levels, whereas women in the control group decreased their perceived parenting knowledge during this period.

Assessment of Labor Knowledge

The amount of time spent on labor in the experimental program was less than that in the control program and its method of presentation was different. It was therefore important to analyze the perceived labor knowledge for both groups. The pre-program mean scores by group were 11.67 (SD 3.47) for the experimental group and 12.39 (SD 3.01) for the control group see Figure 7 . T-test for independent means was used to measure the difference between experimental and control group means. There was no statistically significant difference between the pre-program mean scores for women in the experimental and control groups (t=-1.44 p=0.152).

To determine the effect of group on labor knowledge scores a repeated measures ANOVA was performed on pre-program (Survey One) and post-program scores (Survey Two). Perceived labor knowledge for both groups increased over the time between Survey

One and Survey Two (df 1,168, F=417.857, p=.000. There was no significant difference between the experimental group and control group scores for perceived knowledge about labor (df 1,168, F=2.875, p=.092).

Perceived labor knowledge scores decreased after the birth. A repeated measures ANOVA conducted on the pre-program (Survey One) and postnatal scores (Survey Three) demonstrated that there was a significant increase over time (df 1,168, F=117.213 p=.000). There was no interaction between time and group (df 1,168, F=2.627, p=.107). The mean postnatal score for each group demonstrated that perceived labor knowledge for women decreased slightly after the birth of their baby, but in both groups it remained above the pre-program score.

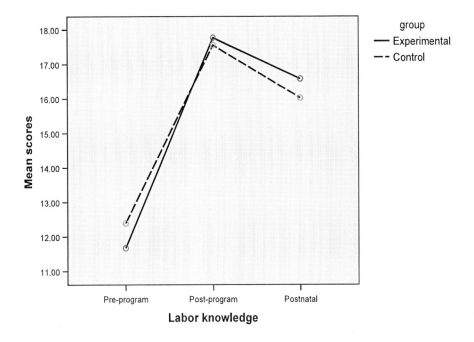

Figure 7. Maternal assessment of perceived labor knowledge by group and time.

Paternal Assessment of Perceived Knowledge

An assessment of perceived knowledge related to issues covered in both experimental and control programs, was performed pre-program, post-program and postnatal. Mean scores demonstrated an increase in assessment of perceived knowledge scores between pre and post-program surveys for men in both programs, with a decrease occurring postpartum.

To determine the effect of group on two aspects of knowledge gained during the antenatal education program the scale was sub-divided. Subscale One related to aspects of parenting knowledge and Subscale Two examined knowledge relating to labor and birth.

Assessment of Parenting Knowledge

Assessment of perceived parenting knowledge was of particular interest because of the differences between experimental and control programs in the amount of time spent on parenting and the different methods used to facilitate learning in this area. The pre-program mean scores for perceived parenting knowledge by group were 12.43 (SD 3.53) for the experimental group and 12.29 (SD 3.29) for the control group. T-test for independent means was used to measure the difference between experimental and control group means. There was no statistically significant difference between the pre-program mean scores for men in the experimental and control groups (t=.266 P=.791).

Perceived parenting knowledge scores increased post-program as shown in Figure 8.. The means scores measured by Survey Two were 16.64 (SD 2.02) for the experimental group and 15.63 (SD 2.29) for the control group. To determine the effect of group on parenting knowledge scores, a repeated measures ANOVA was performed on pre-program (Survey One) and post-program scores (Survey Two). Perceived parenting knowledge for both groups increased over the time between Survey One and Survey Two (df 1,165, F=172.156, p=.000). There was no significant difference between groups over time (df 1,165, F=2.250, p=.135).

Perceived parenting knowledge scores decreased after the birth. Means scores measured by Survey Three were 13.64 (SD 4.44) for the experimental group and 12.82 (SD 3.90) for the control group. A repeated measures ANOVA conducted on the pre-program (Survey One) and postnatal scores (Survey Three) demonstrated that there was no significant increase over time (df 1,165, F=4.509 p=.035) and no difference between time and group (df 1,165, F=0.691, p=.407).

Assessment of Labor Knowledge

The amount of time spent on labor in the experimental program was less than that in the control program and its method of presentation was different. It was therefore important to analyze the perceived labor knowledge for both groups. The pre-program mean scores by group were 9.76 (SD 3.47) for the experimental group and 10.19 (SD 3.13) for the control group. T-test for independent means was used to measure the difference between experimental and control group means. There was no statistically significant difference between the pre-program mean scores for women in the experimental and control groups (t=-.834, p= .406).

To determine the effect of group on labor knowledge scores a repeated measures ANOVA was performed on pre-program (Survey One) and post-program scores (Survey Two). Perceived labor knowledge for both groups increased over the time between Survey One and Survey Two (df 1,165, F=607.489, p=.000) with the difference in experimental group and control group scores not being statistically significant (df 1,165, F=3.596, p=.060). Group did not have an effect on perceived labor knowledge scores.

Perceived labor knowledge scores decreased after the birth as shown in Figure 9. A repeated measures ANOVA conducted on the pre-program (Survey One) and postnatal scores (Survey Three) demonstrated that there was an increase in scores over time (df 1,165, F=333.799 p=.000). There was no difference between groups over time (df 1,165, F=2.544, p=.113). The mean postnatal score for each group demonstrated that perceived labor knowledge for men decreased slightly after the birth of their baby but in both groups it remained above the pre-program score (Survey One).

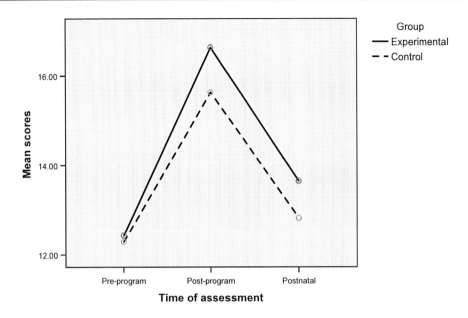

Figure 8. Paternal assessment of perceived parenting knowledge by group and time.

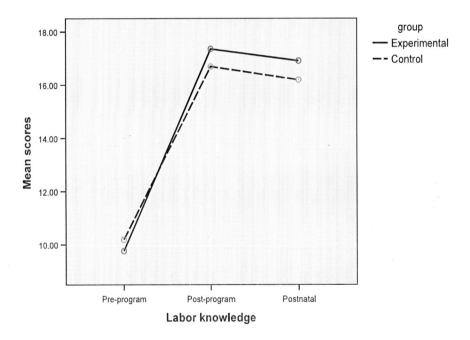

Figure 9. Paternal assessment of perceived labor knowledge by group and time.

DISCUSSION

The aim of this randomized control trial was to test whether women and men who attended the *Having a Baby* would have higher perceived self-efficacy scores eight weeks after the birth, and lower baby worry scores compared with the women and men attending a conventional antenatal education program used as the control. The new *Having a Baby* program was designed from needs assessment data obtained from expectant and new parents in the earlier stage of this project and reported elsewhere [30, 31]. The program was the same length as the conventional program, but the structure and the learning activities were significantly different.

Both women and men in this study were predominantly middle class, English-speaking and educated. Although they were the majority population attending the Royal Hospital for Women, Sydney for the birth of their first baby, the generalization of these results is limited. There are many groups within our multicultural society which may have special needs which have not been identified in this research e.g. adolescents, single women, and those from minority cultures. The teaching and learning methods and topics covered in the program may or may not be suitable for such groups. It is therefore, recommended that the needs of significant minority groups be examined, and the program modified accordingly, so as to encourage these couples to attend and benefit from antenatal education programs.

The results indicate that the women and men who attended the new *Having a Baby* program, compared to those attending the conventional program, had improved perceived self-efficacy and parenting knowledge approximately eight weeks after the birth of their first baby. Both the *Having a Baby* program participants, and those of the conventional program, had similar decreased levels of worry about their baby after the birth of their baby. The reduction in the worry scores of the women and men in the control group was, however, not sufficient to boost their parenting self-efficacy.

Knowledge, skills and experience are related to confidence, which in turn is related to self-efficacy. A strong sense of self-efficacy is necessary for a sense of personal well-being and for persisting in efforts towards success. Persons with greater self-perceptions of efficacy are able to channel their attention and resources to mastering the situation at hand. The results from this study indicate that the *Having a Baby* program, with innovative learning activities such as problem solving and experiential activities, had a beneficial affect on maternal and paternal self-efficacy. The considerable distress currently being experienced by new mothers may have been reduced for these women and men by providing them with the problem solving skills to adapt and adjust to their new life situations. Further research is however is required to determine whether improving parenting self efficacy through childbirth and parenting education can have an effect on family distress and associated health and social outcomes.

This research adds to previous research and not only identifies specific strategies proven to be effective during the childbearing year, but argues the need to refocus regular antenatal education, in particular the labor and birth component. Pregnancy, labor, birth and the early weeks with a baby can and should be regarded as a life transition or life journey. Labor skills can, and should, be presented as life skills. Antenatal education needs to assume a parenting focus and there must be a commitment made to make sessions and topics relevant to the participants for whom they are intended. Today women and men come to antenatal education with a multitude of information from various sources searching to make sense of what they have read, heard and seen; ever more they look to their educator to help in this process. With women and men increasingly coming from nuclear families in many Western countries, contemporary antenatal education is, and needs to be, replacing the informal knowledge networks once available in their local community [33, 34]. This new program went a long way toward doing so.

As specified in the introduction, opinions vary as to how the needs of expectant fathers can and should be met. Although gender-specific activities were a focus of the new *Having a Baby* program, subsequent work now has a male-only facilitated discussion integrated into the program. Similar to the work of Friedewald, Fletcher and Fairbairn [35], this semi-structured discussion explores a range of topics specific to men as fathers. Concurrent to it, the women their own semi-structured discussion on their evolving role as an expectant, and then new, mother with their female educator. Allocated one hour in the program, unpublished data indicates men and women benefit from this peer learning/networking.

At the time of this research consideration was indeed given to designing the Having a Baby program so that it straddled the birth experience, that is it would have had five or six sessions prenatal and two or three sessions postnatal. This structure proved to be difficult for logistical and financial reasons so it did not proceed. The results of this research demonstrate that further work is required with this concept, and indeed in 2009 a Postnatal Parenting program will commence at the Hospital. The aim is to eventually have it as a 'straddled' antenatal-birth-postnatal program.

Finally, the validity of using a randomized controlled trial to measure the outcomes of antenatal education is to be questioned, as it should be for any educational program. With the emphasis on adult learning principles in the experimental program each program would be different. This would not be such an issue with the control program due to its pre-set topics and more didactic approach. The randomization process in this research was effective, and the sample size was effective, so merit can be given to the design.

NOTE

This chapter is, with permission, based on chapters eight and nine of Svensson, J. (2005) Antenatal education: Meeting consumer needs. A study in health services development. Doctoral Thesis, University of Technology: Sydney.

Excerpts of this article are, with permission, from: Svensson, J. et al. Randomised controlled trial of two antenatal education programmes. Midwifery (2007), doi: 10.1016/j.midw.2006.12.012.

REFERENCES

[1]   Svensson, J. 2005. Antenatal Education: Meeting Consumer Needs. A Study in Health Services Development. Doctoral Thesis, University of Technology, Sydney.
[2]   Lamaze, F. 1956. Painless Childbirth. New York: Pocket Books.

[3]   Dick-Read, G. 1944. Childbirth Without Fear. New York: Harper and Row.

[4]   Simkin, P. and M. Enkin, 1989. Antenatal classes, In Effective Care in Pregnancy and Childbirth, I. Chalmers, M. Enkin, and J. Keirse, Editors. Oxford University Press: Oxford.

[5]   Beck, N., et al. 1980. The prediction of pregnancy outcome: Maternal preparation, anxiety and attitudinal sets. *Journal Psychosom Res*. 24 (3): 343-351.

[6]   Bennett, A., et al. 1985. Antenatal preparation and labor support in relation to birth outcomes. *Birth*. 12 (1): 9-16.

[7]   Charles, A.G., et al. 1978. Obstetric and psychological effects of psychoprophylactic preparation for childbirth. *American Journal Obstet Gynecol*. 131 (1): 44-52.

[8]   Davenport-Slack, B. and C.H. Boylan. 1974. Psychological correlates of childbirth pain. *Psychosom Med*. 36: 215-223.

[9]   Spiby, H., et al. 1999. Strategies for coping with labour: Does antenatal education translate into practice? *Journal of Advanced Nursing*. 29 (2): 388-394.

[10] Lee, H. and A. Shorten. 1999. Childbirth education classes: Understanding patterns of attendance. *Birth Issues*. 8 (1): 5-11.

[11] Lumley, J. and S. Brown. 1993. Attenders and nonattenders at childbirth education classes in Australia: How do they and their births differ? *Birth*. 20: 123-130.

[12] Corwin, A. 1999. Integrating preparation for parenting into childbirth education: Part II -- A study. Journal of Perinatal Education. 8 (1): 22-28.

[13] Rolls, C. and D. Cutts. 2001. Pregnancy-to-parenting education: Creating a new approach. *Birth Issues*. 10 (2): 53-58.

[14] Barclay, L., J. Donovan, and A. Genovese. 1996. Men's experiences during their partner's first pregnancy: A grounded theory analysis. *Australian Journal of Advanced Nursing*. 13 (3): 12-24.

[15] Diemer, G.A. 1997. Expectant fathers: Influence of perinatal education on stress, coping and spousal relations. *Research in Nursing & Health*. 20: 281-293.

[16] Schmied, V., et al. 2002. Preparing expectant couples for new-parent experiences: a comparison of two models of antenatal education. *Journal of Perinatal Education*, 11 (3): 20-27.

[17] Galloway, D., J. Svensson, and L. Clune. 1997. What do men think of antenatal classes? *International Journal of Childbirth Education*. 12 (2): 38-41.

[18] Bandura, A. 1986. Social Foundations of Thought and Action: A Social Cognitive Theory. Englewood Cliffs, NJ: Prentice-Hall.

[19] Reece, S.M. and G. Harkless. 1998. Self-efficacy, stress, and parental adaptation: Applications to the care of childbearing families. *Journal of Family Nursing*. 4 (2): 198-215.

[20] Reece, S.M., 1998. Parent Expectations Survey, In Measurement Tools in Patient Edcucation, B.K. Redman, Editor. Springer Publishing: New York. p. 225-232.

[21] Homer, C., et al. 2002. Women's worry in the antenatal period. *British Journal of Midwifery*. 10 (6): 356-360.

[22] Green, J., et al. 2003. Factor structure, validity and reliability of the Cambridge Worry Scale in a pregnant population. *Journal of Health Psychology*. 8 (6): 753-764.

[23] Ohman, S., C. Grunewald, and U. Waldenstrom. 2003. Women's worries during pregnancy: Testing the Cambridge Worry Scale on 200 Swedish women. *Scand J Caring Sci*. 17: 148-152.

[24] Stratham, H., J. Green, and K. Kafetsios. 1997. Who worries that something might be wrong with the baby? A prospective study of 1072 pregnant women. *Birth*. 24 (4): 223-233.

[25] Health Department Victoria. 1990. Having a Baby in Victoria. Melbourne: Health Department Victoria.

[26] NSW Department of Health. 1989. Maternity Services in New South Wales: The Final Report of the Ministerial Taskforce on Obstetric Services in New South Wales. Sydney: NSW Department of Health.

[27] Foley, G., ed. 2000. Understanding Adult Education and Training. 2nd ed. Allen and Unwin: Sydney.

[28] Yalom, I. 1995. The Theory and Practice of Group Psychotherapy. 4th ed. New York: Basic Books.

[29] Svensson, J., L. Barclay, and M. Cooke. 2006. Antenatal education as perceived by health professionals. *Journal of Perinatal Education*. 16 (1): 9-15.

[30] Svensson, J., L. Barclay, and M. Cooke. 2006 The concerns and interests of expectant and new parents: Assessing Learning Needs. *Journal of Perinatal Education*. 15 (4): 18-27.

[31] Svensson, J., L. Barclay, and M. Cooke. 2008 Effective antenatal education: Recommendations of expectant and new parents. *Journal of Perinatal Education,* 18 (4).

[32] Stratham, H., J. Green, and C. Snowdon. 1992 Psychological and social aspects of screening for fetal abnormality durign routine antenatal care. In Research and the Midwife Conference. Manchester: School of Nursing, Unversity of Manchester.

[33] Nolan, M. 1997. Antenatal education: Failing to educate for parenthood. *British Journal of Midwifery*. 5 (1): 21-26.

[34] Zwelling, E. 1996. Childbirth education in the 1990s and beyond. *JOGNN Journal of Obstetric, Gynecologic, & Neonatal Nursing*. 25 (5): 425-432.

[35] Friedewald, M., R. Fletcher, and H. Fairbairn. 2005. All-male discussion forums for expectant fathers: evaluation of a model. *Journal of Perinatal Education*. 14 (2): 8-18.

In: Handbook of Parenting: Styles, Stresses & Strategies   ISBN 978-1-60741-766-8
Editor: Pacey H. Krause and Tahlia M. Dailey   © 2009 Nova Science Publishers, Inc.

Chapter 7

GOODNESS OF FIT BETWEEN PARENTING STYLE AND CHILD TEMPERAMENT: SPECIAL CHALLENGES WITH SLOW-TO-WARM-UP INFANTS

Jessica Stoltzfus and Katherine Karraker

West Virginia University, USA

Morgantown, West Virginia, USA

ABSTRACT

This review focuses on the goodness-of-fit concept, concentrating specifically on how a poor fit between the temperament behaviors of infants and young children and parents' expectations and parenting skills can stress and challenge the parent-child relationship and potentially lead to poor child outcomes. We consider the role of the child, the parent, and the context in establishing, maintaining, and modifying the goodness of fit between children's temperament and their parents' behaviors and in determining child outcomes. We conclude by presenting findings from a recent analysis of 629 mothers and their children that illustrates the special challenges of parenting slow-to-warm-up infants using the goodness-of-fit perspective.

INTRODUCTION

Temperament describes the *way* in which an individual behaves (Chess & Thomas, 1999). It is an inherited, consistent behavioral style that is demonstrated in response to the social and physical environment. Thomas and Chess and their colleagues were among the first to study temperament. From their observations of the typical behaviors of 133 children, they identified nine dimensions of temperament, including activity, rhythmicity, adaptability, approach, threshold of response, intensity, mood, distractibility, and attention span/persistence (Thomas, Chess, Birch, Hertzig, & Korn, 1963), and then defined four temperament categories based on unique combinations of these dimensions: difficult, easy, slow-to-warm-up, and intermediate (Thomas, Chess, & Birch, 1970). The difficult child is high in intensity and activity, low in approach, adaptability, and rhythmicity, and negative in mood. The easy child is mild in intensity, moderate in activity, high in approach, adaptability, and rhythmicity, and positive in mood. The slow-to-warm-up child is mild in intensity, moderate to low in activity, low in approach, variable in rhythmicity, and slightly negative in mood (Thomas et al., 1970). Children who do not fit into one of these groups are assigned to the intermediate category.

Chess and Thomas (1999) also proposed that a good fit between children's temperament and their parents' cognitions and behaviors is critical to children's adaptive social and emotional development. This review focuses on this goodness-of-fit concept, concentrating specifically on how a poor fit between the temperament behaviors of infants and young children and parents' expectations and parenting skills can stress and challenge the parent-child relationship and potentially lead to poor child outcomes. We consider the role of the child, the parent, and the context in establishing, maintaining, and modifying the goodness of fit between children's temperament and their parents' behaviors and in determining child outcomes. We conclude by presenting findings from a recent analysis that illustrate the special challenges of parenting slow-to-warm-up infants using the goodness-of-fit perspective. Because infants with a slow-to-warm-up temperament may be at high risk for later inhibition, which is the tendency to withdraw from new people, places, and things (Kagan, 1994), we focus on the role of a good or poor fit between infants' slow-to-warm-up temperament and their parents' behavior in predicting later inhibition.

THE GOODNESS-OF-FIT MODEL

In general terms, goodness of fit is the result of a match or consonance between the abilities and characteristics of the individual and the demands and expectations of the individual's environment (Chess & Thomas, 1999). When there is consonance between the individual and his or her environment, optimal development is possible. Indeed, goodness of fit is often assessed by examining the outcomes associated with different combinations of individual and environmental characteristics. Chess and Thomas further describe goodness of fit as residing within the *interaction* between the individual and the specific demands and requirements of his or her environment, rather than residing solely within the individual or solely within the environment. For the purposes of our discussion, we focus on parents as the most central and influential aspect of the environment for infants and young children. Thus, a good fit results when certain combinations of child temperament and parenting styles lead to positive child outcomes.

Goodness of fit is the result of dynamic processes that are constantly changing, and is defined within a particular social and cultural context. A good fit in one context may be poor in another. For example, a child who is high in approach, activity, intensity, and sociability will thrive in a preschool environment with other same-aged children, an environment that stimulates the child's joy of being around others and desire for new people, toys, and situations. The preschool environment represents a good fit between the child's temperamental proclivities and his or her surroundings. The same child, once back in the home environment, may become increasingly rambunctious and bored with the familiar surroundings and limited opportunities for social play. Moreover, the child's parents may be too busy, either from household duties such as cooking and cleaning or from caring for siblings, to engage the child in a manner that adequately meets the child's needs. The child's high sociability and activity, behaviors the preschool environment enhanced and cultivated, may result in a poor parent-child fit within the home environment.

As the above example illustrates, a poor fit results when the opportunities and demands of the environment are dissonant with the needs and abilities of the individual. Often, a poor fit results in maladaptive, pathological development (Chess & Thomas, 1999). When a poor fit occurs, neither aspects of the individual nor aspects of the individual's environment are necessarily maladaptive or dysfunctional in and of themselves. Rather, "*the pathology is in the interaction*" (Chess & Thomas, 1999, p. 9). Thus, a poor fit can result from a variety of combinations of child temperaments and parenting styles. Although specific parenting behaviors or child temperament behaviors may not always lead to poor fit and poor outcomes, certain parenting behaviors and child temperament styles are more likely than others to lead to poor fit and poor outcomes. For example, harsh parental discipline and parental criticism generally are associated with poor child outcomes (e.g., externalizing child behavior; Miner & Clarke-Stewart, 2008), and children who are difficult or high in negativity in infancy typically demonstrate higher rates of externalizing, internalizing, and inhibited behaviors in childhood than other children (e.g., behavioral inhibition; Kagan, Snidman, & Arcus, 1998; aggression; Vitaro, Barker, Boivin, Brendgen, & Tremblay, 2006). These parenting behaviors and child temperament styles are considered "vulnerabilities" (Chess & Thomas), as they increase the likelihood of a poor fit. When child temperament vulnerabilities interact with parenting vulnerabilities, a poor fit and poor outcomes are especially likely.

Figure 1 illustrates a number of ways in which child temperament and parenting styles can combine to produce a good or poor fit, and thus good or poor child outcomes. Figures 1a and 1b illustrate simple main effects. In Figure 1a, a particular parenting style (parenting style B in the figure), such as harsh discipline, results in poor child adaptation regardless of the child's temperament. In Figure 1b, a specific child temperament (temperament B in the figure), such as temperamental difficulty, results in a poor outcome regardless of the parenting style the child receives. In both of these cases, goodness of fit is wholly determined by either the parent (Figure 1a) or the child (Figure 1b). Although researchers often report such simple main effects based on group data, they also generally acknowledge that these main effects are commonly moderated by other factors. For example, although many children who are highly reactive in infancy are inhibited in early childhood, a small group of children seem to overcome their initial high reactivity and are uninhibited (Kagan et al., 1998).

Figure 1c illustrates the case when main effects of child temperament and parenting style additively combine. As a hypothetical example, the best fit and outcome may result from the combination of positive parenting (parenting style A) and easy child temperament (temperament A). An intermediate fit and outcome would occur in this example with *either* positive parenting or an easy child temperament, and a poor fit and outcome would occur when poor parenting (parenting style B) combines with difficult child temperament (temperament B). Although this model may apply well to extreme variations in child temperament and parenting style, often these two variables interact in complex and nonadditive ways to produce either a good or poor fit. Figures 1d and 1e illustrate two of the numerous other ways in which temperament and parenting might combine. In Figure 1d, one parenting style (A) leads to a good fit with one child temperament (A) whereas the other parenting style (B) leads to a good fit with another child temperament (B). In Figure 1e, one parenting style (A) fits well with either child temperament (A or B), whereas the other parenting style (B) leads to a good fit with one child temperament (B), but not the other (A).

Simple Effects Model

Temperament	Parenting Style	
	A	B
A	+	-
B	+	-

1a

Simple Effects Model

Temperament	Parenting Style	
	A	B
A	+	+
B	-	-

1b

Additive Main Effects Model

Temperament	Parenting Style	
	A	B
A	+	OK
B	OK	-

1c

Goodness-of-Fit Model

Temperament	Parenting Style	
	A	B
A	+	-
B	-	+

1d

Goodness-of-Fit Model

Temperament	Parenting Style	
	A	B
A	+	-
B	-	-

1e

Figure 1.1a) Parenting style A leads to good infant outcomes regardless of infant temperament. 1b) Infant temperament A leads to good infant outcomes regardless of parenting style. 1c) Parenting style and infant temperament combine additively to produce infant outcomes. 1d) One parenting style combines with one infant temperament to produce good infant outcomes, and the other parenting style combines with the other infant temperament to produce good infant outcomes. 1e) Parenting style affects infant outcomes for one infant temperament but not for another infant temperament.

Numerous examples of good and poor fit have been reported. For example, children with difficult temperament in infancy tend to demonstrate externalizing behavior in middle to late childhood if they receive harsh maternal parenting but not if they receive more positive parenting in infancy (Miner & Clarke-Stewart, 2008; see Figure 1d). Similarly, research has shown that children who are high in negativity in infancy later demonstrate externalizing behaviors if they receive harsh rather than positive mothering and inhibition if they receive positive rather than negative fathering (Belsky, Hsieh, & Crnic, 1998; see Figure 1d). Children without these temperamental vulnerabilities are less affected by a poor fit than children with these temperamental vulnerabilities. For example, temperamentally easy children generally develop adaptively regardless of their parents' parenting style or behaviors (see Figure 1e, parenting style A).

Often, parenting behaviors and child temperament styles that place a relationship at risk for a poor fit are unique, are low in frequency, are unexpected, or violate norms. For instance, Chess and Thomas (1999) present the case of a child born with a characteristically easy temperament (i.e., high adaptability and approach, low intensity, and a predominately positive mood) who also possessed the temperamental vulnerabilities of high distractibility and low attention. Such a child is likely to adapt and develop normally unless features of his or her environment are dissonant with his or her temperamental vulnerabilities. Specifically, if a parent interprets the child's distractibility and inattentiveness as laziness and a lack of responsibility, the parent may require the child to behave in ways that exceed his or her abilities, such as setting up hour-long study sessions. Because such requirements exceed the child's abilities, the child is likely to be unsuccessful at behaving in the way the parent demands. If this mismatch between parental demands and the abilities of the child continues over time, the child is likely to show negative social functioning and may later in childhood, adolescence, and young adulthood demonstrate maladaptive behaviors. In Chess and Thomas's case example, the child's father was derisive and critical of the child. This parental response resulted in a poor fit; the child later demonstrated poor academic performance, and as an adult was frequently unemployed and largely dependent on others. The same child parented differently is likely to develop well. For instance, taking a more adaptive, child-oriented approach, the parent could shape the child's behavior to match the parents' demands by providing small rewards for each successful short interval of studying until the child is able to sit for a longer period of time on his or her own.

In summary, the match or mismatch between the demands of the social environment and the abilities and attributes of the individual produces a good or poor fit and results in adaptive or maladaptive development. Of importance, goodness of fit is identified by the outcome, such as the child's adaptive social functioning in the home or in the broader environment. We now address the processes by which a good fit comes about and either persists or changes.

HOW A GOOD FIT IS ESTABLISHED AND MAINTAINED

A number of specific mechanisms can influence the onset or maintenance of a good fit between a child's temperament and his or her social environment. These mechanisms address the question of "how" a good or poor fit comes about. These mechanisms are categorized for descriptive purposes as relating to the child's role, the parent's role, and the context's role in determining fit.

The Child's Role in Establishing and Maintaining a Good Fit

To a large extent, individuals shape their own environments and are active producers of their environments (Baltes, Reese, & Nesselroade, 1988). Because of the biological basis of temperament, children's temperamentally based behaviors can elicit differential parenting behaviors from birth. In addition to this role of child temperament in eliciting parenting behaviors, genetic similarity between parents and children can facilitate a good fit. Further, an initial good or poor fit may be maintained over time due to the general stability of temperament and the ongoing eliciting effects of particular temperamental styles. However, children also learn to adapt to their environments, and may change the expression of their temperamentally based behaviors due to reinforcement, punishment, and modeling in ways that increase or decrease fit with their parents' behaviors. Across the life span, individuals develop an increasing competency for shaping and selecting their own environments and with increasing precision produce their own development (Lerner & Lerner, 1987). As they get older, children may intentionally influence their parents' behaviors and select the times, places, and activities in which to interact with them.

Effects of Children's Temperament on Others

Children's temperamentally driven behaviors and emotional responses are a source of information to social others (Lerner & Lerner, 1987). The majority of children are born with easy or intermediate temperament styles, which tend to elicit positive parenting behaviors, leading naturally to a good fit and positive child outcomes. Children with more difficult temperaments may be more likely to elicit behaviors from their parents that lead to a poorer fit. For instance, an infant who is predominantly negative in mood and is unable to adapt to new things provides negative feedback to parents who, when introducing the child to new food or toys, experience one failure after another. Such negative feedback can result in a poor fit if the parents are unable to adapt to or understand the child's individuality.

Child effects begin even prenatally, as parents use fetal movement to form a cohesive picture of their infants' personalities (Zeanah, Zeanah, & Stewart, 1990). However, temperament behaviors exert ongoing effects on others as parents continue to perceive their children's individuality beyond the infancy age period and react to their children's temperament in ways that affect parent-child relations. Kingston and Prior (1995) followed children from preschool to middle childhood (i.e., ages 2 to 8 years) and found that children who were temperamentally difficult in early childhood received harsh child-rearing practices from their caregivers and had hostile sibling relations in middle childhood. Moreover, those children with extreme difficulty in infancy were in middle childhood persistently aggressive and were considered at risk for continued social and academic difficulties. Although these results are presented in a main effect model (see Figure 1b), with child behaviors as the mechanism influencing their parents' behaviors and their later outcomes, it is likely that these children's extreme difficulty interacted with the type of parenting they received to result in a poor fit and poor later outcomes. Research has repeatedly shown that harsh and controlling parenting practices are associated with poor later child functioning (i.e., internalizing and externalizing problem behaviors), particularly for children who are highly negative or difficult in infancy (Belsky et al., 1998; Warren & Simmens, 2005), suggesting that these parenting behaviors fit poorly with difficult children's temperament. A better fit and more adaptive developmental trajectory in terms of internalizing and externalizing behaviors may result from parenting behaviors that are patient yet firm with the behaviors associated with their children's extreme difficulty and supportive of their children's characteristics that are more moderate.

The goodness-of-fit model assumes that a person's individual characteristics and behaviors elicit reactions from social others, and that these reactions then provide feedback to the individual and shape his or her further development (Lerner, 2002). For instance, parents tend to respond to high negativity in toddlerhood in either a highly sensitive or in an intrusive (Belsky et al., 1998; Park, Belsky, Putnam, & Crnic, 1997) manner. Highly sensitive parenting is associated with inhibition in these children in early childhood (Belsky et al.; Park et al.), suggesting that this type of parenting does not represent the best fit with the toddlers' negativity. Instead, children high in negativity as infants whose mothers are more intrusive and whose fathers are less sensitive and affectively positive during early childhood (ages 2 to 3 years) are less inhibited at age 3 years than children high in negativity who receive different parenting (Park et al.). Whereas parental sensitivity is beneficial for most children's development, highly negative infants may benefit most from parenting that pushes them to adapt to their environment. Such an example illustrates the goodness-of-fit model (Figure 1d) in that the type of parenting that is associated with good outcomes for some children may be associated with poor outcomes for other children.

Similarity of Child and Parent

An initial good fit or match may naturally occur due to genetic similarity between the child and parent. According to results obtained by behavioral geneticists, 50 percent of the variation among children can be traced to interindividual differences in their genetic makeup and 50 percent can be traced to interindividual differences in their environments (Harris, 1998). Thus, children and parents behave similarly in part for genetic reasons (Harris), so that matching of personality styles and behaviors can occur between children and their parents and result in a good fit. As an example, a parent who is sociable may have a child with the same temperamental proclivities toward approaching and interacting with social others. When the parent spends time with friends or makes new acquaintances the child would be expected to enjoy this social time as well.

Although temperamental behaviors are in part inherited, the inherited genotype may not translate into the child's phenotype, specifically the temperament behaviors that he or she demonstrates. Other factors, such as environmental conditions like nutrition level and exposure to heavy metals, can affect which genes are displayed (Wachs, 2000). Therefore, even though there is genetic similarity between the parent and the child, such similarity does not guarantee that a match will occur, as other factors interact with the genetic material to affect the behavior that is demonstrated by the child.

Not all behavioral similarity between the parent and the child is due strictly to genes. According to Harris (1998), direct genetic effects (like being born temperamentally shy or outgoing, attractive or ugly) have an indirect effect through the way in which others respond to the inherited attributes. Identical twins may be similar in part because of their genes but also in part because they share the attributes associated with their shared genes and thus elicit and receive similar social responses. For instance, a pair of twins may be hesitant to approach others and negative in mood. Social others then respond to these attributes with the same behaviors, perhaps with avoidance. Both children then experience the same learning history from their interactions with others, which may lead to further similarity in their behaviors.

Although heritability correlations are lower for parents and offspring than for identical twins (Plomin, 1990), parents and offspring still share both some genetic and some environmental attributes. For instance, the child of tall and attractive parents likely is also tall and attractive. The child then receives the same (likely positive) responses from others as their parents because of their similar stature and appearance. In response, a child and the parents may behave similarly, which may then influence parent-child fit.

Behavioral similarity between parent and child behaviors that results from genetic similarity between the child and the parent may not guarantee a good fit, however. For example, if an inhibited child is born to parents who are shy, because of the parents' own shyness they may not expose the child to as many novel social situations as would more sociable parents. Thus, the inhibited child may not experience situations that challenge him or her and require changes in his or her shy behaviors. Moreover, the parents would likely not model to the child adaptive ways of interacting with unfamiliar people. In this example, the fit with the parents may appear to be good, but the fit with the broader environment may be poor. Poor developmental outcomes associated with extreme shyness, such as anxiety, depression, and peer rejection (Rubin, 1993), may then result. Such negative outcomes resulting from the interaction between the child's temperament and the child's social environment (i.e., the parents) suggest that this matching has the potential to result in a poor fit between the parents' and the child's behaviors. Note that although the parent and child in this example may find their behavioral similarity to be comfortable and it may lead to a lack of conflict in their interactions, the goodness of fit is determined by the outcome (in this case the child's adaptive social functioning in the broader environment).

Stability of Temperament

Whereas temperament originates in infancy, its influence continues into early childhood and beyond. Temperament tends to be stable over time, particularly after early infancy (Rothbart & Bates, 2006), although it interacts with social and other environmental influences to affect later behaviors and determine personality in adulthood (Goldsmith, Lemery, Aksan, & Buss, 2000; Rothbart & Bates). The stability of temperament largely is due to the inherited and biological bases of temperament, and can result in continuity in goodness of fit across the lifespan (Goldsmith et al.). A recent study by Asendorpf, Denissen, and van Aken (2008) illustrates both the stability of temperament and the ability for individuals to self-select their own environment and be shaped by others. Asendorpf et al. showed that adults who had been highly inhibited as preschoolers (in the top 15% percent of the sample in inhibition) were at age 23 less likely to be in a stable, romantic relationship and more likely to have nonromantic relationships with opposite-sex peers than their uninhibited peers. Moreover, adults who were classified as inhibited in childhood entered the work force 10 months behind adults who were uninhibited in childhood. Such results suggest that highly inhibited individuals self-select into a delayed social interaction trajectory or, alternatively, others consistently respond to their inhibited behavior in a way that shapes their developmental trajectory. Asendorpf et al.'s findings illustrate that continuity in fit can result from stable genetic effects on temperament as well as from stable environments and the continued elicitation of the same behaviors. However, the goodness-of-fit model recognizes that children are able to adapt to their own environments (Chess & Thomas, 1999). Discontinuity in fit can result from the child changing and adapting to his or her social or other environment, through developmental processes, or as a result of his or her learning history.

Children learn to display some temperamentally based behaviors more frequently because they are reinforced, and others less frequently because they are punished. They also model behaviors that they see in others. Parents also often try to shape their children's behaviors to create a better match. For example, Chess, Thomas, and Birch (1965) provide an example of a difficult child whose tantrums in grocery stores and other social scenes was consistently responded to by her parents and others with quiet but firm removal from the situation. The child would quickly calm down in these situations, and, over time, demonstrated fewer tantrums. Although the child continued to be stubborn or uncooperative at times throughout her childhood, she generally adapted well in kindergarten and beyond because of the patient yet firm responses of her parents, relatives, and teachers. In such cases, the temperament of the child does not really change, but the behavioral expression of the underlying temperament changes through the impact of the child's learning history.

Whereas in some cases child behaviors do change as children adapt to their environments, for the most part child behaviors exert a stable, ongoing effect on others in their environment. However, child effects are only one mechanism producing fit. Parents can also play a role in establishing and maintaining a good fit.

The Parent's Role in Establishing and Maintaining a Good Fit

Most parents provide sensitive and competent parenting to their children, which normally leads to positive child outcomes, as this style of parenting produces a good fit for most children's temperament (Figure 1a, parenting style A). On the other hand, a few parents engage in such deficient parenting practices that their children experience very high risk for poor outcomes due to a poor fit (Figure 1a, parenting style B). For example, younger and less mature mothers and mothers who are depressed are less likely than older and non-depressed mothers to provide optimal care (Belsky, 1984). However, in some cases, only particular combinations of child temperament and parenting style are a poor fit and lead to poor outcomes. This section addresses the role of the parent in creating and maintaining a good or poor fit between their parenting style and their child's temperament. Both the cognitions, including perceptions, expectations, beliefs, attitudes, and values, and the behaviors of parents are relevant to this determination of fit (Lerner & Lerner, 1987).

Parenting Cognitions

Parenting cognitions include the attitudes, values, and expectations that parents have regarding their children's behavioral or physical characteristics. Children's abilities to adapt to and meet the expectations of others influence the type of feedback they receive from others and their degree of fit with their social environment (Lerner & Lerner, 1987). For instance, a mother may expect her infant to eat and sleep at approximately the same time each day and may become frustrated with an infant who violates such expectations. Similarly, a teacher may expect his or her students to demonstrate a certain period of attentiveness toward a task and may inadvertently discourage the academic achievement of a child who is hyperactive and inattentive. In these examples, the cause of the poor fit between the child's behaviors and the environment is the expectation of social others, which clashes with the child's temperament.

Parents bring into the infant-parent relationship expectations that may or may not match the child's predispositions. Such expectations may lead to a poor fit unless the infant alters his or her behaviors to achieve a good fit and adapt successfully in the environment that the parents provide. Alternately, the parents may adjust their expectations. For example, in a white middle-class sample of parents and infants (Thomas, Chess, Sillen, & Mendez, 1974), parents expected their infants to demonstrate regular sleep patterns. When the infants violated this expectation by waking frequently at night, resulting in a poor fit, the parents became distressed. The parents then took steps to alter their infants' behavior, attempting to change the poor fit to a good fit (Chess & Thomas, 1999). In many cases, parents' efforts to change challenging infant behaviors are successful, leading to an improved fit. However, sometimes parents' efforts to change their child's behavior to meet their expectations are unsuccessful. In this case, the poor fit is maintained, unless the parents give up on changing the infant and adapt themselves to a difficult behavior. For example, parents whose children engage in frequent and persistent night-waking despite parental attempts to encourage sleeping through the night may have to resign themselves to getting up during the night to assist the infant in returning to sleep (Karraker, 2008). These parents can improve the fit between themselves and their infants by engaging in strategies to reduce their own sleep deprivation, such as daytime napping and sharing night-time child care, and by adapting their own expectations to match their child's sleep behaviors.

Parenting cognitions have been found to affect the fit between infant temperament and parenting during the transition into parenthood. Leerkes and Burney (2007) found that mothers who were high in self-efficacy before their infants were born remained efficacious at 6 months postpartum even when their infants were highly negative and reactive, traits that are typically associated with a poor fit. In this study, the mother's cognitions, specifically her belief in her effectiveness as a parent before her infant was born, may have produced a fit between the infant's temperament and social environment by increasing the mother's positive behaviors toward and involvement with her infant. These mothers may then have received positive reinforcement from their newborn for their interactions and continued to feel competent as a parent. Moreover, high prenatal self-efficacy may have buffered any punishment (e.g., crying, fussing) mothers received from highly negative newborns, so that mothers could maintain their sense of efficacy. In this case, mothers' perceptions acted as the mechanism buffering the effects of infant negativity. In line with a main effects model, self-efficacy is often associated with good outcomes in the context of parenting as well as in a number of other domains, and thus may have more of a main effect than an interactive effect on parental and child behaviors. However, consistent with a differential susceptibility model, maternal self-efficacy may have a particular impact on mothers' parenting when their infants are high in negativity and reactivity, so that high self-efficacy leads to positive parenting of difficult infants and positive child outcomes whereas low self-efficacy leads to poor parenting and poor child outcomes with these children. In contrast, parenting behaviors may be less affected by self-efficacy with an easy infant, and may not be associated with differential child outcomes in this case. This example is most consistent with the model depicted in Figure 1e.

Another way that parent cognitions can influence fit is through the impact of parents' perceptions of their infants' temperament on their behaviors toward their infants. These parental behaviors may then change how infants express their temperamental individuality. For example, Pauli-Pott, Mertesacker, Bade, Haverkock and Beckmann (2003) found that mothers' perceptions of infant positive and negative emotionality preceded the infants' increased behavioral demonstration of these traits in later months. Pauli-Pott et al.'s findings provide a specific example of the mechanism of the parent causing change in the infant: parents' expectations drove their behaviors, which then modified their infants' temperamentally based behaviors through shaping.

Parenting Behaviors

Parents' behaviors play a key role in creating a good or poor fit between themselves and their child's temperament. Certain child temperament behaviors, such as high negativity and low adaptability, may elicit poor parenting behaviors either directly or through their impact on parents' cognitions. These parent behaviors then influence the child's subsequent behaviors in a way that either maintains, increases, or decreases fit.

Not only does the child provide feedback to social others via temperament behaviors, but social others also provide feedback to the child. The goodness of fit concept assumes that the person's individuality elicits reactions from social others, and that these reactions then provide feedback to the individual and shape his or her further development. Moreover, the type of feedback the individual elicits and receives from his or her social environment varies in relation to the individual's ability to adapt and to meet the demands of the specific environment (Lerner & Lerner, 1987). For instance, an inattentive and hyperactive boy with a father who berates such behavior is receiving negative feedback from the father. The child, unable to alter his temperamentally based behaviors, learns that his father does not support his activities. Such a pattern sets the stage for a poor fit. Parents can also model a particular behavior to the child, which may affect how the child demonstrates his or her temperamental style. To reiterate a previous example, if parents of children who are shy or inhibited are also shy, they will demonstrate and model behaviors consistent with this temperament, which will result in similar shy behaviors in the child. In contrast, if parents of a shy or inhibited child are sociable and outgoing, they will model behaviors that are inconsistent with the child's temperament, which may result in the child displaying similar sociability in some situations and changing his or her temperament behaviors.

Not only can children's behaviors change in response to their parents' and caregivers' behaviors, but parents and caregivers can also adapt to their children's behaviors. For example, Chess and Thomas (1999) describe the case of a young mother who was overly stimulating and intrusive with her newborn infant; this infant responded by avoiding eye contact with the mother. Before intervention was needed, however, the mother-child relationship spontaneously began to improve, with the mother demonstrating more appropriate stimulation of the child and the child responding positively (Chess & Thomas). In this case, the parent adapted her behavior to the needs of her child so that a poor fit turned into a good fit. As another example, preschoolers in some locations, particularly in the northern part of the country, are restricted from going outside for free-play during winter months because of the cold and harsh weather. Such a situation represents a poor fit between preschoolers' typical high activity level and need for exercise and their environment. To adapt to this situation, preschool teachers change the children's routine to include "exercise time." The children, guided by their teacher, do activities such as jumping jacks and stretching to allow the children to release some of their energy in an adaptive manner, which enables them to focus on the more learning-based activities that follow in the day. At times, creative methods and insight is required of parents and caregivers in order to attain a good fit between children and their environment.

The Role of Context in Establishing and Maintaining a Good Fit

Attributes of the physical and sociocultural context also influence the degree to which parenting style and child temperament combine to produce a good fit and good child outcomes (Lerner & Lerner, 1987). In addition, because parents are largely responsible for selecting and creating contexts for young children, we also consider in this section the goodness of fit between child temperament and contextual factors. Context is defined as the many influences that are outside of the individual (Dannefer, 1992).

One set of relevant contextual factors includes the physical attributes of the home environment, such as noisiness, crowdedness, and location. Chess and Thomas (1999; Thomas et al., 1974) found that the physical attributes of children's social environment can affect the degree of fit between children's temperament and their parents. In a low-income Puerto Rican sample (Thomas et al.), over half of the parents viewed high levels of activity in their children as problematic, whereas in a middle-class white sample, only one parent considered the behavior problematic. The Puerto Rican sample lived in a dangerous neighborhood and crowded homes. Therefore, the physical properties of the environment did not support the temperamental proclivities of the highly active child. Active children did not have room to play in the home nor were they able to play outside because of the dangerous area in which their families lived. In contrast, most of the white, middle-class sample lived in homes with a high rooms-to-person ratio that were within blocks of a neighborhood park, characteristics that supported the child's ability to play actively without creating tension in the home (Thomas et al.). The same temperament resulted in a different fit depending on the behavioral demands of the environment.

Hane, Fox, Polak-Toste, Ghera, and Guner (2006) provide an example of how the behavioral demands of the environment can affect goodness of fit between children and their parents. They found that mothers perceived their 9-month-old infants as temperamentally prone to distress (suggesting a poor fit) when their infants demonstrated high negativity while the mothers were completing daily home-based activities. However, mothers' perceptions of proneness to distress were not affected by negativity demonstrated during object-oriented play (suggesting a good fit). When feeding or changing the infant or when preparing meals, mothers appeared to be especially likely to notice and be affected by their infants' negative affectivity because such negativity interfered with their ability to complete their tasks efficiently. The same infant behavior did not influence parent-infant fit in another context because of the different behavioral demands of the environment.

A study by Thomas and Chess and their colleagues (Chess & Thomas, 1999; Thomas et al., 1974) illustrates a discontinuity in the quality of fit between child temperament and both parenting and the broader environment resulting from a change in context. Arrhythmic sleep patterns were found to be prevalent in young children in both a middle-class white sample and a lower class Puerto Rican sample. This temperamentally based behavior was considered problematic by the white parents, who took steps to alter the behavior. In contrast, the Puerto Rican parents did not view the behavior as problematic. Because arrhythmic sleep behavior fit or matched the expectations of these parents, no attempts were made by the parents to alter the behavior and the children continued to demonstrate irregular sleep patterns into middle childhood. When the Puerto Rican children entered kindergarten, the expectations of the teachers and principals in their new social environment differed from those of their parents in the home environment. The irregular sleeping pattern interfered with the children's ability to get the amount of sleep that they needed to perform well in school and their ability to get up and get ready for school on time, resulting in a poor fit between the child's temperamental arrhythmicity and the expectations of the social environment. As a result of this poor fit, between ages 5 and 9 years 50 percent of the sample presented problem behavior and were diagnosed with a sleep disorder (Chess & Thomas; Thomas et al.). Such findings illustrate the potential for discontinuity in fit from one age period to another when the context changes but the child's temperamentally based behavior does not.

Study findings also illustrate the importance of considering child gender and physical aspects of the context when evaluating goodness of fit. Matheny and Phillips (2001) evaluated a sample of infants from birth to age 30 months, and assessed relations between infant temperament and characteristics of the home environment. They found that the same environment can interact with the same temperament characteristic differently for boys and girls. Specifically, boys demonstrated high levels of negative emotionality at 24 months if they were raised in noisy, crowded households, whereas girls raised in the same household environment demonstrated more positivity than negativity. This example illustrates that characteristics of certain environments may interact with characteristics of the individual child in ways that make goodness of fit as well as developmental outcomes difficult to predict.

Culture is an important contextual factor that can affect the fit between children's temperaments and their social environment. Goodness of fit is embedded within a particular cultural context in part because culture influences the expectations and beliefs parents have for their children's behaviors (Chess & Thomas, 1999; Sigel & McGillicuddy-De Lisi, 2002). Culture as a context shapes the way parents view a particular behavior and has an orderly effect on the developmental trajectory of the behavior. The same temperament results in a different outcome depending on the culture in which the individual is embedded. Easy temperament in infancy is commonly associated with positive child development, whereas difficult temperament in infancy is often associated with poor child outcomes, such as internalizing and externalizing behaviors (Rothbart & Bates, 2006). This relation, which represents a main effect of a specific temperament on a particular outcome (Figure 1b), exists in part because in western culture, where regularity, predictability, approach, and adaptability are valued by parents, easy infants are likely less frustrating for parents than are difficult infants, who are inadaptable and irregular. However, during a time when resources were limited in an East African sample of Masai infants, difficult infants, who characteristically demonstrate high levels of intensity and negativity, were more likely to demand and receive food from their parents and were thus more likely to survive than easy infants (DeVries, 1984). The poor outcome for easy infants illustrated that difficult temperament fit better with this harsh climate than did easy temperament. The same infant temperament can elicit a good or a poor fit in different cultural contexts, resulting in different child adaptations and outcomes.

The effects of the cultural context on temperament-environment fit can also be attributed to the expectations and attributes of parents and others in particular cultures (Sigel & McGillicuddy-De Lisi, 2002). For example, behavioral inhibition in toddlerhood has different meanings to parents in Canadian culture as compared to Chinese culture (Chen et al., 1998). In China, maintaining order, harmony, and group cohesiveness is important. In this culture, inhibition, which is accompanied by self-restraint, is adaptive and positively valued. In contrast, in Canada, individuality and assertiveness are valued. Because inhibition is characterized by fear and withdrawal, inhibited toddlers are less likely to be assertive in social interactions than are uninhibited toddlers. Therefore, toddler inhibition in Chinese culture results in a good fit, whereas in Canadian culture it does not.

Physical attributes of the environment, behavioral demands of the environment, and cultural attributes all can play a significant role in establishing and maintaining fit between children and their environments. Sometimes cultural factors can be a distal cause and parenting behaviors can be a proximal cause in creating this fit. We next consider the challenges for parents that are associated with two temperament profiles, difficult temperament and slow-to-warm-up temperament, although we acknowledge that the stress and challenge these temperament profiles create for parents may vary with cultural and other environmental attributes.

INFANT DIFFICULT AND SLOW-TO-WARM-UP TEMPERAMENTS AS STRESSORS FOR PARENTS

Sameroff and Chandler (1975) and Bell (1968) were among the first to emphasize that the parent-child relationship is bidirectional, with the parent influencing the child as well as the child influencing the parent. Sameroff and Chandler highlighted the concept that human development is characterized by reciprocal transactions between the individual, including his or her personality and temperament traits, and the environment. In line with this perspective, when evaluating the goodness or poorness of fit between a parent and child, it is important to keep in mind that goodness of fit is in the process or in the interaction. Parenting and temperament, when considered independently, exert main effects on child development. However, certain parent or child characteristics also increase the likelihood of a poor fit and poor outcomes because of their impact on the other member of the dyad. For example, child difficult and slow-to-warm-up temperaments can increase the likelihood of poor outcomes through main effects on children's functioning as well as by decreasing parent-child fit due to the stress for parents of caring for these children. In this section, we review research on children with these two challenging temperament profiles.

Difficult infants are high in negativity and intensity and are low in approach, adaptability, and rhythmicity. These infants demand their parents' attention. They cry loudly and intensely when their parents try to introduce them to new toys, food, and people. Difficult infants are hungry and sleepy at unpredictable times, making it challenging for parents and other caregivers to establish a set, daily caregiving routine. Children who were difficult in infancy continue to struggle to adapt to novelty in childhood. A specific challenge during this age period is entering primary school. Children who are difficult may struggle to adapt to the new challenges associated with school entry because of their slow adaptability. They may also struggle to interact with new peers, teachers, and principals because of their tendency to withdraw from social novelty. Because of their low rhythmicity, difficult children may have difficulty going to sleep and getting up on time for school, which may create conflict in the home environment for parents. A good fit between difficult children and their parents may be challenging for many parents because of the particular behaviors these children present.

Slow-to-warm-up infants also present a distinct set of challenges for their parents. Slow-to-warm-up infants, whose initial hesitancy to approach is paired with a mild rather than a high level of intensity, may be even more likely than difficult infants to continually elicit poor parenting behaviors from their parents and other caregivers. For instance, the parent of the slow-to-warm-up infant may simply ignore the child's hesitancy to approach and low adaptability because these reactions, when paired with a low level of intensity, do not significantly affect the parent's daily functions, whereas the same characteristics, when paired with the difficult infant's high level of intensity, may severely inhibit daily functions and thus motivate the parent to try to alter such behaviors.

Carey and McDevitt (1995) postulate that infant difficult and slow-to-warm-up temperaments are risk factors for a poor parent-child fit. According to Chess and Thomas (1999), "poorness of fit involves discrepancies and dissonances between environmental opportunities and demands and the capacities of the organism, so that distorted development and maladaptive functioning occur" (p. 3). As a result of this dissonance, difficult and slow-to-warm-up infants may elicit and receive poorer parenting behavior than easy and intermediate infants and may therefore be less likely to experience a positive relationship with their parents than infants with a good fit. These temperaments represent specific child vulnerabilities that, especially when paired with parenting vulnerabilities, such as low sensitivity, may lead to a poor fit. A number of studies have explored this link for children with a difficult temperament. For example, Warren and Simmens (2005) investigated relations among infant temperament, gender, and toddler anxiety/depressive (internalizing) symptoms, and found that children who were rated as temperamentally difficult in infancy and received sensitive parenting in toddlerhood demonstrated fewer anxiety/depressive symptoms than children who were rated as temperamentally difficult in infancy but did not receive sensitive parenting. This effect was stronger for boys than for girls, suggesting that temperamentally difficult boys may especially benefit from parenting practices that are high in sensitivity. For infants who were not temperamentally difficult, the level of maternal sensitivity was not associated with their behaviors in toddlerhood; these children were low in anxiety/depressive symptoms regardless of whether they received less or more maternal sensitivity. Such findings illustrate the goodness-of-fit model presented in Figure 1e.

Other research also suggests that some infants benefit more from and are more affected by particular parenting styles than other infants. Park et al. (1997) found that infants whose parents were highly sensitive were more likely than infants whose parents were low in sensitivity to be inhibited in childhood, but only if the infants were high in negativity in infancy. Further, high maternal and paternal negativity (i.e., maternal intrusiveness and paternal insensitivity and lack of protectiveness) led to lowered inhibition in early childhood for highly negative infants only. Park et al.'s findings support the possibility that because both slow-to-warm-up and difficult infants are predominantly negative in mood, they may be more affected by particular parenting behaviors than intermediate and easy infants who characteristically demonstrate a predominantly positive mood. Thus, children who are intermediate and easy appear to have greater resilience than children who are difficult and slow-to-warm-up. This proposal is consistent with a differential susceptibility model highlighted in research by Belsky (1997; Belsky et al., 1998) and others (Bakermans-Kranenburg, van Ijzendoorn, Pijlman, Mesman, & Juffer, 2008). Stright, Gallagher and Kelley (2008) found support for this proposal by showing that first-grade children who were difficult in infancy demonstrated more social competence when interacting with their peers and teachers, had better quality interactions with their teachers, and were rated higher in peer status when they received high quality parenting than children who were difficult in infancy and received low quality parenting. This finding illustrates, in part, the goodness-of-fit model in Figure 1d: children who were difficult in infancy and received high quality parenting performed better than their less difficult peers in terms of their social and academic competence, whereas children who were difficult in infancy but received low quality parenting demonstrated poorer functioning than their less difficult peers who received similar parenting behaviors. Associations between first-grade adjustment and parenting were less strong for children who were less difficult, suggesting that quality of parenting matters less for less difficult children than for difficult children (Stright et al.).

In summary, relations among infant difficult temperament, parenting, and later child behaviors have been empirically investigated. Consistent with the proposed link between certain temperament risk factors and poor outcomes (Carey & McDevitt, 1995), findings have demonstrated the importance of considering the influence of infant difficult temperament in combination with particular concurrent and later parenting practices on the child's later behaviors. In contrast to infant difficult temperament, there is an astonishing lack of research on infant slow-to-warm-up temperament. Relations among infant slow-to-warm-up temperament, parenting, and later child outcomes are just as important to explore as relations among difficult temperament, parenting, and later child outcomes. Such research may help parents and researchers to better understand these at-risk children's behaviors and developmental trajectory.

ILLUSTRATION OF THE SPECIAL CHALLENGES IN PARENTING SLOW-TO-WARM-UP INFANTS

Chess and Thomas (1999) proposed that goodness of fit between infant temperament and parenting behaviors is necessary for adaptive social and emotional development. In line with their proposal, research (Bates, Maslin, & Frankel, 1985; Belsky et al., 1998; Crockenberg & Leerkes, 2006; Sanson, Oberklaid, Pedlow, & Prior, 1991; Warren & Simmens, 2005) has demonstrated that environmental factors, such as parenting, can moderate the relation between infant difficult temperament and related temperament behaviors and later child problem behaviors. The present study examined whether similar relations among slow-to-warm-up temperament, parenting, and later child behaviors are demonstrated.

Inhibition at 24 months was examined for children who were identified at 6 months as having either slow-to-warm-up, easy, or difficult temperaments and as experiencing average or positive maternal parenting styles. Easy temperament was included as a comparison group because of the typical positive outcomes these infants experience relative to difficult infants. Difficult temperament was also included because this temperament is, like slow-to-warm-up temperament, proposed to be a risk factor for poor parent-child interactions and poor later outcomes (Carey & McDevitt, 1995). The child outcome of inhibition was chosen because of the conceptual relation between both the slow-to-warm-up and difficult infant temperaments, which are categorized by low adaptability and a hesitant approach to new things, and the construct of inhibition (Kagan, 1994; Kagan et al., 1998). The general goal of the present analyses was to determine how infants' slow-to-warm-up temperament combines with their mothers' parenting style to predict inhibited behavior in early childhood.

METHOD

Participants and Procedure

Participants were 629 slow-to-warm-up, easy, and difficult infants and their mothers in the National Institute of Child Health and Human Development Study of Early Child Care (NICHD SECC). Mothers ranged in age from 18 to 46, with 35% of the mothers between 24 and 29 years of age and another 35.5% between 30 and 35 years. Eighty-seven percent of the mothers were White, 9.9% were Black, 1.4% were Asian, and 1.3% were identified as "Other." Four percent of the mothers were Hispanic. About half (49.1%) of the infants were male. Additional information on participants, procedures, methods, and materials is available elsewhere (NICHD Early Child Care Research Network, 2001). Infant temperament and parenting data were collected during a 6-month interview with the mother and observation of the mother-infant relationship, and child inhibition data were collected during a 24-month interview with the mother.

Measures

Infant Temperament

Mothers rated their 6-month-old infants' behavioral characteristics with a modified version of the Revised Infant Temperament Questionnaire (RITQ; Carey & McDevitt, 1978). The RITQ is a measure by Carey and McDevitt that was derived from the longitudinal research of Thomas and Chess and colleagues (Thomas et al., 1963, 1970). The NICHD SECC included 56 of the 95 original items for the 6-month questionnaire. The included items assess five of Thomas and Chess's nine dimensions of infant temperament: activity, approach, adaptability, mood, and intensity. A score for each of these five subscales was calculated for each infant by finding the average rating of the items on each subscale (after reverse coding, as needed). Then, each infant was assigned to the slow-to-warm-up ($N = 58$), easy ($N = 488$), difficult ($N = 83$), or intermediate category ($N = 429$), based on these subscale scores. In the current analysis, only slow-to-warm-up, difficult, and easy children were included in analyses.

Child Inhibition

Mothers rated their 24-month-old children's behavioral and emotional characteristics on the Child Behavior Checklist/2-3 (CBCL/2-3; Achenbach, 1992). The CBCL/2-3 contains 99 items that are designed to assess various behavioral and emotional characteristics. The CBCL/2-3 was selected as the measure of child inhibition for the present study because several items seem to capture behaviors typical of inhibited children in early childhood. An inhibition composite score was derived using individual items from the CBCL/2-3 that were selected because they assess behaviors highlighted in research on inhibition in late infancy or toddlerhood. Garcia Coll, Kagan, and Reznick (1984) included withdrawal behaviors, latencies to approach an unfamiliar person, and reluctance to leave mother as behavioral indicators of inhibition in toddlers. Putnam and Stifter (2005) identified toddlers as inhibited when they demonstrated a latency to reach for an unfamiliar toy and maintained a close proximity to their mothers during laboratory tasks. Some researchers have included anxious behaviors such as nail biting, restlessness, hair pulling, and similar behaviors, as measures of inhibition in childhood (Schmidt, Fox, Schulkin, & Gold, 1999) and early adolescence (van Brakel, Muris, Bögels, & Tomassen, 2006). Other findings by van Brakel and colleagues (van Brakel, Muris, & Derks, 2006) suggest that children who are inhibited avoid arousal by not looking closely at aversive stimuli. Items from the CBCL/2-3 that assess these behaviors were included in the inhibition composite along with a few additional items (e.g., doesn't want to go out of home). Selected items are provided in Table 1. Inhibition was reliable at 24 months, Cronbach's $\alpha = .75$.

Table 1. Child Behavior Checklist/2-3 Items Relevant to Inhibition in Late Infancy/Toddlerhood

Item	Loading on Syndrome Scale
3. Afraid to try new things	
4. Avoids looking in the eye	Withdrawn
10. Clings to adults or too dependent	Anxious/Depressed
21. Disturbed by any change in routine	
22. Doesn't want to sleep alone	Sleep Problems
28. Doesn't want to go out of home	
32. Fears certain animals, situations, or places	
37. Gets too upset when separated from parents	Anxious/Depressed
47. Nervous, highstrung, or tense	Anxious/Depressed
68. Self-conscious or easily embarrassed	Anxious/Depressed
73. Shy or timid	Anxious/Depressed
87. Too fearful or anxious	Anxious/Depressed
92. Upset by new people or situations	
98. Withdrawn, doesn't get involved	Withdrawn

Note: From *Manual for the Child Behavior Checklist*/2-3 and 1992 profile, by T. M. Achenbach, 1992, pp. 4-5, 187-188.

Parenting Style

As part of an observational report measure that was used to rate an observer's impression of the entire 6-month home visit, an observer was asked to rate the mother-infant relationship as terrible, poor, fair, good, or excellent on an "overall impression of mother-infant relationship" item (NICHD SECC). This measure was considered in the present study to be a measure of parenting style. It was assumed that mothers who promptly and sensitively responded to their infants' behaviors would receive an impression of mother-child relationship rating of excellent. As the current study included only a single item coded by a single observer at one point in time, no reliability information was available. To obtain the parenting style groups, the variable was split. Very few relationships were rated as poor ($N =$

6; 0.9%) and none were rated as terrible. Therefore, only mother-infant dyads with mother-infant relationships rated as fair ($N = 58$; 9.2%), good ($N = 330$; 52.5%), or excellent ($N = 241$; 38.3%) were included in analyses. Relationships rated as fair or good were considered to indicate an average parenting style and relationships rated as excellent were considered to indicate a positive parenting style.

RESULTS

A 3 (Temperament: slow-to-warm-up, easy, and difficult) x 2 (Parenting Style: average and positive) analysis of variance was performed. The Temperament x Parenting Style interaction was significant, $F(2, 623) = 4.63, p = .01$, partial $\eta^2 = .02$, the Temperament main effect was significant, $F(2, 623) = 31.05, p = .000$, partial $\eta^2 = .09$, and the Parenting Style main effect was significant, $F(1, 623) = 3.91, p = .048$, partial $\eta^2 = .006$. The Temperament and Parenting Style main effects were qualified by the significant Temperament x Parenting Style interaction. To isolate the effect, pairwise comparisons with the Bonferroni adjustment were conducted. Results indicated that children who were slow-to-warm-up at 6 months of age demonstrated significantly more inhibition when their mothers demonstrated a positive parenting style ($N = 22, M = 7.72, SD = 3.97$) than when their mothers demonstrated an average parenting style ($N = 36, M = 5.57, SD = 3.73$). As compared to children who were difficult and slow-to-warm-up at 6 months of age, children who were easy demonstrated overall lower levels of inhibition regardless of whether their mothers demonstrated a positive ($N = 199, M = 4.34, SD = 2.86$) or average ($N = 289, M = 4.78, SD = 3.16$) parenting style and did not differ significantly in inhibition depending on their mothers' parenting style. Similarly, as compared to easy and slow-to-warm-up infants, difficult infants demonstrated overall higher levels of inhibition regardless of whether their mothers demonstrated a positive ($N = 20, M = 7.86, SD = 4.07$) or average ($N = 63, M = 7.17, SD = 3.13$) parenting style and did not differ significantly in inhibition depending on their mothers' parenting style.

DISCUSSION

The present study explored relations among slow-to-warm-up child temperament, the quality of the mother-infant relationship, and child inhibition. Results indicated that a less positive parenting style produced a better fit for slow-to-warm-up infants than did a more positive parenting style. It may be that those mothers who were rated as having an average parenting style behaved in a manner that was at times inconsistent with their infants' temperament. In response, these children adapted in ways that fostered their development and helped to prevent the development of inhibition. As an example, when the slow-to-warm-up infant is distressed by a new toy or unwilling to approach an unfamiliar person, mothers with a less positive parenting style may not react to instantly soothe and calm the child by picking him or her up. The infant's crying and distress would then continue because the parent has not intervened to change the situation for the infant. Instead, the infant must learn to cope with the distressing situation and may consequently demonstrate a more adaptive response when later encountering the same previously distressing scenario. In contrast, mothers with a more positive parenting style may instantly soothe and calm the child by picking him or her up, so that the infant does not develop coping skills. Parenting that challenges the slow-to-warm-up infant's behaviors early in infancy likely creates more stress and challenge in this period for the parent because the negative infant behavior such as crying persists, but is a better fit for slow-to-warm-up infants and ultimately results in better child outcomes in terms of inhibition in toddlerhood.

A goodness-of-fit perspective assumes that the parenting behavior or style that best matches or fits with a child with one temperament type may not be the same parenting behavior or style that best matches a child with another temperament type. Using data on child temperament and the mother-infant relationship, the current findings support this proposal. The slow-to-warm-up child was less inhibited in late toddlerhood when he or she was parented with a less positive parenting style. In contrast, the type of parenting style that mothers demonstrated did not affect the easy or difficult child's level of inhibition. This pattern of results is captured within the goodness of fit model in Figure 1e: Fit between the parenting style and child temperament matters for the behavioral outcomes of one infant temperament but not another.

These findings must be interpreted in light of the study's limitations. The transition from infancy to childhood may require a set of parenting skills not fully captured in our measure of parenting style. Whereas the results highlight the importance of early parenting of the slow-to-warm-up child for his or her later toddler behaviors, more research is needed to understand the parenting factors that affect development in early childhood for children who were slow-to-warm-up in infancy. The findings of the present study also may be limited by the methodology that was used. Child temperament and inhibition were assessed using only maternal report measures. Moreover, mothers' parenting style was based on a single observer's impression of how well the mother and the child interacted together. More research will be needed to conclusively support the importance of fit for the slow-to-warm-up child's later behavioral outcomes.

CONCLUSION

Harris (1998) critiques socialization studies because they make generalizations about causes based on sampling of children and parents' behaviors in isolation from the overall parent-child environment. She asserts that we observe parents' behaviors toward their children and then we label that behavior as overprotective, controlling, permissive, or sensitive. Goodness of fit represents a better way to study the parent-child relationship than typical socialization studies that look just at parents' behaviors toward their children or children's behaviors toward their parents because it makes no a priori assumptions or generalizations regarding whether the parents' behaviors shape the child's behaviors or whether the child's behavior shapes the parents' behaviors. Rather, the goodness-of-fit perspective assumes that the parent-child relationship is bidirectional, with both the child and the parent affecting one another. What is interesting from a goodness-of-fit perspective is whether parents' and children's behavioral tendencies "fit" or "match," and, if there is not a natural match, who or what bends or adapts to create a match.

Life-span theory highlights the concept that development is a life-long process, wherein biology and the context dialectically interact to construct development (Baltes, Lindenberger, & Staudinger, 2006). By linking earlier and later developmental processes, life-span theory aims to identify the individual's plasticity and specify ways to optimize development (Baltes et al.). The goodness-of-fit model illuminates how temperament and personality interact with social factors, such as parenting style as well as the cultural context, to affect development across the lifespan. This model is valuable to life-span developmental research because it shows "how temperament and features of the environment can work together to produce favorable child outcomes" (Karraker & Coleman, 2002, p. 179).

REFERENCES

Achenbach, T. M. (1992). *Manual for the Child Behavior Checklist/2-3 and 1992 profile.* Burlington, VT: University of Vermont Department of Psychiatry.

Asendorpf, J. B., Denissen, J. J. A., van Aken, M. A. G. (2008). Inhibited and aggressive preschool children at 23 years of age: Personality and social transitions into adulthood. *Developmental Psychology, 44,* 997-1011.

Bakermans-Kranenburg, M. J., Van Ijzendoorn, M. H., Pijlman, F. T., Mesman, J., & Juffer, F. (2008). Experimental evidence for differential susceptibility: Dopamine D4 receptor polymorphism (DRD4 VNTR) moderates intervention effects on toddlers' externalizing behavior in a randomized controlled trial. *Developmental Psychology, 44,* 293-300.

Baltes, P. B., Reese, H. W., & Nesselroade, J. R. (1988). *Life-span developmental psychology: Introduction to research methods.* Hillsdale, NJ: Lawrence Erlbaum.

Baltes, P. B., Lindenberger, U., & Staudinger, U. M. (2006). Life-span theory in developmental psychology. In W. Damon & R. M. Lerner (Series Eds.) & R. M. Lerner (Volume Ed.), *Handbook of child psychology: Vol. 1. Theoretical models of human development* (6th ed., pp. 569-664). New York: Wiley.

Bates, J. E., Maslin, C. A., & Frankel, K. A. (1985). Attachment security, mother-child interaction, and temperament as predictors of behavior-problem ratings at age three years. *Monographs of the Society of Research in Child Development, 50*(1-2).

Bell, R. Q. (1968). A reinterpretation of the direction of effects in studies of socialization. *Psychological Review, 75,* 81-95.

Belsky, J. (1984). The determinants of parenting: A process model. *Child Development, 55,* 83-96.

Belsky, J. (1997). Variation in susceptibility to environmental influences: An evolutionary argument. *Psychological Inquiry, 8,* 182-186.

Belsky, J., Hsieh, K., & Crnic, K. (1998). Mothering, fathering, and infant negativity as antecedents of boys' externalizing problems and inhibition at age 3 years: Differential susceptibility to rearing experience? *Development and Psychopathology, 10,* 301-319.

Carey, W. B., & McDevitt, S. C. (1978). Revision of the Infant Temperament Questionnaire. *Pediatrics, 61,* 735-739.

Carey, W. B., & McDevitt, S. C. (1995). *Coping with children's temperament: A guide for professionals.* New York: BasicBooks.

Chen, X., Hastings, P. D., Rubin, K. H., Chen, H., Cen, G., & Stewart, S. L. (1998). Child-rearing attitudes and behavioral inhibition in Chinese and Canadian toddlers: A cross-cultural study. *Developmental Psychology, 34,* 677-686.

Chess, S., & Thomas, A. (1999). *Goodness of fit: Clinical applications from infancy through adult life.* Ann Arbor, MI: Edwards Brothers.

Chess, S., Thomas, A., & Birch, H. C. (1965). *Your child is a person: A psychological approach to parenthood without guilt.* Oxford, England: Viking Press.

Crockenberg, S. C., & Leerkes, E. M. (2006). Infant and maternal behavior moderate reactivity to novelty to predict anxious behavior at 2.5 years. *Development and Psychopathology, 18,* 17-34.

Dannefer, D. (1992). On the conceptualization of context in developmental discourse: Four meanings of context and their implications. In D. L. Featherman, R. H. Lerner, & M. Perlmutter (Eds.), *Life span development and behavior: Vol. 11* (pp. 83-110). Hillsdale, NJ: Lawrence Erlbaum.

DeVries, M. W. (1984). Temperament and infant mortality among the Masai of East Africa. *American Journal of Psychiatry, 141,* 1189-1194.

Garcia Coll, C., Kagan, J., & Reznick, J. S. (1984). Behavioral inhibition in young children. *Child Development, 55,* 1005-1019.

Goldsmith, H. H., Lemery, K. S., Aksan, N., & Buss, K. A. (2000). Temperamental substrates of personality. In V. J. Molfese & D. L. Molfese (Eds.), *Temperament and personality development across the life span* (pp. 1-32). Mahwah, NJ: Lawrence Erlbaum Associates.

Hane, A. A., Fox, N. A., Polak-Toste, C., Ghera, M. M., & Guner, B. M. (2006). Contextual basis of maternal perceptions of infant temperament. *Developmental Psychology, 42,* 1077-1088.

Harris, J. R. (1998). *The nurture assumption: Why children turn out the way they do.* New York: The Free Press.

Kagan, J. (1994). *Galen's prophecy.* New York: BasicBooks.

Kagan, J., Snidman, N., & Arcus, D. (1998). Childhood derivatives of high and low reactivity in infancy. *Child Development, 69,* 1483-1493.

Karraker, K. H. (2008). The role of environment factors in infant night waking. *Journal of Early and Intensive Behavior Intervention, 5,* 108-121. Available at http://www.jeibi.net/

Karraker, K. H., & Coleman, P. (2002). Infants' characteristics and behaviors help shape their environments. In H. E. Fitzgerald, K. H. Karraker, & T. Luster (Eds.), *Infant development: Ecological perspectives* (pp. 165-191). New York: Routledge.

Kingston, L., & Prior, M. (1995). The development of patterns of stable, transient, and school-age onset aggressive behavior in young children. *Journal of the American Academy of Child and Adolescent Psychiatry, 34,* 348-358.

Leerkes, E. M., & Burney, R. V. (2007). The development of parenting efficacy among new mothers and fathers. *Infancy, 12,* 45-67.

Lerner, R. M. (2002). *Concepts and theories of human development.* Mahwah, NJ: Lawrence Erlbaum.

Lerner, R. M., & Lerner, J. V. (1987). Children in their contexts: A goodness-of-fit model. In J. B. Lancaster, J. Altmann, A. S. Rossi, & L. R. Sherrod (Eds.), *Parenting across the life span: Biosocial dimensions* (pp. 377-404). Hawthorne, NY: Aldine de Gruyter.

Matheny, A. P., & Phillips, K. (2001). Temperament and context: Correlates of home environment with temperament continuity and change, newborn to 30 months. In T. D.

Wachs & G. A. Kohnstamm (Eds.), *Temperament in context* (pp. 81-101). Mahwah, NJ: Lawrence Erlbaum Associates.

Miner, J. L., & Clarke-Stewart, K. A. (2008). Trajectories of externalizing behavior from age 2 to age 9: Relations with gender, temperament, ethnicity, parenting, and rater. *Developmental Psychology, 44,* 771-786.

NICHD Early Child Care Research Network. (2001). Nonmaternal care and family factors in early development: An overview of the NICHD Study of Early Child Care. *Journal of Applied Developmental Psychology, 22,* 457-492.

NICHD Study of Early Child Care. (n.d.). *Phase I instrument document.* Retrieved October 1, 2008 from http://secc.rti.org/PhaseIData.cfm.

Park, S., Belsky, J., Putnam, S., & Crnic, K. (1997). Infant emotionality, parenting, and 3-year-inhibition: Exploring stability and lawful discontinuity in a male sample. *Developmental Psychology, 33,* 218-227.

Pauli-Pott, U., Mertesacker, B., Bade, U., Haverkock, A., & Beckmann, D. (2003). Parental perceptions and infant temperament development. *Infant Behavior and Development, 26,* 27-48.

Plomin, R. (1990). *Nature and nurture: An introduction to human behavioral genetics.* Pacific Grove, CA: Brooks/Cole Publishing.

Putnam, S. P., & Stifter, C. A. (2005). Behavioral approach-inhibition in toddlers: Prediction from infancy, positive and negative affective components, and relations with behavior problems. *Child Development, 76,* 212-226.

Rothbart, M. K., & Bates, J. E. (2006). Temperament. In R. M. Lerner & W. Damon (Series Eds.) & N. Eisenberg (Volume Ed.), *Handbook of child psychology: Vol. 3. Socialization, personality, and social development* (6th ed., pp. 99-166). Hoboken, NJ: John Wiley & Sons.

Rubin, K. H. (1993). The Waterloo Longitudinal Project: Correlates and consequences of social withdrawal from childhood to adolescence. In K. H. Rubin & J. B. Asendorpf (Eds.), *Social withdrawal, inhibition, and shyness in childhood* (pp. 291-314). Hillsdale, NJ: Lawrence Erlbaum Associates.

Sameroff, A. J., & Chandler, M. J. (1975). Reproductive risk and the continuum of caretaker causality. In F. Horowitz (Ed.), *Review of child development research* (Vol. 4). Chicago: University of Chicago Press.

Sanson, A., Oberklaid, F., Pedlow, R., & Prior, M. (1991). Risk indicators: Assessment of infancy predictors of preschool behavioral maladjustment. *Journal of Child Psychology and Psychiatry, 32,* 609-626.

Schmidt, L. A., Fox, N. A., Schulkin, J., & Gold, P. W. (1999). Behavioral and psychophysiological correlates of self-presentation in temperamentally shy children. *Developmental Psychobiology, 35,* 119-135.

Sigel, I. E., & McGillicuddy-De Lisi, A. V. (2002). Parent beliefs are cognitions: The dynamic belief systems model. In M. H. Bornstein (Ed.), *Handbook of parenting: Vol. 3. Being and becoming a parent* (2nd ed., pp. 485-508). Mahwah, NJ: Lawrence Erlbaum.

Stright, A. D., Gallagher, K. C., & Kelley, K. (2008). Infant temperament moderates relations between maternal parenting in early childhood and children's adjustment in first grade. *Child Development, 79,* 186-200.

Thomas, A., Chess, S., & Birch, H. G. (1970). The origin of personality. *Scientific American, 223,* 102-107.

Thomas, A., Chess, S., Birch, H. G., Hertzig, M. E., & Korn, S. (1963). *Behavioral individuality in early childhood.* New York: New York University.

Thomas, A., Chess, S., Sillen, J., & Mendez, O. A. (1974). Cross-cultural studies of behavior in children with special vulnerabilities to stress. In D. F. Ricks, A. Thomas, & J. D. Roff (Eds.), *Life history research in psychopathology* (Vol. 3, pp. 53-67). Minneapolis, MN: University of Minnesota Press.

van Brakel, A. M., Muris, P., Bögels, S. M., & Thomassen, C. (2006). A multifactorial model for the etiology of anxiety in non-clinical adolescents: Main and interactive effects of behavioral inhibition, attachment, parental rearing. *Journal of Child and Family Studies, 15,* 569-579.

van Brakel, A. M., Muris, P., & Derks, W. (2006). Eye blink startle responses in behaviorally inhibited and uninhibited children. *International Journal of Behavioral Development, 30,* 460-465.

Vitaro, F., Barker, E. D., Boivin, M., Brendgen, M., & Tremblay, R. (2006). Do early difficult temperament and harsh parenting differentially predict reactive and proactive aggression? *Journal of Abnormal Child Psychology, 34,* 685-695.

Wachs, T. D. (2000). *Necessary but not sufficient: The respective roles of single and multiple influences on individual development.* Washington, DC: American Psychological Association.

Warren, S. L., & Simmens, S. J. (2005). Predicting toddler anxiety/depressive symptoms: Effects of caregiver sensitivity on temperamentally vulnerable children. *Infant Mental Health Journal, 26,* 40-55.

Zeanah, C. H., Zeanah, P. D., & Stewart, L. K. (1990). Parents' constructions of their infants' personalities before and after birth: A descriptive study. *Child Psychiatry & Human Development, 20,* 191-206.

In: Handbook of Parenting: Styles, Stresses & Strategies   ISBN 978-1-60741-766-8
Editor: Pacey H. Krause and Tahlia M. Dailey   © 2009 Nova Science Publishers, Inc.

Chapter 8

MATERNAL EMOTIONAL AVAILABILITY AND INFANT SMILING AND CRYING AT 5 MONTHS OF AGE

G. Esposito[a], P. Venuti[a], S. de Falco[a], and M. H. Bornstein[b]*

[a] Department of Cognitive Science and Education, University of Trento, Italy
[b] Child and Family Research, *Eunice Kennedy Shriver* National Institute of Child Health and Human Development,
National Institutes of Health, Department of Health and Human Services, U.S.A.

ABSTRACT

In this observational study, we examined relations of maternal emotional availability with infant smiling and crying, two behaviors that represent infants' principal social communicative functions. Fifty-four mother–infant dyads were analyzed using two independent observation systems: (a) the infant socioemotional behaviors and (b) the Emotional Availability Scales. The amount of infant smiling differentiated dyads with different levels of maternal emotional availability. The more infants smile, the greater the odds that their mothers will be more emotionally available. By contrast, no association for cry was found with maternal emotional availability. These results are consistent with the burgeoning literature on the Emotional Availability construct that stresses the importance of expressed positive emotions as determinants of the quality of mother-infant interaction.

Keywords: Smile, Cry, Emotional Availability.

INTRODUCTION

By the end of the first half of the first year, infants already command two behaviors that constitute important features of their future social life, namely smiling and crying. Smiling

---

* Correspondence should be addressed to: Gianluca Esposito, Department of Cognitive Science and Education, Via Matteo Del Ben 5, 38068 Rovereto (TN), Italy TEL: +39 0464 483592, FAX: +39 0464 483554; E-MAIL: gianluca.esposito@unitn.it

and crying, as described in attachment theory, are the main behaviours of a primary system in the human species that assures survival of the helpless newborn by alerting others to meet their basic needs and solidifying a link between infant and parent (Bowlby, 1969).These behaviors allow infants to convey their emotional states and needs to their parents effectively (Barnard, Hammond, Booth, Bee, Mitchell, & Spieker, 1989; Trevarthen, 1993, 2003; Bornstein, Gini, Leach, Haynes, Painter, & Suwalsky, 2006). Whereas crying has historically been thought to draw caregivers close, smiling has been thought to keep them near; thus, these two behaviors secure offspring survival and promote development. Because smiling and crying constitute the first signals children use to communicate with their mother, the aim of this study was to assess their association with maternal emotional availability.

Smiling is an automatic reaction, and it is observable beginning in the first week of life (Trevarthen, 2001, 2003). Because the infant's smiles give caregivers pleasure, the smile promotes social interaction. For example, infants' smiles often elicit maternal smiles. Mothers rarely break off bouts of mutual smiling, but instead terminate their own smiling only after their infants have stopped (Messinger & Fogel, 2007).

Crying, especially pain-related cries, stimulates parents to behave rapidly and intently. These biologically determined signals set the stage for other forms of social interaction. Several studies have investigated parents' response to the aversiveness of acoustical features of the infant cry. Cries with higher pitches and irregular temporal patterns are often judged to be unpleasant, annoying, and irritating (Boukydis, 1985; Bisping, Steingrueber, Oltmann, & Wenk, 1990; Esposito & Venuti, 2008) and are associated with negative perceptions of the baby (Dessureau, Kurowski, & Tompson, 1998; Lagasse, Near, & Lester, 2005). Physiological reactions to infant cry include higher skin conductance and heart rate in mothers (Brewster, Nelson, McCanne, Lucas, & Milner, 1998).

In this study, we investigated associations between infants' smiling and crying and maternal *emotional availability*. Emotional availability (EA; Biringen, & Robinson, 1991; Biringen 2000) is a relationship construct that refers specifically to emotional transactions between children and their parents (Aviezer, Sagi, Joels, & Ziv, 1999; Biringen & Robinson, 1991; Bretherton, 2000; Emde, 1980). More specifically, it signifies the quality of emotional exchanges, focusing on partners' accessibility to one another and their ability to read and respond appropriately to one another's communications (Biringen & Robinson, 1991). Mutual understanding and expression of emotions is considered a barometer of dyadic functioning (Biringen, 2000). One dimension of emotional availability is maternal sensitivity. In general, sensitive mothers recognize their infant's cries, interpret them accurately, and respond to them appropriately (Kivijärvi, Räihä, Kaljonen, Virtanen, Lertola, & Piha, 2004). In an optimal situation, the mother reads her infant's cues in ways that increase their mutual pleasure and her enjoyment of her infant (Bromwich, 1976). From the infant's point of view, maternal sensitivity is experienced as a special connectedness with the mother. The interpersonal role of maternal sensitivity is for the child to experience him/herself as worthy, valuable, and interesting to other people (Biringen & Robinson, 1991).

A number of studies have analyzed infants' smiling and crying and maternal emotional availability separately, but few studies have analyzed interconnections between these infant behaviors and dimensions of maternal emotional availability. Studies regarding this interconnection have mainly focused on crying and fussing. Kivijärvi and colleagues (2004) reported an association between maternal sensitivity and amount of infant crying. Maternal sensitivity was assessed using the Parent-Child Early Relational Assessment (PCERA; Burns,

Chethik, Burns & Clark, 1997; Clark, Hyde, Essex & Klein, 1997; Harel, Oppenheim, Tirosh & Gini, 1999). The PCERA provides a phenomenological assessment of the affective and behavioral quality of interactions between the parent and child. Infants of more sensitive mothers cried less than infants of less sensitive mothers at 3 and 12 months of age (see also Hubbard & van IJzendoorn, 1991; Fish, Stifter, & Belsky, 1991; Fish & Crockenberg, 1981).

In this paper, we used observational methods to examine aspects of emotional availability of mothers in relation to two early and paramount social behaviors of their first infants. We hypothesized that, as mothers experience infants' smiles as pleasurable, their tendency will be to be more emotionally available to infants who smile more. According to previous results (Kivijärvi et al., 2004), we also hypothesized that more sensitive mothers would have infants who cry less. Finally, we wanted to investigate which of the two infant behaviors would be more strongly related to maternal emotional availability.

METHODS

Participants

Altogether this study involved 54 mother–infant dyads: infants (M=28, F=26; M age = 155.04 days, SD = 5.08) and mothers (M age = 28.06 years, SD = 4.48). The socioeconomic status of the parents, calculated with the Four-Factor Index of Social Status (SES; Hollingshead, 1975), was broadly middle-class for the Italian population (M = 35.41, SD = 14.83). No statistical differences emerged between boys and girls for infant age, maternal age, and SES. All mothers were at least 18 years of age and married to the baby's father; all infants were firstborn, term, weighed at least 1500 g at birth, only infants, 5 months (157 to 165 days) of age when observed, and healthy at the time of the study.

Data Collection

Each infant-mother dyad was visited in their home by a single female observer, and an hour-long video/audiorecord of the dyad's naturalistic interactions was made. Infants were seen when they were healthy and expected to be awake and alert for at least the hour (on average, infants were awake 99.9% of the recorded time). In all cases, the mother was told that the investigator was interested in observing the infant's usual routine at a time when the mother was at home and solely responsible for his or her care. No other people were present in the home during the visit. Thus, mothers were seen when distractions from other people were minimized and their attention was in principle optimally available to the infant. After a period of acclimation (approximately 15 min) to the recording equipment and the presence of the stranger (McCune-Nicolich & Fenson, 1984; Stevenson, Leavitt, Roach, Miller, & Chapman, 1986), recording commenced. The first 50 min of the record were used for all cases to accommodate occasional momentary interruptions. Conventions were developed and adhered to for recording the infant and mother from distances and angles that maximized the possibility of continuously and reliably coding behaviors of interest. The record of each visit was coded at a separate time. To transform streams of different behaviors of both infants and mothers into appropriate quantitative data (see data scoring) and to ensure reliability the video/audiorecords were coded by multiple coders.

Data Scoring

Two different observation systems with formalized rules were used: (a) Infant socioemotional behaviors (Bornstein et al. 1991) and (b) the Emotional Availability Scales: Infancy to Early Childhood Version (Biringen et al., 1998).

Infant Socioemotional Behaviors

Two infant behaviors were included. *Infant Smile* (IS): When the infant emitted a broad, clear, unambiguous smile. Specifically, (a) the corners of the baby's mouth are extended outward and upward, (b) the eyes "brighten" and are focused, and (c) the eyebrows are relaxed or raised. The mouth may be open or closed. Behaviors such as "half-smiles", "wide-eyed looks", or instances when the baby's face simply "brightens" or appears "happy" without a broad, clear smile were not coded as IS. At least one eye and the mouth must have been visible to code IS. *Infant Cry* (IC): The infant exhibits full-blown distress, including vocalizing, kicking, and facial expressions of distress (i.e., tightly closed eyes, opened mouth) for a duration of at least 5 sec. For IS and IC alike, 3 different scores were calculated: (a) frequency, the number of times the behavior occurred; (b) duration, the total duration of the behavior; and (c) a summary index, the mean standard aggregate of the number of times and total duration of the behavior. Infant socioemotional behaviors were continuously coded, and interobserver reliability was determined using Cohen's (1960) Kappa (k). Coders were trained to achieve, and then monitored to maintain, acceptable levels of agreement, as indexed by $k >$ .70 (Hartmann & Pelzel, 2005). The values for IS and IC were respectively, $k = .72$ and $k = .80$.

Emotional Availability Scales

Emotional availability in the same mother-infant dyads was evaluated independently using the Emotional Availability Scales: Infancy to Early Childhood Version (EAS 3rd ed.; Biringen et al., 1998). These Scales consist of six dimensions concerned with emotional regulation in the parent-child dyad. Four dimensions address the emotional availability of the parent in relation to the child (sensitivity, structuring, nonintrusiveness, and nonhostility), and two address the emotional availability of the child in relation to the parent (responsiveness and involving). In this study, we only used the parent scales. The Sensitivity scale (9 points) was inspired by Ainsworth (Ainsworth, Blehar, Waters, & Wall, 1978) and is designed to assess the parent's contingent responsiveness to child communications, appropriate affectivity, acceptance, flexibility, clarity of perceptions, affect regulation, conflict resolution, and variety and creativity in interaction and play displayed toward the child. Structuring (5 points) assesses the degree to which the parent appropriately facilitates, scaffolds, or organizes the child's interaction, play, exploration, or routine by providing rules, regulations, and a supportive framework without compromising the child's autonomy. Nonintrusiveness (5 points) measures the degree to which the parent supports the child's interaction, play, exploration, or routine by waiting for optimal breaks before initiating interactions, without interrupting the child by being overdirective, overstimulating, overprotecting, and/or interfering. Nonhostility (5 points) measures the degree to which the parent talks to or behaves with the child in a way that is generally patient, pleasant, and harmonious and not rejecting, abrasive, impatient, or antagonistic. (For additional information, see Biringen, 2000; Easterbrooks & Biringen, 2000.) Coding was carried out by two independent coders who were first trained on the EAS to obtain satisfactory interrater reliability with one of the authors of the EAS and then between themselves. Interrater reliability (Biringen, 2005) was assessed using average absolute agreement intraclass correlation coefficients (*ICC*; McGraw & Wong, 1996) on 25% of the interactions coded, and *ICC*s ranged from .84 to .95.

Analytic Plan

We first conducted preliminary analyses of the data. Next, person-level analyses were computed to identify dyads in lower, medium, and higher EA groups. Then, we report descriptive statistics and inferential analysis (applied to frequency, duration, and summary indexes) for the three groups (infants with mothers with lower, medium, and higher levels of EA) for the amount of infant smiling and crying. Separate ANOVAs were employed to test the hypotheses that mothers tend to be more emotionally available when their infants smile more and that more sensitive mothers have infants who cry less. Finally, we used multinomial logistic regression to assess which of the two infant behaviors (smile or cry) is more strongly related to maternal emotional availability.

RESULTS

Preliminary Analysis

Table 1 shows means and standard deviations for the variables analyzed. Distributions of the frequency, duration, and summary indexes of IS and IC and the 4 individual mother EAS were examined for normalcy and outliers. Maternal Nonhostility and Nonintrusiveness showed significantly skewed distributions, no transformations normalized them, and so they were treated as ordinal. Preliminary correlations were conducted to investigate associations between mother age, infant age, and family SES with the infant variables and the maternal EAS scores. Maternal sensitivity was positively correlated with SES ($r = .31$, $p < .05$). Therefore, SES was controlled as appropriate in the main analyses; in specific, the standardized residuals of a linear regression were used for computation. No other significant correlations emerged. In addition, no infant gender differences were found for either infant socioemotional behaviors or EA Scales; therefore, the data are reported for girls and boys combined.

Table 1. Descriptive statistics for infant behaviors and maternal EA

	M	*SD*
IS Frequency	5.41	6.33
IS Duration	11.4	15.32
IC Frequency	14.06	12.39
IC Duration	95.25	119.31
EA Sensitivity	6.97	1.07
EA Structuring	4.32	0.49
EA Nonintrusiveness	4.76	0.46
EA Nonhostility	4.91	0.24

Note: IS = Infant smile, IC = Infant cry, IS duration and IC duration in seconds.

Cluster Analysis of the EA Scales

Person-level analyses were computed using a K-Means Cluster Analysis (Hartigan & Wong, 1979) of the 2 continuous maternal EA Scales. We pooled all dyads into a single analysis so that the clusters would be comparable. The distributions of Nonhostility and Nonintrusiveness were examined in relation to the clusters derived from the other 2 EA Scales. We empirically identified dyads as belonging to three clusters: (1) lower EA, (2) medium EA, and (3) higher EA. Cluster means and standard deviations are presented in Table 2. ANOVAs showed differences among all cluster means.

Table 2. Levels of Maternal EA

	Low EA		Medium EA		High EA		
	M	*SD*	*M*	*SD*	*M*	*SD*	$F_{(2,52)}/\chi^2$
Sensitivity	4.90	0.65	6.57	0.51	7.94	0.41	108.92**
Structuring	3.40	0.22	4.22	0.25	4.79	0.25	77.11**
Nonintrusiveness[a]	40%		56%		81%		3.70*
Nonhostility[a]	40%		56%		100%		13.48*

Note: * $p \le .01$ ** $p \le .001$

[a] Percentage of mothers in the cluster who engaged in more than average Nonhostility and Nonintrusiveness. Test statistic reported is a chi-square.

As an additional check on the validity of our clusters, we used chi-squares and configural frequency analyses (von Eye, 2002) to examine the cluster distributions of mothers who exhibited more than average vs. less than the average hostility and intrusiveness. Mothers who exhibited more than average vs. less than the average intrusiveness, χ^2 (2, n=54) = 3.70, $p \le .01$, and mothers who exhibited more than average vs. less than the average hostility, χ^2 (2, n=54) = 13.48, $p \le .01$, were not equally distributed across clusters.

Maternal Emotional Availability and Infant Smile

Table 3 reports descriptive and inferential analysis for maternal EA and infant smile. Separate ANOVAs were performed on IS (frequency, duration, summary index) controlling SES.

Frequency

No significant interactions emerged for IS frequency. However, a main effect for maternal emotional availability, $F(2, 52) = 3.29$, $p \leq .05$, $\eta^2 = .06$, was found. Simple contrasts indicated that infants of higher EA mothers smiled more than infants of lower EA mothers, M difference $= 6.42$, $SE = 2.96$, $p \leq .05$; no differences emerged either between infants of higher EA mothers and infants of medium EA mothers or between infants of lower EA mothers and infants of medium EA mothers, respectively, M difference $= 3.33$, $SE = 1.73$, ns and M difference $= 3.08$, $SE = 2.99$, ns.

Duration

No significant interactions emerged for IS duration. However, a main effect for maternal emotional availability, $F(2, 52) = 3.42$, $p \leq .05$, $\eta^2 = .08$, was found. Simple contrasts indicated that infants of higher EA mothers smiled for longer periods than infants of medium and lower EA mothers, respectively, M difference $= 8.72$, $SE = 4.19$, and M difference $= 15.03$, $SE = 7.16$, $p \leq .05$. No differences emerged between infants of lower EA mothers and infants of medium EA mothers, M difference $= 6.30$, $SE = 7.23$, ns.

Table 3. Infant smile and cry in relation to emotional availability

	Low EA		Medium EA		High EA		
	M	SD	M	SD	M	SD	$F_{(2,52)}$
IS Frequency	1.00$_a$	1.00	4.09$_b$	4.49	7.42$_b$	7.75	3.29*
IS Duration	1.48$_a$	1.81	7.78$_b$	9.38	16.51$_c$	19.00	3.42*
IS Index	-0.74$_a$	0.48	-0.11$_b$	0.86	0.30$_b$	1.08	2.98*
IC Frequency	12.00	11.60	13.13	15.57	11.81	13.54	0.54
IC Duration	110.06	1.43	83.74	96.25	84.36	101.79	0.30
IC Index	0.03	0.83	-0.03	1.07	0.03	0.97	0.23

Note: * $p \leq .05$ IS = Infant Smile, IC = Infant Cry

Maternal Emotional Availability and Infant Cry

Table 3 also reports descriptive and inferential analysis for maternal EA and infant cry. Separate ANOVAs were performed on IC (frequency, duration, summary index) controlling for SES. No significant interactions or main effects emerged for IC frequency, duration, or the summary index.

Summary Index

No significant interactions emerged for IS summary index. However, a main effect for maternal emotional availability, $F(2, 52) = 2.98$, $p \leq .05$, $\eta^2 = .07$, was found. Simple contrasts indicated that infants of higher EA mothers smiled more than infants of lower EA mothers, M difference = 1.04, $SE = .46$, $p \leq .05$. No differences emerged either between infants of higher EA mothers and infants of medium EA mothers or between infants of lower EA mothers and infants of medium EA mothers, respectively, M difference = .41, $SE = .27$, ns and M difference = .63, $SE = .46$, ns.

Associations between Infant Behaviors and Maternal Emotional Availability

In a final analysis, multinomial logistic regression analysis was used to examine which infant behavior was more associated with maternal emotional availability. Multinomial logistic regression is based on a proportional odds model, assumes only that the dependent variable is an ordinal measure of a continuous construct, and uses the maximum likelihood method to obtain parameter estimates (Long, 1997; McCullagh, 1980; McCullagh & Nelder, 1989). Ordinal regression analysis simultaneously estimates multiple equations depending on the number of levels, and provides only one set of coefficients for each independent variable. Therefore, there is an assumption of parallel regression; that is, that the coefficients for the slopes of the variables in the equations would not differ significantly if they were estimated separately. The final models in each analysis were therefore tested to ensure that they met this assumption (Agresti, 1989; Johnson & Albert, 1999).

For the purposes of logistic regression the given outcome, in our case maternal emotional availability, needs to be ordinal. For this reason we used the three clusters of EA described above, dyads with high, medium, and low levels of EA. In our model, we considered the two infant behaviors (smile and cry), and we controlled the influence of the SES. A main effect was found for infant smile, $\chi^2 (2) = 18.57$, $p \leq .01$, but no significant effect was found for cry, $\chi^2 (2) = 2.10$, ns. In specific, high maternal emotional availability was predicted by infant smiling compared with low maternal emotional availability (OR = -6.77, $p \leq .01$), and compared with medium maternal emotional availability (OR = -1.86, $p \leq .05$).

DISCUSSION

In this observational study, we examined maternal emotional availability and its relations with infant smiling and crying, two behaviors that represent infants' principal social communicative functions. We hypothesized that, as mothers feel pleasure on seeing their infant smile, their tendency would be to be more emotionally available to infants who smile more. We found that the amount of infant smiling differentiates among dyads who display different levels of maternal emotional availability. When an infant smiles more, the odds are that his/her mother will be more emotionally available. This result is consistent with the literature on the Emotional Availability construct (Easterbrooks & Biringen, 2005) that stresses the importance of expressed emotions as determinants of the quality of mother-infant interaction.

Infants did not show many episodes of smiling (about 6 in 50 mins). This limited amount of smiles is probably related to our operational definition of a smile. We did not focus on "half-smiles", "wide-eyed looks", or instances when the baby's face simply "brightens" or appears "happy" because we wanted only to consider behaviors that could be interpreted unambiguously on the parts of both mothers and coders. We note that limiting the numbers of smiling behaviors, which means not taking into account behaviors such as "half-smiles" and "wide-eyed looks", is a conservative approach and lends added weight to our findings.

In accord with the existing literature (Kivijärvi et al., 2004), we hypothesized that more emotionally available mothers have infants who cry less than infants of less available mothers. In general, the amount of crying we observed was no different from levels reported in other studies (Salisbury, Minard, Hunsley, & Thoman, 2001). Although no significant differences were found among the three EA groups, it is important to note that infants in dyads where mothers were more emotionally available (medium or high EA) cried less. Although our results are not statistically significant, their direction agrees with the study of Kivijärvi and colleagues (2004) that reported an association between maternal sensitivity and amount of infant crying; they found that infants of more sensitive mothers cried less than infants of less sensitive mothers at 3 months and 12 months of age. In general, our results can be interpreted in relation to the Emotional Availability framework that describes the emotionally available parent as capable of recognizing, responding, empathizing, and eventually soothing negative emotional signals in the infant (Emde, 1980; Biringen, Robinson, & Emde, 1998).

Finally, we wanted to investigate which of the two infant behaviors was more strongly associated with maternal emotional availability. Logistic regression showed that in our sample smiling was the better predictor of maternal EA. A behaviourally clear expression of positive affect on the part of an infant is more closely linked to a higher level of maternal emotional availability than an infant expression of negative affect. Because mothers feel pleasure in reaction to their infant's smiles, it is possible to hypothesize that mothers of more cheerful (smiling) infants experience more pleasure and are encouraged to be more accessible, attuned, and responsive.

CONCLUSION

Before concluding, we need to consider the balance of limitations and strengths in this study. Although we unearthed an association between maternal emotional availability and a specific infant behavior, we cannot infer who influences whom because as reported in other studies (e.g., Smyke et al., 2007) a cross-sectional design cannot determine direction of effects. Indeed, infant behavior could influence maternal emotional availability as much as maternal emotional availability influences infant behavior. A possible approach to untangle direction of effects might be to measure the level of EA in the same mother with two siblings who differ in their behaviors. Another possible approach could analyze maternal EA in the context of different situations with the same child (when the child expresses different behaviors). A third possible approach that could disentangle direction of effects might employ sequential/contingency analyses. A final possible approach could investigate maternal EA and infant behaviors longitudinally to compare their relative predictive validity on one another. Indeed, obtaining data from two or more time points, and analyzing how later smiling is predicted from prior maternal availability, controlling for prior smiling, in comparison to analyzing how later maternal availability is predicted from prior smiling, controlling for prior maternal availability could lead to a better understanding of direction of effects. Furthermore, because smiling and crying are social responses, the role of temperament in individual differences in the expression of these behaviors should be addressed in future investigation.

In terms of representativeness, we selected all firstborn, typically developing infants of 5 months of age while interacting with their mothers. Examinations of infants of different ages or with special needs; single, separated, or divorced mothers; or fathers might result in different patterns of parent EA-infant behavior associations. In addition, infant behaviors, such as smiling and crying, may present different patterns of expression in presence of other caregivers, such as fathers or grandparents or babysitters, or when in the presence of multiple caregivers at the same time. Furthermore, we studied a sample in one specific country (Italy); it is possible that different patterns of association among maternal EA and infant behaviors would emerge if we considered dyads in other cultures. These restrictions focused the comparisons we undertook; however, these restraints also have implications for the generalizability of the results.

To our knowledge this is the first study to analyze aspects of emotional availability of mothers and their relations with principal social behaviors (smile and cry) of firstborn infants at age 5 months using naturalistic data. For this reason the results might be useful in understanding mother-infant relationships more broadly because they emphasize relations between positive emotions of the infant and levels of emotional availability of the mother.

REFERENCES

Agresti, A. (1989). Tutorial on modeling ordered categorical response data. *Psychological Bulletin, 105*(2), 290-301.

Ainsworth, M. D., Blehar, M. C., Waters, E. & Wall, S. (1978). *Patterns of attachment: A psychological study of the strange situation*. Hillsdale, NJ: Erlbaum.

Aviezer, O., Sagi, A., Joels, T., & Ziv, Y. (1999). Emotional availability and attachment representations in kibbutz infants and their mothers. *Developmental Psychology, 35*, 811-821.

Barnard, K. E., Hammond, M. A., Booth, C. L., Bee, H. L., Mitchell, S. K., & Spieker, S. J. (1989). Measurement and meaning of parent-child interaction. In F. J. Morrison, C. Lord, & D. P. Keating (Eds.), *Applied developmental psychology, Vol. 3* (pp. 40-80). New York: Academic Press.

Biringen, Z. (2005). Training and reliability issues with the emotional availability scales. *Infant Mental Health Journal, 26*, 404-405.

Biringen, Z. (2000). Emotional availability: Conceptualization and research findings. *American Journal of Orthopsychiatry, 70*, 104-114.

Biringen, Z., & Robinson, J. (1991). Emotional availability in mother-child interactions: A reconceptualization for research. *American Journal of Orthopsychiatry, 61*, 258-271.

Biringen, Z., Robinson, J.L., & Emde, R.N. (1998). *Manual for scoring the emotional availability scales* (3rd ed.). Unpublished manuscript, Colorado State University, Fort Collins, CO.

Bisping, R., Steingrueber, J., Oltmann, M., & Wenk, C. (1990). Adult's tolerance of cries: an experimental investigation of acoustic features. *Child Development*, *61*, 1218-1229.

Bornstein, M.H., Gini, M., Leach, D. B., Haynes, O. M., Painter, K. M., & Suwalsky. J. T. D. (2006). Short-term reliability and continuity of emotional availability in mother-child dyads across contexts of observation. *Infancy*, *10*, 1-16.

Bornstein, M.H. et al. (1991). *Manual for observation and analysis of infant development and mother-infant interaction in the first years of life*. Child and Family Research, National Institute of Child Health and Human Development, Bethesda MD 20892-2030.

Boukydis, C.F.Z. (1985) Perception of infant crying as an interpersonal event. In B.M. Lester & C.F.Z. Boukydis (Eds.), *Infant Crying: Theoretical and research perspectives*. Plenum Press, New York.

Bowlby, J. (1969). *Attachment and loss: Vol. 1. Attachment*. New York: Basic Books.

Bretherton, I. (2000). Emotional availability: An attachment perspective. *Attachment & Human Development*, *2*, 233-241.

Brewster, A., Nelson, J., McCanne, T.R., Lucas, D.R. and Milner, J.S. (1998). Gender differences in physiological reactivity to infant cries and smiles in a military sample. *Child Abuse & Neglect*, *22*, 775–788.

Bromwich, R. M. (1976). Focus on maternal behavior in infant intervention. *American Journal of Orthopsychiatry*, *46*, 439–446.

Clark, R., Hyde, J. S., Essex, M. J. & Klein, M. H. (1997). Length of maternity leave and quality of mother-infant interaction. *Child Development*, *2*, 364–383.

TER \h \r 1Cohen, J. F. (1960). A coefficient of agreement for nominal scales. *Educational and Psychological Measurement, 20*, 37-46.

Dessureau, B. K., Kurowski, C. O., & Thompson, N. S. (1998). A reassessment of the role of pitch and duration in adults' responses to infant crying. *Infant Behavior & Development, 21*, 367-371.

Easterbrooks, M. A., & Biringen, Z. (2000). Guest editors: introduction to the special issue: Mapping the terrain of emotional availability and attachment. *Attachment and Human Development, 2*, 123-129.

Easterbrooks, M. A., & Biringen, Z. (2005). The Emotional Availability Scales: Methodological refinements of the construct and clinical implications related to gender and at-risk interactions. *Infant Mental Health Journal, 26*, 291-294.

Emde, R. N. (1980). Emotional availability: A reciprocal reward system for infants and parents with implications for prevention of psychosocial disorders. In. P. M. Taylor (Ed.), *Parent-infant relationships* (pp. 87-115). Orlando, FL: Grune & Stratton.

Esposito, G., & Venuti, P. (2008). How is crying perceived in children with Autistic Spectrum Disorder? *Research in Autism Spectrum Disorders*, *2*, 371-384.

Fish, M., & Crockenberg, S. (1981). Correlates and antecedents of nine-month infant behavior and mother–infant interaction. *Infant Behavior and Development, 4*, 69–81.

Fish, M., Stifter, C.A., & Belsky, J. (1991). Conditions of continuity and discontinuity in infant negative emotionality: Newborn to five months. *Child Development*, *62*, 1525–1537.

Harel, J., Oppenheim, D., Tirosh, E. & Gini, M. (1999). Associations between mother-child interaction and children's later self and mother feature knowledge. *Infant Mental Health Journal*, *20*, 123–137.

Hartigan, J. A. and Wong, M. A. (1979). Algorithm AS136. a K-means clustering algorithm. *Applied Statistics, 28,* 100-108.

Hartmann, D. P., & Pelzel, K. E. (2005). Design, measurement, and analysis in developmental research. In M. H. Bornstein & M .E. Lamb (Eds.), *Developmental Science: An advanced textbook* (Fifth edition; pp. 103 – 184). Mahwah, NJ: Erlbaum.

Hubbard, F. O. A. & van IJzendoorn, M. H. (1991). Maternal unresponsiveness and infant crying across the first 9 months: A naturalistic longitudinal study. *Infant Behavior and Development, 14,* 299–312.

Johnson, V. E., & Albert, J. H. (1999). *Ordinal data modeling.* New York: Springer.

Kivijärvi, M., Räihä, H., Kaljonen, A., Virtanen, S., Lertola, K., & Piha, J. (2004). Maternal sensitivity behavior and infant crying, fussing and contented behavior: The effects of mother's experienced social support. *Scandinavian Journal of Psychology, 45,* 239–246.

LaGasse, L., Neal, A.R., & Lester, B.M. (2005). Assessment of Infant Cry: acoustic Cry analysis and parental perception. *Mental Retardation and Development disabilities: Research Review, 11,* 83-93.

Long, S. J. (1997). *Regression models for categorical and limited dependent variables.* Advanced Quantitative Techniques in the Social Sciences Series 7. Thousand Oaks, CA: Sage Publications. (Chapter 5 - Ordinal outcomes: Ordered logit and ordered probit analysis (pp. 114-147).

McCullagh, P. (1980). Regression models for ordinal data. *Journal of the Royal Statistical Society. Series B: Methodological, 42,* 109-142.

McCullagh, P., Nelder, J. A. (1989). *Generalized linear models* (2nd ed.). New York: Chapman & Hall.

McCune-Nicolich, L., & Fenson, L. (1984). Methodological issues in studying early pretend play. In T. D. Yawkey & A. D. Pelligrini (Eds.), *Child's play: Developmental and applied* (pp. 81-124). Hillsdale, NJ: Erlbaum.

McGraw, K. O., & Wong, S. P. (1996). Forming inferences about some intraclass correlation coefficients. *Psychological Methods, 1,* 30–46.

Messinger, D., & Fogel, A. (2007). The interactive development of social smiling. In Robert Kail (ed.), *Advances in Child Development and Behavior,* 35, 327-366. Oxford: Elsevier.

Burns, K. A., Chethik, L., Burns, W. J., & Clark, K. (1997). The early relationship of drug abusing mothers and their infants: An assessment at eight to twelve months of age. *Journal of Clinical Psychology, 53,* 279–287.

Salisbury, A., Minard, K., Hunsley, M., & Thoman, E.B. (2001). Audio Recording of Infant Crying: Comparison with Maternal Cry Logs. *International Journal of Behavioral Development, 25,* 458-465.

Smyke, A.T., Koga, S.F., Johnson, D.E., Fox, N.A., Marshall, P.J.,Nelson, C.A., Zeanah, C.H., & the BEIP Core Group (2007). The caregiving context in institution-reared and family-reared infants and toddlers in Romania. *Journal of Child Psychology and Psychiatry.* 48 (2), 210 – 218.

Stevenson, M. B., Leavitt, L.A., Roach, M. A., Miller, J. F., & Chapman, R. S. (1986). Mother's speechto their one-year-old infants in home and laboratory settings. *Journal of Psycholinguistic Research, 15,* 451-461.

Trevarthen, C. (1993). The function of emotions in early infant communication and development. In J. Nadel & L. Camaioni (Eds.), *New perspectives in early communicative development* (pp. 48-81). New York: Routledge.

Trevarthen, C. (2001) The neurobiology of early communication: Intersubjective regulations in human brain development. In A. F. Kalverboer & A. Gramsbergen (Eds.), *Handbook on Brain and Behavior in Human Development* (pp. 841-882). Dordrecht, The Netherlands: Kluwer.

Trevarthen, C. (2003). Conversations with a two month-old. In J. Raphael-Leff (Ed.), *Parent-infant psychodynamics: Wild things, mirrors and ghosts* (pp. 25–34). Philadelphia: Whurr Publishers.

von Eye, A. (2002). *Configural frequency analysis: Methods, models, and applications.* Mahwah, NJ: Erlbaum.

In: Handbook of Parenting: Styles, Stresses & Strategies   ISBN 978-1-60741-766-8
Editor: Pacey H. Krause and Tahlia M. Dailey   © 2009 Nova Science Publishers, Inc.

Chapter 9

WORKING CLASS MOTHERING: EXPLORING STRENGTHS AND VALUES[1]

Val Gillies
London South Bank University, London, England, UK

ABSTRACT

Drawing on material from my book (Marginalised Mothers: Exploring Working Class Experiences of Parenting) this paper explores how the experiences and meaning making processes of working class mothers are grounded in specific social and material realities. In particular the focus will be on how these situated understandings allow such mothers to generate crucial resources for their children. This work is based on detailed case study analysis of 14 mothers, all of whom have low incomes, lack formal educational qualifications, and live in disadvantaged communities. I begin by considering the status and significance these women attach to motherhood. In spite of unremittingly negative public portrayals of disadvantaged parents, most of the women forged an extremely positive identity around mothering, emphasising satisfaction, pleasure and competence. In a context of deprivation and struggle, being a mother was valued and prioritised and was characterised by resilience and determination. The significance of home for the mothers in the study is underlined through a focus on the emotional resources made available to children.

INTRODUCTION

Over the last few decades increasing significance has been accorded to parenting as a crucial determinant of children's future behaviour and life chances (Gillies 2008). More specifically, a spotlight has fallen on working class childrearing practices as deficient and perpetuating of a cycle of deprivation. This chapter assumes a critical approach to this debate by drawing on material from a qualitative study of the lived experiences of working class

---

[1] This Chapter draws on material from chapter 6 of my book Marginalised Mothers: Exploring Working-class Experiences of Parenting (pp118-143) published by Routledge in 2007.

mothers in the UK. It will examine the particular challenges of poverty and low social status and will reveal the values and strengths that are generated in response. Highlighted are the crucial cultural and emotional resources that working class mothers provide in enabling their children to survive in a context of material deprivation. In this chapter I explore how demands and pressures are met by working class mothers in the every day course of caring for their children and will draw out the situated nature of their decisions and practices. I will also seek to demonstrate how motherhood generates a positive identity for working class women, symbolising knowledge, self worth, strength, power and resilience.

In particular, public concerns around young and lone mothers will be contrasted with real lived experience to demonstrate how pride, satisfaction and pleasure interrupt and subvert social stigma. In a context of deprivation and struggle, being a mother was valued and prioritised by the women in my research, and was characterised by resilience and determination. I show how crucial (though easily overlooked) home based efforts to repair children's self esteem, protect them from harm and promote their educational and future prospects can be viewed in terms of 'emotional capital'. These emotional investments ensure mothering practices are tailored to reflect the specific challenges faced by working class families on a day to day basis. This chapter draws on material explored in greater depth in the book 'Marginalised Mothers: Exploring Working Class Experiences of Parenting'. The book represents a detailed examination of how working class mothers position themselves within a context of inequality and vulnerability.

THE RESEARCH FRAMEWORK

The material discussed in this chapter is informed by two research studies. The first consisted of an in-depth exploration of 5 white, working class mothers parenting outside of conventional nuclear family boundaries (see Gillies 2007 for more details). The second was a larger study titled Resources in Parenting: Access to Capitals, carried out several years later as part of an Economic and Social Research Council funded project. This latter research had two phases, with the first based on an extensive survey of parents of children aged 8 to 12, and the second involving follow up intensive interviews with 25 mothers and 11 fathers from a wide range of 27 household across England and Scotland. This sample encompassed both white and ethnic minority families. (see Edwards and Gillies 2005 for further details of the research design). The intention with the first, survey phase of the research was to determine consensus or lack of it in parents' publicly expressed norms about appropriate sources of support The second, intensive phase of the research then involved pursuing what resources parents themselves draw on and provide in the complex and specific circumstances that face them in their own lives. Utilising a framework informed by the work of Pierre Bourdieu (1977,1979, 1990), the project conceptualised parenting resources in terms of social, economic, cultural and emotional capital, and thereby centred on social connectedness, material and financial status, values and dispositions, and levels or types of emotional investment in children.

The 5 mothers from the first study and 11 households from the second study were defined as working class on the basis of their access to Bourdieu's core capitals. More specifically all had low incomes, lacked formal educational qualifications, and lived and socialised in disadvantaged communities.

Detailed analysis of the interview data from both studies revealed the extent to which economic, cultural, social and personal resources are interdependent in families (see Gillies 2005, 2006, 2007, 2008a 2008b Gillies and Edwards 2006) . Clear relationships were evident between the resources held by particular parents and the childrearing practices they pursued. Parents in the larger study, with access to middle class resources (like money, high status social contacts and legitimated cultural knowledge) drew on these to consolidate their power and advantage. Previous research has produced similar findings, demonstrating how the minutiae of middle class parenting practice is founded on an active manipulation of social and financial resources to ensure advantage is passed down through the generations (Laureau 2003, Allatt 1993). In this chapter, the understandings and practices of working class mothers are examined to consider the lived reality behind often negative public portrayals.

BECOMING A MUM

> Like it's an important part that now I am like mum, I become a mum, from girl. I become first a lady and after the lady I become mum. It's quite a good change isn't it (Meena – Indian working class mother)

Motherhood entails change in identity for all women. For the mothers in this research it was the source of great pride and self respect with many discussing how having a child marked an important point of transition to adulthood. Several of the mothers were very young when they first became pregnant, but for most their first child was experienced as introducing new depth and meaning to life. Despite prominent negative public portrayals of young motherhood qualitative research has revealed the way such mothers create their own positive meanings around becoming a parent (Kirkman, Harison, Hillier, Pyett 2001, Proweller 2000, Fine and Weis 1998). The example of Sam, a white working class lone mother illustrates the way young motherhood can be experienced as a positive new start in life, enabling powerful self development. Sam had desperately wanted a baby and conceived a child with Kevin soon after leaving school. She described feelings of euphoria when pushing her first child's pram through the park, noting how often people would stop and remark on how beautiful her daughter was.

> She was like the first grandchild on each side…And he (Kevin) absolutely idolised her. Everybody did, you used to take her out on the street and people used to look and stare at her, cos she was so beautiful…Yeah like, she's very, very um. She's special. I don't know. She, cos because she, she brought out a hell of a lot of love in people. People could look at her and say oh she's lovely. She brought out a hell of a lot of love out of people and being the first grandchild as well

Although she had another son by him, Sam's relationship with Kevin was characterised by violent abuse and hardship. Kevin subsequently married another woman some time after Sam threw him out of their house. At the time of the interview she had spent two and a half years coping on her own, but had no regrets over her decision to have children. A new life began for Sam once she was finally able to gain independence as a lone mother. Her proven ability to bring two children up with little support from their father is clearly the source of great pride and satisfaction for her. Being a single mother is depicted by her as difficult and challenging but ultimately very rewarding, providing a number of advantages above dual parenting. In her account Sam describes the process of mothering as a 'job', requiring skill, ability and devotion. Coping alone intensifies the need for competence and efficiency, but it also increases the fulfilment that can be gained from parenting.

Sam's account of becoming a single mother was told as a story of progress and achievement, and was linked to her personal development as an individual. She explained how her decision to give up on Kevin and parent alone marked a powerful subjective change in her, forcing her to become more independent and assertive. A personality change from being in soft to become fiercely self reliant and confident is interpreted as a direct consequence of becoming a mother. According to Sam, commitment to her children (aged six and two at the time of the interview) led her to become more ruthless in securing what she identified as their interdependent needs. She accepts sole responsibility for then and this requires strength and determination. Realisation that she possesses such traits, combined with mounting evidence of her ability to cope alone resulted in a dramatically altered self perception.

This narrative of self development, from, in her words, 'young minded' emotional dependency to capable self determination, constitutes Sam's experience of becoming a single mother. The process of coping alone is presented as self evidently worthy and indicative of strength of character. Consequently Sam appropriates the term 'single mother' to construct a positive self identity as a proficient, independent and responsible individual. Sam is able to articulate this construction despite alternative public representations of single mothers as weak, unable to control their children, and dependent on the state. Her lack of engagement with these negative portrayals underlines the powerful status she attaches to single motherhood. Rather than perceiving her experiences in terms of failure, an assumption commonly superimposed onto the lives of working class lone parents, Sam emphasises her success in achieving the status of being a single mother.

The significance Sam attaches to being a lone mother and the satisfaction and self worth she derives from this status is further emphasised by her determination to remain a lone parent. From Sam's perspective, she and the children have too much to lose by returning to the vulnerability of two parent relationships. As well as stressing her contentment with her current family arrangement, she discussed the advantages of parenting alone, making it clear that she had no intention of risking her independence and control by allowing another man to live with herself and her children. While many of the other mothers in the sample associated financial and practical support with the role of a father, Sam accepted and valued this responsibility as a requirement of lone motherhood. She described Kevin as a 'good father' for continuing to make financial contributions to the children's upbringing, but she also emphasises her own efforts in bringing in and managing money. Allowing another man to take a share in parenting is seen by Sam as risky, and she is anxious to maintain a secure boundary around what she perceived as belonging to herself and her children.

> Cos I like being a single mum, I don't like people interfering like with what I do. Even Kevin if he says anything to me about the kids it gets on my nerves and I think to myself I'm doing my bloody best here and I know I'm doing a really good job.... if he did say I used to

have to take notice but now I don't cos I don't have to. I don't need to. He's married he's got he's own and I've got my own

While she feels satisfied and proud of her efforts as a mother she is acutely aware of her position as vulnerable, and of the need to protect what she has accomplished against the odds. While Sam's fierce determination to parent alone was not shared by other mothers' in the research her dedication and resilience was evident across the sample. The working class mothers in this book prioritised the needs of their children often at great personal expense.

MEDIATING THE EFFECTS OF TRAUMA AND IMPOVERISHMENT

Like Sam, many of the mothers coped with violence and hardship as part of their efforts to nurture, protect and care for their children. These mothers could not conceive of their lives without their children. Moving on without them (as many fathers had done) was simply not a thinkable option. This unspoken but iron commitment sustained them through danger and deprivation, and many felt proud of their ability to parent well in these highly demanding circumstances. But, as the example of Kelly demonstrates, this struggle for survival can be precarious and costly for parents and their children.

Kelly is a white working class mother who lives with her two children Craig (aged 9), Rosie (aged 7) her new partner Terry and his daughter, Jade (aged 7) from a previous relationship. The family live in a rented house in a small town and Terry works as a lorry driver. Kelly had Craig when she was 19 and had always wanted children. Although several of her friends had babies from 14 onwards she had thought it best to wait until she was a bit older. Her relationship with the children's father, Dean was not particularly happy but the family lived together in a small flat and Rosie was born 2 years later. Dean was not working by this time and was becoming increasingly violent and abusive. Eventually, fearing for the children's safety, Kelly fled to a women's refuge. This was a particularly difficult and distressing period for Kelly and the children. Social services became involved and it was discovered that both children had been severely sexually abused. The police were not able to establish who the culprit was, although Dean remains a strong suspect. During this time Kelly and the children lived in fear and grinding poverty. They were forced to relocate to different parts of the country several times, which involved packing up and moving home at short notice. The family struggled to survive on benefits and Kelly often went without food to make sure the children had enough to eat.

Eventually they were able to settle and Kelly's mother and sister moved from the other side of the country to live nearby. Kelly met Terry shortly after and they decided to rent a house and move in together. However, by then Craig's behaviour had become a focus of concern. He has been diagnosed with conduct disorder and his behaviour is often dangerous and out of control. He starts fires, fights, steals and stays out all night. Although for the last few years he has attended appointments with a psychologist his behaviour appears to be getting worse. Teachers at his school will now only allow him to attend mornings because he is so disruptive. Kelly describes a catalogue of incidents and focuses on the week before the interview as an example.

Tuesday morning I was in here and we've got garages across there at the back and I stood at that window and I looked out and all I see was the back of him in flames at the front. So I went running out there because I wasn't sure whether he was on fire or whether he'd set fire to something he was holding. And what he'd done is he'd took a lighter and took a hairspray can and was setting fire to the hairspray can, setting fire to the hairspray can in the air. That was on the Tuesday and so I went into the school and said to them look please just keep him in all day. They said yeah all right we'll try and keep him in. Then on the Thursday he'd come home and he'd bought a [toy] gun from a shop out of all the money that he'd took out of my car. And I've had no guns no toy knives and that's been a rule since they was babies. So they know they're not allowed. So I took it off him on the Thursday and he actually hit me and smashed his room up to the extent that there was no furniture that was actually savable. He had no bed or nothing left.

Kelly is exhausted and overwhelmed, but gets little sympathy or support from Terry who has washed his hands of Craig. From Terry's perspective Craig is 'a little git, end of story'. Terry works long hours and is often away from home and to avoid arguments the couple have agreed not to talk about Craig. Kelly has had lots of professional intervention over the years from social services, Mental health workers, parenting advisors as well as the police and fire brigade. However, with the exception of the emergency services, the support offered has been confined to counselling, advice or therapy with very little practical help. After discovering the sexual abuse social services were able to offer a counselling referral for both children, yet were not able ensure the family had a safe, decent and permanent house to live in. When Craig's behaviour problems emerged Kelly struggled to access and meaningful help and found herself pushed towards inappropriate services such as parenting classes.

I've been to the parent group which is supposed to tell you how to deal with it and that and um that was crap (laughs). Basically. The ideas were good if I had a 4 or 5 year old, but for him things like spending 10 minutes on the chair were supposed to calm him down if he was throwing a tantrum. I if I put him on the chair for 10 minutes he'd just laugh, get up and do what ever he was doing before. I didn't find that very helpful at all...I find that going to the authorities and that just hasn't helped at all. I mean they give me this silly parent book thing and it was just a waste of time. I mean 8 weeks I was going there and we got nothing out of it at all....

Referring Kelly to parenting classes ignores the wider context shaping Craig's conduct. While his disturbed behaviour is most likely rooted in the violence and upheaval shaping his formative years it is Kelly's parenting abilities that are questioned, as opposed to the state's failure to protect a vulnerable young mother and her children. Despite the severity of the problem Kelly has received relatively little useful support from professionals and feels she has been let down. The strain of caring for Craig is immense and she is grateful for any help she can get. Yet despite the difficulties with Craig, Kelly clearly feels she is a good mother and she emphasises her skills in looking after children. When her daughter joined a local children's club (Badgers), Kelly became involved as a parent helper and proudly describes herself as among the most qualified, longstanding helpers in the district. In short Kelly gains great happiness from caring from children, and her life revolves around her own children.

I don't really get much time to myself because Craig, like today he does 9 till half past 12 at school and I've got him here all afternoon. Then in the evening I've got him here. Then other days he don't got to school till quarter past one and he comes home at 3, which doesn't give you a lot of time to go out, even to do shopping or anything. It's just hard work just getting little jobs done....Yeah so the only time I really get to my self is when I'm asleep

Do you think it's important for you to have time on your own?

Not really, cos I do like doing a lot of stuff with kids and that anyway, I can sort of get down to their level and play their games and I sort out craft ideas and things for Badgers and I always get my lot to try it all out before hand anyway. So we do a lot of making things and try new games together and it's not too bad then.

If you manage to get time on your own how do you spend it?

Well I don't really do time on me own. Because if there's no kids around about I'll go round and play with my sisters little boys who's coming up to 2. Or I'll go round and see if my mum's alright, because she's not been very well. So I don't really do time by on my own, I think I'd be quite, what do I do with myself if I did have time to myself....Probably get a job

Mmh what would you like to do?

Work in a nursery (laughs)

The limited period that Craig spends at school is compounding his severely restricted educational development. Kelly expressed particular shock and disappointment that teachers have not been able to provide him with basic reading skills. He is not receiving any special/professional help at school or at home and Kelly is resigned to the prospect of relying on her own efforts to teach him. However, Kelly struggles herself to understand the work that Craig brings home and has instead bought some basic text books to go through with him.

So I don't really get involved with what he's doing at school because he's in so much trouble at school. Sort of school stays at school and I do our bits at home. I've got some special books and things that I've bought and we do them rather than doing what ever he's doing at school.

Links are often made between juvenile delinquency and poor parenting (see Gillies 2000), but the example of Kelly highlights the less visible but central role mothers often play in terms of preventing problems from escalating and continuing to care for children in desperate circumstances. The consistently grim prospects for children looked after by local authorities bares testament to the significance of this role, with care leavers considerably more likely to end up homeless, using drugs and or in prison (Ward, Henderson and Pearson 2003, Robbins 2001, Utting 1997). Far from suggesting any parenting deficit, Kelly's account reveals the extent of energy she devotes to mothering her three children. Also prominent is the pleasure and satisfaction she continues to derive from parenting, alongside the pain and worry. Like the other mothers in this research, Kelly works hard to compensate for the vulnerability and a lack of access to material and economic resources, but this necessitates a prioritisation of particular principles and practices. Kelly's emphasis on home over school is likely to be misinterpreted as a rejection of education as a value because her behaviour does not conform to ideal models of parental involvement. A fundamental concern with ensuring children are equipped to deal with instability, injustice and hardship often clashes with more normative middle class expectations. This is reflected in the different kinds of emotional resources that working class mothers make available to their children in comparison with middle class parents.

VALUABLE FEELINGS: EMOTIONS AS RESOURCES

Despite a general agreement that emotions lay at the heart of family life this crucial dimension of interpersonal relations is often naturalised to a point of invisibility. Some theorists have attempted to illuminate this complex area by exploring how emotions can act as a family resource, drawing on and widening Bourdieu's model of capitals (Reay 2000, 2002, Allat 1993, Nowotny 1981). This work on 'emotional capital' has been valuable in drawing attention to an under theorised parenting resource, but has been characterised by a preoccupation with academic attainment. There is a tendency for existing literature on this topic to equate emotional capital with educational success, viewing it as a resource passed on through parental involvement. To count as emotional capital parental involvement must generate a profit for the child (Reay 2000, 2002). However, this assessment inevitably depends on a value judgement as to what might constitute a 'profit', as is evident in a common conflation between emotional capital as a resource and educational progress as (one particular) outcome (Gillies 2006).

Yet, inevitably interpretations of the best outcome for children are firmly tied to the material and social positions of their parents. Consequently a more flexible understanding of emotional capital is needed to recognise the value of parental investments without imposing middle class values on working class lives. An exploration of the emotions associated with a parent's desire to promote their children's wellbeing and prospects throws light on a range of practices and orientations. This approach allows an appreciation that emotional investments may be directed towards day to day survival as well as maximising future opportunities to get ahead. From this perspective emotional capital can be understood as a resource for crucial short term benefits, as well as more long term investments in children's futures. This avoids a deficit model of working class emotional capital by recognising the crucial yet often hidden resources marginalised parents may generate.

At a broad level the emotions of the mothers in this study were aroused to act as a resource in three main contexts; soothing and boosting children's self esteem, promoting their future interests and protecting and defending them. While these emotional orientations are shared by middle class mothers, practices and investments were highly classed. Attainment at school is recognised as having an important impact on children's self esteem, but while middle class mothers invest heavily in their child's academic success as a marker of worth, working class mothers focus on alternative values to mediate the psychological impact of school failure. As I have argued elsewhere, middle class parents can mobilise formidable economic, cultural and social resources to bolster their child's academic success (Gillies 2005 Gillies 2007). But while most working class mothers would love to see their child do well at school this hope is tempered by a recognition that the odds are stacked against them. Failure is an experience that most working class children must learn to cope with from an early age. Working class mothers are concerned to ensure that children survive without being emotionally crushed and this can be played out in strategies such as a disinvestment from school and a prioritisation of home over school (see Gillies 2006 for a more detailed discussion).

Attempts to boost self esteem are also strongly linked to economic capital. While a large amount of money might be spent on middle class children, emotional significance is more often diverted through the values and aspirations associated with middle class cultural capital. For example, investments might be made in after school activities, extra tuition, 'educational' toys or computer games, or trips to museums. For working class mothers, however, giving is more likely to be associated with a notion of worth and deservingness rather than moral or educational appropriateness. Acquiring a high status or much desired item for a child can convey a range of symbolic meanings, heightened by the scarcity of the financial resources that are required to buy it. The following extract from Julie, an African-Caribbean lone mother, demonstrates the depth of the emotional significance placed on providing something that is desired.

> I've got no money you know, and cos I punch me gas and punch me electric it is difficult and also, you know, I've got like erm the phone, the phone bill, I've got the [playstation] I've got the [playstation] for the children because they're not ones for asking so I feel well, you know, this is like a reward, you know, like for them.....I mean it doesn't bother me whether I get to go on holiday or not but I do think that, you know, definitely for the children because they don't ask to be brought into this world and because they're here I feel that I need to, you know, give 'em things that they haven't got and because like I'm one parent, you know, and yeah they do see the, like, children out there that's got the best this and the best of that but, you know, I do try and provide......

> I. Mm, mm, mm, OK. But what happens if the children really want something but you don't have the money, say like a new pair of trainers or something like that?

> By hook or by crook I'll get it. Yeah, by hook or by crook I'll get it and I don't mean, like, going out there and steal it, I just mean, like, just if it means, like, me not paying a bill, I'd just not pay a bill and do it that way.
> (Julie – African Caribbean, lone mother on benefits)

For Julie, providing things like a playstation or a holiday entails a real struggle that inevitably communicates to her children the extent to which they are valued. For more wealthy parents spending money is a less obviously significant act and consequently there is likely to be a tension between curbing their children's materialism and making them happy. These parents were much more likely to apply codes and norms in relation to buying things for their children like helping the child to save for it, or buying it if it is 'needed' for an educational activity. But when money is scarce treats and gifts are highly meaningful. Much desired items like brand name clothing or a favourite junk food for dinner might make a difficult day at school more bearable for a child, while also communicating a strong message of love and care. Yet from a middle class perspective this might be viewed as an irresponsible extravagance, encouraging consumerism and poor health in a context where money could be better spent.

Emotions expressed by working class mothers are often orientated towards the defence of their children and the safeguarding of justice in terms of rights. Emotional capital in this context could be characterised by anger, outrage and burning feelings of injustice, from which children could draw a sense of their own entitlement and a determination to fight back For example, Julie described how she fought hard to clear her son's name when he was accused of assaulting another boy at school.

> If my child's like done something I'd be so humble, yeah, if he'd done something I'd humble myself yeah? But if I know he's not done anything I'm gonna like support him a hundred and ten per cent, yeah. So I'm saying I went down to the headmaster, you know, to try and like sort this out because it's gone on his record, it's gone in the files so what the headmaster turned round to me and said, Mrs Denis it's not going to go any further in fact Lloyd done it but it won't go any further if when he goes to college, whether it be work, you know, it won't be forwarded to his next employer or, you know, college or whatever, so I'm saying well I don't want it in the filing cabinet because like he didn't do it.

Anxiety to ensure children are protected provoked a number or different reactions and strategies by the mothers in the sample. For example, Kelly explained how she besieged a teacher and drew on social contacts to deal with her daughter's vulnerability to bullies.

> I went in every single day and said to her teacher you know it happened again yesterday. And I done it every single day and I think the teacher just got fed up (laughs). I've got a friend who's a dinner lady at the school as well and so she watched out for her at dinner time and that as well for me (Kelly – White, working class mother)

For other mothers attention was focused on making sure children are streetwise and able to stand up for themselves. The two African Caribbean lone mothers in the study were particularly concerned about the vulnerability and confidence of their daughters at school. Julie expressed anxiety that her daughter might be susceptible to people taking advantage of her.

> Carly's just so so so pleasant, you know, you know, she's erm. Sometimes I do have concerns about Carly's behaviour because, you know, she's so pleasant to the fact that, you know, some people can take advantage of that, you know, of that, you know with one of [pause] because of her nature. I do try and like toughen her up (laughs) because I know what it's like, you know, I know what it's like when you - so I do try to like toughen her up. (Julie – African Caribbean, working class lone mother)

Annette expressed her surprise and pride that her daughter was able to challenge the teacher about her grades.

> She's surprised me with being assertive with a couple if the teachers on grades that she's getting. There was one time when she got a 'C' grade for something that she'd done and the week before she got an 'A' grade for something she didn't consider as good and she actually challenged her teacher, she said "how is it that I got 'A' for that and I spent two hours on this and got a 'C' for it and the teacher was quite taken aback. She said she felt so proud of herself that she challenged her (Annette – African Caribbean, working class lone mother)

Working class emotional capital is plentiful in the home with mothers soothing hurt feelings, bolstering confidence and communicating hopes, fears and expectations that are necessarily shaped by social and economic realities. As I have shown many of the working class mothers in this study were prepared go into school and passionately defend their children to teachers. But on a day to day basis most concentrated on supporting their children outside of this institutional environment. In disputes with other school children it was common for the mothers to approach other mothers in an effort to resolve the issue without involving teachers.

EDUCATIONAL INVOLVEMENT

While mothers in this research often prioritised home above school this does not indicate a lack of interest in children's schooling. Deep concern was expressed about children's future prospects and the mothers worked hard to ensure their children were not left behind in terms of education. Significantly though, their strategies were often less visible because they tended to bypass the school system. As I outlined earlier in this chapter, Kelly's emotional investments, by necessity, circumvented the school system, reflecting the choices available to her. She is aware she can not rely on the school to deal with Craig's disturbed behaviour and low reading age, and she does not have a middle class voice of authority to demand better provision. Attempts by working class mothers to address poor resourcing in schools were not well received, as Louise, a white mother, found when she complained about a seemingly endless stream of temporary supply teachers allocated to her daughter's class. She was told she should be grateful the school were providing her daughter with any teachers at all. Notwithstanding the tight funding dilemmas facing many schools, it is difficult to imagine this statement being made to middle class parents.

While the context is very different, the concern, fears and commitments of the working class mothers in this research are just as valuable and representative of emotional capital as they would be for the parents of academically successful children. Although unlikely to lead to the hard currency of academic qualifications, their efforts represent a highly significant resource in shaping their children's future. Yet the valuable contributions made by working class mothers in terms of supporting their children's education are rarely recognised because they lack the prominence of more middle class approaches. For example, from a middle class professional's point of view Liz, a white working class mother, might be questioned in terms of her commitment to her children's education. Like the most of the mothers in my study, Liz assumes a largely submissive role with respect to day to day school involvement. Contact beyond reports, administrative letters and occasional parents' evenings is rare and associated with being summoned to account for a problem. Yet behind this apparent disinterest there lies considerable anxiety and an everyday labour intensive struggle to ensure school work is taken seriously.

> And I do threaten him if he gets a bad school report, which touch wood he's not had. But they've got a new scheme now. They're getting three a year at the end of every term. So it's not going to be a year before I know what he's up to. Which I'm pleased because I often wonder, you often wonder how they're getting on really. Because the school doesn't ever contact you, it's hearsay isn't it. He says oh yeah I'm doing great. But I mean I do look through his books. Like I was looking through them last night, and um er he gets all agitated you know - put them back, put them back- and you know - Why are you going through my

bag it's all personal. You know he doesn't want you to look at anything and when I ask him things you know how he's getting on at school. He's always yeah okay. And he's quite vague about it.... I mean they always say I moan. But I'm not, I don't think I'm moaning all the time, I just will ask him what he's doing. But it's just, in their eyes it's you're moaning all the time.

While Liz tries to keep herself informed of her oldest son's progress she relies on limited feedback from him and the teachers. She is grateful for the regular school reports as they tend to provide reassurance that her children are not falling behind or misbehaving. She does not have the sense of entitlement or confidence to ask for more detailed information and more importantly she would have little use for it. From Liz's perspective a mother's role is to supervise, push and pull her children in the right direction, while education remains the teacher's domain. This is reinforced by a privacy boundary drawn by her son, who views his mother's scrutiny terms of intrusion. Consequently Liz's efforts to support her son's education at home are characterised by 'nagging' and conflict. For example, Liz describes how she feels she has to chide Adam into doing his homework.

He always has to be pushed though, you know with the homework. I was moaning at him only last night about he homework. He's one of these boys, you've got to be behind him. If the teacher says well I'd like a small paragraph, then he will write a small paragraph. He'll never think there's lots more to write about that I'll go and do a whole page. He's like well she wanted a small paragraph and I've done it (laughs) you know...You know and I always say well there's loads you can write about that. No no that's all she wanted. And I say well, and it annoys me.....And I definitely think that with boys it's just like well I've done the home work, I'm not going to get a detention now. And I'm moaning at him, you just do the minimum that gets you out of trouble. You know and I keep saying to him don't you want to do well at school. He says yeah I do want to do well at school but I don't want to have to keep doing loads of home work. And I said well you're not going to get anywhere if you don't put anything in

Liz admits to 'moaning' and openly acknowledges that Adam's attitude towards his homework annoys her, but she feels a responsibility to keep pushing 'behind him' to ensure he gets the work done. 'Doing the minimum that gets you out of trouble' was identified as a key motive spurring on Adam to do his homework. This resonates with an anxiety Liz expresses about the negative consequences of not following rules, but she is clearly frustrated Adam's reluctance to do the best he can. She plays an active role in persuading, motivating and occasionally pressurising her sons into certain activities for their own good. This responsibility was accepted by Liz as an inevitable feature of mothering, but it was also a source of concern and worry for her.

You know I think, I think definitely since he's been a teenager I've definitely noticed a lack of, um, he's quite, he's not hard work, but he definitely needs that shove all the time. And um he is quite happy to lollop about and TV on and you run around getting things for him. And unless you, like you know, he does ask me to get things. And I say, you know what's wrong with you getting up and getting it. Cos I don't want them all the time being waited on hand on foot. Because when they grow older they're going to find things really difficult. And he is quite um, a lazy boy. And I'm always having to um. I mean now and again he'll do things for me but he's always oh (exhales) you know and a moan and a groan and you know

While Liz is prepared to 'shove' Adam, ensuring he fulfils obligations and takes up opportunities, she is anxious that this approach encourages his laziness. By taking an indirect responsibility for her son's life decisions, she is worried that he is not developing the independence and self sufficiency he will need to carry him through his adult life. Nevertheless, Liz is clear that laziness is considerably preferable to the risks associated with her reduced input. Liz's account of parenting reveals the amount of effort and commitment she feels mothering requires. Yet the emotional labour she undertakes is largely invisible and directed towards aims that are less likely to be understood or shared by the middle classes. Her deep sense of personal responsibility for the actions, choices and decisions made by her children is primarily orientated towards protecting them from the pitfalls and uncertainties of a dangerous world. With middle class children considerably more insulated from these risks, the emotional investments of their parents can afford to centre on conserving and consolidating their advantages. Middle class perspectives are often unable to recognise the particular strengths and benefits of working class parenting practices, and are liable to misinterpret this emotional investment in terms of low aspiration and lack of concern.

CONCLUSION: VALUING WORKING CLASS MOTHERING

Being a good mum comes from being a good person and you've got to be a good person to be a good mum (Sam – white working class mother)

The chapter has explored the rich cultural and emotional resources provided by working class mothers. The women in this study attached a powerful significance to motherhood and cared deeply about their children. Notably the mothers were heavily invested in traditional gendered constructions of motherhood in terms of commitment, devotion and dedication. As other research suggests those publicly constructed as a threat to the stability of the family are the most likely to draw on traditional views about the role of women and set particularly high standards for themselves as mothers (Bullen et al 2000). Being a 'good mother' is inextricably bound up with wider, moral evaluations of the self. Arguably, no other role, or status of existence so comprehensively determines notions of social and personal worth for women. I have suggested that the concept of 'emotional capital' can help to illuminate the classed nature of parenting practices, revealing a contrast between middle class preoccupations with academic performance and working class concerns to keep children safe, soothe feelings of failure and low self worth, and challenge injustice. In the context of poverty, vulnerability and failure, working class children may have precious few resources to draw on other than the emotional capital they access from their mothers.

The mothers' commitment and sense of responsibility was often characterised by personal sacrifice and struggle, yet also generated great pleasure and satisfaction. The was demonstrated by Sam's account of lone motherhood, and also the case study example of Kelly, who remained dedicated to her children through violence, vulnerability, extreme poverty and continued to cope with serious and stressful after effects on her son. Kelly's strength and competence is unrecognised in her interactions with professionals, while her family's more pressing needs for practical support go unmet. The low status accorded to working class mothers ensures the crucial resources they provide are at best overlooked and at worst pathologised. Recognition of this labour demands a much greater appreciation of the varied and situated roles that parents play in caring for their children, alongside a critical deconstruction of the many middle class assumptions that ground contemporary family policy debates.

REFERENCES

Allatt, P. (1993) 'Becoming privileged: the role of family processes', in I. Bates and G. Risebourough (eds), *Youth and Inequality*. Buckingham: Open University.

Bourdieu, P. (1977) *Outline of a Theory of Practice*, Cambridge: Cambridge University Press.

Bourdieu, P. (1979) *Distinction: A Social Critique of the Judgement of Taste*, London: Routledge.

Bourdieu, P. (1990) *In Other Words: Essays Towards a Reflexive Sociology*, Cambridge, Polity Press.

Bourdieu, P. and Passeron, J. (1977) *Reproduction in Education, Society and Culture,* London: Sage.

Bullen, E., Kenway, J. and Hey (2000) New Labour, social exclusion and educational risk management: the case of 'gymslip mums'. *British Educational Research Journal,* 26 (4), 441-456.

Fine, M. & Weis, L. (1998). *The unknown city: the lives of poor and working-class young adults.* Boston, MA: Beacon Press.

Gillies, V. (2008) Childrearing, class and the new politics of parenting, *Sociology Compass*, 2/3, 1079-1095.

Gillies, V. 2008 'Perspectives on Parenting Responsibility: Contextualising Values and Practices', *Law and Society*, 35 (1) 95-112.

Gillies, V. 2007 Marginalised Mothers: Exploring Working Class Parenting, London: Routledge.

Gillies, V. 2006 Working Class Mothers and School Life: Exploring the Role of Emotional Capital, *Gender and Education* 18 (3) 81-295.

Gillies, V. 2005 Raising the meritocracy: parenting and the individualisation of social class, *Sociology*, 39 (5) 835-853.

Gillies, V. (2000) Young people and Family Life: Analysing and Comparing Disciplinary Discourses. *Journal of Youth Studies*, Vol 3, No 2, 211-228.

Gillies, V. and Edwards, R. (2006) A qualitative analysis of parenting and social capital: comparing the work of Coleman and Bourdieu, *Qualitative Sociology Review*, Vol II. Issue 2. (http://www.qualitativesociologyreview.org /ENG/archive_eng.php).

Gillies, V. and Edwards, R. (2005) Resources in Parenting: Access to Capitals Project Report , Families & Social Capital ESRC Research Report No14.

Kirkman, M., Harrison, L., Hillier, L. and Pyett P. (2001) 'I know I'm doing a good job': canonical and autobiographical narratives of teenage mothers. *Culture, Health & Sexuality* 3 (3) 279 – 294.

Lareau, A (2003) *Unequal childhoods, class, race and family life.* Berkeley: University of California Press.

Notwotny, H. (1981) Women in public life in Austria, in C. Fuchs Epstein and R. Laub Coser (eds) *Access to power: cross national studies of women and elites* (London: Sage).

Proweller, A. (2000). Re-writing/-righting lives: Voices of pregnant and parentingteenagers in an alternative school. In L. Weis & M. Fine (Eds.) *Construction sites:Excavating race, class, and gender among urban youth,* 100-120. New York, :Teachers College Press.

Reay, D. (2000) A useful extension of Bourdieu's conceptual framework? Emotional capital as a way of understanding mother' involvement in their children's education? *Sociological Review,* 48 (4), 568-585.

Reay, D. (2002) Gendering Bourdieu's Concept of Capitals?: Emotional Capital, Women and Social Class, Paper given at Feminists Evaluate Bourdieu: International Perspectives Conference, Manchester, 11th October.

Robbins D, 2001, Transforming Children's Services: An Evaluation of Local Responses to the Quality Protects Programme, Year 3, Department of Health.

Utting, W. (1997), People Like Us: The Report of the Review of Safeguards for Children Living Away from Home, London: Department of Health/Welsh Office, The Stationery Office.

Ward, J. and Pearson, G. (2003) Tracking care leavers as they move to independence, ESRC Research Report, http://www.regard.ac.uk/research_findings/R000223982/report.pdf

In: Handbook of Parenting: Styles, Stresses & Strategies   ISBN 978-1-60741-766-8
Editor: Pacey H. Krause and Tahlia M. Dailey   © 2009 Nova Science Publishers, Inc.

Chapter 10

CHILD-PARENT RELATIONS AS A MUTUAL OPPORTUNITY FOR A SIGNIFICANT DEVELOPMENTAL ENCOUNTER WITH THE "OTHER"

Esther Cohen

School of Education, the Hebrew University of Jerusalem, Israel

Neta Ofer-Ziv

Amirim Child Therapy Center, Macabim, Israel

INTRODUCTION

Parenting is a process of creation: the parent's creation of a child, and the child's creation of a parent. This chapter will focus on the notion that this creation arises from the dialectical tension that emerges in the space between parent and child. The basic tension present in parenthood, the tension between parent and child, is a particular example of the basic existential tension existing between a person and an "Other" or, in other words, the tension between one subject and another. This tension between two subjects receives intense expression when the need of the one, at any particular moment, is different from the need of the other. The moment in which this acute dialectical tension between the two is created, which sometimes also involves sharp tension within each subject, is a potential moment of growth and development. Any solution that attempts to eliminate this tension quickly, so that the need of the one overpowers the need of the other, results in the constriction of the space that enables the process of creation and development. The tension between desires, between perceptions and impulses that conflict with each other in the context of intimate relations is not, we claim, a negative element that sullies relationship or mars development, as is sometimes believed. On the contrary, this tension is likely to contribute not only to the development of significant and rich relations, but also to the development of each individual within the relationship. According to this outlook, beneficial parenting does not seek to reduce conflicts or difference, or to avoid them, nor does it view conflict as a "necessary evil," but rather as an opportunity for growth and creativity.

Given the structural hierarchy of relationships between parent and child, the responsibility for containing this dialectical tension, in the early phases of infancy, falls almost exclusively on the parent. Later on, as the child develops, this responsibility is transferred gradually also to the child. The child's developing ability to contain this tension in his relations with his parents and to find creative solutions within himself allows him to participate in a similar process vis-à-vis other children, other people, and as an adult vis-à-vis his or her own children. The parents' responsibility for containing the dialectical tension and preserving it, we esteem, is the most complex psychological task required of a person. Containing this dialectical tension within a more equal relationship is also a difficult task, riddled with failures, as evidenced in relations between intimate couples or between adults in other contexts. This task is more complex in parenting, both because it involves a process of transition from biological union to physical and psychological separation, and also because of the demanding nature of parenting, with all its inherent paradoxes. One such central paradox, which adds to the challenge of containing this dialectical tension, is the tension that parents experience as a conflict between two central tasks: the task of nurturing, which includes sensitive and responsive care, nurturing, protection, and the establishment of love and of trust, versus the task of education and socialization, which includes demands and achievement-oriented training as well as demands for conformity with behavioral, social and cultural standards.

Despite the difficulty involved, enhancing the ability to cope with the containment of dialectical tension in parent-child relations may contribute to the development of individuals with better personal and interpersonal abilities, as well as to the creation of a more ethical society. In this chapter we will attempt to substantiate this claim regarding the importance of preserving dialectical tension between opposites, both from the perspective of developmental and interpersonal psychology and with the aid of psychoanalytic theories, chiefly those of Winnicot (1971), Jessica Benjamin (2005), and LaMothe (2005).

In order to understand the components of a parent's ability to contain dialectical tension, one must focus, we argue, on processes of intrapersonal and interpersonal regulation and how these develop. Several important insights into this issue are offered by integrative developmental theories and innovative research, as presented in the separate works of Daniel Siegel (Siegel, 2004), Schore (Schore, 2001) and Fonagy (Fonagy, 2002). These studies focus on mental and neurobiological regulatory processes as central processes that promote emotional and social development, and are an outcome of attachment processes between parent and child. Certain processes, such as the creation of an internal working model, reflexivity, and creation of meaning are highlighted by this research as significant for developing the capacity for regulation of emotion and behavior. The ability to process emotion, especially in the context of anxiety, is closely tied, we believe, to the capacity of the parents to contain dialectical tension and to create from within this tension. These studies support the argument that ineffective regulation of anxiety and frustration is a dominant factor in "choosing" to break this dialectical tension, which leads to the dichotomizing process of splitting rather than to an integrative process of growth. The loss of the regulatory capacity occurs most significantly in traumatic situations and tends to lead to coping strategies that employ splitting mechanisms (Schore, 2001).

In this chapter we will point to a variety of patterns for coping with situations of conflict, which a parent must adopt in daily life in order to preserve the dialectical tension that promotes processes of emotional and social adaptation in their children. We will demonstrate how the failure to use this variety of patterns, or even the disturbance of the balance between them, presents an obstacle to the development of strong interpersonal abilities, and we will hypothesize that these situations are related to the parents' unregulated levels of anxiety. Finally, we will relate to contemporary characteristics of our culture that diminish the ability of parents to contain dialectical tension, and which increase anxiety and delay the normal development of the parent's and developing child's regulatory capacity. Among these characteristics, we will devote most of our attention to the common belief that suffering and frustration are unnecessary and even damaging to the development of children. We maintain that the effect of these beliefs on parenting explains to a great extent the severe crisis that many parents experience in their relationships with their children. Our discussion thus introduces a different dimension to our understanding of what has been described as the collapse of parental authority in the last few decades (Griffin, 2007).

The conception of parenting, offered in this chapter, integrates ideas and findings from different disciplinary fields, and has practical applications both at the level of individual interventions with parents, and at the level of prevention programs and group interventions.

CONTRIBUTION OF PSYCHOANALYTIC THEORY

Psychoanalytic theory, in its cross-fertilization with phenomenological philosophy, has addressed various forms of the subject's development and being, by introducing and elaborating the innovative notion that a child is a subject who has a rich, complex and vulnerable internal life, which is significantly impacted by his relationship with his parents. Both philosophy and psychoanalysis evolved and underwent changes over time and began to define inter-subjective relations as a topic of inquiry, rather than merely relations between subject and object. In this chapter we will discuss the work of several theorists who have contributed significantly to understanding the special texture of relations that exists in parenting and who have enhanced our understanding of relations occurring in the space between two subjects.

The first psychoanalyst we discuss is Winnicott, who elaborated the idea that something significant occurs in the encounter between two "Others," something that cannot occur within each person separately. Winnicott describes an intermediate space of experience that exists between the mother and the child, which he calls a "potential space," and which is associated with a developmental transition between the symbiosis of early infancy and the acceptance of separateness and difference, as well as of awareness of an external reality that can be shared with others; a transition between feelings of childish omnipotence and reality testing, and the development of the ability to 'use the parent' and to navigate between one's own internal reality to another's. Out of the infant's need to cope with reality, it creates the prototypes of symbolic capacity which allow it to tolerate its being separate and the fact that it is not omnipotent, but rather limited by the reality principle (Winnicott, 1971). The concept of space is a metaphor that refers to the capacities and psychological processes of both child and parent, both of whom have to cope with the issue of separateness and of external and internal reality. Winnicott notes that the collapse or the restriction of the potential space is the result of overwhelming anxiety that derives from lack or from impingement.

The relevancy of Winnicott's concept of space to broader aspects of interpersonal interaction in the course of various life-phases is stressed by LaMothe (2005). He suggests observing the potential space as containing four interrelated dynamic and dialectical processes: surrender versus generation; recognition versus negation; care versus quiescence; disruption versus repair. LaMothe (2005) believes that the collapse of the potential space symbolizes the loss of dialectical tension, which is accomplished by moving toward one pole of such a dialectical pair and distorting it. Consequently there is a diminishing of subjectivity, vitality and agency.

LaMothe elaborates how both poles of each dialectical pair have an important contribution to make as long as the tension between them is preserved. Thus, both the surrender and independent generation of experiences are important, because both attest to personal will and the freedom to choose, despite the limitations of choice. Surrender involves the choice to give oneself to another and is not identical to submission, which occurs when one of the poles takes over forcibly, by denying the other's needs or perspective, and refusing to budge from one's own position in such a way that constructs oneself as omnipotent. Similarly, the binary of care and quiescence contains the conditions necessary for human survival. Just as the human infant requires the care of his parents, on which its life depends, it also requires his parents' restraint and calm, and their avoidance of unnecessary invasiveness, so that it can develop his own ability to cope. By virtue of its parents' overcoming their own anxiety as well as their ability to recognize him or her, the infant can develop trust and mutuality. Its parents' restraint or calm waiting is to be distinguished from neglect or indifference, both of which represents a distortion of this pole, while abandoning the dialectical tension with the pole of recognition.

Similarly, disturbances and disruption in relations between intimates and their repair are essential ingredients for growth, change and intimacy. Not only is it impossible to manage interpersonal relations without disruptions, but without these, life loses its vitality and there is no possibility of creating meaning. Of course disruptions that have no possibility of repair lead to anxiety and to destruction. Maintaining the tension between surrendering to a reality in which disruptions occur, out of a belief that they can be repaired (by each side), allows moments of creativity.

The dynamic of "recognition-negation," noted by LaMothe, and its contribution to understanding intersubjective relations has been thoroughly explored by Jessica Benjamin (2005). Benjamin relies significantly on the concept of recognition that was developed even earlier by Kohut (1985), and argues that a basic challenge of human development is the ability to recognize and accept the 'Other' both as similar and as different from oneself. The recognition of the other's being different (negation) is a necessary condition for experiencing recognition, for there is no meaning to recognition by someone who is identical to me.

Benjamin (2005) begins her book *Bonds of Love* with a beautiful description of a mother gazing at her infant during its first hours of life. In describing this experience she characterizes the basic tension between mother and child, the tension between separateness and belonging, or in our terms, the tension between the opposites that preserve their separateness, but are still connected to each other. From examining maternal experience, Benjamin arrives at the recognition of this tension which is typical of parenting, the tension that is supposed to be contained by the mother – the fact of that the infant is both similar to and different from her. From a theoretical perspective, Benjamin reinforces what Kohut writes about recognition: "…Recognition is not a sequence of events, like the phases of maturation and development, but a constant element through all events and phases. Recognition might be compared to that essential element in photosynthesis, sunlight, which provides the energy for the plant's constant transformation of substance..." (Benjamin, 1988, p. 22). At the same time, she challenges the idea of the self-sufficient subject: "....Thus intersubjective theory, even when describing the self alone sees its aloneness as a particular point in the spectrum of relationships rather than as the original 'natural state' of the individual...I suggest that intrapsychic and intersubjective theory should not be seen in opposition to each other (as they usually are) but as complementary ways of understanding the psyche..." (ibid., p.20).

This idea may be taken one step farther, to say that the meaning of intrapsychic events can only be understood when the perspective that recognizes intersubjective tension is maintained. This tension allows intrapsychic processes the possibility of existing and developing. This conclusion emerges from Benjamin's central argument, according to which recognition, which is an essential process for creating any kind of structure, is possible only in the presence of two subjects, that is, an essential dependency between them must be formed. In Benjamin's words, "The decisive problem remains recognizing the other. Establishing *myself* (Hegel's 'being for itself') means winning the recognition of the other, and this, in turn, means I must finally acknowledge the other as existing for *himself* and not just for me...Only by deepening our understanding of this paradox can we broaden our picture of human development to include not only the separation but also the meeting of minds..." (ibid., p. 36). What Benjamin calls the paradox of recognition, the inherent structural tension between the two subjects, is in essence what we are calling the dialectical tension that defines the space that is created between parent and child. Benjamin goes on to show that this situation invites the risk of a power struggle in which one side attempts to receive recognition at the expense of erasing the other, however, this state of affairs certainly cannot offer a solution. Benjamin makes the argument that when one doesn't surrender to the paradox a new sense of intimacy arises between two people. This feeling does not produce continuous harmony, but provides moments of harmony, which are moments of growth, in which a balance is momentarily struck between the two subjects, rather than a merging.

Benjamin hypothesizes that the reason that the dualistic conception of the individual has been accepted for such a long time (as has the idea of linear progression toward individuation) rather than the alternative conception of intersubjectivity, is because the former notion of the individual sees paradox as a very painful experience, involving constant fear that dependency upon another constitutes a threat for independence, and that the recognition of the other comes at one's own expense. She stresses, that when the conflict between dependency and independence becomes too powerful, the psyche relinquishes the paradox in favor of an opposition.

A significant dynamic is implied here, in which the capacity to contain the paradox and permit a solution that does not relinquish separateness, yet is still aware of the need for recognizing the other, depends upon affective variables regarding the capacity to tolerate suffering and anxiety. This point, already made by Winnicott (1971) is extremely significant and introduces into the discussion the affective parameter which is an inseparable component of the capacity to contain dialectical tension. It would appear, therefore, that what keeps a person from recognizing the other is often the anxiety of becoming obliterated. The truly difficult task of parenting is to be capable of tolerating the dialectical tension between parent and child, including the abundant anxiety that this arouses in both parent and child.

Regulating this anxiety becomes the most decisive factor that enables both a space of interpersonal development and a personal internal space to exist. When anxiety is excessive, the paradox of recognition may be "solved" through a power struggle and a collapse of the dialectical tension. It is important to note, that we are not speaking of repression, or elimination of anxiety, but rather of its regulation.

To illustrate these ideas we have chosen to present an example, derived from daily life, that clarifies the connection between anxiety and parental capacities, and between the ability to contain dialectical tension and inspire development and creativity. At a time when one of the authors of this paper was struggling to put our ideas into writing, she received a phone call from her sister who told her the following story:

> …Last Sunday I really didn't feel well. My partner was overseas and I woke up in the morning with the feeling that I was ill. I got my two-year-old son ready for preschool and he asked for a bag of cornflakes for the road. I gave him the cornflakes in a plastic bag, and to my dismay the bag tore and some of the cornflakes spilled out. We were already in the car on the way to his preschool. My son began to cry and to yell that he wanted to go back home to get some new cornflakes. Merely finding a parking spot near the house is a complicated task, not to speak of getting him out of the car seat, taking him upstairs, etc. The moment he began to yell I knew there was no chance of winning this struggle. In my condition, not feeling well, there was no point in fighting with him. Having no choice and feeling defeated, I took him upstairs, gave him what he wanted and went back on our way to preschool. I understood at the time that there was no chance of winning this battle…A few days later, I already felt much better. I started to work on a lecture I was supposed to deliver, and I was keen to continue work on it. Again we left for preschool, and this time my son forgot a book he wanted to take with him. Again he began to yell 'Home, now!' and it was clear to me that I was not going back, but it was also clear to me that there would be no battle here. I'm not sure how and why I broke out in laughter. My son responded by yelling, I laughed again and added a word. He yelled again and added a word, and we invented a small song in this way. We reached his preschool in an excellent mood. It's amazing how much significance there is to these basic mothering capabilities at every moment…

This example clearly demonstrates the connection between the capacity for regulating anxiety and the ability to allow growth and development. In the first instance, when the mother leaves the house with her child, when she's already feeling weakened, she responds with anxiety to the conflict of wills. In this situation she can do little else but to interpret the situation as a power struggle which one side will have to lose. She understands that in her situation there is no chance of winning, and she therefore gives up in advance. In the second instance, when she is feeling well, the conflict does not threaten her but rather, she is capable of maintaining the dialectical tension. She is capable of remaining in the conflictual state of divergent wills, without experiencing anxiety. At this special moment a new creation emerges in the space between the mother and child—they invent a song together. The conflictual situation does not end with the capitulation of one party, but rather with a new creation that integrates both elements of the conflict (the mother's wishes and the child's wishes). It is important to note, that the creation is born spontaneously the moment the conflict becomes apparent and the mother is capable of containing it without reacting with anxiety. This is not a matter of an orderly process of problem-solving aimed at arriving at an appropriate compromise (which also has value in situations of conflict), but rather of using conflict for expansion, play and creativity in the potential space between two people.

It would appear that in a state of unregulated anxiety a person cannot sustain a significant encounter with the other and also cope with the other's 'otherness' in a manner that enables this expansion. When anxious, one is either limited to defending oneself at the expense of the other, or of relinquishing oneself for the sake of the other. In both cases one misses the opportunity for a beneficial mutual relationship with the other. Regulation of anxiety, therefore, is a necessary element for creating conditions for relating and for growth.

AFFECT REGULATION AND REGULATION OF ANXIETY

Developmental Dimensions

The relationship between parents and children arouses powerful emotions. In families with young children it has been found that conflictual interactions occur anywhere between 3.5 to 15 times in an hour. This high incidence is even greater in families of children who are ill, aggressive, or have special needs. Even in regular families parents report that they experience high levels of anger at their children, which they feel the need to control. At the same time, what stabilizes relations is the fact that parents report a far greater number of positive interactions with their children, as opposed to negative ones (2.5 times as many) (Dix, 1991). Therefore Dix suggests that one can view parental emotions as a reflection of the soundness of parent-child relations, and of children's developmental prognosis. How do parents cope with the task of affect regulation and how do they instill in their children similar capacities?

The process of regulation is viewed today as a fundamental process that characterizes development in general and neuro-psychological and emotional development in particular. The definition of the concept "affect regulation" and the clarification of processes that are associated with this concept are the subject of contemporary and emerging discussion in the research literature (Cole, Martin, & Dennis, 2004). For the purposes of our study we shall adopt the definition of Eisenberg and Spinrad (2004), who consider self-regulation of emotions to be a process of initiating, avoiding, inhibiting, maintaining or shaping the occurrence, form, intensity, or continuation of internal affective states, physiological processes, attentional processes, and motivational states, that are related to emotions or to behavioral manifestation of emotions. All these processes are in service of the realization of personal goals and of biological or social adaptation.

This definition points to the fact that emotional regulation does not mean control or emotional restraint, but rather that it requires the acquisition of a variety of different strategies, some of which increase arousal rather than reducing it, as well as the ability to activate them selectively and appropriately. This definition emphasizes that the internal regulation of emotional states and of behavioral expression is connected also to the regulation of cognitive, motivational, physiological, and attentional processes. **It is important to remember, that the term "regulation" refers to the principle by which a certain balance is maintained between (at least) two opposing variables, and not to a process through which one variable eliminates the other.** Regulation of heat is a process wherein balance is maintained between the rapid movement of molecules and lack of movement of molecules. Many physiological life functions operate according to the principle of regulation, such as the regulation of body temperature through changes in the level of activity, perspiration, and more.

In the realm of human emotional development the primary regulatory system, which is engaged in regulation of anxiety and distress, is the system of attachment. No human creature is born with the ability to regulate its affective reactions by itself; because a human infant is so helpless, it experiences states of distress of alternating intensity and of different provenance. Regulation of these states occurs within the dyad of a caregiver and infant. The theoretical and research literature offers several complementary explanations for the connection between the quality of the parent-infant relationship and the development of affect regulation capacities within the developing child and the mature adult.

The formulators of attachment theory, and chief among them Bowlby (Bowlby, 1973; 1979) assumed that when the changes that occur from moment to moment in an infant, which signal the state it is experiencing, are successfully interpreted and regulated by the caregiver, the infant learns that in situations of distress and arousal it does not fall apart or lose control, and that the presence of an adult will allow it to reproduce a regulated sense of comfort. In addition, the more the infant experiences the presence of an adult as sensitive, caring and protective, the more secure its basis for exploration and expansion becomes. Bowlby (1973) describes the phenomenon of the "safe base" that enables the infant to take the risk of venturing away from the secure zone of parental protection, in favor of the drive for curiosity, daring, and learning; the physical and psychological presence of the parent in the background allows the infant to return to him or her for regulation of states of anxiety or hyper-arousal. The tension between the infant's need for security and its drive to explore, like the child's gradual exposure by the parent to temporary and minor situations of tension, challenges the infant's capacities and new strategies for regulation, which are not dependent upon the parent's immediate physical presence. In this way, the primary innate capacities of attachment develop from clinging, crying, or searching for closeness to more advanced capacities such as communicating through remote "signaling," speech, pursuing, provocation, and more. The child learns to use "transitional objects" and symbolic or other imaginative means of self-comforting. By the end of the first year the child has developed a consistent and stable pattern of attachment, which is based on the accumulation of real experiences. This is, in fact, the "internal working model," which includes the internal representation of the self, the other, and of relationships, and acts as an internalized system of expectations or interpretive schemas of "reality." This system is aroused and is especially salient after the period of early infancy and in situations of distress and anxiety. Children who developed secure attachment experience themselves as worthy of love, support and as competent; they experience the other as someone beneficent who can be trusted. These children manage interpersonal relations with flexibility and pleasure.

Other studies by researchers of attachment theory, such as Ainsworth, Main, and Sroufe and their colleagues (Fonagy, 1999) have brought more clarity to the maladaptive patterns of affect regulation which develop and solidify as part of the personalities of children who did not have the benefit of appropriate affect regulation by a sensitive caregiver.

Children who experienced parental rejection in the process of their first year of life, and whose needs for security and comforting were often denied by a caregiver (children who are classified as anxious-avoidant, in terms of the quality of their attachment), learn to adopt specific defense mechanisms for the purpose of emotional regulation. They tend to protect themselves from dependence and the expected subsequent rejection and attempt to exercise **hyper-control** over their emotions. By denial and avoidance of feelings of anxiety they display behavior of extreme self-reliance, while taking risks, and testing boundaries, or alternately by preemptively reducing their fields of interest and their needs, to avoid entering situations of dependency and distress ("I'm not interested"; "That's stupid"; "Who needs a hug?"). Both strategies are adaptive for the purpose of regulating anxiety under conditions in which it is impossible to rely on an adult to take the role of regulator, but they are maladaptive from a developmental viewpoint, for they limit the development of flexibility and creativity and the scope of significant interpersonal experiences. These solutions do not preserve the tension between the two poles of internal conflict, but result instead in the elimination of one pole (the need for relatedness, warmth and security) in favor of the other (independence, and non-dependency), and as a consequence, in a loss of complexity, flexibility, and range of possibilities.

Another group of children (classified as exhibiting anxious-ambivalent or resistant attachment), who experienced ineffective or inconsistent caring, exhibit **hypo-control** in emotional situations and have difficulty regulating themselves even when experiencing slight distress. They live in a chronic state of signaling distress and of dependency on an adult, and most of their energies are spent in monitoring the connection with the adult, who is always frustrating, because he or she can never satisfy the child. In this attachment pattern one can also observe the inability to contain the conflict between dependency and independence, and a relinquishing of the complexity involved in this effort, in favor of developing dependence alone.

In both groups the regulatory mechanisms that these children adopt do not allow them to successfully preserve the tension between the ability to explore and the ability to calm down by receiving soothing, between the needs for dependency and neediness, and a sense of independence and self-reliance. This situation exacts steep prices in the process of interpersonal development, and in other various aspects of adaptation, especially in coping with situations of stress, as has been demonstrated in a number of longitudinal studies (Cassidy and Shaver, 1999).

An even graver scenario from the perspective of acquiring strategies for affect regulation occurs when a parent constitutes a source of fear and stress for the child. In this type of situation a child may develop "disorganized attachment." This sort of pattern is characterized by an insoluble "freezing" typical of extreme states of fear, because the figure who is supposed to help with regulating fear is also the source of fear. These children exhibit a lack of regulation strategies, and consequently, dissociative characteristics and behaviors; their development is characterized by social difficulties and considerable difficulties with affect regulation.

In his attempt to understand the significant capacities acquired by children through attachment patterns in order to achieve self-regulation, Fonagy (Fonagy 2002; 1999) has argued that the beneficial caregiver helps the infant gradually develop a capacity for "mentalization." This capacity, which enables an individual to think about his or her own behavior, as well as the behavior of others—in terms of feelings, motivations, perceptions and subjective reasons—and to understand it, involves a capacity for meta-cognitive thinking. Fonagy shows in a series of studies that this capacity has critical significance in the formation of a "regulating personality," and that damage to this capacity can result in a borderline personality, and behavior characterized by lack of regulation and eruptions. The capacity to mentalize develops, he claims, out of relationships with caregivers who model this kind of mental activity in relation to themselves and fulfill two central tasks in respect to the infant and the child: first, they respond with empathy to the infant's affective expressions, contain them, reflect back and interpret the child's mental process sensitively, while organizing experience through language and other elements of communication. In addition, they find a way to "signal" to the child their own affective state as individualized adults, who possess a different point of view regarding the current experience, as well as other experiences. Thus, for example, when an infant is frightened, they will mirror, interpret and validate its response and attempt to soothe it, but will preserve a sense of "lightness" in respect to the source of fear, using some or another aspect of the communication (for example, the tone of voice, or facial expression) in order to signal to the child that they themselves were not frightened. Another contribution of parents to young children's mentalization capacities is their use of imaginative-playful modes and "make believe" which contribute to the development of the symbolic and meta-cognitive abilities of the child.

The explanations that have been presented thus far for the development of the capacity for affect regulation are in accord with innovative studies that deal with neuro-psychological-development and explore in particular the conditions in which the capacity for regulation develops both at the level of brain activity, and at the behavioral level.

Daniel Siegel (Siegel, 2001; 2004) proposes that the brain is a "social organism"; that is to say, that its development is dependent not only on genetic determinants, but also on external interpersonal stimulation. Studies show that experiences lead to nervous activity that activates genes which in turn produce proteins that are capable of creating new synapses. It is therefore possible to assume that experiences that occur in the context of attachment relationships fashion neural connections and pathways in the developing brain, especially in regions of the pre-frontal cortex, where signals from different parts of the brain are assembled into integrative functions. When there is good integration coupled with rich differentiation, functioning will be flexible, creative, and stable. The brain must, therefore, receive external beneficial stimulation in order to produce equilibrium and integration between brain regions and especially between two central systems in the brain, which Siegel calls "the low road" and "the high road". The "high road" is enabled when there is good integration between the activity of the neo-cortex, including the prefrontal lobes together with circuits of the limbic system (which is associated with emotion, memory and motivation) and with the low areas (the brain stem which processes information from the body and regulates arousal). This integration enables processes of reflexivity, self-understanding, empathy, sensitive communication and morality. But this integration may become paralyzed at times of physical distress or threat, or more chronically among people who experienced trauma, or as a result of unprocessed mourning, which leads to a state of activity on the "low road."

The "low road" is what stimulates an impulsive behavioral reaction, while the "high road" activates processes of judgment and regulation, manifested in calculated and controlled behavior. Siegel argues that balancing these two systems produces a stable and functional personality, who suffers neither from lack of spontaneity on the one hand, nor from a behavioral lack of control, on the other. Such a balance is achieved, he argues, through coordinated integration of these two systems with the help of the higher regulatory system. This regulatory system creates integration that relies on the creation of meaning that connects together experiences. The ability to attribute meaning and to create a coherent and meaningful narrative, Siegel claims, is developed through a connection with the attachment figure, who attributes meaning to the infant's behavior, emotions, and thoughts, through its endeavors at empathic relating.

Similarly, Alan Schore (Schore, 2001) presents a research survey, showing how the brain structures responsible for regulation, such as the right orbito-frontal cortex, develop correctly in the context of interactions with significant and beneficial others, who assist with regulating levels of arousal, anxiety and distress. The mechanisms of regulation whose functioning he describes are characterized by the fact that they deal with the preservation of equilibrium between two opposing sub-systems, such as the sympathetic and para-sympathetic systems, as well as other systems that are involved with arousal and soothing. He introduces a new angle by illuminating how the setting of boundaries by parents contributes to brain development and regulatory capacities. The evidence he presents substantiates his claim that the setting of boundaries creates for the child a painful but vital experience of shame that is characterized by a low-intensity level of arousal. This state is tied to the increase in levels of corticosteroid and activity of the para-sympathetic system which contribute to the maturing of the orbi-frontal cortex, the brain region associated with emotional regulation and the capacity for behavioral inhibition (Edwards, 2002).

Schore shows how in cases where there is no appropriate external regulation processes of dissociation occur, in which instead of integrating the experience into existing associations and structures, it becomes isolated. Furthermore, Schore stresses, the multiplication of this type of situation produces a more general dissociative pattern, that inhibits the development of regulatory structures, and damages the child's ability to continue to develop higher level structures that are responsible for regulation in interpersonal relationships. Schore explains that the mechanism of dissociation is a primary primitive and inefficient mechanism of auto-regulation, as opposed to the more developed integrative mechanisms, in which regulation is activated through the connection between the child and the attachment figure. He argues that the dissociative mechanism may be more common than what has been realized to date, and might be part of the psychopathology of everyday life.

To tie this discussion to the basic idea that has been presented here concerning the preservation of tension between opposites as opposed to eliminating it, it can be said that preservation and containment of oppositions are expressed on two different levels within the regulatory system. On one level one can see that a necessary condition for the creation of a regulatory system is the existence of two separate subjects (parent and child). On the second level one can see that efficient regulation depends on containing and connecting internal oppositions, and not eliminating them.

Parental Self-Regulation

The topic of the parent's own regulation processes in the course of parenting has been studied to only a small extent, in comparison to the child's self regulation. Most explanations of parental self-regulating capacities are based on attachment theory and its developments, as well as the research inspired by those theories. Fonagy and Target (Fonagy & Target, 2003) claim, based on research evidence, that secure attachment and reflective capacity are an inter-generational accomplishment. In other words, parents who show secure attachment in their adult life, who present a rich and coherent autobiography and who attribute importance to interpersonal relations and to emotions, have most likely been raised as children with secure attachment in early infancy, or acquired it through internal reflective work, or through corrective experiences in life or in therapy. These all helped them develop reflective ability, understanding and non-defensive acceptance of their past, as well as awareness of themselves and of others. Parents exhibiting mature and secure attachment have also a significantly higher chance of raising children with secure attachment. The capabilities that help securely attached parents regulate their emotions successfully are, they claim, their highly developed ability for interpersonal interpretation, and a capacity for acceptance that accords respect to the child as a separate and unique individual.

Parents who have suffered in their past traumatic experiences and have not succeeded in processing them successfully, will have a difficult time coping with anxiety in adult life and consequently in regulating this anxiety in their functioning as parents. Siegel (2003, 2004) also stresses the use of reflective ability and the exploration of one's autobiographical narrative as important factors in the regulation of negative affect that arise in the process of parenting. In his opinion, parents can continue to develop this ability in daily life through education about the neuropsychological processes that are associated with interpersonal relations, as well as through guidance and therapy. Practicing and developing self-awareness in regard to their emotional reactions through the recall of their own past memories is a mental activity that has the potential to help parents understand the reasons for their hyper-sensitivities and, through their parenting, to undertake to emotionally "correct" experiences they underwent as children to their own parents.

A slightly different emphasis on meta-cognitive processes associated with parenting is proposed by Gottman, Katz and Hooven (1997), who deal with emotional communication within the family, and especially with the concept of "meta-emotion." This concept refers to the feelings and stances a parent has in respect to his or her own emotions and their effects on emotional communication in the family. They emphasize that everyone has a set of feelings about feelings, e.g., shame over the fact that one is afraid, or embarrassment over the fact that one is angry, etc. This set is important also in respect to parents' thoughts about their children, and it affects one's ability to teach the child and guide him in managing or coping with his own feelings. Their study shows, that the group of parents who are characterized by a high level of awareness about their emotions, a capacity to discuss them and separate different types of emotions, and an attitude of respect toward feelings without being intimidated by them, is also characterized by children who are more competent at regulating their emotions. These attributes are shown to contribute to children's emotional regulation beyond parental patterns of displaying warmth, acceptance, and a positive attitude.

Dix (1991) proposes that affect regulation in parenting is based on three elements: one's own ability to identity affective states and understand their source; the capacity for estimating what will be the result of expressing emotions in relations with others; self-regulating capacities or strategies of control in expressing emotion. Dix stresses, on the basis of research, that a significant correlation exists between processes of parents' emotional involvement with their child, as well as the quality of this involvement, and parental motivations, cognitions, and attributions. Findings indicate that parents who experience distress in their relations with their children have higher expectations of their children, evaluate the child's intentions in a more negative vein, and their own effectiveness as parents as inferior, in comparison with parents who are able to successfully manage more harmonious relations with their children.

It would appear that the parent's ability to implement means of self-regulation and to use them successfully is also influenced by the child's own characteristics, including his or her temperament, for example. To an even greater degree this ability is influenced by the set of pressures that impinge upon the parent, as on the support systems at the parent's disposal. This set includes intimate relations, familial and communal ties, and socio-economic, social and cultural factors (Edwards, 2002).

In sum, we have seen how a parent's emotional regulation, by means of various mechanisms, shapes the child's ability to produce regulatory structures out of relations with significant others. We have also seen that these regulatory processes are founded on integrative processes that preserve separateness among different elements. In order to fulfill one's role as parent one must not only be able to successfully regulate both one's own emotions, and the child's emotions, but one must also be "marked" unmistakably as an "Other", that is, as an entity possessing separate thoughts and desires. One can estimate, therefore, how complex is the parent's role as someone who must at one and the same time preserve the dialectical tensions between herself and her child and to produce a system of emotional regulation for the child. The parent, therefore, serves in a complex dual role: on the one hand her feelings, opinions and desires constitute a pole that generates tension vis-à-vis the child's feeling, opinions, and desires, but at the same time she is the one who is responsible for producing an emotionally regulated environment that will enable the child to produce internal growth processes, while preserving the internal tension, without resolving it in favor of a primitive defense mechanism (such as dissociation or splitting). The parent needs to transform—in accordance with the child's needs—the balance between these two poles. The more the child grows the more the parent must increase the relative weight of the pole of separateness, without losing the opposite pole of regulating the child's emotional environment. At the end of the maturation process the child must be in possession of structures that enable him to use emotional regulation within interpersonal relations, while preserving dialectical tension vis-à-vis others. At the end of this phase the parent can manage the relations with the child in a more mutual way, when she is no longer solely responsible for preserving the balance within the dialectical tension.

MODELS OF PARENTAL COPING WITH DIALECTICAL TENSION IN EVERYDAY LIFE

What are the types of daily interactions in which mutual contact around situations of difference and conflict between parents and children occur, and which of these successfully contain a productive dialectical tension? How do parents help children build regulatory capacities beyond the stages of early infancy?

We suggest examining parental reactions to situations of conflict by highlighting two basic prevalent patterns: action-oriented reactions and interpretive reactions. Both reaction patterns are significant poles through which parents cope with situations of conflict, while, of course, they sometimes combine both types. An action-oriented reaction is characterized by the fact that the parent decides upon a (re)solution of the conflict and implements it. The interpretive reaction includes explanations of feelings, demands and behaviors, as well as clarification of preferences of different degrees of intensity. In both patterns the end-result of the conflict may vary in relation to the type of conflict resolution strategy employed, as is explicated in the following categorization.

The action-solution pattern may involve conflict resolution through either one of two patterns of dichotomous solutions or through a compromise solution. One dichotomous solution may involve the imposition of the parent's desires upon the child (e.g., "Enough with the television, you're going to bed now"; "If you don't wash your hands you won't get food"; "You have to come home straight after school"). These parental responses are important, because they create the foundation for a sense of separateness, the independent judgment and free will of the parent, which establishes the parent's pole within the dialectical tension. Another dichotomous action-oriented response reflects a capitulation of the parent to the child's desires (e.g., "You're right, there's no school tomorrow, so you can stay awake and watch some more T.V."; "I don't have the strength to argue with you, fine, get your school bag ready tomorrow morning"; "O.K. you convinced me, I'll buy you the game you wanted although it costs much more than I had planned to spend"). These parental responses are important because they establish the child's sense of being separate from the parent, as possessing free desires of his or her own.

The third type of action-oriented solution is not dichotomous, but rather conciliatory. The parent reacts, while holding the dialectical tension, and offers a compromise that takes into account some of the child's desires and some of the parent's desires. In this situation the parent uses sentences like "We can't watch a movie now, but we can do it after dinner"; or "If you allow me to rest for another five minutes, I'll come help you comb the doll's hair." These parental responses are important in that they teach the child methods of interpersonal problem solving, without producing a dichotomous solution. However, compromise patterns are possible only after the dyad has established patterns of the separateness of desires and preferences through the employment of dichotomous patterns of the two previously discussed types. These parental responses are important, however it is important to stress that they are not examples of the creative growth-inducing situations discussed in the paper, because this sort of solution does not create something new but rather constitutes a partial satisfaction of the needs of both sides.

As outlined previously, an additional, but different pattern of parental reactions to conflict situations with their children is the interpretive pattern. Interpretive patterns include indications of reasons for demands, or explanations of feelings and behaviors, as well as clarification of choices and preferences of different degrees of intensity. These patterns nourish the child's internal meta-cognitive and meta-emotional foundation, and develop the child's ability to attribute meaning to his or her own behavior, feeling and thoughts, as well as to those of others. This pattern is activated in a number of typical situations:

- • Situations in which the parent attempts to interpret the child (for example: "You were probably so absorbed in the game in the yard, that you didn't notice and arrived too late for dinner"; "You look so angry that it's difficult to think and talk practically about solving the problem").
- • Situations in which the parent interprets him- or herself to the child (e.g., "I am simply troubled by Grandma's situation, and that's why I'm impatient"; "I really don't like to watch you staring at the television for hours and not doing anything"; "I am offended and disappointed that you didn't tell the truth, it's important to me that we should be able to trust each other").

- • Situations in which the parent interprets the interaction between him or her and the child. (For example: "I came back from work really tired, and you were so excited, more excited than I could take, and that's why I got angry when you jumped on me as soon as I got out of the car"; "You feel very shy when we go out places and that's why you cling to me, but then I lose my patience, and you end up feeling insulted.")
- • Situations in which the parent interprets the behavior of people and of other children to whom the child is exposed (e.g., "I think your friend is sad because you didn't share your game with him"; "Your sister is very angry because she really can't stand it when you go into her room and touch her things"; "Daddy got angry at the driver in the other car because he wasn't driving carefully").
- • Situations in which a parent interprets the behavior of characters in a story, a game or a film.

Parents who successfully connect interpretive patterns to action-oriented patterns enable their children to learn how to integrate reflective abilities and capacities for interpersonal problem solving. A similar idea has been illustrated in an integrative coaching program designed for parents which deals with training in sensitive and effective communication with children (Stollak, 1973).

The coaching sessions train the parents to include in their responses to the child, in recurring situations of conflict, as many of the four following types of message:

- Messages expressing understanding of the child's situation;
- Messages expressing acceptance of the child's feeling or validation and understanding of his or her experience;
- Messages clarifying the parent's position and feelings or the demands of reality vis-à-vis the subject of conflict;
- A message offering a responsible compromise that attempts to combine the needs of the child and the parent, or the demands of reality.

For example: "You disturbed me when I was on the phone, because you had a hard time waiting for me to listen to you. When something feels very urgent and you are excited—it is hard to wait. But I want you to know that it is very annoying when you disturb me in the middle of an important conversation. I'm not willing for it to happen again. Maybe we should agree on a sign, so I'll know when I should cut a conversation short, because you have something important that you want to talk about, and I will do my best to get off the phone as soon as possible."

Of course, in reality, parents cannot dwell upon each conflictual situation and include all of the above messages, but it is important that in the final balance, the child will be exposed to all these messages.

Interpretive responses or compromise problem solving are not performed unilaterally by the parents. They gradually include their children in these actions, by using methods for developing emotional expression, scaffolding for thinking of the interpersonal results of one's behavior, and emotional coaching (Edwards, 2002). In this way parents help their children develop these interpersonal-cognitive capacities and promote their ability to cope with social situations (e.g., "Why do you think your friend is insulted? Think of a way that you can appease him"; "You can't get the game that you chose because it costs 50 dollars, and I only gave you 20 to spend. That's really a bummer. What do you suggest doing?").

Experiencing these interactions is a preliminary condition for the emergence of creative solutions, an occurrence that often appears miraculous, and which we have attempted to highlight in this paper. Creative solutions emerge in situations in which dialectical tension is perpetuated and not resolved neither the parent nor the child knows how to resolve it. Through the suspension of this tension a common solution emerges, the product of a joint creative act. This creation, emerging from the attempt to cope with the tension, without relinquishing either pole, is unique and original, and does not follow the acquired patterns of solving problems through compromises. These situations are the most unique and the most moving moments in a relationship between a parent and a child. They cannot exist without the child having experienced different action-oriented, or interpretive patterns, and their integration. They can and do exist, it goes without saying, within the context of a significant emotional connection. In this situation there is no sense of a winner or of a loser, and not even of a partial victory, but rather a sense of enthusiasm and satisfaction, that arise in connection to the novel integration of the two poles. In the following passage we present an example derived from the parental experience of one of the authors.

When a new baby was born into the family, the eldest child, a seven-year old girl, complained about the fact that her mother was no longer free to respond to her requests for attention, with the promptness and for the duration to which she had been accustomed. The mother expressed understanding of her daughter's frustration, but stressed that because of the baby's young age, often his needs were more urgent, and because her time was also more limited, her daughter might have to wait, or sometimes even forgo her request completely. The dialectical tension remained present, until one day when the daughter demanded the mother's attention while she was busy, the mother suggested that she draw or write something. In response the daughter announced: "I know what I'll do! I'll make a list of all the things I give up to the baby, and when he grows up he'll have to give all those things back to me." With this creative solution the child used the new symbolic capacities of writing she had just acquired and created a new emotional application for them.

Let us now present an additional example, taken from a therapeutic setting, of a solution that emerged from maintaining dialectical tension, when the child was of a more advanced age.

A 13-year-old adolescent announced to his parents one day that he thinks he should leave the house and move to a boarding school. The mother was troubled and very hurt by this and decided to turn to professional counseling to work out for herself what might be the source of her son's distress. The analysis that emerged with her therapist in regard to her relationship with her son, led her to the conclusion that she is unsuccessful at giving him sufficient space. She realized that precisely because she knew so well how to interpret his behavior, and how to explain her positions in such a clear and logical manner (a situation that was sarcastically referred to at home as "Mom is always right") he was left with no room to feel that he was independently choosing his behavior, such that it would express his separateness and uniqueness. The mother was filled with sorrow after reaching this insight, and thought that perhaps her ability, which had been so helpful for her child when he was young, was no longer put to good use. She understood that it would be very difficult for her to change this pattern, and recognized that such a process would certainly not occur rapidly, and therefore her son might be right in desiring to be distant from her during his adolescence. The mother was caught in the midst of a sharp dialectical tension. She understood and sensed her own desire to be close to her child and for him to remain at home, but on the other hand she understood his sense of suffocation and desire to move away. She could not imagine a solution that would be good for both of them, but decided at the encouragement of her therapist, to share her insights with her child. She discussed this with the child and asked him if the way in which she understood the situation made sense to him. The child thought it did, and even shared with his mother the strong urge he had been feeling of late to do things that went against his own values, only so he could feel that he had the courage to be different and not only to be a good kid. The impulses, he told her, were unpleasant, and he felt that they might be explained by what his mother had just described to him as the dynamic of their relationship. The conversation ended with this disclosure, but the issue of the boarding school remained unresolved. Some weeks later the child began to be interested and very active in a radical-anarchist ideological group. This group's ideology inspired passionate arguments between him and his mother, such as the value of government, principles of justice, and more. The issue of the boarding school did not come up again for a long time, but during a casual conversation the child said that he was thinking of putting off the idea for one year, and that he no longer felt such a sense of urgency around it. It seemed as though the tension between mother and son, which had revolved around the child's desire to feel separate and independent, and the mother's inability to enable this, was resolved through the intense arguments surrounding the child's involvement with the radical movement. This solution was a solution that emerged in the space between them, and substituted for the solution that was embodied in the boarding school idea. This solution was enabled only after the mother and child understood the tension in which they were immersed, and due to their ability to contain the sadness and the sense of stuckness that arose from it.

We stressed earlier that in order for this sort of solution to occur, the parents and the child must have experienced in their relationship the entire gamut of both dichotomous and compromise-oriented action-oriented patterns and interpretive patterns, and combinations thereof. The balance between the various solutions and interpretations is an extremely complex skill. A parent must adapt this balance anew with each child because of each child's unique characteristics, and even with the same child over and over again, because of the constant evolvement of the child, the environment, and the parent. When the parent does not succeed in creating an appropriate balance between these elements, the bond between child and parent may be damaged. Sometimes the child contributes in an unconscious way to balancing his parents' different patterns, by adopting coercive action-oriented patterns himself (a child who refuses to go to school, or a teenager who performs a criminal act). These behaviors may provoke the parent into a reflective and interpretive position. They may sometimes stimulate a parent who realizes that he is experienced as too weak, to communicate his own opinions and desires more clearly and decisively and to protect his integrity. Children are even likely to "wage war" continuously against exaggerated dichotomous and coercive behavior on the part of the parents, by acting oppositionally, a pattern that forces parents to begin to consider the possibility of implementing more compromising courses of action. Sometimes the child interprets herself for her parents, or interprets their interactions (for example, "It's not so terrible that I lied to you one time when I was stressed out, and it doesn't mean that every time I'm under pressure I'll lie to you. I have a lot of good reasons for telling you the truth, mostly because it's important to me that you trust me.").

It is important to note, that such a balance is based on a variety of situations of conflict and not on a continuous harmonious state. The balance needs to be struck between different modes of coping with conflict, but not by eliminating or avoiding them. One can identify situations of imbalance in which the parent does not succeed in providing the relationship with the "right diet" (that is, managing conflicts in a sufficiently diverse and appropriate manner), when the child's or parent's behavior becomes chronically dysregulated, or when they work themselves into serious and extremes situations and the capacity for mutuality is damaged. It is important for the parents to be familiar with the complexity of coping patterns between parents and children in situations of conflict, and to understand that each of these behavioral patterns is necessary and appropriate, but not sufficient in and of itself for creating interactions that are conducive to growth. The identification and reinforcement of weakened patterns and the enrichment of new patterns may contribute to the parents' sense of confidence and may reduce anxiety, and thus contribute to a better capacity to regulate interpersonal and intra-personal that arise in the course of their parenting of each child.

No less crucial is that professionals in the fields of education, welfare, and mental health have a good understanding of the complex task of parenting. Instead of emphasizing mistakes and negative instances of coping, the focus should be changed to deficiencies and excesses in the "diet" of coping with the individual child. It is important that these trained professionals know how to help parents understand the importance of conflicts and of managing them, and do not uphold an ideal of harmonious conflict-free relations. It is also important that they know how to support parents, to reduce their anxiety and help them develop regulatory systems that enable them to contain tension, and that they are skillful at analyzing in a convincing manner the difficulties that arise in the system when it is in crisis. Often, the judgmental messages that are conveyed to parents by professionals end up making things even more difficult for the parents. In the next section we will focus on several social and cultural factors that tax parents' ability to contain dialectical tension and to manage conflicts in ways that are beneficial and conducive to growth.

CULTURAL CONDITIONS THAT IMPINGE ON THE CONTAINMENT OF DIALECTICAL TENSION IN PARENTING

Many social and cultural variables make parenting difficult in the present era, in comparison with earlier periods (Goelman, 2005; Taffel, 2006), and are a focus of concern among professionals who deal with children's emotional development. Most worrisome is the reduced amount of spontaneous interpersonal interaction among children, at the expense of an increase of interactions with electronic gadgets, a state of affairs which leads to deficits in emotional and creative development. Parents today suffer from a decrease in practical and emotional support systems. Concurrently, many parents experience a lack of time for coping with conflict situations with their children and therefore avoid the difficult process that occurs in the dialectical space between parents and children.

Here we wish to focus on another significant cultural factor, which we believe is closely tied to the problem of maintaining dialectical tension in the encounter with the other, and this is our culture's attitude toward suffering. The dominant cultural belief today, in regard to suffering is that it is an unnecessary human experience which can be avoided, and that it can even by extremely dangerous. We are not referring to a person's natural tendency to avoid situations that involve suffering and to attempt to escape them, but rather we address the belief that it is possible to lead meaningful and happy lives, without hardly any suffering at all. This conception arises from a natural defensive tendency, already mentioned earlier, to avoid encountering things that are unpleasant, or to produce a "split" in situations that are difficult to contain. This conception has been significantly encouraged and promoted by the development of modern technology, which offers the promise of a life free of effort and suffering. Technology has been successful at making it easier to accomplish distasteful or burdensome tasks, and scientific and especially medical knowledge is indeed making advances in reducing physical and psychological pain. Many people believe that the personal accumulation of wealth, together with technological progress will lead them to a life of well-being and comfort, free of suffering.

In addition, the popularization of psychodynamic psychological approaches that are focused on children has led to a belief that strict, demanding parents, who frustrate their children's wishes, cause psychological damage to their children. These approaches have led to an idealization of the model of the endlessly nurturing parent who provides love, experiences and resources, so much so that the parent's selfhood is erased or destroyed (Cohen & Lwow, 2004). Because of their fear of hurting their children, many parents try to reverse the methods of child-rearing that they themselves experienced (and which they often see as the sources of their problems) and strive to minimize as much as possible their children's suffering or frustration. At the same time, they often work long hours in order to earn enough money to be able to afford all the resources and technologies that they believe will cause their children to be happier and to experience less suffering and effort.

The difficulty of tolerating suffering is an important human trait that motivates people to seek new and important solutions to problems and difficulties. However, fear of suffering and the belief that it is superfluous and dangerous cause people to resolve the dialectical tension in interpersonal relations, and in parenting especially, in a dichotomous fashion, by avoiding it at any cost. As was emphasized before, high levels of anxiety and the inability to regulate it significantly reduce the parent's ability to tolerate dialectical tension and result in the activation of primitive mechanisms of self-regulation such as dissociation. Parents' difficulties at regulating anxiety, which is affected by the abovementioned cultural attitudes concerning suffering, prevent them from equipping themselves with the patience and endurance that parenting requires. They may have difficulty dealing with the boredom of sitting patiently in a mutual game with a child, or with monitoring and maintaining a framework of rules of conduct that has been established with the child. They may find it difficult to regulate their disappointment with the child's achievement, or to tolerate the child's unpleasant reactions, such as anger or opposition. They also find it very difficult to accept diagnoses that are given to a child who has difficulty at school (such as learning disabilities). Therefore they are likely to blow up impulsively and to hurt a child's feelings, or to limit their involvement with the child altogether.

Many parents often fail at containing the child's own suffering or anxiety, even when these are an unavoidable aspect of reality, and part of normal developmental coping challenges. Parents may neglect giving their children immunizations or dental treatment in order to protect their children from suffering. Many children do not succeed at learning how to fall asleep by themselves because their parents cannot tolerate a few minutes of the infant's crying, preventing the child from discovering a mode of self-soothing. Other parents who are fearful of a child's suffering fail at teaching the child appropriate hygiene habits, even up until school age, and the children may exhibit habit disorders such as encopresis. Fear of the child's suffering causes these parents to intervene in order to protect the child from frustrations that arise in interpersonal relations among children (a conflict with a friend), from a learning process or from problem solving (losing a game). The difficulties of children entering adulthood to leave their family home are often tied to their parents' as well as their own fear of meeting the new challenge of coping as an independent person. In all of these cases, and in similar ones, parents protect their child from important developmental frustrations that form the basis of the intra-personal tension that produces meaning, and create higher integrative structures.

The classic case in which parental authority is broken and mutuality in relationships disappears (Cohen & Lwow, 2004) is where a parent cannot tolerate a child's expressions of suffering, in encountering the tension that arises between the child's desires and opinions, and those of the parent. These feelings cause parents to prefer and increase the relative incidence of dichotomous solutions in which they relinquish their desires in favor of their child's. Such situations are more common when the parent or the child exhibit certain sensitivities or weaknesses arising from their experience or life circumstance (e.g., a parent who underwent a traumatic experience of loss, an adopted child, a child who suffers from a medical or mental problem). This situation may acutely weaken the dialectical pole that defines the parent as separate, and as a consequence solutions of compromise are not produced either. This weakening causes a great deal of suffering to the parent, because usually the child will exaggerate his demands and behavior in an unreasonable way. This situation tends to arouse much anxiety for the parent, both in regard to the child and to himself, for he feels as though he has been effaced and rendered helpless vis-à-vis the child. This anxiety may increase the incidence of dichotomous solutions in which the parent subjugates the child and forces the child to relinquish his desires in favor of the parent's, after which the parent feels guilty. This leads to an extremely destructive cycle, in which the relative incidence of dichotomous action patterns of both types increases in comparison with interpretive, creative or compromise action-oriented patterns, and the child's development and functioning are impaired.

It is very important in our opinion not to mistakenly embrace the belief that increasing parental authority by encouraging and increasing the legitimacy of dichotomous solutions, in which the parent imposes his wishes on the child, will offer a solution to this problem. On the contrary, such a process may only exacerbate the dichotomous cycle by promoting the use of mutual coercive tactics (Patterson, 1982) that harm relations and development. Our understanding of parenting, as presented in this chapter suggests that repair of the dichotomous cycle can occur only with a rebalancing of the different mechanisms of conflict resolution, coupled with the development of more sophisticated capacities for performing each type (Cohen & Lwow, 2004). This work on conflict resolution must be accompanied by a process in which a trained professional, by virtue of acting as a containing and soothing figure, helps the parent reduce anxiety, and reinforces the parent's regulatory mechanisms. The structuring and elaboration of regulatory mechanisms occurs in the process of counseling through the creation of new meanings and new understandings in respect to the complexity of parenting, and by transforming cultural attitudes concerning the damage and dangers of exposing children to suffering, toward a view that appreciates some suffering as necessary for any normal developmental process.

SUMMARY AND IMPLICATIONS

In this paper we have presented a view of the human being as a creature who is inherently dependent on the Other for his or her own processes of development and creation. This outlook emerges from the basic understanding that the preservation of oppositions, and not their elimination, is an essential element of life and of development, lying at the foundation of various regulatory processes. Therefore, it appears that a central aspiration of human development ought to be the possibility of maintaining relationships in which the individual's uniqueness can be expressed, while still recognizing the uniqueness of the Other (and without breaking loose of dependency, in the direction of independence). Such a relationship is founded on the constant preservation of dialectical tension, and on the opposition between the need to maintain separateness and independence, and the need for intimacy and dependency. Only a diverse system of patterns of conflict resolution may stabilize such a complex interpersonal state, while engendering processes of creation and growth that enhance the ability to tolerate and to contain the tension between these two vectors.

Such a model does not idealize peaceful and harmonious relations, but rather produces relationships in which vitality is maintained through conflict and vacillations. To combat the influence of frustrating and fantastic models of continual harmony and an effortless life that is free of suffering, professionals and practitioners are called upon to make social interventions concerning the need to develop mechanisms for managing different types of conflict between people. We believe that the recognition of conflicts as essential potential states that are amenable to management with a variety of tools that can promote growth might minimize dichotomizing and splitting processes that are engendered by anxiety, and promote social processes that contain difference and opposition and thus enable creation and development.

The application of these ideas is vital for the domain of parenting, in which the regulatory processes of parents—especially the regulation of suffering and anxiety—exercise a major influence in the development of the affect regulation systems of the child. A parent-child relationship that is conducive to growth is founded on a balanced "diet" of diverse and alternating experiences of coping with interpersonal conflict. Some of these coping experiences reflect dichotomous solutions, and some solutions of compromise; some reflect action-oriented decisions and others represent attempts at interpreting and understanding, while most involve various combinations of these coping patterns. In the professional literature one can find many schemes and suggestions for applying combinations of these types of coping strategies (D'Zurilla & Nezu, 1999).

This chapter emphasizes another variety of conflict resolution that is less familiar in the professional literature as other patterns are. This type of solution emerges when there is no attempt to obscure the conflict or to resolve it, but rather to contain it, while trusting in the importance and stability of the bond. These situations carry potential for the development of creative solutions. In such situations the conflict itself, and the ability to delay active solution-oriented interventions, produces something in the space between the parent and the child that could not have been created by either one separately. This, in our view is the surplus value of being human: the opportunity for a significant emotional and ethical encounter between one person and another, one that engenders the experiences of joy, excitement and intimacy between two people, which would not have been possible under any other circumstance. This encounter serves as the foundation for development and human creativity. It should be stressed that this is an important phase which is only achievable in the context of a relationship that includes a correct proportion of interpersonal experiences involving the various conflict resolution patterns that allow each pole to be stabilized, mutual interpretive processes to be set in motion, and stress to be relieved through compromise-oriented solutions.

Our approach has several implications for therapists who work with parents on children's behavioral problems or with problems in child-parent relationships:

- It focuses the goal of therapy on the enrichment and balancing of patterns of coping with parent-child conflicts instead of aspiring that these conflicts cease to exist. This is a more realistic and constructive focus.
- It minimizes judgmental attitudes toward the parents and reduces guilt. The different patterns that parents employ are all considered important (with the exception, needless to say, of unusual cases of abuse or neglect).
- The challenge presented in the joint work with parents is to map and identify which patterns are not sufficiently in use and which are overused or do not exist at all in the parents' (and child's) repertoire. The balancing of the different patterns is adapted to the child's characteristics, environment and developmental phase.
- It develops parents' affect regulation. When parents find it difficult to adopt a certain coping pattern, one must pay special attention to the parents' affect regulation processes, and especially to regulation of anxiety and tension. The possibility of using the therapist as a "safe base" for these states is vital for parents. In addition, the therapist can help develop mentalizing mechanisms that allow parents to try to understand the sources of their anxiety and tension, as well as the possible causes of the child's behavior. The therapist engages in developing the parent's own interpretive capacities while increasing his or her awareness to personal-historical as well as socio-cultural factors that contribute to the difficulty of affect regulation.
- It provides information and develops parents' understanding of ways to promote self-regulation among children, and educates about the importance of practicing different methods of self-regulation and of regulating the child as important building blocks toward developing a repertoire of parental coping strategies.

Finally, we have argued that the suspension of problem solving at a stage in which interpretive and compromise-seeking capacities can be mobilized, while reinforcing belief in the strength of the bond and of human creativity, may often lead to the creation of a space where unique and creative instances of coping can occur in parent-child dyads and among other family members as well.

REFERENCES

Benjamin, J. (1988). The bonds of love: Psychoanalysis, feminism and the problem of domination. New York: Pantheon Books

Bowlby, J. (1973). Attachment and loss. Vol. 2. Separation: Anxiety and anger. New York: Basic Books

Bowlby, J. (1979). The making and breaking of affectional bonds. London: TavistockCassidy, J. & Shaver, P. R. (Eds.), (1999). Handbook of attachment: Theory, research and clinical applications. New York: Guilford Press

Cohen, E. & Lwow, E. (2004). The parent-child mutual recognition model: Promoting cooperativeness and responsibility in disturbed adolescents who refuse treatment. Journal of Psychotherapy Integration, 14(3), 307-322

Cole, P. M., Martin, S. E. & Dennis, T. A. (2004). Emotion regulation as a scientific construct: Methodological challenges and directions for child development research. Child Development, 75, 317-333

Dix T. (1991). The affective organization of parenting: Adaptive and maladaptive processes. Psychological Bulletin, 110 (1), 3-25

D'Zurilla, T. J. & Nezu, A. M. (1999). Problem solving therapy: A social competence approach to clinical intervention (2nd ed.). New York: Springer Publishing Company

Edwards, M. E. (2002). Attachment, mastery and interdependence: A model of parenting processes. Family Process, 41 (3), 389-404

Eisenberg, N. & Spinard, T. L. (2004). Emotion-related regulation: Sharpening the definition. Child Development, 75 (2), 334-339

Fonagy, P. (1999). Transgenerational consistencies of attachment: A new theory. Paper to the Developmental and Psychoanalytic Discussion Group, American Psychoanalytic Association Meeting, Washington D.C.

Fonagy, P., Gergely, G., Jurist, E.L. & Target, M. (2002). Affect regulation, mentalization and the development of the self. New York: Other Press

Fonagy P. & Target , M. (2003). Evolution of the interpersonal interpretive function: Clues for effective preventive intervention in early childhood. In W. Coates, J. L. Rosenthal & D. S. Schechter (Eds.), September 11: Trauma and human bonds (pp.99-114). Hillsdale, New Jersey: The Analytic Press

Goelman, D. (2005). The 2005 Edge annual question: What do you believe is true even though you cannot prove it? Edge 152—January 4. The Edge Foundation Web site: www.edge.org

Gottman, J. M., Katz, L. F & Hooven, C. (1997). Meta-Emotion: How families communicate emotionally. Mahwah New Jersey: Lawrence Elbraum Associates

Griffin, L.R. (2007). Take back your parental authority without punishment. Berkley Pub. House

Kohut, H. (1984). How does analysis cure? In A. Goldberg (Ed.), Chicago: University of Chicago Press

LaMothe, R. (2005). Creating space: The fourfold dynamics of potential space. Psychoanalytic Psychology, 22, 2, 207–223

Patterson, G. R. (1982). Coercive family process. Eugene, OR: Castalia

Schore, A. N. (2001). The effects of early relational trauma on right brain development, affect regulation, and infant mental health. Infant Mental Health Journal, 22 (1-2) 201-269

Siegel, D. (2001). Toward an interpersonal neurobiology of the developing mind: Attachment relationships, 'mindsight', and neural integration. Infant Mental Health Journal, 22(1-2), 67-94

Siegel, D. (2004). Attachment and self-understanding: Parenting with the brain in mind. In M.Green & M. Scholes (Eds.), Attachment and human survival (pp. 21-35). London: Karnac Books

Siegel, D.J. & Hartzell, M. M. (2003). Parenting from the inside out. New York: Tarcher/Putnam

Stollak, G.E. (1973). What happened today: Stories for parents and children. Dubuque, IA: Kendall/Hunt.

Taffel, R. (2006). The divided self. Psychotherapy Networker. www.psych otherapynet worker.org/jo06_taffel.html

Winnicott, D. (1971). Playing and reality. London: Tavistock.

In: Handbook of Parenting: Styles, Stresses & Strategies   ISBN 978-1-60741-766-8
Editor: Pacey H. Krause and Tahlia M. Dailey   © 2009 Nova Science Publishers, Inc.

Chapter 11

AMOUNT OF TIME IN EXTRACURRICULAR ACTIVITIES IMPACT ON PARENTING AND ADOLESCENT BEHAVIOR PROBLEMS

Andrea D. Mata, Katherine C. Schinka
and Manfred H.M. van Dulmen
Kent State University, Ohio, USA

U.S. adolescents are spending an increasing amount of time in extracurricular activities. Some adolescents who are spending an increased amount of time in extracurricular activities are experiencing behavior problems (i.e. anxiety, stress; Ginsburg & The Committee on Communications and Committee on Psychosocial Aspects of Child and Family Health, 2007). It is not clear, however, why involvement in extracurricular activities is associated with behavior problems for some, but not all adolescents. The purpose of this chapter is to propose a conceptual model to further understand the mechanisms underlying adolescent mental health problems among adolescents who spend increased amount of time in extracurricular activities. The proposed model investigates bidirectional effects among (a) the amount of time an adolescent spends in extracurricular activities, (b) parental stress, (c) parental warmth/control, and (d) adolescent behavior problems.

INVOLVEMENT IN EXTRACURRICULAR ACTIVITIES AMONG U.S. ADOLESCENTS

U.S. adolescents have a great amount of leisure time, and a large proportion of the average U.S. adolescent's leisure time is spent in extracurricular activities. Extracurricular activities are activities that are highly organized, meet regularly, and include an adult leader or supervisor (Mahoney, 2000). Since the 1980's, U.S. adolescents have become progressively busier (Anderson & Doherty, 2005; Hofferth & Sandberg, 2001). Additionally, U.S. adolescents' time use patterns changed from 1981 to 1997 and the amount of time spent in structured sports has doubled (Hofferth & Sandberg, 2001). The average U.S. adolescent currently spends approximately five hours per week participating in extracurricular activities (Mahoney, Harris, & Eccles, 2006). However, participating in at least ten hours per week in extracurricular activities is not uncommon for U.S. adolescents (Shanahan & Flaherty, 2001). Additionally, a subgroup of U.S. adolescents, approximately three to six percent, spends twenty or more hours per week participating in extracurricular activities (Mahoney et al., 2006). The amount of time spent in extracurricular activities by this subgroup of overscheduled adolescents is worrisome because empirical findings indicate that some of these overscheduled adolescents are developing behavior problems (Ginsburg & The Committee on Communications and Committee on Psychosocial Aspects of Child and Family Health, 2007, but see Mahoney et al. 2006 for mixed findings).

There are three explanations of why U.S. adolescents are spending an increased amount of time in extracurricular activities or being overscheduled: 1) research findings indicate that involvement in extracurricular activities is associated with positive developmental outcomes 2) the ideology of what defines a "good parent" has changed and 3) expectations for college admissions in the United States have increased.

POSITIVE DEVELOPMENTAL OUTCOMES ASSOCIATED WITH PARTICIPATION IN EXTRACURRICULAR ACTIVITIES

Participation in extracurricular activities is associated with academic outcomes such as higher academic success (Eccles, Barber, Stone, & Hunt, 2003; Mahoney, Cairns, & Farmer, 2003) and lower rates of school dropout (Mahoney & Cairns, 1997; McNeal, 1995). Participation in extracurricular activities is also associated with additional networking opportunities, including increased connections with adults outside of the family (Hansen, Larson, Dworkin, 2003) and promotion of interpersonal relationships (Larson, Hansen, & Moneta, 2006). Lastly, participating in extracurricular activities is associated with higher levels of self-esteem (Richman & Shaffer, 2000). Empirical findings associated with the positive developmental outcomes related to participation in extracurricular activities have been disseminated to parents. Parents want their children to have these positive developmental outcomes because scientific studies indicate they lead to success later in life. Therefore, parents enroll their adolescents in extracurricular activities with the mentality that more is better—more extracurricular activity participation, the more positive developmental outcomes.

THE IDEOLOGY OF WHAT DEFINES A "GOOD PARENT" HAS CHANGED

The second explanation of why adolescents are spending an increased amount of time in extracurricular activities or being overscheduled is that the idea of what makes a "good" parent has changed (Coakley, 2007). The idea of what makes a "good" parent has changed because during previous generations, parents made their adolescents' schedules fit into their own life styles. Now, however, parents allow their adolescents' schedules to dictate the family's life style (Rosenfield & Wise, 2000). For example, parents may spend less time conducting activities they enjoy and family vacations because their adolescent has dance lessons, basketball practices, cheerleading camps, and other extracurricular activity obligations. Some parents report they do not feel like they are good parents if they are not living a hurried lifestyle and report not being able to slow down because they fear others will perceive them as a bad parent (Ginsburg & The Committee on Communications and Committee on Psychosocial Aspects of Child and Family Health, 2007). Indeed, parents are willing to go to great lengths to insure their adolescents succeed, and many parents enroll their adolescents in many hours and a wide breadth of extracurricular activities (Ginsburg & The Committee on Communications and Committee on Psychosocial Aspects of Child and Family Health, 2007). Therefore, many parents perceive themselves as a good parent if they make huge self sacrifices for their adolescents. Second, parents perceive themselves as a good parent if they know where his or her adolescent is at all times (Coakley, 2007). Parents enroll their adolescents in extracurricular activities because these activities are supervised and thus they know where their adolescent is. Parents who enroll their adolescent in many hours of extracurricular activities per week can rationalize that they are good parents because they (a) made many self sacrifices and (b) they know where their adolescents are at all times.

EXPECTATIONS FOR COLLEGE ADMISSIONS IN THE UNITED STATES HAVE INCREASED

Increased expectations for college admissions also explains why adolescents are spending an increased amount of time in extracurricular activities. College admissions have become increasingly rigorous, and parents perceive that extracurricular activity participation is key in getting into college (Ginsburg & The Committee on Communications and Committee on Psychosocial Aspects of Child and Family Health, 2007). Additionally, adolescents are being told by their guidance counselors that they need participation in extracurricular activities for admission into college. The pressure to become increasingly involved in extracurricular activities has thus led to an increased number of adolescents being overscheduled.

THEORETICAL FRAMEWORK

What is missing in the literature is a conceptual framework that comprehensively assesses how overscheduling affects parental behaviors and consequently adolescent behavior problems. Researchers rely predominately on unidimensional influences of parents when studying adolescents. However, solely investigating the unidimensional influences of parents on adolescent outcomes is too simplistic. Focusing on the unidimensional influences of parents does not attempt to understand the complex picture of the family (Collins, Maccoby, Steinberg, Hetherington, & Bornstein, 2000). The complex picture of the family can be understood by investigating the mutual influence—the bidirectional effects between the parent and adolescent. A bidirectional effect is when the parent's behavior impacts the adolescent's behavior and the adolescent's behavior impacts the parent's behavior. Bidirectional effects were noticed over sixty years ago (Bell, 1979) and are discussed in frameworks including systems theory (Whitchurch & Constantine, 1993) and ecological models (Bronfenbrenner, 1979).

EXTRACURRICULAR ACTIVITIES-PARENTING-ADOLESCENT MODEL

The extracurricular activities-parenting-adolescent (ECA-PA) model conceptualizes why some adolescents are experiencing behavior problems with increased amount of time in extracurricular activities while others are not. The ECA-PA model is depicted in Figure 1. The ECA-PA model shows how the amount of time in extracurricular activities impacts parenting and adolescent behavior problems. The model considers the following constructs: 1) amount of time in extracurricular activities 2) parental stress 3) parental warmth/control and 4) adolescent behavior problems (i.e. internalizing and externalizing). The predicted associations between each of these constructs are discussed below.

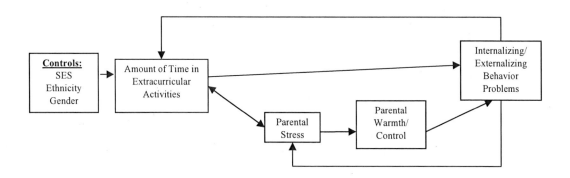

Figure 1. Extracurricular activities-parenting-adolescent model.

The first association in the ECA-PA model is how the amount of time an adolescent spends in extracurricular activities affects parental stress. The ECA-PA model predicts that as the amount of time an adolescent spends in extracurricular activities increases, the stress felt by the parent (i.e. parental stress) increases. Parents rate their adolescents being overscheduled as the third highest parenting difficulty (Roehlkepartain, Scales, Roehlkpartain, Gallo, & Rude, 2002). Additionally, forty-one percent of U.S. parents said their adolescents' schedules made parenting harder (Roehlkepartain et al., 2002). Parents may become more stressed when the amount of time their adolescents are spending in extracurricular activities increases because more time in extracurricular activities adds to a parent's to do list. Parents become stressed because they have to get off from work, pick up their adolescent, feed their adolescent, take their adolescent to the extracurricular activity, stay at the extracurricular activity, bring the adolescent home from the extracurricular activity, make sure the adolescent's homework is done, have the adolescent go to bed, and then start the routine over again the next day (Sidebotham & The ALSPAC Study Team, 2001). This example depicts the day to day hassles of parenting adolescents who are spending an increased amount of time in extracurricular activities. These day to day hassles are strongly associated with parental warmth and control (Creasey & Reese, 1996).

The second association depicted in the ECA-PA model is the association between parental stress and parental warmth and control. The ECA-PA model predicts that as the amount of parental stress increases parental warmth decreases. Parents who are stressed do not parent effectively (Dodge, Pettit, Bates, 1994; Pinderhughes, Nix, Foster, Jones, & The Conduct Problems Prevention Research Group, 2001). Parents who are stressed are more likely to be insensitive towards their children and lack parental warmth (Berk, 2008). Therefore, parents who have adolescents who are spending increased amount of time in extracurricular activities could become more stressed which then lowers their parental warmth towards their adolescent.

The next association in the ECA-PA model is the association between parental warmth/control and adolescent behavior problems. The ECA-PA model predicts that as parental warmth decreases, adolescent behavior problems increase (McKee, Colletti, Rakow, Jones, & Forehand, 2008). Parental control is negatively associated with both internalizing (Galambos, Barker, & Alemida, 2003) and externalizing behavior problems (Fletcher, Darling, & Steinberg, 1995; Rogers, 1999; Pettit, Laird, Dodge, Bates, & Criss, 2001).

The association between amount of time in extracurricular activities and adolescent behavior problems is the fourth association in the ECA-PA model. The ECA-PA model predicts that as amount of time in extracurricular activities increases, adolescent behavior problems will increase. An increased amount of time in extracurricular activities may stress the adolescent who is participating. Some children react to increased time in extracurricular activities with anxiety and signs of stress (Ginsburg & The Committee on Communications and Committee on Psychosocial Aspects of Child and Family Health, 2007). Forty-one percent of adolescents report feeling stressed most or all of the time because all the activities they were involved in (Brown, n.d.). Additionally, adolescents with higher numbers of extracurricular activities were more stressed—those who reported having three or more extracurricular activities doubled the likelihood the adolescent reported being stressed (Brown, n.d.).

The fifth association in the ECA-PA model is the association between adolescent behavior problems and parental stress. The ECA-PA model predicts that as adolescent behavior problems increase, parental stress increases. Adolescent behavior affects parental stress (Abidin, 1976; Sidebotham & The ALSPAC Study Team, 2001). Adolescents with internalizing or externalizing behavior problems increase their parent's parental stress. Parents with adolescents who have behavior disorders reported higher levels of parental stress (Creasey & Reese, 1996; Dumas, Wolf, Fishman, & Culligan, 1991; Fisher, 1990; Mash & Johnston, 1983; Stewart, Deblois, & Cummings, 1980), because adolescent behavior problems adds to the amount of issues parents need to address.

The association between adolescent behavior problems and the amount of time in extracurricular activities is the sixth association discussed in the ECA-PA model. The ECA-PA model predicts that as adolescent behavior problems increase, the amount of time in extracurricular activities increases. Parents with adolescents with behavior problems enroll their adolescents in extracurricular activities because they heard about the positive developmental outcomes associated with participating in extracurricular activities. Parents who have adolescents who are demonstrating internalizing behavior problems enroll their adolescents in extracurricular activities so that their adolescents can expand their social networks and develop friendships with same age peers. Parents who have adolescents who are demonstrating externalizing behavior problems enroll their adolescents in extracurricular activities to help their adolescents express their aggressive tendencies in a more socially appropriate fashion (i.e. sports). This association has no empirical support that we are aware of. However, positive developmental outcomes associated with participating in extracurricular activities are more prominent for adolescents who are at high risk for the development of behavior problems (Mahoney, 2000; Mahoney & Cairns, 1997). Adolescents who had low levels of school involvement and academic competence had lower levels of school dropout if they were enrolled in extracurricular activities. However, adolescents who had low levels of school involvement and academic competence and did not participate in extracurricular activities had higher levels of school dropout.

The final association in the ECA-PA model is the association between parental stress and the amount of time in extracurricular activities. The ECA-PA model predicts that as parental stress increases, the amount of time in extracurricular activities increases. The number of parents experiencing parental stress has increased in the last few decades because there has been a rise in single parent and two working parent households (Shaffer, 2009). These parents are likely to have higher levels of parental stress because they are working many hours. Parents working many hours have to less time to take care of their adolescents and therefore they need child care services. Parents enroll their adolescents in extracurricular activities as an alternative form of child care (Ginsburg & The Committee on Communications and Committee on Psychosocial Aspects of Child and Family Health, 2007). Parents can work and know their adolescent is being supervised by an adult and their adolescent is gaining something from his or her participation.

Given research in the many areas involved with the ECA-PA model, three controls are considered: family socioeconomic status, adolescent gender and family ethnicity. Adolescents who are from a higher socioeconomic status family have higher levels of extracurricular activity participation (Vandivere, Gallagher, & Moore 2004). Controlling for gender is needed for two reasons. The first reason is boys participate in more sports compared to girls; however, girls have higher levels of overall extracurricular activity participation (Eccles & Barber, 1999). The second reason why gender will be controlled for is the model might change slightly depending on the participant's gender—indicating different pathways for males and females. For example, females who have an increased amount of time in extracurricular activities might experience more internalizing behavior problems than externalizing behavior problems, however, boys who have an increased amount of time in extracurricular activities might experience more externalizing behavior problems than internalizing behavior problems. Finally, controlling for ethnicity is needed because different rates of extracurricular activity participation were found depending on the family's ethnicity. European Americans are statistically significantly more likely to participate in extracurricular activities compared to African Americans and Hispanics (Brown & Evans, 2002; Hull, Kilbourne, Reece, & Husaini, 2008).

DISCUSSION

The ECA-PA model moves beyond the question of whether or not U.S. adolescents are overscheduled and attempts to understand the mechanisms underlying overscheduling in extracurricular activity involvement by investigating the associations among (a) amount of time in extracurricular activities (b) parental stress (c) parental warmth/control and (d) adolescent behavior problems. This model can aid in intervention efforts by examining maladaptive associations between amount of time spent in extracurricular activities, parenting, and adolescent behavior problems. Individual families can utilize the model when an adolescent is exhibiting behavior problems due to increased amount of time in extracurricular activities. The adolescent can either decrease the amount of time he or she is participating in extracurricular activities or a family intervention could be conducted. The ECA-PA model will be used to demonstrate what parental and adolescent behaviors are associated with lower levels of adolescent behavior problems within the context of increased amount of time in extracurricular activities. Hopefully, the model can be put into practice by encouraging families to examine the parental and adolescent behaviors associated with adolescent behavior problems and amount of time in extracurricular activities. Families' examination of problematic parent and adolescent behaviors can make them aware and hence foster change.

The findings from testing the ECA-PA model can also aid in prevention practices. The ECA-PA model would suggest what types of families are more likely to have adolescents who experience behavior problems due to increased amount of time in extracurricular activities. Families could compare themselves to the types of families indicated by the ECA-PA model to experience behavior problems and decide the optimal amount of time in extracurricular activities for their family. Families who are informed about the possible negative effects of increased amount of time in extracurricular activities could be prevented from overscheduling their adolescent and reduce the likelihood of their adolescent experiencing behavior problems.

REFERENCES

Abidin, R. (1976). *Parenting skills workbook*. New York: Human Sciences Press.

Anderson, J. R., & Doherty, W. J. (2005). Democratic community initiatives: The case of the overscheduled children. *Family Relations, 54*, 654-665.

Bell, R. Q. (1979). Parent, child, and reciprocal influences. *American Psychologist, 34*, 821-826.

Berk, L. E. (2008). *Infants, children, and adolescents* (6th ed.). Boston: Pearson Allyn and Bacon.

Bronfenbrenner, U. (1979). *The ecology of human development: Experiments by nature and design*. Cambridge, MA: Harvard University Press.

Brown, R., & Evans, W. P. (2002). Extracurricular activity and ethnicity: Creating greater school connection among diverse student populations. *Urban Education, 37*, 41-58.

Brown, S. L. (n.d.). KidsHealth KidsPoll—Are kids too busy. Summary of findings. Retrieved on February 3, 2009, from http://www.nah ec.org/KidsPoll/busy/Busy _Summary_of_Findings.pdf

Coakley, J. (2007). *Sports in society*. New York, NY: McGraw Hill.

Collins, W. A., Maccoby, E. E., Steinberg, L., Hetherington, E.M., & Bornstein, M.H. (2000). Contemporary research on parenting: The case for nature and nurture. *American Psychologist*, 55, 218-232.

Creasey, G., & Reese, M. (1996). Mothers' and fathers' perceptions of parenting hassles: Associations with psychological symptoms, nonparenting hassles, and child behavior problems. *Journal of Applied Developmental Psychology, 17*, 393-406.

Dodge, K. A., Pettit, G. S., & Bates, J. E. (1994). Effects of physical maltreatment on the development of peer relations. *Development and Psychopathology, 6*, 43-55.

Dumas, J. E., Wolf, L. C., Fishman, S. N., & Culligan, A. (1991). Parenting stress, child behavior problems, and dysphoria in parents of children with Autism, Down Syndrome, behavior disorders, and normal development. *Exceptionality, 2*, 97-110.

Eccles, J. S. & Barber, B. L. (1999). Student council, volunteering, basketball, or marching band: What kind of extracurricular involvement matters? *Journal of Adolescent Research, 14*, 10-43.

Eccles, J. S., Barber, B. L., Stone, M., & Hunt, J. (2003). Extracurricular activities and adolescent development. *Journal of Social Issues, 59*, 865-889.

Fisher, M. (1990). Parenting stress and the child with attention deficit hyperactivity disorder. *Journal of Clinical Child Psychology, 19*, 337-346.

Fletcher, A. C., Darling, N., & Steinberg, L. (1995). Parental monitoring and peer influences on adolescent substance use. In J. McCord (Ed.), *Coercion and punishment in long-term perspectives*. New York: Cambridge University Press.

Galambos, N. L., Barker, E. T., & Alemida, D. M. (2003). Parents do matter: Trajectories of change in externalizing and internalizing problems in early adolescence. *Child Development, 74*, 578-594.

Ginsburg, K. R., & The Committee on Communications and Committee on Psychosocial Aspects of Child and Family Health. (2007). The importance of play in promoting healthy child development and maintaining strong parent-child bonds. *Pediatrics, 119*, 182-191.

Hansen, D. M., Larson, R. W., & Dworkin, J. B. (2003). What adolescents learn in organized youth activities: A survey of self-reported developmental experiences. *Journal of Research on Adolescence, 13*, 25-55.

Hofferth, S. L., & Sandberg, J. F. (2001). How American children spend their time. *Journal of Marriage and the Family, 63*, 295-308.

Hull, P., Kilbourne, B., Reece, M., & Husaini, B. (2008). Community involvement and adolescent mental health: Moderating effects of race/ethnicity and neighborhood disadvantage. *Journal of Community Psychology, 36*, 534-551.

Larson, R., Hansen, D., & Moneta, G. (2006). Differing profiles of developmental experiences across types of organized youth activities. *Developmental Psychology, 42*, 849-863.

Mahoney, J. L. (2000). School extracurricular activity participation as a moderator in the development of antisocial patterns. *Child Development, 71*, 502-516.

Mahoney, J. L., & Cairns, B. (1997). Do extracurricular activities protect against early school dropout? *Developmental Psychology, 33*, 241-253.

Mahoney, J. L., Cairns, B. D., & Farmer, T. W. (2003). Promoting interpersonal competence and educational success through extracurricular activity participation. *Journal of Educational Psychology, 95*, 409-418.

Mahoney, J. L., Harris, A. L., & Eccles, J. S. (2006). Organized activity participation, positive youth development and the over-scheduling hypothesis. *Social Policy Report, 20*, 1-31.

Mash, E., & Johnston, C. (1983). Parental perceptions of child behavior problems, parenting self-esteem, and mothers' reported stress in younger and older hyperactive and normal children. *Journal of Consulting and Clinical Psychology, 51*, 86-99.

McKee, L., Colletti, C., Rakow, A., Jones, D. J., & Forehand, R. (2008). Parenting and child externalizing behaviors: Are the associations specific or diffuse? *Aggression and Violent Behavior, 13*, 201-215.

McNeal, R. B., Jr. (1995). Extracurricular activities and high school dropouts. *Sociology of Education, 68*, 62-80.

Pettit, G. S., Laird, R. D., Dodge, K. A., Bates, J. E., & Criss, M. M. (2001). Antecedents and behavior-problem outcomes of parental monitoring and psychological control in early adolescence. *Child Development, 72*, 583-598.

Pinderhughes, E. E., Nix, R., Foster, E. M., Jones, D., & The Conduct Problems Prevention Research Group. (2001). Parenting in context: Impact of neighborhood poverty, residential stability, public services, social networks, and danger on parental behavior. *Journal of Marriage and the Family, 63*, 941-953.

Richman, E. L., & Shaffer, D. R. (2000). If you let me play sports: How might sport participation influence the self-esteem of adolescent females? *Psychology of Women Quarterly, 24*, 189-199.

Roehlkepartain, E. C., Scales, P. C., Roehlkepartain, J. L., Gallo, C., & Rude, S. P. (2002). *Building strong families: Highlights from a preliminary survey from YMCA of the USA and Search Institute on what parents need to succeed.* Retrieved February 3, 2009, from http://www.abundantassets.org/pdfs/BSF-Highlights.pdf

Rogers, K. B. (1999). Parenting processes related to sexual risk-taking behaviors of adolescent males and females. *Journal of Marriage and the Family, 61*, 99-109.

Rosenfield, A., & Wise, N. (2000). *The overscheduled child: Avoiding the hyper-parenting trap.* New York, NY: St. Martin's Griffin.

Shaffer, D. R. (2009). *Social and personality development* (6th ed.). Belmont, CA: Wadsworth.

Shanahan, M. J., & Flaherty, B. P. (2001). Dynamic patterns of time use in adolescence. *Child Development, 72*, 385-401.

Sidebotham, P., & ALSPAC Study Team. (2001). Culture, stress and the parent-child relationship: A qualitative study of parents' perceptions of parenting. *Child: Care, Health and Development, 27*, 469-485.

Stewart, M., Deblois, C., & Cummings, C. (1980). Psychiatric disorder in the parents of hyperactivie boys and those with conduct disorders. *Journal of Consulting and Clinical Psychology, 56*, 909-915.

Whitchurch, G. G. & Constantine, L. L. (1993). Systems theory. In P. G. Boss, W. J. Doherty, R. LaRossa, W. R. Schumm, & S. K. Steinmetz (Eds.), *Sourcebook of family theories and methods: A contextual approach* (pp. 325-355). New York and London: Plenum Press.

Vandivere, S., Gallagher, M., & Moore, K. A. (2004). Changes in children's well-being and family environments. *Child Trends, 18*. Retrieved February 2, 2009, from www.urban.org/UploadedPDF/310912_snapshots3_no18.pdf

In: Handbook of Parenting: Styles, Stresses & Strategies   ISBN 978-1-60741-766-8
Editor: Pacey H. Krause and Tahlia M. Dailey   © 2009 Nova Science Publishers, Inc.

Chapter 12

STRATEGY AND PRACTICE OF SUPPORT FOR MULTIPLE BIRTH FAMILIES: EVIDENCE-BASED CARE AND POPULATION APPROACH WITH HUMAN NETWORK

Syuichi Ooki

Ishikawa Prefectural Nursing University, Ishikawa, Japan

ABSTRACT

In Japan the rate of multiple births has been increasing since 1975 because of the wide spread of fertility treatment. Currently more than 1% of all births are multiples. The rapid increase of multiple births is now a common public health concern in developed countries. Multiple birth babies are more likely to be born preterm and of low birthweight, adding to the many pressures of coping with two or more babies. The nurturing of multiples entails a physically, mentally and economically higher burden than that of singletons, and multiple birth families surely expect appropriate information to facilitate the healthy growth of their children. Multiples tend to lag behind singletons in their physical growth and motor and language development. Multiples are reported to be one of the risk factors for maternal depression and child abuse. Good preparation and advice during or even before pregnancy is essential. After the birth, parents need continuing support and access to care from health professionals who understand their different and special needs. Therefore, there is an increasing need for appropriate information to be provided to parents and health professionals regarding the growth and development of multiples, tips on child bearing, and social resources for families. However, little information is available, especially in Japan. Multidisciplinary collaboration is essential to resolve these themes surrounding multiple birth families. Moreover, population-based or at least large-scale epidemiologic studies to assess the long-term health, social and psychological impact of multiple births on the family, children and society are crucial to provide a scientific basis and to persuade policymakers of the importance of supporting families with multiples.

The author has adopted three main strategies to resolve these problems. The first strategy is monitoring and reanalyzing vital statistics concerning multiple births, and providing an objective macroscopic vision of public health problems related to multiple births. The second strategy is to provide evidence-based information to health professionals and policymakers as well as multiple birth families. A large-scale database of multiples, mainly twins, has been organized since 1984. The third strategy is to construct a human network and family support system at the prefectural level by means of a population-approach method. The goals of these projects are to contribute to the development of welfare programs for families with multiples as well as to coordinate research useful for both maternal and child health and human genetics.

INTRODUCTION

Since the early 1980s the number of multiple births has rapidly increased in all developed countries largely due to the widespread use of inadequately monitored ovulation induction and multiple embryo transfer (Bryan, 2006). Currently, around 3% of live births in Western developed countries are multiple births. Increasing multiple births rates have also been observed in Japan. More than 1% of all births are multiples (Ooki, 2006c).

Although there are similarities to singleton pregnancy and parenthood, the experience of expecting and parenting multiples is undeniably very different. The birth and parenting of multiples always present unique challenges for both families and health professionals. Multiple births are associated with substantial medical, health care, socio-emotional, developmental, educational and economic consequences for both families and society (Denton, 2005b; Leonard & Denton, 2006).

Addressing the causes of the high numbers of iatrogenic multiple births continues to be an urgent challenge. Meanwhile, those caring for multiple-birth children and their families need a fuller understanding of their special problems and needs (Bryan, 2006).

In this chapter the author introduces the current practice of supporting multiple birth families in Japan, where such support has not yet reached the level of many Western countries. Some important topics related to multiple births are concisely described below.

IATROGENIC MULTIPLE PREGNANCY

Multiple pregnancy is the most serious complication of assisted reproductive technology (ART) because of its well-established medical risks and social and economic consequences. Many infertile couples in Japan, with or without their knowledge of the health risks and family impact of a multiple birth, are said to regard a twin pregnancy as the ideal outcome of ART.

Before any treatment for infertility that increases the possibility of a multiple pregnancy is performed, the prospective parents need to be fully informed about the risks associated with multiple pregnancy as well as the practical, emotional and financial impact of parenting multiples (Leonard & Denton, 2006). Health care policymakers and fertility specialists must continue their efforts to lower the rates of iatrogenic multiple pregnancy, especially higher-order multiple gestation.

PREGNANCY AND PARENTING PROBLEMS RELATED TO MULTIPLE BIRTHS

Parents often describe multiple pregnancy as physically and emotionally difficult (Bryan, 2003). The diagnosis of multiple pregnancy frequently comes with a shock as well as happiness.

Parents should be given written information about multiple births including details regarding local and national support organizations (Denton, 2005a). Multiple birth education classes for expectant parents should start early and include the pregnancy. The goal is to educate parents and other family members about the unique aspects of multiple pregnancy and parenthood. Information about prenatal, postnatal and neonatal care should be provided. Building a support network is a vital component (Leonard & Denton, 2006).

Mothers of multiples have been shown to suffer more from lack of sleep and fatigue than mothers of single-born children. Furthermore, depression is more common well beyond the infancy period, probably due at least to social isolation and fatigue (Bryan, 2003). It would not be surprising to find that child abuse is more common in multiple birth families (Tanimura et al., 1990). The rates of divorce are higher in parents of multiples than of singletons.

The development of most multiple birth children will be within the normal range. However, they will face a higher risk of certain longer-term problems including cerebral palsy, learning difficulties and, in particular, language delay. Multiple birth children have also been found to have weaker concentration ability and a higher incidence of attention deficit hyperactivity disorder (Bryan, 2003; Denton, 2005b). The environment of multiples differs in many ways from that of a single-born child and is likely to have a significant effect on the child's development.

Multiple birth families have unique needs, which are still not widely understood or sufficiently addressed by health care and other professionals. A well-trained multidisciplinary team, which provides specific care, parent education and support, is the basis for improving health outcomes for multiple birth family members (Leonard & Denton, 2006).

FINANCIAL IMPLICATIONSFOR FAMILIES

The financial impact of having multiples on families is considerable, with most experiencing a substantial loss in income and an enormous increase in expenditure, especially if the infants are preterm or have complex health needs. Most women leave the work force on reduced or no salary; many do not return to outside employment for months or even years. Withdrawal from the workplace may also result in the mother losing a measure of social status and a protective factor for mental health (Hall & Callahan, 2005; Leonard & Denton, 2006).

Moreover, extra daily life expenditures are required of multiple birth families compared to families with single-born children. The majority of multiple birth families, despite finding their income greatly diminished, do not qualify for subsidized child care or extra financial support. Early in the pregnancy, parents should be encouraged to explore the maternal support resources in their families and communities and to try to seek advice from other multiple birth parents.

THE DECLARATION OF RIGHTS AND STATEMENT OF NEEDS OF TWINS AND HIGHER ORDER MULTIPLES OF COMBO

The Council of the Multiple Birth Organization of the International Society for Twin Studies (COMBO) adopted in 1996 and updated in 2007 the Declaration of Rights and Statement of Needs of Twins and Higher Order Multiples (http://www.ists.qimr.edu.au/Rights.pdf, accessed November 3, 2008).

This statement is a very informative and revealing overview of a variety of socio-psychological and bio-medical aspects of the problems of multiple birth families or multiples themselves. The following six statements are adopted in the declaration.

1. Multiples and their families have a right to full protection, under the law, and freedom from discrimination of any kind.
2. Couples planning their families and/or seeking infertility treatment have a right to information and education about factors which influence the conception of multiples, the associated pregnancy risks and treatments, and facts regarding parenting multiples.
3. A) Parents have a right to expect accurate recording of placentation and the diagnosis of the zygosity of same sex multiples at birth. B) Older, same sex multiples of undetermined zygosity have a right to testing to ascertain their zygosity.
4. Any research incorporating multiples must be subordinated to the informed consent of the multiples and/or their parents and must comply with international codes of ethics governing human experimentation.
5. A) Multiple births and deaths must be accurately recorded, including any fetal losses during the duration of the pregnancy and infant deaths in the first year following delivery. B) Parents and multiples have a right to care by professionals who are knowledgeable regarding the management of multiple gestation and/or the lifelong special needs of multiples.
6. Co-multiples have the right to be placed together in foster care, adoptive families, and custody agreements.

The summary of the 'Statement of Needs' is as follows: twins and higher order multiples have unique: conception, gestation and birth processes; health risks; impacts on the family system; developmental environments; and individuation processes. Therefore, in order to insure their optimal development, multiples and their families need access to health care, social services, and education which respect and address their differences from single born children.

These rights and statements were useful milestones in the development of support systems of families with multiples in Japan.

THREE ASPECTS OF STUDIES ON MULTIPLES

There are three main independent fields of research regarding multiples, as shown in Figure 1. It is important to have a proper understanding of the specific features of scientific research on multiples, especially twins. Twins have been special resources for researchers for a long period. Twins are generally recognized as being a valuable resource not only for research on twin births themselves (the study 'of' twins in the field of obstetrics or biology), but also for research clarifying the relative contributions of genetic and environmental factors on human phenotypes (the study 'by' twins in the field of human genetics). The twin study method, namely the determination of similarities between monozygotic (MZ) and dizygotic (DZ) 'pairs', is an ideal natural experiment in human genetics. Researchers are interested in the kinship between twin pairs rather than twin individuals.

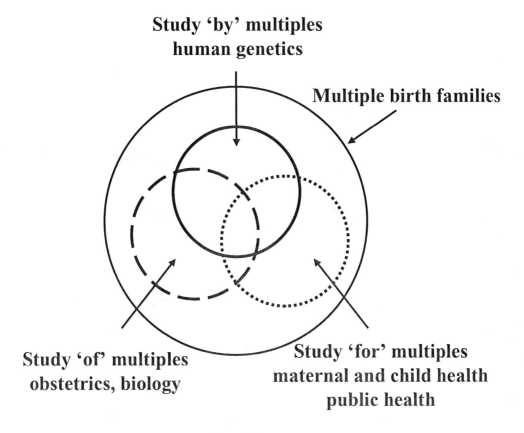

Figure 1. Need for comprehensive research in multiples.

It is only more recently that the special problems and needs of twins and higher-order multiple birth children themselves and of their families, and the need for special research (the study 'for' twins in the field of maternal and child care in public health) have begun to be recognized, although the number of reports is still very small compared to the other two research fields. In other words, twins and their families have been historically mainly subjects of research rather than subjects of care or support.

It is quite natural to think that these three types of studies on twins and multiples as essentially strongly related to one another. The family support practices of families with multiples will become more fruitful if the findings of scientific research concerning twins and multiples in biology, obstetrics, psychology and human genetics are taken into account, in addition to the research on maternal and child care. On the other hand, all research using multiples and their families as subjects should provide benefits for them.

SUPPORT FOR FAMILIES WITH MULTIPLES IN JAPAN

The Japanese Association of Twins' Mothers (JATM) was established in 1967. This organization has predominantly the longest history of activity and the largest number of members of any similar organization serving the multiple birth families throughout Japan. Although its contribution has been enormous, a nationwide systematic support system has not yet been achieved.

There are many small local twins' mothers' clubs or multiples' support groups throughout Japan, although the exact number of such groups is unknown. The reason for this is that they come into existence and disappear in a relatively short time, and no systematic governmental survey has been undertaken. Most of these small clubs do not have a stable foundation in terms of both financial and human resources. Many clubs have had common problems, for example the lack of a successors to a club leadership, relatively short periods of enrollment of the members, etc. There are no meta-clubs or organizations connecting these small clubs throughout prefectures or throughout the nation.

Many Western countries have nationwide organizations to support multiple birth families (Denton, 2005a). There exists no such organization in Japan. Support from local governments, public health centers and municipal maternal and child health care centers are not sufficient. The history of such support is very short; e.g., the first multiple birth families-focused child care class was held in 1991 by a municipal public health center in Amagasaki city.

Moreover, very little information, advice and support is provided by medical institutions. Even if a maternity class regarding multiple pregnancy is held, most of these activities are not followed up with other similar programs in the communities where families live once the mothers deliver the multiples and leave the hospital.

Multiples-focused pregnancy and parent education resources include leaflets, books and other printed materials, videos and DVDs, prenatal childbirth education classes, and online or telephone information and support networks. Valuable peer and professional support may come from local multiples' support groups or health care centers (Leonard & Denton, 2006). Although the situation has gradually improved, there remain very few such resources in Japan.

PUBLIC HEALTH PROBLEMS RELATED TO MULTIPLE BIRTHS IN JAPAN

All of the problems related to multiple pregnancy mentioned above cannot be resolved if they are discussed merely in the context of certain families having problems at the moment or as problems in the narrow sense of clinical obstetrics. The main problems related to the rapid increase of multiple births in Japan can be summarized as follows:

1. Lack or Insufficiency of Information

All kinds of information regarding multiple births is lacking, including evidence-based objective data on, for example, fertility treatment, short- and long-term prognosis of multiples, and medical economics. Qualitative data, for example, tips on the child-rearing of multiples, are also lacking and not fully described and organized. Therefore, health professionals do not know what the problems are. Even if they recognize the problems they do not know how to solve them.

2. Division, Disparity and Inequality of Information

There is very little cooperation and collaboration between families with multiples, medical institutions, administrative agencies, educational institutions and research institutions. This situation leads to division and inequality of information between parties and within each party, for example, between multiple birth families.

3. Delay of Institution of Laws and Guidelines

Governments and academic societies have very few guidelines or policies regarding multiple births, including fertility treatment, compared to Western countries or national or international academic societies. Therefore, the future directions of support for multiple birth families are vague and unclear.

4. Lack of Specialists in Multiple Births

In general, few professional advisors in the fields of pregnancy and the growth and development of children have all kinds of adequate information to answer parents' questions concerning parenting multiple birth children.

5. Shortage of Infrastructure and Social Resources

Social supports for families with multiples are very limited, and not necessarily convenient to use. Moreover, these social resources are very different among municipalities in both quantity and quality.

6. Lack of Mental Support For Multiple Families

Since multiple pregnancy has high risks, the priority is put on the safety of the delivery, and as a consequence mental care for mothers is overlooked. It is also important to improve family competency, including the capacity to make informed decisions, and to empower families.

THE NEED FOR A POPULATION APPROACH AND A HIGH-RISK APPROACH

It is often pointed out that the level of the health conditions of multiple birth families is lower than that of families with single-born children. There is no maternal and child health policy focused on multiple birth families in Japan. *The Maternal and Child Health Handbook*, which is presented by the Ministry of Health, Labor and Welfare (MHLW) to all pregnant women, was designed for singletons and does not mention multiples. These disadvantages and this inequality of information start during pregnancy, or even during fertility treatment. This situation without doubt raises the risks of anxiety, experiencing difficulty and of failure in the child care or parenting of multiples.

The health conditions of multiple birth families are affected broadly by the social, economic, and cultural environment surrounding these families. It is very important to recognize that this situation is not limited to some special families at high risk, but rather applies to most multiple birth families with a variety of risk levels. As a social mechanism, many additional burdens apply to multiple birth families. These situations are not recognized as objective data. Many families do not recognize their risks accurately, and could quickly fall into bankruptcy due to a small, unexpected trigger. Many mothers claim that they can overcome severely difficult periods of parenting multiples through the support of twins clubs, but may fail at parenting and may commit child abuse without such support. There are many families with latent risks. We must change our strategy so that families are fundamentally supported.

Taking all these factors into account, it is obvious that ad hoc individual support without a clear purpose, as is presently available, is insufficient, and a 'population approach' focusing on all multiple birth families would be more effective. According to the population approach, the mortality or morbidity is higher among many people with small risks than among few people with very high risks. Therefore, making the overall situation slightly better would effectively improve the health condition of the total population.

Merely waiting for families to ask for help or to take part in the child care classes is less effective than providing information actively and positively to all multiple birth families. It is important to target families without information, families who have information but cannot utilize it, as well as families who have information and can use it. If the social isolation of mothers is a severe problem not only for the mothers themselves but also for the multiples, general improvements in the community to make it easier for mothers to go out with multiples is an effective approach to the problem.

On the other hand, multiple birth families are obviously a high-risk group in terms of maternal and child health. Moreover, many future risks are predictable during pregnancy or fertility treatment. Appropriate early intervention as a 'high-risk approach' would also be effective.

Community networks for multiple birth families would make both the population approach and the high-risk approach possible.

THREE STRATEGIES

These problems surrounding multiple birth families are never resolved by the efforts of families with multiples alone, even if they create local twins' clubs or groups. A more multidisciplinary collaboration including specialists from each domain involved is essential.

Moreover, population-based or at least large-scale epidemiologic studies to assess the long-term health and the social and psychological impact of multiple births on family, children and society are crucial to provide a scientific basis and to persuade policymakers of the importance of supporting families with multiples. The author has adopted three main strategies.

The first strategy is to monitor vital statistics and ART statistics concerning multiple births, although the latter are very limited in Japan. Monitoring and reanalyzing these statistics provide an important objective macroscopic view of the public health problems related to multiple births.

The second strategy is to provide evidence-based information to health professionals and policymakers as well as multiple birth families. A large-scale database of multiples, mainly twins, was begun in 1984. The primary purpose of this database was genetic epidemiologic twin research. However, it turned out that the data were also a useful resource for the provision of information on many features specific to twins, for example their growth and development, to families with multiples and health professionals. There are many tips for parenting multiples which are derived mainly from experience and intuition. Scientific data will add correct evidence-based information to these experience-based tips.

The third strategy is to construct a human network and family support systems at the prefectural level by means of the population approach method mentioned above, which has recently become one of the mainstream approaches to public health problems in Japan, especially for the prevention of life-style related diseases. It would be very difficult to construct a nationwide family support network quickly. Therefore, prefectural level support networks should be constructed initially.

Although the author may focus mainly on twin pregnancy and parenthood in the following description, the demands associated with higher-order multiples are of course similar but usually greater.

First Strategy: Making Good Use of Vital Statistics and Statistics on Assisted Reproductive Technologies

Background

With multiple births, there is a high risk of preterm births and low birthweight. Preterm newborns account for a high percentage of perinatal mortality, and, if they survive, they are at increased risk for health and developmental problems. Previous studies on the effects of multiple births have shown their significant influence on pregnancy and long-term outcomes. Preterm and low birthweight infants are more likely to require costly intensive care.

The author analyzed the secular trends of the impact of multiple births on low birthweight, premature delivery, stillbirths rates and perinatal and infant mortality rates to clarify the main public health effects of multiple births in Japan.

Outline of Japanese Vital Statistics of Multiple Births

Vital statistics of multiple births within the entire Japanese population since 1951-2007, collected by the MHLW, were gathered and reanalyzed. The numbers of all registered births were obtained according to plurality, birthweight since 1975 or gestational weeks since 1979. As the numbers of babies in multiples were not differentiated, these babies were treated in one category as multiples concerning live births.

Secular Trends of Multiple Births Rates

Recent multiple births rates have been affected mainly by fertility treatments and maternal age (Derom et al., 1993). The secular trends of multiple births rates are shown in Figure 2. Currently, more than 1% of all births in Japan are multiples. About 25 thousands live births are multiples, and the number is still increasing, with singletons constantly decreasing.

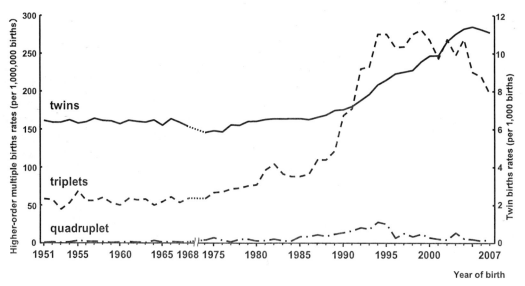

Vital statistics, 2007.

Figure 2. Secular trend of multiple birth rates.

Secular trends of multiple births rates for Japan and seven Western counties (Australia, Denmark, France, Netherlands, Norway, UK (England and Wales) and USA), which were easily available using Web site information (http://www.abs.gov.au/, http://www.dst.dk/uk.aspx, http://www.insee.fr/en/, http://www.cbs.nl/en-GB/default.htm, http://www.ssb.no/english/, http://www.statistics.gov.uk/, http://www.cdc.gov/nchs/, accessed November 12, 2008), were calculated to show the current situation of Japan. The definition of the multiple births rates sometimes differs among countries. Multiple births rates were defined as maternities of multiple births per 1000 total births, including both stillbirths and live births for Japan. It is well known that compared to Caucasians, the Japanese have a biologically low rate of spontaneous multiple births, because of the lower rates of polyzygotic multiples. Percentage increases of the multiple births rates between 1975 and 2006 were calculated for each country. While multiple births rates were very low in Japan compared to Western counties, the percentage increases of the multiple births rates from 1975-2006 was about 100%, close to those of Western countries, as shown in Figure 3. The multiple births rates clearly have been decreasing recently in some countries, suggesting social or medical intervention to reverse the rapid increase of iatrogenic multiple births.

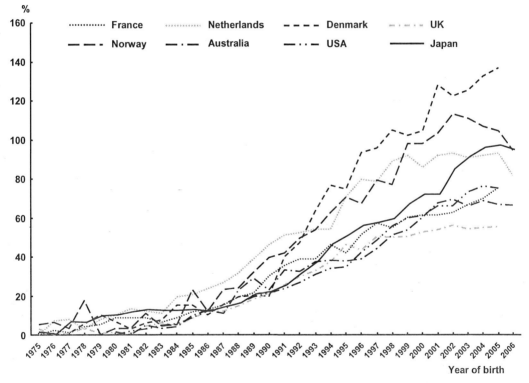

Vital statistics, 2006.

Figure 3. Secular trends of percentage increases of multiple birth rates in Japan compared with seven Western countries.

Low Birthweight and Preterm Delivery

Secular trends of relative risk (RR) and population attributable risk percent (PAR%) were calculated for multiples, with singletons as the reference group concerning low birthweight (LBW: <2,500g) using 1975-2006 vital statistics and premature delivery (before 37 weeks) using 1979-2006 vital statistics. PAR% is an indicator to clarify the public health impact of certain risk factors, and is used to estimate the total contribution of multiples on the LBW and preterm delivery. Attention should be paid to the fact that this indicator is influenced not only by RR, but prevalence of risk factor, namely the multiple births rates.

The proportion of low birthweight infants slightly but constantly increased. Recently, about 70% of multiples were LBW. While the proportion of LBW in multiples was increasing, RR was constantly decreasing, as the percentage of LBW in singletons was slightly increasing. The RR in 2006 was 9.

PAR% of three types of LBW is shown in Figure 4. PAR% tended to increase as a whole during the past 30 years. Recently, PAR% was around 15% as to LBW, 23% as to VLBW (very LBW, <1,500g) and under 19% as to ELBW (extremely LBW, <1,000g).

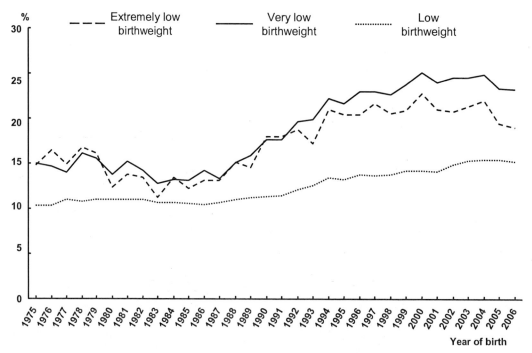

Vital statistics, 2006.

Figure 4. Secular trends of population attributable risk % for birthweight of multiples.

The proportion of preterm delivery before 37 weeks was constantly increasing. About half multiples were delivered before 37 weeks in 2006. As the proportion of preterm delivery of singletons was relatively constant, RR was constantly increasing and reached at 12 in 2006.

PAR% of multiple births for preterm delivery tended to increase linearly for long periods and recently slightly decreased and reached around 20%, as shown in Figure 5.

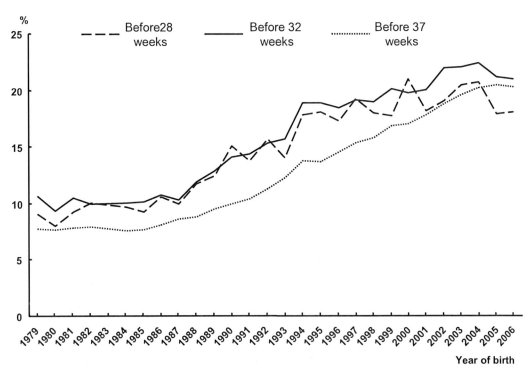

Vital statistics, 2006.

Figure 5. Secular trends of population attributable risk % for preterm delivery of multiples.

Multiple births rates increased about 78% (6.46-11.47) during the 1979-2006 periods. PAR% of multiples for birthweight under 2,500g increased 38% (11.0-15.2%), and for preterm delivery before 37 weeks increased 162% (7.7-20.2%).

Although estimating the intrauterine growth of multiples using the same cut-off point for singletons, namely 2,500g and 37 weeks, can be problematic, the present analyses were performed using this cut-off point according to many previous reports on multiple births.

In an international study, the PAR% of live birth twins before 37 weeks was reported to be 10% (USA) to 19% (France) from 1995–1997 (Blondel et al., 2002). This is in relatively good accordance with the present results in these periods. Another international study (Blondel et al., 2006) showed that the PAR% of live births multiples for preterm delivery before 37 weeks were 18% (Italy) to 25% (Denmark) in 1998–2001. The results of the present study in these periods were 15.7–17.0%, which was slightly lower, partly suggesting the effect of the lower prevalence of multiples in Japan compared to Western countries.

The risks of very preterm delivery (<32 weeks) and ELBW (<1,000g) attributable to multiples are much higher than the risks of overall preterm delivery (<37 weeks) or LBW (<2,500g). Very preterm delivery or low birthweight require intensive care in neonatal units, and are at high risk for neonatal morbidity and developmental problems (Topp et al., 2004). Therefore, the rising number of multiples will increase the burden on neonatal services and health services in general, as well as resulting in higher numbers of children surviving with impairment.

Stillbirths Rates, Perinatal and Infant Mortality

Inasmuch as all these indicators were markedly improved both singletons and multiples, multiples were still 2–5 times higher compared with singleton. The main reason for this elevated perinatal mortality is preterm and very preterm birth, resulting in low and very low birthweight children. Zygosity and chorionisity are important variables. Perinatal mortality and morbidity are definitively elevated in MZ and more specifically monochorionic twins as compared to DZ twins.

But, it is worth noting that prognosis is rather good as to multiples than singletons, if certain period of gestational weeks or birthweight is obtained. According to vital statistics, the infant mortality rate is lower in multiples compared to singletons, if birthweight or gestational age is near the cut-off point of LBW (2,500g) or preterm delivery (37 weeks).

Composition of Maternal Age

Maternal age class of multiple births is higher than that of singletons, as shown in Figure 6. This is because spontaneous multiple pregnancy and iatrogenic multiple pregnancy rates both rise with maternal age.

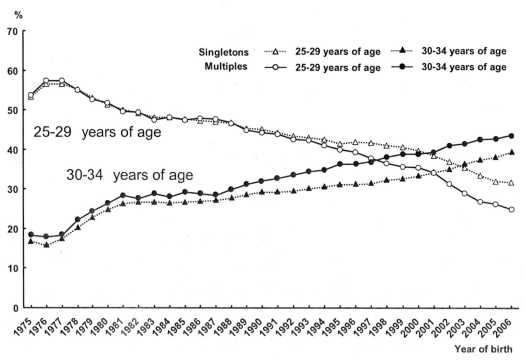

Vital statistics, 2006.

Figure 6. Construction of maternal age class according to plurality.

There are many primiparity mothers of multiple births. It seems that mothers of higher age have many physical and mental burdens for parenting multiples. Moreover, if mothers take fertility treatment, economic burden would be also added. This may be still the case as to fathers.

Statistics on Assisted Reproductive Technologies

ART statistics as to multiple births is very limited in Japan. The number is reported as multiple pregnancy, not real number of still or live births, according to plurality. So the figures presented below were estimation by the author. Using spontaneous multiple births rates according to maternal age class in 1974, when fertility treatment was not yet performed widely, and the all numbers of multiple births, including spontaneous and iatrogenic, according to maternal age class, the secular trends of percentage of multiple births according to pregnancy status was estimated. As to iatrogenic groups, percentage of multiple births by ART was also estimated. Births rates by ART were used as an alternative to multiple births rates by ART. As success rate of singleton births is higher than multiple births, the figure is slightly overestimated in favorer of multiple births by ART. Recently half of multiple births in Japan are estimated to be attributed to fertility treatment, as shown in Figure 7, and the half of multiple births in fertility treatment is attributed to ART. The main effect of higher maternal age was observed concerning iatrogenic rather than spontaneous multiple births.

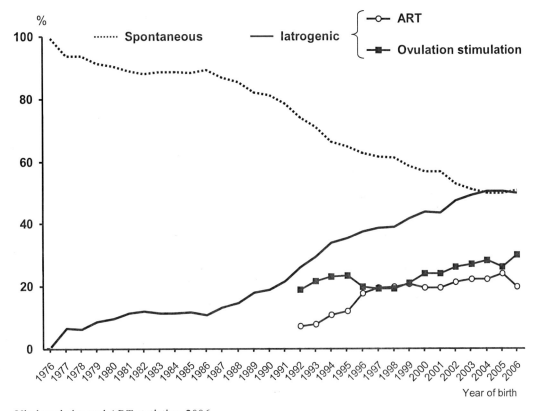

Vital statistics and ART statistics, 2006.

Figure 7. Percentage of spontaneous and iatrogenic multiple births (1974–1975 as reference).

Summary

The present results offer clear evidence of the public health impact caused by the rapid increase of multiple births in Japan. Moreover, these impact can be presented by medical economics (Ettner et al., 1997; Hall & Callahan, 2005; Luke et al., 1996), laws and guidelines on fertility treatment or multiple births (Bryan et al., 1997; Denton, 2005b; Leonard & Denton, 2006), the real situation of families with multiples (Thorpe et al., 1991), and social family support system or maternal and child health policies (Ooki, 2006c).

Second Strategy: Construction of Large-Scale Twin Database and Provision of Evidence-Based Information

Strategies For the Collection of Data On Multiples in Japan

Many countries including some Asian countries are constructing or have constructed large population-based twin registries. No systematic twin registry exists in Japan, however. There are four main types of data included in studies on multiples in Japan (Ooki, 2006c).

First, vital statistics can be obtained (Kato, 2004; Minakami et al., 1999), but it is almost impossible to obtain access to personal information concerning individuals.

Second, data from large hospitals have been used in the field of obstetrics, primarily for the purpose of managing high-risk pregnancies. The collection of obstetric data on multiples is relatively easy with the trade-off of selection bias in favor of high-risk infants.

Third, the Basic Resident Registration of municipalities can be used. This registration reflects the whole population of each area, and serves as a possible source for recruitment of families with multiples. Nevertheless, this method has many weaknesses. To put it briefly, cost-effectiveness is extremely low in the case of multiple birth families.

Fourth, there is a volunteer-based database of multiples, which includes, for example, data from mothers belonging to associations for parents of multiples. It contains more detailed information on the condition of multiples after birth; both vital statistics and hospital data have difficulty addressing this. Although volunteer-based databases may have some selection biases, cost-effectiveness is very high, if data collection is performed properly.

To fill the gap between vital statistics and hospital data, a volunteer-based twin database has been organized and input into computer from 1984 (Ooki & Yokoyama, 2003, 2004; Ooki et al., 2004; Ooki & Asaka, 2005) that is larger and less biased than hospital data and contains more detailed information after birth, a difficulty for both vital statistics and hospital data. The ideal way is to construct more representative, and nationwide database on multiples, which was impossible to obtain in Japan. The present database is the second-best possible method.

Outline of Japanese Database of Multiples in Childhood (JDMC)

The database consisted mainly of three independent groups.

The first group included 1,161 mothers and their twin children living in the Tokyo metropolitan area. All of the twins in this group—the school applicants group—had applied between 1981 and 2007 to the secondary school attached to the Faculty of Education at the University of Tokyo. This school was established in 1948 and adopted a unique entrance system. About 50 pairs of twins aged 11–12 years old who live in the Tokyo metropolitan area take an examination every year, and about 15 pairs are admitted (Ooki & Asaka, 2006). The enrolled twins participate in the twin study of education and related projects. All of the parents of applicants hand in a Twins Protocol Questionnaire, which gathers information on family structure; obstetrical findings on the mothers; the twins' physical growth, motor, language, and mental development; feeding methods; the twins' and parents' medical histories; and any behavioral problems of twins from birth to 11–12 years of age. Zygosity questionnaire was also contained.

The second group—the maternal associations group—consisted of 951 mothers from several associations for parents of multiples throughout Japan. The main contribution was from the JATM, as mentioned previously. Continuous data have been gathered from 2001.

The third group consisted of nearly 1,500 mothers who were recruited by medium or personal communication mainly from 2004, for example books and Web site. The data of this group are not fully input and utilized.

Mailed or hand-delivered questionnaires of nearly the same format were used to collect the data from the first two groups. Most medical findings were obtained from *The Maternal and Child Health Handbook*, which is presented by the MHLW to all pregnant women. The growth data of children based on mass examinations are usually recorded in this Handbook, and it serves as a valuable source of health information for pregnant women, as it contains detailed medical records on pregnancy and delivery, as well as on child care, for children up to six years old. This Handbook also presents the growth standards of weight and height/recumbent length and motor and language developmental milestones every 10 years, e.g., 1980, 1990, and 2000. The author advised the mothers to refer to these records when completing the questionnaire. Although this method seemed to be the most effective way to collect large amounts of data on twins after birth, it did not produce perfect longitudinal data. No information on detailed chorionicity could be gathered.

For the school applicants group, one of the parents of each applicant, usually the mother, participated in a medical interview by two or three interviewers (the author being an interviewer from 1987 on) in which their responses to the questionnaire were checked carefully.

These questionnaire surveys are now in progress. The response rates of the questionnaire were 100% for the school applicants group and more than 70% for the maternal associations group.

Ethical Issues

The methods of informed consent vary according to the subjects. As to school applicants group, the statistical analysis of the data was clearly written in the application document, and the detailed explanations concerning data collection by questionnaire and interview, and blood sampling for zygosity examination and health check were added as another paper from 1999. Moreover, informed consent was obtained from each twin and his or her parents in writing from 2001 on. The data analysis was also permitted by the ethical committee of this school. Zygosity diagnosis using DNA sample was permitted through the ethical committee of the Graduate School of Medicine, University of Tokyo. All the mothers in the maternal associations group cooperated voluntarily in this research, mainly through the presidents of their associations.

Method of Zygosity Determination

There are two types of twins, and they have different origins. MZ twins derive from the division of a single zygote, whereas DZ twins derive from the independent release and subsequent fertilization of two ova. Zygosity determination is the process of determining whether same-sex twin pairs are MZ or DZ.

The three important reasons for determining zygosity at birth are (1) medical, (2) scientific and (3) personal (Derom et al., 2001). Zygosity is particular importance in questions of organ transplantation and inheritance of specific diseases (medical). To determine the relative contribution of genetic and environmental factors to the human traits, comparison of similarity between MZ and DZ pairs is made in the field of human genetics. Accurate zygosity determination is essential (scientific). The question of zygosity has a special importance to the multiples and their families. Each person should be able to identify himself/herself without doubts (personal).

The need for an appropriate method of determining zygosity for use by twins' parents or health professionals have rapidly increased, especially when twins are too young to respond to questions. It is important to offer a simple and proper method to classify zygosity of twins in childhood.

Before the 1970s, macro-and microscopic postpartum placental examination and the study of phenotypic characteristics remained the primary methods of determining zygosity. More recently, however, widespread use of DNA polymorphisms has improved the determination of zygosity (Kyvik & Derom, 2006). Two main methods of zygosity determination of same-sex twin pair are DNA/genetic markers and zygosity questionnaires. Although the accuracy was lower concerning questionnaire method compared to DNA/genetic markers, cost performance is high and less invasive. Therefore, many twin registries adopted this method when epidemiologic studies are performed. Fetal membranes information is obstetrically useful to determine chorionisity rather than zygosity.

Development of Zygosity Questionnaire For Japanese Twins

More than twenty studies have shown that the determination of zygosity in twins based on questionnaires can be done with considerable accuracy, showing that the accuracy of the questionnaires employed is around 95% (Rietveld et al., 2000). The accuracy of the zygosity questionnaire for twins' mothers was re-evaluated using 159 MZ and 65 DZ twin pairs and their mothers (Ooki & Asaka, 2004). The twins were all from the school applicants group from 1985 to 2003. Their accurate zygosity was determined by means of many DNA/genetic markers. It was confirmed that most subjects of the present study did not have much knowledge of their zygosity. The results of zygosity classification using many DNA/genetic markers and zygosity questionnaire were compared.

The questionnaire was divided into two parts. The first part contained 16 items regarding mainly physical similarities at about 1 year of age. According to the answers, the following similarity points were given: 1 (no difference), 2 (do not know), and 3 (clear difference). The three questions of the second part asked mothers whether the twins were 'like two peas in a pod' and whether they were 'mistaken for one another and by whom' at about 1 year of age (Ooki et al., 1993). According to the degree of similarity, 1 to 3 (first two questions) or 1 to 4 (last question) points were allotted. Of all 16 questions of the first part, 'shape of fingers' and 'shape of eyebrow' were selected in addition to the second part three questions, as very informative questions.

The similarity points of five questions were totaled, with distribution from 5 (1,1,1,1,1 for each answer) to 16 (3,3,3,3,4 for each answer). The distributions of summed score according to determined zygosity are shown in Figure 8. The difference of distribution of summed scores between MZ and DZ pairs was clearly seen. If the cut-off point was set between the score 9 and 10, total accuracy was 94.6% (212/224), with accuracy of MZ equal to 95.0%

(151/159) and that of DZ equal to 93.8% (61/65). The determination of the cut-off point can be flexible according to the particular use of the data. A trade-off exists between high accuracy and a high percentage of unclassified pairs. If zygosity determination by DNA/genetic markers was regarded as the gold standard, the accuracy of the zygosity questionnaire was 97.5%, although around 10% (the score 9) of pairs were unclassified.

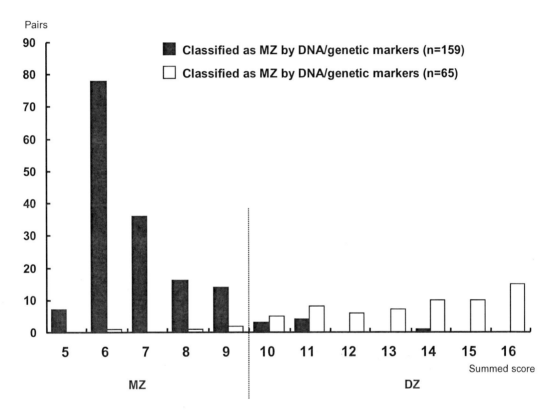

Figure 8. The distribution of summed score with cut-off point according to zygosity.

The results of simple summed score methods of five items showed nearly the same accuracy obtained from logistic regression analysis, suggesting the effectiveness of this simple method in practical use, especially when this questionnaire is used for the purpose of offering zygosity information to twins' mothers and health professionals more easily.

The similarity of twin pairs at about 1 year of age was quite informative (Price et al., 2000). Some items that were useful for zygosity determination in Caucasian samples, such as eye color, hair color, and facial color, were not useful in Japan. Mothers regard their children as similar or dissimilar intuitively and the reasons for their judgment are highly variable.

A limitation of this questionnaire is the retrospective methodology of the mothers' reports, which may be informed by factors other than the twins' resemblance as infants.

The zygosity of the JDMC twins was determined primarily by a questionnaire that was completed by the mothers in both groups. For the school applicants group, zygosity was diagnosed also by the use of many DNA/genetic markers for those twin pairs who were actually admitted to school. This is one of the advantageous features of the present database, as zygosity diagnosis is seldom performed in Japan.

Table 1. Basic Characteristics of Present Database in 2005

		School applicants group	Maternal associations group
N		1140 pairs	951 pairs
Year of data collection		1981-2005	2001-2004
Birth year of twin pairs	Mean ± SD (range)	1979±7 (1968-1993)	1995±4 (1986-2003)
Sex of twin individuals	Male/Female	1065/1215	982/920
Zygosity	Monozygotic	329/405	235/210
	Dizygotic	91/83/72/57	95/109/95/113
	Suspended	29/39	46/31
	Insufficient information	19/16	11/6
Age of twin pairs at data collection (years)	Mean ± SD (range)	119 ±0.4 (11-12)	5.9±3.8 (0-15)
Maternal age at twins birth (year)a	Mean ± SD (range)	29.1±3.9 (19-43)	30.7±3.8 (21-24)
Paternal age at twins birth (year)b	Mean ± SD (range)	31.9±4.7 (19-53)	33.3±4.5 (22-50)
Treatment of infertility	Yes	32(2.8%)	292(30.7%)
	No	1021(89.6%)	640(67.3%)
	Unknown	87(7.6%)	19(2.0%)
Gestational age (weeks)	Mean ± SD	37.5±2.2	36.9±2.3
Parity	1	598(52.5%)	655(68.9%)
	2-5	541(47.5%)	296(31.1%)
	Unknown	1(0.1%)	0(0%)
Neonatal condition	Healthy	1793(78.6%)	1491(78.4%)
	Hyposthenia (not so healthy)	304(13.3%)	205(10.8%)
	Neonatal asphyxia	128(5.6%)	130(6.8%)
	Unknown	55(2.4%)	76(4.0%)

Note: [a]4missing values as to school applicants. [B]14 missing values as to school applicants, 5 missing values as to maternal associations. [C]15missing values as to school applicants, 14 missing values as to maternal associations. SD: Standard Deviation.

Basic Characteristic of JDMC

Birth injuries of mothers or twins, such as placenta previa, placental abruption, coiling of the umbilical cord, neonatal asphyxia, and twin-to-twin transfusion syndrome, were observed to varying degrees. None of these were grounds for exclusion from the following study. In general, it was very difficult to set clear and consistent inclusion/exclusion criteria, as nearly 50% of the present subjects had at least one of the complications, apart from the severity. Moreover, no subjects showed apparent retardation of growth and development at the time of data collection.

The basic characteristics of the subjects including the obstetric findings of the mothers are summarized in Table 1. The numbers of subjects are that of data analyses in 2005.

Representativeness of the Subjects of JDMC

Birthweights were analyzed according to the subject's group and sex (Ooki & Asaka, 2005). Selected percentiles by gestational age were calculated. Smoothing of the growth curves was performed for both groups using a cubic spline function, and the curves compared with the only birthweight norms for twins in Japan (Kato, 2004) calculated by using the vital statistics of around 65,000 pairs of twins.

The number of gestational weeks for the maternal associations group was one week less than that of the school applicants group. The birthweight of maternal associations group was lower than that of the school applicants group, partly reflecting the earlier gestational age. Nevertheless, the smoothed curves of the 50th percentile of the birthweight showed little difference between the school applicants group, the maternal associations group, and the vital statistics (Figure 9).

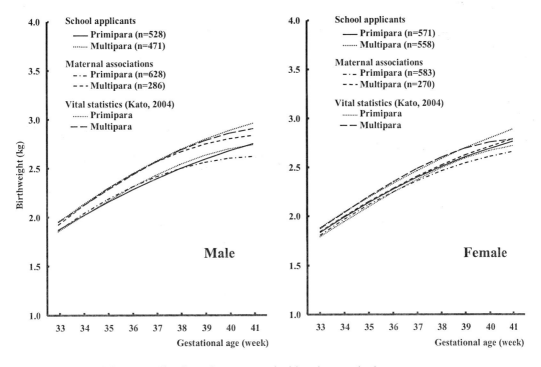

Figure 9. Birthweight percentiles for twins compared with twins standards.

The present subjects were normally developed twins. Therefore, birthweight seemed to be larger than the general twin population. Compared with hospital data, however, the present data more closely reflects real birthweight of the general twin population.

Birthweight discordancy was also analyzed in order to estimate the selection bias through which severely discordant twins are unknowingly excluded from the twin database. For each twin pair, the intrapair relative birthweight difference (RBWD) was calculated as a percentage of the absolute difference of birthweight divided by heavier birthweight (Sadrzadeh et al., 2001). The mean RBWDs between MZ and DZ same-sex twin pairs within each group or between groups were compared to test the selection bias of severely discordant twin pairs.

The curve of the relative cumulative frequency of RBWD according to same-sex pairs and opposite-sex pairs was nearly the same for both groups, and showed that as the 30% level of RBWD, the relative cumulative frequency of both groups reached between 96% and 97%, irrespective of the sex combination of the pairs.

The RBWD of MZ pairs was significantly lower than that of DZ same-sex pairs in both the school applicants group (p=.02) and the maternal associations group (p=.00), whereas no significant difference in RBWD was found between the two groups regarding zygosity and sex combinations. Data on growth and development might be influenced by birth year and recruitment methods. As the RBWD was nearly the same for both groups irrespective of sex combination, there seemed no fatal selection bias of severely discordant twin pairs in the school applicants group.

Features of the school applicants group are as follows: First, both twins were alive and showed no marked growth disturbance at ages 11 and 12 years. Second, the twins lived only in the Tokyo Metropolitan area. Third, all in the group applied to take an entrance examination for a university-affiliated school, which could exclude children with disabilities or low birthweight twins. These features may have an advantage regarding growth and development, although the direct effect of these positive selection biases is difficult to specify.

The total MZ/DZ ratio for the school applicants group was 2.5 (752/306) as of 2007, and that of the maternal associations group was 1.1. The MZ proportion was much higher in the school applicants group, partly reflecting the higher proportion of spontaneous MZ twinning in this period in Japan, but also partly reflecting selection biases based on the sampling process itself whereby MZ pairs are more likely to be applicants.

The mean birth year of the school applicants group was around 16 years earlier than that of the maternal associations group. There was a tendency towards higher maternal and paternal age, higher percentage of primiparity, and considerably higher frequency of treatment using ovulation-stimulating drugs or in-vitro fertilization in the maternal associations group. These reflect recent birth trends in Japan including singleton births.

Many reports have indicated differences between spontaneous and iatrogenic multiples in maternal and birth characteristics such as socioeconomic and educational status, maternal age, gestation, and birthweight (Helmerhorst et al., 2004). The maternal associations group clearly reflected some of these differences. Twins conceived spontaneously had shorter gestations, slightly lower birthweight, and lower maternal ages at birth compared with twins conceived with assistance.

Limitations of the JDMC

The following limitations should be always considered when interpreting findings obtained from present database.

First, the data were obtained from retrospective records, and the methods of measurement were not necessarily consistent. There must be the potential for recall bias.

Second, data collection methods of growth and development are different from national survey conducted by the MHLW, namely retrospective records vs. observation at the mass examination, and cannot be adjusted for.

Third, strict medical criteria regarding the definition of behavior characteristics or breast-feeding were not used. It would have been difficult to obtain correct answers of events that happened for some subjects about years ago.

Fourth, as all data were derived from normally developed twins, the results may have been overestimated. The present data do not necessarily show when twins fully catch up with singletons or the prevalence of clinically significant difficulties in twins.

Fifth, as the birth years of the present subjects ranged from 1968 to 2003, a period of 35 years, yearly trends may be considered.

Sixth, as the control data of singletons were not contained in the present database, the prevalence could not directly be compared between twins and singletons.

Main Evidence Obtained from the JDMC

Main evidence produced by the present database, which was provided to the multiple birth families and health professionals is described in brief. The number of the subjects is slightly different according to the study.

Zygosity Misclassification of Twins At Birth

It has been recognized that many MZ twins are misdiagnosed at birth as being DZ because they have dizygotic placentas (Machin, 1994). In Japan, this problem has been acknowledged several times, though it has never been addressed directly.

The circumstance of zygosity misclassification was estimated by using reports of twins' mothers of four independent participant groups (Ooki et al., 2004). All participants were mothers of same-sex twin pairs. The first group of participants consisted of 564 mothers, who were all members of the JATM (year of data collection; 1989). The second group of participants consisted of 225 mothers of school applicants group (year of data collection; 1997–2003). The third group of participants consisted of 112 mothers of the readers of the quarterly magazine TWINS (Bindeballe Publishing Company in Tokyo, year of data collection; 2001). The fourth group of participants was a further 730 mothers of JATM (year of data collection; 2001–2002). There was no overlap of participants.

The author collected information on zygosity by means of a questionnaire. For the second group of participants, the reported number of placenta was also asked. Reported number of placenta was classified as follows: one, two and 'never told'.

Reported zygosity was classified as follows: 'told MZ', 'told DZ', 'told both MZ and DZ', and 'never told' (including being told 'do not know'). The percentage of told any zygosity, namely MZ and/or DZ, was calculated, as well as by whom it was reported. About 80-90% of mothers were told their children's zygosity by an obstetrician irrespective of participant group. Therefore, the problem of zygosity misclassification appears to occur at birth in maternity hospitals.

The frequency of being told any zygosity at birth was calculated according to the birth year of twins, combining all subjects. Of the total of 1,631 twin pairs, birth year was confirmed for 1,496 pairs (91.7%). From 1960 to 1979, the percentage of mothers told any zygosity was 90.4% (85/94). From 1980 to 1989, the percentage was 80.4% (502/624), and from 1990 to 2002, the percentage was 80.1% (623/778).

Zygosity was determined using five questions of zygosity questionnaire with total accuracy of 98% leaving about 10% of participants unclassified. Zygosity was determined using many DNA/genetic markers, as well as the zygosity questionnaire, for 26% (58/225) of the second group. The second group was divided into two subgroups by the method of zygosity determination. The zygosity determined by questionnaire or DNA/genetic markers and that reported at birth were compared. If mothers were told their children's zygosity not at birth, but later, for example during their children's infancy, those data were regarded as never told. If mothers were told both MZ and DZ separately at birth, they were counted both MZ and DZ according to the number of reported times.

The results of told zygosity according to classified zygosity are shown in Figure 10.

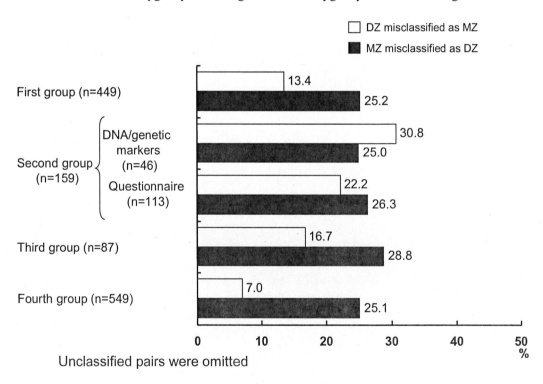

Figure 10. Percentage of zygosity misclassification at birth.

The percentage of MZ pairs who were reported to be DZ at birth was about 25-29% through all samples. There was no significant difference of misclassification ratio concerning MZ misclassified as DZ between all five groups divided by the method of zygosity determination. On the other hand, the percentage of DZ pairs reported to be MZ ranged from

7% to 31% and was sample dependent. In total, MZ pairs who were reported to be DZ was estimated to be 26% (211/824) and DZ pairs who were reported to be MZ was estimated to be 11% (36/333).

The percentage of MZ pairs who were reported to be DZ at birth was about 25-30% through all samples. This percentage was in very good accordance with that of MZ twins having dizygous placenta. According to Machin (1994), the percentage of MZ twins having dizygous placenta is estimated to be between one fourth and one third.As present data were obtained only from twins' mothers, another possibility is that they mistake the told number of placenta for zygosity. This possibility cannot be denied, as information from obstetricians or other medical specialist was not obtained. In Japan there are no data as to the training, knowledge, and opinion of obstetricians in hospitals or clinics regarding multiple births, containing numbers of placenta and zygosity. It seems rather difficult to obtain unbiased data from medical specialist.

Mothers were asked about their interest in their children's zygosity and the reasons. About 70% of mothers showed their interest in their children's zygosity for many reasons. One of the main reasons was their doubt about the zygosity they were told at birth. Although decreasing, about 80% of mothers are told their children's zygosity at birth. Considering all of these issues, medical specialists, who have much more knowledge than parents, should be careful what advice they give parents about zygosity, placenta and related information.

There are several limitations in this study. First, and the largest, was the information bias resulting from the collection of the data only from mothers. Second, the accuracy of zygosity determination using questionnaire is not 100%; therefore, zygosity misclassification by zygosity questionnaire itself could occur.

Growth and Development of Twins

Background

In recent years in Japan, the developmental norms have been examined every ten years (for example, in 1980, 1990, and 2000) and have been presented by the MHLW. The physical growth in utero and after birth, motor and language development of twins in childhood must be evaluated using the standards for the general population, that is, essentially the standards for singletons. According to these measurements, many twins are regarded as having poor growth and development, especially when they are very young, and this causes both the twins and their parents much embarrassment and concern. Appropriate data should be provided to families and health professionals.

(1) Intrauterine Growth of Twins

The subjects consisted of 1,061 twin pairs from school applicants group. Their birth year ranged from 1968 to 1990 (Ooki &Yokoyama, 2003). Because birthweight is the strongest indicator of the risk of perinatal death, birthweight norms are important both for clinical practices and for epidemiologic studies (Glinianaia et al, 2000). It is well known that intrauterine growth of twins differs from that of singletons. Many studies concerning birthweight standards by gestational age have been reported (Ananth et al., 1998; Arbuckle et al., 1993; Buckler & Green, 1994; Glinianaia et al., 2000; Leroy et al., 1982; Ooki & Asaka,

1993; Teng et al., 1994). Other body size parameters at birth, such as birth length (Leroy et al., 1982; Ooki & Asaka, 1993), chest circumference (Leroy et al., 1982; Ooki & Asaka, 1993), and head circumference (Buckler & Green, 1994; Leroy et al., 1982; Ooki & Asaka, 1993) have not been reported as consistently as birthweight. Comparing these characteristics in twins with those of singletons may provide clues about the patterns of twin growth.

Previous studies have been conducted mainly in Western countries. In Japan, relevant factors, such as the perinatal medical system, twins' birth rates, and body size of mothers, differ significantly from Western countries.

Factors that Affect Body Size Parameters at Birth

The variables considered were sex, birth order (first-born or second-born in twin pair), gestational age, maternal and paternal age at twin birth, birth year of twins, parity, zygosity, and presentation, and so on. The results showed that the contribution of gestational age was the strongest (R^2=.31, p=.00 for birthweight, R^2=.30, p=.00 for length, R^2=.25, p=.00 for chest circumference, and R^2=.18, p=.00 for head circumference). Sex and parity also contributed to body size parameters, albeit slightly. The effect of parity was second largest influence on birthweight, though the effect itself was small. Males were heavier and larger than females. Irrespective of sex, body size parameter became larger for multipara than for primipara. The effect of parity on body size parameters, especially on birthweight, was independent of gestational age. An effect of zygosity on birthweight and length was also observed. DZ were larger than MZ, but the effect was not as large. These results were in accordance with previous reports (Blickstein et al., 1995; Ramos-Arroyo et al., 1988).

The Problem Of Missing Data

Body size parameters were analyzed according to the missing data conditions; for example, birthweight was analyzed whether or not birth length was measured. From analyzing the body size parameter data in terms of missing data, it became obvious that birthweight and length were measured more often than chest circumference and head circumference. The number of missing values for birthweight and length were 8 (0.4%) and 134 (6.3%) respectively, whereas the number of missing values for chest circumference and head circumference were 283 (13.3%) and 281 (13.2%), respectively. Two possible reasons were (1) the avoidance of troublesome work, or (2) an emergency circumstance, in which there was no time to measure parameters other than weight and/or length. To confirm the latter possibility, birthweight or birth length was compared according to the missing data condition. Indeed, a significantly light birthweight was observed when the other three items were not measured. No significant difference of length was observed when chest or head circumference were not measured. Thus, birthweight could be underestimated if standards were developed using only subjects with a full set of measurements. To ascertain the possible cause of the absence of certain data, the frequencies of neonatal asphyxia according to the missing data condition were analyzed. In cases in which length, chest circumference, and head circumference were not measured, the frequency of neonatal asphyxia was 14.2% (19/134), 10.6% (30/283), and 10.7% (30/281), respectively. In cases in length, chest circumference, and head circumference were measured, the frequency of neonatal asphyxia was 5.1% (102/1988), 5.0% (91/1839), and 4.9% (91/1841), respectively. These findings strongly suggested that the reason for missing data was an emergency situation; these subjects may include a disproportionate number of unhealthy or at-risk infants. Conversely, chest or head circumference may only be measured for relatively healthy neonates. For these two parameters, it seems important to bear the possibility of positive selection bias in mind.

Correlations of Body Size Parameters

Using subjects that had data on gestational age and all four parameters (n=841 for males and n=962 for females), correlation coefficients of body size parameters were calculated. Gestational age was correlated with weight (r=.576 for males, r=.538 for females), length (r=.555 for males, r=.514 for females), chest circumference (r=.513 for males, r=.492 for females), and head circumference (r=.462 for males, r=.418 for females), in this order for both sexes; the results were in accordance with the regression analyses. Birthweight showed high correlations with length (r=.801 for males, r=.770 for females) and chest circumference (r=.828 for males, r=.810 for females), and a slightly lower correlation with head circumference (r=.691 for males, r=.688 for females). Birthweight in twins was well correlated with birth length and chest circumference, although the correlation between birthweight and head circumference was slightly lower, suggesting a need for growth standards on head circumference.

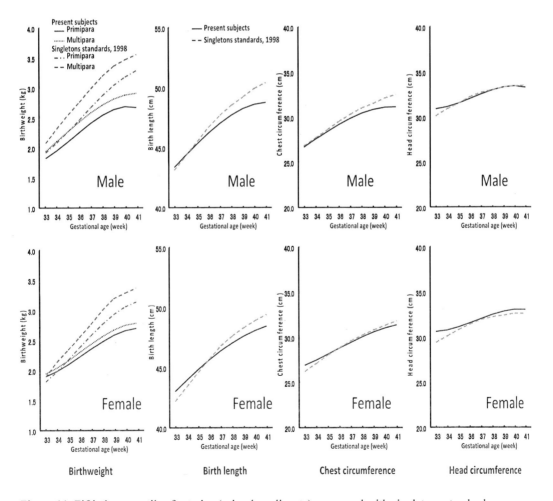

Figure 11. Fiftieth percentiles for twins (school applicants) compared with singletons standards.

Comparison with Singletons

Reference body size parameters at birth were analyzed according to sex. Means, standard deviations, and selected percentiles by gestational age were calculated. Smoothing of growth curves was performed by a cubic spline function and compared with previously reported norms for the general population. The general population standards that were based on hospital data presented (n=1,133) by a research group of the MHLW in 1998.

Smoothed 50th percentile curves are compared with singleton norms (Figure 11). Compared with singletons, the weight deficit started from 33 weeks' gestation and became more marked by the week. Not so markedly as weight, the size deficit according to gestational week was observed primarily in regards to length. No deficit was observed for chest or head circumference.

As to length, about a 1cm deficit was observed at 41 weeks for both sexes. Little has been reported (Leroy et al., 1982; Ooki & Asaka, 1993), as to this parameter; moreover, it has been pointed out (Buckler & Green, 1994) that length is unreliable, with many different measurement techniques. Nevertheless, the results of this study were in accordance with previous reports.

Chest and head circumference were nearly the same as or even larger than those of singletons, partly suggesting the positive selection bias mentioned above. According to Bucker and Green (1994), who analyzed over 5,300 head circumferences of twins, differences in head circumferences between singletons and twins are only evident with gestations longer than 35 weeks, and from 37 weeks' gestation onwards, the mean head circumference of singletons exceeded that of twins by only 5 mm. The deficit of head circumference in twins, though it exists, is certainly not as large as birthweight. This result suggested that neurological development of twins is protected against limited space in utero.

It is said that previous population-based and large hospital-based investigations do not agree with regard to the gestational age at which singleton and twin growth curves start to differ (Glinianaia et al., 2000). Besides, the difference between the results of most of the studies may partly result from the differences in study populations.

It is very important for both multiple birth families and health professionals to recognize that the intrauterine growth of twins is amazingly different from that of singletons. The growth of twins in utero is considerably restricted. Different adoption mechanism of twins from that of singletons may exist, although the system was not well studied and established. The present data offer reference birth size parameters for normal development through infancy, or the upper limit of intrauterine growth norms.

Birthweight Norms of Twins

Although the sample size of this study is not as large as population-based twin studies often performed in Western countries, especially for lower gestational weeks, figures for the 50th percentile of the present curves mostly landed consistently near the norms irrespective of parity and sex, as shown previously in Figure 9..

Birth years of the present sample were distributed over twenty years. It has been recommended that birthweight norms should be updated every 5-10 years (Arbuckle et al., 1993), because secular trends have been observed. In this study, secular trends of body size were not considered, partly because no strong birth year effect was observed by regression analysis.

(2) Physical Growth of Twins in Childhood

Background

There have been many studies on the physical growth of twins in childhood in Western countries (Akerman & Fischbein, 1992; Pettersson et al, 1976; Philip, 1981), including Wilson's detailed summary of the features of twin growth (Wilson, 1986). It is well known that the growth patterns of twins in utero and in childhood are very different from those of singletons (Ooki & Asaka, 1993; Ooki & Yokoyama, 2003). Most studies reported so far regarding the physical growth of twins after birth in Japan had very small samples and therefore only roughly classified age after birth.

There are two important and often confused dimensions to estimating the growth of twins: comparing individual twins versus singletons, and comparing the similarity of the twins within a pair by zygosity. The characteristics of twins' physical growth from birth to 6 years of age were analyzed and growth charts of normally developed Japanese twins were presented in comparison with those of the general population (Ooki & Yokoyama, 2004).

Preliminary Analyses and Data Combination

The subjects were 937 (maternal associations group) and 1,092 (school applicants group) twin mothers and their twin children. Before the data of the two groups were combined, weight and height in both groups were examined in detail (Ooki & Asaka, 2005).

Both birthweight itself according to gestational weeks and the percentage difference in relative birthweight within pairs were nearly the same, as shown previously. Moreover, the two groups were very similar to each other in body weight and height from birth through 6 years of age. For example, the range of body weight difference between the groups at the 50th percentile of the raw data was from -1.30 kg to 1.50 kg. These findings suggested that the groups were not very different, at least in their physical growth. Moreover, in both groups the data seemed to reflect normal physical development of twins in utero and after birth.

It is not always the case that growth charts are developed based on only one group of subjects. Usually, complicated methods of weighting measurements and modifying those measurements according to the number of subjects and so on are part of the development of growth charts.

Factors Affecting Body Size of Twins After Birth

Usually, the growth standards after birth are presented according to sex alone. In the case of twins, at least two additional factors that are not relevant to singletons might also be considered: the birth order in twin pair and their zygosity.

The factors that affected the body weight and height/length of twins at selected ages were confirmed by stepwise regression analysis. The variables considered were sex, birth order in twin pair, gestational weeks, maternal and paternal age upon the birth of the twins, parity, zygosity, presentation, the birth year of the twins, and the group to which the subjects belonged. Of these variables, gestational weeks, sex, parity, zygosity, and birth order in twin pair significantly affected both birthweight and birth length. The birth year of the twins and the group did not meet the 0.05 significance level. Lasting effects of gestational weeks and sex were found up to at least 3 years of age. The effects of gestational weeks rapidly decreased with age, while the effect of sex did not. The contributions of other factors were negligible and mostly disappeared by 6 to 12 months of age. The effects of parity, birth order in twin pair, and zygosity in twins on their birthweight and length, irrespective of gestational age, have been extensively reported. Nevertheless, in the present study those effects were small and mostly disappeared at an early age.

Growth Charts of Twins

The growth standards of the general population do not correct the effects of gestational periods to reflect the actual conditions of physical growth. Therefore, the growth charts for the twins were differentiated only by sex to estimate the difference between the general population and twins.

The selected percentiles of body weight (kg), height/length (cm), and body mass index (BMI: kg/m^2) at each age were calculated on the basis of accurate days since birth, and growth curves were drawn by means of a spline function. BMI is mathematically equal to the Kaup index, which has been widely used in Japan as an index for the physique or obesity of a child younger than 6 years.

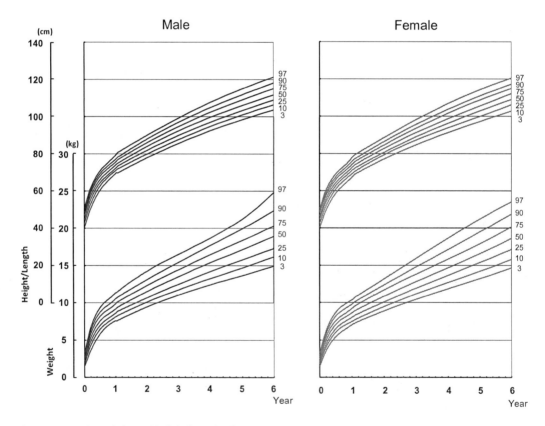

Figure 12. Body weight and height/length of twins by age percentiles from birth to 6 years of age.

The percentile curves of weight, height/length and BMI from birth to 1 year of age and those from 1 to 6 years of age are presented separately for males and females, although all age were combined in Figure 12, and widely distributed for twin mothers' associations and health professionals. It was extremely important to present objective growth charts for twins in childhood using the best available methods as quickly as possible. Moreover, there exists much less information on the physical growth of triplets. The growth charts developed in the present study will be more useful than those of the general population to estimate the growth of higher-order multiples.

The Size Deficit in Twins Compared to Singletons

The size deficit in twins was calculated as the percentage difference between the value of the general population and that of the twins divided by the value of the general population. Size deficits were calculated using the 50th percentile values of the growth standards presented by the MHLW in 1990.

The size deficits of twins in weight and height/length from birth to 6 years of age are presented in Figure 13. The weight deficit of twins was more than 20% at birth relative to the growth standards of the general population. However, the deficit decreased rapidly, to approximately 5% within the first 6 months, and diminished thereafter. The length deficit of the twins was approximately 6% at birth and gradually decreased, reaching about 3% by 7 to 8 months of age. It then decreased slightly thereafter.

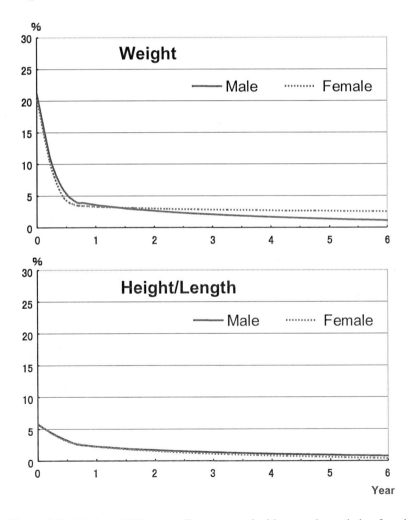

Figure 13. Size deficit of twins at 50th percentiles compared with general population from birth to 6 years of age.

Compared with the general population, the twins' size deficit was greatest at birth but decreased dramatically in the first 6 to 12 months, reaching as little as approximately 2%, around 1 kg for weight and 1 cm for height, by 6 years of age. This finding was consistent with the data reported by Wilson (1986). It was very difficult to determine when or whether twins fully catch up to singletons, as the present study did not use a complete birth cohort containing singletons. Since it is found here that most of the size deficit of twins compared to the general population is gone by 6 years of age, there is no practical necessity for specific growth charts for twins after that age.

Longitudinal Similarity of Body Weight from Birth to Three Years According to Zygosity

Mothers of multiples often concerns about the similarity or dissimilarity of their children within a pair. To clarify longitudinal similarity of body weight, 648 pairs of same-sex twin pairs, consisting of 505 MZ and 143 DZ, were analyzed. As shown in Figure 14, similarity of twins were strongly influenced by zygosity; more than 90% of MZ pairs were similar (percent difference of weight was within 10%), whereas 65% as to DZ. About half of MZ pairs were constantly similar after birth.

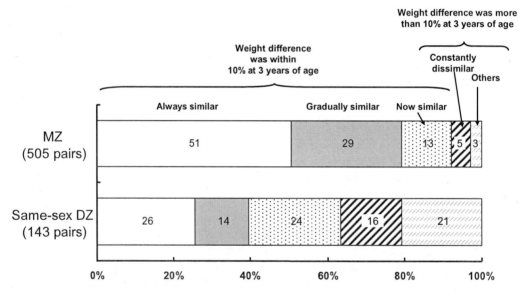

Figure 14. Longitudinal within-pair difference of body weight at birth, 6 months, 18 months, and 3 years of age according to zygosity.

Even if individual twin baby are born small, they rapidly catch up with singletons until one year of age. This rapid weight gain of low birthweight infant is not limited to the multiples. But, MZ pairs become more and more similar by one year of age irrespective of birthweight difference, whereas DZ pairs become more and more dissimilar. This tendency becomes marked with age. This is because MZ twin pairs, who have identical genetic composition, reach to the genetically determined their body weight. On the contrary, DZ twin pairs, whose genetic similarity is only 50%, equal to siblings in general, show variety of similarity. Therefore, if body size similarity of twin pairs were evaluated without considering their zygosity, the results give needless concerns to the parents in some cases.

Caution For Use of Growth Charts

These data were semi-longitudinal rather than complete cross-sectional. Consequently, the range of measurements in each age group becomes smaller than it would be in complete cross-sectional data, such as the standards for the general population. The clinical use of 3rd percentiles and 97th percentiles of this growth charts as indicators of growth retardation is not necessarily appropriate.

(3) Motor Development of Twins

Background

Many studies have shown that twins tend to lag behind singletons in terms of motor development (Chaudhari et al., 1997; Goetghebuer et al., 2003; Peter et al., 1999), although the causes of this delay are not explained simply by the earlier gestational age at birth or the lighter birthweight of twins compared to singletons and appear to be influenced by more complicated factors. The differences between twins and singletons are not limited to the birthweight or gestational periods. For example, the psychosocial environment can also differ between families with twins and those with singletons, and these factors may well influence early development.

Questions Concerning Motor Development

The subjects were 951 (maternal associations group) and 1,131 (school applicants group) twin mothers and their twin children (Ooki, 2006a). Six items regarding motor development milestones, namely, 'maintaining head,' 'rolling over,' 'sitting without support,' 'crawling,' 'pulling up to a standing position,' and 'walking without support,' were selected on the basis of *The Maternal and Child Health Handbook*. The age of attainment of a set of markers of gross-motor development and a within-pair difference were questioned in terms of month. Since data on 'rolling over' was presented by MHLW only from the 1990 survey, there is little data on this measurement.

The Descriptive Statistics

In the statistical calculation, the following adjustment was performed. Because the age given by mothers was by month and each month theoretically contained about 30 days, 0.5 months was added, assuming that the age at the first occurrence of each milestone in each month was normally distributed.

Reports on gross-motor development milestones in twins are very limited because of sampling difficulty. Among the available studies, Peter et al. (1999) and Goetghebuer et al. (2003) reported the attainment of the set of motor development milestones using hospital data of about one or two hundred sets of twins. The results were in accordance with gestational period or birthweight, which the present data showed to be longer and heavier than those reported by Peter et al. (1999) and shorter and lighter than those reported by Goetghebuer et al. (2003). The difference is thought to be associated not only with the measurement methods, but also with the sampling population (hospital data vs. volunteer-based data), cultural factors, racial differences, genetic background, and many other unknown factors.

The age at which various motor development milestones are achieved by singletons varies considerably in the literature. This variation is probably as much due to differences in the definitions of the developmental stages and the methods of collecting data as it is due to differences in the population environment or genetics (Goetghebuer et al., 2003). For example, birth year effects are observed for the norms of the Japanese general population presented by the MHLW, and some of this effect is thought to be related to changes in the definition of the motor development milestones.

Regarding these samples, there was no positive selection bias at least in the normal range of birthweight (Ooki & Yokoyama, 2003), compared with twins' birthweight norms by vital statistics. It is difficult to think that motor development selectively showed a positive selection bias.

Cumulative Frequency Distribution

Cumulative frequency distribution regarding the age at motor developmental milestones was compared with data presented by the MHLW, wherein the values of cumulative relative frequency for selected months after birth were presented. Standards of the general population in 1980, 1990, and 2000 were used as a reference considering the twins' birth year. Cumulative frequency distribution compared with general population norms is shown in Figure 15.

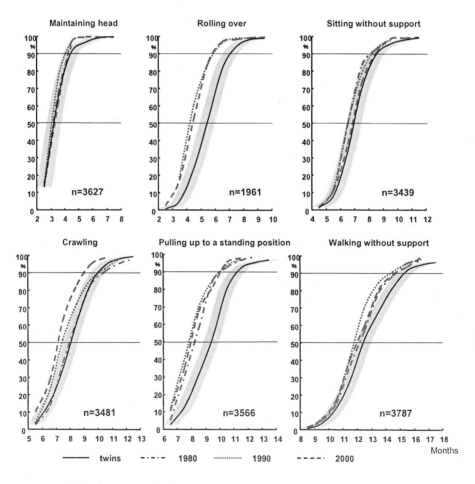

Figure 15. Cumulative frequency distribution of twins for the age of attainment of six motor developmental milestones.

The present data were obtained in terms of month. In general, an interval of about one month was considered. Therefore, both the earliest and the latest patterns were presented; thus, the results are shown as an area. Compared with general population curves, those for the current subjects indicated a delay of about one to two months for 'rolling over' and 'pulling up to a standing position,' whereas no obvious delay was observed for 'maintaining head' or 'sitting without support.' Nevertheless, the months at which cumulative frequency reached about 97–99 percent were nearly the same between twins and the general population.

The first possible explanation for a delay of several months for attaining some motor development milestones was the essential delay of development in twins compared with that in singletons, though the reasons for this delay are complicated and cannot be ascertained directly. Another possible explanation is the difference in the data collection methods between the general population and the present subjects. The present data were based on maternal retrospective reports, whereas developmental norms presented by the MHLW were determined based on observations during health examinations.

Factors Affecting Motor Development of Twins

The quantitative variables considered were gestational age (weeks), birthweight (g), birth year of twins, maternal age at twin birth, and the number of birth injuries if any. The qualitative variables considered were sex, birth order in twin pair, parity, zygosity, method of delivery, and health condition at birth.

The effect of gestational age on the motor development was consistently the largest. The effect of birthweight was also significant for most types of motor development, though the effect itself was not so large compared with that of gestational age. As birthweight is strongly correlated with gestational age, the effect of birthweight was thought to be weakened. In singletons, birthweight, length, and prematurity are recognized risk factors for developmental delay.

The effect of birth year of twins was observed on 'pulling up to a standing position' and 'walking without support' for children in the school applicants group. In this case, recent birth year showed a tendency toward earlier attainment of motor development. This effect was not observed in the maternal associations group. A possible reason is the difference of birth year between the groups. According to the growth standards presented by the MHLW, the age of attainment of motor development milestones by Japanese children in general became earlier from 1980 to 2000, particularly from 1980 to 1990. The present results for the school applicants group may partly reflect this general tendency. As the age of twins at data collection was about 11–12 years for all subjects in the school applicants group, the effect of age at data collection can be ignored. Therefore, the result reflects the birth year effect.

The effect of zygosity and birth order in twin pair is unique to twins. In the present subjects, no birth order effect was observed, as Goetghebuer et al. (2003) reported. On the other hand, the effect of zygosity on 'walking without support' was observed in both groups. The effect of zygosity on body weight of infant twins has been well observed (Ooki & Yokoyama, 2003). In this case, MZ twins are generally lighter than DZ twins because of the intrauterine growth delay. This effect decreases gradually with months after birth and disappears at about one year of age. In the present study, the zygosity effect was observed with regard to 'pulling up to a standing position' for the school applicants group, and 'walking without support' for both groups. In this case, MZ twins were delayed compared with DZ pairs. If this delay is based on the intrauterine growth retardation of MZ twins, the effects may well be observed in the earlier stage of gross-motor development milestones. One possible cause is thought to be the twins' extremely close relationship and relative indifference to the outer world, which is more often observed in MZ pairs. Therefore, the close relationship of MZ pairs, which gradually becomes obvious after birth, may be one of the risks of not only language development (as described later) but also motor development in attaining the ability to walk.

The effect of parity on 'sitting without support,' 'pulling up to a standing position' and 'walking without support' was observed for both groups. In this case, twins of multiparity lagged slightly behind twins of primiparity. According to Goetghebuer et al. (2003), a trend towards slower development in families with more than one sibling was found, suggesting that development could be related to the availability of the mother. In addition, the care given to families with twins may have an impact on development. In a family with twins, the availability of the mother is restricted even without other siblings.

The effect of birth injury, method of delivery and health condition at birth are very complicated regarding twin delivery. At the population level, these effect was weakened, confounded with many other variables. At the case study level, neonates with severe birth injury may well be delayed in total development, including motor development. Moreover, the delay observed in twins could be due to antenatal factors that do not affect birthweight or length, such as the mother being undernourished, reduced space in utero, or lower mobility of the mother during pregnancy.

The difference in development between singletons and twins could also be due to postnatal environment. The effect of parent-child interaction and communication on motor development was suggested (Goetghebuer et al., 2003). For example, maternal verbal stimulation has been shown to be a significant predictor of motor development in infants. Moreover, maternal mental condition or stress is thought to affect the motor development of children. Maternal depression is reported to be significantly associated with poorer infant mental and motor development at one year of age (Murphy et al., 1997). Mothers of premature twins initiated less communication and gave fewer responses towards their offspring than did mothers of singletons (Ostfeld et al., 2000). Some of these risk factors are more frequently observed in twin pregnancy and parenting.

Within-Pair Differences

Within-pair differences in the first appearance of motor development milestones according to zygosity are shown in Figure 16. Irrespective of subject group, MZ pairs were more similar than were same-sex DZ or opposite-sex DZ pairs. This tendency became more obvious as the set of motor development skills advanced. More than half of the DZ pairs showed differences of one month or more in attaining 'walking without support.'

Motor development was obviously similar between MZ pairs compared with that between DZ pairs. Mothers of same-sex twins often did not know the correct zygosity of their children. Therefore, the similarity between MZ twin pairs compared with that between DZ twin pairs suggested a role of genetic background in motor development, even taking into consideration the accuracy of data.

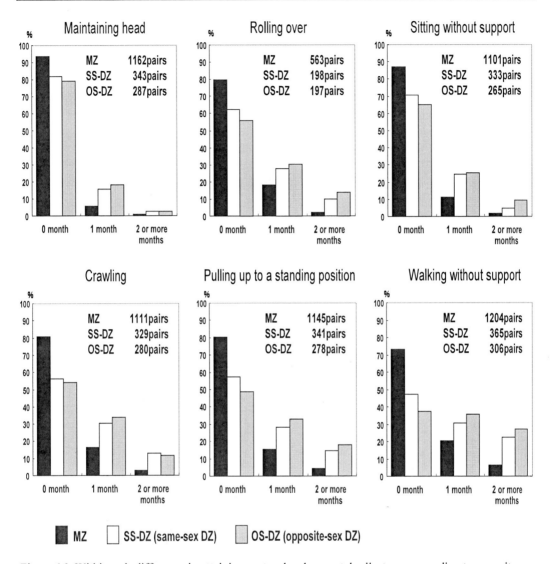

Figure 16. Within-pair difference in attaining motor developmental milestones according to zygosity.

(4) Language Development

Background

It has become a well known fact that twins tend to lag behind singletons in terms of language development (Akerman, 1987; Hay et al., 1987; Rutter et al., 2003; Thorpe et al., 2003; Tomasello et al., 1986), although the causes of this delay are unknown and appear to be complex. The purpose of the present study was to compare language development of twins with that of the general population (Ooki, 2005a). Moreover, some features of language development reported by mothers, which were unique to twins, were also analyzed.

Age at First Spoken Word

With regard to language development, the age at first spoken word was asked about by month. In analysis, only those twins whose first spoken word occurred between 6 to 25 months were used in consideration with the growth standards presented by the MHLW. Therefore, 1,207 answers, representing 614 males and 593 females of maternal associations group, were used in analysis.

In the statistical calculation, the same adjustment as the motor development was performed. Because the data answered by mothers was by month and contained about 30 days internal, 0.5 months was added.

Factors that affect the age at first spoken word of twins were confirmed by stepwise regression analysis. The variables considered were sex, birth order in twin pair, birth complications of mothers or twins, gestational age (weeks), maternal and paternal age at twin birth, parity, zygosity (MZ or DZ), birthweight(g), motor development (age at sitting with head steady), and age of twins at data collection. The results showed that factors affecting the age at first spoken word were sex (p=.00) and motor development (p=.00). In these cases, females and earliness of sitting with head steady showed a tendency toward earliness for the age at first spoken word, though the contributions of these factors themselves were not so large. The birth complications (p=.04) was also selected. In these cases, no birth complications showed a tendency toward earliness for the age at first spoken word.

Though the present data were limited to only maternal reports, considerably significant effects of sex and motor development were observed. On the other hand, no effects of birthweight and gestational age were observed. These factors appeared not so influential regarding the age at first spoken word. Recently, using systematic collection of detailed twin data from the Avon Longitudinal Study of Parents and Children, Rutter et al. (2003) concluded that obstetric/perinatal features do not account for the slower language development in twins relative to that of singletons.

Cumulative Frequency Distribution Regarding the Age at First Spoken Word

Cumulative frequency distribution regarding the age at first spoken word was compared with those presented by the MHLW using above dataset, wherein the values of cumulative relative frequency for selected months after birth were presented. Standards of the general population in 1990 and 2000 were used considering twins' birth year.

Cumulative frequency distribution compared with general population norms are shown in Figure 17. Only the range between 8.5 and 18.5 months is presented, which is how general population norms are presented. Both the earliest and the latest patterns were presented, the same as motor development. Compared with general population norms, that in the maternal associations group was about one to two months delayed. Nevertheless, about 95% of twins had begun speaking one word at 18 to 19 months.

The first possible explanation for this was essential delay of development in twins compared with that in singletons. Another possible explanation derives from the difference in the data collection method between the general population and the present subjects.

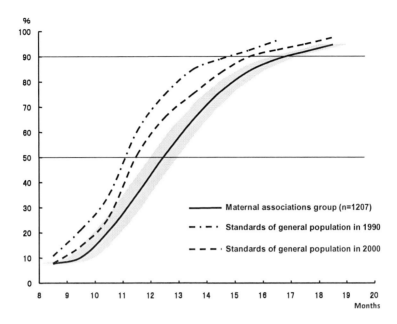

Figure 17. Cumulative frequency distribution of twins for the age at first spoken word compared with standards obtained from the Japanese general population.

Maternal Subjective Estimation of Their Twins' Language Development

For the school applicants group, the following two questions regarding maternal subjective estimation of their twins' language development were asked in addition. The first question was, 'In childhood, was your twin children's language development delayed compared with that of contemporary singletons?' The mothers selected one answer from the following three items: 1 (not delayed), 2 (slightly delayed), and 3 (considerably delayed). Significant sex difference was observed. Considerable degrees of delay in language development relative to that in singletons was reported by 12% of mothers of males and 6% of mothers of females. A slight delay was also reported by 27% of mothers of males and 18% of mothers of females. Considering zygosity, this tendency was obvious with regard to MZ male twins.

The second question was, 'To what degree was the language development of your twin children alike during childhood?' The mothers selected one answer from following three items. 1 (no difference [very similar]), 2 (slight difference), and 3 (clear difference). Maternal estimation of the similarity of language development within twin pairs is shown in Figure 18. A significant influence of zygosity on similarity was observed. About 30% of mothers of same-sex DZ twins reported 'clear difference' in development between children, whereas only 8% in MZ. The delay in males was marked in opposite-sex DZ pairs.

Males were clearly delayed compared with females. This tendency was widely recognized in twins as well as in singletons. The causes were more complicated in twins in consideration of the effect of their co-twin. According to Garitte et al. (2002), apropos of language development, it is more advantageous for a male twin to have female co-twin than a male co-twin. An effect of the sex difference of the co-twin was not clearly observed in this study, partly because of limited questions.

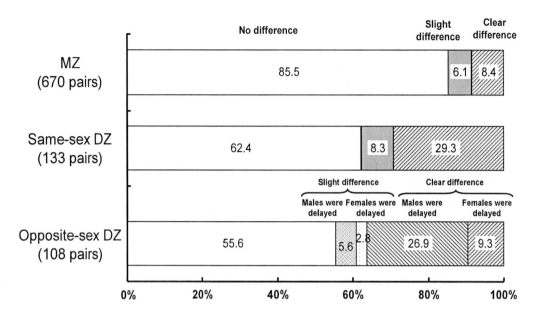

Figure 18. Answers to the question 'To what degree was the language development of your twin children alike during infancy?'

It has been reported that patterns of parent-child interaction and communication have environmentally mediated effects on language and account for twin-singleton differences in language development (Rutter et al., 2003). Language development of twins is very complicated, and is influenced by sex and zygosity in their various combinations. Moreover, the influence of so-called 'twin language' has often been reported (Bishop & Bishop, 1998; Dodd & McEvoy, 1994; Hay et al., 1987). In general twin language is often observed to be used only within certain twin pairs, and it cannot be understood by others. As yet, there is no established definition of twin language. About 40% of twin pairs show twin language, typically occurring in the second year of life and decreasing considerably over the next 16 months (Thorpe et al., 2001). Twin language has more often been observed in males and MZ pairs, causing delay of language development. According to the results of maternal reports, MZ males showed the largest delay relative to development in singletons, which finding partly supports the above findings regarding twin language.

Maternal subjective reports may be very informative concerning total development throughout childhood, as mothers are typically able to observe their twin children more frequently and attentively than anyone else can. Language development in childhood was obviously similar between MZ pairs compared with that between DZ pairs, irrespective of sex combination. Both members of MZ male pairs may be delayed to nearly the same degree, with the result that twin pairs became relatively similar, whereas DZ male pairs of twins may be delayed to varying degrees, with the result that twin pairs became dissimilar. This tendency suggested a role of genetic background in language development. Dale et al. (1998) reported considerable genetic contribution to language development by performing the detailed genetic epidemiologic twin study of the largest sample based on more than 3,000 pairs of twins.

Over the Course of This Study

In general, three main reasons for delayed language development of twins have been suggested: obstetric complications, twin-specific features, and postnatal differences in family interaction.

The present study consisted of two separate analyses of answers to questions of language development for the two independent samples. Nevertheless, the two sets of data showed two common results that have often been reported in the language development of twins. Twins tend to lag behind singletons in terms of language development and this tendency is more marked in male twins.

The age of twins in the maternal associations group varied, and not all of them had reached the stage of childhood at which language development is complete. The author used these subjects as a sample that more adequately represents the general twin population. The twins in the school applicants group had already completed the basic language development of childhood. Therefore, the author used this group to analyze total language development throughout childhood by means of maternal subjective estimation of their children.

(5) Breast-Feeding of Twins

Background

Numerous studies show the superiority of human milk for infants. Although an adequate quantity and quality of milk production has been documented even for high multiples, it seems difficult for mothers rearing multiples to breast-feed for many reasons.

If national data are used for health guidance, many multiples may be regarded as being breast-fed less. The reasons many people give for not starting to breast-feed multiples could be avoided if appropriate support is given by family members and by the medical team, if they are adequately informed.

There have been many studies concerning the breastfeeding of multiples in Western countries. These reports deal with the introduction of the skills or techniques for breast-feeding multiples (Flidel-Rimon & Shinwell, 2006; Gromada & Spangler, 1998; Neifert & Thorpe, 1990), and practical recommendations or guidelines for the specialist (Hattori & Hattori, 1999; Leonard 2003). In contrast, there is little epidemiologic research (Leonard, 2003) that focused on breast-feeding multiples.

Questions Concerning Breast-Feeding

The subjects were 951 (maternal associations group) and 1,140 (school applicants group) twin mothers and their twin children (Ooki, 2008b). Feeding methods were divided into three categories: full breast-feeding, partial breast-feeding (mixed feeding) and formula feeding. The detailed method of feeding and the percentage of breast milk consumed in partial breast-feeding were not obtained. Mothers recorded the duration (starting and ending full month) of each feeding method. The data were organized according to the full month. Therefore, the first 30 days represented 0 months.

The author excluded 159 twins with no data on feeding method. Thus, 4,023 twins (1,969 males and 2,054 females) aged from 1 to 15 years (mean 9.2 years, SD 3.9 years) of 2,018 mothers were analyzed in this study.

To analyze a trend-taking place over more than 30 years, the combination of the two different samples is the second-best possible method.

Breast-Feeding Rates of Twins

Breast-feeding rates were calculated from 0 to 6 full months. To compare the results with the official Japanese data on breast-feeding rates of 1 to 4 full months (1970, 1980, 1990 and 2000 surveys by the MHLW), the birth years of the twins were divided into four groups: 1968–1974, 1975–1984, 1985–1994 and 1995–2003.

In the 1985–1994 birth year period, which contained twins from both the school applicants and maternal association groups, there was no significant difference of feeding method between the two groups for any month.

The breast-feeding rates compared to those reported in Japanese national surveys are shown in Figure 19. The full breast-feeding rates of twins were lower than that of the general population. On the other hand, the combined rates of full and partial breast-feeding were close to those of the general population, except in the 1968–1974 periods.

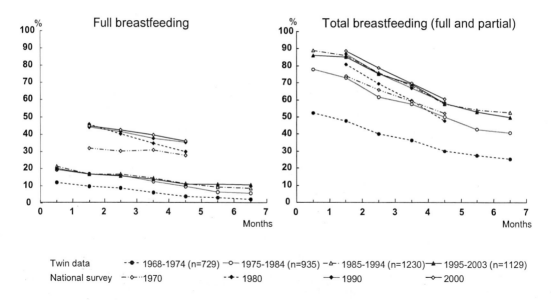

Figure 19. Breastfeeding rates of twins according to birth year group.

The breast-feeding rates of multiples vary considerably in the literature. This wide variation is probably due as much to differences in the definitions of breast-feeding, the methods of collecting data, and the sampling population. In the present study, a simple questionnaire was used to obtain retrospective data. The questions concerning feeding method seemed not so different from those used in the national survey in Japan or in other countries (Leonard, 2003).

In the present sample in the 1995–2003 periods, full breast-feeding rates were 20% and partial breast-feeding rates were 86% at 0 months postpartum, reflecting the importance of the definition of breast-feeding. The breast-feeding rates of twins clearly rose after the 1975 period. The most likely reason for this is that a national campaign of breast-feeding promotion was started in 1975 in Japan, followed by the WHO recommendation on breast-feeding.

Mothers of multiples achieve very high breast-feeding initiation rates as shown in studies of twins' mothers clubs, with rates of 70–90% (Damato et al., 2005; Neifert & Thorpe, 1990). This range, however, may well represent the rates that can be obtained in a highly motivated select group, and demonstrates the importance of support groups.

With regard to whether the breast-feeding rates between singletons and twins differ, several studies have been performed, and conflicting evidence has been reported. Population-based statistics in Wales in 2004 showed that the initiation rate of breast-feeding was 52% for singletons, 40% for twins, and 15% for triples (Flidel-Rimon & Shinwell, 2006).

Epidemiologic studies that have included twins and/or high order multiples other than singletons have constantly shown that twins/multiples are significantly less breast-fed exclusively at discharge and at 4 weeks of age (Ford et al., 1994), at 2–3 months postpartum (Thome et al., 2006) and throughout early childhood. According to the Japanese National Survey 'First Longitudinal Survey of Babies in 21st Century', exclusive breast-feeding rate during first 6 months was 21.5% in singletons (n=45,594) and 1.3% in multiples (n=975). Of many factors associated with exclusive breast-feeding, multiple births were the strongest negative factor for exclusive breast-feeding (Kaneko et al., 2006).

There exist several hospital-based intervention studies with relatively small sample size (less than 100 mothers). Despite an intensive promotion program, it was rare for multiples to be discharged on exclusive breast-feeding. Flidel-Rimon and Shinwell (2005) showed that a dramatic increase in breast-feeding rates in very low birthweight singletons and twins has been noted in recent years (1995-2002), due in no small part to appropriate hospital policies and practices. These reports suggest that if partial breast-feeding was regarded as a success, twins can be breast-fed as successfully as singletons with sufficient assistance and encouragement.

Within-Pair Differences in Feeding Method

The percentage of concordance pares were around 95% in all six months, and constantly higher in MZ than DZ pairs. Complete discordance, namely when one twin is breast-fed and the other twin is formula-fed, was seen in about 1% of cases in each month. Most reports on the breast-feeding of multiples did not consider the differences between individual twins. According to Gromada and Spangler (1998), MZ were more similar than DZ in terms of their styles of breast-feeding, including the length of feedings and time between feedings, which the mothers of twins surely recognize. The present results showed that MZ were more similar than DZ as to feeding method, partly supporting the above indication.

Factors Affecting Breast-Feeding

Maternal and infants' obstetric factors that affected the selection of the kind of breast-feeding of twins were confirmed. Following the previous guidelines for breast-feeding multiples (Gromada & Spangler, 1998; Leonard, 2002) and possible low rate of full breast-feeding, the author regarded full breast-feeding and partial breast-feeding in one category as 'at least some breast milk feeding' (Geraghty et al., 2004) . Multivariate logistic regression analysis was performed according to the birth order in twin pair to avoid overestimation based on the independence of the sib-pair data. As the effect of birth year was thought to be large this variable was always adjusted.

Gestational weeks for first-born twins, maternal age and use of incubator for both first- and second-born twins were selected at 0 months, gestational weeks for first-born twins, maternal age and use of incubator for second-born twins was selected at 3 months, and only gestational weeks for both first- and second-born twins was selected at 6 months.

The effect of gestational age on breast-feeding rates was consistently the largest when the birth year effect was adjusted, as was often pointed out previously. The effect of birthweight was also significant for univariate analyses, especially at 0 months. This effect was not found in the multivariate analyses. As birthweight is strongly correlated with gestational age, the effect of birthweight was thought to be weakened. In singletons, birthweight and prematurity are recognized risk factors for breast-feeding inhibition.

The effect of maternal age at twin birth and the use of an incubator on breast-feeding rates at 0 months were observed. This effect was partly observed at 3 and 6 months. In this case, older mothers and those of twins where an incubator was used tended to breast-feed less. The effect of sex, presentation, zygosity and neonatal asphyxia, which was seen in univariate analyses, was not observed in multivariate analyses.

The effect of birth injury, method of delivery (Caesarean section or not) and health condition at birth (neonatal asphyxia or not) are not observed. These factors are very complicated with respect to twin delivery. Neonates with severe birth injury may well be less breast-fed. For example, breast-feeding multiples after a Caesarean section is not a simple task.

There exist many reports that examine the factors that interfere with the breast-feeding of multiples, with relatively small sample size (Ooki, 2008b). Difficulties with breast-feeding multiples include insufficient prenatal and early postpartum breast-feeding education and support, delayed lactogenesis, insufficient milk supply, problems with latch and positioning, profound maternal fatigue, and parental mental health issues. Prematurity often interferes with breast-feeding (Nyqvist, 2002). More general factors, such as education level, income and smoking were often identified. Moreover, maternal mental condition or stress is thought to affect breast-feeding rates. Feeding infants was found to be significantly more stressful for mothers of twins than singletons. Socioeconomic factors are also likely to be important in breast-feeding. Some of these risk factors have been more frequently observed in twin pregnancies and nurturing.

In addition, maternal affect and/or coping attributes were likely to differ depending upon whether singletons or multiples were involved. There is a possibility that social and psychological factors—for example prenatal education for breast-feeding, mental condition or anxiety, and support from families and medical staff—are more important with respect to breast-feeding multiples than singletons.

The present study focused mainly on maternal and infants' perinatal and neonatal factors, and represents the first attempt to analyze the factors related to breast-feeding twins at the individual twin level. Geraghty et al. (2004) pointed out the essential difference in the definition of breast-feeding between multiples and singletons. Current methods of obtaining breast-feeding data for the mothers of singletons may not adequately describe the breast-feeding behaviors of multiples, because most data do not consider the difference within the pair. The present results suggested that inhibiting factors of breast-feeding multiples may in part differ according to birth order in twin pair.

Behavior Characteristics

(1) Handedness

Background

Left-handedness is a normal variant, but may result from early-life brain damage (Miller et al., 2005). There has been a long-standing debate on the complex correlation of the development of human hand preference with brain lateralization, and occasionally, the correlation of both hand and brain lateralizations with human mental development or diseases.

Twin studies provide a unique opportunity for the discussion of the origin of human handedness for the following reasons. First, twin studies have often been used to analyze the genetic background of handedness. Second, the effects of complications at birth on handedness were examined, as twin births itself is accompanied by many birth stressors or birth complications.

However, several problems have been pointed out regarding the use of twin data. The main issues are whether the prevalences of left-handedness between (1) singletons and twins, (2) MZ and DZ twins, (3) monochorionic (MC)-MZ and dichorionic (DC)-MZ twins, and (4) first-born and second-born twins are equal. The effect of chorion type of MZ on laterality, which depends on the timing of twinning, and is known as 'mirror imaging', in which MC-MZ pairs show a higher discordant rate of handedness than DC-MZ pairs. Including this background, the present study was performed (Ooki, 2005d; 2006b).

Data Collection

The subjects were 951 (maternal associations group) and 1,131 (school applicants group) twin mothers and their twin children. Handedness was assessed using the question, 'Which hand would your twin children predominantly use, if possible, to write a letter?' Mothers identified the direction of handedness from three categories: *right*, *either*, or *left*. The following question, 'Have you attempted to have your twin child change the hand he/she mainly use?' was also asked. The mothers chose from two categories, *yes* or *no*. This question was associated with the permanent change rather than the temporary change of hand preference. If the mothers answered *yes* and *from left to right*, their children were treated as left-handers. In the following statistical analysis, *either* was treated as *left* in accordance with many other twin studies. Information on parental handedness was obtained from the maternal associations group in this study.

Prevalence of Handedness

The results are shown in Table 2. As for the sex difference, left-handedness was more common in males than in females, although not necessarily to a statistically significant degree. Left-handedness was more common in the maternal associations group than in the school applicants group irrespective of sex.

Table 2. Frequencies of behavior Characteristics

	Source	N	Unchanged / Often	Right Changed[a] / Sometimes	Either / Rarely or never	Left	Missing
Handedness Males	S	1057	854(85.3%)	34(3.4%)	29(2.9%)	84(8.4%)	56
Femals	S	1205	1007(86.9%)	31(2.7%)	37(3.2%)	84(7.3%)	46
Males	M	982	691(72.7%)		259(27.3%)		32
Females	M	920	691(77.3%)		203(22.7%)		26
Finger-sucking Males	S	1057	182(18.1%)	224(22.2%)	601(59.7%)		50
Females	S	1205	273(23.6%)	114(19.4%)	660(57.0%)		47
Nail-biting Males	S	1057	56(5.5%)	228(22.3%)	737(72.2%)		36
Females	S	1205	63(5.3%)	247(20.9%)	871(73.8%)		24
Stuttering Males	S±M	1849	16(0.9%)	103(5.8%)	1654(93.3%)		76
Females	S±M	1943	7(0.4%)	61(3.2%)	1818(96.4%)		57
Tics Males	S±M	1789	12(0.7%)	96(6.1%)	1473(93.2%)		208
Females	S±M	1889	5(0.3%)	64(3.8%)	1607(95.9%)		213
Sleeptalking Males	S	1065	22(2.1%)	523(50.4%)	493(47.5%)		27
Females	S	1215	19(1.6%)	618(52.3%)	544(46.1%)		34
Males	M	792	47(6.2%)	427(56.1%)	287(37.7%)		31
Females	M	738	51(7.1%)	392(54.8%)	272(38.0%)		23
Half-sleeping Males	S	1065	7(0.7%)	237(2.31%)	782(76.2%)		39
Females	S	1215	7(0.6%)	265(22.5%)	904(76.9%)		39
Males	M	792	26(3.4%)	274(35.9%)	463(60.7%)		29
Females	M	738	22(3.1%)	213(30.0%)	475(66.9%)		28
Night terrors Males	S	1065	9(0.9%)	75(7.3%)	943(91.8%)		38
Females	S	1215	5(0.4%)	90(7.7%)	1075(91.9%)		45
Males	M	792	17(2.2%)	111(14.7%)	629(83.1%)		35
Females	M	738	19(2.7%)	114(16.1%)	577(81.3%)		28
Nocturnalenuresis Males	S	1065		492(48.8%)	516(51.2%)		57
Females	S	1215		481(41.6%)	674(58.4%)		60
Males	M	792	110(15.2%)	250(34.5%)	365(50.3%)		67
Females	M	738	60(8.7%)	202(29.2%)	429(62.1%)		47

S: School applicants group, M: Maternal associations group

Data were obtained from Ooki (2005b, 2005c, 2005d and 2008a)

The prevalences in the maternal associations group according to four age classes, that is, 1-3, 4-6, 7-9, and 10-15, were 32.6% (191/585), 23.4% (126/539), 20.1% (74/368), and 20.2% (71/352). These prevalences decreased until 7–9 and then stabilized after 7–9.

The prevalence depends on the age of the subjects at the time of data collection, the method of measurement, demographics and other factors. Therefore, the prevalence varies in the reports, which makes it difficult to compare the results.

Cultural pressure to use the right hand has not been very strict recently in Japan, particularly in urban areas. The high prevalence of left-handedness in the school applicants group may be partly related to the fact that the subjects all live in the center of Tokyo.

Compared with other large-scale twin studies, the prevalence of left-handedness (*left* and *either*) in the school applicants group was not high. Using 35 samples of the twin studies to date (with a combined sample size of 21,127 twin pairs) reported by Medland et al. (2006), the author calculated the prevalence in twin individuals to be 12.6% (5,305/42,254). The prevalence obtained in the present study in the school applicants group was not significantly different from this value. Moreover, when both sets of the present data were compared for subjects in the same age group, that is, the 11 and 12 year olds, the prevalences of left-handedness was not statistically different between the two groups.

Regarding whether the prevalence of left-handedness between singletons and twins differs, several studies with large sample sizes have been performed. Of these studies, those of Orlebeke et al. (1996) and Medland et al. (2003) showed that the prevalence of left-handedness in twins is not higher, whereas those of Derom et al. (1996) and Sicotte et al. (1999) showed a high prevalence of left-handedness in twins. In the study of Davis and Annett (1994) for a large adult population (N=33,401), twins were more likely to be left-handed irrespective of age group and sex.

Concordance in Twin Pairs

The results are shown in Table 3. The concordance rates of left-handedness were slightly higher in MZ pairs compared to DZ pairs as a whole, suggesting little or no contribution of genetic factors to this trait. The concordance rates according to zygosity in the present sample was not so different from other large-scale twin studies with more than 1,000 pairs published to date (Neale, 1988; Orlebeke et al, 1996; Medland et al, 2003), though the percentage of discordant male pairs of DZ was higher.

Secular Trend and Age Effect on Handedness

If birth years of school applicants group are divided into two groups, that is, 1968-1980 and 1981-1992, the prevalence increases slightly from 13% (162/1280) to 16% (137/880). Neale (1988) observed a slight increase in the proportion of right-handers in twins with age (range 8-80 years), and regarded this phenomenon as more likely to be associated with a secular trend, namely reduced cultural pressure to become right-handed, than with left-handers becoming right-handers as they age.

The age of the twins clearly affected on handedness in maternal associations group. However, prevalence decreased rapidly with age from 33% (1–3 years) to 20% (7–9 years).

Table 3. Probandwise Concordance Rates of Behavior Characteristics to Zygosity and Sex Combinations

	Source		MZ		DZ		
			MM	FF	MM	FF	OS
Handedness	S	N (pairs)	344	431	102	92	127
			0.18 (16/88)	0.28 (32/116)	0.13 (4/32)	.25 (6/24)	0.13 (4/31)
Finger-sucking	S	N (pairs)	311	393	68	66	112
			0.89 (218/245)	0.81 (280/347)	0.69 (40/58)	0.72 (42/58)	0.66 (56/85)
Nail-biting	S	N (pairs)	311	393	68	66	112
			0.72 (132/184)	0.65 (144/220)	0.41 (14/34)	0.52 (16/31)	0.48 (24/50)
Stuttering	S±M	N (pairs)	512	573	141	148	278
			0.51 (32/63)	0.54 (22/41)	0.10 (2/20)	0.15 (2/13)	0.09 (2/23)
Tics	S±M	N (pairs)	472	518	124	141	248
			0.42 (26/67)	0.30 (14/46)	0.24 (4/17)	0.15 (2/13)	0.29 (4/14)
Sleeptalking	S	N (pairs)	318	387	98	104	124
			0.91 (308/337)	0.90 (400/445)	0.69 (68/99)	.62 (48/78)	0.64 (74/16)
	M	N (pairs)	178	156	98	104	155
			0.88 (200/226)	0.89 (182/205)	0.72 (86/119)	0.73 (90/123)	.70 (136/195)
Half-sleeping	S	N (pairs)	316	389	86	82	124
			0.68 (102/151)	0.77 (138/179)	0.47 (20/43)	0.43 (18/42)	0.53 (30/57)
	M	N (pairs)	179	157	99	104	153
			0.81 (116/143)	0.77 (92/120)	0.67 (46/69)	0.54 (38/70)	0.46 (44/96)
Night terrors	S	N (pairs)	317	387	87	82	124
			0.60 (28/47)	0.68 (42/62)	0.21 (4/19)	0.18 (2/11)	0.36 (8/22)
	M	N (pairs)	177	156	97	103	154
			0.73 (36/49)	0.71 (40/56)	0.38 (12/32)	0.50 (22/44)	0.45 (28/62)
Nocturnalenuresis	S	N (pairs)	312	379	82	83	124
			0.94 (290/310)	0.91 (282/311)	0.76 (52/68)	0.87 (60/69)	0.77 (96/124)
	M	N (pairs)	169	154	94	102	145
			0.85 (148/175)	0.83 (104/125)	0.65 (58/89)	0.64 (46/72)	0.57 (70/123)

S: School applicants group, M: Maternal associations group, MZ: Monozygotic, DZ: Dizygotic, MM: Male-male, FF: Female-female, OS: Opposite sex.

Probandwise concordance rates were cal:culated as 2×C/(2×C+D), where "C" denotes the numbers of affected concordant pairs and "D" denotes the numbers of discordant pairs.

Data were obtained from Ooki (2005b, 2005c, 2005d and 2008a)

This rapid decrease did not seem to be explained by a secular trend or cultural pressure. According to Janssen (2004), handedness changes frequently during normal development and seems to stabilize only at the ages of 3 to 4 years. The higher prevalence of the maternal associations group than the school applicants group seems to reflect the difference in age distribution between the two groups. One possible explanation is that many young twins in the maternal associations group are 'ambidextrous', who were defined as left-handed. The prevalence of ambidextrous subjects in the maternal associations group decreased from 8% (90/1,124) in 1–6 years to 2% (13/720) in 7–15 years. Perhaps many ambidextrous subjects become right-handed as they grow older, although a direct estimation requires longitudinal data.

Factors Associated with Handedness

Multivariate logistic analysis showed that birth year (odds ratio: OR=1.02) and neonatal asphyxia (OR=1.62) were selected in the school applicants group, and sex (OR=1.34), the age of twins (OR=1.56), parity (OR=1.31), gestational age (OR=1.58), and family history (OR=1.82) were selected in the maternal associations group. Unfortunately, the data of family history was not obtained as to school applicants group. Birthweight was not selected, whereas gestational age was selected. The largest OR of the family history was obtained.

Several birth stressors, such as neonatal asphyxia, birth complications, and a short gestational age were associated with left-handedness, although specific determinants were not detected. According to Williams et al. (1992), both infant resuscitation and the birth stress significantly affected the handedness of 5-year-old children. The present study also supports this finding.

The effects of zygosity, chorionicity/placentation, birth order in twin pair, and sex combination on sidedness are problems unique in twins. Many studies of such problems have been performed, and controversial results have been obtained. Regarding the difference in prevalence of zygosity, Sicotte et al. (1999) and Medland et al. (2003) did not observe a difference between MZ and DZ twins, whereas Orlebeke et al. (1996) observed a higher prevalence of left-handedness in MZ twins, particularly males. The present results did not show a zygosity difference in handedness.

The effect of birth order in twin pair has been discussed. According to James and Orlebeke (2002), the hazards associated with being first-born in twin pairs (e.g., trauma) are more closely associated with left-handedness than those associated with being second-born (e.g., hypoxia). Derom et al. (1996) observed a slightly higher prevalence of left-handedness in first-born twins than in second-born twins, but not statistically significant. On the other hand, Elkadi et al. (1999) and Medland et al. (2003) did not observe birth order effects. Moreover, Boklage (1981) observed a 1.8-fold higher prevalence of left-handedness in the second-born members of same-sex discordant pairs. The results were thus inconsistent. The present results did not reveal any association between birth order in twin pair and left-handedness.

As to maternal associations group, the effect of family history was the largest. Familial left-handedness, including families with twin children, has been well established from research performed decades ago (Boklage, 1981). However, they do not provide a conclusive explanation of the causes of left-handedness, as genetic and shared environmental factors were not separated by familial handedness. A recent study by the author (Ooki, 2005d) showed that the etiologies of handedness are mostly attributable to non-genetic factors rather than genetic factors. According to Bishop (2001), who used 150 families with twin pairs, the parent-offspring similarity of handedness was attributed to cultural transmission rather than to genetic effects.

No factors associated with handedness specific to twins were identified, although being a twin itself may have some effects.

(2) Several Behavior Characteristics in Childhood

Background

Finger-sucking, nail-biting, stuttering, tics, sleeptalking, half-sleeping, night terrors and nocturnal enuresis occur often in childhood. As with many complex behavioral traits or disorders, most of children with these behaviors in the population are probably mild in severity. Among young children, partial or complete recovery from such behaviors is common. Parents, however, are frequently concerned about their children's repetitive or stereotyped behavior patterns. Since behavioral characteristics in childhood vary greatly with age, it is desirable to increase the accuracy of information about the age of occurrence and duration using longitudinal data.

Some brief results concerning habitual behaviors of twins were presented in Tables 2 and 3. The results have been reported in detail elsewhere (Ooki, 2005b, 2005c, 2006b, 2008a)

Data Collection

The mothers identified the frequency from four categories: *often, sometimes, rarely or never*, or *don't know*. The frequency of finger-sucking between 0 to 2 years of age, tics and stuttering of 3 or more years of age, and other traits of all years of age were analyzed. As to nocturnal enuresis in the school applicants group, *often* and *sometimes* were not differentiated. The difficult terms such as tics and night terrors were explained in easily understandable language.

2.1) Finge- Sucking and Nail-Biting

Finger-sucking occurs in the early months and peaks at about 18 months to 2 years. Most children stop finger-sucking by age 4, although a few continue to suck their fingers into adulthood. Nail-biting is also a common oral habit in children and young adults, but is a rare habit in children under the age of 3 years. From the ages of 3 to 6 years, there is a significant increase in the number of children who bite their nails (Ooki, 2005c).

Often, finger-sucking is simply a pleasurable activity unrelated to any underlying emotional or other disturbance (Peterson & Schneider, 1991). Finger-sucking before the ages of 4 to 6 is typically not considered problematic, although there are dental concerns (Watson et al., 2002). After this age, however, chronic finger-sucking may lead to dental problems, and problems with peers or parents. The role of anxiety, nervousness, tension or stress in the etiology of nail-biting has been well documented.

Prevalence of Finger-Sucking and Nail-Biting

Finger-sucking was significantly more common in females than in males (Table 2). There was no sex difference in nail-biting. Finger-sucking and nail-biting were not significantly related to zygosity and birth order in twin pair.

The prevalence of behavior characteristics in childhood reported in the literature has been widely divergent. The reason for this variation partly reflects differences across studies in sample characteristics, for example subject age, sampling methods, and subject selection (clinic-based vs. population-based), as well as diagnostic criteria.

Moreover, the influence of cultural variations on finger-sucking (Lubitz, 1992), including the widespread use of a dummy or pacifier, have been pointed out. There have been few reports, however, on the prevalence of these habits in twins. Of them, Bakwin (1971a) reported that 30% (203/676) of twins aged 6 to 18 years engaged in nail-biting. The prevalence of finger-sucking and nail-biting in the present sample was within the range of various reports.

Parent-to-Offspring Transmission of Nail-Biting in Childhood

The nail-biting of the parents when they were children was classified according to the number of parents who had this habit. A strong parent-offspring relationship was observed irrespective of birth order in twin pair. If both parents were nail-biters in childhood, their children showed about a 3 to 4 times higher prevalence of nail-biting than children whose parents had not had this habit. The familial transmission of nail-biting was recognized decades ago. According to Bakwin (1971a), the prevalence of nail-biting in offspring decreases according to the number of parents who were nail-biters during their own childhood. The prevalence in the children of parents who had been nail-biters was almost three times greater than in children whose both parents had not been nail-biters (Bakwin, 1971a). The present results also provided good support for these tendencies.

Concordance in Twin Pairs

All probandwise concordance rates of MZ pairs were higher than those observed in DZ pairs (Table 3), suggesting a genetic contribution to both finger-sucking and nail-biting.

A twin study of nail-biting using large samples has only been performed by Bakwin (1971a). He analyzed 203 twins of 338 same-sex twin pairs who showed nail-biting, and found higher pairwise (not probandwise) concordance rates in MZ pairs than in same-sex DZ pairs. Bakwin (1971b) also performed a twin study of persistent finger-sucking, using the same sample, and found a higher pairwise concordance rate in MZ pairs than in DZ ones.

2.2) Stuttering and Tics

Stuttering and tics are both puzzling and debilitating traits that occur often in childhood. Despite nearly a century of research activity, the etiology of stuttering and tics remains uncertain. Within the last few decades, however, promising findings from behavioral genetic studies have provided evidence that genetic factors may be important in the expression of stuttering and tics in childhood (Ooki, 2005b).

Prevalence of Stuttering and Tics

Stuttering and tics were significantly more common in males than in females (Table 2). Stuttering and tics were not significantly related to zygosity and birth order in twin pair.

The prevalence of stuttering reported in the literature has been widely divergent, from a low of 0.7% to a high of 15.4%. The morbid risk for stuttering is usually cited as 5.0%, a figure reflecting the average across studies. The prevalence of tics has also been divergent, from 2.9% to more than 20% of school children. The prevalence of stuttering and tics was not so different from previous reports. Moreover, the tendency of higher prevalence in males for both stuttering and tics was also in accordance with that observed in singletons, suggesting partly the effects of sex difference on both traits.

Concordance in Twin Pairs

All probandwise concordance rates of MZ pairs were higher than those observed in DZ pairs (Table 3), strongly suggesting the role of genetic background.

The genetic contributions to stuttering (Yairi et al., 1996; Ambrose et al., 1997) and tics (Godai et al., 1976) have long been pointed out. Of these, twin studies have been relatively few in number. Andrews et al. (1991) and Felsenfeld et al. (2000) showed the genetic contribution to stuttering by analyzing a large Australian Twin Cohort.

2.3) Behaviors During Sleep

As pointed out by numerous studies, many habitual behaviors during sleep in childhood, for example sleeptalking, nocturnal enuresis, teeth-grinding, night terrors, sleepwalking are genetically controlled. In the present study the author analyzed four behavior characteristics often seen during sleep in childhood (Ooki, 2008a). These traits are usually, if anything, normal habits in the broad sense, rather than behavioral problems or disorders.

Prevalence of Habitual Sleep Behaviors in Children

Two subject groups (school applicants group and maternal associations group) were analyzed separately so their results could be compared and to provide more information. Significant sex difference was observed only for nocturnal enuresis in both groups, with males showing significantly higher frequencies (Table 2). No traits were significantly related to zygosity according to birth order in twin pair.

The prevalence of behaviors during sleep has varied depending on the report, and it is somewhat difficult to compare the results (Hublin et al., 1998a). As to night terrors, one possible caution is that night crying may have been misclassified into night terrors in younger age children. The prevalences of sleeptalking, half-sleeping (being half-asleep, doughy with sleep, or sleep drunkenness) and night terrors were all higher in the maternal associations group than in the school applicants group in this study, suggesting partly the effects of age difference of both groups. Nevertheless, the frequencies of the present study were not so different from previous reports on the prevalence of these traits, summarized by Hublin et al. (1998a, 1998b, 1999). Moreover, the following results of present study have been observed generally in singletons. First, sleeptalking, half-sleeping, and night terrors occurred in that order of frequency. Second, males showed higher frequencies as to nocturnal enuresis compared to females.

Probandwise Concordance Rates

All probandwise concordance rates of MZ pairs were significantly greater than those observed in DZ pairs, except for nocturnal enuresis of females in the school applicants group (Table 3), strongly suggesting the role of genetic background.

Some Practical Guidelines

(1) Physical Growth, Development and Habitual Behaviors

Twins showed a tendency to lag behind singletons in terms of physical growth and motor and language development in the present successive studies, as many studies have already pointed out. Nevertheless, as twins mature, their development tends to catch up with that of singletons.

According to the interviews with mothers, the following advice was frequently given upon health examinations by health professionals without decisive evidence. 'Because your children are twins, delay of the growth and development compared with singletons, is a natural event', or 'Your children will catch up with singletons sooner or later. Therefore, do not worry'. Surely this advice offers temporary comfort to mothers, but provides no essential solution. Concern about growth and development, especially language development, is one of the most common and most serious questions about their children that parents, especially those of twins, bring to their pediatricians or public health nurses. Although a substantial proportion of delays in twins seemed to resolve themselves in the preschool or early school years.

It does not seem that being twin itself biologically raise the prevalence of habitual behaviors, such as nail-biting, tics, and sleep talking, although the situation of being twin pairs may raise the frequency psycho-socially.

Moreover, MZ pairs are in general more similar than DZ pairs, with variety of degrees, concerning almost all traits of growth, development and habitual behaviors. In other words, DZ pairs show considerable within-pair differences or discordance. Therefore, it is of little meaning when estimating or advising the similarity of twin pairs without considering their zygosity. Thus, the author consider zygosity as one of the key concepts for both genetic studies and maternal and child health care of twins. This result shows apparent fact that human traits in childhood are more or less influenced by complicated genetic as well as environmental factors, some of which for twins are apparently different from those for singletons.

Mothers may feel anxious over the results of two types of comparison: comparison of twins with singletons and comparison between two their children. In the situation of a medical examination of twins, health professionals should be aware that even within twin pairs, growth and development can differ considerably, and the existence of difference or discordance within a pair is usually in itself of little consequence. Moreover, total estimation of growth and development as twin children is essential, which should be take resemblance and difference of twins from singletons into consideration.

(2) Breast-Feeding Multiples

Combined rates of full and partial breast-feeding were close to those of the general population. It was desirable to raise the full breast-feeding rates of multiples while maintaining the total (full and partial) breast-feeding rates by following the above guidelines.

The most influential factor that negatively correlated with breast-feeding from 0 to 6 months was gestational weeks. Antenatal counseling, hospital practice, the attitude of the medical team towards breast-feeding, the expertise of the public health nurse, and national policies on maternal and child health could change the current situation. However, when breast-feeding is not possible, the health professionals must carefully avoid judgmental approaches that may induce guilt, and mothers should not be given the impression that they have to breast-feed exclusively in order to breast-feed successfully (Leonard, 2003).

Third Strategy: Human Network and Population-Based Database Construction in Ishikawa Prefecture

Background

Many countries are constructing or have constructed large population-based twin registries, as mentioned previously. The majority of twin registries throughout the world have been constructed primarily for genetic studies, though several of these registries (Derom et al., 2002) focus on maternal and child health for families with multiples. It appears to be very difficult to achieve a high participation rate from families with very young children in Japan, particularly if researchers perform only a genetic twin study with no feedback for the participants. The nurturing of multiples entails a higher burden physically, mentally and economically than that of singletons, and participants surely expect appropriate information from researchers to facilitate the healthy growth of their twins. Offering information useful for the parenting multiples would be a strong incentive for the parents to participate in such studies.

Given this background, the construction of a population-based database of multiples in childhood at the prefectural level began in 2004 (Ooki, 2006c). The basic idea is population approach/strategy in public health to reduce health risks of multiple birth families. The goals of the registry are to contribute to the development of welfare programs for multiple birth families as well as to co-ordinate research useful for both human genetics and maternal and child health. The well established and sophisticated strategies and methods to recruit twin families into the registry were very useful for the construction of human network and information distribution in this program.

Maternal and Child Health Administration in Japan

Japan consists of 47 prefectures, the basic unit of local government, and about 1800 municipalities. National government policies for the health of mothers and children are planned and administered by the MHLW. This ministry sets goals related to maternal and child health policies and provides technical assistance to local public organizations and other associations.

Public Health Centers (PHCs) were operating in approximately 517 locations in 2008; additionally, the government offices of cities, towns and villages operate other municipal PHCs. These health centers administer independent policies together with the policies and administrative functions delegated or transferred by the MHLW. At present, most of the functions of Maternal and Child Health administration have been transferred from the prefectural level to the municipal level. Typically, a single prefecture has several PHCs, which serve several municipalities within their catchment area. PHCs establish communication and coordination between municipalities with respect to maternal and child health projects in cities, towns and villages, give guidance and advice to municipalities on technical matters, and provide expert maternal and child health services. Each PHC may also have a local PHC, the branch office, if necessary. In other cases, the city defined by law as the 'core city' of the prefecture may also have its own PHC.

Ishikawa Prefecture

Ishikawa Prefecture is located in the middle of the Hokuriku region of Honshu Island in Japan, as shown in Figure 20. The prefecture is long and narrow from the south-west to the north-east. The former feudalism may be reflected in attitudes toward patriarchy, sterility, child nurturing and multiple births in some districts. Kanazawa city, the prefectural capital, is now the center of the Hokuriku area, whereas Noto area is less-populated and accessibility is not necessarily good.

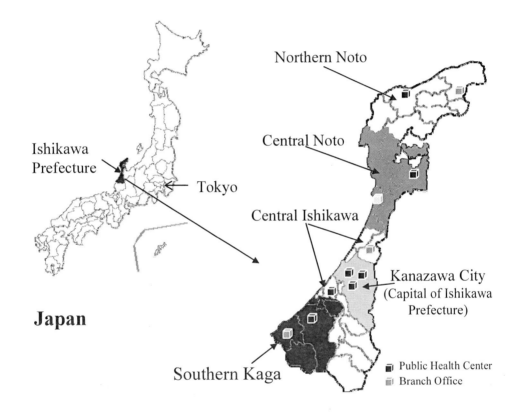

Figure 20. Position of Ishikawa Prefecture in Japan and its five districts.

When this project was initiated in 2004, the total number of municipalities in this prefecture was 39. The population is currently approximately 1,170,000, which is about 1% of the total Japanese population, and Kanazawa City has a population of approximately 450,000. Both the total population and birth rate of this prefecture have been gradually decreasing, while the percentage of people over 65 years of age has been increasing and is now about 20%. The birthrates of this prefecture over the past 10 years have been nearly the same as those of Japan as a whole.

Ishikawa Prefecture has four prefectural PHCs, each with a branch office, and Kanazawa City, the core city, has three PHCs.

Vital Statistics About the Multiple Birth Rates in Ishikawa Prefecture

To obtain an initial outline of total multiple births, secular trends of multiple births in Ishikawa Prefecture were analyzed based on the Japanese vital statistics. The twin birthrate of this prefecture is higher than that of Japan as a whole. The number of multiple births is between 113 and 159 deliveries each year after 1995. This number makes exhaustive identification of newborn multiples and a construction of the population-based registry possible.

Social Support by Governmental and Medical Institutions in Ishikawa Prefecture

Sources of support for multiple birth families and information provided as support by governmental and medical institutions were compiled exhaustively from a mailed questionnaire in June 2004. Recipients were all PHCs in the prefecture, a municipal PHC, and obstetric and pediatric medical institutions. The number of surveyed institutions totaled 417, consisting of 49 governmental and 368 medical institutions.

The number of support associations available to the parents of multiples in this prefecture was ascertained through governmental and medical institutions as well as through personally obtained information, and their activity was investigated.

The response rate was greater than 90% with respect to governmental institutions of health centers, and around 60 to 70% with respect to medical institutions, with the exception of a very low response rate concerning pediatric clinics. This response rate in itself seemed to reflect the interest in or relationship with the multiple birth families. The primary obstetric and pediatric hospital in this prefecture answered the questionnaire. Certainly several municipalities have no or very few families with multiples. No deliveries of multiples are handled at local or small obstetric hospitals or clinics.

The three most important problem areas according to governmental and medical professionals in supporting multiple birth families were the following: the lack of knowledge on multiples among the health professionals themselves (28% = 36/128), the lack of information on the multiple birth families or on the multiple birth itself (20% = 26/128), and insufficient social resources available to multiple birth families (20% = 25/128).

Multiple births deliveries were highly concentrated in the district at several higher-level medical institutions, that is, those that have a neonatal intensive care unit and deal with high-risk pregnancies, as expected.

There are 11 associations for parents of multiples, six in Kanazawa, three in Central Ishikawa, and two in Kaga, which vary in the size of their membership from about 10 to 200 families. The families of approximately 30% to 40% of multiples under 6 years of age are estimated to belong to some kind of association.

The present findings and outline of social support organizations available to families with multiples were important in the development of a closely focused case report and in the construction of an effective human network.

Construction of the Human Network

A human network to support multiple birth families was organized alongside the demographic research and questionnaire survey. This network was constructed with the help of the relationships between families with multiples, support groups for child rearing, governmental and medical institutions, and research institute such as the prefectural nursing university. The Health and Welfare Bureau of Ishikawa Prefecture provided assistance in a positive way: several intensive meetings were held for the purpose of exchanging information between members of associations for the parents of multiples, the medical staff of large hospitals, public health nurses, midwives and twin researchers. Workshops, round-table discussion and other events were also held periodically, about two or three times per year, in both the local and central districts. The workshop program included professional lectures on multiples and meetings where the parents of multiples could meet with each other and exchange experiences. Information of this network was vigorously presented to the mass media, including television stations, newspaper publishing companies, and local bulletins and newsletters. The local mass media was found to be quite effective in advertising this program. Moreover, past research results on multiples by the author were rewritten so as to be easily understood, and were provided in a fact sheet, brochure and leaflet presented to participants in the workshop, family support events, and so forth.

Finally, the 'Ishikawa Support Network for Multiple Birth Families' was founded in July, 2005. The current work was the first attempt in Japan to construct a support network system focused on the multiple birth families at the prefectural level, especially targeted to young children. This network comprises a wide range of members, including families with multiples, maternal and child health authorities of the municipalities, and medical and research institutions. Its aims are to hold workshops, family support events and parenting classes specialized for families with multiples, to facilitate the exchange of information and discussion on maternal and child health policies, and to promote research on multiple births.

The leaflet produced by this network is available in every PHC, municipal PHC and obstetric and pediatric institution, as well as in other places where it would come to the attention of expectant mothers or parents of multiples. All expectant mothers who have submitted a notification of pregnancy receive *The Maternal and Child Health Handbook*, issued by the municipalities. If a woman receives more than one Handbook, this indicates that she is an expectant mother of multiples. It is important to introduce the network to the families of multiples. Public health nurses, who introduce the network during their home visits, accomplish this effectively, especially in rural areas. In some cases, mothers with experience in parenting multiples also visit maternity hospitals.

Multiplied Effect of This Support Network

By constructing a support network at the prefectural level, continuous support, an expansion of cooperation, a wide range of information exchange, support that is carefully crafted according to the characteristics of the region, a reduction of the overburden for specific key persons and expansible support became possible. By belonging to this network, local twin mothers' clubs gain avenues of communication with governmental or medical institutions.

Moreover, the methodologies of social support networks in other fields with more members and longer histories, for example, patients' associations, are applicable.

Other prefectures have constructed, for example Gifu and Hyogo prefectures, or have been constructing and appear to be considering this kind of support network. The Ishikawa support network provides a good model. The experience of the success or failure of the process of constructing a support network will be useful directly or indirectly to other prefectures.

Peer Support Program

A peer support program was started in 2007 jointly with the Supporting Network for the Nursing of Multiples in Japan. This is a home-visit program involving well-trained peer supporters, namely the mothers of multiples. Its main differences with the previous family support provided by local twin mothers' clubs are as follows.

First, the roles of coordinator and peer supporter were clearly divided. Coordinators arrange requests from clients, make support plans, and allot proper peer supporters according to the chief complaints of clients. They usually go along with peer supporter while home-visit, sometimes connect clients to social resources or health professionals of governmental and medical institutions. They also follow up the client and provide mental support for the peer supporter. The main role of the peer supporter is attentive listening to the client, and she also makes an activity log for case conferences. The peer supporter may advise the client, but does not impress her own opinion. In principle, they do not provide household assistance.

Second, an education program by professionals is provided for the coordinator and peer supporter. This education program involves training in basic knowledge on multiple pregnancy and births, parenting multiples, and social resources and training in attentive listening.

Third, since this program is considered one of the activities of the support network, it also incorporates training in systems dealing with clients who are having difficulty or who have emergency needs.

It is very difficult to improve the statistical indicators of maternal and child health quickly, but this approach will achieve results in the future. Periodical meetings for the discussion of anecdotal reports or case conferences are held. Most peer supporters have said that they themselves feel empowered in many instances.

Perspective

These strategies were appropriate for Japanese maternal and child health policies. The population of Ishikawa Prefecture is small compared to that of other major prefectures such as Tokyo, Kanagawa and Osaka. Recently, the number of multiple births in Ishikawa Prefecture has been approximately 100 to 150 every year, which makes an exhaustive support and study of multiples possible. This project stresses the importance of the health and welfare of families with multiples. This strategy is welcomed by the many participants and other involved parties.

CONCLUSION

The impact of fertility treatment on multiple births was pointed out years ago (Derom et al., 1993). The rapid increase in iatrogenic multiple births is now a public health concern in the broad sense, in addition to purely obstetric problems associated with multiples and makeshift support for some families with multiples. Nevertheless, a societal discussion that includes families with multiples, obstetric associations for fertility treatment and those for perinatal management, governmental offices and twin research studies have not occurred, at least in Japan.

The future direction of support for multiple birth families based on community networks is shown in the Figure 21. Previous support systems were mainly focused on the individual or on small numbers of families with urgent needs or those willing to participate in child care classes. This is an approach to resolving problems downstream. However, many problems surrounding multiple birth families are wider social concerns. These problems have more essential background factors such as societal perspectives on fertility treatment, medical economics, perinatal medical systems, the institution of laws and guidelines, and human and social resources. It is necessary to take an approach that is focused on the background factors and wider context to resolve these problems.

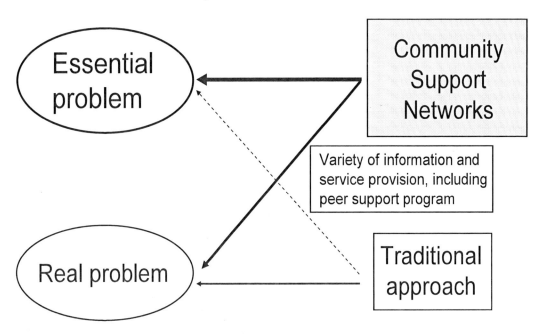

Figure 21. Construction of community support networks and future direction of support for multiple birth families in Japan.

Most data on multiples after birth can only be obtained by volunteer families with multiples. Epidemiologic studies should be performed based on community networks of multiple families and should reflect their real needs and unknown social concerns with appropriate and useful feedback based on scientific evidence. If research which actively involves the multiple birth families concerned is performed routinely, both families and researchers can benefit, and good relationships will be developed. The concept of the community support network seems to be one effective means of providing support for the multiple birth families. Evidence-based care for multiple birth families should be performed. Public health initiatives to resolve the many problems related to the rapid increase of multiple births are expected to be proposed and implemented.

ACKNOWLEDGMENTS

The author gratefully acknowledges the help of Toshimi Ooma in the analysis of the data and the help of Dr. Noriko Kato of the National Institute of Public Health for useful suggestions and information. The author also gratefully acknowledges the help of Dr. Yukiko Amau, the past president of The Japanese Association of Twins' Mothers and many other mothers of twins who helped in the collection of data. The peer support program was a collaborative project with the Supporting Network for the Nursing of Multiples in Japan (Teruko Tanaka, President), Gifu and Hyogo Support Network for Multiple Birth Families. This program was supported in part by a grant-in-aid from the Welfare and Medical Service Agency.

REFERENCES

Akerman, B. A. (1987). The expectation and parentage of twins. A study on the language development of twin infants. *Acta Genet Med Gemellol, 36,* 225-232

Akerman, B. A., & Fischbein, S. (1992). Within-pair similarity in MZ and DZ twins from birth to eighteen years of age. *Acta Genet Med Gemellol, 41,* 155-164.

Ambrose, N. G., Cox, N. J., & Yairi, E. (1997). The genetic basis of persistence and recovery in stuttering. *J Speech Lang Hear Res, 40,* 567-580.

Ananth, C. V., Vintzileos, A. M., Shen-schwarz, S., Smulian, J. C., & Lai, Y. L. (1998). Standards of birth weight in twin gestations stratified by placental chorionicity. *Obstet Gynecol, 91,* 917-924.

Andrews, G., Morris-Yates, A., Howie, P., & Martin, N. G. (1991). Genetic factors in stuttering confirmed. *Arch Gen Psychiatry, 48,* 1034-1035.

Arbuckle, T. E., Wilkins, R., & Sherman, G. J. (1993). Birth weight percentiles by gestational age in Canada. *Obstet Gynecol, 81,* 39-48.

Bakwin, H. (1971a). Nail-biting in twins. *Dev Med Child Neurol, 13,* 304-307.

Bakwin, H. (1971b). Persistent finger-sucking in twins. *Dev Med Child Neurol, 13,* 308-309.

Bishop, D. V. (2001). Individual differences in handedness and specific speech and language impairment: evidence against a genetic link. *Behav Genet, 31,* 339-351.

Bishop, D. V., & Bishop, S. J. (1998). "Twin language": a risk factor for language impairment? *J Speech Lang Hear Res, 41,* 150-160.

Blickstein, I., Zalel, Y., & Weissman, A. (1995). Pregnancy order. A factor influencing birth weight in twin gestations. *J Reprod Med, 40,* 443-446.

Blondel, B., Kogan, M. D., Alexander, G. R., Dattani, N., Kramer, M. S., Macfarlane, A., et al. (2002). The impact of the increasing number of multiple births on the rates of preterm birth and low birthweight: an international study. *Am J Public Health, 92,* 1323-1330.

Blondel, B., Macfarlane, A., Gissler, M., Breart, G., Zeitlin, J., & PERISTAT Study Group. (2006). Preterm birth and multiple pregnancy in European countries participating in the PERISTAT project. *BJOG, 113,* 528-535.

Boklage, C. E. (1981). On the distribution of nonrighthandedness among twins and their families. *Acta Genet Med Gemellol, 30,* 167-187.

Bryan, E. (2003). The impact of multiple preterm births on the family. *BJOG, 110,* 24-28.

Bryan, E. (2006). Best Practice Guidelines. *Early Human Development, 82,* 353-354.

Bryan, E., Denton, J., & Hallett, F. (1997). *Guidelines for Professionals: Multiple Pregnancy,* London: Multiple Births Foundation.

Buckler, J. M., & Green, M. (1994). Birth weight and head circumference standards for English twins. *Arch Dis Child, 71,* 516-521.

Chaudhari, S., Bhalerao, M. R., Vaidya, U., Pandit, A., & Nene, U. (1997). Growth and development of twins compared with singletons at ages one and four years. *Indian Pediatr, 34,* 1081-1086.

Dale, P. S., Simonoff, E., Bishop, D. V., Eley, T. C., Oliver, B., Price, T. S., et al. (1998). Genetic influence on language delay in two-year-old children. *Nat Neurosci, 1,* 324-328.

Damato, E. G., Dowling, D. A., Madigan, E. A., & Thanattherakul, C. (2005). Duration of breastfeeding for mothers of twins. *J Obstet Gynecol Neonatal Nurs, 34,* 201-209.

Davis, A., & Annett, M. (1994). Handedness as a function of twinning, age and sex. *Cortex, 30,* 105-111.

Denton, J. (2005a). Twins and more--1. Some current thinking on multiple births. *J Fam Health Care, 15,* 143-146.

Denton, J. (2005b). Twins and more--2. Practical aspects of parenting in the early years. *J Fam Health Care, 15,* 173-176.

Derom, C., Derom, R., Vlietinck, R., Maes, H., & Van den Berghe, H. (1993). Iatrogenic multiple pregnancies in East Flanders, Belgium. *Fertil Steril, 60,* 493-496.

Derom, C., Thiery, E., Vlietinck, R., Loos, R., & Derom, R. (1996). Handedness in twins according to zygosity and chorion type: a preliminary report. *Behav Genet, 26,* 407-408.

Derom, C., Vlietinck, R., Thiery, E., Leroy, F., Fryns, J. P., & Derom, R. (2002). The East Flanders Prospective Twin Survey (EFPTS). *Twin Res, 5,* 337-341.

Derom, R., Bryan, E., Derom, C., Keith, L., & Vlietinck, R. (2001). Twins, chorionicity and zygosity. *Twin Res, 4,* 134-136.

Dodd, B., & McEvoy, S. (1994). Twin language or phonological disorder? *J Child Lang, 21,* 273-289.

Elkadi, S., Nicholls, M. E., & Clode, D. (1999). Handedness in opposite and same-sex dizygotic twins: testing the testosterone hypothesis. *Neuroreport, 10,* 333-336.

Ettner, S. L., Christiansen, C. L., Callahan, T. L., & Hall, J. E. (1997). How low birthweight and gestational age contribute to increased inpatient costs for multiple births. *Inquiry, 34,* 325-339.

Felsenfeld, S., Kirk, K. M., Zhu, G., Statham, D. J., Neale, M. C., & Martin, N. G. (2000). A study of the genetic and environmental etiology of stuttering in a selected twin sample. *Behav Genet, 30,* 359-366.

Flidel-Rimon, O., & Shinwell, E. S. (2005). Breast-feeding Multiples. In Blickstein, I., & Keith, L. G. Editor, Multiple Pregnancy: Epidemiology, Gestation, and Perinatal Outcome, (Second Edition pp.726-733). New York: Taylor & Francis.

Flidel-Rimon, O., & Shinwell, E. S. (2006). Breast feeding twins and high multiples. *Arch Dis Child Fetal Neonatal Ed, 91,* F377-380.

Ford, R. P., Mitchell, E. A., Scragg, R., Stewart, A. W., Taylor, B. J., & Allen, E. M. (1994). Factors adversely associated with breast feeding in New Zealand. *J Paediatr Child Health, 30,* 483-489.

Garitte, C., Almodovar, J. P., Benjamin, E., & Canhao, C. (2002). Speech in same- and different-sex twins 4 and 5 years old. *Twin Res, 5,* 538-543.

Geraghty, S. R., Khoury, J. C., & Kalkwarf, H. J. (2004). Comparison of feeding among multiple birth infants. *Twin Res, 7,* 542-547.

Glinianaia, S. V., Skjaerven, R., & Magnus, P. (2000). Birthweight percentiles by gestational age in multiple births. A population-based study of Norwegian twins and triplets. *Acta Obstet Gynecol Scand, 79,* 450-458.

Goetghebuer, T., Ota, M. O., Kebbeh, B., John, M., Jackson-Sillah, D., Vekemans, J., et al. (2003). Delay in motor development of twins in Africa: a prospective cohort study. *Twin Res, 6,* 279-284.

Godai, U., Tatarelli, R., & Bonanni, G. (1976). Stuttering and tics in twins. *Acta Genet Med Gemellol, 25,* 369-375.

Gromada, K. K., & Spangler, A. K. (1998). Breastfeeding twins and higher-order multiples. *J Obstet Gynecol Neonatal Nurs, 27,* 441-449.

Hall, J. E., & Callahan, T. L. (2005). 107 Economic Considerations. Blickstein, I., & Keith, L. G. (ed.), In Multiple Pregnancy: Epidemiology, Gestation & Perinatal Outcome. 2nd, pp889-894. Taylor & Francis, New York.

Hattori, R., & Hattori, H. (1999). Breastfeeding twins: guidelines for success. *Birth, 26,* 37-42.

Hay, D.A., Prior, M., Collett, S., & Williams, M. (1987). Speech and language development in preschool twins. *Acta Genet Med Gemellol, 36,* 213-223.

Helmerhorst, F. M., Perquin, D. A., Donker, D., & Keirse, M. J. (2004). Perinatal outcome of singletons and twins after assisted conception: A systematic review of controlled studies. *BMJ, 328,* 261.

Hublin, C., Kaprio, J., Partinen, M., & Koskenvuo, M. (1998a) Sleep talking in twins: epidemiology and psychiatric comorbidity. *Behav Genet, 28,* 289-298.

Hublin, C., Kaprio, J., Partinen, M., & Koskenvuo, M. (1998b) Nocturnal enuresis in a nationwide twin cohort. *Sleep, 21,* 579-585.

Hublin, C., Kaprio, J., Partinen, M., & Koskenvuo, M. (1999) Limits of self-report in assessing sleep terrors in a population survey. *Sleep, 22,* 89-93.

James, W. H., & Orlebeke, J. F. (2002). Determinants of handedness in twins. *Laterality, 7,* 301-307.

Janssen, J. P. (2004). Evaluation of empirical methods and methodological foundations of human left-handedness. *Percept Mot Skills, 98,* 487-506.

Kaneko, A., Kaneita, Y., Yokoyama, E., Miyake, T., Harano, S., Suzuki, K., et al. (2006). Factors associated with exclusive breast-feeding in Japan: for activities to support child-rearing with breast-feeding. *J Epidemiol, 16,* 57-63.

Kato, N. (2004). Reference birthweight range for multiple birth neonates in Japan. *BMC Pregnancy Childbirth, 4,* 2.

Kyvik, K. O, & Derom, C. (2006). Data collection on multiple births -- establishing twin registers and determining zygosity. *Early Hum Dev, 82,* 357-363.

Leonard, L. G. (2002). Breastfeeding higher order multiples: enhancing support during the postpartum hospitalization period. *J Hum Lact, 18,* 386-392.

Leonard, L. G. (2003). Breastfeeding rights of multiple birth families and guidelines for health professionals. *Twin Res, 6,* 34-45.

Leonard, L. G., & Denton, J. (2006). Preparation for parenting multiple birth children. *Early Hum Dev, 82,* 371-378.

Leroy, B., Lefort, F., Neveu, P., Risse, R. J., Trévise, P., & Jeny, R. (1982). Intrauterine growth charts for twin fetuses. *Acta Genet Med Gemellol, 31,* 199-206.

Lubitz, L. (1992). Nail biting, thumb sucking, and other irritating behaviours in childhood. *Aust Fam Physician, 21,* 1090-1094.

Luke, B., Bigger, H. R., Leurgans, S., & Sietsema, D. (1996). The cost of prematurity: a case-control study of twins vs singletons. *Am J Public Health, 86,* 809-814.

Machin, G.A. (1994). Twins and their zygosity. *Lancet, 343,* 1577.

Medland, S. E., Wright, M. J., Geffen, G. M., Hay, D. A., Levy, F., Martin, N. G., et al. (2003). Special twin environments, genetic influences and their effects on the handedness of twins and their siblings. *Twin Res, 6,* 119-130.

Medland, S. E., Duffy, D. L., Wright, M. J., Geffen, G. M., & Martin, N. G. (2006). Handedness in twins: joint analysis of data from 35 samples. *Twin Res Hum Genet, 9,* 46-53.

Miller, J. W., Jayadev, S., Dodrill, C. B., & Ojemann, G. (2005). Gender differences in handedness and speech lateralization related to early neurologic insults. *Neurology, 65,* 1974-1975.

Minakami, H., Izumi, A., & Sato, I. (1999). Gestational age-specific normal birth weight for Japanese twins. Risk of early neonatal death in small-for-gestationalage and large-for-gestational-age twins. *J Reprod Med, 44,* 625-629.

Murphy, M., Hey, K., Brown, J., Willis, B., Ellis, J. D., & Barlow, D. (1997). Infertility treatment and multiple birth rates in Britain, 1938-94. *J Biosoc Sci, 29,* 235-243.

Neale, M. C. (1988). Handedness in a sample of volunteer twins. *Behav Genet,* 18, 69-79.

Neifert, M., & Thorpe, J. (1990). Twins: family adjustment, parenting, and infant feeding in the fourth trimester. *Clin Obstet Gynecol, 33,* 102-113.

Nyqvist, K. H. (2002). Breast-feeding in preterm twins: Development of feeding behavior and milk intake during hospital stay and related caregiving practices. *J Pediatr Nurs, 17,* 246-256.

Ooki, S. (2005a). Language development of Japanese twins in childhood based on maternal reports. *Jpn J Health & Human Ecology, 71,* 12-24.

Ooki, S. (2005b) Genetic and environmental influences on stuttering and tics in Japanese twin children. *Twin Res Hum Genet, 8,* 69-75.

Ooki, S. (2005c). Genetic and environmental influences on finger-sucking and nail-biting in Japanese twin children. *Twin Res Hum Genet, 8,* 320-327.

Ooki, S. (2005d). Genetic and environmental influences on the handedness and footedness in Japanese twin children. *Twin Res Hum Genet, 8,* 649-656.

Ooki, S. (2006a). Motor development of Japanese twins in childhood as reported by mothers. *Environ Health Prev Med, 11,* 55-64.

Ooki, S. (2006b). Nongenetic factors associated with human handedness and footedness in Japanese twin children. *Environ Health Prev Med, 11,* 304-312.

Ooki, S. (2006c). Population-based database of multiples in childhood of Ishikawa prefecture, Japan. *Twin Res Hum Genet, 9,* 832-837.

Ooki, S. (2008a). Genetic and environmental influences on sleeptalking, half-sleeping, night terrors, and nocturnal enuresis in childhood – a study of two Japanese twin samples. *Jpn J Health & Human Ecology, 74,* 130-146.

Ooki, S. (2008b). Breast-feeding rates and related maternal and infants' obstetric factors in Japanese twins. *Environ Health Prev Med, 13,* 187-197.

Ooki, S., & Asaka, A. (1993). Physical growth of Japanese twins. *Acta Genet Med Gemellol, 42,* 275-287.

Ooki, S., & Asaka, A. (2004). Zygosity diagnosis in young twins by questionnaire for twins' mothers and twins' self-reports, *Twin Res, 7,* 5-12.

Ooki, S., & Asaka, A. (2005). Comparison of obstetric and birthweight characteristics between the two largest databases of Japanese twins measured in childhood. *Twin Res Hum Genet, 8,* 63-68.

Ooki, S., & Asaka, A. (2006). Twin database of the secondary school attached to the faculty of education of the university of Tokyo. *Twin Res Hum Genet, 9,* 827-831.

Ooki, S., Yamada, K., & Asaka, A. (1993). Zygosity diagnosis of twins by questionnaire for twins' mothers. *Acta Genet Med Gemellol, 42,* 17-22.

Ooki, S., & Yokoyama, Y. (2003). Reference birth weight, length, chest circumference, and head circumference by gestational age in Japanese twins. *J Epidemiol, 13,* 333-341.

Ooki, S., & Yokoyama, Y. (2004). Physical growth charts from birth to six years of age in Japanese twins, *J Epidemiol, 14,* 151-160.

Ooki, S., Yokoyama, Y., & Asaka, A. (2004). Zygosity misclassification of twins at birth in Japan. *Twin Res, 7,* 228-232.

Orlebeke, J. F., Knol, D. L., Koopmans, J. R., Boomsma, D. I., & Bleker, O. P. (1996). Left-handedness in twins: genes or environment? *Cortex, 32,* 479-490.

Ostfeld, B. M., Smith, R. H., Hiatt, M., & Hegyi, T. (2000). Maternal behavior toward premature twins: implications for development. *Twin Res, 3,* 234-241.

Peter, I., Vainder, M., & Livshits, G. (1999). Genetic analysis of motor milestones attainment in early childhood. *Twin Res, 2,* 1-9.

Peterson, J. E., & Schneider, P. E. (1991). Oral habits: A behavioral approach. *Pediatr Clin North Am, 38,* 1289-1307.

Pettersson, F., Smedby, B., & Lindmark, G. (1976). Outcome of twin birth. Review of 1,636 children born in twin birth. *Acta Paediatr Scand, 65,* 473-479.

Philip, A. G. (1981). Term twins with discordant birth weights: observations at birth and one year. *Acta Genet Med Gemellol, 30,* 203-212.

Price, T. S., Freeman, B., Craig, I., Petrill, S. A., Ebersole, L., & Plomin, R. (2000). Infant zygosity can be assigned by parental report questionnaire data. *Twin Res, 3,* 129-133.

Ramos-Arroyo, M. A., Ulbirght, T. M., Yu, P. L., & Christian, J. C. (1988). Twin study: relationship between birth weight, zygosity, placentation, and pathologic placental changes. *Acta Genet Med Gemellol, 37,* 229-238.

Rietveld, M. J., van Der, Valk, J. C., Bongers, I. L., Stroet, T. M., Slagboom, P. E., & Boomsma, D. I. (2000). Zygosity diagnosis in young twins by parental report. *Twin Res, 3,* 134-141.

Rutter, M., Thorpe, K., Greenwood, R., Northstone, K., & Golding, J. (2003). Twins as a natural experiment to study the causes of mild language delay: I: Design; twin-singleton differences in language, and obstetric risks. *J Child Psychol Psychiatry, 44,* 326-341.

Sadrzadeh, S., Treloar, S. A., Van Baal, G. C., & Lambalk, C. B. (2001). Potential bias regarding birth weight in histrical and contemporary twin data bases. *Twin Res, 4,* 332-336.

Sicotte, N. L., Woods, R. P., & Mazziotta, J. C. (1999). Handedness in twins: a meta-analysis. *Laterality, 4,* 265-286.

Tanimura, M., Matsui, I., & Kobayashi, N. (1990). Child abuse of one of a pair of twins in Japan. Lancet, 336, 1298-1299.

Teng, R. J., Jou, H. J., & Ho, M. M. (1994). Intrauterine growth of twins in Taiwan. *Zhonghua Min Guo Xiao Er Ke Yi Xue Hui Za Zhi, 35,* 266-272.

Thome, M., Alder, E. M., & Ramel, A. (2006). A population-based study of exclusive breastfeeding in Icelandic women: is there a relationship with depressive symptoms and parenting stress? *Int J Nurs Stud, 43,* 11-20.

Thorpe, K., Golding, J., MacGillivray, I., & Greenwood, R. (1991). Comparison of prevalence of depression in mothers of twins and mothers of singletons. *BMJ, 302,* 875-878.

Thorpe, K., Greenwoood, R., Eivers, A., & Rutter, M. (2001). Prevalence and developmental course of 'secret language'. *Int J Lang Commun Disord, 36,* 43-62.

Thorpe, K., Rutter, M., & Greenwood, R. (2003). Twins as a natural experiment to study the causes of mild language delay: II: Family interaction risk factors. *J Child Psychol Psychiatry, 44,* 342-355.

Tomasello, M., Mannle, A., Kruger, A. C. (1986). Linguistic environment of 1- to 2- year-old twins. *Dev Psychol, 22,* 169-176.

Topp, M., Huusom, L. D., Langhoff-Roos, J., Delhumeau, C., Hutton, J. L., Dolk, H., et al. (2004). Multiple birth and cerebral palsy in Europe: a multicenter study. *Acta Obstet Gynecol Scand, 83,* 548-553.

Watson, T. S., Meeks, C., Dufrene, B., & Lindsay, C. (2002). Sibling thumb sucking. Effects of treatment for targeted and untargeted siblings. *Behav Modif, 26,* 412-423.

Williams, C. S., Buss, K. A., & Eskenazi, B. (1992). Infant resuscitation is associated with an increased risk of left-handedness. *Am J Epidemiol, 136,* 277-286.

Wilson, R. S. (1986). Growth and development of human twins. In Falkner, F., & Tanner, J. M. (ed.) Human Growth Vol.3 2nd ed, pp.197-220. Plenum Press, New York.

Yairi, E., Ambrose, N., & Cox, N. (1996). Genetics of stuttering: a critical review. *J Speech Hear Res, 39,* 771-784.

In: Handbook of Parenting: Styles, Stresses & Strategies   ISBN 978-1-60741-766-8
Editor: Pacey H. Krause and Tahlia M. Dailey   © 2009 Nova Science Publishers, Inc.

Chapter 13

THE EFFECT OF FAMILIAL FACTORS ON THE MANAGEMENT OF CHILDHOOD OBESITY

Moria Golan,[1,2] Roni S. Enten[2] and Danit R. Shahar [1,3]*

[1] School of Nutritional Sciences, The Hebrew University of Jerusalem, Rehovot, Israel
[2] Shahaf, Community Based Facility for Eating Disorders, Israel
[3] The S. Daniel Abraham International Center for Health and Nutrition, Ben-Gurion University of the Negev, Beer-Sheva, Israel

ABSTRACT

This chapter reviews the literature, with the addition of some recent unpublished findings from this group's studies, on the relationship between childhood obesity management and family-based factors. The objective was to better understand the impact of socioeconomic status (SES), family size, family functioning and parenting style on the outcomes of pediatric obesity management programs. Original research and reviews published between 1995 and 2008 were identified by searching Medline, PsycINFO, Agricola and Lexis-Nexis. The literature shows that parents from families of lower SES may underestimate the health risk of excess weight to their children; these families may also be less available for the intensive efforts and supportive interaction needed to address excess weight in their children. Moreover, psychological disturbances, lower family functioning and a permissive parenting style were some of the factors reported to be associated with less success in family-based weight loss programs among families from lower SES as well as larger families.

Keywords: childhood obesity management, family-based factors.

* Author for correspondence and reprints
Moria Golan, RD, PhD
Shahaf, Mobile Post Soreq 76829
Kibbutz Naan
Israel
Tel: 972-8-935-1244
Fax: 972-8-934-8953
e-mail: moriag@netvision.net

INTRODUCTION

In recent years, the prevalence of obesity among children and adolescents has increased dramatically in many Western countries and in countries undergoing economic transition, becoming a major global health concern [1,2]. The prevalence of obesity increases with age among both males and females [3], and there is a greater likelihood that obesity developed in childhood will persist throughout the life span [4,5]. The management of childhood overweight and obesity involves multiple contexts that interact with one another. In the case of a child, the ecological niche includes the family and school environments which are, in turn, embedded in larger social contexts including the community and society at large [6]. Cochrane reviews have established that opportunities for prevention are poorly understood and yet are of paramount importance [7]. Consequently, there is an urgent need for research regarding the capacity to influence the development of children's obesity-promoting behaviors [8].

Recent studies suggest that rapid globalization and urbanization are some factors that account for significant shifts in dietary patterns and physical activity levels that tend to increase risks for childhood obesity [9]. Emerging evidence also provides support for the effect of certain parental behaviors on the development of obesity in their offspring. For example, Huang et al. (2006) found that parents may actually pre-program their children's risk for obesity through biological and lifestyle factors such as maternal diabetes, malnutrition, and smoking before they are even born [10]. This, in combination with increasingly sedentary lifestyles and an energy-dense diet—documented in children living in countries of low socioeconomic status (SES) and among impoverished children of the industrialized nations—increases the risk.

Access to 'obesogenic' diets is determined by many factors, including family income and lack of access to healthier alternatives [11, 12, 13]. The obesogenic environment also includes a large amount of time spent watching television and playing computer and video games, since they are both relatively inexpensive forms of entertainment, as well as a proactive means of avoiding danger in outdoor activities in neighborhoods with higher rates of crime [14].

While a number of recent reviews of interventions designed to prevent obesity and obesity-promoting behaviors have been conducted [15, 16, 17, 18, 19] none have focused specifically on the impact of family-based factors. A recent meta-analysis performed by Young et al. [20] suggests that including parents in weight-loss intervention enhances outcomes, however the analysis failed to provide clear insight into which of the many possible aspects of parental influence was modified in the intervention in order to produce the desired weight-loss. Additionally, it was not possible to determine which aspects of the interventions were most important in modifying parental behavior. However, an examination of the studies yielding the largest effect sizes, have shown them to share methodological elements such as including a high level of parental involvement and multiple treatment components.

To enhance the efficacy of obesity prevention programs as well as therapeutic interventions, a more comprehensive understanding of family dynamics, socio-cultural practices, and their relationships with the obesogenic environment is needed. Understanding these relationships may contribute to the development of risk assessment tools that can be used to help clinicians decide who is most likely to benefit from interventions to control body weight and may also assist in tailoring such a program's content to target populations.

Although it is well-documented that the family has a significant impact on children's health behaviors, findings on the relationship between children's weight status, family functioning, and parenting style are inconsistent [20, 21, 22, 23, 24, 25]. The main objective of this review was to assess the impact of family-based factors on the outcome of interventions designed to prevent obesity and/or promote healthy habits among children and adolescents. This chapter reviews the literature, with the addition of some recent findings from this group's studies, on the relationship between the management of childhood obesity and the following factors: socioeconomic status (SES), family size, family functioning, and parenting style, with the objective of enhancing understanding of some of the moderators and mediators that relate to outcome in pediatric obesity management programs.

LITERATURE SEARCH

Original research and reviews published between 1995 and 2008 were identified by conducting a systemic search of Medline, PsycINFO, Agricola and Lexis-Nexis with the following search strategy: (childhood or pediatric obesity) and (management or intervention or prevention) and (SES or parenting or parents* or family size or family functioning). The search was limited to papers printed in English. Literature search was supplemented extensively with source material from bibliographic of included trials.

SOCIOECONOMIC STATUS

Socioeconomic status or SES is a combination of indicators which differ from study to study. Rearing area, family income, and parental education are some of the variables which comprise SES [26] and which may dictate lifestyle behaviors that result in an increased risk for childhood obesity. Numerous studies have demonstrated an inverse relationship between childhood obesity and family income, education, or both [26, 27, 28, 29, 30, 31]. Among American populations, family income often presents a barrier to healthy eating, with children in lower SES groups eating fewer fruits and vegetables and having a higher intake of fat compared with children in relatively higher SES groups [29]. In their 2006 study, O'Dea and Wilson found that low SES contributed to high BMI in children, mediated by the low nutritional quality of breakfast served to them [32]. Conversely, Anderson et al. [31] found that the work intensity of higher SES mothers is also deleterious for their children's overweight status. Another study which examined children from Ukraine, a country undergoing economic transition found that variables associated with higher living standards such as higher social class, higher meat consumption and friendly neighborhoods were associated with an elevated BMI in children [33].

Kaufman & Karpati examined the socio-cultural roots of childhood obesity by exploring low-income Latino families' food practices, embedded in their everyday lives, their urban neighborhood context, and the larger political and economic processes affecting them. The authors stated that in the context of unstable resources, long-standing food insecurity, and poverty, food is of critical value for participating families and anxiety around food is deeply felt and connected to food scarcity. At the same time, food, in contrast with material goods and housing, is an achievable source of gratification for parents and children. The patterns reveal unstable purchase and eating habits that have potentially negative effects on children, including at various times eating less, overeating, and excessive expectations around (often unhealthy) food [30].

The Impact of Parental Education

Many studies have shown that subjects with higher education are more likely to follow healthy dietary and lifestyle recommendations compared with subjects with a lower level of education and or other environmental stressors, which take higher priority in the parent's life [27, 34, 35, 36]. Higher parental education has also been associated with health consciousness in food choices and consumption among offspring [28]. A large German cross-sectional study found [37] that the indicators of parental education were most strongly associated in an inverse manner with children's obesity. The single most important independently-associated factor for a child to be in the 90th percentile or higher of BMI in the screening population in this study was maternal education. Obesity was particularly prevalent in children whose mothers had less than 9 years of education and similar results were found in the case control population, which included only children with German mother-tongue. Of all the variables listed, paternal education and type of maternal occupation were the most influential independent factors in a stepwise forward regression for childhood obesity. There was also a strong dose–response relationship between a composed index of social class and obesity. Children of the lowest social status had a more than three-fold risk of becoming obese than children of the highest social status in the screening population (OR: 3.29, CI: 1.92–5.63).

The Impact of Television Viewing

Another factor which may contribute to poor weight management in low SES children is the frequency with which they watch television. It has been found that low SES and minority children watch more television than white, non-low SES children and are potentially exposed to more commercials which advertise high-calorie, low-nutrient food during an average hour of television programming [38]. Television viewing has also been associated with a more sedentary lifestyle and consumption of energy dense snacks among children [39]. In a study which focused on food consumption during television viewing, it was shown that both on weekdays and weekend days, 17–18% and approximately 26% of total daily energy, respectively, was consumed by children during television viewing [39]. Moreover, in a recent publication, Viner [14] showed that weekend TV viewing in early childhood influences BMI in adulthood, probably due to the accustomed lifestyle that begins early in life. Furthermore, van Zutphen et al. [40] found that children were more likely to be overweight if there was a television located in their bedroom.

SES and the Management of Childhood Obesity

Only a few studies have examined the impact of SES on weight loss programs. Clay et al. (2002) found that only nine out of forty-one articles presenting empirically supported treatments for obesity reported the SES of participant families. Of those nine, the middle class is disproportionately represented. Thus, the association between SES and treatment outcome in childhood obesity is vague [41]. Some investigators did not find SES or level of parental education to be significant predictors for success or failure in weight loss programs [42, 43]. SES was related to children's initial weight status as well as to attrition rate from the weight loss programs [44]. At least part of the association between SES and weight management may be attributed to parents' underestimation of the health risk of excess weight to their children [45], and the difficulty in achieving and maintaining behavioral changes associated with obesity prevention [42, 45, 46,]. Golan et al. (1998) found a highly significant correlation between SES and the improvement in the obesogenic load in the house (r=0.69; p<0.01). The higher the SES, the greater the improvement noted in the obesogenic behaviors (r=-0.4; p<0.05) [47].

Other research has reported that middle and high SES families as well as intact families were able to benefit more from treatment than families sharing other characteristics [44] and it was suggested that if SES is related to success in parent management, then parents of higher SES may benefit more from parent training than those of larger families or those of a lower SES [48].

FAMILY SIZE

Little attention has been given to the impact of socioeconomic conditions in combination with family size on the management of childhood obesity. Epstein et al. [42, 49] reported that children from larger families were less successful in weight management programs and suggested that the inverse relationship may be due to the important role that effective parent management plays in a family-based treatment program [50]. The effect of family size on effective parent management may be due to parental difficulties with time management [39], more negative parent/child interactions, and lower positive display of affect as well as chronic parental stress [50]. Moreover, family size has been inversely related to duration of parental attention, and positively related to negative parent/child interactions [51]. Since the family-based program is time-consuming for the parent, smaller families have to spend more time with the target obese child, in order to increase the effectiveness of programs which emphasize parental attention as an important motivating factor [42, 51].

Family size has also been found to be related to maternal emotional distress. When mother/child behavior patterns were observed, mothers with more children were more distressed, displayed more negative interactions, and had lower positive impact [50]. However, in a review by Dietz [52], it was reported that neither family size nor birth order had a significant effect on either rates or absolute weight loss.

In Golan's group series of intervention studies with obese children (6–11 years of age), an association between family size, SES and outcome in family-based intervention, with the parents as the exclusive agent of change, has been shown. The studies' outcomes have been described previously, however, the psychosocial data was never published [47, 53, 54, 55].

In the first study, sixty obese children were treated with a health-centered approach via child-only intervention vs. parent-only intervention. None of the psychosocial variables (parents' education, occupation, income, number of children) were associated with the rate of attendance in the sessions. However, Pearson correlations showed significance between the number of children in the family and the reduction in obesogenic load. The greater the family size, the lower the reduction in number of obesogenic food items in the house (r=-0.54; p<0.01), and less improvement in the frequency of eating behaviors that promote obesity (reduction in eating while watching television, eating while standing, and eating in negative situations (r=-0.43, p<0.01). The fewer children in the family, the greater the increase in activity level observed among obese children (r=-0.56, p<0.01).

In a second randomized clinical trial [55], thirty-two families with obese children, 6–11 years of age, were randomized into groups in which participants were provided with a comprehensive educational and behavioral program for a healthy lifestyle. These groups differed in their main agent of change: parents only vs. the parents and the obese child. In both groups, parents were encouraged to foster an authoritative parenting style. The association between family size and SES and outcome in health-centered weight management programs was further explored in a population-based study in which 200 parents of 120 children participated in parents-only groups delivered by 20 group facilitators all over Israel. A significant negative correlation was found between family size and improvement in the obesogenic load in this large study as well (r= 0.52; p<0.01).

In conclusion, most of the literature indicates that childhood obesity management is less effective in lower SES, lower education, and larger families, indicating the need to develop innovative strategies to address the difficulties inherited with these variables.

FAMILY FUNCTIONING

The success of the child in the weight loss program may also depend on the family climate, the extent of family functioning, and on the support system within and/or outside the family [56, 57]. Family functioning is a complex set of functional dimensions comprising factors such as relationships (adaptability, cohesion) and communication patterns. Adaptability is the flexibility in the family's rules, roles, and relationships in response to situational and developmental demands and cohesion is the emotional bonding that family members have toward one another. Combining the dimensions of cohesion and adaptability enables identification of 16 types of family systems tested by FACES, a questionnaire which is widely used [58, 59]. The types termed "balanced" predict the best functioning families. In our previously described studies [47, 53, 54, 55], no association was found between family functioning score and outcome in the health-centered weight management program. Most environmental factors did not show any associations with family functioning and children's weight loss [53, 54].

The Impact of Parental Psychopathology

The family climate can be affected tremendously by parents' psychopathology, potentially causing disruptions in parenting practices and reducing the effectiveness of weight management programs. Some studies have revealed that the severity of obesity among children was more highly correlated with the severity of maternal psychiatric symptomology and personality disturbances than with those found in the fathers [60], while other studies did not find association between childhood obesity and adverse maternal or family characteristics such as maternal depression, negative life events, poor general family functioning or ineffective parenting style [60]. Gibson et al. found that children who lost less weight were younger and had an obese mother with a neurotic tendency [61]. However, both the small sample size (49 children) and the absence of a control group of non-obese children limit the ability to generalize these findings to obese children in general. The authors suggest that the mothers' characteristics are more important than those of the fathers in cases of both children's obesity and their success in weight loss programs.

In some cases, psychological disturbances of the mother (such as anxiety or depression) may cause over-feeding of the infant, which may lead to problematic distinction between hunger and satiety later in life. In one study, improved maternal psychopathology accounted for a significant improvement in the Child behavior checklist total problems scale, and internalizing and externalizing problems subscales in obese children [63]. Researchers demonstrated that parental distress had negative effects on child weight loss during the treatment phase and was mediated by their child's level of anxiety and depression. At the two-year follow-up, parental distress affected child's weight change through its effects on the child's social adjustment; children who had more social problems had less successful treatment [49, 63].   Birch et al. [62] also assert that during early infancy, the mother's attitudes can influence the infant's ability to distinguish hunger and satiety.

Along the same lines, a cross-sectional survey by Campbell et al. (2007) found that mothers' eating behaviors such as intake of high energy fluids, sweet and savory snacks and take-out foods was positively associated with boys' intake of these same foods and girls' intake of high energy drinks [64]. The availability of unhealthy foods in the home was positively associated with unhealthy food consumption. Kroller and Warschburger (2008) found that mothers' use of rewarding certain behaviors resulted in a decreased consumption of fruits and vegetables in children aged three to six that they were at higher risk of overweight, and that mothers' pressure upon the children to eat resulted in higher fat intake in the same children. These findings highlight the importance of maternal modeling in order to achieve positive feeding and eating behaviors and outcomes in children [65].

Family Climate

The family climate is also an important factor in the mediation of weight-related problems. Epstein et al. (1994) study found that rates of weight loss for children whose parents were married were significantly greater than for children whose parents were separated or divorced [66].   In addition, higher parents' family satisfaction ratings were associated with successful weight loss among obese children. Family climate variables also have the potential to impede or enhance child weight loss efforts [67]. In one six-month, family-based weight loss intervention among 57 African-American adolescent girls, parents' variables pertaining to life and family satisfaction were the strongest mediating variables [25].

Overall, the literature shows that a child in a weight loss program has a greater chance for success with better family climate, improved family functioning, and less parental pathology.

PARENTING STYLE

Style of parenting may also influence the effectiveness of weight management programs. Parenting style is a critical factor in the development of food preferences [67, 68, 69] and affects children's energy balance by altering patterns of intake. Alteration of patterns of intake can occur when well intentioned but concerned parents assume that children need help in determining what, when, and how much to eat, and when parents impose child-feeding practices that provide children with few opportunities for self-control [70].

Initial evidence indicates that imposition of stringent parental controls can potentiate preferences for high-fat, energy-dense foods, limit children's acceptance of a variety of foods and disrupt children's regulation of energy intake by altering children's responsiveness to internal cues of hunger and satiety [71, 72, 73]. However, researchers have found that parents who restrict access to particular foods, and parents who display high levels of disinherited eating, especially when coupled with high dietary restraint, may foster the development of excess body fat in their children. This association may be mediated by direct parental role modeling of unhealthy eating behaviors, or through other indirect, and probably subconscious, behavioral consequences, such as the suppression of the child's innate regulation of dietary intake [74, 75]. Forcing a child to eat a food will often decrease the liking for that food [76, 77, 78]; for example, authoritarian feeding has been associated with lower intake of fruit, juices, and vegetables [79]. However, frequent exposure to an unfamiliar food, such as a fruit or vegetable can result in increased consumption, liking and preference for that food [80] and children are more likely to eat these foods when they are made available in the home [81].

Consequently, parental insensitivity and/or unresponsiveness to feeding cues from the child might be counterproductive to the development of the child's ability to self-regulate and may have adverse consequences for the development of the child's food preferences and intake [74]. The implementation of successful child behavior change requires fundamental parenting skills, which are the foundation for successful intervention for youths [69]. In addition, specific parenting behaviors such as modeling healthy eating behavior should be emphasized in the management of overweight children.

It has been suggested that in order to prevent weight-related problems, an authoritative parenting and feeding style should be advised [82, 83, 84]. In this parenting style, the parents decide what is served and the child decides how much to eat. Recent results from our studies have shown [53, 55] a significant inverse correlation between permissive parenting and weight loss. The more permissive the mother, the less weight reduction was observed (R=-0.6; p<0.001). It is important to mention that any correlation between the child-feeding practices of the parent and the child's weight might be in part at least a response by the parents to a pre-existing problem of obesity.

Stein et al. [84] found that change in parenting style plays a role in the long-term outcome of family-based behavioral treatments for childhood obesity. In their study, the only parenting variable that was related to the child 1-year percentage overweight change was father's change in acceptance vs. rejection. Hierarchical regressions showed that adding change in acceptance improves the prediction of percentage overweight change. The authors suggest that a change in father's acceptance may indicate a home environment in which all family members are supportive of the healthy behavior changes attempted by the participating child. As a result, weight management intervention should include parenting style, in order to establish a balance between controlling and permissive parenting practices since imbalanced parenting style is often associated with less responsiveness to hunger and satiety cues and less balanced self-control.

PARENTAL ENROLLMENT IN CHILD TREATMENT

Current empirically supported treatments require a commitment of family resources (i.e., time, money, travel) beyond what many low SES families can afford. McCurdy and Daro's model (2001) of parental involvement in family support programs proposes that parental decisions to enroll and remain in a support program is influenced by a variety of outside and personal factors, and suggest a variety of enrollment strategies such as inclusion of the entire and sometimes extended family, with an emphasis on involving the father as well as appropriate staff training to prevent burn-out [85]. The development of treatments that are flexible in their mode of delivery, time of utilization and can be applied in different settings and environment may make such treatments more acceptable and effective.

Lindsay et al. (2006) described a successful program that targeted three- to five-year-old minority children enrolled in Head Start programs in Chicago, used a culturally and linguistically appropriate program utilizing a parental component which addressed the eating and physical activity patterns of the entire family. The program included weekly classes on a variety of health topics, along with weekly newsletters with homework assignments for the whole family. At two years follow up, the experimental group had significantly smaller increases in BMI than the controls [86].

Another two-year intervention described by Lindsay et al. (2006) targeting middle school boys and girls used a school-based program in which sessions on reducing TV viewing and consumption of high fat foods, and increasing fruit and vegetable intake and physical activity were presented in the classroom setting, in conjunction with several family program components addressing the reduction of TV viewing. The girls in the intervention group had a reduced prevalence of obesity and both boys and girls had increased fruit and vegetable intake, reduced hours in front of the TV and reduced total energy consumption. A later analysis also found a reduced risk of disordered eating behaviors among girls [86].

The importance of parenting on childhood overweight and obesity should also be emphasized in the clinical setting where health professionals can help to guide parents in promoting the development of healthy food related behaviors and physical activity in children. At the primary care level, where physicians are more likely to discuss the benefits of weight loss and the risks of obesity and rarely focus on the patient as the center of treatment, training primary care providers and nurses to use a model based on behavioral and motivational strategies and gauging readiness to change suggested by Simkin et al. (2008), may help to overcome barriers such as limited resources [87]. In addition, Luther et al. (2007) suggest clinicians can use Baumrind's parenting typology to assess specific parenting styles, and offer sensible strategies for parents to use at home, to promote positive outcomes found in the literature [88].

CONCLUSION AND RECOMMENDATIONS

The numerous family psychological factors that moderate the management of childhood obesity include the home environment, socioeconomic status, family size, parents' education, and climate in the home. These factors may influence the eating and activity habits of children as well as the extent of sedentary activities.

- *Moderators of obesogenic environment.* Low SES, lower parental education, and larger family size were independent risk factors for overweight children. Lower SES is associated with higher levels of obesogenic environment and sedentary behavior among children.[89, 90, 91, 92, 93, 94]. The fact that young children usually spend more time with their mothers than their fathers might explain the finding that maternal education had a greater influence on childhood obesity than paternal education [31]. At least part of the association between SES and weight management may be attributed to parents' underestimation of the health risk of excess weight to their children, and the difficulty in achieving and maintaining behavioral changes associated with obesity prevention [95]. Adverse economic circumstances, marital conflict and negative life events seem to be much more frequent in families with a lower SES. These parents might be less involved in the lives of their children, which might then lead to more overeating [28].
- *Parenting style.* A permissive parenting style, associated with greater food intake and less weight loss in studies [96, 97], may reflect unstructured parenting, and children in a less structured family environment may have lower self-regulation. Permissive parenting practices with lower parental monitoring of children's TV viewing [96] may account for the higher level of sedentary life style among low SES families. Families with clear communication, adequate behavior control, and structured parenting help regulate their children's healthy behavior [96].
- *Need for parental involvement with health promotion.* The effects of family size on outcome may be operating simply by reducing the amount of time that a parent has to spend with the child in promoting behavior change or as a role model, reducing the effectiveness of parents in effectively managing their children [95, 98, 99, 100, 101].
- *Supportiveness in the home environment.* Supportiveness is important in enhancing adherence to the change in lifestyle. Support may be less available in parents who are less educated and less aware of the importance of healthy lifestyle. A positive parental attitude was associated with greater weight loss compliance [102].
- *Psychopathology* among obese children is in part a function of parental psychopathology, and child and parent psychological problems may interfere with the effect of treatment [66, 97].

Further research is needed to examine family factors associated with adherence, treatment acceptability and outcome. Such exploration can potentially identify variables that could be targeted in order to maintain positive lifestyle changes necessary for successful weight management among obese children and adolescents. Information should be obtained from subjects from diverse socioeconomic and ethnic backgrounds.

SUGGESTIONS FOR FURTHER PRACTICE

There is a need to expand obesity prevention programs beyond the individual child or parent/child dyad. New programs may include kin or a friend in order to effectively target children in their home environment. External validity of treatment studies can be improved by including more diverse samples that represent those for whom the treatment will be used [41]. We recommend addressing childhood obesity with preventive programs that involve and work directly with parents starting at the earliest stages of child development, to support healthful practices as well as provide general parenting skills both in and outside of the home. Given the limited ability of information to induce changes in behavior [13], and the fact that many of the obvious and commonly used parental strategies to encourage healthful eating have an opposite effect to that intended, alternative strategies are needed.

Intervention programs should address child development, training in general parenting skills and other techniques such as motivational interviewing [103, 104, 105] as well as techniques from strategic family therapy to address parents' ambivalence or resistance to change. Policy-makers should address the problem of limited healthful foods and leisure physical activity available to low SES groups, as well as challenge the myriad of child-focused food advertising.

Although findings imply that parents from higher SES groups may benefit more from parent training than those of larger families and from a lower SES level [39], clinicians should find ways to bridge the gap caused by lower SES condition and explore barriers to treatment success. The design of interventions should engage low-income families' perceptions and practices as well as the conditions in which they live [30], and interventions should be tailored to accommodate specific cultural contexts rather than simply using general management guidelines. Interventions should address the unique barriers faced by families with low SES status and should attempt to better target undereducated parents and their young high-risk children.

REFERENCES

[1]   Swinburn B., Egger G., Raza F. (1999). Dissecting obesogenic environments: the development and application of a framework for identifying and prioritizing environmental interventions for obesity. *Prev Med.* 29, 563–570.

[2]   Lobstein, T., Baur, L., Uauy, R. (2004). Obesity in children and young people: a crisis in public health. Report of the international obesity task force childhood obesity working group. *Obes Rev.* 5, 4–10.

[3]   Teixeira P.J., Sardinha L.B., Going S.B., Lohman T.G. (2001). Total and regional fat and serum cardiovascular disease risk factors in lean and obese children and adolescents. *Obes Res.* 9, 432–442.

[4]   Epstein L.H., Wing, R.R., Koeske R., Valoski, A. (1987). Long-term effects of family-based treatment of childhood obesity. *J Consult Clin Psychol.* 55, 91–95.

[5]   Whitaker, R.C., Wright, J.A., Pepe, M.S., Seidel, K.D., Dietz, W.H. (1997). Predicting obesity in young adulthood from childhood and parental obesity. *N Engl J Med.* 337, 869–873.

[6]   Davison, K.K., Birch, L.L. (2001). Childhood overweight: a contextual model and recommendations for future research. *Obes Rev.* 2, 159–171.

[7]   Campbell, K., Waters, E., O'Meara, S., Summerbell, C. (2001). Interventions for preventing obesity in children. *Cochrane Database Syst Rev.* 2, CD001871.

[8]   Campbell, K., Crawford, D. (2001). Family food environments as determinants of preschool aged children's eating behaviors: implication for obesity prevention policy. *Aust J Nutn Diet,* 58, 19–25.

[9]   Adair, L.S., Popkin, B.M. (2005). Are child eating patterns being transformed globally? *Obes Res.* 13, 1281–1299.

[10]   Huang, J.S., Lee, T.A., Lu, M.C. (2006). Prenatal programming of childhood overweight and obesity. *Matern Child Health J.* 11, 461-473.

[11]   Sobal, J. (1991). Obesity and socioeconomic status: a framework for examining relationships between physical and social variables. *Med Anthropol.* 13, 231-247.

[12]   Neumark-Sztainer, D., Story, M., Resnick, M.D., Blum, R.W. (1996). Correlates of inadequate fruit and vegetable consumption among adolescents. *Prev Med.* 25, 497–505.

[13]   Kinra, S., Nelder, R.P., Lewendon, G.J. (2000). Deprivation and childhood obesity: a cross sectional study of 20 973 children in Plymouth, United Kingdom. *J Epidemiol Community Health,* 54, 456–460.

[14]   Viner, R.M., Cole, T.J. (2005). Television viewing in early childhood predicts adult body mass index. *J Pediatr.* 147, 429–435.

[15]   Ammerman, A.S., Lindquist, C.H., Lohr, K.N., Hersey, J (2002). The efficacy of behavioral interventions to modify dietary fat and fruit and vegetable intake: a review of the evidence. *Prev Med* 35, 25–41.

[16]   Doak, C.M., Visscher, T.L., Renders, C.M., Seidell, J.C. (2006). The prevention of overweight and obesity in children and adolescents: a review of interventions and programmes. *Obes Rev.* 7, 111–136.

[17]   Kral, J.G. (2004) Preventing and treating obesity in girls and young women to curb the epidemic. *Obes Res.* 12, 1539–1546.

[18]   Campbell, K.J. & Hesketh, K.D. (2007). Strategies which aim to positively impact on weight, physical activity, diet and sedentary behaviours in children from zero to five years. A systematic review of the literature. *Obes Rev.* 8, 327–338.

[19]   Brown, T., Kelly, S., Summerbell, C. (2007). Prevention of obesity: a review of interventions *Obes Rev.* 8 (Suppl. 1) 127–130.

[20]   Young, K.M., Northern, J.J., Lister, K.M., Drummond, J.A. (2007). O'Brien WH. A meta-analysis of family-behavioral weight-loss treatments for children. *Clinical Psychology Review,* 27, 240-249.

[21] Kinston, W., Loader, P., Miller, L., Rein, L. (1988). Interaction in families with obese children. *J Psychosom Res.* 32, 513-532.

[22] Wilkins, S.C., Kendrick, O.W., Stitt, K.R., Stinett, N., Hammarlund, V.A. (1998). Family functioning is related to overweight in children. *J Am Diet Assoc.* 98, 572–574.

[23] Klesges, R.C., Eek, L.H., Hanson, C.L., Haddock, C.K., Klesges, L.M. (1990). Effect of obesity social interactions, and physical environment on physical activity in preschoolers. *Health Psychol.* 9, 435–449.

[24] Stradmeijer, M., Bosch, J., Koops, W., Seidell, J. (2000). Family functioning and psychosocial adjustment in overweight youngsters. *Int J Eat Disord.* 27, 110–114.

[25] White, M.A., Martin, P.D., Newton, R.L., Walden, H.M., York-Crowe, E.E., Gordon, S.T., Ryan, D.H., Williamson, D.A. (2004). Mediators of weight loss in a family-based intervention presented over the internet. *Obes Res.* 12, 1050-1059.

[26] Cameron, A.M., Frohlich, N. (1995). Socio-economic status and the health of the population. *Med Care,* 33 (12 Suppl), DS43–DS54.

[27] Power, C., Parsons, T. (2000). Nutritional and other influences in childhood as predictors of adult obesity. *Proc Nutr Soc.* 59, 267–272.

[28] Laessle, R.G., Uhl, H., Lindel, B. (2001). Parental influences on eating behavior in obese and nonobese preadolescents. *Int J Eat Disord.* 40, 447–453.

[29] Patrick, H., Nicklas, T.A. (2005). Review of family and social determinants of children's eating patterns and diet quality. *J Am Coll Nutr.* 24, 83–92.

[30] Kaufman, L. & Karpati, A. (2007). Understanding the sociocultural roots of childhood obesity: Food practices among Latino families of Bushwick, Brooklyn. *Soc Sci Med.* 64, 2177–2188.

[31] Anderson, P.M., Butcher, K.F., Levine, P.B. (2003). Maternal employment and overweight children. *J Health Econ.* 22, 477–504.

[32] O'Dea, J.A. & Wilson, R. (2006). Socio-cognitive and nutritional factors associated with body mass index in children and adolescents: possibilities for childhood obesity prevention. *Health Educ. Res.* 21, 796-805.

[33] Friedman, L.S., Lukyanova, E.M., Serduik, A., Shkiryak-Zizhnik, Z.A., Chislovska N.A., Znivchuk, A.V., Oliynik, I., Hryhorczuk, D. (2008). Social-environmental factors associated with elevated body mass index in a Ukranian cohort of children. *Int J of Ped Obesity,* Online 1-10.

[34] North, K., Emmett, P. (2000). Multivariate analysis of diet among three-year-old children and associations with socio-demographic characteristics. The Avon Longitudinal Study of Pregnancy and Childhood (ALSPAC) Study Team. *Eur J Clin Nutr.* 54, 73-80.

[35] Xie, B., Gilliland, F.D., Li, Y.F., Rockett, H.R. (2003). Effects of ethnicity, family income, and education on dietary intake among adolescents. *Prev Med.* 36, 30–40.

[36] Kranz, S., Siega-Riz, A.M. (2002). Sociodemographic determinants of added sugar intake in preschoolers 2 to 5 years old. *J Pediatr.* 140, 667–672.

[37] Lamerz, A., Kuepper-Nybelen, J., Wehle, C, Bruning, N., Trost-Brinkhues, G., Brenner, H. Hebebrand, J., Herpertz-Dahlman, B. (2005). Social class, parental education, and obesity prevalence in a study of six-year-old children in Germany. *Int J Obes.* 29, 373–380.

[38] Kumanyika, S., Grier, S. (2006). Targeting interventions for ethnic minority and low income population. *Future Child* 16, 187–207.

[39] Matheson, D.M., Killen, J.D., Wang, Y., Varady, A., Robinson, T.N. (2004). Children's food consumption during television viewing. *Am J Clin Nutr.* 79, 1088–1094.

[40] van Zutphen, M., Bell, A.C., Kremer, P.J., Swinburn, B.A. (2007). Association between the family environment and television viewing in Australian children. *J Paediatr Child,* 43, 458-463.

[41] Clay, D.L., Mordhorst, M.J., Lehn, L. (2002). Empirically supported treatment in pediatric psychology: where is the diversity? *J Pediatr Psychol.* 27, 325-337.

[42] Epstein, L.H., Wing, R.R., Koeske, R., Valoski, A. (1986). Effect of parent weight on weight loss in obese children. *J Consult Clin Psychol.* 54, 400–401.

[43] Reinehr, T., Brylak, K., Alexy, U., Kersting, M., Andler, W. (2003). Predictors to success in outpatient training in obese children and adolescents. *Int J Obes.* 27, 1087–1092.

[44] Epstein, L.H., Valoski, A., Wing, R.R., McCurley, J. (1990). Ten-year follow-up of behavioral, family-based treatment for obese children. *JAMA,* 264, 2519–2523.

[45] Jain, A., Sherman, S.N., Chamberlin, L.A., Carter, Y., Powers, S.W., Whitaker, R.C. (2001). Why don't low-income mothers worry about their preschoolers being overweight? *Pediatrics,* 107, 1138–1146.

[46] Israel, A.C., Silverman, W.K., Solota, L.C. (1986). An investigation of family influences on initial weight status, attrition and treatment outcome in a childhood obesity program. *Behavior Therapy,* 17, 131–143.

[47] Golan, M., Weizman, A., Apter, A., Fainaru, M. (1998). Parents as the exclusive agents of change in the treatment of childhood obesity. *Am J Clin Nutr.* 67, 1130–1138.

[48] Wrotniak, B.H., Epstein, L.H., Paluch, R.A., Roemmich, J.N. (2005). The relationship between parent and child self-reported adherence and weight loss. *Obes Res.* 13, 1089–1096.

[49] Epstein, L.H., Myers, M.D., Raynor, H.A., Saelens, B.E. (1998). Treatment of pediatric obesity. *Pediatrics* 101, 554–570.

[50] Epstein, L.H., Wing, R.R., Koeske, R., Valoski, A. (1985). A comparison of lifestyle exercise, aerobic exercise and calisthenics on weight loss on obese children. *Behav Ther.* 16, 345–356.

[51] Conger, R.D., McCarty, J.A., Yang, R.K., Lahey, B.B., Kropp, J.P. (1984). Perception of child, child-rearing values and emotional distress as mediating links between environmental stresses and observed maternal behavior. *Child Dev.* 55, 2234–2247.

[52] Dietz, W.H. (1983). Family characteristics affect rates of weight loss in obese children. *Nutr Rev.* 3, 43–50.

[53] Golan, M., Fainaru, M., Weizman, A. (1998). Role of behavior modification in the treatment of childhood obesity with the parents as the exclusive agents of change. *Int J Obes.* 22, 1–8.

[54] Golan, M., Weizman, A., Apter, A., Fainaru, M. (1998). Reliability and validity of the family eating and activity habits questionnaire. *Eur J Clin Nutr* 52, 771–777.

[55] Golan, M., Kaufman, V., Shahar, D.R. (2006). Childhood obesity treatment: Targeting parents exclusively vs. parents and children. *Br J Nutr.* 95, 1008–1015.

[56] Hertzler, A.A. (1981). Obesity – impact of the family. *J Am Diet Assoc.* 79, 525–530.

[57] Barlow, S.E., Dietz, W.H. (1998) Obesity evaluation and treatment: Expert committee recommendations. *Pediatrics,* 102, E29.

[58] Olson, D.H., Russel, C.S., Sprenkle, D.H. (1983). Circumplex model VI: Theoretical up-date. *Fam Process,* 22, 69–83.

[59] Olson, D.H., Russel, C.S., Sprenkle, D.H. (1985). Marital and family therapy: A decade review. *J Mar and Develop.* 55, 179–183.

[60] Favaro, A., Santonastaso, P. (1995). Effects of parent's psychological characteristics and eating behavior on childhood obesity and dietary compliance. *J Psychosom Res.* 39, 145–151.

[61] Gibson, L.Y., Byrne, S.M., Davis, E.A., Blair, E., Jacoby, P., Zubrick, S.R. (2007). The role of family and maternal factors in childhood obesity. *Med J Aust.* 186, 591-595.

[62] Birch, L.L., Fisher, J.O., Davison, K.K. (2003). Learning to overeat: maternal use of restrictive feeding practices promotes girls' eating in the absence of hunger. *Am J Clin Nutr.* 78, 215–220.

[63] Myers, M.D., Raynor, H.A., Epstein, L.H. (1998). Predictors of child psychological changes during family-based treatment for obesity. *Arch Pediatr Adolesc Med.* 152, 855–861.

[64] Campbell, K.J., Crawford, D.A., Salmon, J., Carver, A., Garnett, S.P., Baur, L.A. (2007). Associations between the home food environment and obesity-promoting eating behaviors in adolescence. *Obesity,* 15, 719-730.

[65] Kroller, K. & Warschburger, P. (2008). Associations between maternal feeding style and food intake of children with a higher risk for overweight. *Appetite,* In Press.

[66] Epstein, L.H., Klein, K.R., Wisnieski, L. (1994). Child and parent factors that influence psychological problems in obese children. *Int J Eat Disord.* 15, 151–158.

[67] Dietz, W.H., Gortmaker, S.L. (1984). Factors within the physical environment associated with childhood obesity. *Am J Clin Nutr* 39, 619–624.

[68] Barbarin, O.A., Tirado, M. (1985). Enmeshment, family processes and successful treatment of obesity. *Fam Relat: J Appl Fam Child Stud.* 341,115–121.

[69] Faith, M.S. (2005). Parent-child feeding strategies and their relationships to child eating and weight status. *Int J Obes.* 29, 549–556.

[70] Cullen, K.W., Baranowski, T., Rittenberry, L., Cosart, C., Hebert, D., de Moor, C. (2000). Socio-environmental influences on children's fruit, juice, and vegetable consumption as reported by parents: reliability and validity of measures. *Public Health Nutr.* 3, 345–356.

[71] Fisher, J.O., Mitchell, D.C., Smiciklas-Wright, H., Birch, L.L. (2002). Parental influences on young girls' fruit and vegetables, micronutrient and fat intake. *J Am Diet Assoc.* 102, 58–64

[72] Birch, L.L. (1992). Children preferences for high-fat foods. *Nutr Rev.* 50, 249-255.

[73] Birch, L.L., Fisher, J.O. (1998). Development of eating behaviors among children and adolescents. *Pediatrics,* 101, 539–549.

[74] Birch, L.L., Davison, K.K. (2001). Family environmental factors influencing the developing behavioral controls of food intake and childhood overweight. *Pediatr Clin North Am.* 48, 893–907.

[75] Hood, M.Y., Moore, L.L., Sundarajan-Ramamurti, A., Singer, M., Cupples, L.A., Ellison, R.C. (2000). Parental eating attitudes and the development of obesity in children. The Framingham children's study. *Int J Obe.s* 24, 1319–1125.

[76] Benton, D. (2004). Role of parents in the determination of the food preferences of children and the development of obesity. *Int J Obes.* 28, 858–869.

[77] Birch, L.L. (1979). Preschool children's food preferences and consumption patterns. *J Nutr Educ.* 11a, 189–192.

[78] Birch, L.L. (1979). Dimension of preschool children's food preferences. *J Nutr Educ* 11b, 77–80.

[79] Costanzo, P.R., Woody, E.Z. (1985). Domain-specific parenting styles and their impact on the child's development of particular deviance: the example of obesity proneness. *J Soc Clin Psychol.* 3, 425–445.

[80] Wardle, J., Herrera, M.L., Cooke, L., Gibson, E.L. (2003). Modifying children's food preferences : The effects of exposure and reward on acceptance of an unfamiliar vegetable. *Eur J Clin Nutr* 57, 341-348.

[81] Reinaerts, E., de Nooijer, J., Candel, M., de Vries, N. (2007). Explaining school children's fruit and vegetable consumption: The contributions of availability, accessibility, exposure, parental consumption and habit in addition to psychosocial factors. *Appetite,* 48, 248-258.

[82] Satter, E.M. (1988). Should the obese child diet? In Clark KL, Parr RB, Castelli WP (eds): *Evaluation and Management of Eating Disorders.* Champaign, IL: Life Enhancement Publications, pp 61–75.

[83] Satter, E.M. (1996). Internal regulation and the evolution of normal growth as the basis for prevention of obesity in childhood. *J Am Diet Assoc.* 9, 860–864.

[84] Stein, R.I., Epstein, L.H., Raynor, H.A., Kilanowski, C.K., Paluch, R.A. (2005). The influence of parenting change on pediatric weight control. *Obes Res.* 13, 1749–1755.

[85] McCurdy, K. & Daro, D. (2001). Parent involvement in family support programs: An integrated theory. *Family Relations,* 50, 113-121.

[86] Lindsay, A.C., Sussner, K.M., Kim, J., Gortmaker, S. (2006). The role of parents in preventing childhood obesity. *The Future of Children,* 16, 169-186.

[87] Simkin-Silverman, L.R., Conroy, M.B., King, W.C. (2008). Treatment of overweight and obesity in primary care practice: Current evidence and future directions. *Am J of Lifestyle Medicine,* 2, 296-304.

[88] Luther, B. (2007). Looking at childhood obesity through the lens of Baumrind's parenting typologies. *Orthopaedic Nursing,* 26, 270-280.

[89] Power, C., Moynihan, C. (1988). Social class and changes in weight-for-height between childhood and early adulthood. *Int J Obes.* 12, 445–453.

[90] Sobal, J., Stunkard, A.J. (1989). Socioeconomic status and obesity: a review of the literature. *Psychol Bull,* 105, 260–275.

[91] Gordon-Larsen, P., McMurray, R.G., Popkin, B.M. (2000). Determinants of adolescent physical activity and inactivity patterns. *Pediatrics,* 105:E83.

[92] Danielzik, S., Czerwinski-Mast, M., Langnasw, K., Dibla, B., Muller, M.J. (2004). Parental overweight, socioeconomic status and high birth weight are the major determinants of overweight and obesity in 5-7 year-old children baseline data of the Kiel obesity intervention. *Int J Obes.* 28, 1494–1502.

[93] Speakman, J.R., Walker, H., Walker, L., Jackson, D.M. (2005). Association between BMI, social strata and the estimated energy content of foods. *Int J Obes.* 29, 1281–1288.

[94] Romon, M., Duhamel, A., Collinet, N., Weill, J. (2005). Influence of social class on time trends in BMI distribution in 5-year-old French children from 1989 to 1999. *Int J Obes.* 29, 54–59.

[95] Tuinstra, J., Groothoff, J.W., Van Den Heuvel. W.J.A., Post, D. (1998). Socio-economic differences in health risk behavior in adolescence: do they exist? *Soc Sci Med.* 47, 67–74.

[96] Chen, J.L., Kennedy, C. (2004). Family functioning, parenting style, and Chinese children's weight status. *J Fam Nurs.* 10, 262–279.

[97] Epstein, L.H., Myers, M.D., Anderson, K. (1996). The association of maternal psychopathology and family socioeconomic status with psychological problems in obese children. *Obes Res.* 4, 501–503.

[98] Galey, R.M. (1986). Epistemology, family patterns, and psychosomatics: The case of obesity. *Family Process,* l25, 437–451.

[99] Mellbin, T., Vuille, J.C. (1989). Rapidly developing overweight in school children as an indicator of psychosocial stress. *Acta Paediatr Scand.* 78, 568–575.

[100] Zametkin, A.J., Zoon, C.K., Klein, H.W., Munson, S. (2004). Psychiatric aspects of child and adolescent obesity: a review of the past 10 years. *J Am Acad Child Adolesc Psychiatry,* 43, 134–150.

[101] Zeller, M.H., Saelens, B.E., Roehrig, H., Kirk, S., Daniels, S.R. (2004). Psychological adjustment of obese youth presenting for weight management treatment. *Obes Res* 12, 1576–1586.

[102] Uzark, K.C., Becker, M.H., Dielman, T.E., Rocchini, A.P., Katch, V. (1988). Perceptions held by obese children and their parents: Implications for weight control intervention. *Health Educ Q* 5, 185–198.

[103] Dunn, C., Deroo, L., Rivara, F.P. (2001). The use of brief interventions adapted from motivational interviewing across behavioral domains: A systemic review. *Addiction.* 12, 1725–1742.

[104] Miller, W.R., Rollnick, S. (2002). *Motivational interviewing.* New York: Guilford Press.

[105] Kirk, S., Scott, B.J., Daniels, S.R. (2005). Pediatric obesity epidemic: treatment options. *J Am Diet Assoc* 105, S44–51.

In: Handbook of Parenting: Styles, Stresses & Strategies   ISBN 978-1-60741-766-8
Editor: Pacey H. Krause and Tahlia M. Dailey   © 2009 Nova Science Publishers, Inc.

Chapter 14

THE ROLE OF THE FAMILY IN AUTISTIC SPECTRUM CONDITIONS: THEORY AND PRACTICAL IMPLICATIONS

Lisa A. Osborne[*] and Phil Reed
Swansea University, UK

ABSTRACT

The role of the family in Autistic Spectrum Conditions (ASC) has a controversial history, but current research has identified a number of key relationships between the behaviors of the child with ASC and parenting stress and styles. The current review highlights a number of relationships between parenting stress, parenting behaviors, and child behavior problems in ASC samples, and identifies areas where current research is lacking. In particular, the following concerns need to be addressed: whether high parenting stress levels impact negatively on child outcomes following interventions for ASC; the nature of the relationship between parenting stress and child behavior problems over time; whether parenting stress impacts on parenting behaviors, and the types of parenting behaviors that are influential for subsequent child behavior problems in the context of ASC; whether any association between parenting behaviors and child behavior problems is a direct one; and whether the contact and communication experiences of parents with professionals leading up to, and during, the diagnostic process is of particular significance. The results of such examinations may well have practical implications for the development of future interventions for ASC.

Autistic Spectrum Conditions (ASC) are a collection of five developmental disorders (autistic disorder, Asperger's syndrome, Rett's disorder, childhood disintegrative disorder, and pervasive developmental disorder not otherwise specified), which are typically characterized by deficits in social-emotional reciprocity. They comprise a wide spectrum of

---
[*] Correspondence address: Lisa A. Osborne,
Department of Psychology,
Swansea University,
Singleton Park,
Swansea, SA2 8PP, U.K.

problems, including impairment in social interactions; communication difficulties; limited spontaneous pretend and imaginative play; and restricted, repetitive, and stereotyped patterns of behaviors and interests.

In addressing the problems, and related issues, produced by having a child with ASC, the role of the parents has recently come to the fore; for example, involving the parents with any interventions given to the child has been shown to be important (e.g., Schuntermann, 2002; Stoddart, 1999). Recent initiatives provide good examples of this movement: the EarlyBird scheme (Shields, 2001) and Portage program (Smith, 2000) specifically highlight the need for parental involvement in helping the child with ASC. Recently, Applied Behavior Analytic (ABA) programs have also focused both on the need for parental involvement (e.g., Gabriels, Hill, Pierce, Rogers, & Wehner, Luiselli, Cannon, Ellis, & Sisson, 2000; Harris, 1994), and on the impacts of the intervention on the family as a whole (Hastings & Johnson, 2001). Given these developments, there seems every reason to place the parents clearly in focus when framing an understanding of the impacts of ASC, and when considering the development of interventions for ASC.

Many of these more family-oriented interventions have noted improvements in children's behaviors and functioning as a result of a reduction in parenting stress and an increase in parental coping abilities (e.g., Harris, Handleman, Arnold, & Gordon, 2000; Lovaas & Smith, 2003; Spaccarelli, Cotler, & Penman, 1992; see Brookman-Frazee, Stahmer, Baker-Ericzen, & Tsai, 2006, for a comprehensive review). There are several studies that suggest that teaching positive parenting skills to parents of children with ASC will subsequently reduce their children's challenging behaviors. For example, teaching parents 'mindful parenting' was shown to reduce aggression, non-compliance, and self-injury in their children, and promoted parental satisfaction with their parenting skills as well as with their parent-child interactions (Singh, Lancioni, Winton, Fisher, Wahler, McAleavey, Singh, & Sabaawi, 2006).

Parent-centered approaches such as EarlyBird have targeted the parents directly, rather than the child, and appear to produce gains in children (see Joycelyn, Casiro, Beattie, Bow, & Kneisz, 1998; Sheilds, 2001). Jocelyn et al. (1998) reported the results of a randomized-controlled trial that evaluated a caregiver-based intervention program for children with ASC, in community day-care centers, over a three month period. In this study, both parents and nursery staff were trained in the intervention program. The children in the experimental group demonstrated greater gains in language abilities, and there were significant increases in parents' and nursery staff's knowledge about ASC, greater perception of control on the part of mothers, and greater parental satisfaction.

There are numerous other interventions that target the problems experienced by the parents of children with ASC, such as Behavioral Marital Therapy, Behavioral Family Therapy, and individualized intervention techniques to help families adapt to the chronic stress of living with a child with ASC (e.g., Cherry, 1989; Harris, 1984; 1994; Moes, 1995). Although several programs have noted improvements in parental stress (e.g., Bitsika & Sharpley, 2000), others have noted less obvious benefits (Bitsika & Sharpley, 1999; Kuloglu-Aksaz, 1994). Despite such occasional negative reports, beneficial child outcomes, as a result of combating parental problems, such as stress, suggest that parental stress impacts on children's behaviors. Findings related to these various interventions suggest that improved parent-child interactions occur through promoting low stress in parents during those interactions, and through the development of more positive communication (e.g., Koegel, Bimbela, & Schreibman, 1996). Parents who receive support, that buffers stress, relate better, emotionally, to their children (Boyd, 2002). Thus, these interventions recognize how parental functioning may influence the behaviors of a child with special needs (Harris, 1994), and several studies have noted improvements in the children's behaviors, as a result of a reduction in parental stress,or improvements in communication and interactions (Engwall & Macpherson, 2003; Harris et al., 2000; Lovaas & Smith, 2003).

Thus, it is now becoming more widely recognized that focusing purely on the impacts of interventions on children with ASC, neglects the important and key role that parents play in the management of their child's problems (Harris et al., 2000). The importance of involving, and preparing, parents, in support of their child undergoing intervention and treatment across a range of conditions and illnesses, is gaining recognition. There is growing evidence that such family- or parent-oriented interventions show more robust and consistent benefits than purely patient- or child-focused interventions (see Martire & Schulz, 2007). Thus, a more parent-oriented approach is arguably required to gain a fuller understanding of the systems, dynamics, and mechanisms that are involved, and influential, in the development and treatment of the child with ASC.

FAMILY ISSUES

There is relatively little current research on family influences on ASC, although this area of study is developing. This relative lack of contemporary study is potentially due to the reaction to Bruno Bettelheim's contentious views on the mothers of children with ASC. Bettelheim (1967) claimed that children with ASC had been raised in 'unstimulating' environments during the first few years of their lives, when their language and motor skills were developing. The nature of Bettelheim's claims lead many to believe that some blame was attributed to parents of children with ASC. This lead to strong feeling, and a backlash regarding the direction taken by subsequent research into the area of the family, and there was a reduction of the amount of investigation into the relationship between parental behaviors and the development of children with ASC. Recently, however, there has been some work on the influence of families, and, more specifically, parents, on ASC, and a re-emergence of interest in this area.

Historical Views on the Family and ASC

Kanner (1944) reported on twenty cases of children, who, from infancy, were manifesting marked autistic tendencies. He noted that many of these children lived in families of high academic achievement. Out of the twenty, nine families were listed in the *Who's Who in America*, or in *American Men of Science*, or in both. It was suggested that it is possible that the preoccupation of such eminent academics was with abstract ideas, rather than with people and social relations. This characteristic could be pathologically exaggerated in their descendants, so that their children live within themselves, and show no interest in social relationships whatsoever.

This characteristic social disinterest could be either, or both, genetic or learnt. However, by 1949, Kanner was more clearly swayed in thinking that ASC is a learnt problem. He observed fifty-five children with ASC, and their parents, and noted that most of the children had been exposed to 'parental coldness', and a lack of 'affectionate warmth', from the beginning of life. Their parents tended to be obsessive, and displayed a mechanical attention to their child's physical needs, but not to their emotional and social requirements. The children withdrew from contact with people, but became affectionate towards objects, and obsessed about preserving sameness. Though intelligent, if they used language at all, they did so in a self-directed manner in order to entertain themselves, and not in an interpersonal and communicative way with others. Kanner claimed that the children sought solitude as a form of comfort and escape from their situation, and profoundly avoided all social contact. These observations of Kanner's correspond to those of Asperger (1944), especially regarding the social class of the families observed. Thus, for these two seminal figures in the field of ASC, the functional causes of ASC were primarily to do with the family, and the family dynamics at work.

This view of ASC as being family-related, and socially generated, along with the prevailing Freudian approach to treatment, as well as the salient research of the time on maternal care, deprivation, and attachment (Bowlby, 1951), ultimately lead to Bruno Bettelheim's controversial work and assertions. In 1967, Bettelheim, a Hungarian Freudian Psychologist, who emigrated to the U.S.A., wrote his book: *The empty fortress: infantile autism and the birth of the self.* This book was a case study of three children suffering from ASC, and it documents their Psychodynamic treatment. He wrote about the experiences of the staff members at the Sonia Shankman Orthogenic School in Chicago, of which he was the Director, and, despite wide-spread perceptions to the contrary, Bettelheim takes no explicit stand on the etiology of the disorder of ASC in this book.

Bettelheim's earlier work provides the framework into which he fitted his study of the treatment of ASC. Bettelheim (1950) wrote a book, entitled: *Love is not enough; the treatment of emotionally disturbed children*, in which he describes the care offered at the Orthogenic School for emotionally-disturbed children. The school worked to restore a sense of security in children, whose parents were not capable of maintaining it, by deploying Psychoanalytic methods of treatment, and everyday activities, in order to reduce their anxieties and insecurities. Bettelheim's interest in the problems seen in children that directly resulted from problems of their parents, and their parents' ways of handling particular situations and activities, was later adapted to the study and treatment of ASC by Bettelheim.

Critiques of Family Causes of ASC

The perception of Bettelheim's work on ASC sparked a backlash that shifted the study of the causes of ASC from looking at environmental, experiential, and learnt influences, to examining organic, biological, and 'within-child' factors. This shift in focus has been welcomed, and embraced, by many people, as can be seen in the sentiments expressed on many websites dealing with ASC. For example, an anonymous writer states: "*Luckily, research has been shown that autism is a disease with biological causes, not social ones.*", on the Macalester University Psychology website. Similarly, Lorna Wing (1997) writes: "*Fortunately not everyone had faith in the theory of the emotional causes of autism.*".

Unfortunately, this resultant 'relief' appears to have been misplaced, in that, while it has served to relieve parents of feelings of guilt and blame, it has failed to lead to any substantial methods of management, and treatment, of the children's problems. Some of the backlash against Bettelheim appears to have been of a very personal kind. His book, *The empty fortress: infantile autism and the birth of the self*, was called: "*The empty book*", by his critics (see Gardner, 2000), and the infamous term "refrigerator mothers", that was so widely attributed to Bettelheim, does not appear to be present in any original sources by Bettelheim himself. He appears to have been a victim of a 'smear' campaign that challenged the whole environmental approach to ASC, and, if ousted, could be replaced by one purely focused on its biological origins.

More scientific, and legitimate, concerns were first expressed by Schopler (1971), who flagged the important issue of parents not being used as scapegoats. He questioned whether 'scapegoating' behavior, as outlined by Allport regarding prejudice, was taking place in the study of ASC, and whether it was biasing attitudes against the parents of individuals with ASC. He warned that researchers, in this area, should be aware of, and on their guard against, such negative behavior, and concluded that professionals should examine their motives in classifying parents as primary causes of ASC. This expression of concern was made at the time when ASC was beginning to be associated with genetic, constitutional, and biochemical pre-dispositions.

Bernard Rimland (1964), a Psychologist, and father of a boy with ASC, wrote a book, entitled: *Infantile Autism: The Syndrome and its implications for a neural theory of behavior*, in which he argued that ASC was a biological disorder, not an emotional one. This book marked an enormous change in the way that ASC was perceived, and it impacted greatly on future treatments, and on the direction in which the study of ASC traveled. Once the floodgates were opened by Rimland for biological explanations of the etiology, and nature, of ASC, numerous suggestions were made in the same biological, and 'within-child' vein.

For instance, a biological theory regarding ASC was proposed by Shattock and Lowdon (1991), who suggest that opioid peptides are involved in the development of ASC. They propose that some people have difficulty in breaking down casein (milk and dairy produce), or gluten (wheat and some other cereal products), during digestion. This inability to digest completely these compounds leads to excess amino acids (peptides) crossing into the brain, rather than being disposed of in the urine, and this interferes with normal brain function and activity. This build-up of such peptides results in autistic-like behaviors.

Rutter (2000) has argued for a strong genetic basis for ASC. As well as the purely genetic work that has been conducted in this area, it has been postulated that many autistic traits may have their roots in genetics. For example, Baron-Cohen, Wheelwright, Stott, Bolton, and Goodyer (1997) have argued, on the basis of a sample of 919 replies from parents of children with ASC, that fathers and grandfathers of children with ASC are far more likely to be engineers than the fathers and grandfathers of children without ASC. They suggest that there is, ultimately, a genetic basis for a cognitive phenotype, or certain cognitive approach, that predisposes a person to excel in engineering. Engineering, as an occupation, is over-represented in fathers and grandfathers of children with ASC, and, if that same predisposition to excel in engineering goes too far, it will result in ASC. Baron-Cohen and Hammer (1997) refer to this cognitive style as a reflection of the functioning of the 'male brain', which they believe is biologically determined. However, there is no way of knowing whether these traits are biologically, or environmentally, determined, and their findings have been disputed by many researchers (e.g., Gerrans & McGeer, 2003; Islam, 1998; Wolff, 1998).

In terms of the evidence for family and parent factors producing ASC, it is clear that much of the evidence is quite anecdotal in nature. This hypothesis has also been challenged on the basis of a few reports that have examined the social class and profession of the parents, as suggested by Kanner (1944) and Asperger (1944; and, later, by Baron-Cohen et al., 1997).

Ritvo, Cantwell, Johnson, Clements, Benbrook, Slagel, Kelly, and Ritz (1971), on the basis of previous studies' findings that parents of children with ASC were found to be more emotionally detached, more highly educated, and from higher socio-economic classes, than parents of typically developing children or parents of disturbed children, wanted to investigate these claimed differences. All admissions to a large metropolitan institution were assessed, and seventy-four children with ASC were matched for gender and age with children with various organic, neurotic, and behavioral problems. Parents' educations, and occupations, were used as variables to indicate social class, and the parents were evaluated for age, ethnic origin, social class, and religion. There were no indications apparent in the results of any differences between the parents of the children with ASC and the matched parents on any of the variables for social class. One finding that was statistically significant was that more mothers of children with ASC did not have employment.

Schopler, Andrews, and Strupp (1979), in a state-wide study of 522 families with children with ASC and related communication problems, found no difference in the severity of ASC between the high and low socio-economic status families. They found no significant difference in the cognitive potential of the children, nor did they find any difference in the complexity of their rituals and obsessive maintenance of sameness, but they did find that children from a higher social class had an earlier age of onset of ASC (although the reasons for this finding are unclear).

Despite the fact that both of these above studies did find a slight effect of social class, the findings have been used to dispute the importance of this influencing factor (see Frith, 1989; Wing, 1997). However, even if the claims of Frith and Wing were accepted, they still do not convincingly challenge the theory that there are differences in the parenting style of parents with children with ASC, irrespective of their high, or low, economic status. Bettelheim (1950) made the point that the central relationship between the parents and child is the key factor, and any early, and continuous, difficulties in this relationship could underlie the disturbance in the child. It is not the case, according to Bettelheim, that specific aspects of the child's behaviors are merely influenced by the occupations of the parents (a view more correctly attributable to Kanner). As will be seen in later sections of this review, there are numerous differences between parents of children with ASC, and parents of those without ASC, in terms of their parenting styles, levels of stress, coping strategies, and parenting behaviors. It is difficult to say whether the variations in these parental factors cause the ASC, or are caused by the severity of the ASC and its associated difficulties. Nevertheless, there is a question here to be acknowledged and addressed.

Contemporary Models of Parenting

There are numerous theoretical models proposed to explain parent-child interactions, which suggest that parental stress may influence parenting behaviors, which, in turn, will impact on child behavior problems (e.g., Deater-Deckard, 1998; Hastings, 2002). Levels of parental stress may have an impact on behaviors of children with learning disabilities, and with ASC, and this finding has formed the basis of several theoretical models of parent-child interactions (e.g., Deater-Deckard, 1998; Hastings, 2002; but see Lazarus, 1991, Osborne, 2008, for alternative models).

In the context of learning disabilities, Hastings (2002) presented a theoretical model of the relationships between child behavior problems, parental stress, and parenting behavior (see Figure 1). This theoretical model postulated that child behavior problems influence levels of parental stress, which, in turn, impact on parenting behavior. These parenting behaviors then subsequently feed back into child behavior problems, thus, producing a cyclical model, displaying singular directionality of influence. Due to there being relatively little work conducted in this area, there is currently limited evidence to support, or reject, these suggested links between child behavior problems, parental stress, and parenting behavior, particularly concerning the dynamics within families of children with ASC. However, this theoretical model can be used as a potential springboard for research in this comparatively neglected area, and allows several key areas of potential parental influence, in the context of ASC, to be highlighted and examined (e.g., parental stress, and parenting behavior).

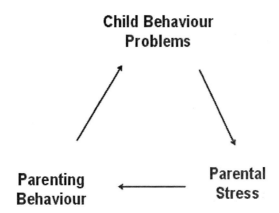

Figure 1. Hastings' (2002) model of parenting.

In support of the use of this theoretical model, a number of studies show that child behavior problems and parental stress do correlate (e.g., Baxter, Cummins, & Yiolitis, 2000; Hodapp, Fidler, & Smith, 1998; Stores, Stores, Fellow, & Buckley, 1998). However, Hastings (2002) claims that two further elements are necessary to substantiate his model. Firstly, the relationship between child behavior problems and parental stress has to be demonstrated as non-spurious, in order to rule out the possibility of other factors, or confounds, having an influence on parental stress. Secondly, temporal precedence should be established for causal directionality, that is, it should be shown that the child behavior problems precede the parental stress.

Several studies have presented data consistent with the view that child behavior problems, and not other factors, are associated with parental stress (e.g., Donenberg & Baker, 1993; Dumas, Wolf, Fisman, & Culligan, 1991; Floyd & Gallagher, 1997). These studies equated child behavior problems across groups; including one developmentally disabled, and one not developmentally disabled, and they demonstrated that there were no differences in reports of parental stress across these behavior problems groups. It should be noted that these previous studies all employed only parent ratings of child behavior problems, and none of these studies employed independent ratings of child behavior problems, such as made by teachers. This is important, as Lecavalier, Leone, and Wiltz (2006) noted that parents and teachers did not perfectly agree on the nature, and severity, of child behavior problems. Although parental stress and parent-rated child behavior problems made each other worse, over a period of a year, there was no such effect when teacher ratings of child behavior problems were used. It may be that high levels of stress in parents are related to an alteration in their perception of the behaviors of their children (see Fong, 1991).

In addition, it is important to establish the temporal precedence between child behavior problems and parental stress, in order to provide some evidence for possible causal directionality. Such evidence could be provided by using a longitudinal study design. Then, the correlations between child behavior problems and parental stress at baseline, and at follow-up, could be used to examine temporal directionality. Hastings (2002) suggested that the correlation between child behavior problems at baseline and parental stress at follow-up should be stronger than the correlation between parental stress at baseline and child behavior problems at follow-up.

However, it should be remembered that this model was developed for learning disabilities, rather than for ASC, and it needs to be considered in the context of the literature on ASC. The above discussion has focused on the methodological issues with regard to establishing the relationship between child behavior problems and parental stress, as there is evidence to suggest that parental stress is important in the context of ASC, and there is little existing evidence for ASC, specifically, to illustrate these methodological points with reference to the other two links in this model.

PARENTING STRESS

Many reports have noted the high degree of stress that parents experience when dealing with their child's problems (e.g., Bebko, Konstantaraes, & Springer, 1987; Shuntermann, 2002). These high stress levels can produce a range of severe problems in the parents. Such problems include depression (Wolf, Noh, Fisman, & Speechly, 1989), and disruption in the context of family life (see Dunn, Burbine, Bowers, & Tantleff, 2001; but see Gabriels et al., 2001). Freeman, Perry, and Factor (1991) found that parenting stress, which was related to specific child behaviors, was also correlated with general levels of parental stress. Koegel, Schreibman, O'Neill, and Burke (1983; see also Donenberg & Baker, 1993) draw a distinction between 'general stress' and 'situation-specific stress' in parents of children with ASC, and suggest that it is plausible that the latter may periodically occur, while finding no evidence of general stress levels being high.

Levels of Parenting Stress

Levels of parenting stress are more highly pronounced in parents of children with ASC, compared to parents of children with almost any other type of disability or health problem (Blacher & McIntyre, 2006; Bouma & Schweitzer, 1990; Dunn et al., 2001; Eisenhower, Baker, & Blacher, 2005; Koegel, Schreibman, Loos, Dirlich-Wilhelm, & Dunlap, 1992;

Perry, Sarlo-McGarvey, & Factor, 1992; Weiss, 2002; but see Holroyd & McArthur, 1976). In a review of current research on parents of children with ASC, Pisula (2003) found that profound parenting stress is reported as being experienced by such parents. For example, Wolf et al. (1989; see also Fisman, Wolf, & Noh, 1989; Sander & Morgan, 1997) found greater stress levels, and more dysphoria and depression, in parents of children with ASC than in parents of children with Down syndrome, and in parents of children without a developmental disability. Similarly, Bouma and Schweitzer (1990) found that ASC contributed significantly more to family stress than did a chronic physical illness (cystic fibrosis). Perry et al. (1992) have also shown this to be the case, in comparison to Rett's disorder.

These elevated levels of parenting stress in parents of children with ASC can be seen clearly by comparing the results of several studies that have all used a common measure of parenting stress (the *Questionnaire on Resources and Stress*; Friedrich, Greenberg, & Crnic, 1983). These various reports have studied parenting stress in the parents of children with: ASC (Osborne, McHugh, Saunders, & Reed, 2008a), Fragile X Syndrome (Backes, von Gontard, Schreck, & Lehmkuhl, 2001), Tubercular Sclerosis (Backes et al., 2001), and Learning Disabilities (Walden, Pistrang, & Joyce, 2000). The resulting levels of parenting stress (broken down by particular domains) can be seen in Figure 2, which shows consistently higher levels of parenting stress in parents of children with ASC, than in the parents of children with the other disorders, across almost all of the measured domains of parenting stress.

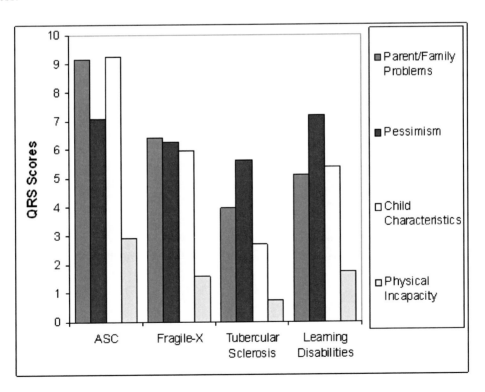

Figure 2. Stress levels of parents of children with various disabilities.

The distribution of parenting stress, across the four domains, in parents of children with each of the different disabilities, can be examined by noting the proportions of the total parenting stress, accounted for by each of the domains of parenting stress, which are shown in Figure 3.

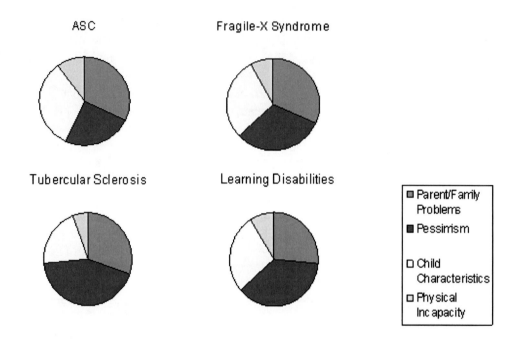

Figure 3. Proportions of parenting stress for the sub-scales of the QRS for various disabilities.

Causes of Parenting Stress

It is reasonably clear that the personalities of parents of children with ASC are not different from the personalities of parents of children with other disabilities, and, indeed, with no disabilities (e.g., Koegel et al., 1983). In fact, the only obvious characteristic that sets this group of parents apart from other parents is their extremely high levels of parenting stress (Blacher & McIntyre, 2006; Dunn et al., 2001; Eisenhower et al., 2005; Hastings & Johnson, 2001; Koegel et al., 1992; Perry et al., 1992; Weiss, 2002). A number of factors have been shown to be related to this elevated parenting stress, including the cumulative effect of long-term parenting a child with ASC (McAdoo & DeMyer, 1977), a number of parental characteristics, such as their coping strategies (Boyd, 2002), and the trigger of the diagnosis of ASC itself (Shuntermann, 2002).

The severity of the child's autistic symptoms is also associated with parental self-reports of stress, with higher levels of stress being reported by parents of children with severe behavioral problems (Bebko et al., 1987; Hastings, 2003; Hastings, Kovshoff, Ward, degli-Espinosa, Brown, & Remington, 2005; Hastings & Brown, 2002; Hastings & Johnson, 2001; Konstantareas & Homatidis, 1989). Kasari and Sigman (1997) found that parents who reported greater levels of stress had children with ASC who were less responsive in social interactions with an experimenter, and less engaged during a social game with the parent. Fong (1991) noted trends toward higher levels of maladaptive behaviors in adolescents with ASC of highly stressed mothers.

Several other factors have been found to contribute towards the high levels of stress in parents caring for children with ASC. Boyd (2002), in a review of the literature, reveals that mothers of children with challenging behaviors, and those mothers who are under greater stress, are more likely to seek social support. Individuals without access to rich social networks tend to report more stress than individuals with good social support, which may be mediated by the parent-perceived expertise of those providing the assistance, and respite (Factor, Perry, & Freeman, 1990; Gill & Harris, 1991; Konstantareas & Homatidis, 1989; Sharpley, Bitsika, & Efremidis, 1997; Weiss, 2002). Additionally, it appears that informal social support is a more effective 'stress-buffer' than formal support for mothers of children with ASC (Boyd, 2002; Hastings & Johnson, 2001).

The perceived presence of social support, along with hardiness, has been found to predict successful adaptation in parents (Weiss, 2002; Wolf et al., 1989), and lack of 'hardiness', and low levels of social support, are predictive of poor adaptation, and worse coping with stress, leading to 'burnout' (Weiss, 2002), and predict depression and anxiety (Boyd, 2002). Maternal- and paternal-stress are associated with the depression of their partner (Hastings et al., 2005). Stress levels may rise, thus, due to a temporary loss of external support from the partner (Hastings, 2003). Likewise, individuals who employ avoidant coping strategies in response to stress, tend to report more feelings of stress and mental health difficulties, compared to those who utilize positive reframing strategies (Dunn et al., 2001; Hastings & Johnson, 2001; Hastings et al., 2005).

Diagnosis of ASC and Parenting Stress

One area that would appear to have a high capacity for the production of stress in parents of children with suspected ASC is their contact and communication with professionals (Brogan & Knussen, 2003; Evans, Stoddart, Condon, Freeman, Grizzell, & Muller, 2001; Goin-Kochel, Mackintosh, & Myers, 2006; Osborne & Reed, 2008; Randall & Parker, 1999). A key aspect of this contact and communication with professionals concerns the process of obtaining a diagnosis of ASC for their child (Brogan & Knussen, 2003; Goin-Kochel et al., 2006; Howlin & Moore, 1997). For example, a large-scale survey by Howlin and Moore (1997) described the experiences of around 1,200 families with children with ASC. Many of these families expressed an early sense of a problem (often by the age of eighteen months), and many sought help from their doctor when their child was as young as two years of age. However, the report indicated that a diagnosis was often not made until the child was six years old, potentially losing the important advantage of early educational intervention.

These findings have been mirrored in several other reports. For example, Goin-Kochel et al. (2006) conducted a web-based survey across five countries, and noted that parent satisfaction with the diagnostic process increased, the fewer professionals they needed to see in order to obtain a diagnosis for their child. Mansell and Morris (2004), in a postal survey of parents in one U.K. Local Education Authority, found that early, and speedy, diagnosis was a key contributor to reducing parental stress (see also Brogan & Knussen, 2003). Both Mansell and Morris (2004), and Oberhein (1996) found that, in general, parents thought that the diagnostic process was a slow, chaotic, and badly-handled procedure. These results are mirrored by those findings obtained from a small set of four interviews conducted with parents in Wales (Midence & O'Neill, 1999). In this study, parents reported difficulty in getting provision for their child, or, indeed, obtaining any form of help and support. However, several of these studies have noted that, on the positive side, the parents, generally, were very appreciative of the help that they did receive (Mansell & Morris, 2004; Oberhein, 1996), and reported relief at obtaining a diagnosis of ASC (Midence & O'Neill, 1999).

In another small-scale analysis, Bartolo (2002; see also Goin-Kochel et al., 2006) noted that the manner of communication between professionals and parents was often problematic. These reported problems invariably revolved around discrepant approaches adopted by professionals across different sites. Other studies have highlighted points of discrepancy, and potential conflict, between the professionals and the parents. Grey (1993; see also Evans et al., 2001, for similar findings) found that points of disagreement between professionals and parents included: the prospect of a cure, the nature of the child's affection, and the uniqueness of the child and how this is related to the possibility of institutionalization.

Thus, diagnosis of ASC for a child is an extremely important event and issue in understanding the potential causes of child behavior problems and prognosis, given its impact on parents (Dale, Jahoda, & Knott, 2006). Diagnosis could be treated, speculatively, as a traumatic event that could induce a state similar to that of Post Traumatic Stress Disorder in parents. Certainly, Klauber (1999) has noted that parents of children with ASC are hyper-vigilant, and sensitive, to feelings of persecution regarding their child's ASC, which would suggest an extreme state of anxiety in this context. This state appears to be present in the extended families of such parents, who also seem to have a proneness to anxiety (Klauber, 1999).

This area is important, as contact with professionals, especially regarding obtaining a diagnosis of ASC, most often comes prior to parents' engagement in a particular intervention program for their child. If the contact with professionals has been particularly stressful, or aversive, this may lead to any subsequent teaching intervention being less successful than it might, otherwise, have been (Robbins, Dunlap, & Plienis, 1991), and may lead to negative feelings, and a lack of trust, concerning those professionals (Brogen & Knussen, 2003).

PARENTING STRESS AND ASC

There have been numerous studies regarding the effectiveness of teaching interventions for ASC. However, parental factors may well influence the effectiveness of such teaching interventions, and studies that focus purely on the impact of teaching interventions in isolation on child outcomes neglect the key role that parents play in the management and treatment of the problems experienced by the child with ASC.

There are two lines of evidence that point to the importance of studying the relationship between parents and the outcomes of teaching interventions for children with ASC. Firstly, parents' mental well-being, and related coping abilities, have been found to influence short-term, as well as long-term, outcomes of teaching intervention programs. Secondly, the levels of stress experienced by parents of children with ASC are enormously high, compared to those experienced by parents of children with almost any other type of disability, or health problem. As a consequence, one parental variable that may affect a child's performance on a teaching intervention is the level of parenting stress.

Role of Stress in General Medical Conditions

The role of stress has been long acknowledged as a powerful force in many medical conditions, and has been shown to influence the outcomes and prognoses for various illnesses and disorders. In the general medical literature, Mazure (1995) claims that stress is a factor in both the development and exacerbation of psychiatric illness, and presents a collection of reviews that investigate stress, different responses to stress, and the interaction of stressors and psychiatric disorders, providing illness prevention strategies. Similarly, Melamed (1995) argues that stress management programs can have a positive influence on immune system responses during treatment and recovery from illness, including life-threatening conditions, like liver transplantation, Stage II and Stage III breast cancer, and following diagnosis of HIV infection.

In childhood disorders, such as diabetes, there has been shown to be a relationship between poor symptom management (diabetic balance) and adverse psychosocial factors, such as family stress (Kaar, 1983; Viner, McGrath, & Trudinger, 1996), and that there is a relationship between illness and family stress (Piening, 1984; see Lloyd, Smith, & Weinger, 2005, for a review). In fact, high family life stress is strongly correlated with the symptoms of diabetes (Viner et al., 1996). In addition, it has been suggested that the interactional styles within the family have an influence over somatic illness, and illness outcome (Tienari, Sorri, Lahti, Naarala, Wahlberg, Rönkkö, Moring, & Pohjola, 1987; Wahlberg, Wynne, Oja, Keskitalo, Anais-Tanner, Koistinen, Tarvainen, Hakko, Lahti, Moring, Naarala, Sorri, & Tienari, 2000). These findings indicate that both physical illness and mental illness can be affected by family influences, such as stress, and interactional and communication styles.

Importantly, Warner and Pottick (2006) reported that nearly 40% of children under the age of six years old, who were admitted to mental health services, were identified as having psychiatric problems that stemmed from family stress. Moreover, Carlson-Green, Morris, and Krawiecki (1995) noted that the best predictors of both children's behavior problems, and their adaptive behaviors, following intervention for pediatric brain tumors, were family and demographic variables, including family stress, maternal coping, and the number of parents present in the home.

Parenting Stress and ASC Outcomes

Given that parenting stress appears to be related to child outcomes and, given that many teaching interventions require long-term, time-intensive, and intrusive access to the family home (see Reed, Osborne & Corness, 2007), and often recruit parents as therapists (Mudford, Martin, Eikeseth, & Bibby, 2001). Mudford et al., 2001), it makes sense to investigate the influence of parenting stress on child outcomes from teaching intervention programs for ASC. A study already mentioned above, relating to pediatric brain tumors (i.e. Carlson-Green et al., 1995), has demonstrated a negative impact of parental stress on child outcomes following an intervention, but not in the context of teaching interventions for ASC.

However, similar findings have been noted for young children with ASC in a family-orientated training program, reported by Robbins, Dunlap, and Plienis (1991; see also Osborne et al., 2008a), in which they explored aspects of family functioning, as they related to the children's progress twelve months later. They found a strong relationship between mother-reported stress and child progress, and, in particular, they noted that high maternal stress can inhibit the success of early interventions. Similarly, Osborne et al. (2008a) presented the results from a community-based study, which examined the influences of early teaching interventions on sixty-five young children who had been diagnosed with ASD. In addition, this study explored the dynamics between the time-intensity of the early teaching interventions (hours per week), and the levels of parenting stress, on child outcomes, when measured nine to ten months after the interventions had first commenced. The intellectual, educational, and adaptive behavioral and social, functioning of the children were all measured. The children in this study were divided into four groups, based on both the levels of time-intensity of their interventions, and on their parents' levels of stress. The study found that there were gains in the intellectual, educational, and adaptive behavioral and social, functioning of the children over the nine to ten month period of assessment, and that there was a positive relationship between the time-intensity of the early teaching interventions and the child outcome gains. It was noted also that high levels of parenting stress counteracted the overall effectiveness of the early teaching interventions. Children whose parents reported higher levels of stress made fewer outcome gains, even when engaged in higher time-intensity interventions, than the children whose parents reported lower levels of stress

In addition to the impacts on the child and the family, stress can impact negatively on the ability of the parents to engage with the child. Konstantareas and Homatidis (1992) examined the self-reported involvement of parents with their children. Parents of non-autistic, but mentally disabled children reported greater involvement with their children than did parents of children with ASC. This difficulty with involvement may also extend to the interventions given to the children (cf. Boyd & Corley, 2001). Other studies have noted that levels of maternal stress are associated with worse maternal well-being, and less engagement in treatments, or intervention programs (Dale et al., 2006). High maternal stress, as well as levels of support received from the intervention programs, and the severity of the child's ASC, predict worse attributions of parental therapeutic self-efficacy (Hastings & Symes, 2002), and greater negative emotional reactions, and more threat-related appraisals to videotaped scenes of adolescents with ASC engaged in everyday activities (Fong, 1991). A relative lack of involvement and engagement with the intervention may exacerbate the stress-related problems experienced by the parents, and lead to the development of a 'vicious circle', or degenerative cycle.

Parenting Stress and Child Behavior Problems

There is evidence that parenting stress correlates both with the symptoms of ASC, and with child behavior problems, and it is important to be able to determine which of these factors is associated most strongly with such parenting stress. The main difficulty is that the severity of ASC symptoms and child behavior problems also correlate with each other, rendering it difficult to separate these two factors (e.g., Eisenhower et al., 2005; Gabriels, Cuccaro, Hill, Ivers, & Goldson, 2005).

Hastings and Johnson (2001; see also Tobing & Glenwick, 2002) report that higher levels of ASC symptomatology (i.e., "severity" of ASC; as measured by the Autism Behavior Checklist) were associated with higher levels of reported parenting stress, as measured by the Questionnaire on Resources and Stress. Similarly, Duarte, Bordin, Yazigi, and Mooney (2005) found that the strongest association in their study was between stress in mothers and having a child with ASC, although, maternal stress increased when the symptoms, poor expression of feeling and emotion, and little social interest, were more severe (see also Baker-Ericzen, Brookman-Frazee, & Stahmer, 2005; Kasari & Sigman, 1997, regarding the effects of child levels of social skills as being a good predictor of maternal stress).

In contrast, several studies present data consistent with the view that child behavior problems, and not other factors, such as the type of disability, or child adaptive behaviors, are associated with parental stress (e.g., Blacher & McIntyre, 2006; Donenberg & Baker, 1993; Dumas et al., 1991; Floyd & Gallagher, 1997; Lecavalier et al., 2006). For instance, Lecavalier et al. (2006) found that child behavior problems were strongly associated with parental stress, especially a specific group of externalised behaviors, such as conduct problems (but adaptive skills were not associated with parental stress). Whereas, Tomanik, Harris, and Hawkins (2004) reported that both child maladaptive, and child adaptive, behaviors correlated with maternal stress. Konstantareas and Homatidis (1989) noted that the best predictor of stress in both parents was child self-abuse, and, for mothers, child hyper-irritability was associated with elevated stress scores. Gabriels et al. (2005) ascertained that parent ratings of their own stress levels were strongly correlated with repetitive behaviors of their children (repetitive behaviors being a form of behavioral problem for many children with ASC). Fong (1991) noted a trend towards higher levels of maladaptive behaviors in adolescents with ASC, whose mothers were highly stressed.

Noh, Dumas, Wolf, and Fisman (1989) found that stress levels were highest in parents of children with behavior and conduct problems, and were slightly greater than those reported by parents of children with ASC. Pisula (1998; 2003) noted that behavioral disorders, and problems related to atypical child behaviors, were the main source of parental stress in mothers of children with ASC. In a ten-year longitudinal study, Gray (2002) noted that, generally, improvements were experienced by most parents of children with ASC in many aspects of their lives. However, less favorable outcomes were reported in families whose children showed violent and/or aggressive behavior problems. The parents in these families continued to experience high levels of parental stress.

As noted above, several studies have equated child behavior problems across groups, including one developmentally disabled and one not developmentally disabled, and demonstrated that there were no differences in reports of parental stress across these groups. For example, Donenberg and Baker (1993) compared children with ASC, children with externalizing behaviors (e.g., hyperactivity and aggression) who did not have ASC, and typically developing children with no significant behavior problems. They found similar higher child-related stress in the parents of the externalizing children and in the parents of children with ASC, compared to the parents of the typically developing children. Dumas et al. (1991) studied reports of parenting stress, child behavior problems, and dysphoria in families of children with ASC, behavior disorders, Down syndrome, and typically developing children. Parents of children with ASC, and parents of behavior-disordered children, reported experiencing higher levels of parenting stress than parents in the other two groups. Mothers of children with ASC, as well as mothers of behavior-disordered children, experienced the highest levels of dysphoria. Although, it should be noted that the parents of the children with behavior disorders reported that their children displayed more intense behavioral difficulties, which were greater in number, than those reported by the parents of all of the other children in the study, including those parents of the children with ASC.

Blacher and McIntyre (2006) found that neither maternal stress, nor depression, were related to the type of disability (intellectual disability, cerebral palsy, Down syndrome, and ASC), once differences in child behavior problems were controlled for. Similarly, maternal stress has been found to be correlated with child behavior problems, but not to correlate independently with adaptive behavior, nor the symptoms of ASC (Hastings et al., 2005). Hence, these studies indicate that the child behavior problems are related to parenting stress, rather than the disability, disorder, syndrome, or condition.

However, this pattern of results is not found in every study, for example, Eisenhower et al. (2005) noted that the type of disability (especially ASC) accounted for maternal stress, even after controlling for levels of child behavior problems. Thus, in some cases, the type of child disability can produce effects on parenting stress, even after differences in child behavior problems, and cognitive levels, have been accommodated. In particular, Eisenhower et al. (2005) conclude that the behavioral differences manifested in children with ASC, compared to children with other disabilities (e.g., Down syndrome, cerebral palsy, and developmental disability), were paralleled by differences in parental stress, such that parents of children with ASC are at increased risk of higher stress, which is contributed to by the characteristics of the ASC itself, over and above any externalizing child behavior problems. Thus, while it appears that there is a large degree of evidence associating externalizing child behavior problems with parenting stress, the influence of the characteristics specific to the ASC itself cannot be ruled out as a factor associated with parenting stress.

Moreover, it remains unclear as to the temporal direction of the influence of these factors on one another. Although it has been widely assumed that child behavior problems, and/or the ASC itself, impact on parenting stress, this view is not strongly supported in the literature. Lecavalier et al. (2006) found that child behavior problems and parental stress exacerbated each other over a period of one year. Thus, suggesting that this relationship is more complicated than the simple unidirectional relationship, as suggested by many models of parenting (see Hastings, 2002). It is worth noting that some studies have shown that significant levels of maternal stress during pregnancy and birth can be associated with ASC, suggesting that stress precedes later problems, and not the other way around (Beversdorf, Manning, Hillier, Anderson, Nordgren, Walters, Nagaraja, Cooley, Gaelic, & Bauman, 2005; Ward, 1990). Although, it may well be that pre-natal stressors could be quite different in nature from those experienced after the birth of the child. Due to the obvious difficulties involved in conducting longitudinal research, there are very few studies that have collected data from several different points across time, and that would allow indication of the temporal directionality of the relationship between parenting stress and child behavior problems. In fact, where these studies do exist, they provide little evidence that child behavior problems predict parenting stress, but rather they tend to indicate that the reverse relationship is stronger (e.g., Robbins et al., 1991).

PARENTING STRESS AND PARENTING BEHAVIORS

The reasons why high parenting stress levels have a negative impact on child behavior problems, and predict worse intervention child outcomes, are currently unclear. There are, however, several possibilities that are worth some mention. On a purely speculative basis, it could be that children with ASC are sensitive to their parents' levels of emotional stress. Perhaps the presence of emotions, such as parenting stress and anxiety, can be sensed by children with ASC, even if they are not fully able to identify those emotional states (Hobson, Ouston, & Lee, 1989). In fact, some people with ASC can be described as over-sensitive to emotional disturbance (Grandin, 1990), and this sensitivity may upset their psychological and emotional equilibrium, and subsequently may affect their behaviors and outcomes. However, there remains very little evidence of any such over-sensitivity to parental emotion in children with ASC.

It could be argued that the parents of children with ASC tend to be more reactive, both in their responses to stressors, and in their parenting styles, which would lead to both high levels of parenting stress, and high resultant levels of child behavior problems. However, this is unlikely, as there is very little evidence for this claim, and there is much research that shows no difference in the personalities, socio-economic statuses, and family backgrounds, of parents of children with ASC, compared to other sets of parents (e.g., Koegel et al., 1983; but see Sanua, 1987).

Possibly the most likely suggestion is that the high levels of parenting stress trigger changes in the parents' ability to patiently accommodate, and respond to, their children's behavior problems. McAdoo and DeMyer (1977) made the point that the continual stress of parenting a child with ASC may lead to changes in the personalities of such parents, and, if this were the case, these changes could have an effect on their parenting behaviors. Holroyd and McArthur (1976) found more family integration problems, reported by mothers of children with ASC, relative to mothers of children with Down syndrome. Certainly, Tienari et al. (1987) found that family interactional styles can have a predisposing influence to, and precipitate, somatic illness, as well as affecting illness outcome. However, over and above the extreme 'burden of care' placed on parents of children with ASC, little is known about their parenting behaviors, let alone whether these parenting behaviors are impacted on by parenting stress.

There is some, though still limited, evidence regarding parenting behaviors *per se*. Rodrigue, Morgan, and Geffken (1990) noted that mothers of children with ASC reported less parenting competence, and less family adaptability, than either mothers of children with Down syndrome, or mothers of children without developmental disability. Powers (2000) suggested that there are three common areas of parenting difficulty for parents of children with ASC. Firstly, there is a risk of over-involvement, or over-compensation, a suggestion supported by the findings of El-Ghoroury and Romanczyk (1999), who reported that parents initiate more play interactions and behaviors with their children with ASC than with their siblings. Secondly, Powers (2000) warned of the 'trap' of over-protectiveness of the child with ASC, or of affording too little autonomy for that child. Thirdly, Powers (2000) highlighted the risk of parental rejection of, or withdrawal from, children with ASC. Nevertheless, there is very little empirical evidence regarding such suggestions, at this point in time.

Similarly, there are few, if any, studies of the effects of parenting stress on the parenting behaviors of parents of children with ASC. There have been some investigations, however, of the effects of parenting stress on parenting behaviors in the general population. For example, Rodgers (1993; 1998) found that parenting stress directly, and indirectly, affected parenting behavior in 85 mothers of young children in Head Start or Kindergarten. Likewise, Kotchick, Dorsey, and Heller (2005; see also Meyers & Miller, 2004), in a longitudinal study of 123 low-income, urban-dwelling, single mothers, noted that higher levels of neighborhood stress had a relationship to greater psychological distress, and detrimental effects on psychological functioning, in the mothers. This subsequently went with less engagement in positive parenting practices, and resulted in poorer parenting over time. Webster-Stratton (1990) found that various stressors seriously disrupted parenting practices, by their influencing some parents to become more irritable, critical, and punitive, and these parenting behaviors, in turn, increased the likelihood that children would develop conduct problems.

Nevertheless, it should be noted that there is a mixed picture presented in this area of research, making more difficult any generalizations from the general population to parents of children with ASC. For example, Greenley, Holmbeck, and Rose (2006) reported variable effects of parenting stress on parenting behaviors, and adaptive parenting, in their study of parents of children with, and without, Spina Bifida. Levers and Drotar (1996), in a review of studies of family and parental functioning in caring for children with cystic fibrosis, noted higher levels of stress in parents of children with cystic fibrosis, compared to parents of healthy children, but they found that parenting behavior, and family functioning, were similar in the two groups. Similarly, Nitz, Ketterlinus, and Brandt (1995) assessed the role of maternal stress, amongst other things, on the parenting behavior of adolescent mothers of healthy infants. Their findings indicated that parenting stress per se did not significantly predict maternal behavior.

PARENTING BEHAVIORS AND CHILD BEHAVIOR PROBLEMS

The above review has suggested that levels of parenting stress may impact on behaviors of children, and lead to subsequent worsening of child behavior problems, and poorer child outcomes following teaching interventions. In order to explain these findings, it has been proposed that high levels of parenting stress can have an impact on subsequent parenting behaviors, which, in turn, impact on child behavior problems, and outcomes. However, although high levels of parenting stress are associated both with subsequently higher levels of child behavior problems, and with later changes in parenting behaviors, it is not known whether parenting behaviors are associated directly with subsequent child behavior problems, and poorer outcomes. It could be that both parenting behaviors and child behavior problems are jointly influenced by parenting stress, but that each of these are not directly impacted upon by one another (see Anthony, Anthony, Glanville, Naiman, Waanders, & Shaffer, 2005; Blader, 2006).

Unfortunately, there is very litlle evidence showing a direct link between parenting behaviors and child behavior problems in the context of ASC. Research reported by Osborne et al. (2008b) explored the relationships between parenting behaviors (which are impacted upon by parenting stress), in parents of children with ASD, and subsequent child behavior problems. The sample deployed by Osborne et al. (2008b) consisted of seventy-two children with ASD (aged from five to sixteen years old), and their parents, who were assessed over a period of nine to ten months. The results of this study noted a relationship between parenting behaviors and subsequent child behavior problems, but only for the parenting behavior of limit setting. It was found that, the better the limit setting abilities of the parents at baseline, the fewer the child behavior problems reported at follow-up, nine to ten months later. Importantly, the parenting behavior of limit setting was found to mediate the relationship between parenting stress and subsequent child behavior problems.

In addition to this direct exploration, there are numerous intervention programs that target the parents of children with ASC. Many of these interventions have noted improvements in the children's behaviors, and functioning, as a result of a reduction in parenting stress, and an increase in parental coping ability (e.g., Harris et al., 2000; Lovaas & Smith, 2003; Spaccarelli et al., 1992; see Brookman-Frazee et al., 2006, for a comprehensive review). There are also several studies that suggest that teaching parenting skills to parents of children with ASC will reduce their children's challenging behaviors. For example, teaching parents 'mindful parenting' reduced aggression, non-compliance, and self-injury in their children (Singh et al., 2006). Nevertheless, these results may not reflect a direct relationship between parenting behaviors and child behavior problems, but could reflect the results of a reduction of parenting stress levels, which, in turn, could have impacted on both parenting behaviors and on child behavior problems, but the latter challenging child behaviors may not have been affected directly via parenting behaviors.

There is, of course, a considerable literature on the effects of parenting practices and strategies in families of typically developing children. Fenning, Baker, Baker, and Crnic (2007) review this substantial literature, and suggest that the parent characteristics of 'warmth' and 'responsiveness' contribute to a more positive, and adaptive, parenting style which, in turn, facilitates a satisfactory social, and emotional, development in the child. On the other hand, low levels of manifest parental 'warmth' correlate with child behavior problems, such as increased externalizing behaviors (e.g., oppositional, and disruptive behaviors). Similarly, a lack of parental 'responsiveness', as seen in over-intrusive interventions, over-controlling, and harsh disciplinary, parenting styles, are, likewise, associated with child behavior problems. Furthermore, Fenning et al. (2007) note that parental emotional expressiveness, in particular, high expressed frequencies of negative affect, especially anger, can act to inhibit empathic responding, reduce levels of emotional understanding, and increase the probability of prolonged and continuing behavioral problems in the child. However, the relevance of much of this parenting literature to the study of children with ASC might be questionable, as an often proposed mechanism for such links between parenting behaviors, and styles, and child behavior problems, and outcomes, is that of imitation (e.g., Bandura, Ross, & Ross, 1961; Fenning et al., 2007). Given the nature of the deficits involved in ASC, the extent to which such parenting findings can be generalized, or applied, to this specific population is unclear.

Some findings that could be relevant, especially as they involve teaching interventions, are those from research conducted on Head Start programs, often involving socio-economically disadvantaged children. In a study by Siantz and Smith (1994), it was found that the parenting styles of the mothers of sixty, three to eight year old, children of Mexican American migrant farm-workers accounted for a significant proportion of the child behavior problems, reported by the mothers. Similarly, Dumas and Wekerle (1995) noted some modest relationship between "dysfunctional parenting" and child behavior problems. However, as these research studies were cross-sectional, and not longitudinal, temporal directionality between these two factors cannot be discerned (see also similar claims made by Jackson, 2000, and by Jackson & Huang, 2000, on the basis of other cross-sectional correlational studies).

On looking at the longitudinal effects of maternal anti-social behaviors and parenting practices on the behavior problems of boys at risk of developing anti-social behaviors, Ehrensaft, Wasserman, Verdelli, Greenwald, Miller, and Davies (2003) noted that lower levels of maternal involvement, and monitoring, and higher levels of conflict between the mothers and sons, contributed to worse subsequent child behavior problems seen one year later. Although the boys' behavior problems were directly worsened by the conduct disorder problems of their mothers, it was established that the effect of parenting was even more contributive to the subsequent child behavior problems. Similarly, Austin, Dunn, Johnson, and Perkins (2004) conducted a longitudinal study, which investigated the impact of families on the behavior problems of children and adolescents with epilepsy. They found that parental confidence in managing discipline of their child at baseline was correlated with child behavior problems at baseline, and also predicted these child behavior problems at follow-up 24 months later. Moreover, decreasing parental confidence in disciplining their child was related to an increase in child behavior problems over time.

Thus, both the study by Ehrensaft et al. (2003) and that by Austin et al. (2004), highlight aspects of limit setting (i.e., monitoring, or managing discipline; see Gerard, 1994) as important parenting behaviors associated with reductions in future child behavior problems. Of course, such behavior management skills are also often emphasized in the context of training programs for parents of children with ASC (e.g., Harris et al., 2000).

SUMMARY

The above review suggests that there are a number of important theoretical reasons for examining the relationships between parenting stress, parenting behaviors, and child behavior problems in ASC samples. The results of such examinations may have practical implications for the development of future interventions for ASC. In particular, the following issues need to be determined: firstly, whether high parenting stress levels impact negatively on child outcomes; secondly, the nature of the relationship between parenting stress and child behavior problems over time, in order to determine the temporal directionality of any such parent-child interactions; thirdly, whether parenting stress impacts on parenting behaviors, and the types of parenting behaviors that are influential for subsequent child behavior problems in the context of ASC; fourthly, that the association between parenting behaviors and child behavior problems is a direct one, and is not the by-product of both of these behavioral elements being impacted upon by additional factors, such as parenting stress; and finally, whether the contact and communication experiences of parents with professionals leading up to and during the diagnostic process is of particular significance. In summary, in addition to identifying areas of research need, this review suggests that the influence of the family, especially the parental levels of stress, should be taken into account when understanding ASC and when designing early teaching interventions for ASC. This is not to apportion blame to the family, but to suggest that helping the parents of children with ASC to reduce their stress levels may also aid the child to achieve greater outcome. Hence, helping the parents will help the child.

AUTHOR NOTE

Correspondence regarding this chapter should be sent to: Lisa A. Osborne, Department of Psychology, Swansea University, Singleton Park, Swansea, SA2 8PP, U.K. (e-mail: l.a. osborne@swansea.ac.uk).

REFERENCES

Anthony, L.G., Anthony, B.J., Glanville, D.N., Naiman, D.Q., Waanders, C., & Shaffer, S. (2005). The relationships between parenting stress, parenting behaviour and preschoolers' social competence and behaviour problems in the classroom. *Infant and Child Development*, 14, 133-154.

Asperger, H. (1944). Die 'aunstisehen Psychopathen' im Kindesalter. *Archiv fur psychiatrie und Nervenkrankheiten*, 117, 76-136.

Austin, J.K., Dunn, D.W., Johnson, C.S., & Perkins, S.M. (2004). Behavioral issues involving children and adolescents with epilepsy and the impact of their families: Recent research data. *Epilepsy and Behavior*, 5, 33-41.

Backes, M., von Gontard, A., Schreck, J., & Lehmkuhl, G. (2001). Parental stress and coping in families with fragile X boys. *Gene Function & Disease*, 2, 151-158.

Baker-Ericzen, M.J., Brookman-Frazee, L., & Stahmer, A. (2005). Stress levels and adaptability in parents of toddlers with and without autism spectrum disorders. *Research and Practice for Persons with Severe Disabilities*, 30, 194-204.

Bandura, A., Ross, D., & Ross, S.A. (1961). Transmission of aggression through imitation of aggressive models. *Journal of Abnormal and Social Psychology*, 63, 575-582.

Baron-Cohen, S., & Hammer, J. (1997). Is autism an extreme form of the "male brain"? *Advances in Infancy Research*, 11, 193-217.

Baron-Cohen, S., Wheelwright, S., Stott, C., Bolton, P., & Goodyer, I. (1997). Is there a link between engineering and autism? *Autism*, 1, 101-109.

Baron-McKeagney, T., Woody, J.D., & D'Souza, H.J. (2002). Mentoring at-risk Latino children and their parents: Analysis of the parent-child relationship and family strength. *Families in Society*, 83, 285-292.

Bartolo, P.A. (2002). Communicating a diagnosis of developmental disability to parents: Multiprofessional negotiation frameworks. *Child Care, Health and Development*, 28, 65-71.

Baxter, C., Cummins, R.A., & Yiolitis, L. (2000). Parental stress attributed to disabled family members: A longitudinal study. *International Journal of Disability Research*.

Bebko, J.M., Konstantaraes, M.M., & Springer, J. (1987). Parent and professional evaluations of family stress associated with characteristics of autism. *Journal of Autism and Developmental Disorders*, 17, 565-576.

Bettelheim, B. (1950). *Love is not enough; the treatment of emotionally disturbed children.* New York: Free Press.

Bettelheim, B. (1967). *The empty fortress: infantile autism and the birth of the self.* Oxford: Free Press of Glencoe.

Beversdorf, D.Q., Manning, S.E., Hillier, A., Anderson, S.L., Norgren, R.E., Walters, S.E., Nagaraja, H.N., Cooley, W.C., Gaelic, S.E., & Bauman, M.L. (2005). Timing of parental stressors and autism. *Journal of Autism and Developmental Disorders*, 35, 471-478.

Bitsika, V., & Sharpley, C. (1999). An explanatory examination of the effects of support groups on the well-being of parents of children with autism: I: General Counselling. *Journal of Applied Health Behaviour*, 1, 16-22.

Bitsika, V., & Sharpley, C. (2000). Development and testing of the effects of support groups on the well-being of parents of children with autism-II: Specific stress management techniques. *Journal of Applied Health Behaviour*, 2, 8-15.

Blacher, J., & McIntyre, L.L. (2006). Syndrome specificity and behavioural disorders in young adults with intellectual disability: Cultural differences in family impact. *Journal of intellectual and Developmental Disabilities*, 50, 184-198.

Blacher, J., Neece, C.L., & Paczkowski, E. (2005). Families and intellectual disability. *Current Opinion in Psychiatry*, 18, 507-513.

Blader, J.C. (2006). Which family factors predict children's externalizing behaviors following discharge from psychiatric inpatient treatment? *Journal of Child Psychology and Psychiatry*, 47, 1133-1142.

Bouma, R., & Schweitzer, R. (1990). The impact of chronic childhood illness on family stress: A comparison between autism and cystic fibrosis. *Journal of Clinical Psychology*, 46, 722-730.

Bowlby, J. (1951). Maternal care and mental health. *Bulletin of the World Health Organization*, 3, 355-533.

Boyd, B.A. (2002). Examining the Relationship between Stress and Lack of Social Support in Mothers of Children with Autism. *Focus on Autism & Other Developmental Disabilities*, 17, 208-215.

Bristol, M. M. (1987). Mothers of children with autism or communication disorders: Successful adaptation and the T-Double ABCX Model. *Journal of Autism and Developmental Disorders*, 17, 469-486.

Brogan, C.A., & Knussen, C. (2003). The disclosure of a diagnosis of an autism spectrum disorder. *Autism*, 7, 31-46.

Brookman-Frazee, L., Stahmer, A., Baker-Ericzen, M.J., & Tsai, K. (2006). Parenting interventions for children with autism spectrum and disruptive behaviour disorders: Opportunities for cross-fertilization. *Clinical Child and Family Psychology Review*, 9, 181-200.

Butow, P.N., Kazemi, J.N., Beeney, L.J., Griffin, A., Dunn, S.M., Tattersall, M.H.N. (1996), "When the diagnosis is cancer: patient communication experiences and preferences", *Cancer*, 77, 2630-37.

Carlson-Green, B., Morris, R.D., & Krawiecki, N. (1995). Family illness predictors of outcome in pediatric brain tumors. *Journal of Pediatric Psychology*, 20, 769-784.

Chakrabarti, S., & Fombonne, E. (2005). Pervasive developmental disorders in Preschool children: Confirmation of high prevalence. *American Journal of Psychiatry*, 162, 1133-1141.

Cherry, D.B. (1989). Stress and coping in families with ill or disabled children: application of a model to pediatric therapy. *Physical & Occupational Therapy in Pediatrics*, 9, 11-32.

Coffman, J.K., Guerin, D.W., & Gottfried, A.W. (2006). Reliability and validity of the parent-child relationship inventory (PCRI): evidence from a longitudinal cross informant investigation. *Psychological Assessment*, 18, 209-214.

Critchley, M., & Earl, C.J.C. (1932). Tuberose sclerosis and allied conditions. *Brain*, 55, 311-346.

Dale, E., Jahoda, A., & Knott, F. (2006). Mothers' attributions following their child's diagnosis of autistic spectrum disorder: Exploring links with maternal levels of stress, depression and expectations about their child's future. *Autism*, 10, 463-479.

Dale, M. (1996). *Working with Families of Children with Special Needs: Partnership and Practice*. London: Routledge.

Deater-Deckard, K. (1998). Parenting stress and child adjustment: Some old hypotheses and new questions. *Clinical Psychology: Science and Practice*, 5, 314-332.

DeMeyer, M.K. (1979). *Parents and Children in Autism*. Washington, DC.: V.H. Winston & Sons.

Donenberg, G., & Baker, B. L. (1993). The impact of young children with externalizing behaviors on their families. *Journal of Abnormal Child Psychology*, 21, 179-197.

Dumas, J.E., & Wekerle, C. (1995). Maternal reports of child behavior problems and personal distress as predictors of dysfunctional parenting. *Development and Psychopathology*, 7, 465-479.

Dumas, J.E., Wolf, L.C., Fisman, S. & Culligan, A. (1991). Parenting stress, child Behaviour problems, and dysphoria in parents of children with autism, Down Syndrome, behaviour disorders, and normal development. *Exceptionality,* 2, 97-110.

Dunn, M.E., Burbine, T., Bowers, C.A., & Tantleff-Dunn, S. (2001). Moderators of stress in. parents of children with autism. *Community Mental Health Journal*, 37, 39-52.

Durate, C.S., Bordin, I.A., Yazigi, L., & & Mooney, J. (2005). Factors associated with stress in mothers of children with autism. *Autism*, 9, 416-427.

Dyson, L., Edgar, E., & Crnic, K. (1989). Psychological predictors of adjustment of siblings of developmentally disabled children. *American Journal of Mental Retardation*, 94, 292-302.

Ehlers, S., & Gillberg, C. (1993). The epidemiology of Asperger Syndrome: A total population study. *The Journal of Child Psychology and Psychiatry and Allied Disciplines*, 34, 1327-1350.

Ehrensaft, M.K., Wasserman, G.A., Verdelli, L., Greenwald, S., Miller, L.S., & Davies, M. (2003). Maternal antisocial behavior, parenting practices, and behavior problems in boys at risk for antisocial behavior. *Journal of Child and Family Studies*, 12, 27-40.

Eisenhower, A.S., Baker, B.L., & Blacher, J. (2005). Preschool children with intellectual disability: Syndrome specificity, behaviour problems, and maternal well-being. *Journal of Intellectual Disability Research*, 49, 657-671.

El-Ghoroury, N.B., & Romancyzk, R.G. (1999). Play interactions of family members towards children with autism. *Journal of Autism and Developmental Disorders*, 29, 249-258.

Engwell, P., & Macpherson, E. (2003). An evaluation of the NAS EarlyBird programme. *Good Autism Practice*, 4, 13-19.

Evans, M., Stoddart, H., Condon, L., Freeman, E., Grizzell, M., & Mullen, R. (2001). Parents' perspectives on the MMR immunisation: a focus group study. *British Journal of General Practice*, 51, 904-910.

Factor, D. C., Perry, A., & Freeman, N. (1990). Stress, social support, and respite care use in families with autistic children. *Journal of Autism and Developmental Disorders*, 20, 139–146.

Fenning, R., Baker, J., Baker, B., & Crnic, K. (2007). Parenting children with borderline intellectual functioning. *American Journal on Mental Retardation*, 112, 107-121.

Fisman, S.N., Wolf, L.C., & Noh, S. (1989). Marital intimacy in parents of exceptional children. *Canadian Journal of Psychiatry*, 34, 519-525.

Fleck, M.P.A., Wagner, L., Wagner, M., & Dias, M. (2007). Long-stay patients in a psychiatric hospital in Southern Brazil. *Rev. Saúde Pública*.

Floyd, F. J., & Gallagher, E. M. (1997). Parental stress, care demands, and use of support services for school-age children with disabilities and behavior problems. *Family Relations*, 46, 359-371.

Fong, P.L. (1991). Cognitive appraisals in high- and low-stress mothers of adolescents with autism. *Journal of Consulting and Clinical Psychology*, 59, 471-474.

Fong, L., Wilgosh, L., & Sobsey D. (1993). The experience of parenting an adolescent with autism. *International Journal of Disability, Development, and Education*, 40, 105-113.

Freeman N. L., Perry A., Factor D. C., (1991). Child behaviours as stressors: Replicating and extending the use of the CARS as a measure of stress. *Journal of Child Psychology and Psychiatry*, 32, 1025–1030.

Frith, U. (1989). *Explaining the Enigma*. Oxford: Blackwell.

Gabriels, R.L., Cuccaro, M.L., Hill, D.E., Ivers, B.J., & Goldson, E. (2005). Repetitive behaviors in autism: Relationships with associated clinical features. *Research in Developmental Disabilities*, 26, 169-181.

Gabriels, R.L., Hill, D.E., Pierce, R.A., Rogers, S.J., & Wehner, B. (2001). Predictors of treatment outcome in young children with autism. Autism, 5, 407-429.

Gardner, M. (2000). The Brutality of Dr. Bettelheim. *Skeptical Inquirer*, Nov.

Gill, M.J., & Harris, S.L. (1991) Hardiness and social support as predictors of Psychological discomfort in mothers of children with autism. *Journal of Autism and Developmental Disorders, 21, 407-416.*

Goin-Kochel, R.P., Mackintosh, V.H., & Myers, B.J. (2006). How many doctors does it take to make an autism spectrum diagnosis. *Autism*, 5, 439-451.

Goodman R (1997). The Strengths and Difficulties Questionnaire: A Research Note. *Journal of Child Psychology and Psychiatry*, 38, 581-586.

Grandin, T. (1990). Needs of high functioning teenagers and adults with autism: Tips from a recovered autistic. *Focus on Autistic Behavior*, 5, 16.

Gray, D.E. (1993). Negotiating autism: Relations between parents and treatment staff. *Social Science and Medicine*, 36, 1037-1046.

Gray D. E. (1994). Coping with autism: Stresses and strategies. *Sociology of Health and Illness*, 16, 275-300.

Gray, D.E. (2002). Ten years on: A longitudinal study of families of children with autism. *Journal of Intellectual and Developmental Disability*, 27, 215-222.

Gray, D.E. (2006). Coping over time: the parents of children with autism. *Journal of Intellectual Disability Research*, 50, 970-976.

Greenley, R.N., Holmbeck, G.N., & Rose, B.M. (2006). Predictors of parenting behavior trajectories among families of young adolescents with and without spina bifida. *Journal of Pediatric Psychology*, 31, 1057-1071.

Handen, B.L., Johnson, C.R., & Lubetsky, M. (2000). Efficacy of methylphenidate among children with autism and symptoms of attention-deficit hyperactivity disorder. *Journal of Autism and Developmental Disorders*, 30, 245-255.

Harris, P.L. (2000). *The work of the imagination*. Malden, MA: Blackwell Publishers.

Harris, S.L. (1984). The family of the autistic child: A behavioral-systems view. *Clinical Psychology Review*, 4, 227-239.

Harris, S.L. (1994). Treatment of family problems in autism. In E. Schopler & G.B. Mesibov (Eds.), *Behavioral issues in autism* (pp. 161-175). New York, NY: Plenum Press.

Harris, S.L., Handleman, J.S., Arnold, M.S., & Gordon, R.F. (2000). The Douglass Developmental Disabilities Center: Two models of service delivery. In J.S.Handleman S.L.Harris (Eds.), *Preschool Education Programs for Children with Autism (2nd ed.)*, (pp 233–260). Austin, TX: Pro-Ed.

Hastings, R. P. (2002). Parental stress and behaviour problems of children with developmental disability. *Journal of Intellectual and Developmental Disability*, 27, 149-160.

Hastings, R. (2003). Brief Report: Behavioral Adjustment of Siblings of Children with Autism. *Journal of Autism and Developmental Disorders*, 33, 99-104

Hastings, R.P., & Brown, T. (2002). Behavior problems of children with autism, parental self-efficacy, and mental health. *American Journal on Mental Retardation*, 107, 222-232.

Hastings, R. P. & Johnson, E. (2001). Stress in UK families conducting intensive home-based behavioral intervention for their young child with autism. *Journal of Autism and Developmental Disorders*, 31, 327-336.

Hastings, R.P., Kovshoff, H., Brown, T., Ward, N.J., Espinosa, F.D., & Remington, B. (2005). Coping strategies in mothers and fathers of preschool and school-age children with autism. *Autism*, 9, 377-391.

Hastings, R.P., & Symes, M.D. (2002). Early intensive behavioral intervention for children with autism: parental therapeutic self-efficacy. *Research in Developmental Disabilities*, 23, 332-341.

Hecimovic, A., Powell, T.H., & Christensen, L. (1999). Supporting families in meetin their needs. In, D.B. Zager (Ed.), Autism, identification, education, and treatment (pp. 261-299). Mahwah: Erlbaum.

Hobson, R.P., & Ouston, J., & Lee, A. (1989). Naming emotion in faces and voices: Abilities and disabilities in autism and mental retardation. *British Journal of Developmental Psychology*, 7, 237-250.

Hodapp, R.M., Fidler, D.J., & Smith, A.C.M. (1998). Stress and coping in. families of children with Smith Magenis syndrome. *Journal of Intellectual Disability Research*, 42, 331-340.

Holroyd, J., & McArthur, D. (1976). Mental retardation and stress on the parents: A contrast between Down's syndrome and childhood autism. *American Journal of Mental Deficiency*, 80, 431-436.

Hoppes, K., & Harris, S.L. (1990). Perceptions of child attachment and maternal gratification in mothers of children with autism and Down syndrome. *Journal of Clinical Child Psychology*, 19, 365-370.

Honey, E., Hastings, R.P., & McConachie, H. (2005). Use of the Questionnaire on Resources and Stress (QRS-F) with parents of young children with autism. *Autism*, 9, 246-255.

Hornby, G. (1995). Fathers'views of the effects on their families of children with Down syndrome. *Journal of Child and Family Studies*, 4, 103-117.

Howlin, P., & Moore, A. (1997). Diagnosis in autism: A survey of over 1200 patients in the UK, *Autism*, 1, 135–162.

Huws, J., Jones, R.S., & Ingledew, D.K. (2001). Parents of children with autism using an e-mail group: A grounded theory study. *Journal of Health Psychology*, 6, 569-584.

Islam, Y. (1998). Is there a link between engineering and autism?: Commentary. *Autism*, 2, 98.

Jackson, A.P. (2000). Maternal self-efficacy and children's influence on stress and parenting among single black mothers in poverty. *Journal of Family Issues*, 21, 3-16.

Jackson, A.P., & Huang, C.C. (2000). Parenting stress and behavior among single mothers of preschoolers: The mediating role of self-efficacy. *Journal of Social Service Research*, 26, 29-42.

Jocelyn, L.J., Casiro, O.G., Beattie, D., Bow, J., Kneisz, J. (1998). Treatment of children with autism: A randomized controlled trial to evaluate a caregiver-based intervention program in community day-care centers. *Journal of Developmental and Behavioral Pediatrics*, 19, 326-334.

Kaar, M.L. (1983). Clinical course of diabetes in children: With special reference to Factors affecting metabolic control. *Acta Universitatis Ouluensis*, 100.

Kanner, L. (1944). Early infantile autism. *Journal of Pediatrics*, 25, 211-217.

Kasari, C., & Sigman, M. (1997). Linking parental perceptions to interactions in young children with autism. *Journal of Autism and Developmental Disorders*, 27, 39-57.

Klauber, T. (1999). The significance of trauma and other factors in work with the parents of children with autism. In A. Alvarez & S. Reid (Eds.), *Autism and personality: Findings from the Tavistock autism workshop* (pp. 33-48). Florence, KY: Taylor & Frances/Routledge.

Koegel, R.L., Bimbella, A., & Schreibman, L. (1996). Collateral effects of parent training on family interactions. *Journal of Autism and Developmental Disorders*, 26, 347-359.

Koegel, R.L., Schriebman, L., Loos, L.M., Dirlich-Wilheim, H., & Dunlap, L. (1992). Consistent stress profiles in mothers of children with autism. *Journal of Autism and Developmental Disorders*, 22, 205-216.

Koegel, R.L., Schreibman, L., O'Neil, R.E., & Burke, J.C. (1983). The personality and family interaction characteristics of parents of autistic children. *Journal of Consulting and Clinical Pdsychology*, 51, 683-692.

Konstantareas, M.M. & Homatidis, S. (1989). Assessing child symptom severity and stress in parents of autistic children. *Journal of Child Psychology and Psychiatry*, 30, 459-470.

Kotchick, B.A., Dorsey, S., & Heller, L. (2005). Predictors of parenting among African American single mothers: Personal and contextual factors. *Journal of Marriage and Family*, 67, 448-460.

Kuloglu-Aksaz, N. (1994). The effect of informational counseling on stress level of parents of children with autism in Turkey. *Journal of Autism and Developmental Disorders*, 24, 109-110.

Kurtz, L., & Derenvensky, J. L. (1994). Adolescent motherhood: An application of the stress and coping model to child rearing attitudes and practices. *Canadian Journal of Community Mental Health*, 13, 5–24.

Lazarus, R. (1991). *Emotions and adaptations*. New York: Oxford University Press.

Lecavalier, L., Leone, S., & Wiltz, J. (2006). The impact of behaviour problems on caregiver stress in young people with autism spectrum disorders. *Journal of Intellectual Disability Research*, 50, 172-183.

Leslie, A.M. (1991). Theory of mind impairment in autism. In A. Whiten (Ed.), *Natural theories of mind: Evolution, development, and simulation of everyday mindreading*. Cambridge, MA: Basil Blackwell.

Levers, C.E., & Drotar, D. (1996). Family and parental functioning in cystic fibrosis. *Journal of Developmental and Behavioral Pediatrics*, 17, 48-55.

Lloyd, C., Smith, J., & Weinger, K. (2005). Stress and diabetes: A review of the links. *Diabetes Spectrum*, 18, 121-127.

Lovaas, O. I., & Smith, T. (2003). Early and intensive behavioral intervention in autism. In E. Kazdin & J. R. Weisz (Eds.), *Evidence-based psychotherapies for children and adolescents* (pp. 325-340). New York: Guilford.

Luiselli, J.K, Cannon, B., Ellis, J.T., & Sisson, R.W. (2000). Home-based behavioral interventions for young children with autism/pervasive developmental disorder: A preliminary evaluation of outcome in relation to child age and intensity of service delivery. *Autism*, 4, 426-438.

Malamud, N (1959). Heller's disease and childhood schizophrenia. *American Journal for Psychiatry*, 116, 215-218.

Mansell, W., & Morris, K. (2004). A survey of parents' reactions to the diagnosis of an autistic spectrum disorder by a local service: access to information and use of service. *Autism*, 8, 387-407.

Marcus L. (1977). Patterns of coping in families of psychotic children. *American Journal of Orthopsychiatry*, 47, 383-399.

Martire, L.M., & Schulz, R. (2007). Involving family in psychosocial interventions for chronic illness. *Current Directions in Psychological Science*, 16, 90-94.

Mash, E.J., & Johnston, C. (1983). Parental perceptions of child behavior problems, parenting self-esteem, and mothers' reported stress in younger and older hyperactive and normal children. *Journal of Consulting and Clinical Psychology*, 51, 86-99.

Mazure, C.M. (1995). *Does stress cause psychiatric illness?* Washington, DC: American Psychiatric Association.

McAdoo, W.G., & DeMeyer, M.K. (1977). Research related to family factors in autism. *Journal of Pediatric Psychology*, 2, 162-166.

McClannahan, L., & Krantz, P. (1994). The Princeton Child Development Institute. In S. Harris & J. Handleman (Eds.), *Preschool education programs for children with autism*. Austin, TX: Pro-Ed.

Meehl, P.E. (1962). Schizotaxia, schizotypy and schizophrenia. *American Psychologist*, 17, 827-838.

Melamed, B.G. (1995). The interface between physical and mental disorders: The need to dismantle the biopsychosocialneuroimmunological model of disease. *Journal of Clinical Psychology in Medical Settings*, 2, 225-231.

Meyers, S.A., & Miller, C. (2004). Direct, mediated, moderated, and cumulative relations between neighborhood characteristics and adolescent outcomes. *Adolescence*, 39, 121-144.

Midence, K., & O'Neil, M. (1999). The experience of parents in the diagnosis of autism: A pilot study. *Autism*, 3, 273-285.

Miles, J., & Shevlin, M. (2001). *Applying regression & correlation: A guide for students and researchers*. London: Sage.

Moes, D. (1995). Parent education and parenting stress. In R.L. Koegel & L.K. Koegel (Eds.), *Teaching children with autism: Strategies for initiating positive interactions and improving learning opportunities* (pp. 79-93). Baltimore, MD: Paul Brookes.

Mudford, O.C., Martin, N.T., Eikeseth, S., & Bibby, P. (2001). Parent-managed behavioral treatment for preschool children with autism: Some characteristics of UK programs. *Research-in-Developmental-Disabilities*, 22, 173-182.

Nitz, K., Ketterlinus, R.D., & Brandt, L.J. (1995). The role of stress, social support, and family environment in adolescent mothers' parenting. *Journal of Adolescent Research*, 10, 358-382.

Noh, S., Dumas, J.E., Wolf, L.C., & Fisman, S.N. (1989). Delineating sources of stress in parents of exceptional children. *Family Relations: Journal of Applied Family and Child Studies*, 38, 456-461.

Oberhein, D. (1996). *The support needs of adults and children with autism and their carers in Kent*. Gillingham: The Kent Autistic Trust.

Osborne, L.A. (2008). A Dynamic Transactional Model of Parent-Child Interactions in Autistic Spectrum Disorders. In P. Reed (Ed.), *Behavioral Theories and Interventions for Autism*. New York: Nova Science Press.

Osborne, L.A., McHugh, L., Saunders, J., & Reed, P. (2008a). Parenting stress reduces the effectiveness of early teaching interventions for Autistic Spectrum Conditions. *Journal of Autism and Developmental Disorders*, 38, 1092-1103.

Osborne, L.A., McHugh, L., Saunders, J., & Reed, P. (2008b). The effect of parenting behaviors on subsequent child behavior problems in Autistic Spectrum Conditions. *Research in Autism Spectrum Disorders*, 2, 249-263.

Osborne, L.A., & Reed, P. (2008a). Parents' perceptions of communication with professionals during the diagnosis of autism. *Autism*, 12, 259-274.

Perry, A., Sarlo-McGarvey, N., & Factor, D.C. (1992). Stress and family functioning in parents of girls with Rett syndrome. *Journal of Autism and Developmental Disorder*, 22, 235-248.

Piening, S. (1984). Family stress in diabetic renal failure. *Health and Social Work*, 9, 134-141.

Pisula, E. (1998). Stress in mothers of children with developmental disabilities. *Polish Psychological Bulletin*, 29, 305-311.

Pisula, E. (2003). Parents of children with autism – review of current research. *Archives of Psychiatry and Psychotherapy*, 5, 51-63.

Pisula, E. (2004). Stress and depression in mothers and the behavior of children with autism in the strange situation. *Przeglad Psychologiczny*, 47, 291-304.

Powers, M.D. (2000). Children with autism and their families. In, M.D. Powers (Ed.), *Children with autism: A parents' guide*, (pp. 119-153). Bethesda, MD.: Woodbine House.

Randall, P., & Parker, J. (1999). *Supporting the families of children with autism*. Chichester: Wiley.

Reed, P., Osborne, L.A., & Corness, M. (2007). The real-world effectiveness of early teaching interventions for children with autistic spectrum disorders. *Exceptional Children*, 73.

Repetti, R.L., & Wood, J. (1997). Effects of daily stress at work on mothers' interactions with preschoolers. *Journal of Family Psychology*, 11, 90-108.

Rimland, B. (1964). *Infantile autism: The syndrome and its implications for a neural theory of behavior*. East Norwalk: Appleton-Century-Crofts..

Ritvo, E.R. Cantwell, D., Johnson, E., Clements, M., Benbrook, F., Slagle, S., Kelly, P., & Ritz, M. (1971). Social class factors in autism. *Journal of Autism and Childhood Schizophrenia*, 1, 297-310.

Robbins, F.R., Dunlap, G., & Plienis, A.J. (1991). Family characteristics, family training, and the progress of young children with autism. *Journal of Early Intervention*, 15, 173-184.

Robinson, E.A., & Anderson, L.L. (1983). Family adjustment, parental attitudes, and social desirability. *Journal of Abnormal Child Psychology*, 11, 247-256.

Rodgers, A.Y. (1993). The assessment of variables related to the parenting behaviour of mothers with young children. *Children and Youth Services Review*, 15, 385-402.

Rodgers, A.Y. (1998). Multiple sources of stress and parenting behavior. *Children and Youth Services Review*, 20, 525-546.

Rodrigue, J.R., Morgan, S.B., & Geffken, G. (1990). Families of autistic children: Psychological functioning of mothers. *Journal of Clinical Child Psychology*, 19, 371-379.

Rutter, M. (2000). Genetic studies of autism: From the 1970s into the millennium. *Journal of Abnormal Child Psychology*, 28, 3-14.

Rutter, M., Lebovici, S., Eisenberg, L., Snezhnevsky, A.V., Sadoun, R., Brook, E., & Lin, T. (1969). A triaxial classification of mental disorder in children. *Journal of Child Psychology and Psychiatry*, 10, 41-61. *Retardation*, 110, 417-438.

Sanders, J.L., & Morgan, S.B. (1997). Family stress and adjustment as perceived by parents of children with autism or Down Syndrome: Implications for intervention. *Child and Family Behavior Therapy*, 19, 15-32.

Sanua, V.D. (1987). Standing against an established ideology: Infantile autism, a case inpoint. *Clinical Psychologist*, 40, 96-100.

Schopler, E. (1971). Parents of psychotic children as scapegoats. *Journal of Contemporary Psychotherapy*, 4, 17-22.

Schopler, E., Andrews, C.E. & Strupp, K. (1979). Do autistic children come from upper middle class parents? *Journal of Autism and Developmental Disorders*, 9, 139-152.

Schopler, E., Reichler, R., Bashford, A., Lansing, M., & Marcus, L. (1990). *Psychoeducational profile* (rev.). Austin, TX: Pro-Ed.

Schuntermann, P. (2002). Pervasive developmental disorder and parental adaptation: Previewing and reviewing atypical development with parents in child psychiatric consultation. *Harvard Review of Psychiatry*, 10, 16-27.

Sharpley, C.F., Bitsika, V., & Efremidis, B. (1997). Influence of gender, parental health, and perceived expertise of assistance upon stress anxiety, and depression among parents of children with autism. *Journal of Intellectual and Developmental Disability, 22,* 19-28.

Shattock, P., & Lowdon, G. (1991). Proteins, peptides and autism: II. Implications for the education and care of people with autism. *Brain Dysfunction*, 4, 323-334.

Shields, J. (2001). The NAS earlybird programme: Partnership with parents in early intervention. *Autism*, 5, 49-56.

Siantz, M.L.de-L., & Smith, M.S. (1994). Parental factors correlated with developmental outcome in the migrant Head Start child. *Early Childhood Research Quarterly*, 9, 481-503.

Singh, N.N., Lancioni, G.E., Winton, A.S.W., Fisher, B.C., Wahler, R.G., McAleavey, K., Singh, J., & Sabaawi, M. (2006). Mindful parenting decreases aggression, noncompliance, and self-injury in children with autism. *Journal of Emotional and Behavioral Disorders*, 14, 169-177.

Smalley, S.L., Tanguay, P.E., Smith, M., & Gutierrez, G. (1992). Autism and tuberous sclerosis. *Journal of Autism Developmental Disorders*, 22, 339-55.

Spaccarelli, S., Cotler, S., & Penman, D. (1992). Problem-solving skills training as a supplement to behavioral parent training. *Cognitive Therapy and Research*, 16, 1-17.

Stoddart, K.P. (1999). Adolescents with Asperger syndrome: Three case studies of individual and family therapy. Autism, 3, 255-271.

Stores, R., Stores G., Fellows, B. & Buckley, S. (1998). Daytime behaviour problems and maternal stress in children with Down syndrome, their siblings, their non intellectually disabled and other intellectually disabled peers. *Journal of Intellectual Disability Research*, 42, 228-237.

Tienari, P., Sorri, A., Lahti, I., Naarala, M., Wahlberg, K.E., Rönkkö, T., Moring, J., & Pohjola, J. (1987). Family environment and the etiology of schizophrenia; implications from the Finnish adoptive family study of schizophrenia. In H. Stierlin, F.B. Simon, & G. Schmidt (Eds), *Familiar realities*. Brunner/Mazel, New York.

Tobing, L.E., & Glenwick, D.S. (2002). Relation of the Childhood Autism Rating Scale—Parent version to diagnosis, stress, and age. *Research in Developmental Disabilities*, 23, 211-223.

Tomanik, S., Harris, G.E., & Hawkins, J. (2004). The relationship between behaviours exhibited by children with autism and maternal stress. *Journal of Intellectual and Developmental Disabilities*, 29, 16-26.

Viner, R., McGrath, M., & Trudinger, P. (1996). Family stress and metabolic control in diabetes. *Archives of Disease in Childhood*, 74, 418-321.

Wahlberg, K.E., Wynne, L.C., Oja, H., Keskitalo, P., Anais-Tanner, H., Koistinen, P., Tarvainen, T., Hakko, H., Lahti, I., Moring, J., Naarala, M., Sorri, A., & Tienari, P. (2000). Thought disorder index of Finnish adoptees and communication deviance of their adoptive parents. *Psychological Medicine*, 30, 127-136.

Walden, S., Pistrang, N., & Joyce, T. (2000). Parents of adults with intellectual disabilities: Quality of life and experiences of caring. *Journal of Applied Research in Intellectual Disabilities*, 13, 62-76.

Ward, A.J. (1990). A comparison and analysis of the presence of family problems during pregnancy of mothers of "autistic" children and mothers of normal children. *Child Psychiatry and Human Development*, 20, 279-288.

Warner, L.A., & Pottick, K.J. (2006). Functional impairment among preschoolers using mental health services. *Children and Youth Services Review*, 28, 473-486.

Webster-Stratton, C. (1990). Stress: A potential disruptor of parent perceptions and family interactions. *Journal of Clinical Child Psychology*, 19, 302-312.

Weiss, M.J. (2002). Hardiness and social support as predictors of stress in mothers of typical children, children with autism, and children with mental retardation. *Autism*, 6, 115-130.

Williams, J. (2006). Learning from mothers: how myths, policies, and practices affect the detection of subtle developmental problems in children. *Child: Care, Health, and Development*, 33, 282-290.

Wing, L. (1997). The history of ideas on autism. *Autism*, 1, 13-23.

Wolf, L.C., Noh, S., Fisman, S.N., & Speechley, M. (1989). Brief report: Psychological effects of parenting stress on parents of autistic children. *Journal of Autism and Developmental Disorders*, 19, 157-166.

Wolff, S. (1998). Is there a link between engineering and autism?: Commentary. *Autism*, 2, 96-97.

In: Handbook of Parenting: Styles, Stresses & Strategies   ISBN 978-1-60741-766-8
Editor: Pacey H. Krause and Tahlia M. Dailey   © 2009 Nova Science Publishers, Inc.

Chapter 15

PARENTING IN THE CONTEXT OF DOMESTIC VIOLENCE: UNIQUE STRESSES AND OUTCOMES

*Erin Gallagher,[1] Alissa Huth-Bocks[1]
and Alytia Levendosky[2]*
[1]Eastern Michigan University, [2]Michigan State University, USA

ABSTRACT

Research shows that 20% to 38% of women experience domestic violence during their lifetime (Tjaden & Thoennes, 2000), and women may be particularly vulnerable to partner abuse during the childbearing years. As such, millions of young children are exposed to DV and are parented primarily by battered women. The notable prevalence of DV indicates that its effect on parenting outcomes requires close examination. As one might expect, existing research has found that DV generally has a devastating impact on parenting capacities (Holden et al., 1998; Levendosky & Graham-Bermann, 2000; 2001).

A few studies that have examined the impact of DV on parenting during the perinatal period have found that parenting is already compromised during pregnancy and shortly after birth as a result of DV (Dayton, Levendosky, Davidson, & Bogat, 2007; Huth-Bocks, Levendosky, Theran, & Bogat, 2004). Similarly, other studies have found that DV negatively impacts mothers' displays of sensitivity, encouragement, and guidance during parent-infant interactions (Sokolowski et al., 2008). These results suggest that DV interferes with an adaptive transition to parenthood and the earliest forms of parenting, which are known to affect long-term childhood outcomes. A number of studies have also found that mothers of preschool and school-age children who are exposed to DV report significantly higher parenting stress compared to non-battered women (Holden et al., 1998; Levendosky & Graham-Bermann, 1998; 2000; Ritchie & Holden, 1998). Parenting stress, in turn, is associated with more negative and less positive parenting behaviors (e.g., Holden et al., 1998, Huth-Bocks & Hughes, 2008) and poor child outcomes (Levendosky & Graham-Bermann, 1998). Not surprisingly, DV is also associated with other parenting deficits such as less supportive behaviors, less parenting effectiveness and child-centeredness (Graham-Bermann & Levendosky, 1998a; Levendosky & Graham-Bermann, 2001), and greater parent-child hostility and aggression (Holden et al., 1998) during the preschool and school-age years, although there appear to be a subset of women who are resilient and don't experience impairments in parenting.

In conclusion, research has demonstrated that DV is surprisingly common among mothers and has deleterious effects on a variety of parenting outcomes in most battered women. This chapter includes a thorough review of the empirical literature documenting the relationship between DV and parenting outcomes beginning in pregnancy and lasting throughout childhood.

INTRODUCTION

Research has documented that 20% to 38% of women experience domestic violence (DV; defined here as male to female partner violence) during their lifetime (Tjaden & Thoennes, 2000), and approximately 12% of women are victims of DV in any given year (Straus & Gelles, 1986). The literature on DV has indicated that it is not unusual for women to experience DV at multiple points throughout their life, such that women may move in and out of violent relationships over time (Bogat, Levendosky, Theran, Von Eye & Davidson, 2003). Notably, research shows that women may be particularly vulnerable to partner abuse during the childbearing years; for example, violence may increase during pregnancy and beyond (Jasinski & Kantor, 2001; Stewart, 1994; Torres et al., 2000). This is not surprising given that individuals tend to be less violent as they age, and therefore, DV tends to occur more frequently early in romantic relationships when women are more likely to become pregnant or have young children (Bradbury & Lawrence, 1999). As a result, millions of young children are parented by battered women (Fantuzzo, Boruch, Beriama, & Atkins, 1997). Because the relationship histories of many of these women are complex, and many women are battered at multiple points in their life (Bogat et al., 2003), it is important to understand the impact of DV on parenting throughout multiple stages of children's lives.

This chapter will review the current literature examining the effects of DV on women's parenting, including descriptions of the numerous ways in which researchers have defined and assessed both DV and parenting across studies. Furthermore, the impact of DV on parenting will be thoroughly examined according to different developmental stages of children, beginning in pregnancy and ending in adolescence.

Definitions and Prevalence

Because this chapter focuses on the impact of DV on parenting, it is first important to distinguish between DV and the construct of marital conflict. While the two constructs may appear similar, considerably more research has examined the consequences of marital conflict, or marital discord, as compared to DV (Cummings, 1994; Emery, 1982; Holden, Stein, Ritchie, Harris, & Jouriles, 1998). In general, marital conflict is considered to be less severe and less threatening to individuals than DV per se. For example, marital conflict may include general disagreements, arguments, and dissatisfaction between partners, but does not necessarily involve threats to an individual's safety or integrity, as typically found in cases of DV.

It is also important to note that in the DV literature, different researchers have defined DV differently across studies by either including or excluding different types of violence. A commonly used definition of DV includes only physical assault, or behaviors that threaten, attempt or actually inflict physical harm (Tjaden & Thoennes, 2000). A second way to define DV is including both physical assault and sexual assault or coercion, including rape by a partner. Finally, a third and less commonly used definition for DV is one that also includes psychological and/or emotional violence, either by itself or in addition to physical and/or sexual violence, such as insulting or degrading comments, vindictive and spiteful behavior, threats to harm the victim and/or the victim's children, or inducing fear of bodily injury or death. Using the above definitions, Tjaden and Thoennes (2000) used data from a National Violence against Women telephone survey of 8000 women living in the United States to examine the prevalence rates of different types of violence perpetrated against women by opposite-sex cohabiting partners. They found that 4.5% of women had experienced forcible rape by a partner within their lifetime, 20.4% of women reported being physically assaulted by a partner, and approximately 78% of women who had experienced a physical assault by a partner also experienced psychological abuse, including threats and a fear of bodily injury or death at the time of the event. Because of the elevated prevalence of DV occurring in homes across the United States, and because 87% of women become parents in their lifetime according to the United States Census Bureau (2007), it is important for the scientific and health-care communities to understand the devastating impact of violence against women on parenting.

It is also important to acknowledge that many different aspects of parenting have been assessed in the DV research literature. Thus, appropriately, parenting is hardly a unitary construct in this literature. For example, some researchers have assessed parental representations of their children (Huth-Bocks, Levendosky, Theran, & Bogat, 2004; Sokolowski, Hans, Bernstein, & Cox, 2007; Theran, Levendosky, Bogat & Huth-Bocks, 2005), parenting stress (Holden et al., 1998; Huth-Bocks & Hughes, 2008; Levendosky & Graham-Bermann, 1998; 2000; Ritchie & Holden, 1998), parenting behaviors (Graham-Bermann & Levendosky, 1998a; Holden & Ritchie, 1991; Holden et al., 1998; Levendosky & Graham-Bermann, 2001; Levendosky, Leahy, Bogat, Davidson & Von Eye, 2006; Ritchie & Holden, 1998; Sokolowski et al., 2007), parent-child relationship quality (Holden & Ritchie, 1991; Holden et al., 1998; Levendosky, Huth-Bocks, Shapiro & Semel, 2003; Ritchie & Holden, 1998), and emotion coaching (Katz & Windecker-Nelson, 2006). Thus, while the research literature has been primarily consistent in finding that DV has a deleterious impact on parenting in homes with children of all ages, and DV is a significant parenting stressor, the aspects of parenting examined has differed across studies.

PARENTING OUTCOMES IN THE CONTEXT OF DOMESTIC VIOLENCE DURING PREGNANCY

Although it has been documented that approximately 1.6% to 20% of women experience DV during pregnancy (Gazmararian et al., 1996), almost no studies have examined the impact of DV on parenting constructs during this particularly vulnerable time. Instead, the vast majority of research has focused on actual parenting behaviors in the context of DV after the child is born because it is typically assumed that this is when parenting most directly impacts children. However, it is known that mothers typically form representations of themselves as mothers (Ammaniti et al., 1992) and representations of relationships with their children by the third trimester of pregnancy (Lumley, 1982; Stern, 1995; Zeanah & Benoit, 1995). Furthermore, these representations are believed to be early precursors to actual parenting behaviors after the birth of the child. For example, representations of the child and the self as a mother may be carried over, or similar to, postnatal representations (Slade & Cohen, 1996; Zeanah, Keener, & Anders, 1986), which, in turn, are likely to impact the mother-child relationship. In other words, how the mother views the child before birth may strongly impact how she views and interacts with the child after birth (Dayton, Levendosky, Davidson, & Bogat, 2007).

In one of the first studies to examine DV and parenting representations, Huth-Bocks et al. (2004) examined the impact of DV during pregnancy on mothers' prenatal representations of their infants and themselves as mothers. Participants were 202 pregnant women between the ages of 18 and 40 who were enrolled in a larger longitudinal study examining risk and protective factors related to DV. In this study, DV was defined as male-to-female verbal, physical, and/or sexual violence. According to this definition, 44% of pregnant women reported experiencing at least one incident of DV during pregnancy; this high prevalence rate was due, in part, to an over-sampling of battered women.

Information about parenting representations (i.e., representations of the infant and the self as a mother) was obtained through a 1-hour structured interview with the mother; mothers' narrative responses were classified into one of three categories: balanced, disengaged-non-balanced, and distorted-non-balanced. Balanced narratives were characterized by the integration of negative and positive affect, richness in detail, and a sense of the mother as connected to her child. Disengaged narratives were characterized by a lack of detail, and emotional and personal distance from the child. Finally, distorted narratives were characterized by inconsistency and contradictions in the mother's responses, an inability to focus on her child, role-reversal, and preoccupation with her child. The mother's responses were additionally coded in this study for representations of the self-as-mother that assessed the mother's feelings about her own competence and self-efficacy in the maternal role, or expectations of herself as a mother. Mothers low on this scale appeared to lack confidence in themselves, whereas mothers high on this scale appeared to be unrealistically self-confident. More balanced mothers were more realistic, acknowledging the challenges of motherhood, but simultaneously feeling competent to provide for the child.

Huth-Bocks et al. (2004) found that women who experienced DV during their pregnancy had more negative and non-balanced representations of their child. More specifically, their thoughts and feelings related to the parent-child relationship appeared less flexible or open to change, less coherent, less sensitive, less accepting, and they had greater perceived infant difficulty, less joy, more anger, more anxiety, more depressed affect, and less feelings of self-efficacy as a caregiver. Thus, battered women were significantly more likely to be classified as having disengaged or distorted representations of their children and their relationship with their children prenatally, while women who had not experienced DV were significantly more likely to be classified as balanced. These findings also held true after the mother's education level and current relationship status were controlled for. Thus, results from this study suggested that parenting, assessed as representations of the child and the relationship with the child, was already compromised before the baby was born in women experiencing DV.

In a follow-up study from the same research group (Theran et al., 2005), the stability of mothers' representations of their infants and relationship with their infants was examined from pregnancy through the child's first year of life in 180 women with data at both time periods. In addition to prenatal and postnatal representations, maternal caregiving was also assessed when the child was 1 year-old through a videotaped free-play interaction between the mother and infant with subsequent scores given for each of the following parenting behaviors: maternal sensitivity (ability to accurately interpret infant's signals), disengagement (lack of connectedness with baby), over-controlling/intrusiveness (interfering with infant's goals), covert hostility (expression of covert hostility), warmth (affection toward baby), and joy (smiling, laughing, enthusiasm). Overall, 71% of the sample had stable parenting representations from pregnancy to the child's first birthday. However, results indicated that women who became non-balanced over the child's first year of life (balanced at pregnancy and non-balanced at follow-up) were significantly more likely to have experienced DV during pregnancy (Theran et al., 2005). In other words, abuse status predicted a negative change in the mother's representations of her child and their relationship between pregnancy and the child's first birthday. Additionally, results indicated that women who changed from having a non-balanced representation of the infant during pregnancy to a balanced representation after birth continued to display less sensitivity toward the child, appeared more disengaged, and showed less warmth than women who had stable balanced representations of the infant over time.

These results suggest that maternal distress possibly related to DV during pregnancy may increase the likelihood that mothers may form non-balanced representations of their infants before and after the child is born. However, while mothers may develop balanced representations of their infants after birth, it appears as though these mothers' parenting behaviors toward their children continues to be negatively impacted by experiencing DV. This study supports the notion that it is likely that the mother-child relationship and parenting may become impaired as a result of negative maternal representations and maternal distress related to an abusive relationship during pregnancy.

Although almost no research has been conducted on the impact of DV on parenting during pregnancy, the results from the two aforementioned studies indicate that, in general, DV appears to have significant negative effects on mothers' representations of the child and of themselves as caregivers during pregnancy (Huth-Bocks et al., 2004), which is likely to translate into less maternal sensitivity and negative representations of the infant during the child's first year of life (Theran et al., 2005). Women who are abused during their pregnancy may have fewer psychological resources, and this may interfere with their ability to tolerate or relate to their infant in a positive manner (Lieberman & Van Horn, 1998). For example, battered mothers may feel overwhelmed by the possibility of caring for another or fear the effects of the violence on their infants. Taken together, these results provide preliminary evidence for DV as a major parenting stressor that may begin before the child is even born.

PARENTING OUTCOMES IN THE CONTEXT OF DOMESTIC VIOLENCE DURING INFANCY

Similar to DV in pregnancy, very little research has been conducted regarding the impact of DV on parenting during infancy. However, as indicated by Theran et al. (2005), the negative effects of DV on parenting during pregnancy may continue into the child's first year of life. Additionally, as mentioned earlier, DV often continues in the lives of families with young children. Thus, it can be assumed that DV occurring in the child's infancy will also have deleterious effects on parenting.

In one of the few existing studies, Levendosky et al. (2006) examined the impact of DV before pregnancy and in the first year of the infant's life on parenting, maternal mental health, and infant externalizing behavior. Participants included 203 women between the ages of 18 and 40. In this study, DV was defined as male-to-female violence, and ranged in severity from mild to severe violence, including threats of violence, physical, and sexual violence. During the infant's first year of life, DV experienced with all partners in the first year postpartum was considered. During the infant's first year of life, 38% of women reported experiencing threats of violence, 21% experienced physical violence, and 8% reported experiencing sexual violence. Parenting was measured through observed maternal behaviors, which were assessed by a 12-minute mother-infant interaction when infants were approximately 1 year of age. Maternal parenting behaviors included sensitivity (the mother's ability to perceive and accurately interpret the infant's signals and to respond appropriately and promptly), warmth (the mother's affection toward the infant), joy (the quality and quantity of the mother's enjoyment during the interaction with the baby), disengagement (mother's connection and involvement with the infant), hostility (the mother's hostile communications and interactions with the infant), and intrusive/controlling behavior (mother's interference with rather than facilitation of infant's goals).

Results from this study indicated that DV during the child's first year of life was significantly correlated with observed maternal parenting behaviors. Mothers who had experienced DV in the first year postpartum were more likely to display hostility and disengagement when interacting with their infants, and they showed decreased warmth and sensitivity toward their infant as well; DV was also associated with poor maternal mental health. In addition, it is notable that this study also found that maternal parenting behaviors mediated the relationship between DV and infants' externalizing behavior at 1 year. Thus, parenting appeared to account for the association between DV and infant outcomes. Overall, these results indicate that, not only is DV often prevalent during the first year after birth in many women, DV negatively impacts parenting during this time. This is not surprising given that mothers' mental health was also found to be compromised as a result of experiencing DV. Furthermore, not only do battered mothers appear to display less positive and more negative behaviors toward their infants, but their problematic parenting behaviors affect infants' externalizing behavior as well.

Another study (Sokolowski et al., 2007) also examined the effects of DV on parenting during infancy. Participants in this study included 100 African-American mothers with children between the ages of 17 and 20 months old. Families resided in housing projects in a large Midwestern city that was characterized by extreme levels of poverty and violence. In this study, DV was defined as male-to-female verbal aggression, including critical and controlling acts, as well as physical violence. Parenting was assessed in two ways: 1) mothers' mental representations of their infants, such as feelings about their relationship with their young child, impressions about their child's personality and behavior, as well as perceived emotional responses to the child assessed through a semi-structured interview, and 2) parenting behaviors from observations of mother-child interactions in three situations including reading the child a book, free play, and a clean-up session. Mothers' parenting behaviors in this interaction task were coded for sensitivity/responsivity and encouragement/guidance.

As expected, mothers' experience of verbal and physical DV with their infants' fathers was significantly related to their parenting representations, such that their narratives contained more guilt, and less sensitivity, involvement, and openness to change regarding their children. In this study, 38% of women had balanced representations of their infants, 36% had disengaged representations of their infants, and 26% had distorted representations of their infants. These findings are consistent with those reported by Theran et al. (2005). The current study also examined the association between mothers' parenting representations and parenting behaviors. Not surprisingly, mothers with disengaged representations were observed to be less sensitive and responsive to their infants, and they used significantly less encouragement and guidance than mothers with either balanced or distorted representations during interactions with their infants.

Both of these studies strongly support a link between DV and mothers' impaired parenting beliefs and feelings. It is possible that mothers' experience of hostility and anger in romantic relationships may transfer over into the parent-child relationship, including views and feelings about this relationship. Furthermore, DV is associated with problematic maternal parenting behaviors, such that mothers who experience DV in their child's first year of life appear to be more hostile and disengaged with their infants (Levendosky et al., 2006) and appear to be less responsive and sensitive toward their infants (Levendosky et al., 2006; Sokolowski et al., 2007). In sum, it seems that DV may render mothers of infant children stressed, distracted, and exhausted in an already emotionally demanding transition to motherhood, and preventing them from being sensitive to their infant's needs at a critical point in child development. Thus, these preliminary studies suggest that the impact of DV on parenting during infancy appears to be particularly problematic for mothers and babies.

PARENTING OUTCOMES IN THE CONTEXT OF DOMESTIC VIOLENCE DURING TODDLER AND PRESCHOOL YEARS

Some of the earliest research conducted examining the impact of DV on parenting involved parents of toddler and preschool-age children. Still, relatively little research has been done examining the effects of DV on parenting with children of this age, even though it has been documented in the literature that DV is most likely to occur in homes with very young children (Fantuzzo et al., 1997).

Several earlier studies using the same sample of participants were conducted (Holden & Ritchie, 1991; Holden et al., 1998; Ritchie & Holden, 1998) in order to examine multiple facets of parenting in the context of homes where DV was present or absent. Participants included 37 battered women and their children [ages 2 to 8; Holden and Ritchie (1998) only examined two groups of younger (ages 2 to 4) and older (ages 5 to 8) children] recruited from a battered women's shelter. The length of time in an abusive relationship ranged from 6 months to 13 years. A comparison group of 37 non-battered women and their children were also included.

In these studies, DV was defined as the use of physical or verbal aggression according to maternal report in response to conflict between the parental dyad. Parenting was comprehensively measured in multiple ways in these studies, including parenting stress, the quality of the mother-child relationship, and specific maternal and paternal behaviors.

Parenting stress was measured by maternal report on a questionnaire according to the degree of stress associated with parenting, such as social isolation, a sense of maternal competence or incompetence, and perception of the child's demandingness. A mother-child observation task was conducted to assess the quality of the parent-child relationship using both a structured play task and a subsequent free-play session. The mother-child relationship was coded for quality of interaction that included the mother teaching her child (instructs, commands, seeks child's opinion), and the overall quality of the interaction (mother versus child initiating, presence of joint play, mother's attentiveness to child's play, and conflict). Finally, maternal and paternal parenting behaviors were assessed according to a computer simulated social situation that simulated a day in the life of a family through a set of 27 vignettes about commonly occurring problems. Mothers were asked how frequently each problem occurred, and how it would be responded to by the mother and the father, including both positive and negative child-rearing practices. Additionally, maternal parenting behaviors were assessed through a questionnaire which inquired about the presence of mother-to-child physical violence, such as throwing something at the child, pushing, kicking, or hitting the child. Finally, children's internalizing and externalizing behavior was assessed through maternal report on a questionnaire.

Results from the Holden and Ritchie (1991) and Holden et al. (1998) studies each indicated that battered women reported experiencing significantly more parenting stress compared to the non-battered women. Next, according to the mother-child observation task, battered women and their children were involved in significantly more conflicts than the comparison group, and battered mothers were less attentive to their child's play. Finally, both maternal and paternal simulated parenting behaviors seemed to be negatively impacted by the presence of violence in the home. Battered mothers indicated that their violent husbands used less reasoning in response to their child's misbehaviors, and were less physically affectionate with their children than comparison fathers. Additionally, mothers of violent husbands indicated that their husbands used spanking as a punishment significantly more often than comparison fathers, and violent husbands were significantly more likely to use power assertive responses to their children's misbehaviors than comparison fathers, according to maternal report. Regarding mothers' parenting behaviors, battered women reported significantly more inconsistent discipline than comparison mothers. In the Holden et al. (1998) study, the authors additionally found that battered mothers reported significantly more aggressive behaviors directed toward their children, including pushing, kicking, or hitting the child, compared to non-battered mothers. Surprisingly, results from this study indicated that battered mothers did not display less affection toward their children or provide less structure in their homes than non-battered mothers. Both studies (Holden & Ritchie, 1991; Holden et al., 1998) found that children of battered mothers exhibited more internalizing behaviors and had a more difficult temperament than comparison children, but the two groups did not differ on the presence of externalizing behaviors. Additionally, Holden and Ritchie (1991) found that the younger group of children (ages 2 to 5) exhibited less internalizing and externalizing behaviors compared to the older group of children.

Overall, the results of these studies indicate that DV has negative consequences for many aspects of parenting among both mothers and fathers in families with young children. The negative impact of DV on many different domains of parenting suggests that DV has a pervasive effect on parenting of young children. While battered mothers did not necessarily display less affection or provide less structure in their homes than non-battered mothers, it is clear that DV is associated with an increase in overtly negative behaviors toward children overall, which in turn, may result in children having an increase in internalizing symptoms, in particular.

The same authors (Ritchie & Holden, 1998) conducted an additional study with a different sample that also examined multiple facets of parenting in homes where DV was present or not present. Participants included 30 battered women and their children (ages 3 to 7) recruited from a battered women's shelter, and a comparison group of 28 non-battered women and their same-age children. In this study, DV was defined as maternal-reported physical violence perpetrated by the father. Parenting was operationalized as parenting stress, and the quality of the mother-child relationship as assessed using a 15-minute observation task that was inherently challenging (the mother was asked to prevent the child from playing with desirable toys). During this observation task, maternal behavior was coded according to maternal attempts at control and affectionate contact. Maternal parenting behaviors were also assessed through the same computer-simulated vignettes about commonly occurring problems in the daily lives of families described above. Child-rearing responses were rated according to the presence of physical affection, positive reinforcement, limit setting, spanking, emotional availability, and inconsistency.

Results from this study indicated that, in general, battered women reported more parenting stress than did comparison women, as found in the previous studies by this research group (Holden & Ritchie, 1991; Holden et al., 1998). Furthermore, parenting stress in both battered and non-battered women was significantly related to more punitive reactions from mothers and less maternal monitoring of their children during the observation task, as well as negatively related to maternal reported physical affection. Higher parenting stress was also related to mothers' tendency to set more limits with their children, use more spanking at home, and use less positive reinforcement. However, it is important to note that this study did not find significant group differences between battered and non-battered on some of women's observed and reported parenting behaviors, which is unlike other studies described so far. The authors speculate that battered women who are able to cope with the stress of DV might be more likely to interact positively with their children, while those experiencing higher degrees of parenting stress may be more likely to have parenting difficulties. The other possibility proposed by these authors is that some mothers experiencing DV may actually engage in positive parenting behaviors in order to compensate for the DV in their homes, which has also been suggested by others (Levendosky & Graham-Bermann, 2000). However, findings generally support the notion that stress from a violent partner relationship may exacerbate the link between DV and parenting in homes with young children.

In one final study (Levendosky et al., 2003) examining the impact of DV on parenting in homes with young children, the mediating role of the mother-child relationship on preschool-age children's functioning was examined. Participants were 103 children and their mothers that were recruited from the community and shelters for battered women. In this study, DV was defined as threats of violence, violent acts, as well as sexual abuse by a partner; in this sample, 43% of women indicated that they had been in an abusive relationship in the last year, and 47% indicated experiencing abuse from their most recent partner.

Parenting was assessed using maternal self-report on a questionnaire asking about effective parenting behaviors, such as the extent to which mothers felt they had control over their child's behavior and the extent to which they kept promises that were made to their child. In addition, the quality of the mother-child relationship was assessed through a 25-

minute observation task in which the mother and child took turns leading the play. Mothers' behavior was coded according to authoritative parenting behaviors during the child-directed play, including maternal self-regulation, intrusive parenting, and demands for self-reliant behavior of the child, as well as negative parenting behaviors during mother-directed play, such as unresponsive play.

Surprisingly, DV was not directly associated with parenting according to the observation task in this study. However, there were both direct and indirect effects of DV on parenting effectiveness according to maternal self-report, but the direct effect was not in the expected direction; more specifically, mothers who indicated experiencing more DV in their homes reported better parenting effectiveness. Additionally, the indirect effect was such that maternal psychological distress (including depression and PTSD symptoms) mediated the relationship between DV and parenting effectiveness, such that higher levels of maternal psychological distress were related to lower levels of parenting effectiveness. Notably, DV was directly and indirectly related to children's behavior problems through maternal psychological distress, including depression and trauma symptoms. Results from this study were contrary to other studies that have examined the impact of DV on parenting in preschool-age children, in that DV was not associated with the quality of parenting or was positively associated with parenting effectiveness, depending on source of information. The authors discuss the possibility that mothers experiencing DV may attempt to compensate for the violence in their homes by being more attentive and responsive to their children, in general. An alternative explanation is that DV may lead to defensiveness on the part of the mother with unrealistic elevated reports of parenting effectiveness. These findings are similar to those of Ritchie and Holden (1998) who also found a lack of expected differences between battered and non-battered mothers.

In conclusion, the majority of research examining the impact of DV on parenting in families with toddlers or preschool-age children has found that DV is associated with more problematic parenting in general. However, there was some evidence that DV was not associated with observed parenting (Ritchie & Holden, 1998), and was possibly related to parenting effectiveness (Levendosky et al., 2003). While the lack of findings between DV and parenting in some studies do not support the vast majority of DV research, the authors of these studies indicated that surprising results may be attributed to the low levels of violence in some community samples, or the tendency for some mothers to compensate for DV in their homes by positively parenting their children or seeing themselves as effective parents. In addition, some mothers may be more resilient or better able to cope with DV than others, further explaining the discrepancies in findings across studies.

PARENTING OUTCOMES IN THE CONTEXT OF DOMESTIC VIOLENCE DURING SCHOOL-AGE YEARS

The majority of research examining the impact of DV on parenting has been done with parents of school-age children. Notably, many researchers have examined the impact of DV on parenting in families with children of a wide range of ages, such as children between ages 4 and 16 (Wolfe, Jaffe, Wilson & Zak, 1985) or children between ages 4 and 14 (Jouriles & Norwood, 1995), to name a few. For the purposes of this chapter, such studies will be reviewed according to the mean age of the children, which typically falls in the school-age range (between 6 and 12). It is important to understand the impact of DV on parenting in families with school-age children because the marital and parent-child relationship become increasingly important as social role models at this age, as children's social relationships outside of the family increase substantially (Grych & Fincham, 1990; MacKinnon-Lewis & Lofquist, 1996; Parker & Asher, 1987). Because there is a substantial amount of literature examining the impact of DV on parenting in homes with school-age children, studies in this section will be grouped according to the aspect of parenting measured.

Parenting Stress

One of the very first studies of DV and parenting examined the effects of DV on maternal parenting stress (Wolfe et al., 1985). These researchers recruited 142 mothers and their 4-16 year-old children ($X = 8.9$) from shelters for battered women and the community. DV was defined as physical violence between partners within the last 12 months. Parenting stress was uniquely assessed as a combination of maternal health, life events, and family crises. In this study, DV was significantly related to maternal parenting stress and children's internalizing and externalizing behavior problems and social competence. Furthermore, results indicated that the impact of DV on children's behavior problems and social competence was partially a function of the degree of maternal stress experienced by the mother. Thus, it seems as though DV is not only associated with maternal stress, in general, but DV is both directly and indirectly correlated with children's social and emotional functioning. This study was important in laying the groundwork for future research on what would show the pervasive effects of DV on other aspects of parenting of school-age children, rather than those limited to parenting stress.

A number of other studies examining the impact of DV on parenting with school-age children measured self-reported maternal parenting stress. In fact, many of these studies used the same questionnaire, the Parenting Stress Index (Abidin, 1983), lending some consistency across studies. Because DV may render parents feeling particularly vulnerable in their home environment, it can be assumed that stress related to their parenting experience may also be increased. Levendosky and Graham-Bermann (1998), for example, conducted a study with 121 women and their children between the ages of 7 and 12 recruited from battered women's shelters and the community. DV was defined as maternal-reported psychological or physical abuse from a male partner during the past year. In this study, parenting stress consisted of both child domain stress (child characteristics seen as stressors, such as difficult temperament) and parent domain stress (parent characteristics seen as stressors, such as personality, investment in parenting, resentment toward parenting). Results from this study revealed that the battered and non-battered women did not differ in their assessment of child domain stress, but women experiencing DV reported significantly more parent domain stress. Additionally, children whose mothers reported high levels of parenting stress exhibited significantly more internalizing and externalizing behavior problems. Thus, it seems as though the presence of violence in the home resulted in mothers experiencing more stress related to their parenting role in particular, which in turn, may have led to less effective reactions toward their children, rendering children more vulnerable to behavior problems.

Similarly, Owen, Kaslow, and Thompson (2006) conducted a study with 139 battered African-American women and their 8 to 12 year-old children recruited from hospitals, shelters for battered women, and health fairs. DV was defined as maternal-reported emotional or physical abuse within the last year from a male partner, and parenting stress was measured as parental distress (distress specifically related to parenting responsibilities), difficult child behaviors (perception of children's emotional and behavioral problems compared to other children), and parent-child dysfunctional interaction (problems relevant to the mother-child relationship). In this study, higher levels of DV were significantly associated with higher levels of parenting stress across all three of the aforementioned parenting stress domains, and parenting stress was directly related to children's internalizing and externalizing symptoms, as found in the previously mentioned study (Levendosky & Graham-Bermann, 1998). Furthermore, parenting stress mediated the relationship between DV and children's internalizing and externalizing behavior problems. This study provides further evidence that DV appears to make mothers more susceptible to feeling stressed in their parental role, which renders children more susceptible to maladjustment.

Some authors have examined the impact of DV on parenting stress in individuals from ethnic/racial minority groups, which is important because of variation across cultures and subgroups around family beliefs and values, which may impact how DV and parenting are perceived. Edelson, Hokoda and Ramos-Lira (2007) examined 44 Latina women and 21 non-Latina women with children between the ages of 6 and 12 that were recruited from various places in the community, but had all reportedly experienced similar amounts of DV in the last year (defined as psychological, physical or sexual abuse from a male partner). These authors were interested in the impact of DV on different facets of the women's mental health, including parenting stress. On the child domain stress subscales, Latina women indicated higher levels of parenting stress, such that these women viewed their children as more difficult to parent compared to non-Latina women. Additionally, Latina women indicated higher levels of parenting stress on the parent domain subscales compared to non-Latina women, such that they reported less parental competence and emotional attachment to their child, and more social isolation. These findings are not surprising given that Latina women had poorer outcomes on measures related to trauma, depression, and self-esteem than non-Latina women. Thus, this study indicates that Latina women experiencing DV had poorer mental health and, in particular, they experienced more parenting stress related to their parental role and viewed their children as more problematic compared to non-Latina women. The authors speculated that because there is a large emphasis on family and gender roles in Latina culture, Latina women who experience DV may find themselves torn between their duty to preserve and maintain the family, and their obligations to protect themselves and their children, resulting in higher levels of parenting stress across parent and child domains.

Other researchers have examined the effects of DV on parenting stress in African American women specifically (Hughes & Huth-Bocks, 2007; Huth-Bocks & Hughes, 2008). The sample in these studies included 190 primarily African-American women with children between the ages of 4 and 12 ($X = 8.3$) who were living in shelters for battered women. DV was defined as maternal-reported psychological and physical aggression toward the mother from her male partner in each study, and parenting stress was measured as parental distress, parent-child dysfunction, and perceptions of difficult child. In these studies, parenting was additionally assessed as self-reported parenting behaviors, including dysfunctional discipline practices such as permissiveness, irritability, and the use of lengthy explanations. Severity of

DV was not directly related to parenting stress in either study; however, parenting stress was related to more ineffective parenting behaviors in both studies, as well as child-reported depressive symptoms (Huth-Bocks & Hughes, 2008). The authors suggested that an accumulation of stressors associated with living in a shelter, in particular, may have taken precedence in causing parenting stress and ineffective parenting behaviors above and beyond distress related to experiencing DV prior to living in the shelter. Thus, while participants indicated experiencing a high level of parenting stress in both studies, the parenting stress did not seem to be associated with DV experience per se.

In general, the aforementioned studies document the association between DV and parenting stress in homes with school-age children. The majority of research shows that DV is associated with higher levels of parenting stress, which may also render parents less effective in their interactions with their children, and children may subsequently experience more behavior problems. These findings were also supported in samples comprised of ethnic/racial minority groups, further indicating the pervasive impact of DV on families of different cultural backgrounds. For example, the latter two studies found that DV was not directly associated with more parenting stress, per se, but parenting stress was consistently associated with ineffective parenting behaviors in African-American battered women. Thus, when parents are removed from the actual environment in which they experienced DV, other stressors such as living in a shelter and being removed from their home, may take precedence over the stress of experiencing DV. This is contrary to the Edelson et al. (2007) study, which found that Latina women experiencing DV appear to have higher levels of parenting stress because there is a large emphasis on family in Latina culture, and these women may find themselves torn between their duty to preserve the family unit, and their obligations to protect their family. In sum, preliminary evidence suggests that family values across cultures may impact the manner in which a woman experiences parenting stress and problematic parenting behaviors in homes with DV.

Parenting Styles

Only one preliminary study has uniquely assessed parenting according to Baumrind's (1971) parenting styles. More specifically, this study (Rossman & Rea, 2005) examined DV in relation to parenting typology, or parenting styles, including Authoritative (neutral, reasoned, consistent, includes child in decision making), Authoritarian (strict, uncompromising, negative, punitive), and Permissive (nonpunitive, unpredictable, inconsistent) styles. One hundred and four mothers and their 5 to 12 year-old children were recruited from battered women's shelters and the community; DV was defined as verbal and physical abuse toward the mother from her male partner. Results indicated that mothers who had experienced DV endorsed significantly more permissive and authoritarian parenting styles (both more ineffective, problematic styles), while non-battered mothers endorsed significantly more authoritative parenting styles, which is known to be the most effective parenting style. For example, battered mothers endorsed greater non-follow-through and non-self-confident parenting strategies than did non-battered mothers, as well as more inconsistency in parenting. Additionally, greater levels of permissive and authoritarian styles were associated with greater child problems of under control, anxiety, and lower school performance. In sum, it appears as though DV is associated with both less effective parenting styles and maladjustment in children across many domains, providing further evidence that DV is a significant stressor in homes with school-age children. It is likely that DV may render parents both overwhelmed and stressed, as also documented in the previously mentioned parenting stress studies, leaving them feeling less confident in their parenting and too exhausted to follow through with their own parental expectations and demands.

Parenting Behaviors

Numerous other studies have measured specific parenting behaviors using multiple methodologies, including maternal report and observation tasks. For example, Hershorn and Rosenbaum (1985) conducted a study with 45 women and their 5 to 15 year-old children ($X =$ 8.46). Fifteen women reported marital violence, 12 women reported maritally discordant (but not violent) marriages, and 18 women reported satisfactory marital relationships without violence. DV in this study was defined as overt marital hostility, including quarrels and sarcasm, and physical abuse. Parenting was assessed as the mother's child-rearing style according to maternal report, in which mothers were asked how they would respond to a number of hypothetical situations in either a rewarding or punishing manner. Surprisingly, battered wives did not report more punitive or punishing child-rearing behavior than did non-battered mothers in this sample, although marital discord and violence were both associated with increased problematic behaviors in children. The authors argued that exposure to DV or marital discord may have a more generalized effect on the behavioral and emotional health of the children than it does on parenting behaviors, suggesting a more direct effect on children. This argument is contrary to other studies, which have primarily concluded that parenting appears to be most directly related to child outcomes in homes with DV.

In a more recent study (Casanueva, Martin, Runyan, Barth, & Bradley, 2008), a large sample of 1,943 families were drawn from the National Survey of Child and Adolescent Well-Being (NSCAW) when children were involved in the child welfare system under the age of 10. DV in this study was defined as physical violence from a partner toward the child's mother in the past year, prior to the past year, or never (no DV). Uniquely, this study assessed maternal parenting behaviors using the Home Observation for Measurement of the Environment – Short Form (HOME-SF), which involves direct observation of the children's home environment during a 45-90 minute home visit. The items were used to create three scales in this study: parental responsiveness, learning stimulation, and spanking. This HOME assessment required both the assessor's observation of the home environment, as well as the mother's verbal report regarding these parenting dimensions. Surprisingly, results from this study found few statistically significant differences in the HOME-SF subscales when examining the three previously mentioned groups of women across the three subscales. However, women who had experienced DV in the past had significantly better HOME-SF total scores than those women currently experiencing DV, indicating that recency of DV is important to consider in terms of possible effects on parenting. Also, parental responsiveness was lower in currently abused women than past victims, but only in mothers of 3 to 5 year-old children specifically. There was no significant group effect regarding spanking between those who had and had not experienced DV. The authors suggested that over time, women may try to compensate for past histories of violence experienced in their home by providing more positive parenting. On the other hand, women being currently abused may be distracted and emotionally overwhelmed; thus, unable to be adequately attuned to their children's needs.

It appears as though women currently experiencing DV may be more at risk for poor parenting behaviors than those who have experienced DV in the past, but women who are able to move on to non-violent relationships may return to non-problematic parenting behaviors.

In another study, conducted as part of a larger study on the topic of interpersonal hostility, stress, and family functioning, Margolin, Gordis, Medina, and Oliver (2003) examined 181 families and their 8 to 11 year-old children, and 65 different mother-child dyads with a 7 to 11 year-old child; each sample was recruited from the community. In this study, DV was defined as husband-to-wife physical and emotional aggression within the last year. Parenting was measured according to mother, father, and child report. Parent-report questionnaires included: child abuse potential, the quality of the parent-child relationship (positive parenting, personal relationship, power assertive parenting) and certain parent dimensions (warmth, consistency, nonrestrictive attitude, sensitivity, structure, reasoning, and discipline techniques). Child-reported questionnaires included: the quality of the parent-child relationship using the same aforementioned parent-reported subscales, and a parent-perception inventory (positive parenting behaviors and disciplining behaviors).

Results indicated that mothers who experienced DV had greater child abuse potential than those who did not experience DV. Additionally, DV was significantly related to mothers' self-reports of power assertive parenting, control tactics, physical punishment, and yelling at their children, and inversely related to mothers' consistency, nonrestrictive attitudes, sensitivity, and structure. For fathers, DV was associated with their reported greater use of physical punishment toward their children, and lower ratings of nonrestrictive attitudes and structure. DV was not associated with child-reported maternal parenting behaviors, but was associated with lower scores for fathers' spending time with the child, talking to the child, assisting the child, showing nonverbal affection to the child, and use of positive reinforcement. Interestingly, according to parent-report, DV in this study was significantly associated with child abuse potential and parenting behaviors in mothers only, but according to child-report, DV was only significantly associated with fathers' parenting behaviors. The authors speculate that for women, DV and child abuse potential is likely related to living in a threatening environment, which results in women feeling hyperaroused, exhausted, and more irritable. For fathers, however, DV appears to be related to an increase in physical punishment and a less structured environment for children.

In sum, the majority of research examining the association between DV and parenting behaviors in homes with school-age children has found that DV is associated with poorer parenting behaviors, although the results from one study (Hershorn & Rosenbaum, 1985) did not support these findings, and suggested that DV has a more direct effect on children's outcomes instead of indirectly through poor parenting behaviors. The aforementioned studies were comprehensive in that multiple methodologies were used to assess parenting behaviors in homes with DV; however, researchers should continue to examine more closely the manner in which DV impacts parenting in homes with school-age children based on different methodologies used (i.e., observation, parent report, child report) and based on the time in which DV occurred in the home (i.e., past versus present). Furthermore, because preliminary findings indicate a difference in maternal versus paternal parenting behaviors in homes with DV, more research is needed to solidify these findings as well.

Parent-Child Aggression or Abuse

Several other studies in the DV literature have defined specific parenting behaviors as parent-child aggression or parent-child abuse (somewhat similar to the prior study that examined *potential* for child abuse), which is considered to be a very harsh form of parental discipline. Examining parent-child aggression seems particularly relevant in homes with DV because child abuse occurs in 35% to 70% of children living in homes with DV (Huth-Bocks, Levendosky & Semel, 2001). For example, McCloskey et al. (1995) examined 365 battered and non-battered mothers and their 6 to 12 year-old children recruited from the community and battered women's shelters. DV was defined as both spousal and parent-child abuse, including verbal, physical and sexual abuse between partners or between parents and the child, based on both parent and child reports. Parenting was assessed based on the mother's report of child-directed abuse. Importantly, mother and child reports of DV were significantly correlated, showing that there is a shared perception about family violence. Results indicated that in homes where mothers were being abused by her male partner, children were more likely to be sexually abused compared to those homes where DV was not occurring. In this sample, nearly all reports of child sexual abuse occurred in homes where DV was occurring. More specifically, in these homes, mothers reported sexual abuse by the male partner in 3.8% of cases, while 1.8% of children admitted to experiencing sexual abuse. In addition, fathers who abused their wives were also more likely to physically or verbally abuse their children, according to both maternal and child report. Findings also showed that children of battered women were significantly more likely to suffer physical abuse by either parent, including being spanked, slapped, or hit with an object. This study also linked DV to children's mental health, including internalizing and externalizing problems, according to the mother's perspective. This is not surprising given that previous research has documented the deleterious impact of any type of child abuse on children's emotional and behavioral outcomes. According to the results from this study, it appears as though DV may be a risk factor for parent-child maltreatment of any kind, including verbal, physical and/or sexual abuse.

Two additional studies (Jouriles & LeCompte, 1991; Jouriles & Norwood, 1995) assessed parenting as mothers' reports of parental physical aggression directed at the child. Jouriles et al. (1991) examined 73 mothers with children between the ages of 5 and 16 ($X = 8.7$), and Jouriles et al. (1995) examined 48 families with children between the ages of 4 and 14 ($X = 8.4$). For each study, the families were recruited from battered women's shelters, and DV was defined in both studies as at least one incident of physical abuse directed at the mother from her male partner within the last year. Both studies examined child gender as a moderator in the association between DV and parents' aggression toward their own children. Jouriles et al. (1991) found that husbands' violence toward wives was significantly correlated with both mothers' and fathers' aggression toward their male child, but not toward their female children. Furthermore, severe marital violence was associated with more severe parent-child aggression for both mothers and fathers in this study. Thus, child gender appeared to moderate the association between DV and parent-child aggression.

Similarly, Jouriles et al. (1995) examined the women living in battered women's shelters according to two groups: those that experienced "more extreme" and those that experienced "less extreme" battering. Results from this study indicated that both mothers and fathers were more likely to behave aggressively with their male children in the "more extreme" battered sample; these results did not hold true for the "less extreme" battered sample or for female children, in particular. According to child-report of parent-child aggression in this study, male children in the "more extreme" battered sample reported more victimization than female children from their mothers, but not from their fathers, but this finding did not hold true for the "less extreme" battered sample. Taken together, both studies indicated that, according to maternal and child report, both mothers and fathers in homes with DV are more likely to be violent toward their male children compared to their female children, and this may especially hold true for those who experience more severe battering. The authors speculated that mothers, in particular, may displace some of their anger they feel toward their husbands onto their male children, or that male children may be more likely to intervene in their parents' marital conflicts more often than girls, resulting in male children being abused themselves.

In a study conducted with a particularly varied sample, Moore and Pepler (1998) examined 113 mothers and children residing in a battered women's shelter, 82 mothers and children residing in a homeless shelter, 82 mothers and children residing in a mother-only home, and 100 children from two-parent non-violent homes. All children were between the ages of 6 and 12. DV in this study was defined as maternal-reported verbal and physical aggression occurring in the home within the last year between parents, and parenting was measured as child-directed verbal or physical violence from a parent within the last year. Results from this study indicated that battered women's shelter family fathers used more verbally aggressive and violent problem-solving tactics, and more physical aggression with their children than fathers in any other group. Additionally, battered women's shelter mothers reported being more physically aggressive with their children compared to mothers in other groups. Thus, it seems as though children from families that were living in battered women's shelters experienced more of this extreme form of harsh parenting compared to other stressed and non-stressed families. It is likely that mothers and children residing in battered women's shelters (displaced from their homes) have been exposed to severe levels of DV. The stress from experiencing severe levels of DV may render mothers more irritable, exhausted, and more likely to aggress against their own children, and may render aggressive fathers more likely to transfer their aggression to their own children as well.

Finally, Levendosky and Graham-Bermann (2000; 2001) conducted two studies with 120 women and their 7 to 12 year-old children recruited from the community and battered-women's shelters. DV was defined as psychological and physical abuse directed at mothers from their male partner in both studies, and also directed at children from their mothers in one study (Levendosky et al., 2001). Levendosky et al. (2000) also measured parenting according to parenting behaviors that occurred during a mother-child observation task, in which the mother and child were asked to spend 10 minutes attempting to resolve one issue about which they had disagreed, and mothers' behavior was coded according to warmth, authority, and depressed mood. Levendosky et al. (2001) further measured parenting as mothers' warmth, control, child-centeredness and effectiveness directed at their children according to maternal report. Levendosky et al. (2000) found that DV significantly predicted maternal warmth toward her child, such that more DV was related to less maternal warmth during the observation task. Levendosky et al. (2001) found that DV was a significant predictor of parenting behaviors, including child-directed abuse and the aforementioned parenting behaviors. In addition, DV was also linked with children's poor social and emotional adjustment in those children that were reportedly abused by a parent, and indirectly linked through maternal psychological functioning, including depression and trauma symptoms.

Overall, the vast majority of research examining the impact of DV on parenting in families with school-age children has found that DV is associated with more problematic parenting in general. Importantly, much of the research conducted with school-age children has also linked DV to maladjustment in children, including more internalizing and externalizing behavior problems, as well as reduced social competence. The link between DV and child outcomes has been established both directly and indirectly, for example, through maternal parenting stress or psychological functioning. The studies examining the impact of DV on parenting in school-age children are unique for a number of reasons. First, multiple facets of parenting have been examined in the context of DV, such as parenting stress, parenting styles, specific parenting behaviors, such as parenting effectiveness and discipline strategies, and finally child-directed violence. Second, many studies used multiple methodologies to assess the domains of parenting, including parent and child-report, parent-child observation tasks, parent-report to hypothetical scenarios that arise when raising children, and even the HOME-SF interview. Some studies also examined differences in parenting according to both maternal and paternal report.

It is also important to recognize that some studies failed to find an association between DV and parenting, unlike most findings in the DV literature. Many authors provided speculations as to why this may have been the case. For example, mothers may attempt to compensate for DV by parenting more positively; alternatively, they may feel a sense of guilt about DV in the home and then may report themselves as more effective parents than they really are. Additionally, there is some preliminary evidence that suggests that male children, in particular, may suffer more parent-directed aggression or abuse than female children in homes with DV. Taken together, it is clear that more research is necessary to solidify the preliminary findings examining the impact of DV on parenting in homes with school-age children. Because of the discrepancies in findings across studies, it is clear that understanding the impact of DV on parenting is complex and multifaceted, and may be impacted by many different variables, including the time at which DV occurred in the home, whether the family has been displaced from their home as a result of DV, child gender, as well as parental characteristics that may be either risk or protective factors in homes with DV.

PARENTING OUTCOMES IN THE CONTEXT OF DOMESTIC VIOLENCE DURING ADOLESCENCE

Interestingly, almost no studies have examined the impact of DV on parenting in homes with adolescent children, which is known to be a time when parenting can be particularly difficult, as adolescents are struggling with increased independence and separation from their parents. In one study, Levendosky, Huth-Bocks, and Semel (2002) examined the impact of adolescent-reported child abuse and mothers' experiences of DV (defined as the presence of psychological, physical or sexual violence within the last year from a male partner) on parenting behaviors, including warmth and effectiveness. The effects of DV and parenting on numerous adolescent outcomes, such as attachment, trauma symptoms, and dating behaviors, were also examined. Participants included 111 adolescents between the ages of 14 and 16 that were recruited from DV shelters, at-risk teen centers, and the community. Although no direct relationship was found between DV and child abuse or parenting behaviors, results showed that DV moderated the association between maternal parenting, including warmth and effectiveness, and adolescent trauma symptoms and positive communication with a dating partner; more specifically, positive parenting was associated with less trauma in both the low- and high-DV groups, but this relation was stronger in the low violence group. Positive parenting was also associated with more positive communication with a dating partner in both groups, but was more highly associated with positive communication in the high-DV group. Results also showed that DV and child abuse were related to a number of adolescent outcomes, including less secure attachment styles, and more depression and trauma symptoms. It is clear from these results that parenting significantly impacts a number of adolescent outcomes, and the presence of high- or low-DV in the home affect the strength of this association.

In one final study examining parenting in the context of DV in homes with adolescents, Stuewig and McCloskey (2005) examined 279 women and their adolescent children as part of a larger longitudinal study examining the impact of DV on children's mental health; participants were recruited from the community and battered women's shelters. DV was defined as physical violence toward the mother from a male partner. Women in this sample appeared to have severe and chronic levels of violence, for example, 62% reported being choked and 69.5% reported being beaten over the 4 years of the study. Parenting was measured initially as parent-reported maternal and paternal harsh parenting practices, including psychological and physical abuse, when the child was school-age, as well as child-reported sexual abuse at the same age. Parenting was later measured as adolescent-reported parental rejection and warmth. Results from this study indicated that DV was not related to harsh parenting or sexual abuse during school-age, nor was it associated with parental rejection or warmth during adolescence. However, DV was found to be associated with internalizing and externalizing behavior problems in children during school-age, as well as with adolescent delinquency problems.

In sum, almost no research has examined the impact of DV on parenting in homes with adolescent children, and neither of the aforementioned studies found DV to be directly associated with parenting. Thus, it is clear that more research is necessary to better understand the impact of DV on parenting in homes with adolescent children, or whether there is such a relationship at all, particularly because children in this age group have a different way of relating to their parents than those children in younger age groups. For example, adolescent youth may be more likely to leave violent situations, and may be more emotionally distant from their parents than younger children. As a consequence, it is likely that the impact of DV on parenting may be different in homes with adolescents compared to homes with younger children.

CONCLUSION

In conclusion, research has documented that many women experience DV during one or more periods of their life (Tjaden & Thoennes, 2000), and women may be particularly vulnerable to partner abuse during the childbearing years (Jasinski & Kantor, 2001; Stewart, 1994; Torres et al., 2000). Consequently, mothers of millions of children experience DV; thus, it is critically important to understand the effects of DV on various parenting capacities across child development, as it is a serious social and public health problem that may require clinical intervention for both mothers and children.

Few researchers have examined the impact of DV on parenting beginning in pregnancy, when parenting beliefs and attitudes begin to take shape, but it has been documented that DV negatively impacts mothers' prenatal and postnatal representations of their children. In turn, problematic representations negatively impact specific parenting behaviors in the first year of a child's life. Research examining the impact of DV on parenting in those families with toddlers, preschool-age and school-age children has been more common. In general, DV appears to be associated with more problematic parenting including greater parenting stress, poorer quality of the mother-child relationship, and specific problematic parenting behaviors of both mothers and fathers, including child-directed abuse. Furthermore, many researchers used multi-informant, multi-method assessment in their studies, making the findings quite robust and comprehensive. Surprisingly, only two studies have examined the impact of DV on parenting in homes with adolescent children, and neither study found DV to be directly associated with parenting. Thus, it is clear that more research is needed to understand the effects of DV on parenting capacities in homes with adolescents, as adolescence can be a particularly challenging time for parents in general.

In sum, DV seems to be a unique parenting stressor faced by a surprising number of parents each year, and may also result in child maladjustment. Consequently, it is important to continue to examine the wide range of effects DV has on parenting and children's outcomes in homes with children of all ages with an emphasis on developmental timing. Since some studies have failed to find an association between DV and parenting, more research is needed to better understand the discrepancies between study findings. For example, more sophisticated models and tests of possible mediating and moderating relationships is called for to advance our understanding of the relation between DV and parenting. In addition, future research should examine the impact of DV on fathers' parenting, as the majority of current research examines only mothers' parenting outcomes in the context of DV. More longitudinal research is also necessary to clarify the association between DV and parenting capacities over time; the vast majority of research has only used cross-sectional data. Finally, it is clear that researchers should specifically examine the impact of DV on parenting capacities during pregnancy, infancy, and adolescence, as these phases of child development have been minimally examined thus far. Existing and future research examining the impact of DV on various parenting domains is essential in guiding appropriate clinical interventions for individuals exposed to partner violence in their homes.

Furthermore, understanding appropriate clinical interventions is essential in aiding and guiding this population. Research has documented that the impact of DV on parenting is complex and multifaceted, and may be impacted by many different variables, including the time at which DV occurred in the home, cultural values, whether the family has been displaced from their home as a result of DV, child gender and age, as well as parental characteristics that may be either risk or protective factors in homes with DV, such as parental psychopathology, general life stress, and access to resources, to name a few. Thus, treatments should not only focus on reducing symptomology in parents and children as a result of exposure to DV, but should also focus on the many latent variables that may influence the outcome of these individuals, including possible protective factors that could lend themselves as strengths for those living in such a stressful situation.

Interventions should also be individually based, and take into consideration the background and cultural context from which families come. In other words, ethnic minority families tend to be over-represented in shelters because of socioeconomic issues; thus, recognizing that African-American women may be more hesitant to ask for help for fear of contributing to negative stereotypes about African-American men, for example, should be taken into consideration. Furthermore, parental psychopathology should be addressed and treated at a very basic level, as both maternal depression and trauma, to name a few, have been found to impact the manner in which mothers cope with DV and their parenting role, which is known to impact children's well-being. Also, because research has documented parenting stress, poor parenting styles, child-directed abuse, and ineffective parenting behaviors to be associated with DV in homes with children of varying ages, it may be helpful to target these issues in the context of parent training programs or community parent education programs. Additionally, providing psychoeducation to families exposed to partner violence may also increase awareness about the long-term impacts of DV on mothers and children. In sum, interventions for these women and children, regardless of the type of setting in which the support might be delivered, will likely be most effective if individualized for them, based upon the severity and types of stresses and needs.

REFERENCES

Abidin, R.R. (1983). Parenting Stress Index clinical manual. Charlottesville, VA. Pediatric Psychology Press.

Ammaniti, M., Baumgartner, E., Candelori, C., & Perruchini, P. (1992). Representations and narratives during pregnancy. *Infant Mental Health Journal, 13,* 167-182.

Baumrind, D. (1971). Current patterns of parental authority. *Developmental Psychology, 4,* 1-103.

Bogat, G.A., Levendosky, A.A., Theran, S., Von Eye, A., & Davidson, W.S. (2003). Predicting the psychosocial effects of interpersonal partner violence (IPV). *Journal of Interpersonal Violence, 18,* 1271-1291.

Bradbury, T.N., & Lawrence, E. (1999). Physical aggression and the longitudinal course of newlywed marriages. In Arriaga, X.B., & Oskamp, S. (Eds.), *Violence in intimate relationships,* (pp.181-202). Thousand Oaks, CA, US: Sage Publications, Inc.

Casanueva, C., Martin, S.L., Runyan, D.K., Barth, R.P., & Bradley, R.H. (2008). Quality of maternal parenting among intimate-partner violence victims involved with the child welfare system. *Journal of Family Violence, 23,* 413-427.

Cummings, E.M. (1994). Marital conflict and children's functioning. *Social Development, 3,* 16-36.

Dayton, C. J., Levendosky, A.A., Davidson, W. S., & Bogat, G. A. (2007, April). *The child as held in the mind of the mother: The impact of prenatal maternal representations on later parenting behaviors.* Poster presented at the biennial meeting of the Society for Research in Child Development, Boston, MA.

Edelson, M.G., Hokoda, A., & Ramos-Lira, L. (2007). Differences in effects of domestic violence between Latina and non-Latina women. *Journal of Family Violence, 22,* 1-10.

Emery, R.E. (1982). Interparental conflict and the children of discord and divorce. *Psychological Bulletin, 92,* 310-330.

Fantuzzo, J., Boruch, R., Beriama, A., & Atkins, M. (1997). Domestic violence and children: Prevalence and risk in five major US cities. *Journal of the American Academy of Child & Adolescent Psychiatry, 36,* 116-122.

Gazmararian, J.A., Adams, M.M., & Pamuk, E.R. (1996). Associations between measure of socioeconomic status and maternal health behavior. *American Journal of Preventative Medicine, 12,* 108-115.

Graham-Bermann, S.A., & Levendosky, A.A. (1998a). Traumatic stress symptoms in children of battered women. *Journal of Interpersonal Violence, 13,* 111-128.

Grych, J.H., & Fincham, F.D. (1990). Marital conflict and children's adjustment: A cognitive-contextual framework. *Psychological Bulletin, 108,* 267-290.

Hershorn, M., & Rosenbaum, A. (1985). Children of marital violence: A closer look at the unintended victims. *American Journal of Orthopsychiatry, 55,* 260-266.

Holden, G.W., & Ritchie, K.L. (1991). Linking extreme marital discord, child rearing, and child behavior problems: Evidence from battered women. *Child Development, 62,* 311-327.

Holden, G.W., Stein, J.D., Ritchie, K.L., Harris, S.D., & Jouriles, E.N. (1998). Parenting behaviors and beliefs of battered women. In G.W. Holden, R. Geffner, & E.N. Jouriles (Eds.), *Children exposed to marital violence: Theory, research, and applied issues* (pp.289-334). Washington, DC: APA.

Hughes, H.M., & Huth-Bocks, A.C. (2007). Variations in parenting stress in african-american battered women. *European Psychologist, 12,* 62-71.

Huth-Bocks, A.C., & Hughes, H.M. (2008). Parenting stress, parenting behavior, and children's adjustment in families experiencing intimate partner violence. *Journal of Family Violence, 23,* 243-251.

Huth-Bocks, A.C., Levendosky, A.A., & Semel, M.A. (2001). The direct and indirect effects of domestic violence on young children's intellectual functioning. *Journal of Family Violence, 16,* 269-290.

Huth-Bocks, A.C., Levendosky, A.A., Theran, S.A., & Bogat, G.A. (2004). The impact of domestic violence on mothers' prenatal representations of their infants. *Infant Mental Health Journal, 25,* 79-98.

Jasinski, J.L., & Kantor, G.K. (2001). Pregnancy and violence against women: An analysis of longitudinal data. *Journal of Interpersonal Violence, 16,* 712-733.

Jouriles, E.N., & LeCompte, S.H. (1991). Husbands' aggression toward wives and mothers' and fathers' aggression toward children: Moderating effects of child gender. *Journal of Counseling and Clinical Psychology, 59,* 190-192.

Jouriles, E.N., & Norwood, W.D. (1995). Physical aggression toward boys and girls in families characterized by the battering of women. *Journal of Family Psychology, 9,* 69-78.

Levendosky, A. A., & Graham-Bermann, S.A. (1998). The moderating effect of parenting stress on children's adjustment in women-abusing families. *Journal of Interpersonal Violence, 13,* 383-397.

Levendosky, A.A., & Graham-Bermann, S.A. (2000). Behavioral observations of parenting in battered women. *Journal of Family Psychology, 14,* 1-15.

Levendosky, A.A., & Graham-Bermann, S.A. (2001). Parenting in battered women: The effects of domestic violence on women and their children. *Journal of Family Violence, 16,* 171-192.

Levendosky, A.A., Huth-Bocks, A.C., Shapiro, D.L., & Semel, M.A. (2003). The impact of domestic violence on the maternal-child relationship and preschool-age children's functioning. *Journal of Family Psychology, 17,* 275-287.

Levendosky, A.A., Huth-Bocks, A.C., & Semel, M.A. (2002). Adolescent peer relationships and mental health functioning in families with domestic violence. *Journal of Clinical Child Psychology, 31,* 206-218.

Levendosky, A.A., Leahy, K.L., Bogat, G.A., Davidson, W.S., & Von Eye, A. (2006). Domestic violence, maternal parenting, maternal mental health, and infant externalizing behavior. *Journal of Family Psychology, 20,* 544-552.

Lieberman, A.F., & Van Horn, P. (1998). Attachment, trauma, and domestic violence: Implications for child custody. *Child and Adolescent Psychiatric Clinics of North America, 7,* 423-443.

Lumley, J.M. (1982). Attitudes to the fetus among primigravidae. *Australian Pediatric Journal, 18,* 106-109.

MacKinnon-Lewis, C., & Lofquist, A. (1996). Antecedents and consequences of boys' depression and aggression: Family and school linkages. *Journal of Family Psychology, 10,* 490-500.

Margolin, G., Gordis, E.B., Medina, A.M., & Oliver, P.H. (2003). The co-occurrence of husband-to-wife aggression, family-of-origin aggression, and child abuse potential in a community sample. *Journal of Interpersonal Violence, 18,* 413-440.

McCloskey, L.A., Figueredo, A.J., & Koss, M.P. (1995). The effects of systemic family violence on children's mental health. *Child Development, 66,* 1239-1261.

Moore, T.E., & Pepler, D.J. (1998). Correlates of adjustment in children at risk. In G.W. Holden, R. Geffner, & E.N. Jouriles (Eds.), *Children exposed to marital violence: Theory, research, and applied issues,* (pp.157-184). Washington, DC: APA.

Owen, A.E., Kaslow, N.J., & Thompson, M.P. (2006). The mediating role of parenting stress in the relation between intimate partner violence and child adjustment. *Journal of Family Psychology, 20,* 505-513.

Parker, J.G., & Asher, S.R. (1987). Peer relations and later personal adjustment: Are low accepted children at risk? *Psychological Bulletin, 102,* 357-389.

Ritchie, K.L., & Holden, G.W. (1998). Parenting stress in low income battered and community women: Effects on parenting behavior. *Early Education and Development, 9,* 98-112.

Rossman, B.B., & Rea, J.G. (2005). The relations of parenting styles and inconsistencies to adaptive functioning for children in conflictual and violent families. *Journal of Family Violence, 20,* 261-277.

Slade, A., & Cohen, L.J. (1996). The process of parenting and the remembrance of things past. *Infant Mental Health Journal, 17,* 217-238.

Sokolowski, M.S., Hans, S.L., Bernstein, V.J., & Cox, S.M. (2007). Mothers' representations of their infants and parenting behavior: Associations with personal and social-contextual variables in a high-risk sample. *Infant Mental Health Journal, 28,* 344-365.

Stern, D.N. (1995). The motherhood constellation: A unified view of parent-infant psychotherapy. New York: Basic Books.

Stewart, D.E. (1994). Incidence of postpartum abuse in women with a history of abuse during pregnancy. *Canadian Medical Association Journal, 151,* 1601-1604.

Straus, M.A., & Gelles, R.A. (1986). Societal change and change in family violence from 1975 to 1985 as revealed by two national surveys. *Journal of Marriage and the Family, 48,* 465-479.

Stuewig, J., & McCloskey, L.A. (2005). The relation of child maltreatment to shame and guilt among adolescents: Psychological routes to depression and delinquency. *Child Maltreatment, 10,* 324-226.

Theran, S.A., Levendosky, A.A., Bogat, G.A., & Huth-Bocks, A.C. (2005). Stability and change in mothers' internal representations of their infants over time. *Attachment and Human Development, 7,* 253-268.

Tjaden, P., & Thoennes, N. (2000). Prevalence and consequences of male-to-female and female-to-male intimate partner violence as measured by the national violence against women survey. *Violence Against Women, 6,* 142-161.

Torres, S., Campbell, J., Campbell, D., Ryan, J., King, C., Price, P., Stallings, R., Fuchs, S., & Laude, M. (2000). Abuse during and before pregnancy: Prevalence and cultural correlates. *Violence and Victims, 15,* 303-321.

Wolfe, D.A., Jaffe, P., Wilson, S.K., & Zak, L. (1985). Children of battered women: The relation of child behavior to family violence and maternal stress. *Journal of Consulting and Clinical Psychology, 53,* 657-665.

Zeanah, C.H., & Benoit, D. (1995). Clinical applications of parent perception interview in infant mental health. *Child and Adolescent Psychiatric Clinicals of North America, 4,* 539-554.

Zeanah, C.H., Keener, M.A., & Anders, T.F. (1986). Adolescent mothers' prenatal fantasies and working models of their infants. *Psychiatry: Journal for the Study of Interpersonal Processes, 49,* 193-203.

In: Handbook of Parenting: Styles, Stresses & Strategies   ISBN 978-1-60741-766-8
Editor: Pacey H. Krause and Tahlia M. Dailey   © 2009 Nova Science Publishers, Inc.

Chapter 16

PARENTING PRACTICES AROUND LEARNING WITHIN LATINO COMMUNITIES: DIVERSITY AND ASSOCIATIONS WITH CHILDREN'S OUTCOMES

Nikki Aikens, Margaret Caspe, Sally Atkins-Burnett, Susan Sprachman and Yange Xue

Mathematica Policy Research, Inc., Princton, New Jersey, USA

Few pictures are as pervasive and powerful in human culture as that of a parent and child together. Whether the child is swaddled on a parent's back in Mongolia, reading a book with her father in the United States (U.S.), or walking through a market with her mother in Kenya, the activities that parents and children share together are a critical component of parenting and how a child comes to know and trust the world. In recent years, researchers have put forward various theories related to parenting. Some investigators have considered parenting styles (e.g., Baumrind, 1971)—that is, dimensions of caregiving that vary along the axes of warmth, nurturance, and responsivity. Other researchers have assessed parents' attitudes, beliefs, and goals related to childrearing, and still others have sought to examine the various categories of parenting practices such as teaching, supporting language, monitoring, and providing resources (Brooks-Gunn & Markman, 2005). This chapter focuses on parenting practices, specifically those related to learning outcomes in the early years.

Parenting practices are the specific activities, tasks, and behaviors parents conduct and direct toward the child. These practices are important to study because they encompass the values, goals, and resources parents organize to make an activity happen, and embedded within them are the emotions and feelings of those engaged in the activity. It is within the context of these adult-scaffolded activities that young children actively internalize and construct the knowledge and skills that are valued within a cultural community (Rogoff, 2003; Vygotsky, 1978). As a result of these practices, participants within communities of shared ethnic, racial and language identities often develop common social interaction styles, practices and scripts (García Coll, et al., 1996; Weisner, 2001).

In the U.S., one of the most critical parenting practices, especially in the preschool years before children enter formal school settings, are the activities parents engage in with their children around learning. We use the term parenting practices around learning to refer to those activities that parents and children take part in together either in the home or community that promote children's cognitive and social emotional development. For example, reading books, telling stories, and counting games are all parent-child activities associated with higher child academic outcomes in the U.S. (Porsche & Snow, 2001). The reconfiguration of U.S. preschools and their increasing emphasis on academics has made it increasingly clear that what parents do to prepare children for formal schooling is of the utmost importance to children's success at the kindergarten level (Lee & Burkham, 2002). However, much of the research that has investigated parenting practices around learning has taken place with White, middle-class groups, without focusing on how other linguistic or cultural groups might engage in these activities, or, the diversity that exists within different racial/ethnic categories in relation to these activities.

The purpose of this chapter is to explore the diversity of parenting practices around learning in early childhood within Latino communities and to understand the factors that relate to such practices. As a roadmap, we begin with a literature review that provides a description of the Latino community and a theoretical framework for our work. We then turn to a discussion of the importance of parenting practices around learning, how these practices might vary between Latino subgroups and within Latino communities and the variables that might be the sources of these variations. In the second section of the paper, we introduce a case study of young Latino children and their families living in Los Angeles County to illustrate the diversity of parenting practices around learning. We conclude with different implications for educators working with young Latino children and families.

Throughout the chapter we contend that the parenting practices related to learning among Latino families are particularly important to study as the number of young Latino children entering preschools is steadily increasing, and educators need to be prepared to effectively work and support these young children and their families. We use the term Latino throughout to refer to peoples and cultures from various regions of the Americas, Spanish-speaking countries in the Caribbean, as well as the part of the U.S. population that traces its descent to the Spanish-speaking Caribbean and Latin-American worlds (Suaréz-Orozco & Paéz, 2002). We acknowledge the tension in the literature which stresses that although racial and ethnic categories are fluctuating constructs created by the social science field at the same time they often have meaning to individuals and groups that help form social identify (Raver, Gershoff and Aber, 2007; Barbarin, 1999). To this extent, we use the term Latino in a broad sense, but also acknowledge that one of the main challenges in researching parenting among U.S. Latinos is to understand the complex, overlapping sources of variation that may lead Latinos to differ among themselves. Nonetheless, even in discussing this complexity we realize that we run the risk of stereotyping groups. That is not our intent. Thus, it is important for the reader to keep in mind that throughout the chapter we will describe the averages or the tendencies of a group to engage in a certain practice, acknowledging that individual and community variations exist.

THE LATINO COMMUNITY IN THE U.S.
AND CONCEPTUAL FRAMEWORK

Latinos currently account for more than 14% of the U.S. population and as such are one of the largest minority groups in the U.S. (U.S. Census Bureau, 2006). Of the growing Latino population, a large proportion (35%) is children. These youngsters are concentrated in regions throughout the country, with California accounting for nearly one third of all Latino children (Hernandez et al., 2008). Children of Mexican ancestry are the most highly represented group, but there is increasing diversity in family origins with many children coming from families of Puerto Rican, Central American or South American descent (Hernandez et al., 2008).

While individual- and community-level variations exist, Latino families are often characterized as upholding cultural values, practices, and beliefs distinguished by a deep sense of loyalty to the family (Arzubiaga, Ceja & Artiles, 2000; Hammer & Miccio, 2004; Rogoff, 2003; Schiefelin & Ochs, 1986; Suárez-Orozco & Paéz, 2002). The expressions "familismo," "respeto," and "educación," which are difficult to define and translate, are frequently utilized to portray Latino cultural convictions towards parenting and child development. These values uphold respect, morality, and cooperation as paramount in one's path through life (Ada & Zubizaretta, 2001; Cooper, Brown, Azmitia, & Chavira, 2005; Harwood, Layendecker, Carlson, Asencio, & Miller, 2002; Jiménez, Moll, Rodríguez-Brown & Barrera, 1999; Reese, Balzano, Gallimore & Goldenberg, 1995). As such, Latino parents create home environments that emphasize close mother-child relationships and interpersonal responsiveness and often adopt practices that promote the ultimate goal of the development of a child's proper demeanor (García-Coll, Meyer, & Brillon, 1995; Harwood, Miller & Irizarry, 1995). In addition, Latino families have been found to lean towards parenting perspectives that are sociocentric; that is, Latino families often place a strong emphasis on the fundamental connectedness of human beings and family members to one another. This is in contrast to what is often experienced in the U.S. mainstream culture— a perspective that promotes the individual as an independent self-contained entity (Harwood, 2001a, 2001b).These perspectives reflect the ways in which parenting practices are shaped by the social and cultural context of the family. In other words, the goals and expectations parents have for their children's development and the strategies they use to achieve those goals are embedded within cultural values, beliefs, and traditions (Gadsden, 2004). Such goals and activities are also shaped by the material resources available to families, including the large economic opportunities and barriers surrounding them. Therefore, exploration of parenting practices and activities cannot be divorced from understanding of the socio-cultural contexts in which families live.

This chapter explores the frequency with which Latino families engage in practices around learning with their children, the factors associated with variations in these frequencies, and how these activities relate to children's early learning outcomes. We situate our chapter in an ecocultural model of human development. This conceptual framework is helpful in understanding how young children's school readiness is affected by their family resources (e.g., parents' educational level, job status, income, immigration status), which shape everyday activities such as play, problem solving and exploration of materials. While exploring these issues, we also maintain a strengths-based approach, which considers the role of culture in learning. This perspective differs from a deficit approach that assumes that certain groups of children and families, typically low-income and ethnic minority, lack certain skills or background knowledge. A strengths-based approach posits that for educators to successfully work with diverse children and families, they need to validate and build on families' cultural identities and culturally specific child-rearing practices (those used outside of school) while also helping families learn the skills and practices that American schools deem important (Moll, et al., 1992). Moreover, educators must do this while also understanding how political, social, or economic systems maintain and propagate social inequalities (Suarez-Orozco, 2001). Thus, educators must be equipped with a repertoire of tools to help parents increase their power and control to shape the learning and educational goals for their children. In short, educators must be able to move beyond the prevailing models of parenting that might presume a universal model of caregiving and instead come to understand the successful workings of diverse families (García Coll & Patcher, 2002). Educators must be willing to share their knowledge with families and support families in finding ways to foster the skills children will need for schooling in the U.S.Yet, educators must also be prepared to learn from families and walk with rather than direct them in supporting children's development.

PARENTING PRACTICES AROUND LEARNING IN THE LATINO COMMUNITY AND MAINSTREAM CULTURE

A growing body of evidence shows that parenting practices around learning relate positively to children's school readiness. School readiness is a general concept that refers to the attitudes, skills and behaviors young children develop that prepare them for entry into kindergarten (National Goals Panel, 1994). For the purpose of this paper we group parenting practices around learning into three general categories (Barbarin & Aikens, in press): (1) direct and intentional learning activities in the home, (2) informal parent-child activities and (3) parent-child activities that occur in the community. Direct teaching includes such activities as telling stories, teaching children letters or words, singing songs, or counting with the child. Informal activities include those that offer opportunities for learning through participation and observation such as taking children on errands, doing household chores together and talking about programs and daily events in one's life. Finally, community activities include outings to libraries, playgrounds, or parks.

In U.S. educational culture, one of the prevailing beliefs is that parents can best prepare young children for formal schooling through specialized direct and intentional child-focused learning activities in the home. From this perspective, families have a responsibility in the out-of-school-time setting to emphasize learning in a context other than productive adult community activities, which in the U.S. might include going to work or paying bills. According to U.S. mainstream cultural norms, parents have a responsibility to promote learning for young children through discrete parent-child activities with a focused goal of academic and cognitive learning as the outcome (Rogoff, 2003). These activities include child-focused conversations in which adults interact with young children in different contexts as conversational partners, alter their speech to promote children's involvement, and focus conversation on child-related topics (Heath, 1982; Ochs & Schieffelin, 1984; Rogoff et al.,

1993). Parents are involved in a direct and child-focused activity when they co-construct stories with their children. Or parents may adopt a "dialogic" style, characterized by the inclusion of many extratextual comments and thought-provoking and comprehension questions throughout the story narration (Whitehurst, 1998). Child-focused activities can also take the form of child play, whereby, for example, a parent enters into dramatic re-enactments with the child or engages in games at the level a child can understand. For example, children of parents who emphasize problem solving and curiosity for learning during play develop long-term individual interests and the ability to attend to tasks for longer periods of time (McWayne, et al., 2004).These activities also include didactic teaching lessons in which parents specifically teach skills they believe are necessary for entry into school (e.g., knowing colors, numbers, letters, etc.). Direct parent-teaching activities—like showing the child how to write words—are linked to children's ability to identify letters and connect letters to speech sounds (Haney & Hill, 2004).

Evidence supports the assertion that young middle class children frequently are involved in these child-focused activities (Heath, 1982) and that these practices are contributing factors that help prepare children for school. These activities are believed to improve child outcomes by actually teaching children the skills and attitudes they need, but these interactions often resemble the teaching style of "school." However, variations occur in the *ways* that parents socialize their children during these types of direct child-centered activities. For example, European American middle class parents often draw their young children into a pattern of speech that imitates the school-like discourse structure of initiation-reply-evaluation (Heath, 1982, 1986; Ochs & Schieffen, 1984; Zentella, 2005). This style closely matches the type of speech that occurs in U.S. schools, thus parents are socializing their children to enter classrooms prepared in the ways of school learning, ready to answer questions, ask questions, and participate in conversations freely.

While we recognize the tremendous diversity found within groups, we summarize here the literature that examines the average practices among Latino families. As a group, immigrant Latino parents might differ from European American middle class parents in the ways they linguistically engage their children. Many Latino parents have a view of learning that focuses on accurate reading of letters, words, and completion of worksheets. Thus, in situations that require direct instruction, parents might focus on discrete, rote learning techniques while asking children to memorize and respond to questions, rather than engaging in back-and-forth dialogue (Gallimore & Goldenberg, 1993).This might be a result of their own educational experiences. In the conversational context, however, research suggests that Latino mothers often emphasize connectedness and social aspects of the story, whereas European American mothers concentrate on organization and linearity (Melzi, 2000). Similarly, when sharing books, low-income Latino mothers living in the U.S. and middle income mothers living in Peru tend to tell rich and engaging stories to children with little interaction and question and answering comments (Caspe, submitted; Melzi & Caspe, 2005). European American mothers, in contrast, often tend to use a co-constructive or dialogic style (Melzi & Caspe, 2005).

However, evidence suggests that direct and intentional child-centered activities are not the only beneficial parenting practices around learning that can occur. Informal and community-based parenting practices lend themselves to what is referred to as learning through "intent participation." Intent participation refers to learning "by observing and listening-in on activities of adults and other children…in anticipation of or in the process of engaging in an endeavor" (Rogoff et al., 2003, p. 178). An emphasis on learning through intent participation fits especially well with the practices of cultural communities that routinely include children in the adult activities that are part of the community's daily life. Learning through intent participation requires children to engage collaboratively with others in shared productive endeavors. For example, a child might watch as his or her mother cleans and folds laundry, observing and paying attention to the separation of colors and the procedures needed to measure water and detergent. Within intent participation, adult-child conversations most often occur primarily for the sake of sharing needed information in the context of ongoing activities, rather than serving as lessons to teach children about talk or to provide disconnected bits of knowledge (Heath, 1983; Ochs & Schieffelin, 1984). The main tool for learning in intent participation is not "scripted" or parent-driven language.

Growing evidence suggests that Latino parents—especially those who have less education and have spent less time in the U.S.—favor an intent participation approach to learning. For example, in a study of first to third grade children observing an adult's demonstration of how to fold origami figures, Mexican American children whose mothers had little experience with school were more likely to observe the adult without requesting further information, compared with both Mexican American and European American children whose mothers had experience with Western schooling (Mejía Arauz, Rogoff & Paradise, 2005). Because of this, these children were more likely to be socialized to learn through observation rather than verbal means. In a different study, Morelli (2003), using time-sampled observations, found that young two- to three-year-old children in middle class European American communities had less frequent access to their parents' work and were more often involved in specialized child-focused activities than were indigenous children in Guatemala. This study sheds light on variations in the extent to which cultures value observation as a style of teaching and learning.

The content of parent-child interactions influences the processes used to help children learn. For example, Valdés (1996) noted that Latino parents place a high value on oral literacy for moral, religious, personal, vocational, and economic reasons. As a result, literacy in the home concentrates on sharing stories with strong moral messages, particularly stories derived from the Bible. These stories are often called "consejos" (Valdés, 1996). Delgado-Gaitan (1990, 2003) in her ethnographic research showed that families have rich oral traditions related to telling stories that account for many activities around learning in the home. Latino parents might also structure language interactions for their young children in culturally influenced ways. For example, Eisenberg (1985, 1999, 2001), in a series of studies, showed that Mexican American mothers rarely structure dyadic conversations with young children. Instead, these mothers encourage children to participate in multi-party conversations that might occur naturally in the home. These patterns of interaction were evident in both low- and middle-income homes.

Such findings might help us understand why numerous studies have noted that reading to children, presumably a more direct and intentional child-focused activity, is not a frequent practice among Latino families in comparison with other racial/ethnic groups. For example, in one analysis of a variety of multi-site studies where 40 to 55 percent of mothers report reading to their toddler every day, Latino mothers were about half as likely to do so (Brooks-Gunn, 2005). This finding was mirrored nationally with the Early Childhood Longitudinal Study-Birth Cohort (ECLS-B) data, in which Latino families of infants under the age of nine months are less likely to read books and share stories with their children than parents from other ethnic backgrounds (López et al., 2007).It was also reflected in the Early Childhood Longitudinal Study-Kindergarten Cohort (ECLS-K) in which Latino families were among the racial/ethnic group least likely to read stories with their kindergartners (West et al., 2000). Other studies with families of toddlers have also mirrored these findings (ACF, 2002; ACYF, 2001). Moreover, Latino families have fewer reading materials in their homes, and typically they also have fewer educationally relevant materials of other types (as indexed by the HOME Learning Scale). These are differences that cannot be explained by access (or lack thereof) to books in Spanish (Brooks-Gunn & Markman, 2005).

VARIATIONS IN PARENTING PRACTICES AROUND LEARNING WITHIN THE LATINO COMMUNITY

When examining the variations in parenting practices we need to keep in mind the demographic characteristics of families and the ways in which these indicators of both available resources and sociocultural experiences influence families. There can be as much variation within as between two groups. To understand the inter-related and overlapping pathways that simultaneously influence parenting practices around learning among Latino families, a number of sources of variation must be disentangled. In this section of the literature review, we attempt to provide a foundation for the variables that have been most frequently examined in the research.

Immigration, Country of Origin, and Years in the U.S.

Although they are all discrete variables, immigration, country of origin, and the number of years living in the U.S. are all factors that have been found to be associated with variations in parenting practices among Latinos. Because they overlap in so many ways, we discuss these factors together. Children of immigrants account for one in four (25%) young children in the U.S., and Latino children are most commonly represented in this group (Hernandez, Denton, & Macartney, 2008). Immigrant status is also associated with socioeconomic factors such as parent education, family economic status, and social integration, all of which may influence the family's resources and parenting practices. Thus, it is important to consider the various pathways by which immigration might impact parenting practices around learning as well as child outcomes. For example, Suarez-Orozco (2002) showed that during migration children are often separated from either one or two parents. This is particularly true for Central American, Dominican and Mexican children. It is unclear how this stressful period and disruption of family ties impacts the ways that parents are able to mobilize resources and time to participate in activities around learning. Moreover, country of origin can be related to impacts on parenting because reasons for migration differ. For example, a family from El Salvador fleeing as refugees may have very different family dynamics from a family migrating from Puerto Rico, an American territory, for better economic opportunities.

Last, the amount of time a family has been in the U.S. is also related to variations in parenting practices around learning. In comparing Puerto Rican families living in Puerto Rico to those living in the U.S., Hammer (2007) showed that mothers who lived on the U.S.

mainland reported teaching their children early literacy-related skills and reading with their children more frequently than did mothers in Puerto Rico. The authors argue that because mothers lived on the U.S. mainland for a longer period of time and were more likely to be educated in mainland schools, it is possible that they were more comfortable and knowledgeable about the skills their children were expected to have when they entered school and were more likely to adopt childrearing goals and values that are more consistent with American school systems.

Level of Education

Parents differ in their educational backgrounds and this variation is associated with differences in parenting practices that influence learning. For example, mothers who are more highly educated tend to talk more with their children which is in turn related to positive child outcomes (Hart & Risley, 1995). Mothers with higher levels of education, regardless of the country in which the education occurred, are generally more familiar with Westernized schooling techniques and have more confidence taking on the teaching roles in the home and intervening in the schools on behalf of their children. Many young Latino children have parents with limited levels of education (Hernandez et al., 2008). Nearly half of young Latino children have parents who are not high school graduates compared to 10% for European-American families. These rates of limited education are even more pronounced in Mexican families (Hernandez et al., 2008; Coltrane et al., 2008). Parents with these limited educational attainments may have little knowledge about the U.S. educational system and may not be able to read and write in either English or their home language. They may hold a different perspective about the value of schooling and the role of parents in supporting children's education. These factors may influence parents' interactions with the school and involvement with their children's learning.

Resources (SES)

Much has been written about how income and poverty influence parenting. Although there are a variety of theories, they all, to some extent, acknowledge that poverty impacts parenting, in part, through material hardship and parenting stress (McLoyd, 1990). Poverty influences the materials, experiences, and services that parents are able to purchase for their children (Yeung, Linver, & Brooks-Gunn, 2002), including factors such as high quality childcare, food, housing and safe neighborhood environments, and stimulating learning materials and activities. Parents who are able to purchase such goods and services are better able to provide opportunities that enhance their child's well-being. Sizeable evidence has established that poverty is strongly associated with less optimal home learning environments. For example, children in low-income households have less exposure to books at home (Evans, 2004; Lee & Burkam, 2002). Additional research suggests that parents' psychological well-being, and, in turn, their interactions and behaviors with their children, are adversely affected by economic hardship (Yeung, Linver, & Brooks-Gunn, 2002). The low family resources, financial stress, and psychological distress associated with poverty may make it more difficult to maintain and enact certain practices that are important for supporting children's early learning.

Latinos, especially Latino children, are overrepresented among the poor nationally (U.S. Census Bureau, 2001). For Latino children, and especially children of Mexican descent, a large part of the poverty gap stems from differences in maternal employment (i.e., Latino mothers have lower employment rates) (Lichter, Qian, & Crowley, 2008). Young Latino children in immigrant families from Mexico, Central America, and the Dominican Republic also are especially likely to have mothers who earn less than twice the federal minimum wage (Hernandez, et al., 2008).

Language and Household size / Demography

Characteristics of the home including language spoken and household size are also important correlates of children's outcomes (Howes, Guerra & Zucker, 2007). The language(s) parents use every day is an important dimension in understanding parenting practices around learning. Language choice and usage is related to a host of factors including parents' connectedness to the community, number of years living in the United States and beliefs around children's development (Howes et al., 2007). However, research has shown that Latino parents who fostered preschool Spanish literacy skills through home literacy activities were more likely to have children with high standardized Spanish reading scores in elementary grades and high English reading achievement in middle school (Reese, Garnier, Gallimore, & Goldenberg, 2000). However, many young Latino children live with a parent who is of limited English proficiency, not speaking English exclusively or very well (Hernandez, et al., 2008). These findings might also influence how parents structure learning tasks for young children, particularly if resources and outreach to parents are not conducted in Spanish. These parents would be isolated from access to programs important for young children.

Moreover, many Latino families have strong connections with extended family (Perry, 2007). Living with many relatives might provide a positive opportunity for young children to interact with many different adults. For example, in one recent study, children's Spanish oral language proficiency was directly related to having extended family members in the same household (Perry, 2007). At the same time, however, household size may be an indication of overcrowding, which can negatively affect children's well-being and health. The number of children in the household also gives some indication of the extent to which parents must divide their attention and could affect both the type and the frequency with which parents engage in learning activities with their children. In this chapter we describe the language or languages families in our sample as well as the number of people living in the home as ways to describe variations in parenting practices around learning.

Parent Depression

Maternal depression poses challenges to parenting and the establishment of a positive parent-child relationship. Depressed mothers tend to be less attentive to, less involved with, and more emotionally disengaged from their children (Bigatti, Cronan, & Anaya, 2001;

Miller, Cowan, Cowan, Hetherington, & Clingempeel, 1993). Studies suggest that economic adversity, stress, and lack of social support are important correlates of parental depression. Poor mothers are more likely to experience psychological distress and a host of factors associated with poor mental health, such as household overcrowding, unemployment and low-wage work, and poor health (Siefert, Bowman, Heflin, Danzinger, & Williams, 2000). In addition, there is an increased risk for depression when mothers lack social support (Reading & Reynolds, 2001). Issues of social support and social isolation may be particularly salient for recent immigrant families. These families may also be exposed to other material and social risk factors that elevate their risk for poor mental health. Research on immigrant Mexican American families in particular shows that depression in this group tends to be high (Gryswycz, 2006).

In summary, research shows that parenting practices around learning are critical for children's later learning and development. However, parents vary in the extent to which they create discrete formal specialized child-focused activities to support children's learning and the extent to which learning occurs through informal and community activities. There is increasing evidence that Latino families, particularly those with lower levels of education and those who have been in the U.S. for shorter periods of time, tend to support children's learning through parenting practices that lend themselves to informal and community opportunities.

DIVERSITY OF PARENTING PRACTICES AROUND LEARNING AMONG LATINO FAMILIES: A CASE STUDY OF LATINO FAMILIES LIVING IN LOS ANGELES COUNTY

In the remainder of this chapter we explore the diversity of parenting practices around learning in early childhood within Latino communities. We draw on data from a descriptive study of preschool children in Los Angeles County to illustrate the diversity in practices and the associations of these practices with different demographic characteristics as well as some differences in the strength of associations with child outcomes. The data we use comes from a study focused on the experiences and developmental growth of children who attended a universal preschool program sponsored by First 5 LA. While the main focus of that study was on describing children's preschool experiences and developmental progress in the year before kindergarten entry, it also included a parent interview with questions about the home environment and community and the informal and formal learning activities that occurred within them. The data in our discussion are drawn from the fall interview of this study, so they represent the experiences of the children and families at the beginning of their involvement in the preschool program and before presumably the preschools influenced parenting behavior. Although attendance in preschool programs has historically been lower among children in Latino families (Hernandez, et al., 2007), the majority of children served by the Los Angeles Universal Preschool (LAUP) is Latino. Moreover, the families represent a range of backgrounds, including characteristics such as economic status, immigrant status, and recency of immigration. Thus, this is a rich data set for exploring some of the issues of diversity within the Latino community in the U.S. We limit our analysis and discussion to the

1,229 families who reported Latino ancestry. Table 1 provides a description of our sample and the diversity found within the community.

Table 1. Parent and Household Characteristics

	Percentage
Mother's Education	
Less than high school diploma or GED	45
High school diploma or GED	21
Some college/Associate's degree	26
Bachelor's degree or more	8
Mother's Employment Status	
Working full Time	40
Working part Time	17
Not in work force	43
Mother Born Outside the U.S.	68
Mother's Time in the U.S. if Born Elsewhere	
5 years or fewer	10
6 to 10 years	31
More than 10 years	59
Mother's Country of Birth if Born Elsewhere	
Mexico	80
Central America	15
Other	5
Mean Number of Persons in Household (Std)	5.2 (1.9)
Household Income Below Federal Poverty Threshold	44
Household Language	
English only	31
Spanish only	16
English primarily	21
Spanish primarily	28
Mean Number of Depressive Symptoms (Std)	3.6 (5.3)

When considering research about associations with Latino families or with newly immigrated families, it is important to also consider the challenges these families may be facing. In the LAUP sample, correlational analyses suggest that parents born outside the U.S., particularly those who recently immigrated to the U.S., had fewer material and social resources (e.g., household income, maternal education) than mothers born in the U.S. (see Table 2). Higher maternal education in this sample was associated with working part- or full-time, fewer household members, and higher household income. Conversely, mothers who were unemployed were more likely to have been born outside of the U.S. and to have lived in the country for fewer years than those born in the U.S. They were also more likely to have more household members and lower household income. Similar to studies of other cultural groups, poor mothers are more likely to have more depressive symptoms. However, no other demographic characteristics were related to parents' depressive symptoms, and the reports of depressive symptoms were lower than those found in studies of other low income populations (ACF, 2006).

Although there are significant relationships observed among parents' demographic characteristics, the strength of the relationships (as measured by the magnitude of the correlation), even when examined as bivariate, is weak for any of the pairs of factors. This points to the unique nature and diversity of our sample on these characteristics. We also caution that our sample might be limited in the degree to which it represents families with challenges similar to the larger population of newly immigrated Latino families. As a case in point, although ten percent of the sample had been in the U.S. for five or fewer years, the families in this sample enrolled their children in a preschool program, suggesting family strengths such as organizational skills, the ability to create family routines and the power to take advantage of community resources. Thus, this sample is likely to under-represent the families with the greatest challenges.

Frequency of Parent-Child Activities

At the start of their child's preschool year, parents engaged in an array of activities, with varying frequency (see Table 3). Contrary to the findings discussed earlier, almost all parents reported engaging in discrete learning activities such as teaching letters, words, or numbers at least once a week. However, the frequency varied among parents and this frequency is related to the mother's education, the household income, and the length of time in the U.S. Once again, the relationships are weak, pointing to the diversity found in each group (see Table 4).

Across the sample, common parent-child activities included talking with children about what happened in preschool, taking children on errands, involving children in household chores, teaching children songs or music, and teaching children letters, words, or numbers. About half of parents reported teaching the child letters, words, or numbers most days of the week, and more than one-third reported teaching the child songs or music most days of the week. Almost all parents in the sample reported talking with children about what happened in preschool most days of the week. About two-thirds reported taking the child on errands, and half involved the child in household chores most days of the week. Notably, none of these activities are dependent on having ongoing access to materials.

Thirty-five percent of parents reported reading to their child every day, and parents reported having an average of 30 books in the home. Nearly two-thirds of children had fewer than 26 books in the home, and a similar percentage had not visited a library within the past month. Families with higher incomes, greater maternal education, and more time in the U.S. reported more frequently reading to their children. The primary language at home was not significantly associated with the frequency with which someone in the home read to their children.

Table 2. Correlation Matrix of Family Characteristics

	1	2	3	4	5	6	7	8	9
1. Mother's education	1.00								
2. Mother at home	-.247**	1.00							
3. Mother born in U.S.	.377**	-.260**	1.00						
4. Mother's years in U.S.	.210**	-.178**	n.a.	1.00					
5. Household size	-.099**	.104**	-.034	.028	1.00				
6. Household income	.376**	-.227**	.357**	.262**	.009	1.00			
7. Household is poor	-.258**	.204**	-.255**	-.213**	-.236**	-.557**	1.00		
8. Spanish only/primarily household	-.050**	.034	-.070**	-.037	-.007	-.060**	.050**	1.00	
9. Parent depressive symptoms	-.009	-.030	.009	.029	.020	-.090**	.141**	.011	1.00

** p≤.01, * p≤.05

Table 3. Parent-Child Activities

Parent-child activity	Percentage			
	Never	1-2 days	A few days	Most days
Told child a story	14.5	33.3	22.4	29.8
Taught child letters, words, or numbers	1.9	26.1	24.5	47.4
Taught child songs or music	16.5	22.9	19.7	40.9
Played a game, sport, or exercised together	11.0	32.8	21.7	34.5
Took child along on errands	3.9	18.1	13.1	64.9
Involved child in household chores	13.6	16.6	18.9	50.8
Talked about what happened in preschool	4.0	4.3	4.8	86.9
Talked about TV programs or videos	30.0	24.1	20.7	25.1
Played counting games	8.5	21.7	28.6	41.2
	Never	1-2 days	3-6 days	Everyday
Read a book to child	4.3	20.5	40.7	34.5
	Never	1-2 times	A few times	Many times
Visited a library	60.3	21.5	12.3	5.9
Visited a playground or park or had a picnic	6.7	30.7	33.7	28.9
Talked about family history or ethnic heritage	44.5	22.2	19.2	14.1
Attended event sponsored by community group	66.5	20.1	10.8	2.6
Attended church, mosque, temple school or activity	28.6	22.3	23.5	25.5
	Mean	SD	Minimum	Maximum
Number of children's books in home	29.9	34.4	0	300

Parents reported rarely visiting libraries, talking about family heritage, and attending community events. In fact, at least half of parents reported never engaging in these activities in the past month. Not being in the workforce was associated with greater likelihood of taking children to religious events, talking about family heritage, and visiting libraries, but was associated with less frequent engagement in some of the other informal activities. Families who spoke Spanish in the household reported more frequently engaging in many of the community activities, including attending religious and community events, talking about family heritage, and visiting playgrounds and parks.

Associations of Family Characteristics with Frequency of Parent-Child Activities

Rather than assume that the parent-child activities would have the same value and meaning across all Latino families, we next decided to examine the associations between individual parent-child activities and different family demographic characteristics.

Table 4. Correlation Matrix of Family Characteristics with Teaching, Informal, and Community Activities

	Mother's education	Mother at home	Mother born in U.S.	Mother's years in U.S.	House-hold size	Household income	Household is poor	Spanish only/primarily household	Parent depressive symptoms
Teaching Activities									
Tell stories	.187 **	.037 *	.180 **	.047 *	-.052**	.149 ***	-.106 **	-.016	-.083 **
Teach letters, words, numbers	.140 **	.003	.089 *	.109 **	-.027	.100 ***	-.088 ***	.012	-.064 **
Teach songs or music	.128 **	.044 *	.132 ***	.043 *	.017	.042 *	-.026	-.013	-.018
Play game, sport, or exercise	.117 ***	.046 *	.085 **	.101 **	-.018	.092 **	-.102 **	-.003	-.083 **
Play counting games	.142 **	-.031	.104 ***	.047 *	-.014	.090 ***	-.080 **	.014	-.035 *
Read book to child	.156 **	.002	.169 **	.134 ***	-.047 **	.150 ***	-.122 ***	-.032	-.073 **
Informal Activities									
Take child on errands	.107**	-.006	.076 **	.045 *	-.026	.001	-.048 **	.008	.038 *
Involve in chores	.160 **	-.097 **	.130 ***	.148 ***	-.104 **	.088 **	-.148 ***	-.018	.027
Talk about preschool	.166 **	-.052 **	.155 ***	.080 **	-.050 ***	.107 ***	-.094 ***	.003	.017
Talk about TV or videos	.087 ***	.009	.039 *	-.047 *	-.057 ***	.013	-.043 *	.002	-.058 ***
Community Activities									
Visit library	.107 ***	.086 **	.047 *	.046 *	-.053 **	-.007	-.030	.029	-.079 **
Visit playground or park	.136 **	-.020	.148 ***	.036	-.057 ***	.080 **	-.039 *	.160 **	-.051 **
Talk about heritage	.015	.096 **	-.074 **	-.130 **	-.066 **	-.009	.005	.133 ***	-.028
Attend community event	.168 **	-.054 **	.114 ***	.098 **	.010	.118 ***	-.072 **	.145 **	-.032
Attend religious event	.039 *	.099 **	-.025	.040	.022	-.043 **	.021	.148 **	-.069 **

** p≤.01, * p≤.05

Table 5. Correlation Matrix of Child Outcomes with Teaching, Informal, and Community Activities

	Expressive vocabulary	Alphabet knowledge	Mathematics	Executive function
Teaching Activities				
Tell stories	.173 **	.142**	.068**	.007
Teach letters, words, numbers	123 **	.076 **	.056 **	-.037 *
Teach songs or music	.072 **	.081 **	.050 **	.028
Play game, sport, or exercise	.089 **	.081 **	.024	.069 **
Play counting games	.147 **	.090 **	.088**	.023
Read book to child	.163 **	.184 **	.107**	.002
Informal Activities				
Take child on errands	.072 **	-.004	.008	-.004
Involve in chores	.166 **	.109 **	.158 **	-.064 **
Talk about preschool	.182 **	.068 **	.164 **	.064 **
Talk about TV or videos	.091 **	.059 **	.093 **	-.028
Community Activities				
Visit library	.092 **	.098 **	.085 **	-.031
Visit playground or park	.133 **	.088 **	.093 **	.014
Talk about heritage	.089 **	.076 **	.099 **	.001
Attend community event	.148 **	.090 **	.087 **	.025
Attend religious event	.061 **	.023	.021	.040 *

** $p \leq .01$, * $p \leq .05$

Correlation analyses suggest that family characteristics were associated with the frequency of parent-child activities in ways similar to those found in studies of other families in the U.S. (see Table 4) (ACF 2006; Lee & Burkam, 2002; West et al., 2000). For example, mothers with more education, who were born in the U.S., and with higher household income were more likely to report engaging in nearly all of the parent-child teaching, informal, and community activities, whereas household poverty and more household members was associated with less frequency of activities. Parent depressive symptoms were negatively associated with a number of activities, including telling children stories; teaching letters, words, or numbers; reading books with children; and visiting libraries. The strongest associations of family characteristics with parenting practices were found among the teaching activities, but even these are weak in magnitude.

ASSOCIATIONS OF PARENT-CHILD ACTIVITIES WITH CHILD OUTCOMES

Correlational analyses indicate that the frequency of parent-child activities was associated with children's school readiness outcomes at the beginning of the preschool year for the full

Latino sample (see Table 5). All parent-child activities were positively associated with children's expressive vocabulary (as measured by the Expressive One-Word Picture Vocabulary Test: English and Spanish-Bilingual Edition (EOWPVT-SBE; Brownell 2000)), and most were associated with children's letter naming skills, which was measured by a rapid letter naming task. For example, children whose parents more frequently told them stories; taught letters, words, or numbers; and read books to them, had better expressive vocabulary skills and could correctly recognize more letters in the fall. More frequent informal and community activities, such as involving children in chores and talking about preschool, was positively associated with children's math skills (as measured by an adaptation of the Early Childhood Longitudinal Study – Birth Cohort (ECLS-B) Mathematics assessment). Reading books to children was also associated with better math skills. Only more frequently playing games, sports or exercising; talking about preschool; and attending religious events were associated with better executive function (Smith-Donald, Raver, Hayes, & Richardson 2007; Blair 2002; Diamond & Taylor, 1996).

ASSOCIATIONS OF PARENT-CHILD ACTIVITIES WITH CHILD OUTCOMES BY LENGTH OF TIME IN THE U.S.

However, both the frequency with which families engage in parent-child activities around learning and the relationships of the activities with child outcomes differs among families in relation to the length of time that they have been in the U. S. More recent immigrants reported more frequent use of counting games, and teaching letters, words, numbers and songs and less frequent use of storytelling and reading to children (see Table 6). With the exception of talking about family heritage, parents who had immigrated more recently reported engaging in all community activities *less* frequently than parents who had been in the U.S. for more than five years. More recent immigrants also reported less frequent involvement in engaging their children during chores than Latino families who had been in the U.S. for longer periods of time, but more frequent involvement with their children during errands and talking about TV. This latter finding is particularly interesting as it suggests that perhaps recent immigrant families view television as a socialization tool.

Involvement in chores provides opportunities for learning particularly for families favoring an intent participation approach. Consistent with this theory, the association between involvement in chores and content-based learning, particularly mathematics, is positive. Moreover, the association is stronger for families in which mothers have been in the U.S. five or fewer years than for families with mothers who have been in the U.S. for longer periods of time. The strength of association between each of the informal activities and mathematics is greater for children who are in recent immigrant families, suggesting that these children may be using intent participation approaches to learning and these activities expose them to mathematics concepts informally.

Table 6. Mean Parent-Reported Frequencies and Variance in Parent-Child Activities

	Mother in U.S. 5 or Fewer Years		Mother in U.S. More than 5 years	
	Mean	Standard Deviation	Mean	Standard Deviation
Teaching Activities				
Tell stories	2.47	1.08	2.55	1.05
Teach letters, words, numbers	3.18	0.90	3.12	0.90
Teach songs or music	2.88	1.05	2.73	1.15
Play game, sport, or exercise	2.60	1.03	2.75	1.06
Play counting games	3.45	0.95	3.33	0.94
Read book to child	2.70	0.99	2.98	0.86
Informal Activities				
Take child on errands	3.45	0.95	3.33	0.94
Involve in chores	2.71	1.19	3.00	1.13
Talk about preschool	3.66	0.87	3.67	0.80
Talk about TV or videos	2.62	1.23	2.35	1.18
Community Activities				
Visit library	1.55	0.89	1.62	0.91
Visit playground or park	2.60	0.96	2.77	0.92
Talk about heritage	2.34	1.14	2.06	1.11
Attend community event	1.33	0.66	1.44	0.76
Attend religious event	2.36	1.07	2.49	1.18

Nonetheless, the negative relationship between involvement in chores and executive functioning is perplexing unless one takes into account the nature of the task used to assess executive functioning and the research on observational learning among Latino cultures. Executive functioning involves "processes that are integral to the emerging self-regulation of behavior and developing social and cognitive competence in young children" (Blair, Zelazo, & Greenberg, 2005, p. 561). For this study we measured executive functioning through a pencil tapping paradigm (Smith-Donald, Raver, Hayes, & Richardson 2007; Blair, 2002; Diamond & Taylor, 1996) in which children were required to inhibit a natural tendency to imitate what the adult does. Although it could be that families who involve their children more in chores are those with more limited resources to support children's executive functioning, it is unlikely given the positive relationships with other cognitive outcomes (that is, mathematics and alphabet knowledge). It is more likely that the negative relationship between involvement in chores and executive functioning can be attributed to a style of learning in line with intent participation. As described earlier, the intent participation approach to learning that Rogoff and others report as evident among more recently immigrated Mexican heritage families relies on the child's carefully observing and imitating the adult behavior. Among children who are accustomed to learning in this way, inhibiting a response would call for greater impulse control than it would for children in families in which the child learns from verbal direction and may discuss, question, or verbally negotiate tasks. The stronger relationships found for more recently immigrated families suggest that this may be a factor in the relationship.

Informal activities are not associated with expressive vocabulary among children in more recently immigrated families. Because children in our study could respond to questions throughout our vocabulary assessments in either English or Spanish, this finding is not related to fluency specific to one language or the other. It is unclear however if these informal activities are instead associated with other language features such as narrative, syntax, grammar, or comprehension. Yet, among families who have been in the U.S. for more than five years, greater use of community activities is positively associated with children's expressive language and cognitive skills. However, this relationship is not noted for families that are more recently immigrated with the exception of library visits. More frequent visits to the library are associated with stronger expressive vocabulary and alphabet knowledge, and the strength of these relationships for library visits is greater than the relationships found in the families with more time in the U.S. This motivation to use the library may be associated with greater understanding of the importance of literacy. Given the absence of a significant positive relationship with the frequency of reading a book to the child, one wonders if the families are using story hours to provide listening experiences for their children. It would be helpful to understand more about the dynamics that undergird these relationships.

In summary, the strength and nature of the associations of parent-child activities with children's school readiness outcomes differed according to the mother's length of time in the U.S. (see Table 7). Associations were found more consistently for families in which the mother had been in the country for more than five years. In fact, for children whose mothers had been in the country for more years, nearly all of the parent-child activities were positively associated with children's expressive vocabulary and ability to recognize letters. The frequency of far fewer activities was associated with children's outcomes for children of more recent immigrants. Similarly, all of the community activities were positively associated with the math skills of children whose mothers had lived in the U.S. for more than five years, but none of these activities were associated with the math skills of children of new immigrants. In addition, the magnitude of the associations of some of the parent-child activities with children's outcomes was stronger for families of new immigrants (e.g., telling stories, visiting libraries, involving children in chores), suggesting that these parent-child activities might be more important for children from recent immigrant families.

CONCLUSION

In this chapter we seek to explore the frequency with which Latino families engage in formal, informal, and community activities that promote learning with their children, the factors associated with the frequency of engagement in these activities and how these parenting practices around learning are associated with child outcomes.

Table 7. Correlation Matrix of Child Outcomes with Teaching, Informal, and Community Activities by Recency of Immigration

	Mother in U.S. 5 or Fewer Years				Mother in U.S. More than 5 Years			
	Expressive vocabulary	Alphabet knowledge	Mathematics	Executive function	Expressive vocabulary	Alphabet knowledge	Mathematics	Executive function
Teaching Activities								
Tell stories	.110	.217**	-.070	-.051	.074**	.099**	.021	-.042
Teach letters, words, numbers	.101	.051	.017	-.073	.118**	.069**	.042	-.058*
Teach songs or music	.110	.108	.094	-.117	.025	.065**	.010	.051*
Play game, sport, or exercise	.087	.040	.102	.130	.081**	.031	.007	.083**
Play counting games	-.075	.124	-.027	-.004	.166**	.111**	.084**	.033
Read book to child	-.134	.185**	-.076	-.069	.133**	.156**	.093**	-.034
Informal Activities								
Take child on errands	.097	-.104	-.195**	-.130	.091**	.017	.019	-.016
Involve in chores	-.130	.183*	.249**	-.192**	.174**	.086**	.141**	-.069**
Talk about preschool	.071	.092	.164**	-.120	.179**	.055*	.156***	.089**
Talk about TV or videos	.029	-.050	.205**	-.111	.083**	.065**	.103**	-.004
Community Activities								
Visit library	.227**	.165*	.007	.083	.099**	.126**	.112**	-.044
Visit playground or park	-.084	.084	.008	-.047	.125**	.083**	.094***	-.038
Talk about heritage	.137	.071	.053	.113	.177**	.093**	.161**	-.007
Attend community event	-.088	.146*	.007	.126	.150**	.078**	.084***	.000
Attend religious event	.213**	.048	.066	-.046	.112**	.063**	.057*	.014

** p≤.01, * p≤.05

First, our exploration supports the idea that Latino parents of preschoolers are engaged in a variety of weekly and monthly activities with their children. In line with research supporting the notion that Latino parents might favor informal parenting practices around learning (Rogoff, 2003), we see a trend by which the activities occurring most frequently in Latino homes were talking with children about what happened in preschool (86.9% of parents engage in this most days), taking children on errands (64.9% of parents engage in this activity most days), and involving children in household chores (50.8% of parents engage in this most days). Although our data do not explicitly provide a qualitative picture of what occurs during these activities, the emotions shared or the language used, it is probable that it is within these more adult-centered activities that young Latino children are developing the observational skills used and valued. Parents demonstrated less frequent engagement in community activities such as visiting libraries and attending community events. Parents also engaged in less frequent joint book reading and owned fewer books than did parents of kindergartners nationally. For example, in the ECLS-K, 45 percent of parents reported reading to their children every day (West & Germino-Hausken, 2000). In addition, the ECLS-K found that the majority of parents of kindergartners reported having more than 25 children's books in the home. [1] When parents engaged in more direct and formal parent-child activities, they more frequently engaged in activities that were not dependent on material resources. Nearly half of parents reported teaching children letters, words, or numbers most days of the week. This emphasis is consistent with other literature suggesting a heavier emphasis on rote skills such as letter knowledge as important for school readiness among low-income and minority parents (Nord, Lennon, Liu, & Chandler, 1999).

Second, there is variation in the frequency of parents' engagement in activities with their children. Consistent with the larger research literature, family resources importantly shape Latino parents' practices and engagement with their children around learning. Parents with more sociodemographic risks, such as recency of immigration, lower education, and less household income were less likely to frequently engage in many learning activities, suggesting that a multitude of factors are in play when considering how frequently parents engage their children in activities around learning. Also of interest, parental depression is associated with household income and poverty status, but not other demographic characteristics, such as immigrant status or recency of immigration. This may suggest other sources of social support available among families.

Finally, the results of our exploration suggest that the number of associations between activities and child outcomes is greater for those mothers who have been in the U.S. for five years or more, but the strength of the significant association for more recently immigrated families is stronger than for the comparable coefficients of families who have been in the country longer. This important finding suggests that something qualitatively changes over time that alters the link between parenting practices around learning and children's outcomes. It is unclear, however, what this change is. Is it that mothers in the U.S. for five years or more engage in activities in a qualitatively different fashion? Is it that they have acquired more economic resources? Is it that after having lived here for more than five years, they are more

---

[1] The ECLS-K provides nationally representative estimates on the frequency of parent-child activities among families with kindergartners at the start of the kindergarten year. Comparisons of parenting practices with data from the ECLS-B may provide a more appropriate comparison because parents' frequency of activities with kindergartners may differ from frequency with preschoolers. However, published data on parent-child activities from the preschool wave of the ECLS-B are not currently available.

established and have more supports in place and thus are able to spend time with their children in different ways? Or perhaps it is that over this period of time, parents come into more contact with U.S. schools and other families, giving them a better sense of what skills are valued in American schools.

It is important, however, to consider this analysis in light of several limitations. First, although we included in our interview representative informal activities that parents might engage in (e.g., going on errands, doing chores), these activities by no means capture the universe of informal activities that exist. In fact, this work may potentially be ignoring an equally or more significant set of parenting practices around learning. That is, there might be other things that parents do that we are not tapping into adequately with the questions included in our survey. Thus, future work, perhaps led by rich ethnographic studies, can attempt to uncover those practices that Latino parents engage in that are even more strongly associated with child outcomes, as well as to investigate strengths-based approaches for building on the teaching practices these families employ. For example, educators might ask families how they could incorporate more literacy-enriching practices into daily parent-child activities such as the chores children are asked to do.

Moreover, in our study, we limited our discussion of child outcomes to those that are language-based and cognitive in nature, although we did include discussion of an executive functioning task. We did not measure many of the social-emotional outcomes that research shows are among the school readiness outcomes that are most important to Latino families (Barbarin, et al., 2008). There might be other types of outcomes that are associated with parenting practices that we have also not explored. In addition, we used an exploratory analysis and examined many bivariate associations to understand the nature and diversity of practices. We did not adjust for the multiple comparisons, and it is possible that the relationships identified as significant are spurious. Multivariate analyses (with adjustments for multiple comparisons) can begin to further shed light on the nature of the relationships we find in this paper.

Overall, this chapter contributes to the growing body of work that documents that Latinos are not a monolithic group. They are a diverse group, varying on a number of factors related to education, immigration and socio-economic status. That is, we cannot attribute the variation in parenting practices around learning to culture or country of origin alone, but must also consider economic and material conditions. Our findings are not just academic in nature, but also provide important insight for educators who work with young Latino children and their families. Results from the ECLS-K show that nationally Latino children enroll in kindergarten at younger ages and are less likely than other children to have been involved in any early childhood programs. Going forward, it is important to make early childhood opportunities available to families and encourage families to access these opportunities. In cases where young Latino children have less access to early childhood programs than their peers, whether due to availability or family choice, it is even more critical to support families in preparing children for school-like ways of interaction, while also respecting what is learned through less formal methods. When working with Latino families, particularly those who are not native to the U.S. and have been in the U.S. for shorter periods of time, teachers should discuss and model with families how to build on the use of informal activities as contexts for learning. Schools must also become much better equipped to implement curricula and teaching practices that are more culturally appropriate in accommodating the teaching styles of diverse families. It is in this way that educators will walk with families in supporting young Latino children's development.

ACKNOWLEDGMENTS

The research reported in this paper was supported by First 5 LA. We would also like to express our gratitude to the families who participated in this study.

REFERENCES

Administration for Children and Families. (2006). *Head Start Performance Measures Center Family and Child Experiences Survey (FACES 2000) technical report.* Washington, DC: U.S. Department of Health and Human Services.

Administration for Children and Families. (2002). *Making a difference in the lives of infants and toddlers and their families: The impacts of Early Head Start—final technical report.* Washington, DC: U.S. Department of Health and Human Services.

Administration on Children, Youth, and Families. (2001). *Building their futures: How Early Head Start programs are enhancing the lives of infants and toddlers in low-income families.* Washington, DC: U.S. Department of Health and Human Services.

Ada, A. F., & Zubiarreta, R. (2001). Parent narratives: The cultural bridge between Latino parents and their children. In M. de la Luz Reyes, & J. J. Halcon (Eds.), *The best for our children: Critical perspectives on literacy for Latino students* (pp. 229-243). New York: Teachers College Press.

Arzubiaga, A., Ceja. M., & Artiles, A. J. (2000). Transcending deficit thinking about Latinos' parenting styles: Toward an ecocultural view of family life. In C. Tejeda, C. Martinez, Z. Leonardo, & P. McLaren (Eds.), *Charting new terrains of Chicana (o)/ Latina (o) education.* (pp. 93-106). Cresskill, NY: Hampton Press.

Barbarin, O. A., & Aikens, N. (in press). Parental practices and children's early language and literacy: Helping parents to help their children. In O. Barbarin & P. Frome (Eds.), *The Handbook of Developmental Science and Early Education: Translating Basic Research into Practice.* Guilford Press: New York, NY.

Barbarin, O. (1999). Social risks and psychological adjustment: A comparison of African American and South African children. *Child Development, 70,* 1348-1359.

Barbarin, O. A., Early, D., Clifford, R., Bryant, D., Frome, P., Burchinal, M., Howes, C., & Pianta, R. (2008). Parental conceptions of school readiness: Relation to ethnicity, socioeconomic status, and children's skills. *Early Education & Development, 19*(5), 671-701.

Baumrind, D. (1971). Current patterns of parental authority. *Developmental Psychology Monograph, 4,* 1-103.

Bigatti, S. M., Cronan, T. A., & Anaya, A. (2001). The effects of maternal depression on the efficacy of a literacy intervention program. *Child Psychiatry and Human Development, 32,* 147–162.

Brooks-Gunn, J., & Markman, L. B. (2005). The contribution of parenting to ethnic and racial gaps in school readiness. *The Future of Children, 15*(1), 139-168.

Coltrane, S., Parke, R. D., Schofield, T. J., Tsuha, S. J., Chavez, M., & Lio, S. (2008). Mexican-American families and poverty. In D. R. Crane & T. B. Heaton (Eds.), *Handbook of families & poverty*. Los Angeles: Sage Publications.

Cooper, C. R., Brown, J., Azmitia, M., & Chavira, G. (2005). Including Latino immigrant families, schools, and community programs as research partners on the good path of life (el buen camino de la vida). In T. Weisner (Ed.), *Discovering successful pathways in children's development: New methods in the study of childhood and family life* (pp. 359-386). Chicago: University of Chicago Press.

Delgado-Gaitán, C. (1990). *Literacy for empowerment: The role of parents in children's education*. New York: Falmer.

Downey, G., & Coyne, J. C. (1990). Children of depressed parents: An integrative review. *Psychological Bulletin, 108*, 50–76.

Eisenberg, A. R. (1985). Learning to describe past experience in conversation. *Discourse Processes, 8,* 177-204.

Eisenberg, A. R. (1999). Emotion talk among Mexican-American and Anglo-American mothers and children from two social classes. *Merrill-Palmer Quarterly, 45*, 259-277.

Eisenberg, A. R. (2002). Conversations within Mexican descent families: Diverse contexts for language socialization and learning. *Hispanic Journal of Behavioral Sciences, 24*(2), 206-224.

Evans, G.W. (2004). The environment of childhood poverty. *American Psychologist, 59*(2), 77-92.

Farver, J. M., Xu, Y., Eppe, S., & Lonigan, C. J. (2006). Home environments and young Latino children's school readiness. *Early Childhood Research Quarterly, 21,* 196-212.

Gadsden, V. L. (2004). Family literacy and culture. In B.H. Wasik (Ed.), *Handbook of family literacy*. New York: Lawrence Erlbaum Associates.

Gallimore, R., & Goldenberg, C. (1993). Activity settings of early literacy: Home and school factors in children's emergent literacy. In E. Forman, N. Minick, & C. A. Stone (Eds.), *Contexts for learning: Sociocultural dynamics in children's development* (pp. 315-335). New York: Oxford University Press.

García-Coll, C., Akiba, D., Palacios, N., Bailey, B., Silver, R., DiMartino, L., & Chin, C. (2002). Parental involvement in children's education: Lessons from three immigrant groups. *Parenting: Science and Practice, 2*(3), 303-324.

García-Coll, C., Meyer, E., & Brillon, L. (1995). Ethnic and minority parenting. In M. H. Bornstein (Ed.), *Handbook of parenting: Biology and ecology of parenting* (pp. 189-209). Mahwah, NJ: Lawrence Erlbaum Associates.

Garcia, C. C., & Pacheter, L. M. (2002). Ethnic and minority parenting. In M. H. Bornstein (Ed.), *Handbook of parenting: Social conditioning and applied parenting* (2nd ed., vol. 4, pp. 1-20). Mahwah, NJ: Lawrence Erlbaum Associates.

Hammer, C. S., Rodriguez, B. L., Lawrence, R., & Miccio, A. W. (2007). Puerto Rican mothers' beliefs and home literacy practices. *Language, Speech, and Hearing Services in Schools, 38*, 216-224.

Hammer, C. S., & Miccio, A. W. (2004). Home literacy experiences of Latino families. In B. H. Wasik (Ed.), *Handbook of family literacy* (pp. 305-328). Mahwah, NJ: Lawrence Erlbaum Associates.

Haney, M. H., & Hill, J. (2004). Relationships between parent-teaching activities and emergent literacy in preschool children. *Early Child Development and Care, 17*(3), 215-228.

Hart, B., & Risely. T. B. (1995). *Meaningful differences in the everyday experience of young American children.* Baltimore, MD: Paul. H. Brookes Publishing Company.

Harwood, R. L., Miller, J. G., & Irizarry, N. L. (1995). *Culture and attachment: Perceptions of the child in context.* New York: The Guilford Press.

Harwood, R., Leyendecker, B., Carlson, V., Asencio, M., & Millar, A. (2002). Parenting among Latino families in the U.S. In M. H. Bornstein (Ed.), *Handbook of parenting: Vol. 4: Social conditions and applied parenting* (2nd ed.) (pp. 21-46). Mahwah, NJ: Lawrence Erlbaum Associates.

Harwood, R. L., Handwerker, W. P., Schoelmerich, A., and Leyendecker, B. (2001). Ethnic category labels, parental beliefs, and the contextualized individual: An exploration of the individualism-sociocentrism debate. *Parenting, 1*(3), 217-236.

Heath, S. B. (1983). *Ways with words: Language, life, and work in communities and classrooms.* New York: Cambridge University Press.

Hernandez, D. J., Denton, N. A., & Macartney, S. E. (2007).Young Hispanic children in the 21st century. *Journal of Latinos and Education, 6*(3), 209–228.

Howes, C., Guerra, A. W. & Zucker, E. (2007). Cultural communities and parenting in Mexican-heritage families. *Parenting: Science and Practice*, 3(7), 235-270.

Lee, V. E., & Burkam, D. T. (2002). *Inequality at the starting gate: Social background differences in achievement as children enter school.* Washington, DC: Economic Policy Institute.

Lichter, D. T., Qian, Z., & Crowley, M. L. (2008). Poverty and economic polarization among children in racial minority and immigrant families. In D. R. Crane & T. B. Heaton (Eds.), *Handbook of families & poverty.* Los Angeles: Sage Publications.

Melzi, G. (2000). Cultural variations in the construction of personal narratives: Central American and European-American mothers' elicitation styles. *Discourse Processes, 30*(2), 153-177.

Melzi, G., & Caspe, M. (2005). Cultural variations in mother's storytelling styles. *Narrative Inquiry, 15*(1), 101-125.

McWayne, C., Hampton, V., Fantuzzo, J., Cohen, H. L., & Sekino, Y. (2004). A multivariate examination of parent involvement and the social and academic competencies of urban kindergarten children. *Psychology in Schools, 41*(3), 363–377.

Miller, N. B., Cowan, P. A., Cowan, C. P., Hetherington, E. M., & Clingempeel, W. G. (1993). Externalizing in preschoolers and early adolescents: A cross-study replication of a family model. *Developmental Psychology, 29*, 3–18

Morelli, G. A., Rogoff, B., & Angelillo, C. (2003). Cultural variation in young children's access to work or involvement in specialised child-focused activities. *International Journal of Behavioral Development, 27*(3), 264–274.

Moll, L. C., Amanti, C., Neff, D., & González, N. (1992). Funds of knowledge for teaching: Using a qualitative approach to connect homes and classrooms. *Theory into Practice, 31*, 132-141.

Perry, N. J., Kay, S. M., and Brown, A. (2007). Continuity and change in home literacy practices of Hispanic families with preschool children. *Early Child Development and Care, 178*, 99-113.

Porsche, M. V. (2001). Parent involvement as a link between home and school. In D. K. Dickinson & P. O. Tabors (Eds.), *Beginning literacy with language* (pp. 291-312). Cambridge, MA: Paul Brookes Publishing.

Raver, C. C., Gershoff, E. T. & Aber, J. L. (2007). Testing equivalence of mediating models of income, parenting, and school readiness for White, Black and Hispanic children in a national sample. *Child Development, 78*(1), 96-115.

Reading, R., & Reynolds, S. (2001). Debt, social disadvantage, and maternal depression. *Social Science and Medicine, 53*, 441–453.

Reese, L., & Gallimore, R. (2000). Immigrant Latinos' cultural model of literacy development: An evolving perspective on home-school connections. *American Journal of Education, 108*(2), 103-134.

Rogoff, B. (2003). *The cultural nature of human development.* New York: Oxford University Press.

Rogoff, B. (1990). *Apprenticeship in thinking: Cognitive development in social context.* New York: Oxford University Press.

Rogoff, B., Paradise, R., Mejía Arauz, R., Correa-Chávez, M., & Angelillo, C. (2003). Firsthand learning through intent participation. *Annual Review of Psychology, 54*, 175-203.

Schieffelin, B. B., & Ochs, E. (Eds.). (1986). *Language socialization across cultures.* Cambridge, UK: Cambridge University Press.

Siefert, K., Bowman, P. J., Heflin, C. M., Danzinger, S., & Williams, D. R. (2000). Social and environmental predictors of maternal depression in current and recent welfare recipients. *American Journal of Orthopsychiatry, 70*, 510–522.

Snow, C. E., Burns, S. M., & Griffin, P. (Eds.). (1998). *Preventing reading difficulties in young children.* Washington, DC: National Academy Press.

Suárez-Orozco, C., & Suárez-Orozco, M. (2001). *Children of immigration.* Cambridge, MA: Harvard University Press.

Suárez-Orozco, M. M., & Paéz, M. M. (2002). *Latinos: Remaking America.* Berkeley: University of California Press.

United States Census Bureau. *Household income rises, poverty rate unchanged, number of uninsured down.* Retrieved August, 26, 2008.

Valdés, G. (1996). *Con respeto: Bridging the distances between culturally diverse families and schools.* New York: Teachers College Press.

Vygotsky, L. S. (1978). *Mind in society: The development of higher psychological processes.* Cambridge, MA: Harvard University Press.

Whitehurst, G. J., & Longigan, C. J. (1998). Child development and emergent literacy. *Child Development, 69*, 848–890.

West, J., K. Denton, and E. Germino-Hausken. (2000). *America's kindergartners: Findings from the Early Childhood Longitudinal Study, kindergarten class of 1998-99, fall 1998.* NCES 2000-070 (revised). Washington, DC.

Yeung, W. J., Linver, M. R., & Brooks-Gunn, J. (2002). How money matters for young children's development: Parental investment and family processes. *Child Development, 73*(6), 1861-1879.

In: Handbook of Parenting: Styles, Stresses & Strategies   ISBN 978-1-60741-766-8
Editor: Pacey H. Krause and Tahlia M. Dailey   © 2009 Nova Science Publishers, Inc.

Chapter 17

PARENTING STYLES IN ADOLESCENCE: THE ROLE OF WARMTH, STRICTNESS, AND PSYCHOLOGICAL AUTONOMY GRANTING IN INFLUENCING COLLECTIVE SELF-ESTEEM AND EXPECTATIONS FOR THE FUTURE

Silvia Moscatelli and *Monica Rubini*

University of Bologna, Italy

ABSTRACT

A large corpus of evidence shows the effectiveness of authoritative parenting, in comparison with authoritarian, neglectful, and indulgent educational styles, on adolescents' personal and social development. However, few studies have examined the influence of authoritative parenting on adolescents' social identity and future plans. In this contribution ($N = 400$) we examined the role of warmth, strictness, and autonomy granting – the core dimensions of parenting– in influencing adolescents' social identity, measured as family collective self-esteem, and expectations for the future, in terms of stable intimate relationships and fulfillment of personal goals. We also tested the role of family collective self-esteem in mediating the influence of parenting style dimensions on expectations for the future. Besides confirming that authoritative parenting leads to better outcomes than the other educational styles, this study sheds light for the first time on the distinct contribution of different parenting dimensions on adolescents' social identity and expectations for the future.

---

* Correspondence concerning this chapter should be addressed to:
Silvia Moscatelli
Dipartimento di Scienze dell'Educazione, Via Filippo Re, 6, 40126 Bologna, Italy.
E-mail: silvia.moscatelli@unibo.it

Over the past five decades, research on child rearing has identified the core dimensions of parenting style – warmth, strictness/supervision, and psychological autonomy granting – and consistently showed that authoritative style is associated to psychological well-being and social development in childhood and adolescence (for reviews, see Steinberg, 2001; Steinberg & Silk, 2002). The present paper contributes to this issue by presenting a study where family is conceptualized as a social group, which contributes to adolescents' social identity (Tajfel & Turner, 1979). Specifically, it analyzes the relationship between each dimension of parenting style and family collective self-esteem, a concept which taps adolescents' judgments on the value of their family and importance of their family membership for their self-concept (Luhtanen & Crocker, 1992). Second, it examines whether and how warmth, strictness/supervision, and psychological autonomy granting influence adolescents' expectations for the future, in terms of self-fulfillment and of having stable intimate relationships. Finally, it tested whether the effects of parenting style dimensions are mediated by family collective self-esteem.

PARENTING STYLES IN ADOLESCENCE

Since early '70s, research on the practices of child rearing has largely demonstrated that high levels of parental responsiveness, together with high levels of demandingness, are related to positive developmental outcomes in children (e.g. Baumrind, 1971; Maccoby & Martin, 1983) Specifically, the combination of high levels of responsiveness and demandingness underlines the so-called authoritative parenting, characterized by high degrees of support and acceptance, continuous promotion of dialogue and discussion within the family, and also by clear expectations and behavioral norms ruling the child's behavior. On the basis of adolescents' ratings of their parents on the two dimensions, other three parenting styles have been identified (Baumrind, 1978; Lamborn, Mounts, Steinberg, & Dornbusch, 1991). Authoritarian parents demand obedience and conformity, and do not appreciate children's autonomy and independency. They are low in responsiveness and support to the child, and favor punitive, forceful disciplinary measures over dialogue. Indulgent (or permissive) parents are very responsive and adopt supportive behaviors towards their child; on the other hand, they give the child a high degree of freedom, do not fix many rules and do not promote discipline. Finally, neglectful (or indifferent) parents are very low in responsiveness and spend little time in interacting and dialoguing with their children; at the same time, they are low in demandingness and fail in providing behavioral standards and rules.

A large corpus of research has demonstrated that adolescents reared in authoritative homes are more psychologically competent, more socially skilled, report less symptoms of depression and anxiety, and score higher on self-esteem and self-reliance measures in comparison with their peers who live in authoritarian, indulgent, or neglectful homes. They are also more successful in school, and less likely to engage in deviant behavior or to take drugs (cf. Steinberg, 2001; Steinberg & Silk, 2002). Interestingly, Steinberg, Lamborn, Darling, Mounts, and Dornbush (1994) reported that differences in adjustment associated to different parenting styles were either maintained or increased one year later the first data collection (Lamborn et al., 1991). Specifically, the results of this follow-up study pointed out that adolescents from authoritative families were those who maintained previous levels of high adjustment, whereas adolescents from neglectful families showed a clear decline in their already disadvantaged situation. Although Harris (1995) has questioned the direction of the relationship between parents' behavior and adolescent adjustment, and has contended that parents have much less influence on their children than other socialization agents as peers, both longitudinal and experimental studies have proved the impact of parenting practices on teenagers' development (Collins, Maccoby, Steinberg, Heterington, & Bornstein, 2000; Steinberg & Silk, 2002).

Trying to understand why and how authoritative parenting leads to such positive developmental outcomes in adolescence, Steinberg, Elmen, and Mounts (1989; see also Gray & Steinberg, 1999) further specified the distinctive features of authoritativeness, and underlined the role of three core dimensions: parental warmth or acceptance (similar to responsiveness), parental control and strictness (similar to demandingness), and psychological autonomy granting. The combination of these dimensions create a positive, harmonious climate at home, where adolescents can have experience of a certain degree of autonomy, but are never left on their own: They are given standards, limits, and guidelines, and have the opportunity to develop self-reliance and competence within a supportive context (Steinberg & Silk, 2002). Family discussion and negotiation, characterized by continuous give-and take verbal exchanges, promote the child's intellectual development, which in turn is associated to the development of psychosocial competence (Rueter & Conger, 1998). Additionally, a good parent-child relationship and a positive climate within the family lead adolescents to disclose spontaneously information about their lives to their parents (Fletcher, Steinberg, & Williams-Wheeler, 2004; Stattin & Kerr, 2000), and enhances parental influences on the child (Darling & Steinberg, 1993).

Thus, whereas early psychoanalytic views considered adolescence as a period of "sturm und drang", and even emphasized the importance of family conflicts as a necessary condition which allows adolescents to detach from their family, recent approaches see adolescence as a period of transition for the child and his/her parents, which requires relationship changes and achieving of a new equilibrium within the family (Steinberg & Silk, 2002). The important point, however, is that a supportive climate in the family, the existence of clear rules and limits, together with the opportunity of discussion and negotiation offered by authoritative parents, may help the child and the family as a whole to reach positive outcomes without rendering the transition too much difficult or traumatic for the actors involved.

Notwithstanding the large variety of variables considered in studying the influence of authoritativeness, up to now there is no evidence on whether and how authoritative parenting affect adolescents' social identity. Tajfel and Turner (1979) conceptualized social identity as a part of self-concept deriving from one's membership in a social group, in terms of knowledge, value and emotions related to that membership. It can be argued, by considering family as a particular type of social groups where members have different roles and status, that family membership, like memberships in larger groups or categories often studied in the literature (e.g., ethnicity, nationality), contributes to adolescents' self-concept by influencing not only specific aspects of their personal identity such as competence or sociability, but also by affecting their social identity. In line with this contention, this study examines whether social identity, in terms of collective self-esteem (Luhtanen & Crocker, 1992), varies among adolescents from authoritative, authoritarian, indulgent, and neglectful families. It also analyzes the contribution of the three core dimensions of an effective, authoritative parenting

– warmth, strictness/supervision, and psychological autonomy granting – on adolescents' collective self-esteem. Second, this study extends the research on the positive effects of authoritative parenting by focusing on adolescents' expectations for the future, in terms of self-fulfillment and of achievement of stable intimate relationships, and analyzes the possible role played by collective self-esteem in explaining the impact of authoritative parenting on these outcomes. Indeed, since collective self-esteem is associated with psychological adjustment (Luhtanen & Crocker, 1992), it is hypothesized that family collective self-esteem will mediate the relationship between authoritative parenting and adolescents' expectations for the future in terms of life plans.

METHOD

Sample and Procedure

400 students (16-18 years old, 47% males and 53% females) attending the forth class from five different types of secondary schools (humanities and sciences gymnasium, technical, and vocational schools) in a medium-size town in North Italy filled in a self-report questionnaire. 97% of fathers and mothers had Italian origins. Since 7 students failed to provide complete data, data from 393 students were included in the analyses.

Headmaster and teachers were explained the aims of the research and asked their consensus to let their students take part in the research. Parents were then informed about the study and asked to contact the school within one month if they wished their child did not participate to the research. No parents withheld the consensus (cf. Lamborn et al., 1991). A month later, two researches administered the questionnaire during classes; all students attending the classes agreed to complete the questionnaire.

Measures

Authoritative Parenting

To capture the three components of parenting - warmth, strictness/supervision, and psychological autonomy granting - we employed existing measures of parenting styles (Steinberg et al. 1989; Gray & Steinberg, 1999). The warmth scale, consisting of 5 items (α = .77), assesses the extent to which parents are perceived as responsive, loving, and involved (e.g., "I can count on my parents to help me out if I have some kind of problem"). The psychological autonomy granting scale (4 items; α = .84) measures the extent to which parents encourage the adolescent to express individuality within the family (e.g., " My parents push me to think in an independent manner").

Finally, the strictness/supervision scale (8 items; α = .85) includes items assessing parental monitoring, in terms of parents' attempt to know the child's activities (e.g., parental knowledge (e.g., "How much do your parents try to know where you go at night") as well as of parents' actual knowledge of them (e.g., "How much do your parents really know where you go at night"). For all measures, the response scale ranged from 1 (*not at all*) to 5 (*very much*).

Collective Self-Esteem

To capture the extent to which belonging to one's own family contributes to adolescents' social identity, eight items from Luhtanen and Crocker's (1992) collective self-esteem scale were selected and adapted to family membership. Specifically, we employed the *private* collective self-esteem items to assess adolescents' personal judgment of their family (e.g., "I feel good about my family"), and the *importance to identity* items, which measure the importance of one's family membership to one's self-concept (e.g. "Belonging to my family is an important part of my self-image"; $\alpha = .83$). The response scale range from 1 (*strongly disagree*) to 5 (*strongly agree*).

Expectations for the Future

In order to measure expectations for the future, 9 items were developed. Items tapped expectations for one's own future in terms of self-fulfillment (e.g. "I see the future as a time when I will able to fulfill myself) and expectations of having satisfying intimate relationships (e.g., "My future plans include stable and satisfying couple relationships"). The response scale ranged from 1 (*not at all*) to 5 (*very much*). A preliminary factor analysis confirmed the distinction between the two factors (expectations of self-fulfillment, 5 items, $\alpha = .76$; expectations of stable intimate life, 4 items, $\alpha = .60$).

RESULTS

Collective Self-Esteem and Expectations for the Future as a Function of Parenting Style

First, to examine specific differences in collective self-esteem and expectations for the future due to the parenting style adopted within each family, families were assigned to authoritative, authoritarian, indulgent and neglectful style. Following Lamborn et al.'s (1991) procedure, scores on the warmth/acceptance and strictness/supervision dimensions were used to classify families, whereas scores on the psychological autonomy dimension were not considered since they are less effective in differentiating among the four parenting styles.

Thus, the sample was trichotomized on the two dimensions, which were considered simultaneously (cf. Maccoby & Martin, 1983): Namely, authoritative families ($N = 67$) were those who scored in the upper tertiles on both dimensions; authoritarian families ($N = 29$) were in the lowest tertile on warmth but in the highest tertiles on strictness; indulgent families ($N = 29$) were in the highest tertile on warmth but in the lowest tertile on strictness; finally, neglectful families ($N = 77$) were those who scored in the lowest tertiles on both dimensions. 199 families fell into one of the four groups. This designation of families as one type or another is of course sample specific; in order to ensure that the families represent distinct categories, families who scored in the middle tertile on either of the dimensions were not considered (cf. Lamborn et al., 1991).

A series of one-way ANOVAs, with parenting style as independent factor, was then conducted. Parenting style significantly affected collective self-esteem, $F(3, 198) = 29.76, p = .000$, expectations of self-fulfillment, $F(3, 198) = 4.83, p = .003$, and expectations of positive intimate relationships, $F(3, 198) = 10.96$, $p = .000$. As shown in Table 1, authoritative families scored higher than all the other three family groups on collective self-esteem, and scored higher than authoritarian and neglectful families on expectations of self-fulfillment. Finally, they significantly differed from neglectful families on expectations of stable intimate relationships. It is also interesting to note that adolescents living in neglectful families obtained lower scores on collective self-esteem in comparison with adolescents brought up in authoritative, authoritarian, or indulgent families.

Table 1. Mean scores of collective self-esteem and expectations for the future as a function of parenting style

	Authoritative Parenting	Authoritarian Parenting	Indulgent Parenting	Neglectful Parenting
Collective Self-Esteem	4.23a (.48)	3.56b (.58)	3.83b (.55)	3.19c (.85)
Expectations of Self-Fulfillment	3.95a (.56)	3.56b (.59)	3.94a,b (.65)	3.60b (.77)
Expectations of Stable Intimate Relationships	4.18a (.42)	3.87a,b (.60)	3.89a,b (.67)	3.61b,c (.69)

Note. Standard deviations are in parentheses. Within rows means with different subscripts are significantly different at p<.05.

Warmth, Strictness/Supervision, and Psychological Autonomy Granting as Predictors of Collective

Self-Esteem and Expectations for the Future

A series of regression analyses was conducted to examine the contribution of the three dimensions of parenting on collective self-esteem and on expectations for the future, and to test the mediating role of collective self-esteem. Following Baron and Kenny's (1986) procedure, mediation is verified when: First, the independent variables (warmth, strictness/supervision, and psychological autonomy granting) affect the mediator (collective self-esteem); second, the independent variables affect the dependent variables (expectations of self-fulfillment and expectations of stable intimate relationships); and third, when the mediator and the independent variables are entered as predictors in the same regression equations, the influence of the independent variable is reduced or becomes non-significant.

Thus, we examined the influence of the authoritative parenting dimensions on collective self-esteem. The analysis showed that warmth ($\beta = .44$, $p = .000$), strictness ($\beta = .09$, $p = .038$), and psychological autonomy granting ($\beta = .21$, $p = .000$) were all associated to collective self-esteem, $R^2 = .40$, $p = .000$, although warmth was clearly the strongest predictor. Afterwards, we tested whether the three dimensions of parenting affect expectations for the future. As shown in Table 2, when expectations of self-fulfillment were considered as dependent variable, warmth turned out to be the only significant predictor. As regards expectations of stable intimate relationships, it was significantly predicted by the three dimensions of authoritativeness. We also examined the relationship between the mediator and each dependent variable. The analyses showed that collective self-esteem predicted both expectations of self-fulfillment and expectations of stable intimate relationships.

Table 2. Results of the mediation analyses

	Expectations of Self-Fulfillment	Expectations of Stable Intimate Relationships
Parental Warmth	.18**	.19**
Parental Strictness/Supervision	-.03	.13*
Psychological Autonomy Granting	.08	.11**
R^2	.05***	.09***
Family Collective Self-Esteem	.26***	.38***
R^2	.07***	.14***
Parental Warmth	.09	.04
Parental Strictness-Supervision	-.04	.10*
Psychological Autonomy Granting	.04	.07
Family Collective Self-Esteem	.20**	.28***
R^2	.08***	.16***

Note: Values for predictors are beta weights.
* $p < .05$; ** $p < .01$; *** $p < .001$.

Finally, we tested whether collective self-esteem mediated the effects of parenting dimensions on expectations for the future. Considering expectations of self-fulfillment as dependent variable, when we entered the mediator into the regression equation, the effect of warmth became non-significant, whereas the relationship between the mediator and the dependent variable was still significant. As regards expectations of stable intimate relationships, entering the mediator into the regression equation reduced the effects of parental warmth and psychological autonomy granting to non-significance, whereas the effect of parental strictness/supervision was reduced but still significant. Thus, it can be concluded that overall, collective self-esteem mediated the influence of authoritative parenting on adolescents' expectations for the future.

DISCUSSION

The findings of the present study contribute to deepen knowledge on authoritative parenting by taking into consideration how parenting style influences adolescents' social identity and expectations for the future. First, they showed for the first time that adolescents grown up in authoritative households display higher collective self-esteem: Namely, they place more value on their family, are more proud and happy of being part of it, and consider their family as more important for their self-concept in comparison with their peers who live in authoritarian, indulgent and neglectful homes. Regression analyses further specified this evidence by revealing that, although all the three dimensions of parenting are related to collective self-esteem, warmth, and to a lesser extent psychological autonomy granting, are the better predictors of such a positive outcome. It is also important to note that, in this study, adolescents from neglectful families were those who scored lower on collective self-esteem, also in comparison with those belonging to authoritarian and indulgent families. Thus, it seems that, if authoritative families provide the highest contribution to adolescent social identity, what it is really dangerous, for a child, is growing up in a context where a low support and acceptance goes with little demandingness and absence of discipline.

Second, our findings revealed that adolescents who live in authoritative families have more positive feelings and are more confident about their future: They have higher expectations of being able to fulfill themselves than their peers brought up in authoritarian and neglectful families, and think that they will have satisfying intimate relationships to a higher extent than children from neglectful families. Thus, even though in this case the differences between the four parenting groups are not so clear-cut, in that not all the predicted comparisons were significant, overall these findings support the impact of authoritativeness on adolescents' adjustment. Again, it is worth to note that neglectful families provide the worst conditions for the child's development of positive expectations for the future, at least as regards expectations of having satisfying stable intimate relationships. Findings of the regression analyses showed that parental warmth was the only predictor of expectations of self-fulfillment, whereas all parenting dimensions were significantly related to expectations of stable intimate relationships.

Finally, our findings support the hypothesis that collective self-esteem mediates the influence of authoritative parenting on adolescents' expectations for the future. In other words, it is possible to contend that the more parents are able to create a warmth, supportive and accepting climate within the family, to ensure the child the opportunity to experience autonomy providing at the same time clear rules, limits and behavioral standards, the more the child will judge his/her family as worth and will base his/her social identity on this particular group membership; in turn, this relationship with the family will help the child to represent him/herself in the future in a positive, optimistic way.

To sum up, this study provides for the first time evidence that parenting style affects adolescents' future plans and expectations. Thus, this study, by conceptualizing family as a social group, contributes to widening the evidence on parenting style (cf. Steinberg, 2001; Steinberg & Silk, 2002) by underlining that, among the processes through which authoritativeness works, a crucial role is played by the enhancement of adolescent family collective self-esteem. Moreover, the evidence we gathered allows to contend that family collective self-esteem can be considered as an important source of support in dealing with the uncertainty of the future. Further research could pursue this line of thought in order to test whether family collective self-esteem is at the basis of pro-active behavior in achieving one's own goals.

REFERENCES

Baron, R. M., & Kenny, D. A. (1986) The moderator–mediator variable distinction in social psychological research: Conceptual, strategic, and statistical considerations. *Journal of Personality and Social Psychology, 51,* 1173–1182.

Baumrind, D. (1971). Authoritarian vs. authoritative parental control. *Adolescence, 3,* 255 - 272.

Baumrind, D. (1978). Parental disciplinary patterns and social competence in children. *Youth and Society, 9,* 239-276.

Collins, W.A., Maccoby, E., Steinberg, L., Heterington, E.M., & Bornstein, M. (2000). Contemporary research on parenting: The case for nature *and* nurture. *American Psychologist, 55,* 218-232.

Darling, N., & Steinberg, L. (1993). Parenting style as context: An integrative model. *Psychological Bulletin, 113,* 487-496.

Fletcher, A.C., Steinberg, L., & Williams-Wheeler, M. (2004). Parental influences on adolescent problem behavior: Revisiting Stattin and Kerr. *Child Development, 75,* 781-796.

Gray, M., & Steinberg, L. (1999). Unpacking authoritative parenting: Reassessing a multidimensional construct. *Journal of Marriage and the Family, 61,* 574-587.

Harris, J.R. (1995). Where is the child's environment? A group socialization theory of development. *Psychological Review, 102,* 458 - 489.

Kerr, M., & Stattin, H. (2000). What parents know, how they know it, and several forms of adolescent adjustment: Further support for a reinterpretation of monitoring. *Developmental Psychology, 36,* 366-380.

Lamborn, S.D., Mounts, N.S., Steinberg, L., & Dornbusch, S. M. (1991). Patterns of competence and adjustment among adolescents from authoritative, authoritarian, indulgent, and neglectful families. *Child Development, 62,* 1049-1065.

Luhtanen, R., & Crocker, J. (1992). A collective self-esteem scale: Self-evaluation of one's social identity. *Personality and Social Psychology Bulletin, 18,* 302-318.

Maccoby, E., & Martin, J. (1983). Socialization in the context of the family: Parent-child interaction. In E.M. Hetherington, P.H. Mussen (Eds.) *Handbook of Child Psychology: Vol. 4. Socialization, Personality, and Social Development* (p. 1-101). New York: Wiley.

Rueter, M., & Conger, R. (1998). Reciprocal influences between parenting and adolescent problem-solving behavior. *Developmental Psychology, 34,* 1470-1482.

Steinberg, L. (2001). We know some things: Parent-adolescent relationship in retrospect and prospect. *Journal of Research on Adolescence, 11,* 1 - 19.

Steinberg, L., Elmen, J.D. & Mounts, N.S. (1989). Authoritative parenting, psychosocial maturity and academic success among adolescents. *Child Development, 60,* 1424 - 1436.

Steinberg, L., Lamborn, S.D., Darling, N.S., Mounts, N.S. & Dornbusch, S.M. (1994). Over-time changes in adjustment and competence among adolescents from authoritative, authoritarian, indulgent and neglectful families. *Child Development, 65,* 754 - 770.

Steinberg, L., Lamborn, S.D., Dornbusch, S.M. & Darling, N.S. (1992). Impact of parenting practices on adolescent achievement: Authoritative parenting, school involvement, and encouragement to succeed. *Child Development, 63,* 1266 - 1281.

Steinberg, L. & Silk, J.S. (2002). Parenting adolescents. In M.H. Bornstein (Ed.) *Handbook of Parenting* (pp. 103-133). Mahwah, NJ: Lawrence Erlbaum Associates.

Tajfel, H., & Turner, J.C. (1979). An integrative theory of intergroup conflict. In W.G. Austin, & S. Worchel (Eds.), *The Social Psychology of Intergroup Relations* (pp. 33–47). Monterey, CA: Brooks/Cole.

In: Handbook of Parenting: Styles, Stresses & Strategies   ISBN 978-1-60741-766-8
Editor: Pacey H. Krause and Tahlia M. Dailey   © 2009 Nova Science Publishers, Inc.

Chapter 18

PREDICTORS OF MATERNAL AND PATERNAL PARENTING STRESS IN CENTRAL AMERICAN REFUGEE FAMILIES WITH ADOLESCENT OFFSPRING

Noorfarah Merali
University of Alberta, Edmonton, Alberta, Canada

ABSTRACT

Despite their strong presence in North America, Central American refugees have been identified as the most critically understudied Hispanic group. Relatively little is known about their cultural and familial adaptation (Dona & Berry, 1994; Guarnaccia, 1997; Organista, 2007). The cultural life of Central Americans is centered on the family and community rather than on the rugged individualism of North American society. Family and community relationships tend to have a hierarchical power structure with associated mores for interaction, in contrast to an egalitarian arrangement (Hernandez, 2005; Organista; Sue & Sue, 2008). Transmission of the culture of origin to one's children is a key focus among Central American families (Hernandez; Organista). Refugee parents have been found to have a heightened attachment to their heritage culture due to the forced rather than voluntary nature of their resettlement process in the host society (Roizblatt & Pilowsky, 1996). However, intergenerational cultural transmission may be compromised by the pressures that adolescents experience to assimilate with peers in the new socio-cultural environment. Parents may use youth's behavior and ethnic identity to gauge the effectiveness of their parenting ability and strategies, with signs of weak ethnic identity or Western cultural influence generating stress in the childrearing process (Baptiste, 1993; Hernandez; Sue & Sue). Existing research suggests that Central American mothers and fathers may play different roles in the cultural socialization of children (Harwood, Leyendecker, Carlson, Asencio, & Miller, 2002; Phinney & Vedder, 2006; Sue & Sue), implying a possible variance in indicators of adolescents' cultural stance that may serve as predictors of stress for parents of each gender.

This chapter describes a research study investigating relationships between parenting stress and adolescent ethnic identity development, adolescents' openness to behavior changes towards Western norms, and adolescents' age of migration among 100 Central American refugee families. Close to one-third of the participating parents reported high or clinically significant stress levels. Stepwise Multiple Regression Analysis revealed that in combination, adolescents' age of arrival in Canada and level of openness to behavior changes towards Western norms accounted for 37 percent of the variance in mothers' stress scores. Adolescent ethnic identity development was the only significant predictor of fathers' stress levels, accounting for 12 percent of the variance in fathers' stress scores. Relationships between these variables and maternal and paternal stress are discussed considering each parent's role in adolescents' cultural socialization. Recommendations for assisting with the parenting process across two cultures are also presented.

INTRODUCTION

In the 2006 national census, Hispanics/Latinos ranked among the five most highly represented ethnic minority groups in Canada, and they were identified as one of the nation's fastest growing ethnic populations (Statistics Canada, 2006). Hispanics are also currently the largest ethnic minority group in the United States (U.S. Census Bureau, 2000). The Hispanic community in North America consists of both immigrants and refugees (Harwood et al., 2002; Hernandez, 2005; Organista, 2007). Berry (2006) distinguishes between these two types of migrants. Immigrants are individuals who voluntarily move to another country seeking better educational, economic, or social opportunities, with the intention of permanent residence or citizenship. In contrast, refugees face forced displacement and resettlement due to social or political upheaval in their countries of origin that threatens personal and family security. Refugees may intend to permanently reside in the country of asylum or fantasize about an eventual return to their homelands once conditions improve (Berry). The largest immigrant group among the Hispanic community is Mexicans, whereas the largest refugee group among this community is Central Americans (Guarnaccia, 1997; Organista).

Central Americans include people who have come to North America fleeing political violence in their home countries of El Salvador, Guatemala, Nicaragua, Honduras, and Belize (Guarnaccia, 1997; Hernandez, 2005; Sanchez, 2003). The cultural transition process in a new society has been found to be particularly challenging for refugee families from cultures distinct from the host culture (Roizblatt & Pilowsky, 1996). This has been attributed to the combination of parents' heightened attachment to the ideals of their home countries under conditions of forced resettlement and the opposing pressures that adolescents experience to assimilate in the school environment. Despite their strong presence in North America, Central Americans have been identified as the most under-researched Hispanic group (Dona & Berry, 1994; Guarnaccia; Organista, 2007). Difficulty engaging their participation in research has been attributed to the fact that many members of this community in the United States sought asylum as undocumented or illegal refugees, fearing that participation in research may lead to identification or deportation (Organista). The present study was an attempt to address the gap in existing research on the cultural adaptation of Central Americans in North America. It aimed to examine factors related to the stress of parenting across two cultural worlds (the home and host societies), which collided through forced relocation from political violence. The study was conducted in the Canadian context.

The Acculturation Context

Berry (2006) described acculturation as the process of socio-cultural transition whereby immigrants and refugees make two related decisions: (a) a decision about the degree to which they will retain their own culture and ethnic identity, and (b) a decision about the degree to which they will interact with and adapt to members of other ethno-cultural groups. Berry emphasized that the nature of an individual or family's cultural transition experience depends heavily on the characteristics of the society of resettlement and existing policies related to diversity. Berry, Westin, Virta, Vedder, Rooney, and Sang (2006) developed a taxonomy of 13 societies of settlement based on the percentage of immigrants included in those societies and the nature of national policies related to immigration. They calculated each country's score on a diversity index taking into account: (a) variability in population ethnic origins, (b) language variance, and (c) homogeneous versus heterogeneous population subgroups. The diversity index scores ranged from 0.65 to 1.42. According to Berry et al., 19 percent of the Canadian population consists of immigrants/refugees. The official national policy of multiculturalism encourages maintenance of one's heritage culture, intergroup contact and tolerance, and simultaneous acquisition of either of the two official languages (English or French). Among the 13 countries included in their taxonomy, Canada had the highest score on the diversity index (1.42), suggesting the greatest level of population heterogeneity in ethnic and cultural make-up.

There are currently 360,235 members of the Hispanic community residing in Canada (Statistics Canada, 2006). The majority of them, 219,440 individuals, are first generation immigrants/refugees, having been born outside of Canada and faced with the process of acculturation upon their relocation. The majority of Central American refugees in Canada are from El Salvador (59,145), Guatemala (18,205) and Nicaragua (11,150), with smaller numbers having migrated from Honduras (5,845) and Belize (240) (Statistics Canada).

Central American Cultural Life

The Hispanic culture that Central Americans practice differs from North American culture in a number of fundamental ways. One of the key differences is in the emphasis on familism rather than individualism (Organista, 2007; Sue & Sue, 2008). Familism is a central value of the Hispanic culture (Chun & Akutsu, 2003; Harwood et al., 2002; Hernandez, 2005; Sabogal, Marin, Otero-Sabogal, VanOss Marin, & Perez-Stable, 1987). It consists of three dimensions: (a) a perceived obligation to assist the family, (b) a belief that the family should be a source of social support, and (c) a belief that family members should be the primary referents for an individual's values and behavior (Sabogal et al.). In relation to the family's cultural transition process in North America, parents are expected to be the guides or role models for the maintenance of culturally appropriate behavior among their offspring. Organista describes two terms that are commonly used among the Hispanic community to refer to youth, which clearly reflect how their diversion from following parental role modeling of traditional behaviors is viewed: "Bien educado" refers to youth who are perceived to be raised properly in accordance with traditional values. In contrast, "Mal criado" refers to youth who are perceived as being poorly raised and as having lost their traditional culture to North American influence (p. 143). The emphasis on familism rather than individualism in the Hispanic culture also deemphasizes personal autonomy among youth in favor of respect for parental authority and family obligations (Fuligni, Tseng, & Lam, 1999; Harwood et al.).

A major difference in relationships among Central Americans from North American cultural norms is their hierarchical structure. "Respeto" or respect is shown by deference to the authority of individuals with higher status in relationships either by parenthood, birth order, or gender (Organista, 2007, p. 143). Avoidance of conflict and unassertive communication are often emphasized in the socialization of children (Hernandez, 2005; Organista; Sue & Sue, 2008). In terms of the daily cultural life of Central Americans, Spanish language use, religious practice in the form of Catholicism, and affiliation with other members of the Hispanic community is strongly encouraged (Organista; Hernandez; Sue & Sue).

Developmental Tasks of Parents and Adolescents

According to Erikson's (1963, 1968) theory of psychosocial development, the key developmental task of mid-life is to make a valuable contribution to the lives of future generations. Difficulties making one's contribution can precipitate task-related stress. The mid-life stage in Erikson's model represents the age bracket of most parents of adolescents, for whom this task translates into an attempt to provide their children with the skills needed to become successful members of society. For immigrant and refugee parents, a central part of the parenting process is the transmission of their cultural heritage (Baptiste, 1993; Santisteban & Mitrani, 2003). If they find this developmental task to be challenging, parenting stress is likely to result.

Parents' primary developmental task interacts with the developmental task of their adolescents. For adolescents, the key developmental task is the establishment of a consolidated identity. Achievement of an identity involves exploration of a variety of values and behaviors, with the result of making a conscious commitment to a chosen way of being (Erikson, 1963, 1968). For immigrant and refugee adolescents, the task of achieving a consolidated identity involves examining and resolving their attitudes towards their own cultural group and the majority group in the host nation (Berry, 2006; Phinney, 2003). These two components of identity are labeled ethnic identity and civic identity, respectively (Berry; Phinney).

When adolescents make behavioral changes towards Western norms, parents often report that they feel ineffective in the transmission of their cultural heritage; they tend to express distress about losing the authority to influence their children (Baptiste, 1993; Hernandez, 2005; Merali, 2004; Roizblatt & Pilowsky, 1996; Sue & Sue, 2008). These reactions occur despite the fact that cultural change does not preclude retention of one's ethnic identity or integration of the home and host cultures (Berry, 2006; Phinney, 2003). In their cross-sectional study of three generations of Hispanic adolescents (using a mixed sample of Hispanic groups), Perez and Padilla (2000) found that although adolescents tended to display a greater orientation towards the host culture over time and across generations, they still maintained allegiance to Hispanic family values.

In a qualitative study conducted by Merali (2004), Central American refugee parents reported close parental monitoring of their adolescents' behavior to assess their degree of culture retention and assimilation into the host culture. When they perceived their adolescents' Hispanic ethnic identity to be weakening due to the adoption of behaviors characteristic of Western norms modeled by their peers, they reported increasing their direct supervision of youth. This occurred by spending more time with them and taking on a chaperone role when the youth interacted with non-Hispanic peers. In addition, the parents reported countering the youth's exposure to North American culture outside of the home with informal, cultural and religious education in the home context. Central American parents in the Merali study utilized various terms to describe the stress they experienced when they perceived their adolescents to be losing their culture, such as sadness, agony, fear, craziness, and desperation.

Parent Gender and Youth's Age of Arrival in Canada

Existing research suggests that mothers and fathers may play different roles in the cultural socialization of children (Harwood et al., 2002; Phinney & Vedder, 2006; Organista, 2007; Sue & Sue, 2008). In the gendered division of labor in Hispanic and Central American families, mothers tend to be cultural role models for traditional behavior, whereas fathers tend to be the actual enforcers of culturally appropriate behavior. A number of studies reviewed by Harwood et al. (2002) compared the behaviors of Central American mothers and mothers of other Hispanic subgroups with mothers of European or North American backgrounds. In these studies, the Hispanic mothers were found to attend closely to child behavior and coach child behavior in appropriate directions by focusing on their own behaviors and thoughts rather than on those of the child (Harwood et al.). Fathers tend to be the primary authority figures and disciplinarians in the Central American family (Hernandez, 2005; Organista; Sue & Sue). However, there may be greater sharing of authority among acculturated dual-career families, and more child discipline on the part of mothers of infants (Harwood et al.; Hernandez). In a recent large-scale study of family cultural adaptation among a mixed ethnic sample including Central American refugees, Phinney and Vedder (2006) found that fathers played a greater role in restricting adolescents' rights and behavior and emphasizing family/cultural obligations than mothers.

The level of cultural role modeling and discipline required to facilitate the intergenerational transmission of the family's cultural heritage and some level of adaptation to the new environment may vary with an adolescent's age of arrival in the host society. Older children may face greater challenges in integrating into established peer groups in the host culture school system without being open to some cultural changes or adjustments, which could prompt parental reactions (Padilla, 2006). However, at the same time, older youth may have had the greatest entrenchment in their own culture, making the integration process difficult and warranting additional parental guidance and assistance (Padilla). Padilla posited that adolescents who arrive in the host society at later ages may pose greater challenges for parents. The advanced cognitive development that accompanies increasing age may increase their likelihood of questioning parental authority and teachings and the pressures coming from the host society.

Purpose of the Study

Since the central developmental task of the life stage of parenthood involves intergenerational cultural transmission among refugee families, it is plausible that both mothers' and fathers' levels of parenting stress may be related to their adolescents' ethnic identity development, acceptance of North American behavior patterns, and age of arrival in Canada. However, it is possible that fathers' stress levels may be more vulnerable to fluctuations in youth's identity development, given their more direct role in heritage culture maintenance. The purpose of this study was to predict parenting stress levels of Central American refugee mothers and fathers based on their adolescents' ethnic identity development, degree of openness to North American behavior patterns, and adolescents' age of arrival. The study also aimed to investigate possible gender differences in the relationships between these variables and their predictive value in contributing to parenting stress. The results would inform recommendations for family interventions to assist Central American refugee parents with the parenting process across two cultural worlds.

METHOD

Participants

Recruitment and Study Criteria

The research participants were recruited through immigrant-serving agencies and Hispanic cultural community associations in two major Canadian cities. Bilingual and bicultural (English and Spanish-speaking) settlement/community workers in these settings were provided with one-page study descriptions to distribute to Central American refugee families who met the criteria for inclusion in the study. There were three criteria for involvement in this research: (a) refugee status, (b) being first generation immigrants (i.e., both the parents and adolescents were foreign-born), and (c) the family includes an adolescent between the ages of 12 and 18. The study descriptions included the names and contact information of these bicultural workers who were hired as research assistants. Potential participants were instructed to contact them to arrange convenient dates, times, and locations for questionnaire administration. Study descriptions were created in both English and Spanish. The process of forward and backward translation (Larson, 1984) was used: One staff member at the local Language Bank translated the English version of the study description into Spanish, and another bilingual expert reproduced the English version from the first language variant. Inconsistencies in meaning were resolved through consensus in developing a final version of the study information to communicate to potential participants.

Family Socio-Demographic Characteristics

The obtained sample consisted of 100 Central American refugee parent-adolescent dyads (200 individual participants). Their countries of origin included El Salvador (40%), Nicaragua (19%), Guatemala (13%), Honduras (18%) and Belize (10%). The Central American refugees had resided in Canada for an average of 12 years ($SD = 7$), although their level of tenure in the host society ranged from 1 year to 15 years. The mean ages of the parent and adolescent participants were 41.78 years ($SD = 6.70$) and 14.00 years ($SD = 1.79$), respectively. The ages of participating adolescents varied from 12 to 18.The parents' age of arrival in Canada ranged from 20 to 58 ($M = 29.49$, $SD = 10.66$). The adolescents' age of arrival in Canada ranged from 1 to 17, with the average age of arrival of the Central American adolescents being 8.15 years ($SD = 4.53$).

Sixty-seven of the participating Central American refugee parents were mothers and 33 were fathers. Among the participating mothers, there was a fairly even distribution of those participating in the study with their adolescent daughters and those participating in the study with their sons (37 same gender parent-adolescent dyads versus 30 opposite-gender parent-adolescent dyads). Similarly, approximately half of the fathers were partaking in the study with their adolescent daughters (16), whereas the other half were partaking in the study with their sons (17).

The average family size of the study participants was 4 members ($SD = 1.23$). On average, the parents tended to have 2 children, with one of them being an adolescent ($SD = .63$). Seventy of the participating parents were married, 22 were separated or divorced, 2 were widowed, and 6 were single parents. The number of years of schooling that the parents had completed ranged from 0–25 years, with an average of 13 years of education ($SD = 4.34$). At the time of the study, the majority of the parents were working full-time (59 parents). Nineteen of the parents were employed on a part-time basis, 11 were unemployed, and 11 were students.

Of the 78 parents who were employed, 19 (24.36%) were working in professional occupations such as medicine, nursing, accounting, and computer programming. Eleven (14.10%) of them were working in semi-professional roles, such as data entry and records management, home-care assistants, and laboratory assistants. The remaining employed parents were working in skilled trades, such as carpentry, mechanics, or seamstress positions (15: 19.23%), or in manual labor positions (33: 42.30%).

Materials

Assessment of Parenting Stress

The Central American parents completed the Incompetence Scale of the Stress Index for Parents of Adolescents (SIPA; Sheras, Abidin, & Konold, 1998). The 8 items are written at a fifth-grade reading level. They solicit self-evaluations of one's parenting ability and difficulty controlling, influencing, and handling adolescent behaviour on a 5-point Likert scale (Strongly Disagree to Strongly Agree). The items directly address various ways in which existing literature suggests that parents engaged in the parenting process across two cultures may perceive their authority and control over children changing as a result of acculturation into the host society. The scale includes an item examining parents' degree of self-blame about not being able to influence adolescent behavior as well, which could capture a reduction in parenting self-efficacy if attempts to transmit the family's cultural heritage to adolescent offspring are unsuccessful. Some items on the scale are reverse scored, and the scale is scored using a scoring template developed by the test creators (Sheras et al., 1998). The minimum and maximum scores on this scale are 5 and 40, respectively. Higher scores on the SIPA indicate higher parenting stress levels (Swearer, 2001).

Reviews of the scale properties across studies identify an internal consistency coefficient above .80. Evidence of its validity comes from inverse correlations with scores on the Family Adaptability and Cohesion Scales (FACES-III), as well as from different frequencies of mental health service use among parents with high and low stress scores (Jones, 2001). The instrument was developed in English and has recently been translated into Spanish. In the present study, an assessment of the internal consistency of the Spanish version of the SIPA 8-item scale resulted in a Cronbach's alpha of .80, attesting to equivalent psychometric properties of the English version.

Assessment of Adolescent Ethnic Identity Development

Adolescent participants completed the Revised Multigroup Ethnic Identity Measure (MEIM; Roberts, Phinney, Masse, Chen, Roberts, & Romero, 1999). The MEIM assesses ethnic identity development. It conceptualizes ethnic identity as a continuous variable involving exploration of one's cultural heritage through questioning, learning about, and practicing cultural traditions, values, and behaviors, with the result of making a commitment to a personalized, positive ethnic identity (Phinney, 2003; Roberts et al., 1999). The 12 items directly match this conceptualization. The measure is scored by obtaining the mean item score across the 12 items. Mean item scores range from 1 to 4. Higher scores on the measure reflect a strong sense of attachment with and commitment to the heritage culture, whereas lower scores reflect a weak identification with one's cultural heritage (Phinney, 2003).

Roberts et al. (1999) obtained evidence of the instrument's construct validity among an ethnically mixed sample including 253 Central Americans; factor analysis grouped the items into two distinct but interrelated factors: Exploration and Active Involvement in Ethnic Group, and Affirmation, Belonging, and Identity Commitment. An assessment of the internal consistency of the measure yielded a Cronbach's alpha of .81 among the research sample (Roberts et al.). The MEIM was recently translated into Spanish. In the present study, an assessment of the internal consistency of the Spanish version of the 12-item MEIM yielded a Cronbach's alpha of .88, attesting to its high reliability.

Assessment of Parents' and Adolescents' Openness to Behavior Changes Towards Western Cultural Norms

The Behaviour Questionnaire (Merali & Violato, 2002) was used to evaluate the Central American refugee parents' and youth's openness to shifts in adolescent behavior in the direction of North American ways of being. This instrument consists of 24 items addressing prototypical behavioral shifts that adolescents often make during the acculturation process in the host society. The behavioral shifts cover the areas of individualistic/autonomous behaviors (such as moving out on one's own prior to marriage or spending more time with friends than family), interaction patterns (including interaction with members of other cultures and genders and adopting assertive communication methods), friendship and dating preferences, and Western cultural participation (e.g., English language use, use of popular media, etc.). The items were developed with reference to the literature on immigrant and refugee families, and in consultation with 14 bicultural psychologists, social workers, and settlement workers spanning 7 different cultural groups. The bicultural consultants included a psychologist and settlement worker from the Central American refugee community.

Respondents are asked to indicate the degree to which they perceive each behavior to be acceptable on a 5 point Likert scale; a rating of 1 represents a judgement that the behavior is completely unacceptable, whereas a rating of 5 represents a judgement that the behavior is completely acceptable. For the purpose of this study, respondents were asked to rate the degree to which their parent or adolescent views the behaviors to be acceptable in addition to reporting their own behavior judgements. Therefore, each of the 24 items on the Behaviour Questionnaire had two 5 point Likert scales attached to it, one with a "What You Think" heading and another with a "What Your Parent or Teen Thinks" heading, as utilized in a study by Merali (2002). The maximum and minimum scores for each of these rating scales across the 24 items on the Behaviour Questionnaire are 120 and 24, respectively.

Having both parents and adolescents provide self-ratings on the Behaviour Questionnaire as well as providing their perceived ratings for the other family member allows for the calculation of two additional scores: (a) a perceived intergenerational difference score, and (b) an actual intergenerational difference score. The perceived intergenerational difference can be calculated by subtracting the total Behaviour Questionnaire self-rating score from the estimated total score for the other family member. The actual intergenerational difference is calculated by subtracting the parent's total self-rating score from the adolescents' total self-rating score of openness/acceptance of cultural change. These scores provide important descriptive information about family dynamics during the cultural transition process by differentiating between parents' and adolescents' appraisals of intergenerational discrepancies in acculturation in the family and family realities (Merali, 2002).

The Behaviour Questionnaire is available in English and Spanish, as well as in a number of other languages. A factor analysis of the Behaviour Questionnaire yielded 4 factors consistent with the item topics described above (Merali, 1996). Merali and Violato (2002) conducted a reliability assessment of the instrument across 7 different cultural and language groups. They found that the Behaviour Questionnaire has high internal consistency. They obtained Cronbach's alphas ranging from .91 to .93 across the language groups, including Spanish (Merali & Violato).

Obtaining Family Socio-Demographic Data and Informed Consent

Both parent and adolescent participants also completed a Family Information Form addressing their status on demographic variables. On this form, respondents were asked to list the first and last names of all immediate family members to facilitate accurate matching of parent and adolescent data sets. An Informed Consent Form was administered to participants prior to the completion of the Family Information Form and all other study questionnaires.

Translation of Study Materials and Accommodation of Participants' Language Preferences

The Family Information Form and Informed Consent Form were submitted to assessors at the local Immigrant Language and Vocational Assessment Centre for modification. The assessors simplified the language used to ensure comprehension by individuals with low levels of English proficiency. They also suggested changes in wording that would facilitate clear and accurate translation of study materials into Spanish. The materials were translated using the process of forward and backward translation described earlier (Larson, 1984). Both

English and first language versions of all study materials were made available to participants to account for variable levels of first and second language proficiency.

There was significant variability in participants' comfort and literacy in English and Spanish across the two generations. This was elucidated by the fact that 84 of the 100 Central American refugee parents chose to complete the study questionnaires in Spanish, whereas 83 of the 100 participating adolescents chose to complete the study questionnaires in English.

Procedure

Pernice (1994) reported that refugees are most receptive to participating in research when the research occurs in contexts that are already familiar to them. Inclusion of members of their own cultural communities in study implementation can also facilitate involvement. Such conditions seem to offset skepticism about the principal investigator's intentions based on refugees' lack of familiarity with social science studies, and fears about how research participation may affect their immigration status or risk of deportation (Pernice). Taking these findings into account, questionnaire administration primarily occurred on-site at the immigrant-serving agencies or cultural community associations from which participants were recruited. Two bilingual and bicultural (Hispanic) members of the staff at each agency/association were hired as research assistants; one individual was responsible for administering study materials to parents, whereas the other individual was responsible for concurrently administering them to adolescents.

On-site questionnaire administration was scheduled on an individual basis with each parent-adolescent dyad, with the parent and adolescent completing the questionnaires in different rooms. The dates and times of the questionnaire administration process were arranged according to participants' convenience. A small proportion of Central American families (20 parent-adolescent dyads) requested that the questionnaires be administered through a home visit. The bilingual research assistants accommodated their requests and followed the same procedure separating parents and adolescents in different rooms for questionnaire administration.

In each questionnaire administration session, the bilingual research assistants introduced themselves and provided a brief overview of the purpose and nature of the study as addressed in the Informed Consent Form. They also made it clear that both English and first language versions of all study materials would be available. They informed the participants that they would be present to answer any questions throughout the procedure and explained that adolescents' questionnaire responses would not be shared with their parents and vice versa. After participants signed the Informed Consent Forms and parents also signed their adolescents' consent forms, the Family Information Form and the other study questionnaires were provided to each participant according to his/her language preference.

The research assistants provided an orientation to responding to Likert scale items prior to having the parent or adolescent complete each questionnaire. This orientation utilized a few sample items from each instrument to demonstrate anchors for the highest rating, lowest rating, and ratings ranging around the mid-point of the scale. Tran (1993) found this type of orientation to help refugees who are unfamiliar with survey research better understand the response process and to utilize a wider range of scale responses. The orientation process can help to prevent limited responding using only the highest or lowest points of the scale or biased responding.

The questionnaire explanation and administration process took approximately half an hour for each parent-adolescent dyad. Upon the parent and adolescent's completion of the questionnaires, each family member was given a small remuneration of $10 for study participation. The obtained data was coded and scored by a graduate research assistant, and was subsequently analyzed by the principal investigator.

RESULTS

Descriptive Information

Parenting Stress Scores
Central American refugee parents' scores on the SIPA scale used for this study ranged from 9 to 33, with an average score of 21.02 (SD = 5.42). Scores at or below 23 are considered to represent normative levels of parenting stress, whereas scores of 24 and 25 suggest a high degree of parenting stress, and scores from 26 and up indicate clinically significant stress levels according to published norms for this scale (Sheras et al., 1998). Sixty-seven of the 100 parents in this study had parenting stress scores at or below 23, 10 had scores of 24 or 25, and 23 of the parents had stress scores ranging from 26 to 33. Therefore, one-third of the Central American refugee parents who participated in this study reported high or clinically significant levels of parenting stress.

A separate examination of mothers' and fathers' parenting stress scores revealed similarities in stress levels. Central American refugee mothers' parenting stress scores ranged from 9 to 33, with an average score of 21.25 (SD = 5.56). Forty-five of the 67 mothers in the study had parenting stress scores at or below 23 (67%). Four mothers (6%) had scores between 24 and 25, and the remaining 18 mothers (27%) had scores in the high or clinical range. Central American refugee fathers' parenting stress scores ranged from 9 to 31, with an average score of 20.58 (SD = 5.18). Twenty-three of the 33 fathers had parenting stress scores at or below 23 (70%), whereas 10 (30%) had scores reflecting high or clinically significant stress levels.

Adolescent Ethnic Identity Scores
The average mean item score on the MEIM for the Central American refugee adolescents who participated in this study was 3.14 (SD = .49), suggesting that overall, the youth had a fairly strong identification with their ethnic heritage. Their mean item scores ranged from 1.83 to 4.0, the maximum score on the measure. Their average score of 3.14 is consistent with the level of ethnic identity development of adolescents from this cultural group who participated in Roberts et al. (1999) study, which was an average score of 3.03 across 253 Central American youth.

Besides the numerical items on the MEIM, there are a few open-ended items asking respondents to label their ethnic identity and to identify the labels their parents would use to describe themselves. These items yield important insights about how the youth and their families are perceived to situate themselves between the heritage culture and the surrounding host culture. These items are worded as: "I would describe myself and my ethnicity as:" and "My father/mother considers himself/herself to be:" Respondents are provided with a number of options that reflect a sole identification with one's heritage culture, a sole identification with the host culture (Canadian culture in this study), or identification with both cultures, as indicated through selection of terms such as Central American Canadian, Latino Canadian, or Hispanic Canadian.

Forty-six of the 100 adolescents who participated in this study self-identified as bicultural, choosing either one of the following three labels: Latino Canadian (30), Hispanic Canadian (10), or Central American Canadian (6). The next most common form of self-identification among the youth was based on the heritage culture, with 32 of them identifying themselves as either Latino (13), Hispanic (11), or Central American (8). Twelve of the adolescents identified themselves as Canadian, whereas the remaining 10 adolescents selected "other" or "multiple", suggesting the possibility of them having a mixed heritage that may affect their self-identification patterns.

Parents' and Adolescents' Openness to Behavior Changes Towards Western Norms

The Central American refugee parents' self-rating scores on the Behaviour Questionnaire ranged from 35 to 99, with a mean of 63.94 (SD = 13.86), suggesting a moderate degree of openness to cultural change on the part of their children. The parents rated their adolescents' Behaviour Questionnaire scores to range between 41 to 120, with a mean of 84.01 (SD = 16.53). Thus, the parents perceived the adolescents in the family to be much more receptive to making changes towards Western norms than the parents were; the average degree of perceived discrepancy about cultural change in the parent-adolescent dyad based on parents' perspectives was 20.46 points (SD = 14.45) on the Behaviour Questionnaire.

The Central American adolescents' self-rating scores on the Behaviour Questionnaire ranged from 44 to 114, attesting to the variability in their acceptance of behavioral shifts towards the host culture. The average self-rating score of the adolescents was 85.17 (SD =16.19), reflecting a fairly open stance regarding making changes towards Western norms. This mean score is very close to parents' estimates of their adolescents' acceptance of cultural change above. The adolescents rated their parents' Behaviour Questionnaire scores to range between 37 and 108, with an average score of 68.43 (SD = 13.78), which is very close to the parents' self-reported views. The average discrepancy in openness to cultural change that the adolescents perceived to exist in the parent-adolescent dyad was 17.69 points on the Behaviour Questionnaire (SD = 12.64). The calculation of the actual intergenerational difference in acceptance of behavior changes towards Western norms in each parent-adolescent dyad yielded an average difference score of 22.92 points (SD=15.37) on the Behaviour Questionnaire.

Multiple Regression Analysis Findings

Stepwise Multiple Regression Analysis was utilized to separately predict maternal and paternal parenting stress scores among the Central American refugee sample based on: (a) adolescents' ethnic identity scores on the MEIM, (b) adolescents' Behaviour Questionnaire self-rating scores, and (c) the youth's age of arrival in Canada. In the Stepwise Multiple Regression procedure, variables that meet statistical criteria for having a significant relationship with the dependent variable and other variables in the regression equation are entered into the equation one at a time, and variables that do not contribute to the prediction of the dependent variable are removed. The criterion for variables entering the equation to predict the dependent variable is a probability value of the F of $< = .05$ and the criterion for removing a variable from the prediction equation is a probability of F being $> = .10$. The Stepwise procedure provides the most insight and understanding about the most important variable or combination among a set of variables that can account for variability in the dependent variable (Tabachnick & Fidell, 1996), in this case, parenting stress scores.

The Stepwise Multiple Regression Analysis to predict Central American refugee mothers' parenting stress began with adolescents' Behaviour Questionnaire self-rating score, followed by the addition of their age of arrival in Canada. Adolescents' MEIM scores were excluded from the regression due to a failure to meet criteria for strength of their relationship with maternal parenting stress scores. The correlation between maternal stress and adolescents' ethnic identity scores on the MEIM was almost non-existent (r (65) = -.06, p = .62). In the final two-variable regression model, the multiple correlation between adolescents' Behaviour Questionnaire self-rating scores, age of arrival in Canada, and maternal parenting stress scores was $R=.63$. The adjusted R^2 was 36.5, suggesting that a combination of adolescents' age of arrival in Canada and degree of openness to cultural changes towards Western behaviors accounted for approximately 37 percent of the variance in Central American mothers' stress scores, F (2, 64) = 11.06, $p < .001$. An examination of the t-test results for these two variables suggested that each variable independently significantly explained some unique variance in mothers' stress scores, t (64) = -2.87, $p < .01$ for adolescents' Behaviour Questionnaire self-rating scores and t (64) = 2.21, $p < .05$ for adolescents' age of arrival. An examination of the nature of the relationships between the variables revealed that the variables were also related to each other: Adolescents' openness to making behavioral changes towards Western norms on the Behaviour Questionnaire was inversely related to their age of arrival in Canada (r (65) = -.41, $p <.05$) and had a mild inverse relationship with maternal stress (r (65) = -.20, $p <.05$). Adolescents' age of arrival in Canada was strongly positively associated with their mothers' stress scores (r (65) =.53, $p <.01$), suggesting that mothers of adolescents who were older at the time of migration were experiencing greater levels of distress in the parenting process.

The Stepwise Multiple Regression Analysis to predict Central American fathers' parenting stress scores began with the entry of their adolescents' ethnic identity scores on the MEIM and concluded at that step. The other two variables did not add any predictive power to understanding fathers' stress levels. Adolescent ethnic identity scores were a significant predictor of fathers' parenting stress scores, F (1, 31) =5.13 $p < .05$, such that lower levels of youth ethnic identity development related to higher levels of parenting stress (r (31) = -.38, $p < .05$). Adolescent ethnic identity development scores accounted for approximately 12 percent of the variance in fathers' stress levels, according to the adjusted R^2 value. Although adolescents' degree of openness to cultural change on the Behaviour Questionnaire was positively correlated with fathers' stress levels (r (31) = .36, $p < .05$), this variable appeared to only relate to fathers' mental health through its inverse relationship with ethnic identity development scores. The more open adolescents were to behavior changes towards Western cultural norms, the weaker their sense of ethnic identity (r (31) =-.37, $p < .05$), and the more concerning was this situation for their fathers. Adolescents' age of arrival in Canada was not significantly related to fathers' stress levels (r (31) = .16, $p = .37$).

CONCLUSION

The parenting process across two cultural worlds imposes significant challenges for both mothers and fathers. The fact that one-third of the Central American refugee parents who participated in this study reported high or clinically significant levels of parenting stress, and that similar proportions of mothers and fathers reported high stress levels, attests to the prevalence of parenting difficulties. The specific parenting stress scale used assessed difficulties influencing, controlling, and managing adolescent behavior. It also assessed parental self-blame and guilt for inappropriate adolescent behaviors or ineffective parenting strategies. The experience of parenting stress as expressed by self-report is affected by parental factors, child factors, and factors related to the nature of the parent-child relationship (Sheras et al., 1998). Refugee parenting efforts may be complicated by parents' own level of acculturation into the host society. Factors such as their level of English language proficiency, familiarity with and ability to independently access/interact with host society systems, like the school and health care systems, and degree of interaction with members of other groups, may impact their degree of parental authority versus reliance on children for help (Padilla, 2006). Low levels of integration into the host society on the part of parents may also exacerbate fears about losing youth to the surrounding culture (Padilla). Differences between parents' and adolescents' openness to cultural change towards Western behaviors, which were reported in the descriptive information section, may contribute to increased conflict in the parent-adolescent relationship (Baptiste, 1993; Hernandez, 2005; Sue & Sue, 2008). Intergenerational conflicts may be a source of stress for parents (Baptiste; Hernandez; Sue & Sue).

This study specifically examined the relationship between child factors and parenting stress. Specifically, it examined how two different indices of adolescents' cultural stance related to maternal and paternal parenting stress: Adolescents' levels of openness to behavioral changes towards Western norms and their level of ethnic identity development. It also examined how the demographic variable of adolescents' age of arrival in Canadian society related to parenting stress levels. Given that parenting stress is affected by parent, child, and parent-child interaction factors, the fact that a combination of adolescents' level of acceptance of behavioral changes towards Western norms and their age of arrival accounted for 37 percent of variance in mothers' stress scores is substantial. Hispanic mothers are often positioned as role models for culturally appropriate behavior, and have been found to attend to and more closely monitor youth behavior than mothers of European descent (Harwood et al., 2002). Therefore, it is not surprising that mothers' stress levels heightened in relation to adolescents' acceptance of departures from the heritage culture, rather than being related to their level of ethnic identity. In the case of mothers, there was a stronger relationship between age of arrival of adolescents in Canada and mothers' stress levels. This suggested that older adolescents may pose particular challenges for mothers in their attempts to facilitate the youth's adaptation into the new cultural environment while simultaneously encouraging cultural maintenance. Padilla (2006) discussed the integration challenges of youth who are older at the time of migration and the challenges that less acculturated parents may have in helping them to thrive in the new society.

The adolescent factor of ethnic identity development was inversely related to fathers' reports of parenting stress, accounting for approximately 12 percent of the variance in fathers' stress scores. Since previous research has highlighted the role of fathers as the enforcers of the heritage culture identity among youth (Organista, 2007; Sue & Sue, 2008), weak attachment to the ethnic culture may lead fathers to feel ineffective in the parenting role. This study has uncovered the unique contributions of different indicators of adolescents' cultural stance and demographic characteristics on maternal and paternal parenting stress in relation to the gendered division of labor in Central American families. The research findings suggest that parents may gauge their parenting efforts on indicators of adolescents' cultural integration into the home and host cultures.

FAMILY INTERVENTIONS

The prevalence of high parenting stress among the sample and the relationships between parenting stress and indicators of youth's cultural integration into the home and host cultures suggest the need for family intervention to promote better personal and cultural adaptation. Little support exists to enable refugee parents to work in collaboration with their adolescents to achieve their developmental task of maximizing home culture transmission, while facilitating youth's developmental task of becoming bicultural (Padilla, 2006). Supple, Ghazarian, Frabutt, Plunkett, and Sands (2006) found that pairing family ethnic socialization with harsh discipline for departures from culturally appropriate behavior decreases rather than increases adolescents' affirmation of their ethnic heritage. In contrast, a combination of family ethnic socialization and a high level of parental involvement in adolescents' lives was found to be significantly positively associated with youth's affirmation of their Hispanic culture (Supple et al.). Also, as Perez and Padilla (2000) reported in their research study described earlier, even when adolescents take on some of the values and behaviors of the host society, they still retain core Hispanic cultural values. As refugee parents, Central American parents may be particularly attached to their countries of origin and heritage culture since their migration was involuntary, making it more difficult to accept adolescents' cultural shifts towards the host society (Hernandez, 2005).

There are two newly developed family interventions that appear to be very applicable and potentially helpful for assisting Central American refugee parents with effective parenting across two cultural worlds if used in combination. The first is the Culture and Migration Dialogue Technique (Hernandez, 2005). As Hernandez describes:

> This approach emphasizes a psychohistorical account of the family's migration experience. Beginning with an exploration of the family members' lives before migration and the circumstances surrounding their decision to leave their country, they recount their migration experience. They talk about the social and economic changes they have experienced through the process of adaptation and acculturation, and about losses (p. 189).

This approach ties together a family's experience of involuntary migration due to socio-political upheaval in their country of origin and the personal and cultural adjustment process that has followed in the host society. It can serve to make parents' and adolescents' initial stance towards their home and host culture explicit, and to promote mutual understanding of these initial cultural viewpoints.

The second intervention that appears potentially beneficial in reducing parenting stress and in promoting youth's successful bicultural adaptation among Central American refugee families is the Entre Dos Mundos (Between Two Worlds) bicultural family skill building program. This program was developed by Bacallao and Smokowski (2005) specifically for use with Hispanic immigrant families across cultural subgroups. Three of the guiding principles of the program relate directly to the findings of this study: (a) intervention with families should aim to reduce parents' anxiety about losing their adolescents to the host culture, (b) it should aim to promote youth's bicultural identity development to ensure their success in the surrounding society, and (c) intervention should strengthen family cohesion by increasing parents' and youth's empathy for each other's viewpoints and integration challenges. The program involves eight lessons that bring groups of family members together to discuss the process of cultural adaptation in a new society and actively generate solutions that will promote effective coping. Issues covered in the lessons include the specific worries parents have about their adolescents and vice versa, and what each family member can do to reduce these worries on other family members' parts. For example, youth who have adopted some behaviors characteristic of the host society may express to their parents their retention of Hispanic values of familism and respeto. Another issue covered is how parents and youth communicate when cultural conflicts arise in the family. They work to identify ways that differences in cultural perspectives can be more effectively negotiated. The family problem solving that occurs could lead to decreased use of authoritarian parenting methods and more parent-child collaboration to increase adolescents' affirmation of their ethnic heritage. Ways of balancing demands across both cultures and those stemming from adolescents' immersion in the host society school system are also addressed. Avenues for increasing parental involvement in various areas of adolescent participation outside of the family, such as schools, peer groups, and community associations, are also explored (Bacallao & Smokowski).

LIMITATIONS

The present study has two limitations. First, the study employed a relatively small, non-random sample. Many studies of refugees use non-probability samples; randomly-selected individuals may feel obligated to participate on the basis of cultural norms surrounding respect for authority (Pernice, 1994). Since Central Americans have been difficult to access for research participation, the fact that the sample still included refugees from various countries of origin within Central America and varying socio-demographic profiles would serve to provide useful information about this group's experiences. Nevertheless, the sample characteristics and size could limit the generalizability of the research findings to all members of the Central American refugee community.

Second, the use of self-report measures may elicit socially desirable responses. However, reports of high parenting stress among the research participants suggest that their responses were not limited by concerns about self-presentation or the stigma associated with experiencing difficulties in the parenting process. Similarly, the fact that Central American youth's ethnic identity scores were similar to scores for this ethnic group obtained in other research studies supports the authenticity of their responses.

DIRECTIONS FOR FUTURE RESEARCH

Central American refugees have a strong presence in North America. It is extremely important to develop a better understanding of their familial and cultural adaptation to promote their successful integration into the host society. Central Americans may face unique parenting challenges associated with their refugee status and cultural differences between their home culture and the host culture. The level of stress they experience during the parenting process may vary with adolescents' age of arrival in Canada and indices of their integration into the home and host cultures. Interventions such as the Culture and Migration Dialogue Technique (Hernandez, 2005) and the Entre Dos Mundos (Bacallao & Smokowski, 2005) program may help to minimize the occurrence of parenting stress in the intergenerational cultural transmission process. Future studies should evaluate the effectiveness of these interventions in reducing parenting stress among Central American refugee families.

ACKNOWLEDGMENTS

This study was funded by a Standard Research Grant from the Social Sciences and Humanities Research Council of Canada.

REFERENCES

Bacallao, M. L., & Smokowski, P. R. (2005). "Entre Dos Mundos" (Between two worlds): Bicultural skills training with Latino immigrant families. *The Journal of Primary Prevention, 26,* 485-509.

Baptiste, D. A. (1993). Immigrant families, adolescents, and acculturation: Insights for therapists. *Marriage and Family Review, 19,* 341-363.

Berry, J. W. (2006). Contexts of acculturation. In D. L. Sam & J. W. Berry (Eds.), *The Cambridge handbook of acculturation psychology* (pp. 27-42). New York: Cambridge University Press.

Berry, J. W., Westin, C., Virta, E., Vedder, P., Rooney, R., & Sang, D. (2006). Design of the study: Selecting societies of settlement and immigrant groups. In J. W. Berry, J. S. Phinney, D. L. Sam, & P. Vedder (Eds.), *Immigrant youth in cultural transition: Acculturation, identity, and adaptation across national contexts* (pp. 15-46). Mahwah, NJ: Lawrence Earlbaum Associates.

Chun, K. M., & Akutsu, P. D. (2003). Acculturation among ethnic minority families. In K. M. Chun, P. B. Organista, & G. Marin (Eds.), *Acculturation: Advances in theory, measurement, and applied research* (pp. 95-120). Washington, DC: American Psychological Association.

Dona, G., & Berry, J. W. (1994). Acculturation attitudes and acculturative stress of Central American refugees. *International Journal of Psychology, 29*(1), 57-70.

Erikson, E. (1963). *Childhood and society.* New York: W. W. Norton.

Erikson, E. (1968). *Identity: Youth and crisis.* New York: W. W. Norton.

Fuligni, A. J., Tseng, V., & Lam, M. (1999). Attitudes toward family obligations among American adolescents with Asian, Latin American, and European family backgrounds. *Child Development, 70,* 1030-1044.

Guarnaccia, P. J. (1997). Social stress and psychological distress among Latinos in the United States. In I. Al-Issa & M. Tousignant (Eds.), *Ethnicity, immigration, and psychopathology* (pp. 71-94). New York: Plenum Press.

Harwood, R., Leyendecker, B., Carlson, V., Asencio, M., & Miller, A. (2002). Parenting among Latino families in the U.S. In M. H. Bornstein (Ed.), *Handbook of parenting* (2nd ed., pp. 21-46). Mahwah, NJ: Lawrence Earlbaum Associates.

Hernandez, M. (2005). Central American families. In M. McGoldrick, J. Giordano, & N. Garcia-Preto (Eds.), *Ethnicity and family therapy* (3rd ed., pp. 178-191). New York: Guilford.

Jones, E. L. (2001). Review of the stress index for parents of adolescents. *The Mental Measurements Yearbook* (14th ed., pp. 1186-1188). Lincoln, Nebraska: Buros Institute of Mental Measurements.

Larson, M. L. (1984). *Meaning-based translation: A guide to cross-language equivalence.* Lanham, MD: University Press of America.

Merali, N. (1996). *Immigrants' perceptions of the degree of acceptability of acculturated adolescent behaviours.* Master's Thesis. Division of Applied Psychology, University of Calgary, Calgary, AB.

Merali, N. (2002). Perceived versus actual parent-adolescent assimilation disparity among Hispanic refugee families. *International Journal for the Advancement of Counselling, 24,* 57-68.

Merali, N. (2004). Family experiences of Central American refugees who overestimate intergenerational gaps. *Canadian Journal of Counselling, 38,* 91-103.

Merali, N., & Violato, C. (2002). Relationships between demographic variables and immigrant parents' perceptions of assimilative adolescent behaviours. *Journal of International Migration and Integration, 3*(1), 65-82.

Organista, K. C. (2007). *Solving Latino psychosocial and health problems: Theory, practice, and populations.* Hoboken, NJ: John Wiley & Sons.

Padilla, A. M. (2006). Bicultural social development. *Hispanic Journal of Behavioral Sciences, 28,* 467-497.

Perez, W., & Padilla, A. M. (2000). Cultural orientation across three generations of Hispanic adolescents. *Hispanic Journal of Behavioral Sciences, 22,* 390-398.

Pernice, R. (1994). Methodological issues in research with refugees and immigrants. *Professional Psychology: Research and Practice, 25,* 207-213.

Phinney, J. S. (2003). Ethnic identity and acculturation. In K. M. Chun, P. B. Organista, & G. Marin (Eds.), *Acculturation: Advances in theory, measurement, and applied research* (pp. 63-82). Washington, D.C.: American Psychological Association.

Phinney, J. S., & Vedder, P. (2006). Family relationship values of adolescents and parents: Intergenerational discrepancies and adaptation. In J. W. Berry, J. S. Phinney, D. L. Sam, & P. Vedder (Eds.), *Immigrant youth in cultural transition: Acculturation, identity, and adaptation across national contexts* (pp. 167-184). Mahwah, NJ: Lawrence Earlbaum Associates.

Roberts, R. E., Phinney, J. S., Masse, L., Chen, Y., Roberts, C., & Romero, A. (1999). The structure of ethnic identity of young adolescents from diverse ethnocultural groups. *Journal of Early Adolescence, 19,* 301-323.

Roizblatt, A., & Pilowsky, D. (1996). Forced migration and resettlement: Its impact on families and individuals. *Contemporary Family Therapy, 18,* 513-521.

Sabogal, F., Marin, G., Otero-Sabogal, R., VanOss Marin, B., & Perez-Stable, E. J. (1987). Hispanic familism and acculturation: What changes and what doesn't? *Hispanic Journal of Behavioural Sciences, 9,* 397-412.

Sanchez, M. (2003). *Understanding how torture affects the health and integration process of refugees.* Paper Presented at the Sixth National Metropolis Conference (National Centres of Excellence for Research on Immigration and Integration), Edmonton, AB, March 24, 2003.

Santisteban, D. A., & Mitrani, V. B. (2003). The influence of acculturation processes on the family. In K. M. Chun, P. B. Organista, & G. Marin (Eds.), *Acculturation: Advances in theory, measurement, and applied research* (pp. 121-136). Washington, DC: American Psychological Association.

Sheras, P. L., Abidin, R. R., & Konold, T. R. (1998). *Manual for the Stress Index for Parents of Adolescents.* Washington, D.C.: Psychological Assessment Resources Inc.

Statistics Canada. (2006). *Canadian Population Census Reports.* Retrieved October, 2008, from http://www.statcan.ca/

Sue, D. W., & Sue, D. (2008). *Counseling the culturally diverse: Theory and practice* (5th ed.). Hoboken, NJ: John Wiley & Sons.

Supple, A. J., Ghazarian, S. R., Frabutt, J. M., Plunkett, S. W., & Sands, T. (2006). Contextual influences on Latino adolescent ethnic identity and academic outcomes. *Child Development, 77,* 1427-1433.

Swearer, S. M. (2001). Review of the Stress Index for Parents of Adolescents. In B. S. Plake & J. C. Impala (Eds.), *The Mental Measurements Yearbook* (14th ed., pp. 1188-1189). Lincoln, Nebraska: Buros Institute of Mental Measurements.

Tabachnick, B. G., & Fidell, L. S. (1996). Using multivariate statistics (3rd ed.). New York: HarperCollins.

Tran, T. V. (1993). Psychological traumas and depression in a sample of Vietnamese people in the United States. *Health and Social Work, 18,* 184-194.

U.S. Census Bureau. (2000). *Overview of race and Hispanic origin.* 2000 Census brief. Retrieved November 13, 2008 from: http://www.census.gov/prod/2001pubs/c2kbr01-1.pdf

In: Handbook of Parenting: Styles, Stresses & Strategies   ISBN 978-1-60741-766-8
Editor: Pacey H. Krause and Tahlia M. Dailey   © 2009 Nova Science Publishers, Inc.

Chapter 19

IMMIGRATION EFFECTS ON PARENTING, STRESS, AND RISKY SEX AMONG HISPANIC IMMIGRANT YOUTH

Elizabeth Trejos-Castillo[1] & Alexander T. Vazsonyi[2]

[1]Texas Tech University, Department of Human Development and Family Studies
Texas Tech University, Lubbock, TX, USA
[2] Auburn University, Department of Human Development and Family Studies
Auburn University, Auburn, AL, USA

ABSTRACT

For decades, there has been the generalized view that cultural differences from the country of origin and the host country threaten family relations and exacerbate the risk for immigrant youth to engage in unhealthy and risky behaviors. It has been argued that immigrant families' values, beliefs, and parenting practices are different from the ones found in the host country or are forced to change during the process of adaptation to the host culture, thus, affecting children's developmental outcomes (Isralowitz & Slonim-Nevo, 2002; Nauck, 2001). In the particular case of Hispanic immigrant youth, alarming official statistics on risky sexual behaviors appear to support this notion. Hispanic youth are reported to be at an increased risk for STDs, having sexual intercourse before age 13, and having four or more sexual partners (CDC, 2000; YRBS, 2004). Yet, limited scholarship exists on how parenting processes and perceived stress (e.g., limited social networks, unreceptive school environment) predict risky sexual behaviors across generations of Hispanic immigrant adolescents.

Using a subsample from the National Longitudinal Study of Adolescent Health (Add Health; Waves I & II), the current study examined the potential changes over time in parenting practices (e.g., monitoring, support, and communication) and stress (e.g.,

---

[1] E. Trejos-Castillo. Assistant Professor of Human Development and Family Studies at Texas Tech University. Department of Human Development and Family Studies. Texas Tech University, MS 41230, Lubbock, TX 79409-1162 USA. E-mail: elizabeth.trejos@ttu.edu

[2] A. T. Vazsonyi. Professor of Human Development and Family Studies at Auburn University. Department of Human Development and Family Studies. Auburn University, 284 Spidle Hall, Auburn AL 36849 USA. E-mail: vazsonyi@auburn.edu

psychological well-being, perceived social support, perceived school stress) across 1st and 2nd generation immigrant Hispanic youth (N= 2,016) and their relationships to risky sexual behaviors. Even though GLM results show that maternal parenting and stress constructs indeed changed over time, changes were not significantly different across generational groups. In addition, maternal monitoring, maternal support, and measures of stress emerged as key predictors of risky sexual behaviors across both 1st and 2nd generation Hispanic immigrant youth over time, whereas no moderation effects were found by immigration status on developmental processes across generational groups. Therefore, findings suggest that even though cultural adaptation to the host culture might represent a stressful process as documented by previous literature (e.g., Pérez & Padilla, 2000; Rueschenberg & Buriel, 1989), immigration and stress do not appear to significantly affect parenting behaviors over time or their links to risky sexual behaviors across generations of Hispanic immigrant youth.

Key Words: Parenting, Stress, Risky Sexual Behaviors, Hispanic Immigrant Youth

ACKNOWLEDGMENTS

This research uses data from Add Health, a program project designed by J. Richard Udry, Peter S. Bearman, and Kathleen Mullan Harris, and funded by a grant P01-HD31921 from the Eunice Kennedy Shriver National Institute of Child Health and Human Development, with cooperative funding from 17 other agencies. Special acknowledgment is due Ronald R. Rindfuss and Barbara Entwisle for assistance in the original design. Persons interested in obtaining data files from Add Health should contact Add Health, Carolina Population Center, 123 W. Franklin Street, Chapel Hill, NC 27516-2524 (addhealth@unc.edu). No direct support was received from grant P01-HD31921 for this analysis.

INTRODUCTION

During immigration, individuals are exposed to the cultural patterns of the host culture that may influence the values, beliefs, and norms based on countries of origin; thus, immigrants face the challenge of clinging to their cultural heritage, whereas having to adapt to and assimilate into a new culture. As a consequence, it has been argued that immigrant families' values and parenting practices that differ from the ones found in the host country are pressed to change during the process of adaptation to the host culture (Isralowitz & Slonim-Nevo, 2002; Nauck, 2001). Thus, the immigration process has been described as a particularly challenging and stressful experience (e.g., language acquisition, need to establish new relationships and social networks) that might negatively impact the individual's psychological well-being and potential assimilation into the host-culture, thus placing the individual at a greater risk for the development of multiple problem behaviors and adjustment difficulties (Harker, 2001; Portes & Rumbaut, 1996).

In general, available findings still remain inconclusive about the causes and incidence of adjustment problems in immigrant youth; for the most part, current studies can be classified into two main perspectives. On one hand, some scholars advocate for group differences in developmental processes in individuals from different ethnic and racial backgrounds (Murad, Joung, Van Lenthe, Bengi-Arslan, & Crijnen, 2003; Nauck, 2001; Isralowitz & Slonim-Nevo, 2002). For instance, Majumdar (2005) examined risky sexual behaviors by ethnicity/race using the National Longitudinal Study of Adolescent Heath (Add Health). Results showed that the percentage of youth who reported not using contraception during recent intercourse was highest among Asians (46%) followed by Hispanics (42%). In addition, Hispanic teenagers were 50% more likely than European American s to not use any contraceptive method during recent intercourse; however, after adding individual, familial, and extra-familial factors, the effect was no longer significant. Other studies have also documented differences by ethnicity/race in risky sexual behaviors, such as inconsistent condom use (O'Donnell, O'Donnell, & Stueve, 2001; Murphy & Boggess, 1998; Sneed, Morisky, Rotheram-Borus, Ebin, et al., 2001) and multiple sexual partners (Barone, Ickovics, Ayers, Katz, Voyce, et al., 1996), particularly among Hispanic youth. In the case of immigrant youth, adjustment problems are thought to be exacerbated by the process of immigration and associated changes in family values and parenting practices; unfortunately, scholarship has been plagued by the bias that immigrant youth, especially Hispanics in the United States represent a high risk population, one that is at risk for the development of multiple behavior problems (Gil, Wagner, & Vega, 2000; Santiesteban, Coastworth, Briones, & Szapocznik, 2002). Moreover, some studies have overemphasized the difficulties and problems that these adolescents face when trying to adapt to a new culture and thus, risky sexual behaviors in Hispanic immigrant youth are commonly interpreted as a sign of failure to adapt to the current living circumstances; similar levels of adjustment problems in European-American adolescents, on the other hand, are attributed to other causes (Dihn, Roosa, Tein, & Lopez, 2002; Gil, Wagner & Vega, 2000; Santiesteban et al., 2002; Vega, Gil, Warheit, Zimmerman, & Apospori, 1993).

A second perspective advocates for similarities in developmental processes among individuals from different ethnic/racial groups (Foner, 1997; Fuligni, 1998; Neto & Barrios, 2000; Kwak, 2003). This line of research proposes the existence of "universal" patterns in the relationships between adjustment and problem behaviors in immigrant as well as native families and argues for the existence of no differences in developmental processes. For example, Rowe, Vazsonyi, and Flannery (1994) found evidence that "developmental processes in different ethnic and racial groups were statistically indistinguishable" (p. 409) in a sample of N=3,392 Blacks, N=1,766 Hispanics, N= 8,582 European American s, and N=906 Asians. Langer, Warheit, and McDonald (2001) examined risk (e.g., age, gender, ethnicity/race) and protective factors (e.g., attitudes towards condom use, religious values) related to risky sexual behaviors using a multiethnic sample (N = 338) of Hispanics (72%), non-Hispanic European American (19.8%), and African-American (8%) undergraduate students. Langer and colleagues report no significant differences in rates of risky sexual behaviors among African-American and Hispanic youth in comparison to European American adolescents. Other scholars have also provided evidence supporting the idea that the process of immigration represents a 'shared experience'; in other words, that this process is experienced at a similar level by all immigrant populations in terms of settlement, assimilation, and adaptation to the new culture as well as the receptivity of the host country toward newcomers (Vega, 1995; Portes & Rumbaut, 1996; Phinney, Horenczyk, Liebkind, & Vedder, 2001; Kwak, 2003).

Although there have been some empirical and theoretical advances in our understanding of Hispanic immigrant child socialization and behavioral outcomes, most of the existing knowledge is based on studies of middle-class European American families. Furthermore, the limited literature on parenting practices and sexual behaviors on Hispanic youth has focused primarily on examining those behaviors in comparison to other ethnic/racial youth and thus, has introduced multiple confounds that do not allow for conclusive evidence (Cabassa, 2003; Hovell, Sipan, Blumberg, Atkins, Hofstetter, et al., 1994). Thus, given the scarcity of literature on Hispanic immigrant youth, the current chapter aims to shed some light on a long-term controversy that portrays immigrant families and adolescents at a disproportionately higher risk for negative developmental outcomes by contributing to an area of scholarship that has remained neglected and unexplored. More specifically, this chapter examines how parenting processes may vary across generations as a function of the adaptation to the host culture and associated stress (e.g., psychological well-being, perceived social support, perceived school stress) as well as its potential impact on risky sexual behaviors among immigrant Hispanic youth.

WHY STUDY PARENTING AND RISKY SEXUAL BEHAVIORS AMONG HISPANIC IMMIGRANT YOUTH?

Recent statistics document that one in five children in the United States is born to immigrants (Census Bureau, 2005). According to official data, the Hispanic population grew almost 10% from 2000 to 2002, representing the largest minority group, even larger than the African-American population. Thus, Hispanics currently represent about half of the total number of immigrants entering the United States and account for about 12.5% of the total U.S. population (Census Bureau, 2003). At the same time, population projections for immigrant adolescents estimate that the number of individuals aged 14-24 will increase between 2000 and 2020, with a larger growth among Hispanics (NCES, 2005). As a result, it is expected that 14-17 years old Hispanics will increase by 34%, while the number of African American adolescents—the second largest ethnic minority group in the U.S.—will increase only by 7%. This remarkable increase of Hispanic immigrant families has propelled new trends in research to understand the unique problems and behavioral characteristics of this immigrant population (Crosnoe, López-González, & Muller; 2004; Harker-Tillman, Guo, & Mullan Harris, 2004; Kao, 2004; Villaruel, Langfeld, & Porter; 2002). One area of scholarship that has gained more attention by researchers during the last decade is the role that family and parenting behaviors play in Hispanic youth's sexual behaviors.

Parenting processes are generally described as specific goal-directed attempts by the parent to socialize the child and adolescent (Steinberg & Silk, 2002). Developmental theorists such as Patterson (1982) and Baumrind (1978) have argued that it is the family as the primary socialization institution that represents the 'model' which reinforces or discourages children from engaging in risky behaviors. Furthermore, Dittus, Jaccard, and Gordon (1999) and Kotchick, Shaffer, Forehand, and Miller (2001) have argued that the role of family is central for the sexual socialization of children and youth. Previous research has extensively documented parenting processes such as monitoring, support, and communication as important determinants of risky sexual behaviors in youth (Fasula & Miller, 2006; Jenkins &

Smith, 1991; Kurdek & Fine, 1994; Loeber & Stouthamer-Loeber, 1986; Stanton et al., 2000). Parental monitoring has been widely acknowledged as a protective factor against STDs (Capaldi, Stoolmiller, Clark, & Owen, 2002; Small & Luster, 1994) and by increasing condom-use skills (Stanton et al., 2000), reducing teen pregnancy (Miller, 1998), and predicting number of sexual partners and frequency of condom use among youth (Weber-Shifrin, 2003). Parental support—often conceptualized as parental responsiveness, involvement, and family connectedness (Upchurch, Aneshensel, & Mudgal, 2001)—has also been documented as an important predictor of delayed and less frequent sexual intercourse, frequency of condom use, and pregnancy (Markman, Rortolero, Escobar-Chávez, Parcel, Harrist et al., 2003; McNeely, Shew, Beuring, Sieving et al., 2002; Ream & Savin-Williams, 2005).

In addition, parental communication has been identified as an important factor related to age of first sexual intercourse and having had sex (Karofsky, Zeng, & Kosorok, 2001; Murry-McBride, 1996; Stanton et al., 2000); however, findings from other studies have been inconclusive (DiIorio, Dudley, Soet, & McCarty, 2004; Fasula & Miller; 2006, Rodgers, 1999). It is possible that the lack of associations may be due to design and measurement problems as described by Jaccard et al. (2002). Another potential explanation suggested by Jaccard and Dittus (1993) and Whitaker and Miller (2000) is that the effect of parental communication may interact with peer norms, which in turn, may exert an influence on the adolescent's sexual experiences. In addition, as Hovell, Sipan, Blumberg, Atkins, Hofstetter et al. (1994) point out, the lack of association between parental communication and risky sex in youth may be also due to the fact that communication may have initiated or improved after parents suspect that the adolescent has already initiated sexual intercourse.

In the case of Hispanic families, a recently growing body of research has documented the important role that the family plays in the socialization of Hispanic children. Hispanic families have been characterized by strong cultural beliefs and values of respect, conformity to parents' and elders' authority, expectations about premarital sex as well as the obligation and loyalty of the individual to the family, thus, representing a central element in Hispanic adolescents' sexual experiences (Barrera, Biglan, Ary, & Li, 2001; Calzada & Eyberg, 2002; Vélez-Pastrana, Gónzalez-Rodríguez, & Borges-Hernández, 2005). However, a main limitation of the available literature in parenting processes on Hispanic youth is the lack of consensus and consistency in the operationalization of parenting constructs.

Therefore, whereas some researchers have conceptualized parenting processes in Latino families as "familism[3]" (Romero, Robinson, Haydel, Mendoza, & Killen; 2004), family importance (Gorman-Smith et al., 1996), bonding and pride (Vega et al., 2003), family functioning (Forehand, et al., 1997), and family cohesiveness; others studies have conceptualized parenting behaviors as, for example, communication, monitoring, support (Nichols-Anderson, 2001). Furthermore, parenting in Hispanic youth and families has been studied by examining individual parenting constructs in isolation (Ramírez et al., 2004; Vega, 1990). In summary, the literature on risky sexual behaviors stresses the importance of examining the role of the family and parenting behaviors in explaining these behaviors among youth; however, less attention has been paid to examining developmental processes across

---

[3] Familism can be described as "attitudes, behaviors, and family structures operating within an extended family system" (Velez-Pastrana et al., 2005, pp. 779).

different generations of immigrant youth and whether parenting practices and youth sexual behaviors may vary as a result of the immigration process.

Parenting, Stress, and Risky Sexual Behaviors: Does Immigration Matter?

Traditionally, research on immigrant families and adolescents has mostly adopted the classical model of assimilation; that is, the process of adaptation to the host culture is assumed to follow a linear progression during which immigrants gradually adopt new values and behaviors while discarding the ones from their culture of origin. This approach has also largely supported the erroneous conceptualization of newly immigrants as "in deficit," (e.g., few marketable job skills, Zea, Diehl, & Porterfield, 1996; low-income, descending economic mobility, and lack of education, Suárez-Orozco & Suárez-Orozco, 2001; Coastworth, Maldonado-Molina, Pantin, & Szapocznik, 2005) suggesting that only through the adaptation to the culture and a longer residence, will immigrants be able to make developmental and socioeconomic progress; thus, the second and subsequent generations would do 'better' compared to the 1st generational groups.

Developmentally, adolescents are at a stage of identity formation, which, under the circumstances of immigration might be critically challenged by demands coming from the community (e.g., social capital, Hovey & King, 1996; Pong, Hao, & Gardner, 2005; social support, Levitt, Lane, & Levittt, 2005; Kung, Castaneda, & Lee, 2003) and the school environment (e.g., Romero & Roberts, 2003; Padilla, 2006). As suggested by Stress Theory, the need to adapt to a different culture may lead to problems negotiating competing norms and values from the host country with their parents and thus, might result in negative effects on the adolescent's psychological well-being placing them at a higher risk for adjustment problems (Afable-Munsuz & Brindis, 2006; Zhou, 1997). In addition, immigration may influence how parenting practices evolve to meet and accommodate those needs in children; thus, the parent-child relationship of first-generation immigrant youth may experience more tension and may go through more active processes of negotiation due to the disparity in foreign versus host culture values (García et al., 1996; Vega et al., 2004). For 2nd generation youth, however, the host culture represents their native culture; therefore, the second-generation parent-child relationship can vary substantially compared to the first-generation in terms of cultural continuity and quality (Kwak, 2003; Szapocznik & Kurtines, 1980).

Contrary to the classical "deficit" model, other researchers have documented that a higher degree of adaptation to the American culture translate into greater risky sexual behaviors and sexual activity reported by 2nd generation Hispanic youth when compared with their 1st generation counterparts (CDC, 2001; Villaruel, Langfeld, & Porter; 2002). Evidence has also been provided that second-generation Hispanic youth tend to report higher involvement with peers and other activities outside the family (e.g., school events) that appears to influence whether adolescents defy authority, including parental efforts directed at behavioral control (Rueschenberg & Buriel, 1989; Wall, Power, & Arbona, 1993). Furthermore, a third line of research has advocated for the so called "revisionist theories" of immigrant adaptation to the host culture by providing evidence that rates of adjustment problems among immigrant youth are not substantially greater than those of European American youth or youth from other racial and ethnic backgrounds (Fuligni, 1998; Mullan Harris, 1999; Neto & Barrios, 2000; Phinney et al., 2001). In sum, as exemplified by the previously discussed scholarship, there is a pressing need for further understanding the etiology of risky sexual behaviors among immigrant Hispanic youth and its relationship to parenting efforts across generational groups as well as determining the role, if any, that immigration status plays on developmental processes in youth.

Hypotheses

The extant evidence indicates that immigrant parents often socialize their children in a way that "prepares" them to cope with the host culture whereas at the same time, they also tend to emphasize values and norms from their own culture of origin (Kwak, 2003; Raeff, 1997; Zayas & Solari, 1994). Thus, differences in parenting processes across generational groups as well as adolescent stress (e.g., psychological well-being, perceived social support, and perceived school stress) have been attributed to the immigration and adaptation processes to a host culture. Studies have also documented that these factors are less salient in the second and subsequent generations of immigrant youth, simply because they are born into the host culture, and thus, their culture of origin (Kwak, 2003). Once adaptation stressors decline for first and subsequent generation immigrant youth, it is expected that parental constructs will decrease; as a result, higher adaptation to the host culture may be related to greater risky sexual behaviors reported among 2nd generation immigrant youth, but not among 1st generation adolescent (Jeltova, Fish, & Revenson, 2005).

Based on this evidence, it is expected that parenting constructs and stress would be discontinuous in first-generation immigrant families but not in second-generation immigrant youth, where they would remain largely stable; thus, it is expected that the stability of parenting and stress between T1 and T2 would be moderated by immigration status. Second, although differences in parenting practices across generations and its association to risky sexual behaviors in Hispanic youth remain inconclusive, multiple studies suggests marked differences in risky sexual behaviors across first and second-generation immigrant youth (Jeltova et al., 2005). Thus, it was expected that associations among parenting constructs and risky sexual behaviors would be greater among first than second-generation youth.

METHODS

Sample

Participants for the study were selected from The National Longitudinal Study of Adolescent Health (Add Health) using the following criteria: self-identified Hispanic origin, country of birth (Hispanic/Latino country or U.S.A), and age (13-16 years old). Only individuals available at Wave I and Wave II were included in the longitudinal sample. The final sample (N = 1,968) included n=391 1st generation and n=1,577 2nd generation Hispanic immigrant adolescents. Data collection procedures were established by the institutional review board of the University of North Carolina at Chapel Hill (see Harris, Halpern, Entzel, Tabor, Bearman, et al., 2008); as recommended by Chantala and Tabor (1999), appropriate sample weights were applied for data analyses.

Measures

Demographics

Demographic information on age, sex, family structure, socio-economic status, and ethnicity was provided by the participants.

Parenting Processes

Recent studies using the Add Health data set have acknowledged greater response rates from mothers and/or primary female caretakers than fathers or male caretakers (Hawkins, Amato, & King, 2006). In addition, extant evidence suggests that Hispanic mothers are more actively involved in children socialization than Hispanic fathers (Marín & Marín, 1990; Zayas, 1994); thus, only maternal parenting processes were used in the current analyses. *Maternal Monitoring* was assessed by seven dichotomous items (e.g., "Do your parents let you make your own decisions about the people you hang out with"; Harris, 1999). Due to the lack of scalar properties, items were recoded and summed to compute an overall index of monitoring, which ranged from 0 to 7, where 7 indicated a high level of monitoring; thus, no Cronbach's alphas are reported. *Maternal Support* was assessed using five items (e.g., "how close do you feel to your mother"; Harris, 1999; Ream & Savin-Williams, 2005). Though all items were measured by a 5 point Likert-scale, response categories for the first two items ranged from 1= not at all to 5=very much, whereas responses to the last three items used a 1= strongly agree to 5= strongly disagree scale. All items were recoded so that a high score reflects high support; see Table 2 for reliability estimates). *Maternal Communication* was assessed by four dichotomous items (e.g., "talk about someone you are dating, or a party you went to," Willgerodt & Thompson; 2005); an overall index of maternal communication ranging from 0 to 4 was computed (4 indicated a high level of communication).

Stress

As discussed by Padilla (2006), the transmission and adoption of cultural practices of the host culture take place for the most part in the surrounding community and school environments. At the same time, the immigrant adolescent faces the developmental challenge of constructing a personal identity that not only should incorporate elements of the culture of origin but from the host culture as well. Given the complexity of the immigration phenomenon, stress is better understood by examining multiple factors that affect the adolescent as suggested by previous scholarship (Levitt et al., 2005; Short & Johnston, 1997); thus, the current study included three sub-scales to measure stress: psychological well-being, perceived social support, and perceived school stress. *Psychological Well-being* was measured by 10 items (e.g., "you cried frequently", Meadows, Brown, & Elder, 2006) rated on a 4 point Likert-scale (0=never or rarely to 3=most of the time or all the time); inverse variables were reversed coded so that a higher number would reflect higher psychological well-being. *Perceived Social Support* was measured by eight items (e.g., "how much do you feel that adults care about you?" Harker, 2001) rated on a 5 point Likert-scale (1=at all to 5=very much). *Perceived School Stress* was measured using 8 items (e.g., "how often have you had trouble getting along with other students," McNeely, Nonnemaker, & Blum, 2001; Nooney, 2005) using a 5 point Likert-scale (0=never to 4=every day).

Risky Sexual Behaviors

A composite of six items was used to measure risky sexual behaviors (Upchurch, Lillard, Aneshensel, & Li, 2002; Ream & Savin-Williams, 2005). Each item was dichotomized to reflect high and low risk (e.g., "no" was recoded as 1 = high risk; "yes" was recoded as 0 = low risk); items were summed to compute an index that included five risky sexual behaviors: age of first sex, contraceptive use, type of contraceptive use, STDs, and multiple partners.

Immigration Status was measured based on the adolescent's citizenship status and on his/her parents' country of birth (Crosnoe et al., 2004; Gordon-Larsen et al., 2003). Generational groups were classified as 1st generation (i.e., foreign born) and 2nd generation (i.e., U.S. born).

Plan of Analysis. Preliminary analyses included descriptive statistics (Table 1), reliability estimates (Table 2), and correlations among the main constructs. Due to the complex data design, appropriate data weights were applied and nesting effects were examined prior to conducting the main analyses as recommended by Add Health data analyses procedures (Chantala & Tabor, 1999; Harker, 2001). Consistent with previous studies using Add Health, no significant school clustering effects were found in the study sample on the main constructs (Crosnoe et al., 2004). Next, a series of repeated measures ANOVA were completed to test for changes over time in maternal parenting and stress constructs using a General Linear Model (GLM), where 'time' (T1 & T2) was the within subjects factor, 'group' (immigration status) was the between subject factor, and 'time X immigration status' was the interaction term. A final set of analyses included hierarchical regressions to test the relationships among maternal parenting constructs, stress, and risky sexual behaviors as well as potential moderation effects by immigration status in these relationships. Hierarchical analyses were completed by entering controls in a first step followed by maternal parenting constructs in a second step; stress constructs were added in a third step and interaction terms to test moderation effects by immigration status were included in a final step.

RESULTS

Results of demographic variables are presented in Table 1. First generation immigrant youth were slightly older (15.6 years) than 2nd generation youth (15.2 years) and reported a significantly lower level of maternal education and household income; thus, demographic variables were included as controls in all subsequent analyses. All study variables were significantly correlated in the expected direction[4].

---

[4] Correlation table is available upon request.

Table 1. Demographic Variables by Generational Groups

| | Hispanic Immigrant Youth N = 2,016 | | |
	1st Generation n = 402	2nd Generation n = 1,614	
Age (mean)	15.62	15.24	t: 34.07***
Sex			χ^2: .003
Male	49.3	49.2	
Female	50.7	50.8	
Family Structure			2.38
Biological parents	50.0	51.7	
Biological mother only	28.4	27.8	
Step families	11.2	9.2	
Other	2.7	3.7	
Maternal Education			26.07***
Less than high school	47.8	35.7	
High school diploma or GED	28.9	35.0	
More than high school (some college)	12.2	19.7	
College or post-graduate schooling	9.7	9.5	
Annual Family Income			68.58***
$15,000 or less	30.1	18.3	
$16,000 to $34,000	25.6	26.0	
$35,000 to $59,000	7.2	19.3	
$60,000 or more	4.2	11.6	

Note: *p < 0.05, **p < 0.01, ***p < 0.001. Participants were given the option to answer "does not know/does not apply"; these figures are not included in the table and make up the difference between the sum of all categories and 100%.

Results from the General Linear Model (GLM) analyses showed that the time effect for maternal monitoring (F [1, 1626] = 39.34, p <.000), maternal support (F [1, 1679] = 9.23, p <.002), and maternal communication (F [1, 1556] = 11.18, p <.001) were significant indicating that those parenting constructs changed over time.

Table 2. Reliability, Means, and SD Estimates for Maternal Parenting Constructs, Stress, and Risky Sexual Behaviors by Immigration Status at T1

	Items (range)	1st Generation Hispanic Immigrant Youth			2nd Generation Hispanic Immigrant Youth		
Parenting Constructs		α	M	SD	α	M	SD
Maternal Communication	4 (0-4)	+	1.8	1.3	+	1.9	1.2
Maternal Monitoring	7 (0-7)	+	2.5	1.7	+	2.2	1.5
Maternal Support	5 (1-5)	.78	4.5	.82	.85	4.5	.83
Stress Constructs							
Psychological Well-Being	4 (0-3)	.78	4.6	1.4	.69	3.5	1.6
Perceived Social Support	8 (1-5)	.63	3.9	1.3	.66	3.7	1.2
Perceived School Stress	7 (0-4)	.82	3.6	1.7	.81	4.2	.98
Risky Sexual Behaviors	5 (0-5)	+	.65	.88	+	.72	.95

Note: + These measures are indexes created with dichotomous items instead of continuous items; thus, no psychometric properties are reported.

More specifically, maternal monitoring and maternal support significantly decreased from T1 to T2 whereas maternal communication increased significantly from T1 to T2 (see Figures 1, 2, and 3). The test for the interaction between time and group did not reach statistical significance for maternal parental monitoring (F [1, 1626] = .441, p<.507), maternal parental support (F [1, 1679] = .067, p<.795), or maternal parental communication (F [1, 1556] = 1.46, p<.228). The results indicate that even though all maternal parenting constructs seem to change over time, these changes are not significantly different across 1st and 2nd generation Hispanic immigrant youth.

In the case of stress constructs, GLM results provided evidence of no significant changes over time in psychological well-being (F [1, 1679] = .113, p <.736) and perceived social support (F [1, 1665] = .801, p <.736); however, a significant increase was found for perceived school stress (F [1, 1679] = 4.35, p <.037). Furthermore, the by group interaction term was not significant for psychological well-being (F [1,665] = .064, p< .801), perceived social support (F [1,679] = .712, p< .399), or perceived school stress (F [1,679] =.712, p< .399). These results provided evidence that generational groups were not differently affected by changes in these constructs from T1 to T2.

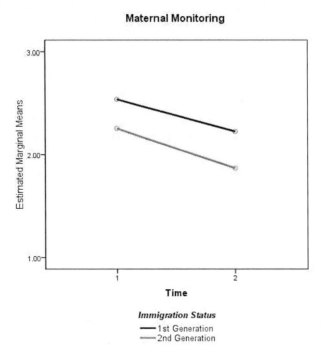

Figure 1. Changes in Maternal Monitoring T1 to T2 by Immigration Status.

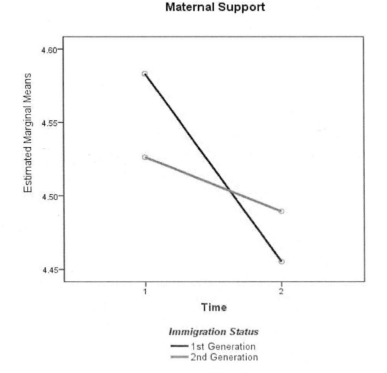

Figure 2. Changes in Maternal Support T1 to T2 by Immigration Status.

Maternal Communication

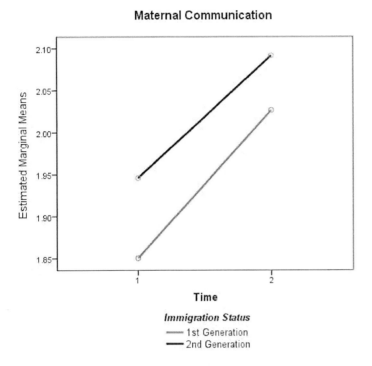

Figure 3. Changes in Maternal Communication T1 to T2 by Immigration Status.

Adolescent Psychological Well-being

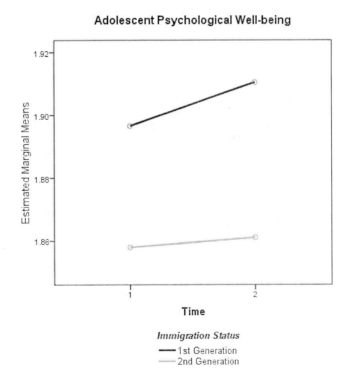

Figure 4. Changes in Adolescent Psychological Well-being T1 to T2 by Immigration Status.

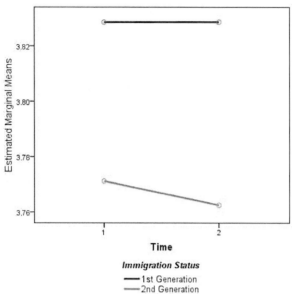

Figure 5. Changes in Adolescent Perceived Social Support T1 to T2 by Immigration Status.

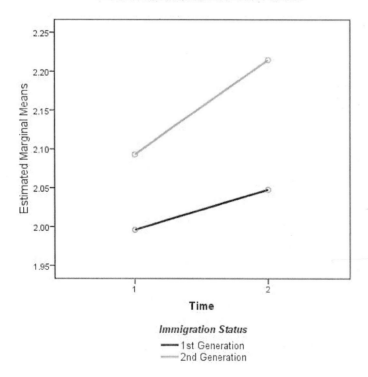

Figure 6. Changes in Adolescent Perceived School Stress T1 to T2 by Immigration Status.

The following set of analyses examined the unique contribution of maternal parenting and stress constructs at T1 on risky sexual behaviors at T2 in the total sample. Results from the hierarchical regression analyses showed that demographic variables explained 4% unique variance in risky sexual behaviors. Maternal parenting variables explained an additional 2% of variance; stress constructs also explained an additional 2% of variance. With the exception of maternal monitoring ($\beta = .50$, $p < .919$), maternal parenting variables, namely, maternal support ($\beta = -.490$, $p < .012$) and maternal communication ($\beta = -.268$, $p < .021$), significantly predicted risky sexual behaviors at T2. Similarly, psychological well-being ($\beta = -.488$, $p < .01$), perceived social support ($\beta = -.962$, $p < .01$), and perceived school stress ($\beta = -.579$, $p < .00$) significantly predicted risky sexual behaviors at T2. Results from moderation tests showed significant effects by immigration status on psychological well-being ($\beta = -.240$, $p < .03$), perceived social support ($\beta = -.561$, $p < .00$), and perceived school stress ($\beta = -.249$, $p < .01$).

To determine whether moderation effects were statistically significant across groups, post-hoc analyses were conducted to examine for significant differences in regression coefficients using unstandardized coefficients and standard error terms (Baron & Kenny, 1986; Cohen & Cohen, 1983), along with an adjusted alpha $= .01$ $(.05/5 = .01)$ for multiple sample comparisons. Thus, z scores lower than 2.58 ($p < .01$; two tailed) provided no evidence of significant differences. The results revealed that moderation effects by immigration status were not statistically significant for psychological well-being ($z = 1.27$), perceived social support ($z = 2.07$), and perceived school support ($z = 1.88$).

Table 3. Time 1 Maternal Parenting and Stress Constructs Predicting Risky Sexual Behaviors T2

Risky Sexual Behaviors T2 Total Sample

Steps	Variables	b	SE	β	p	ΔR^2
1	Demographic Variables					.04
	Maternal Monitoring	.50	.13	-.01	.91	.02
2	Maternal Support	-.49	.19	.63	.01	
	Maternal Communication	-.27	.11	-.54	.02	
	Psychological Well-being	-.48	.14	-.58	.01	.02
3	Perceived Social Support	-.96	.28	-.76	.00	
	Perceived School Stress	-.57	.16	-.78	.00	
	Immigration Status	.25	.86	.04	.64	.01
	Monitoring X Immigration Status	-.01	.03	-.06	.13	
	Support X Immigration Status	-.27	.10	-.98	.09	
	Communication X Immigration Status	-.14	.06	-.56	.19	
4	Psychological Well-being X Immigration Status	-.24	.08	-.57	.00	
	Perceived Social Support X Immigration Status	-.56	.15	-.53	.00	
	Perceived School Stress X Immigration Status	-.24	.08	-.69	.00	

Notes: Scores presented are from the final step.

CONCLUSION

American youth are initiating sexual activities at progressively younger ages, declining from about 15 years in age during the 1980s to around 13 years during the 1990s (CDC, 2005; O'Donnell, O'Donnell, & Stueve, 2001)—the Centers for Disease Control reports that out of 158 national schools surveyed in 2004, 46.7% of all high school students reported having had sexual intercourse (CDC, 2005). Epidemiological evidence shows that about 900,000 15-19 year old adolescent females become pregnant in the U.S. each year—78% of those are unwanted pregnancies. This represents the highest rate of teenage pregnancy among industrialized nations (CDC, 2000). Official statistics also document that there are an estimated of 4 million cases of sexual transmitted diseases (STDs) per year among 10-19 year old adolescents and about 6 million cases of STDs among 20-24 year old young adults, that at least one third of males report having had sex before they entered middle-school, and that one-fifth of females have had their first sexual intercourse before they left eighth grade (CDC, 2001; 2005). Furthermore, during 2003, approximately 4,000 youth were diagnosed with AIDS, accounting for about 12% of the total population diagnosed with the illness in that year (CDC, 2005).

The alarming trends in STDs, HIV, and unplanned pregnancies among teens seem to identify ethnic/racial minority youth and immigrant youth (CDC, 2000; 2005). However, across empirical scholarship, the results remain inconclusive; more specifically, the available literature can be generally divided into two main types of findings: differences and similarities in developmental processes. The difference perspective has largely attributed differences in behavioral outcomes among youth based to their ethnicity/race and culture of origin (Dihn et al., 2002; Gil, Wagner, & Vega, 2000), whereas the similarity perspective argues that despite ethnic/racial or cultural backgrounds, adolescents experience similar developmental processes (Kagitçibasi; 2005; Dmitrieva et al., 2004). Thus, despite some significant interactions between ethnicity/race and risky sexual behaviors, most previous studies suggest that race and other demographic variables do not explain risky sexual behaviors because these behaviors are determined by an array of other intervening factors such as the family, individual characteristics, community, and school contexts among others (Aneshensel, Becerra, Fielder, & Schuler, 1990; Eamon & Mulder, 2005; Flores, Eyre, & Millstein; 1998).

As exemplified by the aforementioned gaps in current scholarship on risky sexual behaviors among youth, this area of research warrants additional exploration, not only to better understand the etiology of such behaviors from a more inclusive perspective, but also to further our knowledge on how minority and immigrant youth might experience similar or different developmental trajectories. To date, even though empirical evidence has identified parenting processes as key predictors of risky sexual behaviors among Hispanic youth, only a handful of studies, most of them cross sectional, have examined the etiology of risky sexual behaviors with a particular focus on the family. In addition, almost no studies have taken into consideration potential generational differences and stress effects which may account for observed differences in risky sexual behaviors.

In trying to overcome these previous shortcomings, the current chapter included multiple parenting constructs (e.g., maternal monitoring, maternal support, and maternal communication) and three indicators of perceived stress (psychological well-being, perceived social support, and perceived school stress) to examine their longitudinal effects on risky sexual behaviors in Hispanic youth. By comparing 1st and 2nd generation groups, the chapter also aimed to add to the growing literature on ethnic minority and immigrant youth and to shed some light on the dynamics of developmental processes in immigrant adolescents.

Although the findings suggest that maternal parenting practices do change over time as previous scholars have documented (García et al., 1996; Vega et al., 2004; Zayas & Solari, 1994), the changes do not differ by generational status. The observed similarities in changes of parenting across generations provide some evidence that core family values among Hispanic families appear to remain largely stable across generations and thus, changes in parenting might be more related to developmental issues that might not differ from the ones experienced by families with adolescents from different ethnical/racial backgrounds (Varela, Vernberg, Sanchez-Sosa, Riveros, Mitchell et al., 2004). With the exception of maternal monitoring, maternal parenting constructs (maternal support and maternal communication) significantly predicted risky sexual behaviors across generational youth. This finding may be related to the particular characteristics of the Hispanic family which has been described to exert a high emphasis on obedience, respect, and obligations toward elders as well as more restrictive values in terms of premarital sexual exploration (Pérez & Padilla, 2000; Raffaelli & Ontai, 2001; Vélez-Pastrana et al., 2005). Thus, assuming that these values are present in both groups of immigrant families, this may prevent both first and second generation Hispanic youth from engaging in risky sexual behaviors.

Another potential explanation may relate to the broadly established link between parenting and sexual behaviors in youth, where positive parenting practices (e.g., high levels of monitoring, closeness, or support) have been found to considerably delay sexual intercourse and lower sexual risk taking behaviors among youth (Hovell et al., 1994; Luster & Small, 1994; Miller, 2002; Rose et al., 2005). In addition, the relationship between positive parenting and lower levels of risky sexual behaviors has been well established across different ethnic groups (Kotchick et al., 1999; Meschke et al., 2002). For example, Ream and Savin-Williams (2005) has suggested that the lack of change in parenting (e.g., support, communication) between Waves I and II in the Add Health data set may have positively impacted youth in the sense that it prevented them from engaging in risky sexual activities at Wave II. Finally, these findings are concurrent with some previous studies but not with others; this is not surprising given the inconsistencies reported by extant scholarship that call for a closer examination of parenting trajectories across generational groups of immigrants.

It is important to clarify that some empirical evidence supports differences in parenting related to immigration status in Hispanic immigrant parents (e.g., Romero et al., 2003; Zapata & Jaramillo, 1981); these differences have been documented to be associated with language acquisition patterns and parents' ethnic identity. However, these differences have not been documented to be associated with risky sexual behaviors among Hispanic immigrant youth. Furthermore, though some evidence supports the idea of immigration status effects on immigrant Hispanic sexual behaviors, there is not a clear agreement in the literature as to how these constructs are related to risky sexual behaviors among Hispanic immigrant youth; thus, whereas some studies report that less acculturated Hispanic youth are less sexually active (Driscoll et al., 2001), other studies provide evidence that first generation Hispanic youth are less likely to use condoms (O'Donnelle, O'Donnelle, & Stueve, 2001).

Contrary to the significant results found for changes in parenting processes over time, the results show that stress indicators, with the exception of perceived school stress, did not change over time. It is possible that, as suggested by Padilla (2006), stress at school might seem more noticeable to immigrant youth as a result of the continuous transmission of cultural values of the host culture and the development of relationships with native individuals. The same dynamics to a lesser extent might occur at home and in the community but it is at school were youth more actively engage in the assimilation and adaptation to the American culture (e.g., English language acquisition, role modeling, cultural expectations).

Similarly to the results of parenting processes, stress indicators were not significantly different across generations of immigrant youth; this finding underscores the importance of further exploring the effects that immigration might or might not have on immigrant families and youth across multiple domains. Immigration is a complex phenomenon that is often interpreted from a pessimistic and deficit view informed by biases and assumptions that do not necessarily reflect the characteristics of the immigrant individuals. Though scarce, however, some empirical studies have pointed out that immigrant populations tend to be strongly connected to networks that provide plenty of psychosocial resources that serve as buffers against socioeconomic difficulties as well as negative emotional and behavioral outcomes (Golding & Burnam, 1990).

In general, the lack of significant effects by immigration status on parenting, stress constructs, and risky sexual behaviors across generations of youth further suggests that even though differences might exists in terms of stress and cultural assimilation into the host culture as documented by previous literature (e.g., Pérez & Padilla, 2000; Rueschenberg & Buriel, 1989), the immigration process does not appear to influence how parents parent across generations. Overall, the findings show that parenting processes and their relationships with risky sexual behaviors in Hispanic immigrant youth did not differ by generational groups. This represents an important insight supported by a growing body of literature that argues for similarities in developmental processes across ethnic and racial groups (Dmitrieva et al., 2004; Kagitçibasi; 2005; cf., Lansford, Deater-Deckard, Dodge, Bates, & Pettit, 2004).

Although the present chapter provides significant insights, limitations are also important to be acknowledged. More specifically, the analyses rely solely on self-reported data which might be biased. In addition, two of the parenting measures (maternal monitoring and maternal communication) were dichotomous and lacked psychometric properties. Finally, though longitudinal, the sample used in this chapter included two points in time; thus, results should be cautiously interpreted in reference to longitudinal associations.

Future Directions

An important goal of this chapter was to add to the extant literature on parenting practices in Hispanic youth. Though the authors were able to accomplish this goal in part by examining three parenting process, namely, monitoring, support, and communication, it is important to acknowledge that future studies need to consider additional ones (e.g., closeness or conflict) that are cited in the current parenting literature (Galambos, Barker, & Almeida, 2003). In addition, measurement problems experienced with parenting constructs (e.g., dichotomized variables) can be overcome by including more sound parenting measures in future studies (e.g., multiple items, continuous variables and scales). As suggested by previous studies, it is possible that engagement in risky sexual behaviors among the Hispanic youth population may be particularly related to specific behaviors such as condom use (O'Donnelle et al., 2001;

Sneed et al., 2001) or age of first sexual intercourse (Upchurch et al., 1998). Thus, future research efforts should also test individual indicators of risky sexual behaviors (e.g., condom use, multiple sexual partners, age of first sexual intercourse, etc.).

It is also possible that adolescents may have not perceived changes in parenting processes over time even though parents may have "intended" to socialize their children in a different way in response to the assimilation and adaptation process parents themselves experience as suggested by previous studies (Romero, Cuellar, & Roberts, 2000). Future research should collect data on parenting processes from the parents' point of view in addition to the adolescent one in order to more closely examine potential immigration effects on parenting processes across generations of immigrant youth.

REFERENCES

Afable-Munsuz, & Brindis, CD. (2006). Acculturation and the sexual and reproductive health of Latino youth in the United States: A literature review. *Perspectives on Sexual and Reproductive Health, 4*, 208-219.

Aneshensel, C.S., Becerra, R.M., Fielder, E.P., & Schuler, R.H. (1990). Onset of fertility-related events during adolescence: A prospective comparison of Mexican American and non-Hispanic White females. *American Journal of Public Health, 80*, 959-953.

Baron, R. M., & Kenny, D. A. (1986). The moderator-mediator variable distinction in social psychological research: Conceptual, strategic, and statistical considerations. *Journal of Personality and Social Psychology, 51*, 1173-1182.

Barone, C., Ickovics, J. R., Ayers, T. S., Katz, S. M., Voyce, C. K., & Weissberg, R. P. (1996). High-risk sexual behaviors among young urban students. *Family Planning Perspectives, 28*, 69–74.

Barrera, M., Biglan, A., Ary, D. & Li, F. (2001). Replication of a problem behavior model with American Indian, Hispanic, and Caucasian youth. *Journal of Early Adolescence, 21*, 133-157.

Baumrind, D. (1978). Parental disciplinary patterns and social competence in children. *Youth and Society, 9*, 239-276.

Cabassa, L. J.(2003). Measuring acculturation: Where we are and where we need to go. *Hispanic Journal of Behavioral Sciences, 25*, 127-146.

Calzada, E.J., & Eyberg, S.M. (2002). Self-reported parenting practices in Dominican and Puerto Rican others of young children. *Journal of Clinical and Adolescent Psychology, 31*, 354-363.

Capaldi, D. M., Stoolmiller, M., Clark, S., & Owen, L.D. (2002). Heterosexual risk behaviors in at-risk youth men from early adolescence to young adulthood: Prevalence, prediction, and association with STD contraction. *Developmental Psychology, 38*, 394-406.

Chantala, K., & Tabor, J. (1999). Strategies to perform a design-based analysis using the Add Health data. *Add Health Paper Series.* Carolina Population Center. Retrieved April 2006: http://www.cpc.unc.edu/addhealth.

Centers for Disease Control and Prevention (2000). *Young people at risk: HIV/AIDS among America's youth.* Retrieve: 01/21/2006. www.cdc.gov/hiv/pubs/facts/youth.htm.

Centers for Disease Control and Prevention. (2001). *Sexually Transmitted Disease Surveillance,* Retrieved: 03/05/2006. www.cdc.gov/hiv/pubs/facts/youth.htm.

Centers for Disease Control and Prevention. (2005). HIV/AIDS among youth. Retrieve: 05/15/2006. www.cdc.gov/hiv/pubs/facts/youth.htm.

Cohen, J., & Cohen, P. (1983). *Applied multiple regression/correlation analysis for the behavioral sciences.* Hillsdale, NJ: Lawrence Erlbaum Associates, Inc.

Coastworth, D.J., Maldonado-Molina, M., Pantin, H., & Szapocknik, J. (2005). A person-centered and ecological investigation of acculturation strategies in Hispanic immigrant youth. *Journal of Community Psychology, 33,* 157-174.

Crosnoe, R., López-González, L., & Muller, C. (2004). Immigration from Mexico into the math/science pipeline in American education. *Social Science Quarterly, 85,* 1208-1226.

Dinh, K. T., Roosa, M. W., Tein, J., & Lopez, V. A. (2002). The relationship between acculturation and problem behavior proneness in a Hispanic youth sample: A longitudinal mediation model. *Journal of Abnormal Child Psychology, 30,* 295–309.

DiIorio, C., Dudley, W.N., Soet, J.E., & McCarty, F. (2004). Sexual possibility situations and sexual behaviors among young adolescents: The moderating role of protective factors. *Journal of Adolescent Health, Volume 35,* 528-539.

Dittus, P.J., Jaccard, J., & Gordon, V.V. (1999). Direct and nondirect communication of maternal beliefs to adolescents: Adolescent motivations for premarital sexual activity. *Journal of Applied Social Psychology, 29,* 1927-1963.

Dmitrieva, J., Chen, C., E., Greenberger, E., & Gil-Rivas, V. (2004). Family relationships and adolescent psychosocial outcomes: Converging findings from Eastern and Western cultures. *Journal of Research on Adolescence, 14,* 425-447.

Driscoll, A. K., Biggs, M. A., Brindis, C. D., & Yankah, E. (2001). Adolescent Latino reproductive health: a review of the literature. *Hispanic Journal of Behavioral Sciences, 23,* 255-326.

Eamon, M. K., & Mulder, C. (2005). Predicting antisocial behavior among Latino young adolescents: An ecological systems model. *American Journal of Orthopsychiatry, 75,* 117-127.

Fasula, A.M., & Miller, K.S. (2006). African-American and Hispanic adolescents' intentions to delay first intercourse: parental communication as a buffer for sexually active peers. *Journal of Adolescent Health, 38,* 193-200.

Flores, E., Eyre, S.L., Millstein, S.G. (1998). Sociocultural beliefs related to sex among Mexican American adolescents. *Hispanic Journal of Behavioral Sciences, 20,* 60-83.

Foner, N. (1997). The immigrant family: Cultural legacies and cultural changes. *International Migration Review, 31,* 961-974.

Forehand, R., Miller, K.S., Dutra, R., & Chance, M.W. (1997). Role of parenting in adolescent deviant behavior: Replication across and within two ethnic groups. *Journal of Consulting and Clinical Psychology, 65,* 1036-1041.

Fuligni, A. J. (1998). Authority, autonomy, and parent-adolescent conflict and cohesion: A study of adolescents from Mexican, Chinese, Filipino, and European backgrounds. *Developmental Psychology, 34,* 782-792.

Galambos, N.L., Barker, E.T., & Almeida, D.M. (2003). Parents do matter: Trajectories of change in externalizing and internalizing problems in early adolescence. *Child Development, 74,* 578-594.

Garcia, C., Lamberty, G., Jenkins, R., McAdoo, H., Crnic, K., Wasik, B., et al. (1996). An integrative model for the study of developmental competencies in minority children. *Child Development, 67*, 1891-1914.

Gil, A.G., Wagner, E.F., & Vega, W.A. (2000). Acculturation, familism, and alcohol use among Latino adolescent males: Longitudinal relations. *Journal of Community Psychology, 68,* 857-863.

Golding, J.M. & Burnam, A.M. (1990). Immigration, stress, and depressive symptoms in a Mexican-American community. *Journal of Nervous and Mental Disorders, 178*, 161-171.

Gorman-Smith, D., Tolan, P.H., Zelli, A., & Huesmann, L.R. (1996). The relation of family functioning to violence among inner-city minority youth. *Journal of Family Psychology, 10*, 115-129.

Guilamo-Ramos, V., Jaccard, J., Pena, J., & Goldberg, V. (2005). Acculturation-related variables, sexual initiation, and subsequent sexual behavior among Puerto Rican, Mexican, and Cuban youth. *Health Psychology, 24*, 88-95.

Gordon-Larsen, P., Mulan Harris, K., Ward, D.S., & Popkin, B.M. (2003). Acculturation and overweight-related behaviors among Hispanic immigrants to the US: The National Longitudinal Study of Adolescent Health. *Social Science & Medicine*, 57, 2023-2034.

Harker, K. (2001). Immigrant generation, assimilation, and adolescent psychological well-being. Immigrant generation, assimilation, and adolescent psychological well-being. *Social Forces, 79*, 969-1004.

Harker Tillman, K., Guo, G., & Mullan Harris, K. (2006). Grade retention among immigrant children. *Social Science Research, 35*, 129-56.

Harris, K.M., Halpern, C.T., Entzel, P., Tabor, J., Bearman, P.S., & Udry, J.R. (2008). The National Longitudinal Study of Adolescent Health. http://www.cpc.unc.edu/projects/addhealth/design.

Hawkins, D.N., Amato, P.R., and King, V. (2006). Parent-adolescent involvement: The relative influence of parent gender and residence. *Journal of Marriage and Family 68*, 125–136.

Hovell, M.F., Sipan, C.L., Blumberg, E.J., Atkins, C.J., Hofstetter, R. & Kreitner, S.M. (1994). Family influences on Latino and Anglo adolescents' sexual behavior. *Journal of Marriage and the Family, 56*, 973-986.

Hovey, J.D., & King, C. (1996). Acculturative stress, depression, and suicidal ideation among Immigrant and Second-Generation Latino Adolescents. *Journal of the American Academy of Child & Adolescent Psychiatry, 35*, 1183-1192.

Isralowitz, R. E. & Slonim-Nevo, V. (2002). Substance use patterns and problem behaviors among immigrant and native-born juvenile offenders in Israel. *Addiction Research and Theory, 10*, 399-414.

Jaccard, J. and Dittus, P. (1993). Parent–adolescent communication about premarital pregnancy. *Families in Society, 74*, 329–343.

Jaccard J., Dodge, T., & Dittus, P. (2002). Parent-adolescent communication about sex and birth control: a conceptual framework, *New Directions for Child and Adolescent Development,* 97:9–41.

Jeltova, I., Fish, M. C., & Revenson, T. A. (2005): Risky sexual behaviors in immigrant adolescent girls from the former Soviet Union: Role of natal and host culture. *Journal of School Psychology, 43*, 3-22.

Jenkins, J. M., & Smith, M. A. (1991). Marital disharmony and children's behaviour problems: Aspects of a poor marriage that affect children adversely. *Journal of Child Psychology and Psychiatry, 32,* 793–810.

Kagitçibasi, C. (2005). Autonomy and relatedness in cultural context: Implications for self and family. Journal of Cross-Cultural Psychology, 36, 403-422.

Kao, G. (2004). Parental influences on the educational outcomes of immigrant youth. *International Migration Review, 38,* 427-449.

Karofsky, P.S., Zeng, L., & Kosorok, M.R. (2001). Relationship between adolescent–parental communication and initiation of first intercourse by adolescents. *Journal of Adolescent Health, 28,* 41-45.

Kotchick, B.A., Dorsey, S., Miller, K.S., & Forehand, R. (1999). Adolescent sexual risk-taking behavior in single-parent ethnic minority families. *Journal of Family Psychology, 13,* 93-102.

Kotchick, B. A., Shaffer, A., Forehand, R., & Miller, K. S. (2001). Adolescent sexual risk behavior: A multi-system perspective. *Clinical Psychology Review, 21,* 493–519.

Kung, W.W., Castaneda, I., & Lee, P.J. (2003). Stress, social support, and coping as predictors of depression level: Differences between native-born and immigrant Mexican-Americans. *Journal of Immigration & Refugee Services, 3,* 62-80.

Kurdek, L. A., & Fine, M. A. (1994). Family acceptance and family control as predictors of adjustment in young adolescents: Linear, curvilinear, or interactive effects? *Child Development, 65,* 1137-1146.

Kwak, K. (2003). Adolescents and their parents: A review of intergenerational family relations for immigrant and non-immigrant families. *Human Development, 46,* 115-136.

Langer, L., Warheit, G.J., & McDonald, L. P. (2001). Correlates and predictors of risky sexual practices among a multi-racial/ethnic sample of university students. *Social Behavior and Personality, 20,* 101-119.

Lansford, J.E., Deater-Deckard, K., Dodge, K.A., Bates, J.E., & Pettit, G.S. (2004). Ethnic differences in the link between physical discipline and later adolescent externalizing behaviors. *Journal of Child Psychology and Psychiatry, 45,* 801-812.

Levitt, M.J., Lane, J.D., & Levitt, J. (2005). Immigration stress, social support, and adjustment in the first postmigration year: An intergenerational analysis. *Research in Human Development, 2,* 159-177.

Loeber, R., & Stouthamer-Loeber, M. (1986). Family factors as correlates and predictors of juvenile conduct problems and delinquency. In M. Tonry, & N. Morris (Eds.), *Crime and justice: An annual review of research,* Vol. 7. Chicago: University of Chicago Press.

López-González, L. (2005). Immigration from Mexico, school composition, and adolescent functioning. *Sociological Perspectives, 48,* 1-24.

Majumdar, D. (2005). Explaining adolescent sexual risks by race and ethnicity: Importance of individual, familial, and extra-familial factors." *International Journal of Sociology of the Family 31,* 19-37.

Marín, G., & Marín, B.V. (1991). *Research with Hispanic populations.* Newbury Park, CA: SAGE.

Markman, C.M., Rortolero, S.R., Escobar-Chaves, S.L., Parcel, R.H., & Addy, R.C. (2003). Family connectedness and sexual risk taking among young urban youth attending alternative high school. *Perspectives on Sexual and Reproductive Health, 35,* 174-179.

McNeely, C.A., Shew, M.L., Beuhring, T., Sieving, R., Miller, B.C., Blum, R.W. (2002). Mothers' influence on adolescents' sexual debut. *Journal of Adolescent Health, 31,* 256-265.

Meadows, S.O., Brown, S.J., & Elder, G.H. (2006). Depressive symptoms, stress, and support: Gendered trajectories from adolescence to young adulthood. *Journal of Youth and Adolescence, 35,* 93-103.

Meschke, L. L., Bartholomae, S., & Zentall, S. R. (2002). Adolescent sexuality and parent-adolescent processes: Promoting healthy teen choices. *Journal of Adolescent Health, 31,* 264-279.

Miller, B.C. (1998). Families matter a research synthesis of family influences on adolescent pregnancy. National Campaign to Prevent Teen Pregnancy, Task Force on Effective Programs and Research, Washington, DC (1998).

Mullan Harris, K. (1999). Health risk behaviors among adolescents in immigrant families. Paper presented at the second biannual meeting of the Urban Seminar Series on Children's Health and Safety entitled "Successful Youth in High-Risk Environments", Harvard University.

Murad, S. D., Joung, I. M. A., Van Lenthe, F. J., Bengi-Arslan, L. & Crijnen, A. A .M. (2003). Predictors of self-reported problem behaviors in Turkish immigrant and Dutch adolescents in the Netherlands. *Journal of Child Psychology and Psychiatry, 44,* 412-423.

Murphy, J. J., & Boggess, S. (1998). Increased condom use among teenage males, 1988-1995: The role of attitudes. *Family Planning Perspectives, 30,* 276-280, 303.

Murry-McBride, V. (1996). An ecological analysis of coital timing among middle-class African American adolescent females. *Journal of Adolescent Research, 11,* 261-279.

Nauck, B. (2001). Social capital, intergenerational transmission and intercultural contact in immigrant families. *Journal of Comparative Family Studies, 32,* 465- 490.

National Center for Education Statistics (NCES). (2005).Youth indicators. Trends in the well-being of American youth. Department of Education. Retrieved005/15/2006 http://nces.ed.gov/programs/youthindicators/index.asp

Neto, F. & Barrios, J. (2000). Predictors of loneliness among adolescents from Portuguese immigrant families in Switzerland. *Social Behavior and Personality, 28,* 193-206.

Nichols-Anderson, C.L. (1997). The effects of parental practices and acculturation upon sexual risk taking among Latino adolescents. Dissertation. Oklahoma State University.

Nooney, J.G. (2005). Religion, stress, and mental health in adolescence: Findings from Add Health. *Review of Religious Research, 46,* 341-354.

O'Donnell, L., O'Donnell, C. R., & Stueve, A. (2001). Early sexual initiation and sub-sequent sex-related risks among urban minority youth: The reach for health study. *Family Planning Perspectives, 33,* 268-275.

Padilla, A.M. (2006). Bicultural social development. *Hispanic Journal of Behavioral Sciences, 28,* 467-497.

Patterson, G. R. (1982). *Coercive family processes.* Eugene, OR: Castalia.

Perez, W., & Padilla, A. M. (2000). Cultural orientation across three generations of Hispanic adolescents. *Hispanic Journal of Behavioral Sciences, 22,* 390-398.

Phinney, J. S., Horenczyk, G., Liebkind, K. & Vedder, P. (2001). Ethnic identity, immigration, and well-being: An interactional perspective. *Journal of Social Issues, 57,* 493-511.

Planos, R., Zayas, L.H., & Busch-Rossnagel, N.A. (1995). Acculturation and teaching behaviors of Dominican and Puerto Rican mothers. *Hispanic Journal of Behavioral Sciences, 17*, 225-236.

Pong, S. , L. Hao, & Gardner, E. (2005). The roles of parenting styles and social capital in the school performance of immigrant Asian and Hispanic adolescents. *Social Science Quarterly, 86*, 928-950.

Raeff, C. (1997). Individuals and relationships: Cultural values, children's social interactions, and the development of an American individualistic self. Developmental Review, 17, 205-238.

Raffaelli, M., & Ontai, L. L. (2001). She's 16 years old and there's boys calling over to the house: An exploratory study of sexual socialization in Latino families. *Culture, Health and Sexuality, 3*, 295–310.

Ramírez, J.R., Crano, W., D., Quist, R., Burgoon, M., Alvaro, E.M., & Grandpre, J. (2004). Acculturation, familism, parental monitoring, and knowledge as predictors of marihuana and inhalant use in adolescents. *Psychology of Addictive Behaviors, 18*, 3-11.

Ream, G.L., & Savin-Williams, R.C. (2005). Reciprocal association between adolescent sexual activity and quality of youth-parent interactions. *Journal of Family Psychology, 19*, 171-179.

Rodgers, K.B. (1999). Parenting processes related to sexual risk-taking behaviors of adolescent males and females. *Journal of Marriage & the Family, 61*, 99-109.

Romero, A.J., Cuéllar, I., & Roberts, R.E. (2000). Ethnocultural variables and attitudes toward cultural socialization of children. *Journal of Community Psychology, 28,* 79-89.

Romero, A.J., & Roberts, R.E. (2003). Stress within a bicultural context for adolescents of Mexican descent. *Cultural Diversity and Ethnic Minority Psychology, 9*, 171-184.

Romero, A., Robinson, T., Haydel, K, Mendoza, F., & Killen, J. (2004). Associations among familism, language preference, and education in Mexican-American mothers and their children. *Journal of Developmental & Behavioral Pediatrics, 25*, 34-40.

Rose, A., Koo, H. P., Bhaskar, B., Anderson, K., White, G., & Jenkins, R.R. (2005). The influence of primary caregivers on the sexual behavior of early adolescents. *Journal of Adolescent Health, 37*, 135-144.

Rowe, D. C., Vazsonyi, A. T., & Flannery, D. J. (1994). No more than skin deep: Ethnic and racial similarity in developmental process. *Psychological Review, 101*, 396-417.

Rueschenberg, E., & Buriel, R. (1989). Mexican American family functioning and acculturation: A family system perspective. *Hispanic Journal of Behavioral Sciences, 11*, 232-244.

Santiesteban, D.A., Coastworth, J.D., Briones, E., & Szapocznik, J. (2002). Investigating the role of acculturation, familism, and parenting practices in Hispanic youth behaviors problems. *Journal of Family Psychology, 17*, 121-133.

Short, K.H., & Johnston, C. (1997). Stress, maternal distress, and children's adjustment following immigration: The buffering role of social support. *Journal of Consulting and Clinical Psychology, 65*, 494-503.

Small, S. A., & Luster, T. (1994). Adolescent sexual activity: An ecological, risk factor approach. *Journal of Marriage and the Family, 56*, 181-192.

Sneed, C.D., Morisky, D.E., Rotheram-Borus, M.J., Ebin, V., Malotte, C.K., Lyde, M., & Gill, J, K. (2001). 'Don't know' and 'didn't think of it': Condom use at first intercourse by Latino adolescents. *AIDS Care, 13*, 303-308.

Stanton, B. F., Li, X., Galbraith, J., Cornick, G., Feigelman, S., Kaljee, L., & Zhou, Y. (2000). Parental underestimates of adolescent risk behavior: A randomized, controlled trial of parental monitoring intervention. *Journal of Adolescent Health, 26*, 18-26.

Steinberg L., & Silk, J.S. (2002). Parenting adolescents. In: Borsntein (Ed.), *Handbook of parenting* (pp.103-134). Mahwah, New Jersey: Lawrence Erlbaum Associates.

Suárez-Orozco, M., &Suárez-Orozco, C. (2001) *Children of immigration.* Cambridge, MA: Harvard University Press.

Szapocznik, J., & Kurtines, W. (1980). Acculturation, biculturalism, and adjustment among Cuban Americans. In A. M. Padilla (Ed.), *Acculturation: Theory, models and some new findings* (pp. 139-157). Boulder, CO: Westview.

Upchurch, D. M., Aneshensel, C.S., & Mudgal, J. (2001). Sociocultural contexts of time to first sex among Hispanic adolescents. *Journal of Marriage and Family, 63*, 1158-1169.

U.S. Census Bureau (2003). The Hispanic population. Retrieved: 02/07/05. http://www.census.gov/prod/2001pubs/c2kbr013.pdf#search='Census%20Bureau%20Hispanics%202001'

Varela, R.E., Vernberg, E.M., Sanchez-Sosa, J.J., Riveros, A., Mitchell, M., & Mashunkashey, J. (2004). Parenting style of Mexican, Mexican American, and Caucasian-Non-Hispanic families: Social context and cultural influences. *Journal of Family Psychology, 18*, 651–657.

Vega, W.A (1995). The study of Latino families. In R. Zambrana (Ed.), *Understanding Latino families: Scholarship, policy, and practice* (p 3-17). Thousand Oaks, CA: Sage.

Vega, W.A., Gil, A.G., Warheit, G.J., Zimmerman, R.S., & Apospori, E (1993). Acculturation and delinquent behavior among Cuban American Adolescents: Toward an empirical model. *American Journal of Community Psychology, 21*, 113-125.

Velez-Pastrana, M.C., Gonzalez-Rodriguez, R.A., & Borges-Hernandez, A. (2005). Family functioning and early onset of sexual intercourse in Latino adolescents. *Adolescence, 15-37.*

Villaruel, A.M., Langfeld, C., & Porter, C.P. (2002). Sexual behavior of Latino pre-adolescents and adolescents: The relationship of acculturation and generational history. *Hispanic Health Care International, 1*, 24-30.

Wall, J.A., Power, T.G., & Arbona, C. (1993). Susceptibility to antisocial peer pressure and its relation to acculturation in Mexican-American adolescents. *Journal of Adolescent Research, 8*, 403-418.

Weber-Shifrin, E. M. (2003). Parental monitoring and risky sex: The impact parental efficacy and perceived parental attitudes. Dissertation, Northwestern University, Department of Clinical Psychology. Evanston: Illinois.

Whitaker DJ, Miller, K.S, & Clark, L. F.(2000). Reconceptualizing adolescent sexual behavior: beyond did they or didn't they? *Family Planning Perspectives, 32*, 111-117.

Willgerodt, M. A., & Thompson, E. A. (2005). The influence of ethnicity and generational status on parent and family relations among Chinese and Filipino adolescents. *Public Health Nursing, 22*, 460-471.

Youth Risk Behavior Surveillance (2004). Morbidity and Mortality Weekly Report 53 / No. SS-2. Retrieved: 02/04/05. http://www.cdc.gov/mmwr.

Zapata, J.T., & Jaramillo, P.T. (1981). Research on the Mexican-American family. *Journal of Individual Psychology, 37*, 72-85.

Zayas, L.H. (1994). Hispanic family ecology and early childhood socialization: Health implications. *Family Systems Medicine, 12*, 315-325.

Zayas, L. H., & Solari, F. (1994). Early childhood socialization in Hispanic families: Culture, context, and practice implications. *Professional Psychology: Research and Practice, 25*, 200-206.

Zea, M.C., Asner-Self, K.K., Birman, D, & Buki, L.P. (2003). The abbreviated multidimensional acculturation scale: Empirical validation with two Latino / Latina samples. *Cultural Diversity and Ethnic Minority Psychology, 9*, 107-126.

Zhou, M. (1997). Growing up American: the challenge of confronting immigrant children and children of immigrants. *Annual Review Sociology, 23*, 63-95.

INDEX

C

G

H

I

M

N

Q

R

U

V